Aboriginal Economy & Society

Australia at the Threshold of Colonisation

Ian Keen

OXFORD

UNIVERSITY PRESS

OXFORD

UNIVERSITY PRESS

253 Normanby Road, South Melbourne, Victoria 3205, Australia

Oxford University Press is a department of the University of Oxford.
It furthers the University's objective of excellence in research, scholarship,
and education by publishing worldwide in

Oxford New York

Auckland Bangkok Buenos Aires Cape Town Chennai
Dar es Salaam Delhi Hong Kong Istanbul Karachi Kolkata
Kuala Lumpur Madrid Melbourne Mexico City Mumbai Nairobi
São Paulo Shanghai Taipei Tokyo Toronto

OXFORD is a trade mark of Oxford University Press
in the UK and in certain other countries

National Library of Australia
Cataloguing-in-Publication data:

Keen, Ian.
    Aboriginal economy and society: Australia at the threshold of colonisation.

    Bibliography.
    Includes index.
    ISBN 0 19 550766 5.

    1. Economic anthropology—Australia. 2. Aboriginal Australians—Economic conditions.
    3. Hunting and gathering societies—Australia. I. Title.

306.30994

Typeset by OUPANZS
Printed through Bookpac Production Services, Singapore

Cover photo: Kuuku-Ya'a man hunting dugong in an outrigger canoe (D. F. Thomson, TPH2873,
reproduced courtesy of Mrs D. M. Thomson and Museum Victoria).

Acknowledgments

Spouses often appear last in the acknowledgments; so first I thank Libby Keen for her companionship and intellectual support.

Many Yolngu people have instructed me about their homeland and culture; I thank especially the late Bariya, the late Dja:wa, the late Dha:thangu, and Jimmy Wululu for sharing their knowledge. I learned much about nineteenth-century Gippsland economy and society while conducting research on behalf of Mirimbiak Nations Aboriginal Corporation; I am grateful to many Gunnai/Kurnai people for their hospitality, especially Sandra Mullett, who guided me round the region.

The publication of this book is in no small measure the result of encouragement and gentle prompting on the part of Jill Henry, then of Oxford University Press, who saw the proposal through its initial stages. The publication team at Oxford University Press have been patient, helpful, and efficient; I thank Debra James, who shepherded the book through the publication phase, Chris Wyness for his advice, Tim Campbell for his meticulous editing of the text, and Racheal Stines and Kerry Cooke for the excellent design and typesetting.

The Faculties Research Fund of the Australian National University (funded by the Australia Research Council) provided essential funds to support travel and research within Australia. Sue Fraser of the Department of Archaeology and Anthropology was always generous with her time in administering those funds and in supporting the research in other ways. The National Museum of Ethnology (Minpaku) in Osaka and the Japanese Ministry of Education provided generous financial support and hospitality during my time as a Visiting Professor in 2000–01. I thank Shuzo Koyama and Masatoshi Kubo for sponsoring my visit, and Nobuhiro Kishigami for looking after me.

Heather McDonald's assiduous search for materials provided the backbone of the project. I also thank Virginie Branchut and Felicita Carr for research assistance, and Tracey Dalitz for checking the references.

The staff of a number of museums and archives in Australia have been very generous with their time and expertise: the Australian Institute of Aboriginal and Torres Strait Islanders, Museum Victoria, the Western Australian Museum, the South Australian Museum, the State Library of Australia, the library of the University of Western Australia, and the J. S. Battye Library in Perth. Particular thanks are due to Lindy Allen, Mary Morris, Rosemary Wrench, and their colleagues at Museum

Victoria, and to Sandy Toussaint for advice about resources in Western Australia. For giving me access to their PhD theses I am grateful to Laurent Dousset, Annette Hamilton, Mike Pickering, Tony Redmond, and Fredric Viesner.

During my time in Japan many colleagues at the National Museum of Ethnology (Minpaku), as well as members of the Australian Studies Group from other universities and organisations, provided intellectual stimulus and hospitality. The museum administrative staff provided support with unfailing politeness and cheerfulness. My neighbours in Inokodani, Mr and Mrs Anno, were extraordinarily helpful in guiding an illiterate foreigner through the Japanese banking, postal, and retail systems, and were generous in their hospitality, as were the Kishigami family. Thanks also to the Yoshigoshi family in Nagasaki for a memorable Christmas.

At the University of Queensland, Leonn Satterthwait and Judith Cameron participated in an early phase of the research on which this book is based. A number of Australian colleagues have given me moral support and encouragement at times when my resolve has flagged; I thank especially Rosita Henry, Tim Rowse, Peter Sutton, and Bob Tonkinson, and anonymous reviewers of the proposal for this book for Oxford University Press. Colleagues at the Australian National University made helpful comments and suggestions about the proposal at various stages of its inception: I thank Don Gardner, Julie Gorrell, Chris Gregory, Francesca Merlan, Frances and Howard Morphy, and Nicolas Peterson.

Several scholars have responded to seminars and papers with comments and invaluable information, and to specific requests: I thank Kim Akerman, Christina Birdsall Jones, Tamsin Donaldson, Laurent Dousset, Coral Dow, Britte Duelke, Beth Gott, Patrick McConvell, Paul Memmott, Mike Pickering, Tony Redmond, Alan Rumsey, Elizabeth Williams, participants in the anthropology, history and Centre for Cross-cultural Research seminars at the Australian National University, colleagues at the Ninth International Conference on Hunting and Gathering Societies in Edinburgh (2002), and participants in the Archaeology and Linguistic Conference in Canberra (2002).

For their comments on parts of the manuscript I am grateful to Harry Allen, Jeremy Beckett, Athol Chase, Caroline Bird, Tamsin Donaldson, Laurent Dousset, Coral Dow, Beth Gott, Peter Hiscock, Francesca Merlan, Nicolas Peterson, Tony Redmond, Bruce Rigsby, Alan Rumsey, Peter Toner, Bob Tonkinson, and Frederic Viesner. The two anonymous readers for Oxford University Press made very helpful suggestions for improvements to the text as a whole.

For assistance with photographs and other illustrations I thank John Dallwitz, Ian Dunlop, Lea Garam at the South Australian Museum, the National Library, Nicolas Peterson, the Powerhouse Museum, John Stanton, Mrs D. H. Thomson, and Museum Victoria. Thanks also to Ian Hayward for drawing the maps for Chapter 2, Chris Clarkson for advice about map sources, and Dave McGregor for technical assistance.

Contents

List of Figures

List of Maps

List of Plates

List of Tables

A Note on Orthographies

Generally speaking, I have retained the orthographies used in the original sources. It is too hazardous for a non-linguist to attempt to construct a consistent orthography from the older spellings. Where linguists have developed orthographies—such as for the Western Desert, Kimberley, and northeast Arnhem Land languages—I have used these. The disadvantage for the reader is that the spellings do not always provide a reliable guide to pronunciation. Older sources tend to use the letter 'u' ambiguously: to signify the short 'a' (similar to the sound in 'hat') and the 'u' sound as in 'put'. A. W. Howitt used 'ū' for the sound as in 'put' (I have simplified this to 'u'), and 'ŭ' to signify the sound as in 'hat'. 'Gn' at the beginning of a word denotes the sound 'ng' as in 'sing'. K. Langloh Parker attempted to render Yuwaaliyaay sounds into an English orthography, and the early sources for the southwest use a wide variety of spellings.

Modern orthographies, including those for the Western Desert language, Wangaaybuwan (neighbours of Yuwaaliyaay people), Sandbeach languages (Umpila, etc.), Ngarinyin and Yolngu languages, employ similar conventions; the following is a rough guide (adapted from Yallop 1982):

b, p	voiced as in *sober*, unvoiced as in *soapy*
dh, th	voiced as in *the*, unvoiced as in *through*
d, t	voiced as in *lady*, unvoiced as in *sooty*
rd, d̲, rt, t̲	as in American English *cord*, or *court*
dj, dy, tj, ty	voiced as in *hard yakker*, unvoiced as in *not yet*
g, k	voiced as in *go*, unvoiced as in *joker*
'	glottal stop as in London dialect *wa'er* (*water*)
m	as in *mother*
nh	similar to the *n* sound in *tenth*
n	as in *no* or *ten*
rn, n̲	similar to *rn* in American English *corn*
ny, nj	similar to *ni* in *onion* and Spanish *ñ*
ng	as in *sing* ('gn' at the beginning of a word in early orthographies)
l	as in *lift*
rl, l̲	as in American English *curl*
rr, r	rolled *r* as in Scottish *Mary*
r, r̲	as in southern English *Mary*
rd, d̲	as in American English *cord*
w	as in *winter*
y	as in *yes*
i	as in *bit*
i:, ii	long *i* as in *machine*
u	as in *look*
u:, uu	long *u* as in *coop* ('o' represents 'uu' in some Yolngu orthographies)
a	between the *a* sound in *pat* and the *u* sound in *mud*
a:, aa	long *a* as in *father*
e	as in *peck*

e:, ee	long *e* as in *Cairns*
o	as in *lock* but more like *o* in Japanese *miso*
o:, oo	long *o* as in *hawk*, but more like *ō* in Japanese *'sō desu ka!'*
ai, ay	diphthong as in *glide*
au, aw	diphthong as in *loud*

Introduction

To what extent did Aboriginal economy and society vary across Australia at the time of British colonisation, and in what ways? This book attempts to answer these questions by comparing the economy and society of seven very different regions of the continent as they were at the threshold of colonisation. A comparison of this kind is long overdue. Previous studies have concentrated on single topics, such as kinship, social organisation, religion, or ecology, or made somewhat broader-based comparisons but of only two or three areas. Overviews of Aboriginal culture and society have sampled variation in several institutions—kinship, religion, local groups, and so on—in a piecemeal way. This book reconstructs the economy and society of seven regions at the threshold of colonisation, and systematically compares them in order to bring out their similarities and differences.[1]

There are several reasons for undertaking this exercise. First, the comparison will illuminate the character of each region, as well as bringing out differences between them. Second, it will counter certain prevalent stereotypes: people tend to assume that Aboriginal cosmologies conformed everywhere to the concept of 'Dreamtime' or 'the Dreaming', and assume that Aboriginal people everywhere organised themselves into 'clans' if not 'tribes'. A third reason is that a reinterpretation of regional ethnographies, especially the rather fragmentary sources on the southeast and southwest, will assist other studies, such as histories of colonisation and analyses of social change. Finally, the book will serve as an introduction to and overview of Aboriginal economy, society, and culture before they were altered by colonisation.

At the threshold of colonisation

The much used category of 'traditional' culture or society is problematic. Contrasted with 'modern' it places contemporary ways of life in the past, and it implies there was

1

a period before European colonisation when people lived unchanging 'traditional' lives—aspects of which continue in the present—and were somehow outside history.[2]

'The threshold of colonisation' does not imply an unchanging 'traditional' past, for it is likely that the invention and diffusion of technologies and social forms were ongoing processes. Recent developments in archaeology and linguistics have opened the way to a much more dynamic picture of Australia before 1788. They make it possible to think of reconstructions of modes of Aboriginal social life and culture as historically located, rather than implying a timeless domain of a people 'without history'.[3]

Australia was not divided into a mosaic of separate societies before 1788, as the maps of Aboriginal 'tribes' imply. People engaged in *networks* of interaction both within the continent and across its boundaries in the north. For 300 years before European exploration Yolngu people of northeast Arnhem Land had regular contact with Macassan trepangers, and for millennia the Torres Strait had formed a corridor for relations between Aboriginal people and Melanesians.[4] Thus Aboriginal forms of social life were not static but dynamic. Nevertheless, the British colonisation of Australia began a much more radical process of social change than did contact with the Macassans, and, importantly, had very different kinds of effects in different places. For the purposes of this book, it would not make sense to compare, say, Arnhem Land in the 1920s with Gippsland in the 1920s, for by this point the latter had been changed very radically by white colonisation, while the former had not. It makes more sense to compare Arnhem Land in the 1920s with Gippsland in the 1820s (as reconstructed by Howitt). The British colonisation of Australia, as well as the later internal colonisation of the continent, effectively occurred at different times in different places, and with varying degrees and kinds of impact; so the 'threshold of colonisation' is not a specific period, but is relative to place.

In some regions colonisation had quick and devastating effects, radically transforming the lives of Aboriginal people within a few decades. This was the case in Gippsland, the home of Kŭnai people, from the 1830s onwards. In areas remote from European centres of population, such as the Western Desert and northeast Arnhem Land, the impact occurred much later, with a more gradual and less radical effect. The nature of the colonisation process also affected the conditions for subsequent knowledge of the modes of social life that existed at the time of colonisation. Later in this chapter I shall briefly introduce the main ethnographers of each region and their approaches to anthropology, as well as the historical circumstances of their research.

The approach to economy and society

A work such as this cannot include everything; it has to be limited in scope yet full enough to be meaningful. To this end the book focuses on the economy, because just about all aspects of Aboriginal culture and society had a bearing on this aspect of social life. This will make it possible to be broad yet concise, and will allow me to explore the relationships between environments, technologies, economy, and society. But there is room for a systematic treatment of Aboriginal economy in its own right. A few excellent monographs on community economies that interact with the wider market economy have been complemented by many smaller-scale studies and broad overviews. Reconstructions of pre-colonial economies, however, have been confined to a few general works by geographers and economists.[5]

As well as describing the environmental conditions under which people lived their lives and the resources upon which they drew, this book will use two main analytical frameworks. The first is the analysis of 'institutional' forms and practices, including such topics as identity, cosmology, totemism, kinship, marriage, and governance. The second is the analysis of economic relations and processes, including the control of the means of production, the organisation of production, distribution, exchange, and consumption. I shall examine how the various domains or institutional fields in terms of which people organised their lives were implicated in the economy: for example, the involvement of cosmology in the ownership and control of access to land and technology, and the implications of kinship relations for the organisation of production and exchange.

Environmental conditions and constraints

Part I of the book surveys the environment, resources, technology, population density, and pattern of settlement and mobility of each of the seven regions. Anthropologists have usually discussed such matters as aspects of 'ecology', a long-standing topic of research in Australia. Intensive studies began with the ecological research of Donald Thomson in Cape York Peninsula and Norman Tindale in the Western Desert. Studies have looked at various aspects of relations between people and the environment, such as the seasonality of resource availability and patterns of movement, modes of subsistence in relation to the environment, and the control of access to land, water, and resources. I shall treat these 'ecological' aspects as integral to economy: environments constitute arenas of human action and being, they yield resources to be exploited, and they impose constraints and provide enabling conditions for practices.[6]

Institutional fields

Part II of the book compares variants in the forms of 'institutional fields'. Institutions are domains of coordinated ideas, actions, events, organisation, and roles that Anthony Giddens refers to as 'the more enduring features of social life'.[7] Examples in English-speaking countries are family, religion, education, economy, law, and government. Structural-functionalist anthropologists took these and related institutions to have universal application, but the sensitivity of cultural anthropology to the categories and descriptions employed by the people themselves (so-called 'emic' categories) highlighted problems of translation arising out of the application of these institutional categories to the cultures of non-English-speaking peoples. The rather more flexible concept of 'social field', with its focus on discourse as well as fields of social relations, has displaced the concept of institution somewhat—I shall put them together.[8]

The categories of institutional field used in this book probably overlap only partially with Aboriginal ones. A concept such as 'cosmology' certainly does not capture all the meaning of *rom* in Yolngu languages or *tjukurrpa* in Western Desert languages, but it does enable me to describe aspects of them. The word 'kinship' as construed here closely coincides with the range of senses of the Yolngu term *gurruṯu*. The ideal would be to describe such fields according to Aboriginal categories, then compare them through the use of these analytical concepts. However, few of the ethnographic writings drawn on for this book record just how people labelled the broad domains of social life. Nevertheless, similarities between ethnographic descriptions such as kin relations in the seven regions are sufficient to make the domains proposed here workable.

Aspects of economy

'Economy' refers to the production, distribution, exchange, and consumption of the material means of life, how they articulate with other valued items, particularly through exchange, and the organisation of these processes. This is what has been called a 'substantivist' approach to economy, in contrast with a 'formalist' approach. According to formalist definitions the economy is about the choices people make in the allocation of scarce resources to desired ends. The formalist definition makes sense in the context of market economies, in which the flow of money largely defines the boundaries of the economy. It reflects liberal ideologies that emphasise individual freedom and the capacity to make choices, rather than the constraints of social and political structures, which are emphasised by a political economy approach. In societies or sectors in which the economy is not defined by the market but is 'embedded' in other institutions, a formalist definition in terms of choice takes in too much and a substantivist approach is more useful. The approach of this book is substantivist in that it takes the subsistence sector as its focus. It works out from that focus to include other valued items linked to subsistence production, distribution, and exchange, and assesses the implications of institutional forms and processes for the organisation of various aspects of economy.

What kind of economies did Aboriginal people practice? In one view they were the antithesis of capitalism because they limited demand. In his article 'The original affluent society' (reprinted in his book *Stone Age Economics*), Marshall Sahlins sought to counter the picture of the hunter–gatherer economy as a struggle for existence in marginal environments by depicting it as an economy of limited 'wants'—in contrast with the unlimited wants of capitalist societies depicted in J. K. Galbraith's *The Affluent Society*. For Sahlins, hunters and gatherers lived in the 'original affluent society' just because they were not struggling to satisfy endlessly expanding desires. In the face of limited means they followed the 'Zen road' to affluence of limited wants. Productive capacity met relatively stable wants more than adequately, making available very generous amounts of leisure time. This analysis rests in part on Sahlins's equation of 'economy' with subsistence; the unlimited 'wants' in market economies, however, include far more than subsistence needs.[9]

Sahlins wrote from an avowedly substantivist point of view. Noel Butlin, an economist, argues from a formalist perspective that Aborigines allocated time and resources to all sorts of things, including education and religious life. If we include such values, then Aboriginal 'wants' were not as restricted as Sahlins suggests, and included religious knowledge as well as the sexual and productive services of spouses and children's spouses.

From another perspective, economies like those of Aboriginal people stand as the antithesis of capitalism in being 'gift economies' as opposed to 'commodity economies'. Goods in gift economies do not become commodities when exchanged, and possessions are not private property; instead, transfers take the form of 'inalienable gifts' that retain their links with the donor even after being given. Discussions of gift exchange in the works of Chris Gregory, Annette Weiner, and Maurice Godelier do much to clarify relations of exchange in Australia as well as New Guinea. These writers understand the realm of inalienable possessions and the sacred to be a source of social order and of the value of inalienable gifts, which connect in turn to the more mundane items of everyday distribution. I shall discuss inalienable gifts and possessions in detail in Chapter 12.

This, in brief outline, is the analytical framework I shall bring to bear on the each case study, but how should the comparisons be approached?

Why compare?

In comparing the economy and society of the seven regions my purpose is mainly descriptive and analytical—to map and describe variation in the seven regions in order to shed light on the character of each region, and to bring out their similarities and differences. But some aspects of the resulting patterns demand explanation. In anthropology comparative methods have been recruited to explain connections within and between social or cultural systems.

Comparative analysis has a long history in social and cultural anthropology; indeed, some see it as the essence of the discipline. Nineteenth-century scholars such as E. B. Tylor and Lewis Henry Morgan used comparison and classification of cultural traits to assign them to stages in hypothetical evolutionary sequences. Studies in North America by Franz Boas and his students, including A. L. Kroeber, examined the distribution of cultural traits, related cultural areas to environmental variation, and sought to trace historical connections between cultural areas.[10]

Another broad approach to comparison involves the selection of a number of 'variables' or traits, the systematic analysis of similarities, differences, and correlations between them, and the construction of explanations to account for the correlations. Using a strong system model of society, variation can be construed as resulting from 'transformations' of a prototype or a set of common principles. Lévi-Strauss's analysis of Aboriginal and other kinship systems is an example of this approach. Structural comparisons of societies or regions, such as Marshall Sahlins's study of stratification in Polynesia, can be combined with the construction of long-term historical trajectories drawing on archaeological and linguistic data. A recent exercise of this latter kind is P. V. Kirch and R. C. Green's *Hawaiki*, which reconstructs a prototypical society from the diversity of languages and societies. This method would be difficult to apply to Australia because of the web of cross-cutting connections over many millenia. However, archaeologists and linguists are constructing more limited histories.[11]

I employ a limited comparative analysis to explain some aspects of economy and society that appear to have been linked (Chapter 13). The examination of systemic connections between different aspects of economy and society will suggest some of the conditions under which certain social and cultural forms were able to develop, will reveal some important differences, and will bring out some of the dynamics of these systems. However, because of the small sample the conclusions can only be tentative, although they could be tested against a wider sample and if necessary modified or rejected.

In their introduction to a recent volume on comparison in anthropology, Fox and Gingrich raise the issue of globalisation; they contend that it is inappropriate in a globalising world to treat 'societies' as unconnected case studies. In relation to a reconstruction of modes of social life as they were before the changes brought about by colonisation this objection has less relevance. Nevertheless, we should not assume that the regions compared were discrete, bounded 'societies', for they partook in a continent-wide social network.[12]

The case studies

Each case study draws on the earliest substantial ethnography to be written for the region, illuminated by more recent research. All ethnographic research necessarily took place after British colonisation and settlement had brought about change in Aboriginal societies, so in all cases inferences have to be made about the period prior to colonisation. The ethnographies were shaped not only by the particular social circumstances of the research but by the theoretical and analytical frameworks that inform them. The ethnographic writings on which this book draws reveal the influence of a variety of anthropological paradigms, for the most part evolutionist and functionalist, though in some cases no specific theory at all. But recent research helps us to assess and if necessary reinterpret such work.

Much fuller details of Aboriginal economy and social life exist for some regions than others, and there is little quantitative data on production and consumption or even on the ecology of resources. Information about Gippsland and the southwest is the most fragmentary among the regions studied here. Nevertheless, while there are gaps, sufficient information has been recorded about the southeast and southwest for meaningful comparisons to be made.

What are to be the geographical units of analysis? Since the literature on Aboriginal social life and culture tends to be cast in terms of discrete 'tribes' or peoples such as 'the Kurnai', 'the Aranda' and 'the Walbiri', there is little choice but to begin with such categories. However, several critiques have cast doubt on the validity of a cellular model of Aboriginal sociality. It should not be assumed that these names refer to societies or localised 'social systems', especially given the degree of heterogeneity of both ecologies and cultural forms documented for some regions.[13]

The peoples and regions (see Map 1.1) are as follows:

- Kŭnai people of Gippsland, eastern Victoria[14]
- Yuwaaliyaay people, and their neighbours, of the Darling/Barwon River in northern New South Wales
- Pitjantjatjara people, and their neighbours, of the Western Desert
- Wiil and Minong people of the south coast and hinterland of the southwest region of Western Australia
- 'Sandbeach' people of eastern Cape York Peninsula—the case will focus on northern Sandbeach people (speakers of Umpila and related languages)
- Ngarinyin people, and their neighbours, of the northwest Kimberley; and
- Yolngu people of northeast Arnhem Land.

These names are of varying kinds: *Kŭnai* and *Yolngu* are from the word meaning 'human being', *Pitjantjatjara* distinguishes people by the word they use for 'come/go', and *Yuwaaliyaay* distinguishes people by their particular word for 'no'. Wiil means 'northerners' while Minong is a regional identity. Ngarinyin is the proper name of a language and Sandbeach refers to coastal people.

Map 1.1   The seven case studies

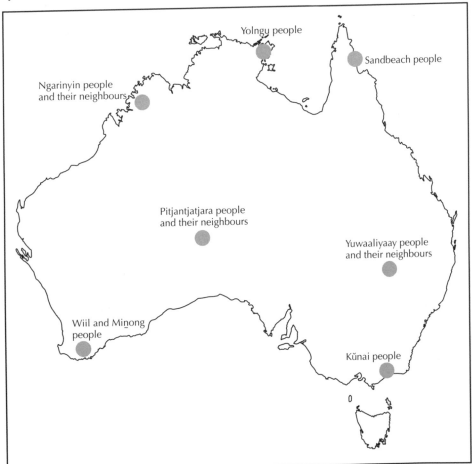

Why have I chosen to study these particular regions? First, the ethnographic record needed to include information on ecology, technology, and resources; the work of Donald Thomson, Norman Tindale, Richard Gould, and Nicolas Peterson pointed me in certain directions. Second, I wanted to include case studies in the southeast and southwest as well as the tropical north and the centre; the work of A. W. Howitt on Kŭnai culture, K. Langloh Parker on Yuwaaliyaay speakers, and the several studies of Wiil and Mi̱nong people appeared to present the richest material on these regions. Third, the case studies needed to encompass broad variation in environments and resources, and needed to sample the known variation in language families and institutional forms; the cases chosen do this. Where possible I also chose regions whose ethnography I was already familiar with, notably northeast Arnhem Land (Yolngu) and Gippsland (Kŭnai).

The seven regions contrast in a number of ways. First, they have very different environments, from the temperate regions with uniform rainfall, through the arid interior, to the tropical zone with a seasonal, monsoon climate. Second, they have contrasting resource bases, from rich estuarine and lacustrine resources of the southeast, through riverine and grassland resources, to the scarcity of water in the arid zone and the rich marine and terrestrial products of the tropical coasts. Third, they represent different language families, both of the very widespread family of languages that linguists call Pama-Nyungan and the very varied non-Pama-Nyungan language families of the northwest of the continent. Fourth, they sample contrasting social-organisational features, from patri-moieties and patri-groups to gender and generation moieties.

Kŭnai people

The people A. W. Howitt called 'Kŭrnai' (Kŭnai, Ganai, or Gunnai) inhabited the major part of what is now known as Gippsland, in eastern Victoria. They exploited the rich resources of the rivers, forests, grass-plains, and lakes, and of the dunes and beaches of the long coastal barrier. Their country formed a crescent between mountains to the north and sea to the south, from Cape Liptrap in the west to Cape Howe in the east, including the lower Snowy River. Westward lay the country of speakers of the Boonwurong language, and to the east, Bidawal (or Maap) people. To the north, in the mountains and on the tableland, lived speakers of Yaitmathang and Ngarigu languages (see Maps 1.1, 2.1, 5.1, and 5.2). The plentiful resources made it possible for Kŭnai to live at quite high population densities by Aboriginal standards.

Geographical barriers isolated Kŭnai people from their neighbours, hemmed in as they were by the mountains to the north, which are snowy in winter, and by swamps and dense scrub to the west. They also differed in language and social organisation from their northerly and westerly neighbours, being culturally closer to Bidawal people along the coast to the east, with whom they had most contact. We shall see that they had quite distinctive institutions—especially their forms of kinship, marriage, and cosmology.[15]

Of the seven peoples in the case studies, Kŭnai experienced the most devastating onslaught from white colonisation, beginning in 1828 with the establishment of whaling stations on Wilsons Promontory, followed by farms throughout the region from the 1830s. By the 1860s, when anthropological research began, the colonial infrastructure was fully in place in Gippsland, with Sale as the regional centre. The Kŭnai population had been decimated by killings and disease, reduced from more than 2000 to less than 200, the majority living at the Lake Tyers Mission (established 1861) and Ramahyuck Mission (1863).

Much of the written evidence regarding the Kŭnai way of life comes from two sources: the published and unpublished writings of the magistrate, administrator, and self-taught geologist and anthropologist A. W. Howitt, and those of the missionary John Bulmer. As well as teaching himself geology, Howitt became an amateur anthropologist and a correspondent of the American anthropologist Lewis Henry Morgan, whom he furnished with information about Australian Aboriginal cultures of the southeast, drawing in turn on his own correspondents. Howitt derived his analytical framework primarily from Morgan's evolutionist scheme. Howitt and Bulmer based their understanding of Kŭnai custom on information from Kŭnai men and women who were living and working on the missions and stations of Gippsland. They included Tulaba Billy McLeod, Mary McLeod, Long Harry Turlburn, Bobby Brown Bundawal, and Big Joe Tankowillin.[16] This book draws on more recent botanical, linguistic, archaeological, and historical research to complement and reinterpret the work of Howitt and Bulmer.

Pitjantjatjara people and their neighbours

The Western Desert is a vast region with a sparse Aboriginal population. It forms part of the arid zone of Australia, with very low and very variable rainfall. We shall see that the search for water dominated Aboriginal relations with the environment, and enforced great mobility. Nevertheless, people were able to exploit a wide variety of terrestrial resources.

Western Desert people identified themselves by local ways of speaking labelled by a characteristic dialect word. These languages formed a chain of dialects of a single Western Desert language, and the related language identities were rather open and overlapped. Indeed, Western Desert cultures were quite similar across the region. The country of Pitjantjatjara and their immediate neighbours included the Rawlinson, Petermann, Warburton, Tomkinson, Mann, Musgrave, and the Everard Ranges and adjacent plains (see Maps 1.1, 2.2, and 5.3).

Although white incursions into the country of Pitjantjatjara people and their neighbours began in the 1870s, the number of cattle in the centre of the continent increased rapidly between 1930 and 1950. Aboriginal people began to settle on stations and government settlements from the 1930s, encouraged by prolonged drought starting in 1926. But many groups, the subject of censuses by Jeremy Long in the mid 1960s, continued to live away from stations and settlements. Thus the 'threshold of colonisation' came late in this region.[17]

The relatively slow pace of social and cultural change enabled anthropologists to carry out research up until the 1970s among people living in the bush as well as on stations and settlements. No one researcher dominates the ethnography of Pitjantjatjara people and their immediate neighbours; after surveys by Spencer and

Gillen, the early work (in the 1930s) of Norman Tindale included studies of ecology, while the Berndts' research at Ooldea in the early 1940s provides the closest to a general ethnography of the region. This book draws on more recent research, such as the work on ecology and economy by Richard Gould and Annette Hamilton, as well as the rich corpus of ethnography of other regions in the Western Desert.

Yuwaaliyaay people and their neighbours

Yuwaaliyaay belonged to a cluster of closely related languages spoken in the region of the Darling/Barwon River and its tributaries. (The Barwon River is the upper extension of the Darling River.) Yuwaaliyaay speakers and other Darling River peoples had access to the resources of rivers and swamps as well as those of the grasslands and woodland, in an environment in which floods alternated with droughts. Darling/Barwon River peoples combined a riverine economy with cereal exploitation on a substantial scale, unlike people of the Murray River to the southwest, for whom seeds were not so important. This semi-arid region allowed only a low population density, higher along the major rivers.

The country associated with the Yuwaaliyaay language lay on the north and northwest side of the Darling/Barwon River, near what is now the border between New South Wales and Queensland, from Brewarrina in the west, probably to what is now the town of Mungindi in the east. The country associated with the closely related Yuwaalaraay language seems to have lain to the north of the Yuwaaliyaay area, including what is now the town of Nindigully on the Moonie River, north of the Queensland border. Gamilaraay country lay on the east side of the Barwon River, and Wayilwan country lay to the south. On the Bokhara River to the west lived speakers of Murruwarri and Barranbinya languages (see Maps 1.1, 2.3, and 5.4). Yuwaaliyaay people participated in the extensive and rather unbounded social network of the Darling River basin.

White incursions into the grasslands to the west of the Great Dividing Range began in the 1820s. Aboriginal people of the Barwon River region faced a massive onslaught in the late 1830s, having already been devastated by smallpox, which spread ahead of the frontier. Nevertheless, as a result of living and working on cattle and sheep stations, the Yuwaaliyaay and their neighbours were evidently able to reproduce many aspects of their way of life into the twentieth century. At Bangate Station, during the last two decades of the nineteenth century, Catherine Parker (who wrote as K. Langloh Parker) recorded customs and myths, accompanied women on their foraging activities, and documented methods of food production. Aboriginal people living at Bangate Station who provided Catherine Parker with information included Boodtha, an elderly woman who became a *wirreenun* (healer) after the loss of a grandchild; Beemunny, an elderly blind woman who told her stories about ancestors; and Yudtha Dulleebah, an old man who instructed her about the significance of the Bora initiation ceremony, fearing it would die with him. I have drawn on Parker's work in this book.

Also useful was the research of R. H. Mathews and others of the same period on the language and rituals of other peoples of the broad region, as well as anthropological, archaeological, and linguistic research carried out in the twentieth century, including that of A. R. Radcliffe-Brown. Harry Allen's PhD thesis on Darling River ecology complements Parker's ethnography to make a rounded case study possible.[18] I also draw on the biography of Jimmy Barker, a Murruwarri man.

Wiil and Minong people

Ethel Hassell gave the name 'Wheelman' to the people whose country was occupied by Jerramungup Station on the upper Gairdner River, near the south coast of the southwest. Wil or Wiil means 'north' in some dialects of the southwest, and Wiilman apparently means 'northerners'. Their coastal neighbours to the south, including what is now Albany, were Minong people (see Maps 1.1, 2.4, 5.5, and 5.6). Because of the fragmentary quality of the research on this region, I draw on the ethnographic sources for both peoples; taken together they make possible a coherent if generalised picture.

The southwest has a unique environment for Australia. The westerlies bring winter rains that water the fertile corner, which is backed by the arid zone to the east. Wiil and Minong people lived toward the more arid side of this fertile region in country of heath and mallee, estuaries and beaches and rugged cliffs, near the eastern extremity of the forest. The population density was probably quite high on the coast, but sparser inland. The southwest forms a distinct culture-area, with closely related dialects and cultural forms.

Of the peoples studied in this book, Minong people probably experienced the earliest prolonged contact with white people, with the establishment of the King George Sound settlement in 1826. Intensive farming of wheat, fruit, market-garden produce and dairy cattle grew rapidly around the main centres, including Albany, and the pastoral industry expanded from the 1840s. The gold rushes of the 1890s further stimulated the influx of population. Aboriginal people in the areas of pastoral settlement fared better than those on whose country intensive cultivation and urban settlement occurred (such as Kŭnai people). Like Yuwaaliyaay people, Minong people were able in the third quarter of the nineteenth century to adapt their social structures to accommodate their relationships with the invading farmers.[19]

The earliest ethnography of the region dates from the first few years of the King George Sound settlement. It takes the form of journals, including those by Captain Collett Barker, commander of the settlement, as well as published observations, such as the excellent ethnographic sketch by Scott Nind. Ethel Hassells's research among Wiil people took place during the two decades from 1870 when she lived on the sheep station at Jerramungup under similar circumstances to Catherine Parker. Her ethnographic writing remained unpublished until it was revised for publication in 1934 and 1936 by the American anthropologist D. S. Davidson. Daisy Bates's travels through Western Australia came at a later date. Her first period of research was 1904–10. An immigrant from Ireland, she worked as a journalist and then for the West Australian Government documenting Aboriginal languages and customs across the state. Her manuscript remained unpublished until 1985, when an abridged version appeared as a book edited by Isobel (Sallie) White. The work includes fragmentary but essential ethnographic information about the southwest, including the Albany region.

The young Mi̱nong man Mokaré provided information to both Barker and Nind. Ethel Hassell names many of the men and women with whom she was acquainted; they include Winmar, Yilgar, Gimbuck, Tupin, and the 'magician' Buckerup. Bates drew on information from Ngalbaitch, a Jerramungup woman, and from Wandinyilmernong and Nebinyan, both Albany men.

The writings of Nind, Barker, Hassell, and Bates make it possible to construct quite a full picture of Wiil and Mi̱nong economy and society. This task is assisted by some excellent recent reconstructions by archaeologists and historians based on the early sources.[20]

Sandbeach people

'Sandbeach people' is a broad expression used by people of eastern Cape York Peninsula, between Temple Bay in the north and Princess Charlotte Bay in the south, to contrast themselves with the 'on top' people of the hinterland. People of this area spoke (and speak) a number of distinct languages, but shared a common orientation towards the sea, as well as technology centred around the hunting of dugong and turtle (see Maps 1.1, 2.5, and 5.7).

This region has a tropical, monsoon climate, with very high summer rainfall and some winter rains. A distinguishing feature of the environment is the shallow coastal water between the mainland and the reefs and cays, exploited for turtle and dugong hunting in outrigger canoes. People of this region also drew on the rich flora and fauna of the coast, estuaries, rivers, and forests of a rather narrow strip between the coast and the ranges. This environment supported a relatively dense population.

The people of the northern two thirds of the region, between Temple Bay and the Stewart River, spoke a cluster of closely related dialects, similar also to the Kaantju language of the hinterland. Most of the available ethnographic information concerns speakers of Kuuku Ya'u and Umpila languages. People to the south of the Stewart River spoke several languages that differed from the northerly ones. This book concerns the more northerly people who shared *kaapay* and *kuyan* patri-moieties and common initiation ceremonies, and who spoke closely related languages. Donald Thomson and others depict the culture of these peoples as somewhat homogeneous.

Sandbeach people formed regular relations with Europeans from the 1870s, when they provided crews for luggers, but it was not until 1925 that they began to be settled on missions, mainly at Lockhart River.[21] Thomson carried out research on a small community living at the mouth of the Stewart River in the late 1920s and at Lockhart River mission. People who gave information to Donald Thomson include Charlie 'Bamboo' Johnson, Big Johnny, Old Charlie Koiyan, and Old Fred Pur'wa. This book also draws on Athol Chase's study of Lockhart in the late 1970s, which in part draws on the memories of old people to reconstruct pre-mission life; I also draw on recent linguistic research by David Thompson and Bruce Rigsby.

Ngarinyin people and their neighbours

The peoples focused on in this case study are speakers of Worrorra, Wunambal, Gamberre, and Ngarinyin languages of the northwest Kimberley. Their languages belong to a very diverse collection of non-Pama-Nyungan languages spoken in the north and northwest of the continent. These peoples form part of what anthropologists have recently identified as the *wanjina-wunggurr* bloc, whose people subscribe to doctrines about these ancestral beings, associated with distinctive rock paintings throughout the region. People of the region also join in the *wurnan* exchange network, linking marriage to the exchange of goods and sacred objects.

Their country in the northwest Kimberley lies within the tropics, with a monsoon climate of high summer rains and rather dry winters. For the most part this country has a very rugged topography of sandstone uplands, cut by rivers and without extensive coastal plains but with a rugged coast (see Maps 1.1, 2.6, and 5.8).

Captain Grey's party had a hostile encounter with Aboriginal people in 1837, and in the early 1880s sheep stations spread in the west Kimberley, later encroaching on Ngarinyin country, while mineral prospecting continued. Hostilities and punitive raids, as well as introduced diseases, took their toll on the Aboriginal population. Missions in the regions began in 1912, and the Ngarinyin and their neighbours also moved to cattle stations and reserves.[22]

The early anthropological research on which this case study is primarily based dates from the 1920s and 1930s, conducted by the missionaries J. R. B. Love and Theodore Hernandez. Research by the anthropologist A. P. Elkin and members of the Frobenius expedition, including Helmut Petri and Theodore Lommel, dates from the same period. I also draw on research conducted from the 1960s up to the present that, because of the degree of cultural continuity, illuminates and fills out aspects of the earlier ethnography. It includes reconstructions of plant use and ecology and technology by Valda Blundell and Ian Crawford, as well as studies of art, cosmology, kinship, language, and relations to land by Alan Rumsey and Tony Redmond. Writings by Aboriginal people from the region include works by the late David Mowaljarlai.

Yolngu people

Northeast Arnhem Land in the Northern Territory comprises a large triangle of land that forms the northwest corner of the Gulf of Carpentaria. It is the home of people formerly known as 'Murngin' in the anthropological literature, and now as 'Yolngu', the word for 'person'. The region has a distinctive culture and group of languages, markedly different grammatically from neighbouring ones. Yolngu languages are of the Pama-Nyungan family (mainly suffixing languages), but they are surrounded by non-Pama-Nyungan families of languages (mainly prefixing). To the west live speakers of Gijingarli and Dangbon languages, to the southwest speakers of Rembarrnga and Ngalkbon languages, and to the south of Ngandi and Nunggubuyu languages. (see Maps 1.1, 2.7, and 5.9)

Northeast Arnhem Land experiences a tropical monsoon climate, with high summer rainfall and a dry winter. The many islands, headlands, bays, and estuaries contain a rich environment of beaches, mangroves, and, in some places, rocky cliffs. Mainland habitats include plains and swamps, rivers and forested upland, while the shallow coastal waters are ideal hunting grounds for marine reptiles as well as dugong. This environment has supported a relatively dense population, especially along the coast and estuaries.

Yolngu people had regular contacts with Macassans, who visited their shores from the early eighteenth century to collect and process trepang in the wet season. After there had been unsuccessful attempts to establish cattle stations in the region, and violent encounters between Yolngu and Japanese pearlers, the Methodist Church established missions in the region starting in 1923. The isolation of the Yolngu people and their neighbours protected them from the worst onslaughts of colonisation, and the tolerant policies of the Methodist missions slowed the pace of social and cultural change.[23]

The anthropological research of W. L. Warner from 1926 to 1929 and Donald Thomson's research in the following decade recorded a way of life apparently little changed from the period before British colonisation. Warner's monograph relies heavily on information from Harry Makarrwala, a leader of the Wan.gurri patri-group who Yolngu identify in their oral tradition as the 'first Aboriginal missionary'. Rraywala, a Mildjingi man from the Glyde River, was one of Donald Thomson's main Yolngu companions. In order to supplement, reinterpret, and contextualise these early findings, I have drawn on research from World War II to the present by a large number of anthropologists, linguists, and archaeologists. As in the northwest Kimberley, the anthropological research in northeast Arnhem Land has traced gradual social and cultural transformations.

The sources

It will already be apparent that this work draws on several kinds of ethnographic sources. First are ethnographies or ethnographic sketches written before the advent of professional anthropology, by interested observers such as Scott Nind and K. Langloh Parker. Second are those of early amateurs with academic connections—A. W. Howitt, for example, corresponded with the evolutionist theorist L. H. Morgan. Third is the work of professionals trained in the natural sciences, but with some training in anthropology, such as Donald Thomson and Norman Tindale. Fourth is work by professionally trained anthropologists like W. L. Warner, and, finally, I am drawing on the recent research of scholars in a variety of disciplines—archaeologists, anthropologists, ecologists, historians, and linguists—whose work can help us to interpret the earlier writings. Each category of sources has advantages, but also brings its own particular problems of interpretation.

We have seen that in the case of the Yuwaaliyaay people and their neighbours, and the Wiil and Minong peoples, Aboriginal modes of life displayed a marked continuity through the early pastoral era, with gradual changes in social practices, especially as the Aboriginal population declined and the density of white settlement increased.

The main ethnographies derive from early colonial contact, and then the late nineteenth and early twentieth centuries, before the era of professional anthropology. An advantage of early observers' reports is that they include details of life on the frontier, and reflect broad interests that would have been edited out of work from a narrower professional framework. The main interpretive problem for this project stems from the fragmentary and unsystematic nature of these reports. Writings of the later colonial observers resulted from informal research at Aboriginal camps on cattle and sheep stations, so I have to take into account the effects of colonial life. For example, there is little fighting in Parker's book, either because of the station context or her self-censorship.

Partly because of the intensive farming and the density of white settlement, Kŭnai people suffered massive loss of life through violence and disease, reducing the population to less than 10% of its former size by 1870. The ethnography of Howitt was largely a reconstruction of past life-ways drawing on the memories of older people as well as on records of continuing practices such as marriage, and doctrines such as ancestral narratives. The evolutionist framework that informed Howitt's work encouraged systematic recording and analysis of institutions such as kinship and 'local organisation', and he kept his descriptions rather separate from his evolutionist interpretation. But his project of reconstruction led him to edit out what he thought were intrusions from mission life, and he relied heavily on people's memories of the past. Howitt's accounts of some institutions, especially 'local organisation', require reinterpretation both to deal with the internal inconsistencies and to take account of more recent understandings and analogies with other regions.

The advantage of work by people trained in the natural sciences is that it is a good source of ecological information, although it can incorporate anthropological frameworks rather uncritically. The main issues of interpretation arising from the work of professionally trained anthropologists are that they are late in colonial/postcolonial trajectories, and particular paradigms strongly shape (and limit) their interpretations. However, within their fields of interest these works tend to be the most thorough and systematic. Anthropological research has continued through to the present, especially in the Western Desert and the tropical north, documenting social and cultural change as well as continuing practices. Recent ethnographic inquiries therefore shed light on the past, as does historical, linguistic, and archaeological research in other regions.

The sources are very uneven, both in the range of topics covered and the thoroughness of that coverage. I have reinterpreted some descriptions and terminology in the light of more recent anthropological understanding of Aboriginal cultures and sociality. Quite often information on a certain aspect of economy and society is simply unavailable for a given region. There is no possibility of recovering the whole texture of Minong social life of the early nineteenth century—all we have are some oral traditions and the writings of Scott Nind, Collett Barker, Daisy Bates, and a few others. Their language provides the grid through which we can imagine Minong life, and the gaps remain unfillable, except by analogy and inference. This work is a compilation of those uncertain guides, each constructed in a distinctive language, each incomplete to a greater or lesser degree. The 'findings' then must be tentative, susceptible to revision in the light of new evidence or a re-reading of the old, and in the light of criticism of the categories, conceptual schemes, and theories that inform them.

Outline of chapters

Part I of the book begins with Chapter 2 on environments and the resources on which people drew. Following chapters move on to the technologies used, the patterns of movement and settlement, and the human populations these environments supported.

The chapters of Part II outline institutional fields: the framing of broad identities in terms of language and totems, kinship and marriage, cosmologies and quasi-technologies ('sorcery', 'magic', and healing), and governance. They draw out the implications of practices within these fields for the organisation of economy, further explored in the third part of the book. Part III is about economic relations and processes. The chapters describe the variation in the control of the productive means, especially land, waters, and technology; the organisation of production; distribution and consumption; exchange, and what has been called 'trade'.

The introductions to the chapters and the glossary should make the book accessible to students and general readers as well as a specialist audience. The reader may approach the book in one of several ways. You could begin with the first and last chapters, which provide an overview of the argument and summarise the findings. Each chapter of Parts II and III begins with an introduction to a topic and a discussion of theoretical and analytical issues, before surveying that aspect in all seven regions. Each of these chapters can be read independently. The ethnography of a particular region can be traced through the relevant sections of the chapters of Parts II and III, and Table 13.10 summaries the key features of each region. The concluding chapter draws the comparisons together, suggests some explanations for the variation between regions, and reviews some of the issues that have arisen in the book. Note also that an Australian National University–supported web site for this book (at http://arts.anu.edu.au/aeastc/) provides a range of suppletmentary materieals, including short regional ethnographies and detailed descriptions of the technology of several regions.

Further reading

For an overview of approaches to economy in Aboriginal societies, see Chris Anderson's chapter in *Social Anthropology and Australian Aboriginal* Studies, edited by R. M. Berndt and Bob Tonkinson (1988); and for an analysis of the economy of an Aboriginal 'outstation', see Jon Altman's *Hunter-Gatherers Today* (1987). Recent works in the anthropology of economy include *Observing the Economy* by Gregory and Altman (1989), *New Directions in Economic Anthropology* by Susan Narotzky, and *Cultural Economies: Past and Present* by Rhoda Halperin (1994). James Woodburn's elaboration of the distinction between immediate and delayed return systems has been influential in studies of hunter–gatherer peoples; see, for example, his 'African hunter–gatherer social organization: Is it best understood as a product of encapsulation?' (1988).

On the place of the concepts of institution and field in social analysis, see, for example, Mary Le Cron Foster's and Simon Roberts's contributions to *The Companion Encyclopedia of Anthropology* (2002), Anthony Giddens's *The Constitution of Society* (1984), and Pierre Bourdieu's *Distinction* (1992). For further reading on comparison in anthropology, see the works cited in Chapter 13, which continues the discussion of this theme.

Notes

1   Examples of overviews of Aboriginal social life and culture include *The Australian Aborigines: How to Understand Them* by A. P. Elkin (1954), *The World of the First Australians* by Ronald and Catherine Berndt (1981), and Ken Maddock's *The Australian Aborigines: A Portrait of their Society* (1972, 1982). For comparisons between the north and the centre see Hamilton (1980, 1981a). Studies of Aboriginal kinship and social organisation include Radcliffe-Brown (1931), Elkin (1931b, 1932), Scheffler (1978), Shapiro (1979), and Turner (1980), and studies of Aboriginal religion include Berndt (1974). Chase and Sutton (1987) compare the ecologies of three regions of Cape York Peninsula.

2   Peter Sutton's recently coined contrast between 'classical' and 'post-classical' social formations (1986) avoids some of the problematic connotations of the category 'traditional', but it retains the dichotomy.

3   The expression 'people without history' is drawn from Eric Wolf (1982).

4   Norman Tindale published his tribal maps in 1974 (Tindale 1974).

5   General works on Aboriginal economy include Butlin (1993), Dingle (1988), and Lawrence (1968). Community studies include those by Altman (1987) and Anderson (1984).

6   See Anderson (1988) for a review of approaches to Aboriginal economy. For discussions of ecology and economy in anthropology, see Ellen (1982) and Narotzky (1997).

7   See Giddens (1979) on institutions; see also Bourdieu (1977).

8   On the concept of 'institution' in anthropology and sociology see Foster (2002: 367) and Giddens (1984); on social fields see Bourdieu (1992), Moore (1979: 55), and Roberts (2002).

9   See Sahlins's book *Stone Age Economics* (1972).

10   See, for example, Kroeber (1939) on natural and cultural areas of North America.

11   See Kirch and Green (2001) on Polynesia, and McConvell and Evans (1997) on Australia.

12   See Fox and Gingrich (2002) on comparison in anthropology.

13   For critiques of cellular models see, for example, Sutton (1978) and Keen (1995).

14   I have retained Howitt's orthography of Kŭnai words for consistency, but deleted the 'r' in 'Kŭrnai', which Howitt seems to have used to lengthen the vowel (from *a* to *aa*). Howitt used a 'u' with a diacritic to denote the vowel sound in, for example, 'cut'; linguists usually represent this sound with the letter 'a'. Aboriginal people of the region spell the name 'Kurnai' or 'Gunnai'; Hercus's spelling is *ganai* (1986).

15   See Howitt (1880: 233) on Kŭnai relations with Bidawal.

16   On Howitt's relations with Aboriginal people see Attwood (1986; 1989: 71–2). On the social history of the region see Attwood (1986, 1989), Harris (1988), and Pepper and D'Araugo (1985).

17   See Layton (1986: 51–118) on the history of this part of the Western Desert.

18   On the history of the Darling/Barwon region see Goodall (1996: 31–2). The most infamous incident was the Myall Creek massacre.

19   See Haebich (1985) on the social history of the southwest.

20   Reconstructions of the ecology and society of the region include those by Bird (1985), Bird and Beeck (1988), Ferguson (1987), Le Souëf (1993), Meagher (1974), and Meagher and Ride (1979).

21   On the social history of the Sandbeach region see Chase (1978, 1989) and Rigsby and Chase (1998).

22   On the social history of the northwest Kimberley see Blundell (1975 vol. I: 32–58).

23   See RM and CH Berndt (1954) on the social history of northeast Arnhem Land. See MacKnight (1976) on the Macassans in Arnhem Land.

PART I

Ecology

Environments and Resources

Introduction

This chapter examines the diversity of plant and animal species that the people of each region used, the environments in which they were found, their habitats and seasonality.

Environmental determinism

Environmental features are among the determinants of human action. To say this is not to propose a crude environmental determinism that explains features of society and psychology according to ecology and climate, for environmental features determine some aspects of social life more directly than others: more directly in the case of seasonal movement by hunters and gatherers, less directly in the case of institutional forms such as marriage. Moreover, the ways in which environmental features affect human actions and institutions depend on the instruments, techniques, knowledge, values, and forms of organisation that people bring to bear on them. Features that people are least able to change, such as rainfall and the presence of the sea, constrain and modify human behaviour to the greatest degree. These do not determine social forms in a simple way, for very different social institutions have developed in similar environments. However, as we shall see, certain environmental features do provide conditions for the development and reproduction of certain practices.[1]

I have sketched here what has been called a 'possibilist' position on the relationship between environment and society, according to which the environment imposes limiting conditions or boundaries on human action and social relations rather than 'causing' them. The relation between human practices and resources, however, is a mutual, interactive one. We shall see that Aboriginal people managed resources through a number of means (using fire, for example), with profound short- and long-term effects, shaping Australian landscapes. People's activities had effects on environments, not all of them intended, and these effects altered the conditions that enabled and constrained particular human activities.[2]

Australian environments

The case studies sample the diverse range of environments in Australia. Geographers divide the Australian land mass into three zones: the Shield, which comprises the western and central portions; the Highland Zone, which is the eastern sector, including Tasmania; and, in between these two zones, the Lowland Zone, which runs from the Gulf of Carpentaria in the north to the mouth of the Murray River in the south. This chapter will sample all of these areas. But certain *general* features of Australian environments are important to an understanding of Aboriginal relations to land and resources.

Perhaps the most significant feature of Australian environments is the overall aridity of the continent, and its susceptibility to regular droughts driven by the El Niño southern oscillation. La Niña–related rainfall causes widespread flooding in eastern Australia and is associated with a greater frequency of cyclones in the tropical north than in El Niño phases.

Various factors, including the summer monsoon in the north and winter westerlies in the southwest, result in a general pattern of moister coastal regions and hinterlands, tailing off to a very arid interior. In between, the semi-arid belt is much more extensive in the north and east than the south and west. Tables 2.1 and 2.2, which will be referred to throughout the chapter, show the variation in mean rainfall and temperature in the seven regions.

Average annual rainfall is less than 300 millimetres over half the area of Australia, and summer temperatures are very high over much of the continent. The low average rainfall and high evaporation rate inland, as well as the absence of permanent snowfields, means that water does not remain long on the surface. Permanently flowing rivers are largely confined to eastern and southeastern catchments; flow varies greatly along the courses of these rivers (by a factor 11,000 for the Darling River), and local floods alternate with droughts. Water courses over most of the continent are intermittent, and about a third of the continent lacks coordinated surface drainage, notably on the Shield. Half the land mass has no surface water draining to the sea. In the north, most run-off occurs in summer when the rivers flood.[3]

A second general feature of Australian environments is the fire-resistance and fire-dependence of many Australian plants. These qualities are related to the cycle of droughts, which enhances the likelihood of wildfires caused by lightning or human action. Plants and animals have adapted both to drought and to fire. In the case of spinifex, for example, fires release nutrients and clear away old plants, allowing new ones to germinate; these plants in turn promote burning through the flammable oil in their leaves. Many plants depend on fire to reproduce: for example, fire induces seed release in eucalypts. The Aboriginal use of controlled burning, in what Rhys Jones called 'fire-stick farming', modified these effects greatly. (See Chapter 3 for more on the use of fire.)

Ecology and seasonality

Many of the studies on which this chapter draws examine the range of food species, the habitats in which they were found, and their seasonality; Donald Thomson and Norman Tindale pioneered this kind of research in Australia. I will be drawing on their work in the sections on Pitjantjatjara, Sandbeach, and Yolngu resources.

The location and seasonality of resources greatly affected the organisation of production, for people had to move to the locations of food resources; the degree, range, and seasonality of mobility varied greatly in Australia. The limited storage, and more or less immediate consumption, of foods meant that food species had to be available 'in the field' all year round. People of each region could choose from very many species, but some were more abundant than others, and people valued some foods more than others; less-preferred foods served as buffers against the shortage of popular ones. The suite of technologies was important too: food-procurement technologies determined what resources people could obtain, and transport technologies dictated the range and speed of movement (see Chapter 3).

Table 2.1   Rainfall in the seven regions

Region	Highest monthly mean (mm)	Lowest monthly mean (mm)	Annual mean (mm)	Variability index
Gippsland				0.5
Orbost	85.9 (Jun)	57.5 (Feb)	851.9	
Omeo	72.2 (Oct)	45.9 (Apr)	682.1	
Sale	63.0 (Oct)	41.5 (Jul)	607.3	
Wilsons Promontory	121.4 (Jul)	46.3 (Feb)	1059.8	
Darling/Barwon River				1.25
Brewarrina	51.8 (Jan)	22.2 (Aug)	413.2	
Walgett	63.3 (Jan)	27.4 (Dec)	477.8	
Western Desert				1.75
Gibson Desert	45 (Feb)	5 (Jul, Sep)	231	
Warburton	28 (Feb)	4 (Jul, Sep)	ca 215	
Ernabella	43.7 (Jan)	11.9 (Sep)	274.9	
Southwest				<0.5
Albany	145.3 (Jul)	23 (Jan)	934.3	
Bremer Bay	—	—	625	
Kojonup	89.6 (Jun)	13.6 (Jan)	533.5	
Lake Grace	57 (Jul)	13 (Jan)	354	
Eastern Cape York Peninsula				0.75
Lockhart River airport	442.1 (Mar)	17.8 (Sep)	2159	
Northwest Kimberley				0.75
Kuri Bay	392.8 (Jan)	1.3 (Aug)	1373.7	
Gibb River	193 (Jan)	1 (Aug)	757	
Fitzroy Crossing	153.2 (Jan)	1.4 (Aug)	541.1	
Northeast Arnhem Land				<0.75
Milingimbi	256.6 (Jan)	0.5 (Aug)	1156.6	
Yirrkala	262.5 (Jan)	3.3 (Sep)	1317.9	

Source: Commonwealth Bureau of Meteorology (2003)

Table 2.2   Temperatures in the seven regions

Region	Hottest month: Mean daily max. (°C)	Hottest month: Mean daily min. (°C)	Coolest month: Mean daily max. (°C)	Coolest month: Mean daily min. (°C)	Highest max. temp. (°C)	Lowest min. temp. (°C)
Gippsland						
Orbost	25.5 (Feb)	13.5 (Feb)	14.7 (Jul)	4.2 (Jul)	45.2 (Jan)	−3.2 (Jul)
Sale	26.1 (Feb)	13.0 (Feb)	13.8 (Jul)	3.6 (Jul)	—	—
Wilsons Promontory	20.5 (Feb)	14.7 (Feb)	12.2 (Jul)	8.3 (Jul)	41.1 (Jan)	−0.6 (Jun)
Darling/Barwon River						
Brewarrina	36.1 (Jan)	20.4 (Jan)	18.1 (Jul)	4.3 (Jul)	48.9 (Dec)	−4.2 (Jul)
Walgett	35.5 (Jan)	20.5 (Jan)	17.5 (Jul)	4.4 (Jul)	48.0 (Jan)	−3.8 (Jul)
Western Desert						
Ernabella	34.6 (Jan)	19.9 (Jan)	17.8 (Jul)	3.4 (Jul)	43.0 (Jan)	−7.6 (Jul)
Southwest coast						
Albany	22.9 (Feb)	15.3 (Feb)	15.6 (Jul)	8.0 (Jul)	38.9 (Mar)	2.7 (Aug)
Bremer Bay	24 (Jan)	15 (Jan)	16 (Jul)	8.0 (Jul)	—	—
Southwest hinterland						
Kojonup	29.5 (Jan)	13.2 (Jan)	14.4 (Jul)	5.9 (Jul)	44.2 (Jan)	−3.5 (May)
Lake Grace	30.0 (Jan)	13 (Jan)	ca 15 (Jul)	ca 6 (Jul)	—	—
Eastern Cape York Peninsula						
Lockhart River	31.5 (Jan)	23.6 (Jan)	27.0 (Jul)	19.2 (Jul)	40.2 (Nov)	3.3 (Jul)
Northwest Kimberley						
Kuri Bay	34.2 (Apr)	26.1 (Dec)	31.2 (Jul)	18.8 (Jul)	42.9 (Nov)	7.0 (Jul)
Northeast Arnhem Land						
Milingimbi	33.6 (Nov)	24.5 (Jan)	28.8 (Jul)	18.2 (Jul)	39.6 (Nov)	7.5 (Jul)
Yirrkala	30.5 (Dec)	24.9 (Dec)	27.5 (Jul)	20.3 (Jul)	37.8 (Dec)	12.5 (Jul)

Source: Commonwealth Bureau of Meteorology (2003)

The relation between animal and vegetable resources

The relative contribution of animal and vegetable foods has been the subject of some controversy. In 1964, Mervyn Meggitt proposed that 70–80% of the Aboriginal diet in central and northern Australia consisted of vegetable foods. On the basis of more recent and more extended fieldwork in north-central Arnhem Land, Betty Meehan and Rhys Jones concluded that 40–50% of the diet by weight of Anbarra people consisted of flesh, predominantly fish, rising to 80–90% in the late dry season, when vegetable foods declined. These figures are consistent with an early (but limited) study of the Kunwinjku people of western Arnhem Land by Margaret McArthur, and with Nicolas Peterson's study of Yolngu people at Mirrngadja in northeast Arnhem Land. Apart from this information on Arnhem Land, the only other useful data on food production in any of the regions discussed in this book is from Richard Gould's studies of the Western Desert; there is considerable difference between the findings for these two areas. This issue of animal versus vegetable foods relates in part to the difference between men's and women's production, for women produced the bulk of vegetable foods, as well as the bulk of small game, crustaceans, and invertebrates.[4]

With these broad features in mind, I turn now to the case studies. They survey environmental conditions and the ethnographic evidence regarding water supply, the range of food resources, the habitats in which they were found, and their seasonality. (For an overview see the conclusion to this chapter, and Tables 13.1 and 13.2 in the last chapter of the book.)

Kŭnai people

Kŭnai people lived (and their descendants remain) in an environment with a temperate climate and high rainfall, with summer and winter rains (Map 5.1 shows the region the Kŭnai occupied). They enjoyed the rich resources of estuaries, lakes, swamps, plains, rivers, and forest.

Land forms

What is now called Gippsland lies in eastern Victoria at the southern end of the Great Dividing Range, between 37° and 39° south and about 146° and 149° east. It consists of a crescent of foothills, alluvial plains, and coastal plains bounded to the south by sea and to the north by elevated tablelands (nearly 2000 metres at their highest) characterised by low relief and wide shallow valleys. Broad in the west, the coastal plain becomes narrow to the east as it passes the Gippsland Lakes, and almost peters out near the mouth of the Cann River. The Strzelecki Range rises from the coastal plain in the southwest of the region, near Wilsons Promontory, which encloses deep bays. The long coastal sand-barrier is an important geographical feature, and gave rise to the extensive lakes, which are flooded estuaries, into which most of the major rivers flow. An exception was the Snowy River, which, before the construction of the hydro-electric scheme, had the heaviest flow of Gippsland's rivers. It flooded regularly with the spring thaw, fed by the melting snow of the Snowy Mountains.

Climate

Gippsland has a temperate and moist climate, with a long, warm (sometimes hot) summer and a cool winter, and with a gradual transition from the warmer and drier lowlands to the cooler and wetter highlands (Tables 2.1 and 2.2).[5] Rainfall in Gippsland is seasonally quite uniform; it is moderate on the plains and increases with altitude and from west to east. Frequent heavy downpours result in rapid rises in the short coastal rivers and streams, and flooding of low-lying country such as (in former times) the Snowy River flats. Importantly, variability is relatively low in

Gippsland (less than 0.5), but long-term variations include El Niño droughts about every five years or so; the Avon River dried up during the 1967–68 drought.

The narrow coastal belt has generally mild temperatures because of the moderating influence of the sea. Temperatures rise on the plains, then decrease with altitude, with severe winter frosts and snow in country above 600 metres (see Table 2.2). Gippsland enjoys a comparatively long growing season: nine months on the coast and seven months in the tablelands.

Habitats and resources

As Map 2.1 shows, the Gippsland environment was very diverse, from montane and wet forests on higher land, down to the grass-plains, lakes, and swamps, and the long coastal barrier. The very diverse plant communities were (and some remain) host to many species of animals and birds, including a very wide variety of edible species.

Map 2.1   Gippsland vegetation

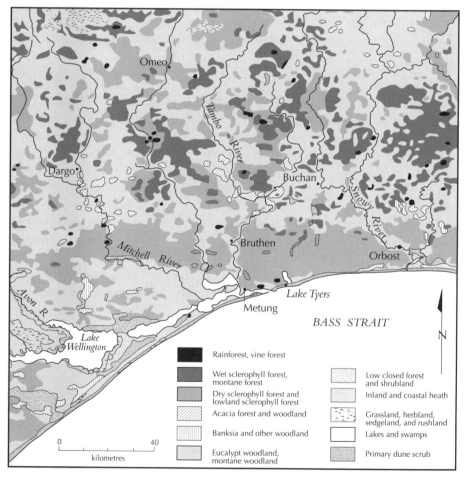

Source: Commonwealth of Australia (2003)

Gippsland is generally a well-watered place, though subject to drought. Lakes and rivers abound, and in some years flooding creates an abundance of water. Along the coastal dunes, people could obtain fresh water from small swamps and by digging.

Beth Gott's research shows that the staple foods were 'roots' of various kinds, which constituted 32% of the plant species recorded as being used for food in Victoria. These had the advantage of being available longer through the year, and reproduction through root propagation enabled a large amount to be collected within a small area. I will begin with the region around the Snowy River in the east of Kŭnai country.[6]

Some food resources grew in a wide range of habitats—for example, edible roots, rhizomes, and tubers, such as Austral bracken, the fibrous root of which was roasted and the starch beaten out, and 'blackfellow's bread' (*Polyporus mylitlae*), an edible fungus that was occasionally eaten. The *Geranium* species with edible roots grew in dry forest, rainforest, gully, grassland, and alpine habitats. Edible seeds or nuts, as well as fruits, could be obtained in many habitats. Fruits included cherry ballart (*Exocarpos* sp.), coprosma, and kangaroo apple (*Solanum vescum*). Kŭnai men would have found emus in a range of forest habitats, from coastal banksia woodland to riparian forests.

High up on the margins of Kŭnai country are the montane woodlands, tableland forests, and sub-alpine vegetation of snow gum (*E. pauciflora*) and other species. Together with the alpine habitats, these yielded plants with edible roots such as the bulbine lily, grass lily, and yam daisy. But rather few kinds of mammal and reptile inhabited the higher country.

Recent research describes a wide variety of plant communities in the east Gippsland forests. Patches of various kinds of dry forest, dominated by several species of *Eucalypt* (such as silvertop), covered the dissected foothills and inter-montane basins up to about 1000 metres or so. Various tree species dominated in the rain-shadow valleys, on the rocky outcrops, and on the moister slopes and gullies, with tall mountain ash prolific at higher elevations. Paperbarks and tea-trees lined the rivers. Patches of cool temperate rainforest occur at elevations over 500 metres, with dry rainforest in the rain-shadow valleys and lower gullies. Lowland forest with yellow stringybark or silvertop covered the foothills up to 200 metres (about 20 kilometres inland), and coastal grassy forest clothed the lower land. (Because of the nature of the source maps, Map 2.1 generalises these categories.)

In the dry forests, tuberous herbs, including the lilies, orchids, bindweed, clematis, *Geranium* species, *Hypoxis* species, and yam daisy, provided year-round staples. Fruits included the cherry ballart. Pith and leaves of the tree-ferns (*dagal, karak*), eaten raw or baked, as well as *Dicksonia australis*, seem to have been particularly important in the diet, as were various greens, less readily available in the forests of higher altitudes. The manna gum (*E. viminalis*) and other species produced sugary pellets that could be collected from the ground, and were home to lerp, the shells of small sap-sucking insects that were also a source of sugar. A number of large reptiles inhabited the woodlands and forests, including those of the river-banks (riparian forests).

The lowland forest, rain-shadow woodland, and moist and montane forests provided habitats for a number of larger macropods, as well as small mammals. The box/ironbark woodland and rocky outcrop scrublands were home to few mammals, with the rain-shadow woodlands intermediate in richness of species. The dry forests of the foothills and inter-montane basins were home to a similar range of bird species.

In the wet forests, food staples were in short supply; tree ferns and bracken would have been the best source of food, and seasonal fruits could have been obtained in these habitats. The wonga pigeon, several kinds of cockatoo, and other birds were found in the riparian forests.

Heathlands, with their rich complement of shrubs, sedges, and orchids, spread along the boundaries of the river flats and east across the coastal plains, with patches in the open forest inland. Species of *Caladenia* and *Diuris* orchids provided edible roots. The fairly dense vegetation of the wet heathland provided continuous cover for ground-dwelling mammals, including the potoroo and black wallaby, which presumably were harder to hunt in this habitat. Among the birds of the coastal heathland were quails and cockatoos.

The river flats of the Snowy River, which extended about 20 kilometres up the river from the mouth, flooded in most years following the melting of snow in the high country, in some years creating a huge supply of water. Near the mouth of the Snowy River a complex web of swamps, creeks, and small lakes carries salt-marsh and estuarine-wetland vegetation.

Aquatic habitats provided important plant staples. *Typha* (bulrush), regarded as the most important staple, and water ribbons, were unsuited to rapid rocky streams, requiring some soil or mud in which to take root. Bulmer recorded a wide range of aquatic bird species eaten by Kŭnai people, who exploited the wetland habitats for larger water birds and their eggs; they especially valued swan eggs. The important reptile of the wetlands was the snake-necked tortoise, used for both its flesh and eggs. People also ate coastal and marine birds such as cormorants, shags, sea eagles, and gulls.

Many species of fish were present, at certain stages of their life-cycle, in the estuaries, lakes, rivers, and creeks, adapted to varying salinity; they were of economic importance in different seasons. Some fresh-water species, found in the lakes, spent part of their life-cycle in the estuaries, where they spawned or developed. Rivers and inland wetlands were home to the platypus and eastern water rat as well as fish.

The dunes above the long, sandy beaches carry several complexes of coastal vegetation, dominated by coastal tea-tree and coast wattle. To the east of the Snowy River estuary the coastal dune barrier separates Lake Corringle from the sea, and rocky points form the nodes of shallow bays, rich in shellfish.

The coastal forests provided a source of edible acacia gum, which was mixed with water as a drink, as well as eucalyptus gums. Mistletoe provided edible fruits, and nectar could be obtained from flowering plants such as honey-pots and banksias. Common bittercress was eaten in coastal areas, while pigface in the primary dune scrub provided greens, seeds, and a sweet red fruit, and acacia (wattle) gum could also be found in these habitats.

Many types of mammal lived in the coastal sclerophyll forest. The smallest mammals and reptiles were in the dune scrub and coastal banksia woodland, but larger mammals also foraged here. Among the invertebrates, grubs (*krang*) could be obtained from several kinds of tree.

Table 2.3   Some Kūnai food resources through the year   ■ = available

	Jan	Feb	Mar	Apr	May	Jun	Jul	Aug	Sep	Oct	Nov	Dec
Vegetable foods— Roots and tubers												
Wetland varieties:												
• Typha (bulrush)			■	■	■							
• Other wetland varieties								■	■	■		
Coastal varieties	■	■									■	■
Vegetable foods—Fruits												
Lacustrine fruits								■	■	■		
Coastal varieties:												
• Kangaroo apples and other species	■										■	■
• Pigface		■	■									
Fish												
Lacustrine fish								■	■	■		
Eel, mullet, flounder											■	
River fish					■	■	■					
Mammals												
Forest—wallaby, kangaroo, etc.	■	■			■	■	■				■	■
Birds												
Waterfowl—swans, ducks								■	■			
Megapodes—emu										■	■	■
Cockatoos and other parrots								■	■	■		

A marked feature of the beaches along much of the Gippsland coast, although not east of Lake Tyers, is that they form part of the sand barrier, giving ready access to marine as well as lake and estuary species. Kŭnai people exploited the occasional beached whale, and killed seals on the beach. Shellfish and crustacea (including crabs, rock lobster, freshwater crayfish, and freshwater mussels) provided a more regular food supply.[7]

The west of the region presented a similar range of habitats. In addition, the long chain of lakes formed by the coastal barrier (130 kilometres long, from Lake Tyers in the east to Jack Smith Lake in the west) was a prominent feature, together with the extensive plains, which included areas of grassland.

Grassland habitats are not well described in the literature as they have been replaced by farmlands, but small perennial herbaceous plants survived best in open forests and plains. Many of the forest plants with edible roots and tubers were to be found in the grasslands, as well as *Hypoxis* species (yellow star and golden weather-glass). Echidnas and long-nosed bandicoots lived in these habitats, and the grasslands presumably also supported bustards and emus (which were valuable for eggs as well as meat), as well as large mammals. The extensive lakes and swamps of this part of Gippsland were rich in fish, fowl, and aquatic plants. Wetland and coastal resources would have been similar to those of the east. Further west, near Wilsons Promontory, people used canoes in the coastal water to visit the islands for mutton birds and shellfish.[8]

Foods according to season

How Kŭnai people scheduled their foraging is not recorded in detail, but it has been possible to reconstruct a generalised account of the seasonal availability of some major resources from the ethnographic and ethnobotanical sources. Table 2.3 shows that summer foods included fish of the lakes, such as eel, mullet, and flounder, and vegetable foods of coastal habitats, such as kangaroo apples and various roots and tubers (including *Typha* species). Kangaroo apples appear in profusion after fire, so Kŭnai people may have deliberately managed them through burning off. Eels appeared in such profusion in some years that people came down from the hills to the lakes to catch them. In the late summer people hunted macropods as well as emu in the forests, and small mammals became more common in the diet. People preferred to harvest *Typha* (bulrush) in the autumn when the tubers were at their most nutritious. Winter foods included fish from the rivers as well as mammals of the forest and plains. In spring people relied on fish from the lakes once more, various fruits, wetland vegetable foods, waterfowl and other birds. The movement of people reflected the seasonality of resources (see chapter 4).

Pitjantjatjara people and their neighbours

We now move near to the centre of the continent on the Shield, where the Pitjantjatjara and their neighbours lived, and still live, within the belt of maximum aridity, between about 20° and 30° south, and 125° and 135° east (see Map 5.3). The environment and resources of this region, on the southern fringe of the arid zone's 'grain belt', were very different from those of the southeast, much sparser.

Land forms

The Western Desert lies on the extensive plateau that forms part of the Western Shield of Australia, within the region of uncoordinated drainage. It rises to more than 300 metres in height, with ranges over 600 metres. Mountain desert predominates in the sandstone and granite Warburton, Tomkinson, Petermann, Mann, and Musgrave Ranges, rising to 1254 metres at Mount Morris. These ranges and the adjacent plains are the home of Pitjantjatjara-speaking people and their neighbours. They lie between about 23° and 25°70' south, and about 125° and 133° east. The vast areas of the Gibson Desert to the west and the northern part of the Great Victoria Desert to the south consist of flat or broadly undulating sand-plains and sand-ridge desert. Parallel sand ridges, up to 30 metres high, lie about 400 metres apart along the line of the prevailing winds, stabilised by vegetation.

Shield deserts lie to the north of the ranges, in the country of the Pintupi people. These deserts are an ancient, stable sand surface with extensive sand and stony laterite plains of low relief, with rocky plains and mesas. Disconnected drainage systems centre on salt-lakes such as Lake Mackay, Lake Hazlett, and Lake Amadeus. Occasional flooding occurs along lines of 'river lakes'.[9]

Climate

The Western Desert is very arid, with a mean annual rainfall of 275 millimetres at Ernabella but less than 200 millimetres in the Gibson Desert, which is the driest region (see Table 2.1).[10] The summer rains, influenced by the northwest monsoon in the north of the region, take the form of heavy showers, while the winter rains are often a cold, light drizzle, with occasional hail-showers and, very rarely, snow in the west. Rainfall is *extremely variable,* both in terms of total rainfall from year to year and in the same month in successive years, with a variability index of nearly 2.0. It also varies greatly from place to place across the desert. Because rains are irregular, often falling in local showers, one area may become green and fertile while an adjoining area remains dry. Overall, effective rainfall in the region is low.

The region experiences very hot summers and warm winters (see Table 2.2). The lack of cloud cover creates strong contrasts between diurnal and nocturnal temperatures; in July, temperatures can drop to several degrees below zero at night, rising to an average of 27°C in the early afternoon. Relative humidity is low, varying on average from 25% to 40% during the year.

Habitats and resources

Over 100 species of plant were potential sources of food in the west of the Western Desert (comprising about 35% of the recorded flora), of which 20 to 40 were sig-

nificant staples. People especially prized quandong (*Santalum acuminatum*) for its suc-
culence and sweetness. Many supplementary foods added variety and could be used
if the staples became scarce, and some species continued to be productive even in
conditions of low rainfall. Importantly, people could manipulate the distribution of
Solanum and other species through the use of fire, and the spreading of seed ensured
predictable patches of resources (see Chapter 3).[11]

Pitjantjatjara people preferred to have some meat in their diet, but game was
rather scarce. People regularly hunted more than a dozen species of animal, and
game included adult birds, nestlings, and reptiles (a particularly reliable source of
food). As well as meat, people ate honey ants, white ants, grubs, and the eggs of birds
such as emus, eagles, and bustards. Dingoes and ravens were eaten only when other
game was scarce.

Two characteristics of the desert fauna are particularly important from the point
of view of foraging. One is that many species live in burrows or shelter under rocks,
so they have to be extracted by digging. Another is that population sizes, especially
of the small mammals, are very erratic. Ephemeral plants appear and insects proliferate after rains; seed and insect-eating mammals also multiply, sometimes in plague
proportions, and, with them, carnivores. Conversely, as the resources at the bottom
of the food-chain diminish, so do the populations higher up. These fluctuations
added to the uncertainty of life in the desert.

Writers on Western Desert peoples agree that the scarcity of water was the main
constraint on population, and the search for water dominated relations with the land,
necessitating constant movement (Plate 2.1). There are no flowing rivers in the
region. Indeed, few parts of the Western Desert have continuous river channels: most

Plate 2.1   A Pitjantjatjara boy digging for water in rock crevices in the Mann Ranges, July 1933
(photograph by Norman Tindale, courtesy of the South Australian Museum Archive)

drainage lines are less than 40 kilometres long. The scattered surface waters vary in the degree to which they persist, from permanent springs to ephemeral clay-pans. The summer rains replenish the water table, fill the rock-holes, and put water in the sandy creek beds. What Bob Tonkinson writes about people of the Lake Disappointment region applies also to the Pitjantjatjara people and their neighbours: they looked to well-known sources of water (such as sheltered rock-holes, soaks in creek beds, and wells in the sand-hills and rocky areas), the location of which was recorded in stories. The presence of herbs in the clay-pans signalled the presence of water. Wells, up to seven metres deep, sometimes even more, tapped subterranean waters, though few of the wells were obvious to the eye. Local rains filled the ephemeral rock-holes. Western Desert people could also obtain water from certain plants. In the west of the region people were able to name at least one water source for every 230 square kilometres on average. But the distribution of surface water depended on the very variable rainfall, and so varied through the year and from one year to another.[12]

I am drawing here on Fiona Walsh's study of Mardu plant use (in the west of the Western Desert) to fill out the picture provided by Tindale and Gould.[13] She classifies habitats into ranges, sand-plains, and wetlands. Mardu people made further discriminations: sand-plain (*laanga*), sand-dune (*tali*), clay-pan (*linji*), and salt-lake (*warla*). Within these land forms Mardu named plant associations by reference to the dominant species—such as *janparrakurru*, or 'having *janparra*' (hard spinifex, *Triodia basedowii*)—and named some places by the species available there, such as 'bush-yam place'. Plant resources tend to be more habitat-specific than animals. (See Map 2.2 for vegetation in the Petermann Ranges–Lake Amadeus area.)

The shield desert includes belts of dense mulga scrub, and extensive areas of spinifex. River red gums grow along the intermittent streams in breakaway country. The sand-plains carry low open-hummock grassland of spinifex, with patches of soft grass, hakea, and low mulga, or woody shrubs. Some of the plains are of more gravelly 'buckshot', vegetated with spinifex, woody shrubs, and tall trees, or belts of mulga on heavier gravels; and on top of the sand ridges is open shrubland of *Grevillea stenobotrya*. The dominant vegetation of the sand ridges of the Gibson Desert is mulga woodland, with mixed acacia shrublands and some desert oak woodland between the sand ridges. Small areas of coolabah woodland are found, with a few salt-lakes and some samphire vegetation.[14]

These habitats provided edible seeds, fruits, and lerp. The Pitjantjatjara category *mirka* included mulga and eucalypt galls, acacia resin, and insect exudations. Among the insect foods were the larvae of cossid moths ('witchetty grubs'), wasp galls, lerp, especially important in dry periods, termite aeletes, and ant eggs. Among the native mammals in the sand desert were many species of native rats and mice, carnivorous marsupials, seed-eaters such as bandicoots, and insect-eaters. Animals protected themselves from the sun and wind during the day, many were nocturnal, and many sheltered in burrows and had to be dug out.

Turning to the ranges, the mountain desert is mainly covered in acacia scrub and shrubland, with a few ghost gums, while spinifex clothes the more expansive areas. Eucalypts, acacias, and other kinds of tree grow in the rocky water-courses, and on the slopes is low, open woodland of acacias. The slopes near the ranges support rather

Map 2.2 Vegetation of the Petermann Ranges–Lake Amadeus region of the Western Desert

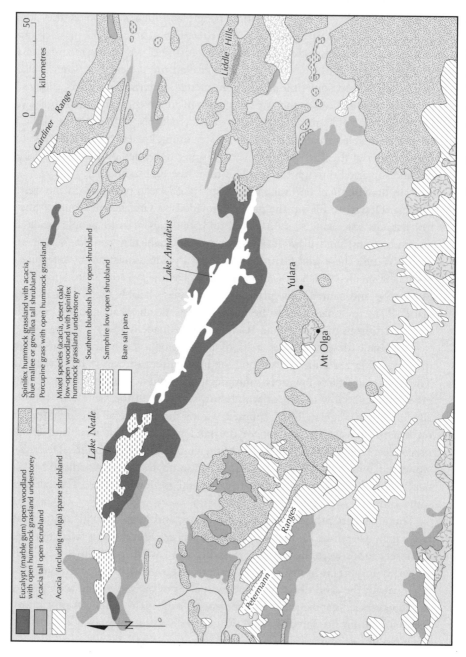

Source: Conservation Commission of the Northern Territory (1991)

Plate 2.2   A woman winnowing purslane seed (*Portulaca oleracea*) in the Warburton Ranges, August 1935 (photograph by Norman Tindale, courtesy of the South Australian Museum Archives)

denser vegetation of mulga or mallee with an understorey of soft grass and spinifex. In the deep gorges, permanent pools and soaks maintain pockets of water-dependent vegetation, and provided dependable water resources for humans. Mammals take advantage of the rocky outcrops and sheltered ravines as havens from predators and sources of water, and they formed a ready supply of game.

Fiona Walsh found the smallest number and least-diverse range of plant species in the ranges. However, people targeted the ecotones between the ranges and sand-plains, as well as between wetlands and sand-plains, as areas for collecting resources. The many lizards there include the perentie, a large desert monitor.

What Walsh refers to as 'wetlands' are ephemeral and depend on local rainfall. Wetland vegetation varies greatly as a result of local rainfall and burning off, but the greatest number and diversity of food-plant species are to be found in this habitat, especially in the few years after burning. Plant resources included seeds of annual grasses and trees, tubers, and fruits. Two species of tuber could be collected in large quantities from wetlands, while roots of five other species provided food in dry periods.

Foods according to season

Pitjantjatjara and their neighbours recognised four main seasons according to Tindale (I have revised his terminology):

- *kuḻi*, 'hot weather'—about early December to late February
- *yukiripirri*, 'green time'—about March to mid May, when the clay-pans filled with water
- *nyinnga*, 'cold time'—roughly from mid May to late July
- *piriya*, 'warm and steady wind from the north and west'—the dry season, roughly August to November.

These were not strictly calendrical, for their timing depended on the weather, although people also noted the heliacal rising of the Pleiades—*kungkarangkalpa*, the Seven Sisters.[15]

Richard Gould has recorded the seasonal availability of various foods used by Ngaatjatjarra people (see Table 2.4). As a result of highly localised variation in rainfall, the same plant staples became available at different times in different years. And since there are no predictable seasons when edible plants might be expected to ripen, food species did not appear in a stable seasonal pattern. However, in the early months of the year the supply of fruits and seeds became generally scanty, and tubers were not at their best. Meat, especially reptiles, would have been especially important.[16]

In late summer the fruits of *Canthium latifolium* ripened, together with edible seeds of *Chenopodium rhadinostachyum* (goosefoot), and these were staples. In mid-winter, fresh *Solanum* and quandong fruits (*Santalum acuminatum*) as well as edible seeds provided the main staples (see Plates 2.2, 2.5).

Productivity of animal and vegetable foods

There is a dramatic contrast between animal and vegetable foods in Gould's data about productivity. Between July 1966 and July 1970, groups of 8 to 14 people gathered about 5430 grams of vegetable staples per person per day, and only 826 grams of meat, which thus formed about 15% of produce by weight. Reptiles contributed over half the meat. In her research at a camp at Everard Park (see Map 5.2), Annette Hamilton found that each person in the camp received about 160 grams of meat per day. Ngaatjatjarra people expressed a strong preference for meat in spite of (or perhaps because of) its short supply.[17]

Using large wooden bowls, grindstones, and a source of water, Mardu women (in the west of the Western Desert) could harvest *Yakirra australiensis* at the rate of at least 490 grams per hour, and they preferred to harvest and process foods in large quantities to increase efficiency. One woman in Walsh's study harvested 50 fresh and 100 dried *Solanum diversiflorum* fruits in an hour, amounting to 1.01 kilograms. (This implies that five hours work per day was required to attain the average yields recorded by Gould). In a related study, O'Connell and Hawkes found that Alyawarra women produced returns in the range of 750–5,200 kilocalories per person per hour (about 0.5–1.7 kilograms) collecting *Ipomea* roots, *Solanum*, and acacia seeds in the sand-hills. Returns of *Vigna* roots, larvae of cossid moths, and lizards from the mulga woodland were lower—about 200–800 kilocalories.

Yields of some vegetable staples were greater in drought years than very wet years, due to the preservation of fruits through desiccation, as in the case of quandong. The effects of prolonged drought, however, have not been studied. Indeed, Walsh believes

Table 2.4 Pitjantjatjara people and their neighbours: ■ = available
Food resources through the year

Food staple	Kuḻi (hot weather)		Yukiripirri (green time)			Nyinnga (cold time)			Piriya (warm north-west wind)		Kuḻi (hot weather)	
	Jan	Feb	Mar	Apr	May	Jun	Jul	Aug	Sep	Oct	Nov	Dec
WET YEAR (1966–67)												
Vegetable foods— Edible seeds												
Wanguṉu (*Erogrostis eriopoda*)			■	■	■	■						
Kalpaṟi (*Chenopodium rhadinostachyum*)		■	■	■								
Vegetable foods— Ground and tree fruits												
Fresh *kampuṟarpa* (*Solanum centrale*)					■	■	■					
Dried *kampuṟarpa* (*Solanum centrale*)	■	■										
Ngaṟu (*Solanum chippendalei*)	■	■	■									
Yawalyuru (*Canthium latifolium*)		■	■	■								
Wayaṉu, 'quandong' (*Santalum acuminatum*)						■	■	■				
Yiḻi, 'wild fig' (*Ficus sp.*)								■	■	■		
Mammals and birds												
Mainly large macropods and emus	■											■
DROUGHT YEAR (1969–70)												
Vegetable foods—Ground and tree fruits												
Ngaṟu, bush tomato (*Solanum chippendalei*)	■								■	■		
Yiḻi, 'wild fig' (*Ficus sp.*)	■			■	■	■						
Wanguṉu (*Erogrostis eriopoda*)				■	■	■						

Source: Gould (1980)

Gould's assessment was skewed towards vegetable foods because of the particular conditions that existed during his research—periods of high rainfall had increased the availability of plant foods.[18]

On the eastern end of the 'Aboriginal grain belt', Yuwaaliyaay people had some types of resources in common with Pitjantjatjara, but added the resources of rivers, swamps, and flood-plains.

Yuwaaliyaay people and their neighbours

> The guides assured us the Narran was not far off, although we had understood when at the Barwan that the distance was 25 miles from these springs. We passed over very good ground, and found the country to improve as we advanced. We were conducted through the most open parts of scrubs by our guides ... We crossed one or two slight elevations wholly composed of compact felspar in flocks—forming ridges resembling an outcrop of strata, whereof the strike always pointed N.W. and S.E. Various curious new plants and fruits appeared; amongst others a solanum, the berry of which was a very pleasant-tasting fruit. The plant was a runner and spread over several yards from one root. There was also a fruit shaped like an elongated egg; it appeared to be some Asclepiad, and was called by the natives 'Doobáh'. They ate it, seeds and all, but said it was best roasted.
>
> Charles Sturt, *Two Expeditions into the Interior of South Australia*, vol. 1, pp. 84–5

The country of the Yuwaaliyaay people occupies the corner between the Culgoa and Darling/Barwon River, between latitudes 29° and 30° south and longitudes 147° and 149° east, in the middle of the Darling River Basin in the Lowland Zone (see Map 5.4). The Darling/Barwon is a region of clay-plain and river flood-plain, arid by comparison with Gippsland and with much more variable and unpredictable rainfall.

Land forms

The Darling Basin region lies below 150 metres, and is generally flat with low hills on the eastern and western margins. The Barrier Range and smaller ranges form the western boundary of the basin, while the low, wooded foothills of the Great Dividing Range shape its eastern boundary, with isolated outcrops on the plain. The tributaries of the Darling/Barwon River have their sources between the Blue Mountains in the south and the Warrego Range in the northwest (an expanse of some 1300 kilometres) resulting in a very variable flow. Many of the rivers and creeks have high banks, and many are intermittent, drying up completely in drought conditions. Increases of flow and the highest water levels in the Darling/Barwon River occur in late summer and late winter to spring, and June is the time of lowest water, but the time of greatest flow varies greatly from year to year.

The river was the southern limit of Yuwaaliyaay country and an ecological focus for Yuwaaliyaay people and their neighbours (see Map 5.4). The Narran River in the middle of Yuwaaliyaay country, reduced to a chain of waterholes in dry conditions, feeds into the extensive Narran Lake on the north side of the Barwon River.[19]

Climate

The region lies near the eastern limit of the semi-desert and on the boundary of the arid zone; there is a mean annual rainfall of 400 millimetres at Brewarrina, and of less to the west and rather more to the east (Table 2.1). It has a degree of seasonality, about 1.3:1, with rather more rain in the summer than the winter. Importantly, variability is quite high, at 1.25. (This compares with a variability index of about 0.50 in Gippsland and the southwest, and 2.00 in the Simpson Desert.) Susceptible to frequent floods, the region is also very drought-prone, having experienced five periods of prolonged drought between 1885 and 1965. Periods of drought tend to be followed by above-average rainfall and floods that cover large areas of the back country with water, sometimes lasting for years, and causing fish and fowl to proliferate. There is effective rainfall for less than four months of the year.

Summers in the region are hot and winters cool: Bourke experienced a high of 52.8°C in 1877. The median frost period is about 60 days (Table 2.2).

Habitats and resources

The food resources of the region were those of rivers and swamps, grassland and woodland, conditioned by the very variable climatic conditions (see Map 2.3 for the vegetation of the region). As in Gippsland, edible roots and tubers had an important place in the diet, but in the upper reaches of the Murray–Darling basin the widely dispersed seeds of grasses, and of some tree species, constituted one of the main vegetable staples. In this region the root foods included a species of yam.[20]

The amount and location of water in the Darling/Barwon River region depended greatly on the cycle of flood and drought, which also affected patterns of movement (covered in Chapter 4). With a rise in the river level and local rains, the extensive plains would be flooded. During dry periods the ephemeral rivers shrank to series of pools, and the Darling/Barwon became brackish. In the absence of surface water, alternative sources included water trapped in the galls of eucalypt trees.

Open woodland and grassland were the predominant forms of vegetation in the region, but there were very variable plant communities. Trees occurred as dense stands, separated by wide areas of grassland, or thinly spaced, separated by grasses, small shrubs and herbs. Grasslands formed a major component of the vegetation between the trees, with tussocks of Mitchell grass, as well as other grasses. These grasses also formed the ground layer in woodland areas.[21]

People combined burning off of the grasslands, so they could hunt small game, with the harvesting of seed. As in the Western Desert, some animal and reptile species had to be dug out of burrows—wombats, rat kangaroos, hopping mice, and goannas. Stick-net rats could be extracted using fire. Few possums were to be found on the lower Darling River, and the same seems to have been true of the Darling/Barwon River, although Parker thought them to have recently disappeared.

Map 2.3 Vegetation of the Darling/Barwon River region

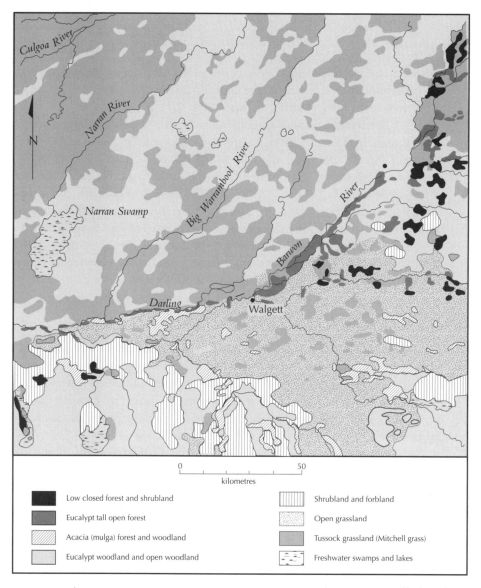

■ Low closed forest and shrubland	▥ Shrubland and forbland
■ Eucalypt tall open forest	▦ Open grassland
▨ Acacia (mulga) forest and woodland	▦ Tussock grassland (Mitchell grass)
▤ Eucalypt woodland and open woodland	▦ Freshwater swamps and lakes

Source: Commonwealth of Australia (2003)

A number of plants provided greens and fruits in the poplar box (*Eucalyptus populnea*) and mulga (*Acacia aneura*) woodlands. Women steamed some types of yam with damp grass in an earth oven, heated with hot stones. Other root foods, such as 'thistle', pigweed, and crowfoot, were eaten raw. As in other regions, people ate grubs and termite aeletes, which are rich in fat. Acacia gums provided second-preference foods, and were also used as adhesives and as a medicine for wounds and sores.

As well as the Darling/Barwon River, Yuwaaliyaay country included a substantial swamp, now called Narran Lake, fed from the north by the Narran River. Waterways supported several plant communities. Aquatic plants included *Typha* (bulrush), the roots of which were most starchy in late summer and autumn, though used all year, and *Tryglochin procera*, which produces a rhizome with root tubers.

Rising water levels attracted nomadic species of waterfowl, such as ducks, which then left when the waters fell. A flood brings in thousands of water birds, and breeding followed a suitable rise in water levels. The wetlands also provided a habitat for a variety of reptiles and amphibia, including frogs and long-necked tortoises.

An abundance of fish could be caught in the Darling/Barwon River, in its tributaries, and on the flood-plain after rain, aided by the use of the large stone fish-traps (at Brewarrina), large nets, and fish-spears. Nets could yield individual hauls of cod of 135–225 kilograms, as observed by Eyre among Paakantji people. However, the river was generally unproductive in winter months because of a reduced flow of water and low temperatures (under $10^{\circ}C$ is likely at times). Freshwater mussels, which bury themselves in the mud during droughts, could most readily be obtained in wet conditions, and people probably gathered yabbies (small freshwater crayfish) in large numbers when the plains flooded.[22]

Kangaroos and emus were attracted to the rivers after a flush, but tended to head up country and into the scrub after light rains. In cool, damp, spring weather, kangaroos moved into the hills for feed. Like people of the lower Darling River, the Yuwaaliyaay and their neighbours caught wallabies with nets.[23]

Foods according to season

Yuwaaliyaay people and their neighbours could obtain several kinds of greens, such as trigonella and nasturtium plants, all year round, depending on conditions. Root foods tended to be available all year, as did pigface and warrigal cabbage (see Table 2.5).

Summer foods included grass seeds, roots of *Typha* (bulrush) and other species, and various fruits. Native millet (*Panicum decompositum*) grows in summer and seeds from December to April. When stooked, however, the grass may be kept green until as late as July, as Thomas Mitchell observed on the Narran River.[24]

Some of the grasses remained harvestable for seed through autumn and into winter. Of the root foods, several, including *Geranium* species, were primarily winter resources. The availability of tree resources such as the acacias depended on local conditions as well as season.

In winter, people became more dependent on non-riverine foods, such as large mammals, yabbies, and birds, as well as foods from several shrubs and trees and a variety of root foods.

Spring to late summer is generally regarded as the best time for fishing for native freshwater species. Rises in water levels induce plankton blooms, especially on the backwaters and flood-plains, creating a suitable environment for young fish. However, Sturt observed during a dry summer in 1846 that people had fished out the pools and were living on herbs and roots, and he found the Darling River to be very saline.[25]

Table 2.5 Yuwaaliyaay food resources through the year

■ = plentiful   ▨ = available

Food staple	Jan	Feb	Mar	Apr	May	Jun	Jul	Aug	Sep	Oct	Nov	Dec
Vegetable foods—Roots and tubers												
Cumbungi, bulrush (*Typha* sp.)	■									■	■	■
Water ribbons (*Triglochin procera*)				▨	■	■	■	■	■	▨		
Yams (*Dioscorea* sp.)	Incomplete information											
Pigweed, purslane (*Portulaca oleracea*)	Incomplete information											
Crowfoot (*Ranunculus* sp.)	Incomplete information											
Geranium sp.				▨	■	■	■	■	■	▨		
Picris sp., *Cucumis* sp.				▨	■	■	■	■	■	▨		
Boehavia sp.	Incomplete information											
'Thistle top' (?*Sonchus* sp.)				▨	■	■	■	■	■	▨		
Vegetable foods—Seeds												
Grasses:												
• Native millet (*Panicum decompositum*)	■	■	■	■	▨					▨	■	■
• Love grass (*Eragrostis* sp.)	■	■									■	■
• Brittlegrass (*Setaria* sp.)	■											
• *Aristida* sp. and *Stipa* sp.				▨	■	■	■	■	■			
Aquatic fern spores:												
• Nardoo (*Marsilea drummondii*)	■	■	■	■	▨	■	▨			▨	■	■
Shrubs:												

Table 2.5 Continued

Food Staple	Jan	Feb	Mar	Apr	May	Jun	Jul	Aug	Sep	Oct	Nov	Dec
• Purslane, pigweed (*Portulaca* sp.)	■	■									■	■
• Saltbush (*Chenopodium* sp.)				▨	■	■	■	■	■	■		
• Goosefoot (*Atriplex* sp.)				▨	■	■	■	■	■	■		
• Flax plant (*Linum marginale*)				▨	■	■	■	■	■	■		
Trees:	Incomplete information											
• Mulga (*Acacia* sp.)	▦	▦	▦	▦	▦	▦	▦	▦	▦	▦	▦	▦
• *Amaranthus* sp.	▦	▦	▦	▦	▦	▦	▦	▦	▦	▦	▦	▦
• Kurrajong (*Brachychiton populneus*)												
• *Pittosporum phillyreoides*				▨	■	■	■	■	■	■		
Vegetable foods—Fruits												
Native orange (*Capparis* sp.)	Incomplete information											
Portulaca sp	■	■									■	■
Sonchus sp.	■	■									■	■
Quandong (*Santalum acuminatum*)	Incomplete information											
Nitraria sp.	■	■									■	■
Vegetable foods— Leaves, greens												
Pigface (*Carpobrotis* sp.)	▦	▦	▦	▦	▦	▦	▦	▦	▦	▦	▦	▦
Sonchus sp.	Incomplete information											
Warrigal cabbage (*Trigonella* sp.)	▦	▦	▦	▦	▦	▦	▦	▦	▦	▦	▦	▦
Nasturtium sp.	▦	▦	▦	▦	▦	▦	▦	▦	▦	▦	▦	▦

Table 2.5 Continued

Food Staple	Jan	Feb	Mar	Apr	May	Jun	Jul	Aug	Sep	Oct	Nov	Dec
Portulaca sp.	■	■									■	■
Fish and crustacea												
Freshwater crayfish	▒	▒	▒	■	■	■	■	■	▒	▒	▒	▒
Freshwater mussels	▒	▒	▒	▒	▒	▒	▒	▒	▒	▒	▒	▒
Mammals												
Kangaroos	▒	▒	▒	■	■	■	■	■	▒	▒	▒	▒
Small mammals (possums, etc.)	▒	▒	▒	■	■	■	■	■	▒	▒	▒	▒
Birds												
Emu	▒	▒	▒	■	■	■	■	■	▒	▒	▒	▒
Reptiles												
Long-necked tortoise (*Chelodina longicollis*)	■	■	■								■	■

Yabbies could be dug out of their holes in cold weather, but were more easily obtained in summer by dragging a net across the muddy bottom of a lagoon.

On the whole, reptiles and amphibia seem to have been more easily obtained in the warmer months. Frogs spend winter under rocks and logs, emerging during milder spells, while long-necked tortoises and other reptiles were unobtainable in that season. People seem to have relied more on hunting mammals and emus in the autumn and winter months. Depending on conditions, emus usually nested from May to August, when they and their eggs were vulnerable, with an average clutch of seven (and a range of 5–20).

Wiil and Minong people

For the fourth case study we move to the south coast of the southwest region of Western Australia. This is the country of Minong people, and, in the hinterland, Wiil people. Their country lies between about 33°30' and 35° south, and 117°30' to 119° east (see Maps 5.5 and 5.6).

Land forms

Most of the southwest is an extension of the Great Western Plateau of the Shield. The plateau has an altitude of about 300 to 400 metres, broken by flat-topped ironstone-capped hills and scattered granite outcrops. It too lies in the region of uncoordinated drainage, in which creeks drain into numerous shallow, seasonal lakes, salt-lakes and clay-pans. The south-coast sand-plain forms an intermediate zone between the plateau and the coast, but with no sharp topographical boundaries. The land gradually falls to the coast from about 300 metres at Lake Grace, broken by the Stirling, Barren and Russell Ranges, which form a chain of hills with summits up to about 1100 metres high. Short rivers, including the Fitzgerald and Hammersley, cut through deep gorges to drain into the sea. The coast is rugged, with steep cliffs and jagged headlands in which are hidden small rocky coves divided by wide crescentic bays and sandy beaches. Sand-bars across the river mouths have formed flooded river basins such as King George Sound, the home of Minong people.[26]

Climate

The Mediterranean climate of the southwest is seasonal, with winter rains born on the westerly winds from April or early May, and dry summers. Rainfall is highest along the western scarp and along the southwest coast, decreasing as one moves east and northeast. Table 2.1 shows a marked difference in mean annual rainfall between, on the west side of the south coast, Albany (934 millimetres) and, on the east side, Bremer Bay (625 millimetres), and between coast and hinterland (354 millimetres at Lake Grace). The length of the summer dry season increases from nearly four months at Albany to more than six months at Bremer Bay, and more than seven at Lake Grace. Annual variability is low at 0.50 between Albany and Bremer Bay, but the reliability of rainfall also decreases towards the east. Because of the lower temperatures, the moisture index is higher overall than on the Darling/Barwon River, in spite of similar average annual rainfall.[27]

The warm, dry summers have a mean maximum of 30°C in the hinterland, but lower on the coast (Table 2.2). The cool, moist winters bring widespread frosts on the plateau between May and September, especially in July and August. Snow falls for a short period in the Stirling Ranges in most winters, and extremes include violent hail storms as well as floods.

Habitats and resources

Wiil people at Jerramungup people lived on the boundary of the heathy south-coast sand-plain and the inland southwest vegetation zone in which mallee forest and woodland predominated before clearing for farming. At King George Sound and its hinterland the vegetation was transitional between the jarrah-marri and karri forest to the west and the mallee and mallee-heath to the east (see Map 2.4).

Drawing on Caroline Bird's analysis, I have classified the habitats into salt-lakes; dry (heathy) sand-plains; moist, seasonally inundated environments; and coastal/

Map 2.4   Vegetation of the south coast of the southwest

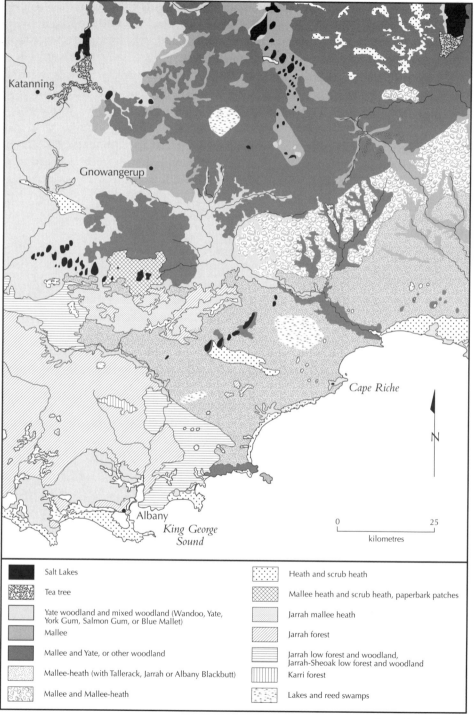

Katanning

Gnowangerup

Cape Riche

N

Albany

King George
Sound

0   25

kilometres

	Salt Lakes		Heath and scrub heath
	Tea tree		Mallee heath and scrub heath, paperbark patches
	Yate woodland and mixed woodland (Wandoo, Yate, York Gum, Salmon Gum, or Blue Mallet)		Jarrah mallee heath
	Mallee		Jarrah forest
	Mallee and Yate, or other woodland		Jarrah low forest and woodland, Jarrah-Sheoak low forest and woodland
	Mallee-heath (with Tallerack, Jarrah or Albany Blackbutt)		Karri forest
	Mallee and Mallee-heath		Lakes and reed swamps

Source: Beard (1976, 1979)

estuarine habitats.[28] The region had many permanent sources of fresh water, but the summer dry season imposed stresses on water supplies, particularly inland, where less rain fell than on the coast. Scott Nind reported in 1831 that 'large districts are abandoned for want of water'. People could obtain water all year round by digging in the coastal sand-dunes and by climbing trees to get water from the tree excrescences. Freshwater lakes and swamps remained sources of water for most of the year, while the winter-wet lakes and swamps on the coastal sand-plain and the intermediate zone yielded a supply in winter. Fresh water became trapped in semi-permanent pools of the perennial rivers, but became brackish as the season advanced, while soaks and springs occurred on alluvial flats. Inland, supplies of fresh water became trapped in 'gnamma holes' (rock-holes) in granite outcrops.[29]

Between 70 and 100 kilometres inland, on the watershed between the Swan–Avon basin and the south-coast rivers, mallee with patches of mallee heath clothed the gently undulating sand-plain, with patches of eucalypt woodland, dominated by tallerack (*Eucalyptus tetragona*) in the major valleys and the many small lakes and salt-pans. On granite soils falling gradually from the watershed towards the coast, mallee-heath became more prominent in a complex mosaic with mallee, and yate (*E. lehmanni*) woodland grew in the valleys.

A wide range of vegetable resources could be obtained on the dry sand-plain. Vegetable foods included some herbs, such as kangaroo paw and fringe lily, and a number of shrubs. The much less productive salt-lake environments also yielded herbs with tuberous roots. Mobile animals such as kangaroos, wallabies, and emus occupied a wide range of habitats.

The Stirling Range carried distinctive vegetation—thickets of banksias, dryandras, other flowering trees, and some grass trees on the summits. The plain to the south of the Stirling Range carried almost continuous jarrah-marri forest, with patches of banksia woodland and mallee-heath, and tea-tree and paperbark swamps in the valleys. Wandoo woodland intervened in the lower-rainfall area to the southwest. The broken plains to the west and north of King George Sound were covered by a mosaic of jarrah-marri forest, casuarina woodland, eucalypts, and mallee, with reedy swamps in the valleys. Nearer the coast in the west of the region the many small circular lakes and swamps and steep-sided trenches cut by the rivers were home to yate woodland accompanied by paperbark scrub, with mixed eucalypt woodland dominant in the lower valleys.

Bill Ferguson points out that the woodland around and through the forest, with its dense understorey, was a much richer and more accessible source of plant foods. People kept the woodland corridors open by burning off (see Chapter 3).

In the complex of granite bosses and sand-hills along the coast east from King George Sound to Bremer Bay, heath covered the hills, with some clumps of trees and a wide variety of shrubs and herbaceous plants. Swamps and lakes formed by the dunes carried melaleuca, shrubs, and sedges.

The wetlands of the hinterland, estuaries, and coast provided a wide variety of food plants, including lilies, vines, orchids, herbs, and aquatic herbs. In their breeding season, from late winter to spring, waterfowl congregated in large numbers on

Table 2.6 Wiil and Minong vegetable foods through the year

■ = available

Vegetable Food	Jan	Feb	Mar	Apr	May	Jun	Jul	Aug	Sep	Oct	Nov	Dec
Roots and tubers												
Kangaroo paws (*Anigozanthus* spp.)	■	■	■	■	■	■	■	■	■	■	■	■
Pale lily (*Caesia parviflora*)	■	■	■	■	■	■	■	■	■	■	■	■
Burchardia multiflora	■	■	■	■	■						■	■
Venus fly-traps (*Droseraceae* spp. (six spp.))	■	■	■	■	■						■	■
Clematis spp.	■	■	■	■	■	■	■	■	■	■	■	■
Chocolate lily (*Dichopogon strictus*)	■	■	■	■	■	■	■	■	■	■	■	■
Bloodroot (*Haemodorum spicatum*)	■	■	■	■	■	■	■	■	■	■	■	■
Orchidaceae	■	■	■	■	■	■	■	■	■	■	■	■
Pelargonium australe	■	■	■	■	■	■	■	■	■	■	■	■
Native parsnip, etc. (*Platysace* spp.)	■	■	■	■	■	■	■	■	■	■	■	■
Twining fringe lily (*Thysanotus patersonii*)	■	■	■	■	■						■	■
Water ribbons (*Triglochin procera*)	■	■	■	■	■	■	■	■	■	■	■	■
Bulrush (*Typha domingensis*)			■	■	■							
Wurmbea dioica	■	■	■	■	■							■
Seeds												
Acacia acuminata	■	■	■								■	■
A. microbotrya	■	■	■	■							■	■
A saligna	■	■	■								■	■

Table 2.6 Continued

Food Staple	Jan	Feb	Mar	Apr	May	Jun	Jul	Aug	Sep	Oct	Nov	Dec
Quandong (*Santalum Acuminatum*)	X	X							X	X	X	X
Zamia nuts (*Macrozamia riedlei*)			X									
Sandalwood (*S. spicatum*)									X	X	X	
Nectar												
Banksia spp.									X	X	X	
Dryandra sp.												
Fruits												
Billardiera erubescens	X	X									X	
Carpobrotus sp.			X									X
Epacridaceae spp. (ca 20 spp.)						X	X	X				
Weeping cherry (*Exocarpos sparteus*)	X										X	
Pronaya elegans	X											
Quandong (*Santalum acuminatum*)	X								X	X		
Blue-bell creeper (*Sollya heterophylla*)	X	X	X	X								
Leaf base												
Grass tree (*Xanthorrhoea preissii*)						X	X	X	X	X	X	
Gum												
Yate (*Eucalyptus occidentalis*)	X	X										X
Wattle (*Acacia* spp.)	X	X	X								X	
Suckers												
Western Australian Christmas tree (*Nuytsia floribunda*)	X											X

Source: Bird (1985). I have included the species marked by Bird (1985:136) as recorded in the southwest, but only those that she relates to habitats; she indicates eight further species, recorded as food plants elsewhere in Australia, that grow in this region.

the wetlands. Other wetland fauna included frogs, gilgies, and long-necked fresh-water tortoises. Snakes and lizards had a wide distribution, being particularly common in swamps.

The scrub behind the foreshore was rich in wallabies. Men caught fish with spears in rivers, bays, and inlets. Both men and women caught fish by hand and cooperated in making fish weirs. People do not seem to have eaten shellfish, and ignored the oyster beds in King George Sound. Seals could be found in shallow coastal waters, and they were occasionally clubbed or speared, but the people, lacking watercraft, did not travel out to the seal colonies on the islands near the coast. Stranded whales provided a seasonal food for a large number of people, especially at Bremer Bay and on Doubtful Island.

Seasonality

Bird has reconstructed the seasonal availability of resources from the coast to the hinterland, and I have supplemented her data with Scott Nind's and Collet Barker's information (see Tables 2.6 and 2.7). The table generalises what were in fact variable seasons.[30]

Among the many root foods some could be harvested all year but were most nutritious at certain times of year. The orchids were most nutritious in summer, but hard to find. A variety of seeds (primarily acacia) and fruits ripened during the summer months. Banksias and dryandras provided nectar in early summer, and acacia gum became available. This was the season for gathering termite eggs and larvae. People fished with fish weirs at the end of December, and conducted fire-drives for kangaroo in the summer months. Salmon runs occurred along the coast in summer. People trained dolphins to 'herd' fish into the shallow waters, where they could be speared (a practice that also occurred in Moreton Bay in Queensland).[31]

Late in the summer dry season (late March to May), the scarcity of water led people to gather in large camps at the permanent waters of the coast and wetlands, and people climbed trees to get water from the tree excrescences. Nind reports that coastal residents procured fish 'in the greatest abundance' in late summer (*pourner*), lighting fires on the shore to attract them. Also at this time of year men hunted kangaroos by surrounding them.

The supply of seeds dwindled by the late dry season but a variety of root foods remained available, as did several kinds of fruit. Edible fungi came into season. As the swamps dried up, frogs and gilgies became available, and waterfowl became concentrated on the remaining waters. Large and small game gained in importance, especially possums, and in the rivers the fish were running.

During the wet winter (June–July) people generally dispersed to take advantage of seasonal water sources—in depressions on the coastal plain and watersheds, in river pools and creeks. People sometimes gathered in large numbers to hunt kangaroos, wallabies and emus, and to fish in the estuaries.

Kangaroos, at their fattest in June, were particularly valued in the winter months. A variety of root foods became available, as did fruits of the heathlands (especially

Table 2.7 Seasonal availability of fish of the southwest coast

■ = available

Fish	Jan	Feb	Mar	Apr	May	Jun	Jul	Aug	Sep	Oct	Nov	Dec
Western blue groper (*Achoerodus gouldii*)	■	■	■	■	■	■	■	■	■			
Yellow-eyed mullet (*Aldrichetta forsteri*)			■	■	■	■	■	■				
Australian salmon (*Arripis trutta esper*)			■	■	■	■						
Australian ruff (*A. georgianus*)					■							
Australuzza novae-hollandiae	■	■										■
Snapper (*Chrysophrys unicolor*)			■									
Chidoglanis microcephalus						■	■	■				
Flathead mullet (*Mugil cephalus*)			■	■	■	■	■	■				
Mylia butcheri	■											■
Phyllichthys punctuata	■	■										■
Bluefish (*Pomatomus saltator*)			■	■	■							
Tarwhine (*Rhabdosargus sarba*)	■	■										■
Sciaena antartica	■	■	■	■	■	■	■	■	■	■	■	■
Yellowtail (*Seriola grandis*)										■	■	■
Samson fish (*S. hippos*)										■	■	■
Sillago sp.		■										
Usacaranx georgianus												

Source: Bird (1985)

Table 2.8 Seasonal availability of animal foods of the southwest coast

■ = available

Food	Jan	Feb	Mar	Apr	May	Jun	Jul	Aug	Sep	Oct	Nov	Dec
Mammals												
Kangaroos			■	■	■	■	■					
Brush kangaroos									■	■	■	
Wallabies	■											■
Possums	■				■	■	■					■
Bandicoots					■							■
Kangaroo rats					■							■
Birds												
Emus, emu eggs				■	■	■						
Parakeets, cockatoos	■								■	■	■	■
Black swans	■											
Australian ravens					■							
Other young birds										■	■	
Reptiles												
Lizards, lizard eggs	■									■	■	■
Snakes	■										■	
Fresh-water tortoises	■				■	■	■					■
Amphibia												
Frogs			■	■								
Insects												
Larvae			■									

Source: Bird (1985)

Epacridaciae). Nesting birds and their eggs became prey in the wetlands, while larger game diminished in importance. Roots remained an important staple, and some fruits were coming into season. As the wet season came to an end Minong people returned to the coast to get a few fish in calm weather, and they gathered roots there too.

Gatherings for communal activities began in the early dry season (November–December) as people moved back to the coast or to the permanent wetlands. This was the season for communal wallaby hunts, and reptiles and possums were also important foods. Banskia and dryandra flowers began to yield nectar, and acacia seeds and a variety of roots became available. People also hunted young birds and took their eggs.

Sandbeach people

The east coast of Cape York Peninsula has a tropical monsoon climate of high rainfall, hot, wet summers, and drier winters. The lush forests and littoral zone provided rich terrestrial and aquatic resources, while the estuaries and shallow coastal waters, with their reefs, islands, and cays, yielded a wealth of marine resources (exploited through the use of outrigger canoes), in strong contrast with the southwest.

Land forms

The country of Sandbeach people lies between 12° and $14^\circ 30'$ south, and between 143° and 144° east (see Map 5.7).[32] The low, rugged mountains of the McIlraith Range, the Iron Range, and adjacent ranges, mainly of granite, vary in elevation from about 500 metres in the south to about 200 metres in the north. They border the narrow coastal plain of old sand-dunes to form the western boundary of Sandbeach country. Several short rivers drain the eastern side of the ranges, running swiftly east to the sea. The rivers provide a wide range of habitat types, including pools, falls, runs and glides, rapids, oxbow lakes and billabongs, waterholes, backwaters, lagoons, and feeder streams. Each provides a range of micro-habitats. The inner marine zone consists of shallow water, sandbars, cays, and fringe reefs, together with estuaries and beaches, while the outer marine zone consists of small islands and outer reefs.

Climate

Eastern Cape York Peninsula is hot and very wet; most rain falls in the summer, but there is still significant, though variable, winter rainfall (a mean of 17.8 millimetres in September, the lowest month). Average annual rainfall exceeds 2000 millimetres at Lockhart River (Table 2.1). The summer rains begin in November on average, and taper off through May, when the southeast trade winds bring dry air. In contrast with the arid zone, rainfall is highly reliable, with an index of 0.75. The region is hot in summer and warm in winter; minimum temperatures can fall below 10°C, while summer maximums regularly reach more than 40°C (Table 2.2).[33]

Habitats and resources

The Sandbeach region supports mainly open forest, woodland, and heathland. However, extensive rainforests grow between the Pascoe River, to the north of the Sandbeach region, and Rocky River in the south (see Maps 2.5, 5.7).[34]

Map 2.5   Vegetation of the Nesbit River region, eastern Cape York Peninsula

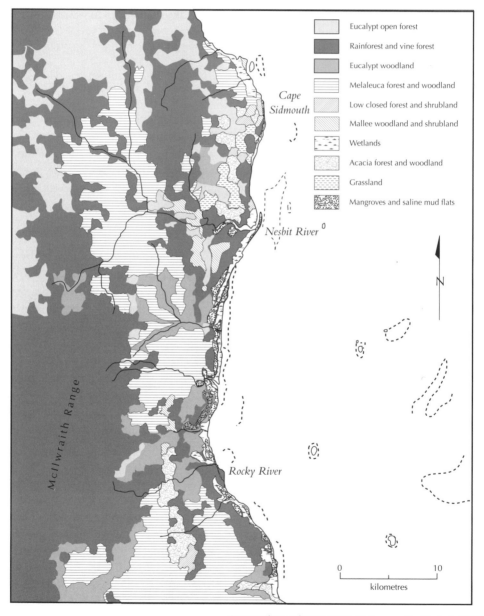

Sources: Chase and Sutton (1987), Commonwealth of Australia (2003)

Athol Chase and Peter Sutton classify Sandbeach habitats into four zones: coastal hinterland, coastal dune, inner marine and outer marine. Umpila people classified the land and waters into five zones, from the deep sea to the high ranges:

- *ngaachi kanichi*—on-top place
- *ngaachi paalachi, yi'achi*—behind/middle place
- *ngaachi malngkana*—beach place, or 'sandbeach'
- *ngaachi kuytu acha*—shallow saltwater place
- *ngaachi kuytu kulu*—deep saltwater place

On the east coast of Cape York Peninsula, the swales, pans, and swamps of Sandbeach country fill to capacity in the summer wet season and the short rivers run full. Most surface water disappears towards the end of the dry season, when Aboriginal people would dig for water behind the dunes, but pools persist in some rivers as well as in permanent lagoons. People also collected water from paperbark trees using a bailer shell.[35]

Vegetation types between the McIlwraith Range and the sea are quite varied. From the edge of the coastal strip to about 10 kilometres inland, and up to about 100 metres elevation, areas of low melaleuca woodland are interspersed with open forest and low open forest dominated by stringybark (*Eucalyptus tetrodonta*), coastal vine forest, and some grassland, especially in the Lockhart River valley. This is the vegetation of the coastal sand-dunes, with their deep podzol soils; it forms a rather unstable ecosystem. Shallow freshwater lakes occur in depressions in the dunes.

Vine forest covers the peaks of the Iron Range, and at higher elevations, north of Massey Creek, moist evergreen (notophyll) vine forest begins to dominate on the slopes and plateaux, interspersed with open forest in the northern part of the McIlwraith Range. Semi-deciduous (mesophyll) vine forest lines the rivers, giving way to layered open forest dominated by stringybark and other species. From Lloyd Bay north to Cape Weymouth, coastal vine forest comes down to the shore, while extensive mangroves cover the Lockhart River delta.

The hinterland forests, swamps, rivers, and patches of grassland were a source of vegetable foods, wood for spears, bark for various implements, and grass for baskets. Wild honey and macropods were found in the open forest, and in the rainforest there were mountain yams and fruits. The small and isolated grass-plains of the coastal hinterland were home to wallabies and other small animals, as well as such birds as ibises and quails; larger birds, such as emus, inhabited a range of habitats.

Dry-season fruits of a variety of trees and shrubs could be obtained in the riparian vine forest and the rainforest scrubs of the coastal dunes. Of particular importance in this region, the prolific wongai plum (*Manilkara kauki*) grew in dense groves along the beaches and estuaries. Vine-forest birds, including the cassowary, the scrub or brush turkey, and the jungle fowl, were important for their eggs, and the riverine vine forests were home to cuscuses and echidnas. Macropods also entered these habitats, and small mammals could be found.

Freshwater swamps and lagoons contained aquatic plants and waterfowl, especially from the late dry season (August). Aquatic fish, eels, and freshwater tortoises were other important resources.

Plate 2.3   Two Western Desert women wet-milling grass seed (photograph by Norman Tindale, courtesy of the South Australian Museum Archives)

Along the coastal strip, from 2 to 4 kilometres in width, lie patches of mangroves and salt-flats. Mangroves and dune scrub were a source of pods and fruits, vines and tubers. Yams became available in larger quantities at the end of the wet season, especially *Dioscorea sativa*.

Shellfish and fish species could be garnered from the beaches and the estuaries, while turtle eggs were seasonally available on the beaches. The saltwater environment yielded shellfish, crustaceans, several varieties of turtle, especially the green turtle, and dugong, which forage on sea grass in the shallow coastal waters. The eastern Cape York Peninsula region is rich in fish.

The islands support vegetation types similar to those on the coastal dunes. Some yams and fruits could be gathered on the islands, and birds including Torres Strait pigeons (*Ducula spilorrhoa*) could be hunted, for their eggs as well as their flesh. Of particular importance in this zone are mangroves and sea grasses, the food of dugong and turtle. The mangroves grow in sheltered bays, coastal inlets, and creeks, on the sheltered side of islands, and on inner reef platforms. They are a source of fruits and pods, and provide habitats for shellfish and crustacea, as well as nurseries for many species of fish.

Foods according to season

Sandbeach people recognised six main seasons marked by the prevailing winds, by rain and storms, and by heat and dryness:

- *ngurkitha*, 'northwest wind'—about February to April, the time of the monsoon rains
- *kiitha kuutulu*, 'southwest wind'—about April to June, the end of the monsoon rains
- *kaawaalu*, 'southeast winds'—the early dry season, from about June to August
- *kayimun*, 'hot sun' or 'dry'—mid-to-late dry season, from about August to November
- *matpi pa'inyan*, 'cloud build-up'—roughly from November to December, a time of impending storms
- *malantachi*, 'stormy weather' or 'storm time'—from about December to February.

While people hunted several kinds of bird and animal throughout the year, land resources, including those of freshwater habitats, were highly seasonal in contrast with marine resources, although seasons varied from year to year (see Table 2.9). However, vegetable foods of one kind or another could be gathered all year round.

Chase and Sutton point out that outrigger canoes, capable of carrying up to six or seven people, allowed people to extend their hunting, fishing, and shellfish gathering to the more remote islands, cays, sand-bars and reefs that lie 12 kilometres or more out to sea. In the saltwater marine environment, fish, shellfish, crustaceans, and the large green turtle and dugong could be taken opportunistically in all seasons, although the condition of the prey (its 'fatness', among other qualities), weather conditions, the tide, and the clarity of the water affected the ability to hunt and fish.

With the beginning of the summer wet season (*malantachi*), when movement became difficult, people relied on second-preference vegetable foods, including mangrove pods and fruits. Mullet provided an important wet-season estuarine resource. Lockhart River people who spoke to Athol Chase remembered the wet season as a hard period, not only because of the reliance on less-palatable foods and the extra work involved, but also because of the crowded and wet conditions in the large wet-season residence groups. At the end of the wet season, towards the end of July, women harvested yams in large quantities in the coastal dune scrub.

The yam called *thampu* (*Dioscorea sativa*) remained important through the dry season (*kaawaalu*). Fruits and berries of the coastal dunes, riverine vine forest, and estuaries could be harvested from the middle of the dry season. In the same period, groups travelled inland in search of vegetable foods, wood for spears, bark for implements, and grass for baskets. Large schools of estuarine fish, including beach salmon (*Eluetheronema tetradactylum*), moved from the estuaries into the muddy shallows along the coast to feed on the influx of shrimp.

Starting in June, after the wet-season rains, flocks of nutmeg pigeons (*Miristacivora spilorrhoa*) nested on the islands closest to the shore. People caught large quantities of adult birds, young birds, and eggs in canoe raids to the islands.

In the late dry season (*kayimun*, late October and November) large shoals of mullet arrived in the estuaries; people speared them from the shallow sand-bars at the mouths of creeks and rivers. During the same period, people combed the beaches for turtle eggs. In November, as the strong, constant southeast winds dropped and the seas became calmer, men searched continually in their outrigger canoes for green turtles, which were mating, and for the more elusive dugong. With the end of the monsoon in June, estuarine fish migrated into the muddy shallows along the coast.

Table 2.9 Sandbeach food resources through the year

■ = plentiful   ▦ = available   ░ = available from time to time

Food	Malantachi ('storm time')		Ngurkitha ('northwest wind')		Kiitha Kuutulu ('southwest wind')	Kaawaalu ('southeast wind')			Kayimun ('hot sun')		Matpi pa'inyan ('cloud build-up')	
Food staple	Jan	Feb	Mar	Apr	May	Jun	Jul	Aug	Sep	Oct	Nov	Dec
Vegetable foods—roots and tubers												
Yams			▦	▦	■	■	■	■	▦	▦		
Wild arrowroot and other tubers	■	■	▦					■	■	■	■	■
Vegetable foods—Fruits												
Nonda plum								░	■	▦		
Manilkarra plum									▦			
Other coastal fruits	░							▦	▦	▦	▦	▦
Mangrove fruits	■	■	■	░	■						░	▦
Shellfish	░	░	░	░	░	░	░	░	░	░	░	░
Fish												
Ray	■	░								■	■	■
Threadfin salmon			▦	■	■	▦						
Mullet	▦	▦	░	░	░	░	░	░		■	■	
Freshwater products												
Freshwater fish, eels, tortoises	▦					▦	▦	▦	■	■	■	■
Rainforest products	▦					▦	▦	▦		■	■	
Reef products												

Table 2.9 Continued

Food	Malantachi ('storm time')		Ngurkitha ('northwest wind')		Kiitha Kuutulu ('southwest wind')		Kaawulu ('southeast wind')		Kayimun ('hot sun')			Matpi pa'inyan ('cloud build-up')	
Food staple	Jan	Feb	Mar	Apr	May	Jun	Jul	Aug	Sep	Oct	Nov	Dec
Fish, shellfish, crustacea	dark	dark	dark				dark	dark	dark	dark	dark	dark
Mammals												
Macropods	light	light	light	light	light	light	light	light	medium	light	light	light
Cuscus	dark	dark	light	light	light	light	light	light	light	light	light	light
Small mammals	light	light	light	light	light	light	light	light	light	light	light	light
Dugong	medium	light	light	light	light	light	light	light	light	light	medium	medium
Birds												
Cassowary	light	light	light	light	light	light	light	light	light	light	light	light
Megapodes							medium	medium	medium	light	light	light
Torres Strait pigeon	medium								dark	dark	dark	dark
Reptiles												
Land reptiles	light	light	light	light	light	medium	light	light	light	light	light	very light
Marine turtles	medium	light	light	light	light	light	light	light	light	light	light	light
Eggs												
Megapode eggs	dark	medium									dark	dark
Turtle eggs								medium	light	light	dark	medium
Insects												
Wild honey	medium						medium	medium	medium	dark	dark	dark

Source: Chase and Sutton (1987:78)

Waterfowl flocked to the swales and lagoons from around August, when falling water levels encouraged prolific growth of aquatic plants. As the country dried out, people burned off the small and isolated grass-plains of the coastal hinterland during game drives for wallabies and other small animals. The disturbed insects and grubs attracted birds such as the ibis, and the burning also encouraged new growth. At the end of the dry season, with the creeks, rivers, and waterholes at their lowest, people sought cuscuses, cassowaries, and echidnas in the riverine vine forests, and fished for eels, tortoises, and freshwater fish, often using poisons. The mounds of the scrub turkey and the jungle fowl yielded incubating eggs.

Ngarinyin people and their neighbours

Also living in the tropical zone, Ngarinyin people and their neighbours drew on a similar range of foods as Sandbeach people, but differed in relying on resources from the rugged sandstone uplands. Ngarinyin speakers and their Worrorra, Wunambal, and Gamberre neighbours lived (and still live) in the northwest Kimberley in the northwest of the continent, between about 14°30' and 16°30' south and 124° and 127° east (see Map 5.8). This is a region with a tropical monsoon climate; a rugged coast of inlets, peninsulas, and islands; and a high sandstone hinterland.

Land forms

The Kimberley is an isolated region of mountains bounded by the Timor Sea to the north, the Ord River to the east, the Fitzroy River to the south, and the Indian Ocean to the west. Adjacent to the Fitzroy River in the southwest of the region lie extensive grassland and woodland plains, giving way in the northeast to the limestone Napier Range, with its many caves and waterholes, and the Oscar Range. The quartzite and sandstone King Leopold Range rises to 936 metres at Mount Ord, which is drained by the Lennard, Isdell, and Fitzroy Rivers. To the north and east is the high, rugged Kimberley plateau of quartzite (and of sandstone to the west); it rises to 778 metres at Mount Hann (see Map 5.8). To the south lies sand-ridge desert covered with spinifex. On the smoother basalt hills and plains of the Camden Peninsula to the west, laterite capping forms flat-topped mesas.

The rivers have etched deep valleys, up to 300 metres deep, that become long inlets on the west coast. This coastline has many bays and inlets, though rather few sandy beaches, and breaks up to form numerous offshore islands. The very extensive tidal range (up to 12 metres) creates fast tidal currents and whirlpools between the coast and the islands.[36]

Climate

Like eastern Cape York Peninsula, the Kimberley region has a tropical monsoon climate; 90% of its rain falls between November and April, brought on the northwest winds, while the remainder of the year is relatively dry, unlike at eastern Cape York.

Mean annual rainfall forms a cline across the Kimberley from northwest to south-east—1370 millimetres on the coast, higher on the Mitchell Plateau, and falling to about 750 millimetres at Gibb River. The southeast trade winds between April and November bring generally dry conditions and cooler nights. Annual variability is low on the coast (0.7 at Kuri Bay), higher at Gibb River (0.92); dry-season variability is very high, especially on the coast (see Table 2.1).

The region is prone to frequent tropical cyclones that come mainly between January and March, and generally cross the coast from the northwest. A dozen major cyclones moved over the hinterland between 1910 and 1971. The region is also very hot, with mean summer temperatures over 35°C. Winter minimum temperatures can fall below 5°C on the higher points of the plateau, but generally remain over 20°C on the coast (Table 2.2).

Habitats and resources

In a good wet season there was, of course, no shortage of water. If necessary, people could dig for water behind the beaches on the coast. On the offshore islands fresh-water sources were located at the back of the beaches and in the inter-tidal zone, which was used at mid or low tide.[37]

Each habitat type carried a specific range of food resources (see Map 2.6).[38] The vegetation of the Mitchell Plateau is predominantly high-grass savannah woodland, dominated by an alliance of stringybark and woollybutt on the deeper soils, with bloodwood (*E. dichromophloia*) together with stringybark on the shallower soils. The grass layer consists mainly of annual sorghum species, which grow up to two metres high, with some spinifex. On the sandstone scarps and gorges are communities of broad-leaved and mainly deciduous trees, including species of boab tree (*Brachychiton* spp.), which are important both economically and culturally.

The volcanics and dolerite of the Camden Peninsula have a similar vegetation to the Mitchell Plateau. A different mix is found on the streams and levees, where ghost gums are the principal trees, while river red gums and longleaf paperbarks fringe the rivers. Interspersed with the woodland are open grassy glades, and vine thickets grow in sheltered places. Particularly significant for food in the open wood-land were the cycad palms and cabbage palms in the understorey, as well as various fruits. The basaltic hills nearer the coast, with their pockets of rich clayey soils, sup-ported root foods.

Fringing the rivers towards the west, where rainfall is higher, are species of *Terminalia* and *Ficus* as well as melaleucas, acacias, and other trees; pandanus palms are common on the banks of the larger rivers. The vine forests on deep clay near per-manent fresh water were host to vegetable foods year-round.

Leached sands above the river flats, supporting open forest of eucalypts, acacias, and grevilleas, were a source of acacia gum, fruits, and round yams. A variety of root foods could also be found in boggy sand at the foot of hills. People would find long yams (*Dioscrorea elongata*) and other roots in the scrub near the river banks under river gums and kurrajong trees. This habitat provided a similar range of fruits as the vine forests, as well as the kurrajongs, figs, and buchanania.

Source: Beard (1978)

Map 2.6   Northwest Kimberley vegetation

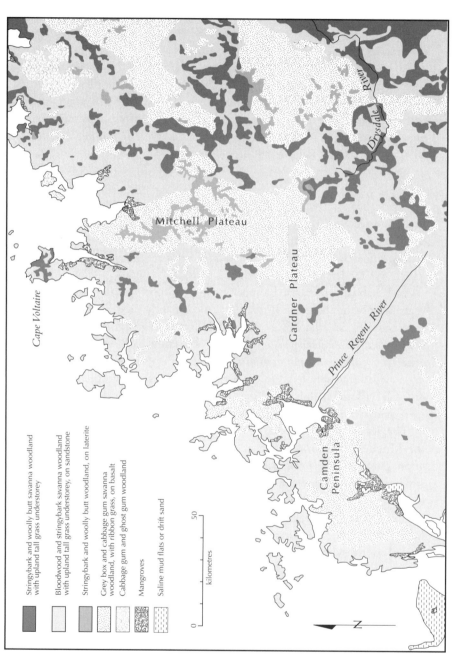

Stringybark and woolly butt savanna woodland
with upland tall grass understorey

Bloodwood and stringybark savanna woodland
with upland tall grass understorey, on sandstone

Stringybark and woolly butt woodland, on laterite

Grey box and cabbage gum savanna
woodland, with ribbon grass, on basalt

Cabbage gum and ghost gum woodland

Mangroves

Saline mud flats or drift sand

kilometres

0   50

N

Cape Voltaire

Mitchell Plateau

Gardner Plateau

Prince Regent River

Camden
Peninsula

Drysdale River

In spite of the poor soils, the dunes and the sandy banks of the freshwater rivers were rich in food species, including several seed-bearing tree species, such as the boab tree, and vines with edible roots. These foods would also be found at freshwater springs adjacent to the sea—rich environments with dense patches of rushes and pandanus palms. The outstanding food plant there was *Flemingia involucrate*, with its long, slender roots.

Flood-plains, clothed with open forest and a grassy understorey, provided the habitat for various root foods, including *Typhonium liliifolium*, whose caustic bulb was made edible with careful preparation. A variety of *Solanum* produced one of the few dry-season fruits of the region. On grassy patches on the black-soil plains the main food plant was pandanus, the source of large clusters of nuts; a freshwater crab could also be obtained in this habitat. Freshwater pools were home to plant foods, especially during the dry season, including water lilies and rushes with edible roots, tubers, and stalks.

There are extensive saline mud-flats around Montgomery Island, and at the head of George Water (the mouth of the Glenelg River, see Map 5.8). On the coast, mangroves grow on tidal mud in sheltered bays, inlets, basins, and estuaries. Ian Crawford writes that the people of this region, unlike Sandbeach people, did not eat plant foods from mangroves, but the mangroves did yield shellfish, teredo worms, and crabs.

The islands are clothed in spinifex and acacias on stony soils, but vine scrub, a source of yams and fruits, grows behind the dunes on some islands. Sue O'Connor's studies of island archaeology and ethnography on the west coast show that the islands were not permanently settled; instead, people visited them from the coast, as they do today, leaving few archaeological traces because of the winds and storms. When visiting the islands, people relied on food that came from the beach, reefs, and tidal pools. Women and children fished with short spears (and in recent times with lines baited with crabs), collected fruits, and dug for yams in the scrub behind the dunes, where fruit trees also grew. They also collected shellfish, especially oysters and chiton (*Acanthopleura spinosa*). The men hunted turtle and dugong, and caught large fish in deep waters from boats (the double raft in the past), from rocky platforms, or from the edge of deep pools at low tide. O'Connor remarks that people only ventured away from the beaches to dig for yams; given the paucity of fauna there was no reason to venture further. The islands are home to a few species of small rodents, sasyurids, and reptiles. Breeding colonies of birds tend to be confined to the coastal margins.

Seasonality

The Ngarinyin and their neighbours took the flowering of certain plants, as well as other events, as indicators that certain foods were in season:
- *Verticordia cunnignhamii* flowers—oysters, crabs, turtle eggs
- woollybutt (*Eucalyptus miniata*) flowers—crabs, hermit crabs
- bush almond (*Terminalia* sp.) flowers—*gadai* fish, parrotfish, stingray livers
- *Vitex glabrata* flowers—bream

- march flies—freshwater crocodile eggs
- fast-running clouds—turtle eggs.

Table 2.10 shows the more common vegetable foods through the year, but a wide variety of other species were also eaten. Seasonal availability varied from year to year.

At the height of the summer wet season the rivers flooded, and flatter ground became waterlogged. These were lean times, as the previous season's root foods had rotted and the new ones had not yet formed. Kangaroos and other game supplied most of the food, although heavy rain made hunting difficult. As Table 2.10 shows, a variety of plant foods were available, mainly fruits (such as 'bush apple', some figs (*Ficus*), and species of *Buchanania*) and kurrajong seeds. On the coast, red mullet moved to shallow waters in summer. The many species of lizard occupied a wide range of habitats, and some species were available at all times of year; lizards were hunted by both men and women.

The rains eased around late February, but food had not yet become plentiful. Some root foods were coming into season and fruits could still be gathered—the 'native grape' and the blackberry tree (*Vitex glabrata*) ripened as well as some seeds and nuts, including boab and 'bush almond'. Wallabies could be trapped in caves and rock shelters at this time, while bandicoots could be found in hollow logs, and were hunted by women as well as men. Frilled lizards came down to the ground in the wet season, and emus fed on white berries, making them easy to stalk.

In the late wet season (about April) a wide variety of root foods, including the important *Dioscorea* yams and lily tubers, began to reach maturity, ending the lean time of the wet season. The winds began to turn to the southeast.

In the dry season (May to August) the southeast trade wind blew steadily. Men burnt off the long grasses and spinifex, while women collected roots and some fruits and seeds, including roots of water plants. The plentiful supply of food allowed people to congregate to perform major ceremonies. Dry-season foods included tubers, edible gum (which was mixed with other foods), and boab nuts. Bark from river gums was burned to make ashes, to be mixed with food or tobacco. This was the favoured time for hunting possums, for they were fatter, and Johnston's crocodiles, more easily captured in the billabongs. Freshwater species of shellfish were also easier to collect in the billabongs in the dry season, although most shellfish could be gathered throughout the year.

In the 'hot time' (September to November) root crops began to become scarce and hard to find. People burned off the grassland in communal drives for kangaroos, wallabies, smaller marsupials, reptiles, emus, and quails—some men set a fire while others waited with spears and clubs. The first rains would regenerate the vegetation, attracting marsupials and larger birds, which would be stalked by individual hunters. Crocodile eggs became available from October.

As the rainy season approached (mid November to late December) the weather became very hot and humid, with frequent lightning and some small storms. Many of the edible fruits had ripened, compensating for the shortage of root foods.

The main difference from the Sandbeach region is the reduced emphasis on marine resources for inland groups, although coastal resources were similar if more challenging to obtain.

Table 2.10 Ngarinyin people and their neighbours: Vegetable food resources through the year

■ = available

Vegetable Food	Jan	Feb	Mar	Apr	May	Jun	Jul	Aug	Sep	Oct	Nov	Dec
Roots and tubers												
Native grape (*Ampelocissus acetosa*) root					■	■	■	■	■	■	■	
Water lily (*Aponogeton elongatus*) tuber						■	■	■				
Buchanania florida (tree) root				■								
Green plum (*Buchanania oblovata*) root					■	■	■	■				
Ground creeper (*Boerhavia diffusa*) tuber	■	■	■	■	■							
Cartonema parviflorum tuber				■	■	■	■	■	■	■	■	
Kapok bush (*Cochlospermum fraseri*) root	■	■	■	■	■							
Water lily (*Colocasium antiquorum*) rhizome; caustic before cooking									■			
Commelina ensifolia root					■	■	■	■	■	■	■	
Curculigo ensifolia root					■	■	■	■	■	■	■	
Cyperus sp. bulb					■	■	■	■	■	■	■	
Round yam (*Dioscorea bulbifera*); requires cooking to make edible					■	■	■	■	■	■	■	■
Long yam (*D. transversa*) tuber					■	■	■	■	■	■	■	■
Rush (*Eleocharis sphacelata*) tuber					■	■	■	■	■	■	■	
Spike rush (*Eriosema chinense*) root					■	■	■	■	■	■	■	
Flemingia involucrate root					■	■	■	■		■	■	
Native rosella (*Hibiscus rhodopetalus*) root					■	■	■	■	■	■		
Hypoxis marginata bulb										■	■	■

Table 2.10 Continued

Vegetable Food	Jan	Feb	Mar	Apr	May	Jun	Jul	Aug	Sep	Oct	Nov	Dec
Ipomoea graminea tuber					■	■	■	■	■	■	■	
Bush potato (*Microstemma tuberosum*) bulb; mixed with green ants	■	■	■	■								
White waterlily (*Nymphaea* sp.) tuber and stem					■	■	■	■	■	■	■	■
Operculina brownii tuber				■	■	■	■	■	■	■	■	■
Tacca leontopetaloides tuber; cooked twice				■	■	■	■	■	■	■	■	■
Vigna sp. root				■	■	■	■	■	■	■	■	■
Vigna lanceolata root; at base of boab				■	■	■	■	■	■	■	■	■
Seeds and nuts												
Acacia tumida					■	■	■	■				
Boab tree (*Adansonia gregorii*)		■	■	■								
Kurrajong (*Brachychiton* sp.)											■	■
Kurrajong (*B. diversifolium*)											■	■
Kurrajong (*B. paradoxum*); gum can be stored											■	■
Turpentine tree (*Canarium australianum*)					■	■	■	■	■	■		
Cycad palm (*Cycas media*)									■	■		
Pandanus sp.									■			
'Bush almond' (*Terminalia* sp.)	■	■	■	■	■	■	■	■			■	■
Grasses (seldom used)												
Chrysopogon sp.					■	■	■					
Panicum delicatum					■	■	■					

Table 2.10 Continued

Food Staple	Jan	Feb	Mar	Apr	May	Jun	Jul	Aug	Sep	Oct	Nov	Dec
Fruits												
Native grape (*Ampelocissus acetosa*)				■	■	■						
Buchanania florida											■	
Buchanania obovata (sun-dried and stored)											■	
Cayratia trifolia					■	■	■	■	■	■	■	
Native cucumber (*Cucumis melo*)					■	■	■	■				
Syzigium sp.	■	■										
Little bush apple (*Syzygium armstrongii*)									■	■		
Bush apple (*Syzygium grandis*)									■	■		■
Rock fig (*Ficus platypoda*)					■	■	■	■				
Ficus racemosa	■										■	■
Milky plum (*Persoonia falcate*); pulverized or sun-dried, mixed with gum	■										■	■
Securinega sp.	■	■									■	■
Wild tomato (*Solanum dioicum*)					■	■	■	■				
Green plum (*Vitex glabrata*); ripe fruit can be sun-dried											■	■
Pith and shoots												
Boab tree (*Adansonia gregorii*)				■	■							
Fan palm (*Livistona* spp.)	■	■	■	■	■	■	■	■	■	■	■	■

Source: Crawford (1976)

Yolngu people

The region east of Cape Stewart and north of the Walker River is the home of speakers of Yolngu languages (see Map 5.9). With a tropical monsoon climate and plentiful resources, the northeast Arnhem Land environment is extremely varied, from habitable offshore islands divided from the mainland by narrow channels and shallow coastal waters, through inland swamps and plains, to rocky uplands. The northeast Arnhem Land environment and resources bear quite a strong similarity to those of eastern Cape York Peninsula and the Kimberley, but differ because of the presence of the great inland Arafura Swamp. Like Kŭnai and northwest Kimberley people, Yolngu people practiced a wide variety of local economies.

Land forms

Northeast Arnhem Land consists of a wedge-shaped peninsula of about 35 000 square kilometres between approximately $11°$ and $13°30'$ south and $134°30'$ and $137°$ east. It extends northeast, dividing the Gulf of Carpentaria from the Arafura Sea. The northern coast is broken by bays, inlets, and strings of islands. The eastern coast of the peninsula cuts southwest from Gove Peninsula to the mouth of the Roper River. Inland, rugged sandstone country rises to about 350 metres. Ranges run north and northeast into the sea to form small peninsulas, dividing deep bays and breaking up to form chains of islands.

Rivers meander north, draining the expansive Arafura Swamp into the Glyde River; their broad catchment area separates the ranges to the east from the high sandstone country to the west. The swamp forms a large, shallow lake of approximately 1300 square kilometres at the height of the wet season, drying out to form a black-soil plain; it is bounded on its northwest and northeast sides by well-marked escarpments which form something of a bottleneck either side of the estuary.

In the east of the region many creeks flow through deep rocky gorges fringed with cabbage palms (*Livistona* sp.) and pandanus thickets. The creeks and rivers flood in the wet season, sometimes violently, but subside during the dry season to leave deep permanent waterholes, as well as some chains of billabongs and lagoons near the main rivers. Many of the tidal estuaries meander through mangrove-covered islands and mud banks and open out into wide mouths.[39]

Climate

Like in eastern Cape York Peninsula and the northwest Kimberley, the Arnhem Land monsoon climate shows a marked contrast between wet and dry seasons. Most of the average 1150–1300 millimetres of rain (on the coast) falls between January and March, born on the northwest winds; the rain tapers off in April, but there are a few winter showers. In March the winds shift to the southeast to initiate the dry season, which extends from about April to October or November. Tropical cyclones bring violent winds and localised torrential downpours, but a major cyclone directly affects any one area only rarely. The variability of the annual rainfall is less than 0.75 (Table 2.1).

June and July have relatively cool nights, with lows of about 17°C. From late August onward the day and night temperatures increase, with an average daily maximum of about 34°C and average nocturnal temperatures of about 25°C in November (Table 2.2). Then the winds veer to the northwest, and increasingly frequent thunderstorms herald the onset of the wet season.[40]

Habitats and resources

Northeast Arnhem Land is awash with fresh and brackish water during the wet season and early dry season. However, the flood-plains dry up by the late dry season, leaving some permanent lagoons, swamps, and billabongs. The permanent springs in the mangroves and on some beaches were important in the Yolngu cosmology as well as for drinking and bathing; some were reserved for older men. People dug wells in the coastal dunes, and sometimes obtained water trapped in the bark of paperbark trees by cutting the bark.

Ecologists (such as Specht) describe several kinds of vegetation community (see Map 2.7).[41] The higher terrain, with its laterite soils, supports open forest (_diltji_, or 'back' country) of stringybark (_Eucalyptus tetrodonta_) and woollybutt (_E. miniata_), with a grassy understorey and variably distributed stands of cycad palms (_Cycas media_), _Livistona humilis_ palms, cyprus pine, bloodwoods, ironwood, acacias, cabbage palms, and grevilleas. The stands of cycad palms were a major resource. Wallabies inhabited the margins, while emus and antilope kangaroos grazed in the deeper parts of the woodland. These large mammals and birds tended to become localised as the country flooded in the wet season. People also valued this environment as a source of honey from native bees.

The sandy detritus between the black-soil plains and the laterite uplands carries a low savannah woodland with grassy understorey. This habitat supports trees bearing edible fruits and seeds, while the bark and sap of other trees were also useful.

The slopes of the escarpment and the river banks support stands of monsoon rainforest with a relatively clear understorey. Cabbage palms (_Livistona_ sp.) and pandanus thickets line the creeks of the rocky gorges. Clumps of vine forest, from a few dozen square metres to a square kilometre in extent, stand on the margins of freshwater swamps and behind coastal dunes. Mainly deciduous trees dominate the vegetation, some providing wood for dugout canoes as well as fibre. Palms such as _Carpentaria acuminata_ yield edible pith. The most important food resource in this habitat was the yams, most readily found in the early dry season before the vines withered and became hard to find. Fruits included some from the sandy fan-delta complex. The vine forest gives cover to wallabies, goannas, carpet snakes, and the mound-building jungle fowl. Its plants provided spear shafts, fish poisons, dyes, and vines for the wicker work used in fish-traps.

Dense blady-grass (_Imperata cylindrica_), which can grow to a height of two metres, covered a greater part of the coastal and estuarine plains, making them impenetrable until they were burnt off in the dry season. Stands of paperbark trees (_Melaleuca leu-_

Map 2.7   Northeast Arnhem Land vegetation

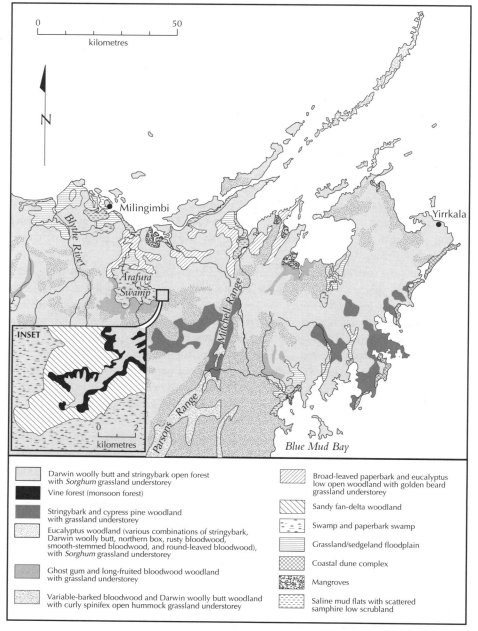

Source: Conservation Commission of the Northern Territory (1991)

cadendra and dwarf paperbark) grew where the swamps remained moist for much of the year. The plains became inaccessible during the height of the wet season, covered as they were in *Sorghum stipoideum*, a grass that reaches a metre or more in height. As the waters receded people could gather wild rice and spike rush (see Plate 2.4).

Plate 2.4   Yolngu women digging *rakay* (spike rush) in the dry season (photograph by D. F. Thomson, TPH977, courtesy of Mrs D. M. Thomson and Museum Victoria)

Edible roots and tubers grew on the margins of swamps and in deep depressions, home also to reptiles such as *Varanus gouldii* and the long-necked tortoise.

Freshwater swamps and lagoons were home to a variety of edible water plants, including waterlilies and spike rush. Fish, of course, proliferated in these environments, which ranged from freshwater to brackish depending on the season and the state of the tides. Many species of fish, including barramundi and various kinds of catfish, tolerated a range of conditions from fresh to salt. Men caught these in various types of fish-trap, or speared them in pools (in the late dry season), and stunned them using fish-poison. Freshwater mussels provided food, and mudfish became isolated in chains of pools along perennial rivers and streams. Water birds proliferated on the shrinking waters as the dry season progressed, with goose eggs (especially of magpie geese) later becoming a major resource at the height of the wet season. Long-necked tortoises buried themselves and their eggs in the mud, to be dug out in the late wet season to mid dry season.

Mangroves line much of the coast and the islands, and the estuaries and their creeks. Occasionally broken by sandy beaches or rugged cliffs, they give way to extensive saline mud-flats and black-soil grass-plains. The mangroves provided a breeding and feeding habitat for forty edible species of fish. The mangrove jack, javelin fish, and bream could be caught with tidal barriers and fish traps, or with fish-spears. The mangroves yielded mud crabs, shellfish, and the water monitor, and birds, including ibises, egrets, herons, and cormorants.

Old channels behind coastal dunes supported spike-rush swamps, while thickets of monsoon forest and pandanus palms stood on older dune systems further inland. The poor soils of the dunes supported fruit trees, including the tamarind trees introduced by the Macassan trepangers. At or above the high-tide line there was *Morinda citrifolia*, which provided wood for smoking pipes, and hibiscus, which was used for spear shafts and fibre for the heavy rope used in hunting turtles and dugong. In the waters trapped behind the dunes stood pandanus palms, with their edible kernels and leaves that were essential for making implements and clothes, as well as vine thickets, some on old middens. Casuarinas gave valuable shade. People also sought the eggs of marine turtles on the beaches.

Some twenty species of edible fish could be found in the shallow coastal waters, including whiting, mullets, and stingrays. As among Sandbeach people, men hunted marine turtles and dugong in the shallows using dugout canoes; their canoes did not have outriggers but sometimes were equipped with a woven pandanus sail. The thirty edible species of shellfish were another a major resource.

The offshore reefs and rocky islets provided homes for marine life and seabirds. The habitats and resources on the larger islands were similar to those on the mainland, but lacked large rivers.

Seasonality

An inland year

In this region resources had a marked seasonality. The Yolngu recognised six or seven seasons, distinguished by the presence or absence of thunder and rains, the state of the vegetation, and the direction of winds. The timing and intensity of seasons varied from year to year. I draw first on Nicolas Peterson's and Donald Thomson's descriptions of Yolngu ecology to summarise the seasonal availability of food resources around the Arafura Swamp.

In the early wet season (*dhuludurr* or *barramirri*, meaning 'northwest monsoon winds', in the Gupapuyngu language) vegetable foods were in short supply because of the waterlogged ground, and access to swamp foods became difficult. Cycad palm nuts (*ngathu*), which were pounded, leached to remove toxins, and made into a bread, constituted an important staple in some areas. People hunted large game, but the wind and rain made fish hard to catch.

At the height of the wet season (*gunmul, waltjanmirri*), usually from January to March, food remained in short supply. Seasonal fruits from the sandy fan–delta and vine forest tided people over until the yams become available again. The winds veered to the west and southeast. *Mayaltha* was the time when the new, 'soft' shoots (*marrayalnggi*) appeared, from about March to April.

From late March through April, at the end of the wet season (*midawarr*) the southeast wind (*dhimurru*) began to blow, but conditions remained hot and humid with scattered showers. The grass remained long and rank but the flood-waters began to retreat. The abundant vegetable foods included yam staples from the monsoon forest. In April, products of the sandy soils (such as *Discorea transversa* and *D. bulbifera*) became available to supplement the yams. Fish and shellfish became abundant, and as the waters receded people engaged in cooperative fish drives using fish traps, weirs, and nets.

Large mammals and birds, such as emus, bustards, kangaroos, and wallabies, were easy to hunt because of the noisy wind and the long grass in which hunters could hide. Honey was available from about February through to July. Men hunted magpie geese and collected their eggs, as well as those of other water-birds, and people dug out long-necked tortoises and their eggs from the swamps.

The flowering of the *gadayka* or stringybark tree (*Eucalyptus tetrodonta*) and the rise of an incessant southeast wind marked the onset of the dry season, which usually lasted from late April to August. People called the months from May to July 'cold-weather time' (*dharratharramirri*). The swamps and plains gradually dried out, and people systematically burnt off the grass of the plains and forest to make travel easier and to reduce the number of mosquitoes and poisonous snakes. Burning off was accompanied by communal hunting drives for kangaroos, bandicoots, and goannas. Residents of Mirrngadja on the southeast side of the Arafura Swamp lived on the sandy fan–delta complex during this period (see inset, Map 2.7). As the weather became hotter (*rarrandharr*, 'when the ground is hot'), leaves withered and got burnt in the fires, making plant foods hard to find. But by late August swamp products again became abundant, especially waterlilies (*dirrpu*, *Nymphaea* sp.). From August, nuts from the stands of cycad palms in the open forest provided a staple, as did rush corms.

People fished in the remaining shallow waters of the plains and saline mud-flats, using grass barriers, nets, and fish spears. Among the most valued fish were saratoga (*Scleropages leichhardtii*) and catfish (*Neoarius australis*). Mudfish (*Oxyeleotris lineolatus*) became important toward the end of the dry season as the rivers turned into chains of shallow pools.

Women gathered long-necked tortoises and their eggs from the sandy fan–delta, providing staple foods from the end of the wet season to the middle of the dry season. Amphibians and reptiles also became important foods from April to October; they were found in or near fresh water and in sandy soils, such as those alongside large rivers. Honey continued to be available.

In the late dry season, through September and October, the wind veered to the northeast (*lunggurrma*). Lightning struck frequently, and the first thunder could be heard (*wulmamirri*, 'thundery'). The yam vines were harder to find but certain staples became available in large quantities, including lilies, cycad palm nuts, and, later, rush corms (*Eleocharis dulcis*). Fish became easy to catch, being concentrated in the shallow waters, and reptiles were an important food.

Bread made of cycad palm nuts and rush corms from the estuarine plains became staple vegetable foods in the late dry season. People caught such reptiles as file snakes (which were isolated in reedy lakes, pools, and streams), long-necked tortoises, Macleay's water snake, and the olive python. People stunned fish with poison and also caught water-birds.

In the 'pre-wet' (*ngurru-waḻtjan*), from late October to early December, when heat and humidity increased to their maximum and violent thunderstorms became more frequent, the wind veered to the northwest (*barra*), heralding the monsoon. The first rains came at *dhuḻudurr*. Bread of cycad palm nuts continued to be a staple food until March in some areas. Many species of fruit again became plentiful, including green plum (*Vitex glabrata*) and the white berries of *Flueagga microcarpa*. Birds, amphibians, and reptiles such as file snakes remained important through November.

A coastal year

Betty Meehan and Rhys Jones lived with Anbarra people on the north-central Arnhem Land coast in the early 1970s; their research shows that the diet of the people on the coast differed most significantly from that of the inland people in containing a large component of marine foods.[42] The coastal people also relied more on store-bought foods than did inland people at the time of Thomson's and Peterson's research. The marine foods they ate included fish, stingrays, crabs, and shellfish such as saltwater mussel and cockles (*Anadara granosa*); all these foods were cooked in large quantities in steam ovens for the end of a ceremony. Men performing in a secret phase of a ceremony ate more red meat than others, and women and children supplied large quantities of cycad-palm-nut bread and shellfish, and sometimes flour damper (unleavened bread cooked in ashes), to the men at the ceremony ground. Wet-season fruits included lady apple (*Syzygium suborbicularis*) and Indian mulberry (*Morinda citrifolia*).

During the mid-to-late dry season at Kopanga (August–December in 1972), people collected fruits including cocky apple (*Planchonia careya*), blackberry tree, or green plum (*Vitex glabrata*), and lady apple (*Syzygium suborbicularis*), as well as pandanus nuts, yams, and spike rush. Wallabies, goannas, long-necked tortoises, shellfish from brackish and salt waters, stingrays and other fish, and crabs provided the flesh component of the diet, while mangrove worms and honey added variety.

As the rains eased and the land began to dry up, women foraged in the hinterland to add new foods to the diet: spike rush, yams, fruits (including *Mimusops elengi*, a medicinal plant), waterlilies, young goannas (*Varanus* spp.), and long-necked tortoises. Men hunted for wallabies as well as ducks, magpie geese, and other birds, and put their large fish-traps into operation, one on a creek near the shore, 2 kilometres to the west of the camp. They caught mainly barramundi.

While hinterland resources remained important to coastal people, they relied much more on sea foods, but the seasonal round was similar in the two environments.

Table 2.11 North-central Arnhem Land vegetable foods through the year

■ = plentiful   ▨ = available

Vegetable Food	Dhuludhur	Gunmul— wet season	Midawarr— late wet season	Dharratharra mirri ('cold weather')— dry season			Rarrandharr ('hot ground')	Lunggurrma ('northeast wind')		Wulmamirri ('thundery')	
	Jan	Feb	Mar	Apr	May	Jun	Jul	Aug	Sep	Oct	Nov	Dec
Roots and tubers												
Waterlilies (*Nymphaea*, ca three spp.)			▨	■	■	■	▨					
Spike rush (*Eleocharis dulcis*)					▨	■	■	■	■	▨		
Long yam (*Dioscorea transversa*)				■	■	■	■	■			■	■
Round yam (*Dioscorea bulbifera*)				■	■	■	■	■			■	■
Polynesian arrowroot (*Tacca leontopetaloides*)				▨	▨	▨	▨					
Sweet potato vine (*Ipomea* sp.)												
Water ribbons (*Triglochin procera*)				▨	▨	▨	▨	▨				
Wild mung (*Vigna vexillata*)							▨	▨	▨			
Bush grape (*Cayratia trifolia*)											▨	▨
Boerhavia diffusa								▨				
Typhonium angustilobum											▨	▨
Scirpus littoralis (a reed)									▨	▨	▨	▨
Seeds and nuts												
Terminalia carpentariae						▨	■	■				
Pandanus spiralis									■	■	■	▨
Peanut tree (*Sterculia quadrifida*)									■	■		

Table 2.11 Continued

Vegetable Food	Dhuludhurr	Gunmul—wet season	Midawarr—late wet season		Dharrathara mirri ('cold weather')—dry season			Rarrandharr ('hot ground')	Lunggurma ('northeast wind')	Wulmamirri ('thundery')		
	Jan	Feb	Mar	Apr	May	Jun	Jul	Aug	Sep	Oct	Nov	Dec
Wild rice (*Oryza rufipogon*)			■	■	■							
Fruits												
Blackberry tree (*Vitex glabrata*)											■	
Lady Apple (*Syzygium suborbiculare*)	■	■										■
Indian mulberry (*Morinda citrifolia*)	■	■	■	■	■	■	■					■
Pouteria sericea					■	■						
Mimusops elengi						■	■	■				
Cocky apple (*Planchonia careya*)									■	■	■	
Ficus racemosa						■	■					
Bluebell creeper (*Sollya heterophylla*)	■	■	■						■	■	■	■
Pith												
Palm (*Carpentaria acuminata*)										■		
Fan palm (*Livistona humilis*)	■	■	■									

Sources: Jones (1980) and Meehan (1982)

Animal and vegetable foods

Betty Meehan found that, at an Anbarra outstation during 1972–73, animal foods and sea foods made a similar contribution to the diet as they had before the availability of flour, rice, and sugar. She estimates that vegetable foods would have constituted 31% of the diet by weight (57% of the kilocalories, 20% of the protein) before food from stores became available, considerably less than in Gould's study of the Western Desert. Men probably ate more flesh than females because they often cooked and consumed large quantities of fish at dinner camps before returning to

Table 2.12 North-central Arnhem Land animal, reptile, and bird foods through the year

■ = plentiful   ▨ = available

Food	Jan	Feb	Mar	Apr	May	Jun	Jul	Aug	Sep	Oct	Nov	Dec
Shellfish												
Shellfish in general	■	■	■	■	■	■	■	■	■	■	■	■
Species thrown up by monsoon storms	■	■										
Mangrove species						▨	■	■	■	■	■	▨
Fish												
Fish caught by spear, hook, or net	■	■	■	■	■	■	■	■	■	■	■	■
Fish caught in fish-traps			▨	■	■	■	■	▨				
Mammals												
Wallabies	▨					▨	■	■	■	■	■	■
Birds												
Geese									▨	■		
Reptiles												
Goannas						▨	■	■	■	■	■	▨
Freshwater tortoises								■	■	■	■	■
Marine turtle eggs		■	■	■		▨						

Source: Jones (1980) and Meehan (1982)

the home base. Mature women ate less overall, for they shared their food, especially with children. Altman comes to similar conclusions about production in an eastern Kunwinjku outstation nearby. He adds that women could produce up to five kilograms per day of yams, which is comparable with the figures on Western Desert women's production rates.[43]

In marked contrast with Gould's remarks about the unreliability of men's hunting, Altman notes the predictability of the production of animal food and fish in Arnhem

Land, enhanced by the use of fish-traps and nets. He thinks that the use of shotguns did not greatly increase the chances of success over the use of spears and spear-throwers.

Comparisons and conclusions

This chapter has drawn on a range of studies to reconstruct the environmental conditions of each region, the food and water resources, and the resources' habitats and seasonality. These are summarised in Table 13.1.

Four broad resource zones

The seven regions belong to four broad zones distinguished according to climate and biota (see Table 13.2).

Kŭnai people exploited southeastern coastal flora and fauna, in their case centred around lakes and estuaries as well as forests and plains. They depended on a diverse range of food species; the important staples were root foods of various kinds—Austral bracken, tuberous herbs, orchids, and aquatic plants such as Typha. Seeds were not a dominant feature of their diet. Fish and waterfowl played as important a role here as among Yuwaaliyaay people and the people of the tropical north, and some marine resources were readily obtainable along Ninety Mile Beach.

Two of the case studies—Pitjantjatjara and Yuwaaliyaay—lie in what Mulvaney and Kamminga call the 'Aboriginal grain belt' of the semi-arid and arid zones, the importance of which Norman Tindale has pointed out.[44] Fish were unavailable in the arid zone of course, and grass seed became important as a staple, linked to seed-grinding technology. Other characteristic plant foods included the *Solanum* species as well as quandongs and wild figs. Small reptiles stand out among the animal foods, with large mammals much more rare and harder to catch. On the western edge of the grain belt, Yuwaaliyaay people also had access to the flora, fish, and fowl of rivers, wetlands, and woodlands.

The heath and mallee that Wiil and Miɲong people lived among provided a different diet again, a diverse mix of herbs, lilies, orchids, and shrubs, along with forest and wetland game and many fish. The zamia nut required processing to render it edible. The main contrast with people of the northern coast (and indeed other coasts) was the relative absence of shellfish in the diet. Seals were the main marine mammal in the diet, with an occasional beached whale.

The fourth zone, what Rhys Jones called the Australian 'tropical savanna' region, has a tropical monsoon climate and a band of characteristically northern flora and fauna.[45] The dominant climatic factor controlling the vegetation is the seasonal variation in rainfall: most of the rain falls in the summer months, brought by the northwest monsoon, and hence most plant growth occurs in these months. Eucalypt woodland forms the main structural component of the vegetation. The typical staple foods of this broad zone included the yam species (*Dioscorea elongata* and *D. rotunda*, the second of which required careful preparation), rush corms, the toxic cycad palm nut (which needs extensive leaching to be edible), and the tropical fruit trees. On the coasts, the marine turtles and mammals played an important part in the diet, as did many kinds of fish and shellfish.

A notable characteristic of all the case studies is the very broad range of food species on which people drew, and the availability of at least some foods throughout the year. In Fiona Walsh's view, survival necessitated the maintenance of a broad resource base, avoiding reliance on any one species because that species might have become unproductive under adverse conditions.[46]

Seasonality

All the case studies display some seasonality in resources. However, seasonality varied from year to year, especially in the Western Desert (Pitjantjatjara and their neighbours) and the Darling/Barwon River region (Yuwaaliyaay and their neighbours). Nevertheless, except in times of exceptional drought, the diversity of food species provided an adequate diet throughout the year in all the regions; as certain staples dropped out so others came into season. Less popular foods, such as mangrove pods, provided a fallback when the desirable foods failed. Certain seasons and conditions imposed regular stresses; for example, the early wet season brought difficulties in the tropical north until the yam staples matured. Moreover, the regular droughts brought by El Niño could have devastating effects. The seasonal cycle also had an impact on residence and the possibility of conducting various activities (covered in Chapter 4); for example, most major ceremonies in the tropical north took place at the end of the dry season, when people concentrated around main waters.

Biomass and resources

What does not show up in the case studies is the quantity of foods available in relation to area, related in part to biomass. We can indirectly infer the range of variation in biomass from estimated population densities (see Chapter 4). The densities are expressed here (Table 2.13) as persons per 100 square kilometres; also shown is the mean annual rainfall for each area. However, the relation between population density and rainfall is far from straightforward: the very high densities are associated with coastal or lacustrine resources and those of the Darling/Barwon River, which are brought in from outside the region.

Table 2.13 Population densities, rainfall, and external sources of resources

People	Estimated population density (persons/100km2)	Mean annual rainfall (mm)	External sources of resources
Pitjantjatjara	0.5–1.25	215–31	None
Yuwaaliyaay	1.7–3.1	413–78	Darling/Barwon River
Will/Minong	2–20	625–934	Coastal waters, river basins
Kŭnai	2.5–20	607–1060	Coastal waters, lakes
Ngarinyin	4–25	757–1374	Coastal waters
Yolngu	5–50	1157–1318	Coastal waters
Sandbeach	7–40	2159	Coastal waters

Moreover, the relation of biomass to food resources is complex. In areas of high primary biomass, such as tropical rainforests, plants invest more energy in structural maintenance and the capture of sunlight than in growing the parts that are edible for humans—namely, those to do with reproduction (seeds and fruits) or storage (tubers, etc.). Animals tend to be small, few in number, and located in the treetops; the large animals are widely spaced. In areas of low primary biomass, on the other hand, plants invest less energy in structural maintenance and growth, and more in seeds and fruits. In dry environments many plants with a relatively low primary biomass have large tubers—an adaptation to drought and fire. Hence, primary biomass tends to be inversely correlated with the effective amount of edible plant food, and inversely related to faunal abundance and distribution. To take an example from the case studies, the primary productivity of the Sandbeach environment was high, because tropical rainforest covered a substantial part of the land. Vegetable foods were relatively scarce in this habitat, and were concentrated along the coastal sand-dunes, mangroves, and riverine vine-forests, where they were abundant. Sandbeach people also exploited many riverine and marine resources.[47]

The production of animal and vegetable foods

The two case studies (Pitjantjatjara and their neighbours, and Yolngu) that covered the mix of animal and vegetable foods revealed some key differences. The high degree of reliance on animal foods, especially large game and fish, in the tropical north (about 43% of the diet by kilocalories, 69% by weight) contrasts strongly with the relatively minor place of animal foods in the diet in the Western Desert (about 15% by weight in Gould's study); however, the limited scope of the research may have skewed the findings somewhat.

The distribution of resources in relation to environmental conditions

Complementing seasonality and biomass, an aspect of the geography of resources not discussed in this chapter is variation in the mobility and distribution of resources. Leonn Satterthwait has pointed out that wetlands concentrate birds and some mammals, pulling them in from a wide area (see Chapter 3), and Louis Binford has examined the implications for human residence and mobility of the degree to which resources are localised (see Chapter 4). Some of the variables relevant to such a study are the degree of mobility of resources, the degree to which they are clumped or scattered, and the degree of variability through time (or the degree of predictability).[48]

Further reading

This chapter has touched on several issues and debates in anthropology and related disciplines. On explaining relations between environments, technology, culture, and the organisation of society see Roy Ellen's *Environment, Subsistence, and System: The Ecology of Small-scale Social Formations* (1982). On the relationship between ecological and economic analysis see Rhoda Halperin's *Cultural Economies Past and Present* (1994).

On the general features of the Australian environment and the impact of humans upon it, Tim Flannery's *The Future Eaters* (1997) is a provocative study, and R. L. Heathcote (1994) provides a sound introduction.

Classic studies of the impact of the seasonality of climate on resources and human resource-use in the tropical north include Donald Thomson's *The Seasonal Factor in Human Culture* (1939) and Nicolas Peterson's 'Camp site location amongst Australian hunter-gatherers' (1973). W. E. H. Stanner outlined a program for research on Aboriginal human ecology in his 'Aboriginal territorial organisation' (1965), taken up in the 1970s by the Cape York ecology project supported by the Australian Institute of Aboriginal Studies. This chapter and other chapters draw on some of the results of that project in the work of Athol Chase, Peter Sutton, and John Von Sturmer.

On the debate over the relative contribution of animals and vegetable resources, see the references in the endnotes to works by Mervyn Meggitt, Betty Meehan (formerly Hiatt), Richard Gould, and Jon Altman.

Notes

1   On environmental constraints see Torrence (2001: 85–7).

2   Rose (2000) gives an account of the concept of enabling conditions. See Ellen (1982: 74) on the concept of ecological system, and pp. 21–51 on possibilism.

3   For a description of the general characteristics of the Australian environment see Heathcote (1994: 15–52).

4   On the relative contribution of animal and vegetable foods see Gould (1969a), Hiatt (1967; 1970), McArthur (1960), Meggitt (1964), Jones and Bowler (1980: 19–20), Meehan (1980), and Peterson (1973).

5   On the Gippsland climate see Land Conservation Council of Victoria (1974: 15–16, 19–21, 54; 1982: 50–55, 62) and Hotchin (1990: 18–19).

6   On Gippsland vegetation see Land Conservation Council of Victoria (1974; 1982; 1985), Stearns (1984), and Woodgate et al. (1999). The main sources on Aboriginal food species of the Gippsland region on which I have drawn are Bulmer (in Smyth 1878; 1994), Dow (1997), Gott (1982; 1998; 1999; 2001), Hotchin (1990), Howitt (Papers, SLV Box 8 ms 1053(b)), and Wesson (1991). Coral Dow and Beth Gott have provided information in comments on drafts of this section.

7   See Hotchin (1990: 134–5, 196, 199) for an account of the marine resources mentioned in the early literature, and for an interpretation of the archaeological record; see Coutts et al. (n.d.: 47) on the archaeology of Wilsons Promontory.

8   On the lakes region and Wilsons promontory see Coutts et al. (n.d.: 46), Coutts (1967: 236), and Hotchin (1990: 117). On herbs of the plains see Gott (2000: 4).

9   On Western Desert land forms see Leeper (1970) and Davey (1969).

10   Gentilli (1978) discusses the Western Desert climate.

11   The sources on which I have drawn regarding Western Desert food resources and their habitats include Gould (1980) and Walsh (1990). On fauna in general see Davey (1969), and on Pintupi resources see Myers (1986).

12   On Western Desert water resources see Gould (1969a: 62), Tonkinson (1991), and Walsh (1990: 27–9).

13   See Walsh (1990: 31) on Mardu resources.

14   On Western Desert vegetation see Burbidge et al. (1976) and Burrows et al. (1987).

15   Tindale (1972: 233) records Pitjantjatjara seasons; however, I have corrected some of his terms after consulting with Laurent Dousset and Fredric Viesner, and checking Douglas's *Dictionary of the Western Desert Language* (1977).

16   On the seasonality of Western Desert resources see Gould (1980: 64), Tonkinson (1991), and Walsh (1990).

17   These figures compare with Gould's finding (1967: 59) that following a hunt each person's share averaged 3.3 to 4 kilograms (1.5 to 1.85 pounds), each portion further shared with up to ten people.

18   See Gould (1967: 58–9; 1980: 64, 66) on yields of plant and animal foods, Hamilton (1979: 208) on meat, and Walsh (1990) on Mardu women's productivity.

19   Allen (1972: 2–3) describes land forms in the Darling Basin.

20   For food resources of the Darling/Barwon River region I have drawn on Allen (1972), Dunbar (1943–44: 175, cited in Allen 1972: 81), Frith and Calaby (1969: 92), Frith (1967: 11), Gott (2001), Parker (1905: 110, 116), and Teulon (in Curr 1886 Vol. 2: 201)

21 On the vegetation of the Darling/Barwon region see Allen (1972), Carnahan and Deveson (1990), and Helman (1986).

22 On crayfish see Beveridge (1883: 49–50), cited in Allen (1972: 70). Beveridge was writing about the Murray River, but presumably the upper Darling was similar in this regard. Eyre's observation is mentioned in Gould (1980: 95).

23 On net hunting see Parker (1905: 108).

24 See Mitchell (1839: 90–8) on stooking grass.

25 On rivers and their resources in the Darling/Barwon River region see Allen (1972: 68), Lake (1975; 1978), and Sturt (1849 vol. II: 117–8).

26 On the land forms of the region see Chippendale (1973) and Bird (1985).

27 See Beard (1976), Chippendale (1973), and Gentilli (1978) on the Albany–Bremer Bay region climate.

28 This section on habitats and resources draws on Bird (1985: 131–5), Ferguson (1987), Meagher (1974: 60), and Meagher and Ride (1979: 73–4). Beard (1976; 1979) and Hutton (1981: 230) describe the vegetation of the Albany–Bremer Bay region.

29 On the water resources of the Albany–Bremer Bay region see Bird (1985: 130–1) and Ferguson (1987: 124).

30 On the range and seasonality of Wiil and Minong resources see Barker (1992: 22 January, 22 April, 3 October, 5 October 1830), Bird (1985), Green (1989: 14, 16, 20, 35), and Nind (1831: 36).

31 Caroline Bird (pers. com.) found historical sources on the herding of fish using dolphins in the Southwest; Jay Hall (1984) has found evidence of cooperation between humans and dolphins in southeast Queensland, and of similar practices in other parts of the world.

32 On eastern Cape York Peninsula land forms see Lavarack and Godwin (1987: 203).

33 On the habitats and climate of the Sandbeach region see Chase and Sutton (1987), Biggs and Philip (1995), Danaher (1995), Horn (1995: 21, 49), Isbell (1980a; 1980b), Keast (1981: 1702–3), and Lavarack and Godwin (1987: 204–5). Chase (1980b: 150) reports Sandbeach categories of the environment.

34 The section on Sandbeach habitats and resources draws mainly on Chase and Sutton's work on habitats and seasonality (1987: 77–9), Thomson's research (1933: 457–8), and Thomson's photographic collection on Sandbeach plant and animal resources (held in the Museum of Victoria, Melbourne).

35 See Thomson (MV Thomson photographic collection 2942–6).

36 On northwest Kimberley land forms see Crawford (1976) and O'Connor (1993).

37 On northwest Kimberley water resources see Crawford (1976), and on those of coasts and islands see O'Connor (1993).

38 Beard (1978: 55–63) describes northwest Kimberley vegetation; on the west coast and the islands see O'Connor (1993). The main sources on food resources, their habitats, and seasonality for the northwest Kimberley are Crawford (1976) and Blundell (1975 vol. II), and for the coast, O'Connor (1993). There is also some information in Love (Papers, 1936: 15)

39 On northeast Arnhem Land land forms and habitats see Meehan (1982), Thomson (1948a), Peterson (1973), and Specht (1958).

40 On the northeast Arnhem Land climate see Camm and McQuilton (1987: 24) and Powell (1982).

41 On vegetation in northeast Arnhem Land see Thomson (1948a), Peterson (1973), and Specht (1958).

42 I have drawn on the research of Jones (1980) and Meehan (1982) regarding north-central Arnhem Land coastal resources.

43 On the relative contribution of men and women to eastern Kunwinjku and Anbarra diets see Altman (1987: 94, 149–51) and Meehan (1982: 93–5).

44 See Mulvaney and Kamminga (1999) and Tindale (1974: 99) on the 'Aboriginal grain belt'.

45 See Jones and Bowler (1980) on the 'tropical savanna'.

46 On the necessity for a broad resource base see Walsh (1990: 28–9).

47 This discussion draws on Kelly (1995: 122–5).

48 See Lee (1988) on the implications of abundance, scarcity, clumping, and distribution of resources in the ecology of primates.

Technology

[L]iving principally on wild roots and animals, he tilled this land and cultivated
his pastures with fire.

Edward Curr, *Recollections of Squatting in Victoria* (1883)

Introduction

By 'technology' I mean primarily material instruments ('hardware') and the techniques for employing them. This includes objects such as containers, tools, and
facilities (e.g. fish-traps) and their uses; chemical processes such as the use of plant-
poisons and the reduction of toxicity by leaching; and the use of fire in a variety of
ways. Material technologies include not only tools, but knowledge of what tools to
use and alternative ways of using them. As Bamforth and Bleed note, people need to
be knowledgeable about such matters as how and where to obtain tools, where and
at what time of year particular activities are best undertaken, and how work should
be organised.[1]

The technologies that Aboriginal people brought to bear on the resources
reviewed in the last chapter were based on hand tools and implements, stone tool-
making technology (in conjunction with shell knives, bone, etc.), and human power
rather than animal power or fossil fuels. Fire was an important instrument for managing environments, manufacturing, food-processing, and heating. The overall
character of a suite of technologies is governed in part by what might be called the
'technology of technologies'—that is, the very basic processes used in the harnessing
of energy, the appropriation of raw materials, and the conversion of raw materials.[2]

It is fair to say that anthropology as a discipline has neglected the study of technology. The evolutionists of the nineteenth century took technologies as markers of
stages in social and cultural evolution, but the social anthropology that developed in
the twentieth century out of French sociological theory neglected technology almost
entirely. Technology reappeared in the materialist anthropology of Leslie White and
his successors, who worked in the mid twentieth century in the United States, but
their approach is now largely out of fashion. The anthropology of technology has
burgeoned recently in France, and some lone voices (such as Bryan Pfaffenberger,

Paul Lemmonier and Tim Ingold) have tried to arouse interest in technology in English-speaking anthropology. Descriptions of Aboriginal technologies have been relegated to appendices of ethnographies (such as in Warner's *A Black Civilization*) or made the subject of special studies under the heading of 'material culture'. With some exceptions, archaeologists working in Australia have largely confined their studies to stone and bone implements and not the full suite of tools and implements; this is because of the nature of the material remains. Among those who have explored the relationship between Aboriginal technology and the organisation of social life are Leonn Satterthwait, in his pioneering study of net-hunting, and Annette Hamilton, in her examination of men's and women's tools and implements (Hamilton's interest reflected her neo-Marxist orientation in the late 1970s and early 1980s).[3]

Certain similarities in the technologies and techniques of the seven regions will become apparent, but we will also encounter marked variation.

General features of Aboriginal technologies

An important dimension of any technology is the knowledge people bring to bear in using it. Aboriginal people acquired, shared, and transmitted knowledge about raw materials, the construction and use of items of equipment, the seasonality and distribution of resources, and methods for tracking game and finding plants and other food. Complex knowledge is implied in all of the following categories of technologies and techniques.

Energy

With wood as their main fuel, Aboriginal people used fire for a wide variety of purposes: to warm themselves and cook their food; to shape and harden raw materials in the manufacture of implements; to produce smoke to act as an insect repellent and deodorant; to burn off the forest understorey and grasslands in order to manage plant resources, encourage re-growth (and so attract game), and enhance mobility; and for ritual purposes. People made fire with fire-drills and fire-saws, but also carried firebrands from place to place, and equipped canoes with clay hearths.[4]

Aboriginal people were unassisted by domesticated animals, and so their mobility was limited during rainy seasons in the tropics, and during floods in other regions. However, they did use some non-human energy sources to help with transport: Yolngu people used (limited) wind power for propelling dugout canoes (sometimes fitted with a sail), a technology adopted from Macassan visitors from Sulawesi, and people harnessed water power to the extent of riding on the flow of a river or, as in the western Kimberley, the tide.

Portability

A corollary of hunting and gathering as a mode of subsistence is the relative mobility of people, who have to move to the places where food resources happen to be located. As Shott points out, mobile groups are likely to minimise transport costs by making tools portable, so that the degree of portability of implements is likely to increase with a people's mobility. The costs of portability will be weighed against replacement costs, however—a durable axe, for example, may be worth carrying. Not only portability but greater costs of supply may have led to a preference for multi-functional implements. Sandbeach and Yolngu people used more specialised and diverse containers, tools, and weapons compared with the people of the arid zone, where implements tended to be fewer in number and multi-functional, enhancing portability. Rather fragile temporary shelter could be quickly and easily erected. However, coastal people who visited the islands off the west Kimberley coast left stone rings as the bases of shelters, to be reused on subsequent visits, while Yolngu people built substantial timber platforms in their wet-season camps.[5]

Raw materials

Aboriginal people drew on a very wide range of raw materials from the environment: animal, vegetable, and mineral products. These materials were shaped and manipulated, but underwent little of the physical and chemical conversion that is found, for example, in pottery- or iron-making. The selection of raw materials reflected people's perceptions and experience of their suitability for a particular purpose, whether to provide a fibrous quality for string, a sharp edge, or malleability suitable for shaping into a container. The processing of raw materials included the heating of wood to bend it into shape, the flaking and retouching of stone, assisted by the use of heat in many areas, the grinding of stone edges, the mastication of plant material to make fibre for spinning, and the heating of ochres to change their colour.

Tool-making tools

Tool-making tools and techniques are those employed in the manufacture of other tools, weapons, and facilities. Typically, Aboriginal tool-making equipment included stone hammers and wooden mallets; bone awls for sewing and basket-making; shell and stone chisels, scrapers, and knives; edge-ground and hafted stone axes and adzes; drills and augers, often made of a marsupial's lower jaw and teeth; and spindles used to make string. Simple looms assisted in the making of knotted or looped string bags, nets, and items of apparel (see Plate 3.1).

Some of these tool-making tools also served as production equipment—knives for butchering and hafted stone hatchets for extracting grubs or mangrove worms from wood.

The main manufacturing techniques used by people of the seven regions included:
- stone knapping
- grinding and abrading stone
- bone and wood carving
- the conversion of plant material into fibre by chewing
- spinning fibre into rope and string between the palm of the hand and the thigh, or with the use of a frame

Plate 3.1   A Sandbeach woman working at a loom (photograph by D. F. Thomson, TPH3559, courtesy of Mrs D. M. Thomson and Museum Victoria)

- the twining of leaf fibre for baskets and mats
- looped and knotted string techniques for bags and nets
- the preparation of skins for cloaks and bags, including tanning with acacia bark
- folding and sewing bark for containers and watercraft
- stone wall construction
- various wood-working techniques, including tied-pole construction for house frames, fish-traps, etc., wickerwork for fish-traps, and, in the west Kimberley, wooden nails for raft construction
- timber-hollowing techniques
- bark, foliage, and grass cladding techniques for shelters.

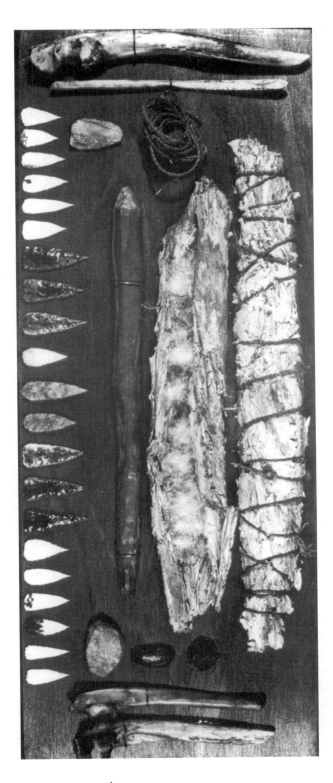

Plate 3.2   Tool-kit for making Kimberley points (H. R. Balfour collection XP780, courtesy of Museum Victoria)

Transport

Everywhere in Australia transport on land relied solely on human power, although networks of tracks and paths aided travel on foot. On water, most coastal and riverine peoples in this study (notably excluding Mi<u>n</u>ong people) used bark canoes that had folded and tied or sewn ends and timber gunwales and stringers, and that were propelled by a long stick or carved paddle (see Plate 3.3). On the coast of eastern Cape York Peninsula, hollowed timber canoes were equipped with outriggers (Plate 3.7), and in northeast Arnhem Land they had a woven sail. Canoe styles reflected their adaptation for use in, for example, grassy swamps (northeast Arnhem Land) or reedy lakes (Gippsland). People also used swimming logs and rafts.

These watercraft enabled people to gain access to resources unobtainable on foot or obtainable only with difficulty. They extended the foraging range not only to islands, reefs, and cays, but along the banks of rivers and into swamps. Yolngu goose-egging by canoe is a prime example, and the wooden canoes with outriggers used by Sandbeach people probably enhanced access to the coastal waters, with their very high tidal range, as did the double rafts of the west Kimberley coast, constructed with wooden dowels.

Communication

The main medium of communication was, of course, speech. Message sticks, whose use has been recorded in many areas, were not writing in the sense of encoded speech; rather, designs seemed to have indicated the bearer's identity and perhaps the topic of the message, such as an impending ceremony. Many peoples used hand signs

Plate 3.3   Kŭnai men in bark canoes, Lake Tyers (courtesy of Nicolas Peterson)

to convey information about such matters as what game had been caught and which relatives were present. People could communicate with others who were within sight but out of earshot. Warlpiri people and their neighbours employed a complete language of hand signs equivalent to speech; it was used by widows in mourning, who were forbidden to speak for a period after their husband's death.[6]

The wider dissemination of information relied on travel by foot and watercraft in conjunction with memory and speech. Its speed of diffusion depended in part on the number of hearers at any one time, on population density, the structure of social networks, and the control of information flow between social networks. In the arid zone, with a population density only 1% of that of the tropical coasts, the flow of information would have been very slow. While 'smoke signals' seem to be a product of the European imagination, people certainly created indexical signs of their presence in the form of smokes and other traces.

Song, dance, and visual forms, important in the organisation of social life, may also be regarded as modes of communication, with complex information conveyed mimetically, iconically, and through metaphor and symbolism. Some have suggested that myths and songs encoded information about the location of water sources in a way that enhances memory. Certainly the encoding of secret religious knowledge in visual representations and language constituted the basis of an important mode of governance in many Aboriginal societies.[7]

Production technologies—tools, weapons, and facilities

In referring to Aboriginal production implements, writers typically highlight just the digging stick and spear, but many other tools, weapons, implements, and facilities were also important. The small hand-held production tools and implements included 'simple machines' in McCarthy's classification. The use of the spear with a spear-thrower comprised a system of levers.[8] Operation of larger facilities, both portable and fixed, required several people. They included nets and traps, both tended and untended, for the capture of animals, birds, and fish, and canoes. The total assemblage varied from region to region, but certain categories remained constant, with variations in materials and construction. The following schema adapts Leon Satterthwait's categories:

Extractors
Hardwood digging stick (all regions)
Edge-ground axe (except for Wiil/Minong)
Kodj hammer–hatchet (Wiil/Minong)
Wooden bowls and spear-throwers used as shovels (Pitjantjatjara)

Entrainers
Concealors
• hides
• branches
• body paint (to conceal odour)
• wind noise

Attractors
- emu lures, such as feathers (Yuwaaliyaay)
- body-odour to attract shrimps (Kŭnai)

Threateners
- simulation of a hawk's flight (with a thrown piece of bark) and its call

Immobilisers

Weapons
- harpoons
- spears, with or without spear-throwers (see Plate 3.4)
- throwing sticks
- clubs
- return and non-return boomerangs

Facilities
- nets, hand-held frame-nets, ground-nets, and long nets for fishing, fowling, and hunting
- traps, including tidal traps of stone and brush, and traps of wicker or of timber and bark (see Plates 3.6 and 3.8)
- pitfalls and snares, such as nooses to catch emus

Retrievers

Fish-hooks (bone or shell) and gorges
Harpoons
Nets, mats

Food-preparation

Grindstones and mullers
Mallets
Graters
Winnowing bowls
Sieves
Leaching techniques
Ovens and other cooking techniques

Food-handling equipment

Spatulas and spoons

Containers
- net-bags and skin bags
- twined baskets (sedge, pandanus)
- dishes and bowls (folded or sewn bark, carved wood, see Plate 2.8)
- water-containers (bailer shells, closely twined baskets, bark buckets (Ngarinyin), carved wood, skin bags)

A feature of Aboriginal technologies not brought out by a classification scheme of this kind is creativity in the use of raw materials as 'instant' tools. For example,

Plate 3.4   A Ngalia man armed with a spear and spear-thrower stalking a feeding kangaroo (photograph by Norman Tindale, courtesy of the South Australian Museum Archives)

in a commonly reported case a person would pick up a pebble or a discarded stone artefact for immediate use. Bob Tonkinson describes the manufacture of grass circlets by women, made to carry dishes on the head. I once observed a Yolngu man swiftly tear and fold a piece of paperbark into a temporary water-carrier.[9]

Gathering techniques included digging, especially for 'root' foods, chopping invertebrates out from wood, and picking fruits and seed-heads. Hunting techniques included the following:

- taking animals or birds in the open, on land or water, by hand or with weapons, sometimes using lures
- using fixed facilities such as traps and nets
- climbing trees to retrieve honey or such animals such as possums or geese
- digging and smoking animals out of holes
- tracking and stalking, using hides and disguises (such as ochres) to hide body odour.[10]

Combined with various techniques, each of the tools and implements mentioned above had properties that enhanced human powers. For example, Leonn Satterthwait shows that the often considerable labour input in net manufacture and hunting paid off in the form of increased returns. Many observers have commented on the large catches of birds, animals, and fish using nets. Where water sources were scarce, locus-based hunting (where game comes to a place such as a waterhole) could in effect harvest an entire region. In density-based hunts (where hunters drove game within a given area) the catchment area, and hence the catch, could be increased greatly with the addition of more hunters around the perimeter. Net hunts could provision large groups if the catch lasted several days, and their results were reasonably certain. Large kills would deplete resources, but Aboriginal people probably controlled their frequency, scheduling large hunts and moving from country to country. Moreover, burning off grassland increased the productivity of the land in absolute terms by providing more feed for mammals and birds.[11]

Storage

A number of ways of storing food have been reported.[12] Kŭnai people may have preserved flesh through desiccation by cooking and smoking, consistent with recent reports of the smoking of eel flesh in Western Victoria. Pitjantjatjara, Yuwaaliyaay, and Wiil people stored food 'in the field' in the form of desiccated fruits left on the plant. They also dried fruits such as *Solanum* (bush tomato) and *Santalum* (quandong) on skewers (after removing the bitter seeds in the case of *Solanum*), or pulverised them into storable balls. Pitjantjatjara people and their neighbours stored meat short-term by thoroughly cooking it, wrapping it in leaves, and placing it in a tree, while Yolngu people pounded meat with *Buchanania obovata* (green plum) and red ochre. Yuwaaliyaay people stooked wild millet, and stored considerable quantities of grass and tree seeds in skin-bags. According to Parker, the seeds were common property of a group of women. Wiil people stored black-wattle seeds in skin bags. Minong people at King George Sound stored fish for a few days in paperbark wrappings. People not only stored foods but also tools and raw materials. For example, Peter Hiscock describes a cache of stone artefacts placed in a pit in Western Queensland.[13]

Plate 3.5   Minong camp above King George Sound, smoke from burning-off in the middle distance (*Panorama of King George's Sound* by Robert Havell, Rex Nan Kivell collection 759, courtesy of the National Library of Australia)

Shelter and clothing

The complexity and uses of shelter varied from region to region depending on the environmental hazards, such as wind, rain, and mosquitoes (see Plate 3.5). People built small, relatively temporary wind-breaks, and huts of light timber, clad with bark, grass, or leaves. A closed shelter or a smoky fire, sometimes both in combination, afforded alternative protection against mosquitoes in northeast Arnhem Land. Where mobility was greatest or the weather clement, minimal shelter such as a simple wind-break sufficed.

The use of skin cloaks and rugs marks a major division in the case studies. People of Gippsland and the Darling/Barwon River wore sewn possum-skin cloaks, while people of the southwest made cloaks from kangaroo skins. Those of the other areas wore minimal apparel—as genital covering, for decoration, as a sign of mourning, as decoration for rituals, or as a marker of adult status. The multi-purpose conical *ngan-marra* mat of northeast Arnhem Land, made from twined pandanus, combined the functions of apron, bassinet, sunshade, mosquito net, and work surface. As well as controlling temperature and providing protection it had moral and symbolic import.

Medical technologies

People of each region employed a wide range of medicines, for the most part plant-based, including infusions and poultices. And I include many Aboriginal healing techniques under the heading of 'quasi-technologies' (Chapter 7), for they involved the supposed extraction of objects injected into the body by dangerous enemies; they were supported by doctrines about ghosts and spirits and the magical powers of objects.

Governance

Military weapons took substantially the same form as hunting weapons, although they were often specialised. In some regions men used boomerangs for fighting but seldom hunted with them. The broader techniques differed of course—for example, people used speech to goad and enrage, and also had techniques to intervene and calm. Several ethnographies (such as W. Lloyd Warner's *A Black Civilization* (1937) and Donald Thomson's 'The joking relationship and organised obscenity in north Queensland' (1935)) describe the range of strategies used, but I will not go into detail about them here.

Socialisation and governance practices also involved hardware in conjunction with symbolic instruments. Initiation, the most formal of the socialisation practices, included the use of material culture items such as musical instruments, complex body decoration, portable objects, masks, and ritual grounds. The control of ritual and religious knowledge involved symbolic instruments associated with 'totemism' (see Chapter 8).

Organisation

All these technologies imposed organisational requirements (see Chapter 10). To state the obvious, only one person could comfortably use a single digging stick; its use was essentially an individual task, although several users could work in parallel. Similarly, only one person could use a particular spear at any time, but several users could hunt or fight in concert. Firepower depended on numbers as well as the rate at which each fighter, perhaps aided by a bystander, could recover and throw spears. Some facilities and techniques, such as large nets and the hunting of dugong from an outrigger canoe, required a more complex division of labour and coordination of tasks.[14] Chapter 10 shows a similar range of teams, differing according to size and gender composition, in the seven regions.

Hunter–gatherers or 'fire-stick farmers'?

Were these the technologies of hunters and gatherers? Indeed, where is the dividing line between foraging (hunting, gathering, and fishing) and farming as modes of subsistence?

According to one view, expressed by Robin Horton, foraging has a number of distinctive features. It involves minimal interference in, and control of, the reproduction of food species. Foragers use an extensive range of species for food rather than relying on just a few species. Foragers move to the location of prey species in their natural habitats instead of closely controlling the location of domesticated plants and animals. A contrasting view is that hunters and gatherers were not simply parasitic, killing and collecting opportunistically, but manipulated the environment and its resources. Aborigines *managed* lands, waters, and their resources.

The use of fire to manage environments has attracted the most attention. As Bill Gammage has recently put it, Aboriginal people managed the whole of Australia—its land, water, plants, and animals. They used fire in a precise and controlled way to hunt, signal, clear tracks, and pattern habitats. They used fire to modify vegetation, and so attract animals and make their behaviour more predictable, and to nurture the habitats of food plants. Commentators generally agree on the importance of frequent, low-intensity burns, and patch-burning, in reducing the impact of wild fires resulting from the build-up of fuel, and in encouraging diversity, so enhancing the availability of food species. Aboriginal people burned off the grasslands and understory to encourage regrowth and attract game animals. For example, in the southeast firing helped regenerate tuberous perennial herb plants of open forest and plains by releasing nutrients into the soil and removing shade. Burning every three years or so would have ensured the optimal supply. Resinous spinifex is unpalatable to macropods; young spinifex, on which small marsupials thrived, could be provided by selective burning, and kangaroos are attracted by green kangaroo grass, which grows after firing.

The effects of fire on plants used for food have been summarised by Beth Gott and John Mulvaney. Firing of cycad groves ensured a bountiful harvest some months later, and all the trees tended to ripen at the same time. Rhizomes and fronds of edible bracken became more plentiful after a fire. Fire ensured fertile conditions for *Solanum centrale* (bush tomato) to flourish on desert dunes after rains. Kangaroo apples (*Solanum vescum*) were abundant in the first year after fire, and required regular burning for continued food production. Fiona Walsh found that in the Western Desert the successional species *Grevillea* aff. *eriostachya* grew in mono-specific stands, to which the Mardu women of her study would make long diversions across less productive country. Burning increases plant diversity in sand-plain habitats, but diversity declines as successional species become established. Walsh found highly diverse and rich-resource species in this kind of habitat; 70% regenerated after fire, and many persisted for several years.

Bill Gammage has suggested that the use of fire created distinctive kinds of landscape:
- grassy paddocks within forests
- grass plains clear of trees but with good soil, leaving trees on poor soil
- open forests with a clear understorey
- edges between plains where animals ate and open forest where they sheltered
- belts of trees or scrub intersecting plains
- copses as shelter and seed stock.

Aboriginal people 'set cool fires in spring to burn swamp and copse edges gently, and hot fires in autumn to destroy regenerating thickets; cool fires to burn grass in patches and hot fires to burn edges in what is left'. For example, in eastern Cape York Peninsula people burned after the first rains to push back the melaleuca by destroying suckers and seeds.[15]

Fire regimes were not the same in every part of Australia. Yaitmathang people of Omeo in north Gippsland, for example, are reported to have been rather sparing with fire, perhaps because of the nature of their upland forests. Certain areas had to be avoided. In northeast Arnhem Land people began to burn off as early as mid-March, continuing through the year until the rains came. They burned each area at least once every three to four year, but avoided stands of vine-forest, sacred sites, stores of sacred objects, and hollow-log coffins left standing after secondary burial. In the southeast, wet sclerophyll forests are unlikely to have been deliberately burned.[16]

But Aboriginal people propagated vegetable foods not only through the use of fire. There are records of direct intervention in the reproduction of some species; the best documented are the replanting of yam-tops in the tropical north and on the west coast, and seed planting in several regions—of purslane, bunya nuts, shrubs, grasses, and *Solanum*. People broke off the top of the yam after harvesting and replanted it, to ensure the next season's growth. People of the east coast dug the soil and separated tubers of yam daisy (*Microseris scapigera*) with its radish-like roots, leaving some in the soil, so promoting their growth and spread. Beth Gott shows that the continual digging of roots thinned them out and made room for new growth, aerated the soil, and turned in litter and ash.

Those living on certain Queensland rivers cultivated grubs by cutting saplings and piling them onto mud banks, and elsewhere people prepared grass trees (*Xanthorrhoea* sp.) to encourage the growth of grubs. In the Channel country in southwest Queensland, women attracted bees to a preferred location by moving a scented bush. Aboriginal people domesticated the dingo in some regions as an aid to hunting. Norman Tindale reports a form of animal husbandry: on the Atherton Tableland Aboriginal people captured young cassowaries, then tethered and fattened them to be food.

Perhaps the most elaborate example of environmental control recorded in Australia is the complex system of eel canals in western Victoria, designed to guide eels from swamps into wicker traps; people smoked and stored the eels. Alastair Campbell suggests that the eel canals may also have been used to irrigate plants and attract birds and fish. Indeed, people of the Roper River in the Northern Territory dammed streams to prevent lagoon and vine-forest areas from drying out in the dry season, to attract birds, and to encourage the growth of plant foods.[17]

These practices change our picture of Aboriginal hunting, gathering, and fishing as a mode of subsistence. It involved a more radical intervention in the ecology than was recognised earlier, and, as Beth Gott remarks, the boundary between foraging and farming is blurred. The writings of David Harris are particularly relevant here; he constructs a continuum from dependency on wild plants and animals to dependency on domesticated ones. Even where production of wild plant-foods and animals dominates, it may be combined with cultivation involving small-scale clearing of vegetation and minimal tillage, and/or the taming, protective herding, or free-range management of animals. Larger-scale clearing and systematic tillage comes further along the continuum. 'Agriculture' involves more or less exclusive cultivation of domesticated plants, livestock raising by settled farmers, or transhumant or nomadic pastoralism

But what counts as a 'domesticated' plant or animal? As Tim Ingold points out, some peoples have husbanded plants and animals little different from their 'wild' counterparts; it is a matter of the relative scope of human involvement in 'establishing the conditions for growth'—that is, their intervention in reproduction. In light of these discussions, although I have used the expression 'hunters and gatherers' to characterise Aboriginal subsistence practices, it might be more appropriate to classify Aboriginal subsistence production as that of hunter–gatherer–cultivators.[18]

With these general features of technologies outlined, I will now describe some of the particular characteristics of each region's technology.

Kŭnai people

Kŭnai people used what K. L. Hotchin calls a general east-coast tool kit, but with particular adaptations to local materials and resources, especially those of the lakes and rivers. Notable features included bone rather than shell for fish-hooks (made by women out of kangaroo leg-bone), the many types of fighting clubs, the fish-spear with two bone tines, and cloaks or rugs of possum skin, suited to the cold winters of the southeast. Other characteristics included the use of a hand-net and long set-net of sedge, stretched between canoes to catch fish, brush fences and nets for capturing water-fowl, sedge net-bags, and a bark canoe used mainly on the lakes and estuaries. The hunting and fighting spear had a head of multiple stone flakes set in resin—similar to the 'death spear' of the Sydney region. Grass-seed grinding was apparently absent in this region.[19]

Pitjantjatjara people and their neighbours

Western Desert technology differed from that used in coastal regions in a number of obvious ways, such as the absence of marine and inland aquatic technologies including large facilities. Hunters did use stone or brush hides to hunt large game (Plate 3.4) and platform-hides in trees—for example, overlooking a waterhole. Wooden containers replaced net and twined ones. Another distinctive characteristic was the prominence of wet seed-grinding in the food-preparation technology, making the muller and grind-stone of particular importance, as among Yuwaaliyaay speakers (Plates 2.2 and 2.5). Hunters poisoned rock-holes with *pituri* (native tobacco, *Duboisia hopewoodii*). Pitjantjatjara technology came high on the portability index, with several multi-functional tools, most notably the dish-shaped spear-thrower incorporating an adze.[20]

Yuwaaliyaay people

A number of features of Yuwaaliyaay technology were distinctive: a fire-saw rather than a fire-drill for fire-making; the use of five types of hunting spear (with wooden heads, barbed and unbarbed); several kinds of net, some very large, for catching fish, birds, and animals; large stone fish-traps on the Darling/Barwon River at Brewarrina (see Plate 3.6) as well as weirs across streams; and the exploitation of grass seed and other seed on a large scale, using seed-grinding technology and techniques, with the grain stored in skin bags. Like Kǔnai people, the Yuwaaliyaay and their neighbours wore cloaks of kangaroo skin in winter. They imported stone axe-heads and grass-tree resin from other groups.[21]

Plate 3.6   Stone fish-traps on the Darling/Barwon River at Brewarrina (photograph by Henry King, Tyrrell Collection; courtesy of the Powerhouse Museum, Sydney)

Wiil and Mi<u>n</u>ong people

Although they used it for bait, people of the southwest did not eat shellfish, apparently because estuarine fishing was so productive, and they used no watercraft except for swimming logs. A couple of features of their stone technology were the double-headed or single-headed *kodj* (axe), used as a hammer as well as hatchet, and the *taap* (saw-knife of hafted flakes). People used spears and tidal traps of stone walls and brush for fishing, but no nets or fish-hooks. Sea mammals were exploited opportunistically, and hunters did not try to access island-sea colonies. Skin bags replaced the twined baskets of the north, and kangaroo-skin cloaks (in contrast with the possum-skin cloaks of the southeast) offered protection against the cold and the winter rain. Commentators stress the use of dingoes for hunting in this region. People ground acacia seed for oil (used for body decoration) and for food. Modes of storage included storing *Santalum* fruits on the living plant. Caroline Bird recorded traditions of storing eggs by painting them with emu fat and caching them.

Like people of the tropical north, Wiil and Mi<u>n</u>ong people used complex food-processing techniques to render bloodroot (*Haemodorum spicatumi*) and fruits of zamia nuts (*Macrozamia riedlei*) edible. Edward Grey describes how women collected nuts in March, left them to soak in a shallow pool for several days, then stored them in rush-lined pits, after which the pulp was edible, either raw or roasted.[22]

Sandbeach people

Sandbeach people made more than 12 types of spear and harpoon, the latter used in conjunction with rope for catching dugong and turtles. Men used hollowed-timber canoes with single and double outriggers on estuaries and coastal waters, especially for dugong and turtle hunting (see Plate 3.7). The use of fishing nets but not traps has been recorded, although people beyond the Sandbeach region to the south used stone fish-traps. No boomerangs were used. In this region women applied labour-intensive techniques for removing toxins from cheeky yams (*Dioscorea rotunda*) and mangrove fruits, including pounding and leaching. Containers included twined baskets and knotted string bags.[23]

Ngarinyin people and their neighbours

The stone technology in the northwest Kimberley region was remarkable for the fine, pressure-flaked spear-points, together with the associated tools—bone and wood rods for pressure-flaking, and sandstone anvils (see Plate 3.2). The spear-heads found their way through exchange networks to the Western Desert, where they were hafted as knives for use in circumcision. Other features included the fire-hardened one-piece wooden spear for fishing, and the double-layered log raft (the logs joined by hardwood pegs) used in the estuaries and on the coast, where the tidal range is 9–12 metres. The coastal people, known as 'tide riders', took advantage of

Plate 3.7   Kuuku-Ya'u men hunting dugong in an outrigger canoe (photograph by
D. F. Thomson, TPH2873, courtesy of Mrs D. M. Thomson and Museum Victoria)

tidal currents of up to 10 knots to travel to the islands, up to 16 kilometres from the
coast, and between the islands. A raft could carry several people, dingoes, and raw
materials. Sue O'Connor remarks that, while flimsy, the rafts did not easily overturn
and sink. Kimberley people not only possessed the technology and techniques for
drilling wood, but also drilled holes in stone beads with a stone point. Containers
included a sewn-bark bucket, sealed with beeswax.

On some offshore islands are the remains of stone house-structures. People covered a round drystone base, up to one metre high and with an entry, with a
superstructure of spinifex and paperbark thatch, the latter brought from the mainland
by raft. Stone and brush fish-traps across inlets resembled those of the southwest and
of northeast Arnhem Land. O'Connor has found no evidence of the use of lines,
hooks, or nets for fishing before recent decades.[24]

Yolngu people

Yolngu technologies included an elaborate variety of spear types, some used solely as exchange items; a variety of fish-traps, some complex (see Plate 3.8); and *lipalipa* dugout canoes adopted from the Macassans, used with a woven pandanus sail (but no outrigger). Men used a specialised bark canoe with a pointed prow for hunting goose and goose-egging in the reedy Arafura Swamp. The availability of iron (beaten into spear-heads and hatchet-heads) pre-dates European and Chinese settlement of the Northern Territory; it was brought by the Macassan trepangers who visited Arnhem Land each wet season, probably beginning in the early eighteenth century. Men made dugout canoes using iron-headed hatchets.

Men and women used a variety of twined pandanus baskets, and women employed a twined conical *ngaṉmarra* mat as an apron, work surface, mosquito net, and bassinet. A two-storey bark house with a smoky fire below provided protection against mosquitoes. Food-processing techniques included the labour-intensive pounding and leaching of toxic and irritant plants, especially cycad-palm nuts, an important source of food at the end of the dry season.[25]

Conclusions

Table 13.3 in the concluding chapter summarises some of the characteristic regional technologies. The suite of technologies varied according to climate, terrain, and resources, as well as such factors as the presence of mosquitoes. Some variations are not readily explained by environmental factors—a case in point is the absence of the spear-thrower among Yuwaaliyaay and Pitjantjatjara people. Barry Cundy suggests that the use of spear-throwers made it easier for less skillful users to throw accurately rather than increasing the speed and distance of the throw, so that in the hands of a good hunter the spear was no less effective without the spear-thrower.[26]

We have seen that the degree of mobility partly explains elaboration and portability—the multi-functional Western Desert implements maximised portability, whereas the complex technologies of Sandbeach and Yolngu people, including several types of spear and harpoon, reflected their relative sedentism—although we have seen that portability is not related to mobility alone.

The range of resources reviewed in the previous chapter, and the technologies and techniques brought to bear on them, make the boundary between hunting–gathering and farming quite fuzzy. An extensive literature discusses the use of fire to foster new growth in order to attract animals, and to create habitat diversity. Other studies highlight the use of irrigation on a limited scale, practices that approximate fish-farming, and techniques for the propagation of food plants. People managed resources as a whole through the deliberate shaping of habitats, and aided the reproduction of some species through direct intervention in reproduction.

The next chapter examines the ways in which people scheduled their access to resources, how they moved around the country in order to gain access to those resources, the kinds of groups people formed, and the density of populations.

Plate 3.8 Yolngu *gurrka-gol* fish-trap (photograph by D. F. Thomson, TPH740, courtesy of Mrs D. M. Thomson and Museum Victoria)

Further reading

Overviews of Aboriginal technologies can be found in Leonn Satterthwait's 'A comparative study of Aboriginal food-procurement technologies' (1980) and John Mulvaney and Johann Kamminga's *Prehistory of Australia* (1999).

The main issues canvassed in this chapter are the relation of hunting and gathering to farming, and the use of fire by Aboriginal people. In an earlier debate, archaeologists and geographers asked why Aborigines did not adopt farming: see, for example, 'New Guinea and Australian prehistory: The "Neolithic problem"' by J. Peter White (1971) and 'Struggle for the savanna' by Rhys Jones and Jim Bowler (1980). David R. Harris's 'Subsistence Strategies across the Torres Strait' (1977), on the transition from foraging to farming across the Torres Strait, has been influential; Robin Horton reviews the issue in his recent book *The Pure State of Nature* (2000)

Recent research and writing has questioned whether Aborigines were simply 'hunters and gatherers' at all. Key works on this topic include John Mulvaney's 'The end of the beginning: 6000 years ago to 1788' (1987), Beth Gott's 'Use of Victorian plants by Koories' (1993), and Fiona Walsh's 'Spatial and temporal use of plants and resource management' (1990).

The literature on the use of fire by Aborigines is very extensive; the pioneering works are Rhys Jones's 'Fire-stick farming' (1969) and Sylvia Hallam's *Fire and Hearth* (1975). Recent studies include those of Beth Gott (2000) and Thomas Vigilante (2002). Tim Flannery discusses the issue in *The Future Eaters* and Robin Horton offers a sceptical view in *The Pure State of Nature* (2000).

Notes

1   For discussions of technology see Bamforth and Bleed (1997: 111) and Torrence (2001: 74).

2   I draw on Hugill's (1993) analysis of technologies in European history for this approach to the technology of technologies. Torrence (2001) remarks that tools that are only powered by human labour have a limited capacity to maximise energy returns.

3   On the anthropology of technology see Gibson and Ingold (1993), Lemonnier (1992), Pfaffenberger (1992), and White (1943). For examples of analyses of Aboriginal technologies see Hamilton (1980) and Satterthwait (1980). For an example of a description of Aboriginal material culture see Sutton (1993).

4   On fire-making see Davidson (1947).

5   Satterthwait (1980) discusses the relationship between portability and complexity in Aboriginal technologies, and Hiscock (in press) discusses risk; see also Shott (1986, cited in Bamforth and Bleed 1997: 111).

6   See Kendon (1988) on Warlpiri sign language.

7   On the encoding of religious knowledge see Keen (1994), Morphy (1991), and Munn (1973).

8   On the definition of machines see McCarthy (1982), Gregory and Altman (1989: 125), and Mumford (1947).

9   See Tonkinson (1991: 50) on instant tools. In the anthropology of technology 'affordances' refers to the suitability of an object for uses not foreseen when it was originally designed (see Pfaffenberger 1992).

10   Oliver (1989: 16) had a useful summary of hunting techniques.

11   On intensification see Lourandos (1983). See Satterthwait (1987: 618–20, 626–7) on the productivity of net-hunting.

12   On Kŭnai preservation of flesh by smoking see Hotchin (1990: 139–41). RM and CH Berndt (1945: 68), Gould (1980: 68) and Tonkinson (1991) discuss Western Desert dessication, and Myers (1986: 74) discusses the drying of fruit. On Wiil storage in the field see Bird and Beeck (1988: 117), and on Wiil seed storage see Hassell (1936: 690). Nind (1831: 33) describes storage of fish among Miṉong people. Thomson (1949: 23–4) describes Yolngu short-term storage of dried fruit, sometimes mixed with pounded kangaroo meat.

13   See Hiscock (1988; in press) on the storage of stone artefacts.

14   On the organisation of net-hunting see Satterthwait (1987).

15   The quotation is from Gammage (2002: 9).

16   On the Aboriginal use of fire see Allen (1983: 53–4), Flannery (1997: 217–36), Gammage (2002), Gott (2000: 6–8; 1993: 196), Hallam (1975), Horton (2000), Latz and Griffin (1978: 80), Jones (1969), Lewis (1982: 61), Mulvaney (1987: 88–9), Walsh (1990: 31), and Vigilante (2002). On the use of fire at Omeo see Helms (1896). Langton (2002) reported on the use of fire in eastern Cape York Peninsula. Nicolas Peterson (pers. com.) pointed out the protection of hollow-log coffins in northeast Arnhem Land.

17   On the propagation of foods see Atchison (1998), Builth (2001), Campbell (1965: 207–10), Gott (1982; 1993), Lourandos (1983), McConnel (1957, cited in Campbell 1965: 208), Mulvaney (1987: 88–9), Tindale (1962), and Walsh (1990). On the forager–farmer debate see Allen (1983), Horton (2000: 98–100), and Jones (1975: 28).

18   On the fuzzy boundary between hunting–gathering and agriculture see Gott (1993: 196), DR Harris (1996), Ingold (1996), Klappe (2002), Spriggs (1996). The quote from Ingold is from page 21.

19   See Hotchin (1990), Bulmer (in Smyth 1878 vol. I: 389), and Howitt (Papers, B8 F5, AIATSIS ms 69) on Kŭnai technology in general, and Howitt (1904: 772) on the technology of fire production. Shell fish-hooks were typical of the New South Wales coast (Mulvaney and Kamminga 1999: 291–2). On the 'death spear' see Mulvaney and Kamminga (1999: 292–3).

20   On Western Desert technologies see Brokensha (1975), Gould (1967: 42–4), Hayden (1977), and Tindale (1974).

21   For descriptions of the technologies of the Yuwaaliyaay and their neighbours see Parker (1905) and Teulon (in Curr 1886). On the Brewarrina fish-traps see Dargin (1976) and Mulvaney and Kamminga (1999: 34).

22   On Wiil and Miṉong technologies see Ferguson (1981) and Hassell (1936). Mulvaney and Kamminga (1999: 293) discuss the neglect of shellfish. The account of emu-egg storage is from Bird (pers. com.). On the processing of zamia nuts see Grey (1841 vol. 2: 295).

23   On Sandbeach technologies see Donald Thomson (unpublished field-notes: MV DT Files 190: 14.10.32, October 1932; Files 191, 192, 195, 196, 256; Thomson photographic collection 2813–3624; 1933: 485), Thompson (1988), Thorpe (1928), West (1964), and Worsnop (1897: 95–6). Bruce Rigsby (pers. com.) provided information about fish-traps.

24   Northwest Kimberley technologies are described by Akerman (1975; 1979a; 1979b), Mulvaney and Kamminga (1999: 239, 240, 325–6), and O'Connor (1987; 1993). Akerman (1979b) shows that Kimberley people heated the stone so it could be flaked more readily.

25   On Yolngu technologies see Thomson (MV Thomson photographic collection 720–1136), Warner (1937: 471–504). On Macassan influence on technologies see MacKnight (1976).

26   On spears and spear-throwers see Cundy (1980).

The Seasonal Round: Population, Settlement, and Mobility

Introduction

A fundamental feature of hunter–gatherer–cultivator modes of subsistence is that people have to move to the location of resources, wherever they happen to be. The ways in which Aboriginal people moved around the country, the degree of mobility, the range of movement, the size and dynamics of residence groups, and the density of populations are the topics of this chapter.

Rainfall (among other environmental features) indirectly affected the density of the human population, as well as patterns of movement, through its effect on food and water resources and on the terrain. People of the arid Western Desert, for example, could only occupy the land at a very low population density, they had to move long distances in their constant search for water, and the unpredictability of resources made seasonal movement irregular. They responded with a system of economic, social, and ritual cooperation across a wide region. The rich coastal resources of eastern Cape York Peninsula, by way of contrast, allowed for a much higher population density. There is a connection between population density and patterns of settlement and mobility—because people could live more sedentary lives on resource-rich coasts and rivers—and social identities had a more localised and differentiated quality where population densities were higher. But a number of factors came into play in structuring settlement and mobility: foraging strategies, transport and housing technologies, the availability of water, the difficulty of the terrain, and social factors such as land ownership.

As Marshall Sahlins has pointed out, foragers living together even in modest numbers quickly reduce the food resources within a convenient range of their camp. They may remain in the same place only by absorbing the increase in effort incurred in foraging further afield or by accepting a decline in real terms in the form of less plentiful supplies, or a decline in the quality of food. At some stage it is going to pay a group to move in order to exploit a fresh area. The size and mobility of groups depends in part on the density, distribution, mobility, and nutritional value of resources. Groups may split or some residents leave when stress on local resources and competition cause social tension.[1]

The archaeologist Louis Binford distinguishes between two broad patterns of mobility: that of 'foragers' and that of 'collectors'. This scheme relies on a distinction between the movement of a whole residence group (residential movement) and the movement of one or more individuals for the purpose of hunting and gathering (logistical movement). Foragers move as a group to the location of food resources; they are generally highly mobile residentially and expend little effort in logistical movement. Collectors generally make few residential moves, and those they do make are often to locations valued as much for their water or firewood resources as their food resources; they move to these locations as a group. They use frequent and long logistical forays to bring resources back to the residence group. The distribution of resources is important in generating these patterns. A homogeneous distribution of resources leads groups to disperse to resource locales. Where resource distribution is patchy it pays people to aggregate in central places, sending out foraging parties on relatively long forays. Aboriginal people tended to conform to Binford's 'collector' model; they formed home bases and shared their produce within and made logistical forays from these home bases. However, the degree of mobility and the size of residence groups varied greatly, as we shall see.[2]

Worldwide comparative studies show that the higher the density of food resources the fewer moves a residence group has to make per annum. Having more localised food resources, including aquatic ones, leads to greater sedentism, while a greater reliance on land mammals may lead to higher mobility. But other resources, such as firewood and water, also influence patterns of movement; in desert environments especially the availability of water is a key determinant. Such 'water-tethered' foragers tend to make use of all the exploitable resources around a water source before moving.

Robert Kelly notes a general pattern in the tropics: people forage on dispersed resources around a camping place (a central location), then move to the centre of a new foraging area, although territorial constraints may limit movement. People move their home base when they judge the length of logistical forays to be too great; a 20–30 kilometre round trip appears to be a common maximum in comparative studies. (It tends to be the length of women's logistical forays that determines residential movement, according to Kelly.) However, the costs of longer foraging distances may be met with higher-value foods, such as large mammals. But transportability is an issue—it may pay to move to a home base nearer the location of bulky foods rather than carrying them for a long distance. With lower average resource-returns overall, the foraging area and travel distance increase and residential movements become more frequent. Moreover, the proportion of food-producers to dependants (the dependency ratio) affects the necessary return rate. Thus, hunters and gatherers must weigh the costs of continuing with a low rate of return and increasing foraging distances against the costs of moving the whole residence group. The distance to the next desirable camping place will be a factor in the calculation.

Binford has suggested that the need to maintain information about resources over a wide area also motivates mobility, although the need for information depends on the degree of resource fluctuation. Mobility also helps to maintain social connections, and hence insure against variability in resources, and to instruct children.

We shall see that people of the arid Western Desert moved their home base frequently, whereas the larger residence groups of Sandbeach people and coastal Yolngu (and neighbouring Anbarra) people, highly dependent on marine and estuarine resources, moved only a few times each year. In a more complex strategy, people formed temporary residence groups away from the larger home base, making logistical forays out from the temporary camps. The small dry-season residence groups of Sandbeach people seem to have been of this kind. Inland residence groups in northeast Arnhem Land split up into smaller groups in the dry season and were more mobile, but re-aggregated for the wet season.

Producers and dependants

In the case of hunters and gatherers the proportion of residents who are productive affects the number of people who can reside together and share food. Not everyone in a residence group produces food on a significant scale; non-producers include the very young (perhaps 30–50% of those under 15), the old, and the sick. Also, if men refrain from performing tasks seen as women's work, then their productive lives are likely to be shorter than women's because of the physical demands of hunting. According to a general model proposed by Bruce Winterhalder, in a residence group of 25 people only seven or eight (28–32%) will be producers. It pays to reside in a group larger than a family, for the presence of several producers evens out variability in production caused by differences in skill, the unpredictability of resources, sickness, and age.[3]

Residing in a group evens out the risk of coming back empty-handed. Thus, Eric Smith proposes, men will join a hunting party if they stand to achieve a higher return rate than if they hunt alone. Fred Myers suggests that the probability of bringing back a game animal increases with the number of hunters because more hunters can cover a greater area. Moreover, a fairly constant supply of meat could be maintained without the same individuals having to go out every day. Smith notes, however, that although adding people to a hunting party will increase returns up to a point, they will fall off with the addition of still more hunters.

Social factors that affect the size of residence groups include the need to train young hunters, recreation, and mutual aid. Living in a group also benefited women: one woman could stay in camp to look after children and old people while others foraged and shared the return; group living also conferred the advantage of safety and protection from attack. However, countervailing forces were at work. The constraints on large groups living together for long periods included not only an increase in the ground that had to be covered (and hence the time that had to be spent) in foraging forays, but also the conflicts and pressures resulting from the need to share within a large group. All residents had some claims on each other, Myers remarks, so that large groups produced conflicts of loyalty as well as continual impositions on a person's generosity. Such pressures may have diminished incentives to hunt and led to the dispersion of larger groups.

Excluding small hunting camps and large, temporary aggregations for ceremonies, the mean sizes of residence groups in regions of Australia remote from white settlement were between about 14 and 33, with ranges of 8–22 in Cape York Peninsula (as observed by Lauriston Sharp in the 1930s) and 18–63 for mainland Arnhem Land. Larger figures have been recorded for some areas but firm data on the size of residence groups and the ratio of producers to dependants is available for only a few of the case studies in this chapter.[4]

Social boundary defence

Theorists of risk link the forces that determine movement to the structure of 'land tenure'—the control of access to land and waters and their resources. Where there are dense resources and predictable returns the cost of 'boundary defence' is less than the benefit and people will tend to guard exclusive territories. This kind of system prevailed on the northwest coast of North America. But where there are sparser, more unpredictable resources it pays people to permit reciprocal but controlled access to resources. What Elizabeth Cashdan terms 'social boundary defence' achieves this end. Here, people differentiate between those with unequivocal rights in a given area and those who ought to obtain permission to visit an area and use its resources. People of all seven case studies in this book had some form of 'social boundary defence', but the degree of exclusivity varied between regions, and with the kind of resource in question (see Chapter 9).[5]

Population densities

Measures of the population density of hunters and gatherers can only be approximate, especially as mobility increases. One way to calculate it is from the average size of land-holding groups (country groups) in relation to the average area of their land in a given region. But this device takes no account of the fact that members of such groups were normally dispersed. Moreover, they did not have exclusive membership in all regions, but had overlapping affiliations. What of coastal groups whose countries include coastal waters, reefs, and islands? Generally speaking, the estimates upon which the case studies draw consist of counts of the Aboriginal populations of very broad areas, such as the whole of Gippsland. This evens out the effects of seasonal movement but neglects variation within the region. We shall see that early estimates varied greatly, by as much as a factor of five in one case. In many regions populations had been affected by smallpox before the colonial onslaught, and by the time officials or others began to make their counts, other diseases as well as frontier violence had taken their toll.

Noting that 'tribes' as mapped by Norman Tindale occupied smaller areas on the coasts than inland, Jo Birdsell made a bold attempt to correlate Aboriginal population densities with mean rainfall. He assumed that tribes had an average size of 500, so that population density could be calculated from a tribe's area, at least on average across a region. His resulting graph allowed one to read off population density from mean rainfall, at least in the absence of resources not directly related to rainfall, such as those of coastal waters and large rivers. However, the tribal model has since been invalidated (see Chapter 5). Moreover, the assumed average size of tribes rests on an assumption about the the pre-colonial population that has been strongly challenged: many archaeologists now believe it to have been much larger than the 300 000 that A. R. Radcliffe-Brown estimated (his minimum figure). Nevertheless, the independent estimates reviewed in this chapter suggest that broad language identities (such as Ngarinyin) and regional identities (such as Miṉong) did apply to a few hundred people in each case, giving one a rough guide to the *order* of population density. The estimates in this chapter, then, are tentative and should not be taken to be hard data.[6]

The case studies outline these estimated population densities, and the patterns of residence, movement, and settlement in the seven regions.

Kŭnai people

Chapter 2 described Gippsland as a region of high, year-round, and quite regular rainfall, with rich resources, especially around the lakes and estuaries and along the coastal barrier.

Human population

Given the moderately high rainfall and the rich resources of the coast, estuaries, and lakes, one would expect there to have been a relatively large Aboriginal population in Gippsland. Contemporary estimates of the 1843–44 population vary from 1000 to 5000, among which the less speculative counts were of around 1500. It is possible that Kŭnai people were affected by the smallpox epidemics that now appear to have spread from the north coast of the continent, apparently brought by Macassan visitors, but the predominant view is that they were not (although an influenza epidemic in the late 1840s did affect the population). The fact that rainfall in Gippsland, while moderately high, is substantially lower than in eastern Cape York Peninsula (850 millimetres at Orbost but only 600 millimetres at Sale) leads me to be sceptical about the very high population estimates, but local densities around the lakes, estuaries, and larger rivers are likely to have been very high (of the order of one or two people per square kilometre). Population densities would have been medium to high across the plains and in the foothills up to 200 metres (one person per 6–12 square kilometres), and lower at higher elevations.[7]

Settlement and mobility

We shall see that 'country groups' held areas of land and waters. There were perhaps more than 30 of them across Gippsland, holding an average area of about 700 square kilometres; groups around the lakes held smaller areas—about 100 square kilometres.

But each individual had rights to use the land and waters of several groups through various kinds of connection, including patrifiliation and place of birth.[8]

Knowledge of Kŭnai patterns of settlement and movement is hazy, based largely on Bulmer's reminiscences of life at and around Lake Tyers Mission, and occasional observations by others, during a time of social turmoil. Early reports mention residence groups of 30, 100, and 200 people in the 1840s and 1850s, although some of these groups were travelling to or from Melbourne. We do not know how many residence groups there were within each country group's area (or 'country') or how they were clustered. The proper names of the countries and groups, as well as what Howitt records about their location, suggest that in some cases residence focused on a core area near key resources where people preferred to live for at least part of the year. The valley at Buchan would have been such a place, and the land around Lake Tyers another. But the multiple identity of some groups suggests a scattering of residence groups among adjacent locations, especially along the coastal dunes.[9]

It is not likely that Kŭnai people regularly moved around the country in large groups. Rather, individuals and small family groups would have moved from one residence group to another. Individuals and families travelling to the country of other groups could visit relatives and gain access to particular resources in particular seasons. For example, people from some of the groups around the lakes (Wurnŭngatti, Waiung, and Binnajerra people, and some from further west) came to Metung for the fishing. These groups were of at least three distinct, broad regional identities: Krauatŭn.golung (of the east), Brabrolung (central), and Tatŭn.golung (lakes and coastal barrier) (see map 5.2). It may be that those who lived together in a residence group pursued similar strategies at each season.[10]

Since people lived in contrasting environments, seasonal mobility must have varied. Bulmer briefly describes the seasonal round of people living at Lake Tyers.[11] People favoured emu meat in the early summer, after the birds had eaten a food called *belka* and were fat. In summer, when the fish were running, people moved to the beach, the river mouths, and the entrances to the lakes, where they lived in rather temporary camps, and made short trips into the forests to hunt mammals such as wallabies. People fished at night with lights and fish-spears for eels, mullet, and flounder. They also ate vegetable foods and fruit, including kangaroo apples, which could be found in the gullies adjacent to the lakes' entrances through the coastal barrier. This was the time of year for major initiation ceremonies, when neighbouring groups gathered at a location such as the mouth of the Nicholson River. Groups also moved down from the hills to the lakes when the eels were prolific.

More mobile in the autumn, people visited other groups and put on ceremonies. They relied more on foods of the forest, including mammals such as possums, koalas, and kangaroos.

In winter, groups of people moved up-river, where they lived in more substantial grass-thatched huts and bark huts; they caught fish with nets and hooks, and garnered forest resources including mammals and birds. In late winter to early spring they moved back to the wetlands.

In spring, when people were living in temporary camps by the wetlands, they collected various vegetable foods, such as *Typha* (bulrush), and fruits. Wildfowl, including ducks and black swans, were available in large numbers and were vulnerable because it was moulting season. People killed cockatoos and other parrots, which were sitting on their eggs, as well as fledglings and moulting birds. Fish became plentiful in the lakes just before they opened to the sea. Bulmer writes this of the people in spring: 'Their well fed bodies being well greased with fish fat, they shone from head to foot'.[12]

Other observers have described similar patterns for the lakes further to the west. In summer and autumn people moved close to the outlets of lakes to fish for eels, then in winter they moved to the hills. In spring they lived among the reeds by swamps and lakes, fishing for eels as they began migrating downstream.[13]

The concentration of country groups around the northern lake shores, the coastal barrier, and the islands in the lakes suggests a more sedentary pattern, although people may have alternated between coast and lakeside. George Augustus Robinson remarked in June 1844 that the lakes, being 'the chief rendezvous of the natives contiguous to the coast are unsurpassed by any in the colony ... the Aborigines may be termed Ichthyophagist'. According to archaeological evidence, people lived on the beach and dunes near reliable sources of fresh water, exploiting shellfish, fish (using nets), birds, and terrestrial fauna. They formed 'main camps' as well as short-term residence groups that hunted or foraged for specific resources, such as shellfish. Further west, near Wilsons Promontory, people used canoes in the coastal water to visit the islands for mutton-birds and shellfish.[14]

It may be that some forest groups moved north up the mountains in the summer to exploit bogong moths, a prolific source of food that drew hundreds of people together. However, Josephine Flood has found no positive evidence of Kŭnai participation with other peoples. Ngarigo people of the Monaro tablelands joined Yaitmathang people of Omeo and their neighbours to feed on moths in the Bogong Mountains (see Map 5.1). Bidawal (or Maap) people, eastern neighbours of Kŭnai people who had connections with Ngarigu people to their northwest, may well have participated. It is possible that Kŭnai people of the upper Snowy River also took part, for they were close neighbours of Bidawal groups.[15]

As for short-term strategies, the archaeological evidence, as KL Hotchin interprets it, is consistent with the existence of short-term residence groups formed away from larger ones as home bases. Similarly, Howitt reports that if men killed large animals a long way from camp, they butchered and cooked them before returning.[16]

To sum up, the evidence suggests a general pattern of residence on the coast and by lakes and swamps in summer, moving inland in autumn then further up-river for winter, returning in spring to the coast and wetlands. People of the Gippsland Lakes and coastal barrier may have been more sedentary than those of the Snowy River.

Pitjantjatjara people and their neighbours

In the arid region of the eastern Western Desert, with its very low population density, the availability of water dictated the high mobility of the people. In spite of seasonal trends, the very variable, localised, and unpredictable rainfall led to somewhat erratic movement.

Human population

Low and very variable rainfall imposed the main limiting factor on human population density. Estimates of the Aboriginal population at the time of initial European colonisation vary from the very low figure of about one person per 200 square kilometres to about one person per 80 square kilometres. The density was perhaps higher in and around the ranges, with their permanent as well as ephemeral waters, than on the sand and shield deserts, but was still very sparse compared with coastal regions.[17]

Settlement and mobility

Western Desert people do not seem to have divided country into discrete areas owned by clearly defined groups. Neighbours agreed more or less on the location of ancestral places and their significance, but individuals varied in the ways they clustered places into larger 'countries'; these countries overlapped. The group of people responsible for a given place or cluster of sites did not take the form of a clearly defined descent group. Rather, individuals formed attachments to sites through a number of connections, such as place of conception or birth. These multiple connections, as well as other links derived from the long journeys of totemic ancestors, gave each individual a claim on places across a wide region.

Pitjantjatjara people and their neighbours classified residence groups into 'large camps' (*ngura pulka*) and 'small camps' (*ngura tjukutjku*). The maximum recorded size of a camp in the 1870s was 150. In the 1930s, explorers saw a groups of about 33 in the Petermann Ranges and another of about 130 people on the Hull River, preparing for a ceremony. Norman Tindale mapped a very large residence group of some 250 people at Konapandi in June 1933, perhaps residing together for a ceremony. It consisted of 40 shelter groups, each with a common wind-break protecting them from the southeast breeze. The plan does not indicate how they may have clustered into camps, but the shelter groups appear to have comprised four couples, 20 nuclear families, five polygynous or extended families (one with no male), one female on her own, one single male, five bachelors' camps, and three groups of girls or women. Because of drought, Strehlow and Duguid encountered only small groups in the Petermann Ranges in 1939.[18]

Censuses taken in the 1950s and 1960s revealed rather smaller residence groups in the Western Desert than in the resource-rich coastal areas. The mean size of residence groups in these censuses was 13.6 people, with a range of four to 28; two-thirds of the groups lay in the range from four to 13. There was no detectable seasonal pattern in the numbers. Residence groups consisted of from one to six camps of single men or monogamous or polygynous families. Larger aggregations would have formed at certain times for ceremonies; Scott Cane has reviewed reports for the Western Desert region as a whole and these large aggregations ranged in size from 100 to 300 people.[19]

Above all it was the availability of water that dictated movement.[20] People moved according to the direction in which they could see rain falling, the location of known staples, and the trend of known lines of waterholes (wells, soakages, and ephemeral rock-holes). In one common strategy, a group visited an area where it had recently rained and concentrated on small soakages while they lasted, foraging around them in an 8–16 kilometre radius (one day's walk). Then the group would move to a more permanent waterhole nearby, and eat all the staples around it. The group with whom Richard Gould lived moved their home base nine times in a period of three months, over an area of about 3000 square kilometres, rather smaller than the individual range of a young man in the biographical narratives recorded by Fred Myers. Pitjantjatjara people preferred to camp in open country, where breezes blow more steadily from one direction—so that they did not have to move wind-breaks constantly—and where they could more readily detect approaching strangers.

Patterns of movement showed some seasonality, but the seasons were not strictly calendrical, for the onset of rains in particular varied greatly from year to year, as did the amount (and time) of rain. But the general picture from several researchers is as follows. Summer rains, roughly from March to May, filled the clay-pans with water and replenished the rock-holes, and the country turned green. Groups split up and became highly mobile, gathering seeds and hunting game attracted to the waters. People could take advantage of the water resources by moving to the outer limits of their usual range, away from permanent waters. Pintubi people (to the north of the Western Desert region) aggregated at times into larger groups to gather seeds.

Mid-May to August was 'cold time'. Winter rains would replenish the water supplies. Groups of medium size (up to 20 people) became moderately mobile, but gathered into larger groups for ceremonies at the large waters or fragmented into small groups depending on local conditions.

As temperatures rose and the country dried out towards the 'dry time', groups tended to coalesce around the more reliable waters, which were reaching their maximum size, although occasional rains replenished rock-holes and pools. (Gould recorded a group of 107 people living at Wanampi well east of Warburton in December 1966, living almost wholly on kangaroo meat.)

Movement became minimal, and groups of 10 to 30 people remained at the permanent waters for the summer before the rains came in the 'hot time', with its occasional thunderstorms. Pintupi groups reached 50 strong. Pitjantjatjara people lived in round huts covered in spinifex at this time, replacing the mulga wind-breaks.

There is some information on the details of foraging strategies. For example, Yankunytjatjara women living at Everard Park (Map 5.3) would choose a place where resources were known to be located and move as a group to that area. They would fan out along a creek-bed; each would take a different tree, excavate the roots, and call to their companions with information about the tree. After a pause to eat, two women might move to examine trees in a nearby area, calling the others if they looked promising. Women would not return to the same place during the same season. Figure 4.1 shows in schematic form the Western Desert pattern of mobility.

Thus movement in the Western Desert was to a degree seasonal, but depended very much on conditions that varied from year to year. The same can be said for Yuwaaliyaay people and their neighbours.

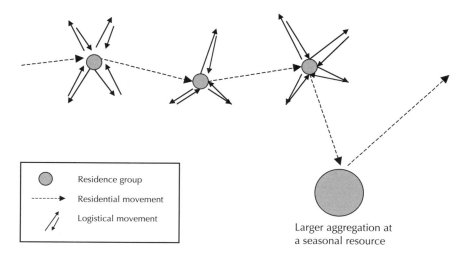

Figure 4.1   Movement of Western Desert residence groups

Yuwaaliyaay people and their neighbours

In the Darling/Barwon River region, the cycle of flood and drought, together with the semi-arid environment, provided the main constraint on population, settlement, and mobility.

Human population

The archaeologist Harry Allen remarks that the human population around the Darling River was adapted to drought years: 'strenuous efforts could support most people during bad seasons and very little effort would support everyone during normal and good seasons'. Based on early sightings of Aboriginal groups, he calculated the population density in relation to the length of river frontage. The result was a summer population of about one person per 0.8–1.6 kilometres of river, and a winter population of less than one person per 3.2 kilometres of river. Winter conditions induced more than half the population to live away from the river. Translated into numbers of people in relation to the area associated with Yuwaaliyaay and Yuwaalaraay languages, the overall density, including the hinterland, would have been medium-low to low—possibly about one person per 30–60 square kilometres. Taking into account the effects of smallpox, which preceded white settlement, and the likely presence of people away from the Barwon River (on the Narran River, for example), the density may well have been higher.[21]

Settlement and mobility

Yuwaaliyaay people of the semi-arid grassland and woodland region of the Darling/Barwon River gave proper names to areas of land or 'countries' (*nguremba*), although it is not clear to what extent these countries were discrete and clearly bounded. Comparisons with neighbouring Gamilaraay, Muruwila, and Murruwarri people suggest that the region associated with the Yuwaaliyaay language included six or seven countries, each with an average area of about 2000 square kilometres. Individuals had an attachment to and took the identity of their country of birth, but each person had access to several countries by virtue of a variety of links (see Chapter 9).[22]

White explorers recorded groups along the Darling and Barwon Rivers of widely varying numbers:

Small groups	1–30 people	51%
Middle-range groups	30–50 people	6%
	50–70 people	22.5%
Large groups	70–100 people	20.5%

It is evident from Harry Allen's map of explorers' sightings that the residence groups along the Barwon River in the country of Wangaaybuwan people and their neighbours were generally smaller than those down-river. The size of residence groups varied with the seasons to some extent. In summer they averaged about 45 residents. In autumn their size fell to less than 30 people on average, and half were of 10 people or less. In winter the mean size was less than half that of summer—about 13. The largest groups occurred in spring, when 20% of them had more than 90 people.[23]

In drought years, when the river fell to very low levels and became saline, some residence groups in the region grew very large. In early February 1829 Sturt visited a residence-group camp of some 70 grass-thatched huts on the south bank of the Darling River between the Warrego and Culgoa Rivers, at the conjuction of Murruwarri and Waangaybuwan country. The Aboriginal people he met were sick with a skin disease, very likely smallpox. He thought each hut capable of sleeping a dozen people or more, but presumably each one was the camp of a family group, a widow or widower, or a bachelors' group, and some huts may have been abandoned because of the death of an occupant, as was customary in Aboriginal communities. If most huts were occupied then there may have been more than 100 residents, perhaps gathered for a ceremony—indeed, Sturt observed people painted in red ochre, yellow ochre, and white clay for mourning.[24]

Seasonal movement

Yuwaaliyaay people and their neighbours, living in a region with highly variable and unpredictable weather and a regime of drought and flood, seem to have been rather more mobile than the Kŭnai. Little direct evidence is available about movement, but Harry Allen has reconstructed seasonal movement patterns for the Darling River region using the evidence of travellers such as Sturt and Mitchell. He outlines a general pattern in which large numbers lived along the riverbanks in the summer in groups of variable size, spreading more widely to include the back country in winter, when the river was cold, low, and least productive. Residence groups along the riverbanks were largest on average in spring, whereas only small groups lived on the river in winter, as we have seen. A winter flood could, however, alter this pattern.[25]

Indeed, the variability of rainfall and river-flow, both in timing and extent, complicated the pattern. Drought gradually reduced people's mobility: as temporary water sources dried up or became too salty to drink, people had to move to more permanent waters (such as springs), living in small groups, or had to move from one temporary source to another. Vegetable foods became scarce, and people fell back on second-preference foods, such as acacia gum. Attracted to the same waters, large animals became easier to catch (e.g. with nets), while drought affected reptiles and small mammals rather less. Short falls of rain allowed people to be more mobile temporarily, and skin water-bags made journeys of one to two days possible. The river remained a source of water, but probably not a good source of food.

Rains, on the other hand, attracted game into the back country following the growth of feed. An explosion of aquatic resources—plants, fish, and fowl—followed the floods, leading people to disperse across the countryside, again hunting with nets. It seems likely that people situated their home bases on higher ground not prone to flooding, both along the Darling River and in the hinterland. People moved short distances when refuse built up around their site, or if a resident died.

Spring and summer fisheries, at their height after a rise in the level of the river (a 'flush') attracted people in large numbers to the riverbank. In such circumstances observers saw groups of up to 100 people (and larger down-river). Large numbers of people congregated away from the main river as well, to exploit the summer harvest of grass seed on the riverbanks and plains. In Yuwaaliyaay country the Narran Swamp and the Narran River, reduced in times of drought to a few waterholes, complicated the overall pattern. Appleton has found archaeological evidence to suggest that people lived a somewhat sedentary life on the shores of the Narran Swamp, where seeds and shellfish were significant in the diet.

To sum up, a general pattern of movement to the riverbanks in spring and summer, and up-country in winter, was complicated by the substantial but unpredictable rains and floods, which drew people to rich resources in the back country as well as the major rivers, and by drought, which necessitated aggregation around the permanent springs and waterholes.

Wiil and Minong people

Chapter 2 showed that Wiil and Minong people lived in a region of moderate rainfall, most of which fell in the winter, but that coastal groups had access to plentiful resources, especially fish.

Human population

Estimates of the size and density of the Aboriginal population at the time of European colonisation range from medium to medium-low. Several writers estimate the overall density along the south coast and its hinterland at one person per 25 square kilometres or a little less. The population density seems likely to have been medium in the hinterland (within the range of one person per 25 to 50 square kilometres), but higher at estuaries and inlets, where average rainfall was higher and communities had ready access to estuarine and coastal-wetland resources (perhaps one person per 5 square kilometres at King George Sound, at least at some times of year, as Bill Ferguson suggests).[26]

Settlement and mobility

Patrifilial groups (i.e. those whose members took their identity from their fathers and fathers' fathers) held countries defined by sites associated with their totemic ancestors. But, as in other regions, people had access to many countries because of links of kinship and marriage, and relationships formed through initiation journeys (see Chapter 8).

Minong people at King George Sound located their huts in sheltered spots near water. The orientation of huts ensured that the opening was leeward, with a fire kept burning in front, but so arranged that people did not overlook their neighbours (see Plate 3.5). A residence group usually had six to eight beehive huts (*mia*), but observers saw some larger ones. People came together in aggregates of up to 26 huts to exploit major resources in certain seasons. Nind estimated that residence groups usually numbered about 20 and rarely exceeded 50, although 26 huts suggests close to 100 residents.[27]

Seasonal movement

Some older sources suggest a pattern of summer on the coast and winter in the hinterland, but later studies propose a more complicated story. The following account puts together reconstructions by Caroline Bird and Sue Le Souëf.[28]

In the summer dry season (December to February) people aggregated at wetlands, both on the coast and on the uplands of the wheat belt (as it now is). People congregated at reliable water sources, including soaks, rock-holes, inland wetlands, and coastal freshwater lakes and swamps. There they exploited a wide range of foods from large home bases. On the coast, people gathered in large groups to exploit fish, freshwater crayfish, and tortoises, and they caught the occasional seal. They also hunted mammals and other reptiles, and they burned off the understorey. Residence groups consisted of up to about 90 people.

In autumn (March to May) people started to move inland from the coast to catch large quantities and varieties of fish and amphibians, and to hunt large mammals.

With the first rains of winter (June to August), which flushed out the accumulated salts and replenished the water supplies, people dispersed into smaller groups to occupy home bases in well-drained areas near the more ephemeral water sources, including rock pools, river pools and winter-wet depressions. They took advantage of creeks and seasonal water sources in depressions on the coastal plain and watersheds. When local resources allowed, the people would form larger groups to exploit the resources.

During winter, people had moved further inland to live in small, dispersed residence groups; well-established paths linked King George Sound to other places along the coast, and to Kojonup and Burungup inland. People hunted large and small mammals, fished in the rivers, now full of water, and collected vegetable foods. The most common camp size of six to eight huts accommodated up to 30 residents. People also fished in the closed bays on the coast, and may sometimes have met in large numbers, as Eyre observed for the 'Murraymin' people further west.[29]

At the beginning of the dry season in spring, as water sources dried up and became increasingly saline, larger groups formed once again, although home bases at soaks, permanent river pools, and small swamps varied in size. In the late dry season (late March to May) the scarcity of water led people to gather in large groups at permanent waters on the coast and in the hinterland. The move back to the coast began in spring, when people lived together in larger numbers exploiting young birds and birds' eggs, roots and grubs, banksia nectar, and occasionally fish.

Mokaré was a young Minong man who befriended a number of British residents in the early years of King George Sound. Bill Ferguson infers the extent of Mokaré's family's movement around the country, using information from British visitors Mokaré took with him on various occasions. They moved across a region extending 70 kilometres north of King George Sound and 120 kilometres along the coast. The family frequented Pillenorup, at the foot of the Stirling Range, but probably went no further north.[30]

To sum up, people in this region of medium to medium-low population density gathered at the coastal and inland wetlands in the summer dry season. In early winter, smaller groups formed at the ephemeral waters, with some larger groups gathering to fish. In the spring, coastal groups moved back to the coast, and in the early summer larger groups gathered at the permanent waters, both inland and nearer the coast. However, the information is insufficient to clearly distinguish between the movement of coastal and hinterland groups.

Sandbeach people

Moving to the tropical zone, the Sandbeach people on the east coast of Cape York Peninsula lived in much more sedentary residence groups.

Human population

Athol Chase bases his estimates of Aboriginal population densities in the early colonial period on an assumption about the average size of patri-groups and on the mapping of patri-group countries. The result is a medium to very high density of one person per 2.5–3 square kilometres on the coast, and about one person per 14 square kilometres in the hinterland west of the ranges. These figures, which are comparable with estimated densities in similarly rich environments (such as the Arnhem Land coast) are high for Australia.[31]

Sandbeach people divided land and waters among named patrifilial groups. A cluster of ancestral sites defined each 'country'; a country consisted of a strip extending from the hills to the west across the seashore to incorporate some reefs, cays, and islands. An individual had formal rights in their mother's country as well as their father's country, and also had access to certain others. People of adjacent patri-group countries shared rather settled dry-season and wet-season residence groups. Nevertheless, in order to exploit the seasonal and localised resources people had to be mobile to a degree.

Settlement and mobility

Each Sandbeach residence group consisted of several camps of nuclear, polygynous, and extended families, as well as a bachelors' camp. In the 1970s Athol Chase, in the company of some of the older Lockhart River residents, mapped the former locations of wet- and dry-season camping places. An estimated population of 800 people, divided among 32 patri-groups, suggests the following average sizes:

- 20 dry-season residence groups—40 residents each
- 12 wet-season residence groups—67 residents each
- 90 small dry-season residence groups—nine residents each.

But this assumes that people used all of the recorded localities at the same time, so the numbers may actually have been higher. Large temporary aggregations for ceremonies in the late dry probably involved several hundred people each; they were made possible by the availability of plentiful vegetable foods at that time of year.[32]

Sandbeach people thought of themselves as belonging to the beach and sea; indeed, they lived on the beach for most of year.[33] Given their high dependency on marine resources, one would expect them to have had relatively low residential mobility, and the ethnographic accounts support this view. Individual men, however, were highly mobile (logistically), travelling from their home base on the beach to pursue dugong and turtles out at sea, especially in the summer months. Groups of women travelled short distances from the home base in pursuit of vegetable foods (concentrated along the coast and rivers), fish, shellfish, crustacea, and small mammals and reptiles. The location of the home bases allowed residents to constantly survey the sea and estuaries, to act rapidly when an opportunity arose (for example, when a turtle or dugong was seen), and also to access resources on the shore. People made only short forays inland, such as trips in the late dry season to poison fish in freshwater pools and to gather fruit from the riverine vine forests. They also moved up and down the coast to take account of small-scale variations in the availability of resources.

The wet season, from about February on, confined people to a few large residence groups of about 70 people each; they lived on the beach and were protected from the rain and clouds of mosquitoes by bark-thatched huts. People of two or three contiguous patri-group countries of the same language lived together, together with people of other countries. Flooded creeks, rivers, and channels constrained movement, and people relied on the nearby mangroves and dune scrub for their staples. Athol Chase recorded the location of 12 major wet-season residence groups among 32 coastal patri-groups: each stood in a relatively dry place, with access to basic food and water resources and a usable path (*kayan*) to inland and other beach areas (Figure 4.2).[34]

During the dry season people lived in 'main camps' averaging 40 or more residents. Chase recorded the former sites of 20 such residence groups among 32 patri-groups.

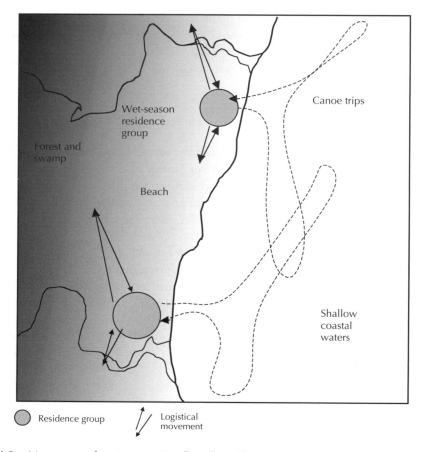

Figure 4.2   Movement of wet-season Sandbeach residence groups

As Lockhart River people remembered them in the 1970s, a 'big mob' of 'country-men' or 'kin' resided at each place. Residents included a core of close kin and often some more distantly related visitors from other places along the coast.

Each residence group lived at a river mouth or headland, in a sandy place such as a river bed. The camp stood close to a supply of water that remained fresh all year and a large stand of mangroves (a source of shellfish), and in a good place from which to hunt dugong and turtle. Each camp had an extensive midden. People dug wells to obtain water if necessary. During the early dry season, when water was plentiful and the num-ber of residents was greatest, people moved their camp spot short distances (about 500 metres), not just to exploit new resources but also when the old camp got dirty. During bad weather, people retreated from the fore-dune to the wooded sand ridges.

These main camps appear to have been home bases from which residents went on forays inland during the dry season, as individuals or in small family groups, for-aging and burning off the grasslands in game drives. They also garnered marine resources, using outrigger canoes to explore the coastal waters and reefs. Individuals and groups occasionally left their residence group to visit other groups, and some-times changed residence.

As the dry season progressed, small groups foraged more widely, for the resources of the forests, swamps, and rivers, staying at temporary home bases along the estuaries and rivers as well as the waterfront. Chase and Sutton show the location of 24 small dry-season residence groups among seven countries. At least six of these residence groups were associated with the Umpila language; ten were situated alongside an estuary, river or creek, with a concentration on the Nesbit River.

There seems to have been some tension in the dry season between the need for a large, stable residence group (a central place of residence) and for small, mobile groups that could hunt and forage for the seasonal, rather localised resources that became available. Dunes and riverine vine forests yielded seasonal vegetable foods, evenly distributed along the coast and rivers. Short-term home bases provided access to some edible fruits inland as well as fish, waterfowl, and other game, apparently compromising between men's and women's needs. Women foraged out of the smaller dry-season residence groups, collecting the more dependable and evenly spread vegetable resources within the coastal strip and along the estuaries and rivers, while the men travelled further for the seasonal, localised game.

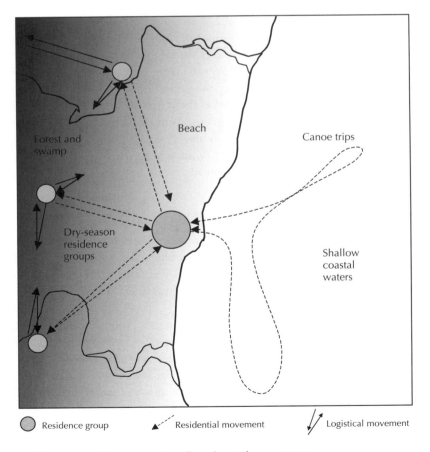

Figure 4.3 Movement of dry-season Sandbeach residence groups

In the late dry season, when the wongai plum (*Manilkara kauki*) came into fruit, people gathered in large numbers at coastal ceremonial grounds for initiation ceremonies. Chase and Sutton recorded two main ceremony grounds among the Umpila groups, while Stewart River people attended initiation ceremonies to the south. Figure 4.3 depicts Sandbeach dry-season patterns of mobility in schematic form.

To sum up, Sandbeach people lived at high population densities, and formed wet-season residence groups, constrained in their movement, on the beach. These groups grew in the dry season, but some residents moved inland to make small temporary camps, foraging more widely as the season progressed, and they formed larger groups around major resources for major ceremonies.

For the next case study, we remain in the tropical zone but move west to the northwest Kimberley, with its monsoon climate, and the rugged sandstone country of Ngarinyin and Worrorra people.

Ngarinyin people and their neighbours

Human population

Estimates of the Aboriginal population of the Kimberley region in the 1930s ranged from 6000 to 7000; by this time, however, the people had been much affected by disease and infertility, so the population was likely to have been considerably larger before white settlement. Estimates of the pre-colonial and early-twentieth-century population of the Kimberley range from about 10 000 to 30 000, at densities of one person per 12 to 35 square kilometres. A medium (one person per 10–25 square kilometres) to medium-low (one person per 25–50 square kilometres) population density seems likely in the hinterland, with a higher density along the coasts and inlets, where marine and estuarine resources could be garnered.[35]

Settlement and mobility

Among the Ngarinyin people and their neighbours, patrifilial totemic groups held areas of land, divided into the two patri-moieties. But individuals had access to a variety of countries, including their mother's and father's mother's countries, their namesake country, and the country from which their spirit came at the time of conception (see Chapter 9).

According to Valda Blundell, Ngarinyin residence groups were flexible in size and composition—from a single family unit to larger groups—but little has been recorded about the size of residence groups at different times of the year. People did describe several kinds of residence group set-up to Blundell: camping alone (*lanja*), a 'big mob' (*barlangarra*), people of one group visiting another, and a large group gathered for a ceremony.[36]

Ian Crawford provides the best reconstruction of seasonal movement in the northwest Kimberley, in his study done with residents of Kalumburu mission, who were presumably speakers of the northern dialects (Gamberre, Miwa, Kwini, and Milawila) as well as Wunambal. I shall take his account as at least indicative of Ngarinyin, Worrorra, and Wunambal patterns. The Aboriginal terms for seasons recorded by Crawford come from the northern dialects rather than Ngarinyin or Worrorra; I retain his spellings.[37]

With the beginning of the summer rains, people moved away from the rivers to higher ground. But fruits and seeds, some of which could be stored, ripened in abundance along the rivers, and game proliferated on the flood plains. Some roots came into season in the basaltic hills, as well as shoots of *dangana* palm.

During the wet season (*wundju*), through January and February, rains fell almost daily and occasionally a cyclone would strike. The rivers flooded and the flatter ground became waterlogged. People built paperbark or stringybark huts on higher ground, or lived in caves and rock-shelters. This was a time when vegetable staples were in short supply. People relied on hunting primarily, although continuous heavy rain sometimes made hunting impossible. During this period inlanders would visit relatives on the coast (such as their wife's people, mother's people, or father's sisters) for seafood.

As the rains eased in February and March (*maiuru*), food remained in short supply, but yams ripened around April (*bande maya*) and reached maturity when the southeast trade winds began to blow at the end of April (*golururu*).

In the dry season (*yirma*), from May to August, when the southeast trade winds blew steadily, people moved down from the hills and rocky country to live in the valleys near rivers and freshwater pools. Men burnt off the long grass and spinifex to enhance access and to stimulate regrowth in order to attract game, combining the burning off with hunting drives. Women collected roots, fruits, and seeds from the habitats with sandy soils, and by June or July they had begun to dig up root crops in the alluvial plains and on the banks of creeks and rivers. The abundance of food allowed people to perform major ceremonies. It was in this season that coastal people visited people of the hinterland, for root crops were scarce in the poorer sands of the coast. The waters had receded by late August and September, when women gathered the tubers of waterlilies.

In the hot season (*yuwala*), from September to November, root crops became scarce—plants that had not been harvested became difficult to find. People poisoned the shrinking pools to catch fish, and some fruits ripened. People congregated in large residence groups at permanent waters. From mid November to late December, as the rainy season (*djaward*) approached, lighting flashed and small rain storms occurred. Many of the edible fruits ripened, so that food again became plentiful.

On the coast and the islands people camped regularly in the same spot on the dunes above the high-tide line, using wind-breaks at times of high wind or moving into more sheltered spots. Coastal people visited the islands, leaving the remains of their shelters and other paraphernalia for future visits; they seem not to have lived on them permanently.

To sum up, in this region of medium to medium-low population densities, residence groups formed on high ground in the wet season but moved down to the valleys at the end of the wet season; in general the people were quite mobile, but congregated in large numbers for major ceremonies. As the country dried out, people gathered around the permanent waters, moving up-country with the first rains.

Yolngu people

Although detailed research into Yolngu land use came rather late, when only a few groups still lived permanently away from the missions, Yolngu ethnography nevertheless provides a relatively detailed picture of pre-mission patterns of settlement and mobility and their diversity. The Arnhem Land climate, with its seasonal cycle of flood and drought, necessitated a similar annual round to that of the Ngarinyin people and their neighbours.

Human population

Yolngu population densities appear to have been comparable to those of other Aboriginal peoples living in well-watered coastal environments. Estimates of the early-twentieth-century Yolngu population fall between 1500 and 3000. A Yolngu population of about 2500 in the late nineteenth century and early twentieth century seems plausible, but it probably fluctuated markedly under the impact of smallpox and other diseases brought by the Macassan trepangers, from the early eighteenth century onwards, and later by Europeans. The population density of northeast Arnhem Land as a whole may be estimated at about one person per 14 square kilometres, a medium–high figure. Densities generally would have been highest (perhaps in the high range of one person per 4 to 6 square kilometres) on islands with permanent fresh water, around the Arafura Swamp, along estuaries, and on the coastal plains. In some places along the coast and on estuaries the population density was higher still, while inland densities fell to about one person per 20 square kilometres. Higher densities than in the northwest Kimberley are to be expected because of the extensive and very productive wetlands and shallow coastal waters.[38]

Settlement and mobility

Yolngu people divided their land and waters into named countries, each defined by one or more focal ancestral places. In areas of rich resources, quite well-defined boundaries separated countries, each of which was owned by a named patri-group (described as a 'sib' or 'clan' in the literature). As in other regions, individuals had use rights in a number of countries, including their mother's, mother's mother's, and spouse's countries. Studies describe residence groups ranging from small groups of 20 or so people to groups of more than 100 gathered for a major ceremony.

It is not clear whether people situated a wet-season residence group on every patri-group's country, or if they were rather more sparsely distributed than this, as in eastern Cape York Peninsula.

Coastal groups[39]

W. Lloyd Warner based his anthropological research at the Methodist Mission on the island of Milingimbi, which is separated from the mainland by a narrow, mangrove-lined channel. His account of settlement and mobility reflects the coastal location of his research. According to Warner, the residence group fell to its smallest size in the wet season, when it consisted for the most part of a few males related as brothers or brothers-in-law, plus their wives and children. In the early dry season, when the mosquitoes had subsided and the spear grass had been burned off, these groups coalesced into residence groups of 30 to 40 people (or more at the time of a ceremony) and included close and more distant relatives. With the abundance of local resources at the end of the dry season, groups coalesced still further for major ceremonies.

Betty Meehan's description of an Anbarra coastal community in the early 1970s makes for a useful comparison, even though the community depended partly on the township of Maningrida. This 'outstation' community, living at the mouth of the Blyth River, consisted of people whom the Yolngu called Burarra; they were close neighbours of eastern Yolngu groups. Thirty to forty people lived a relatively sedentary life near the beach in the wet season gathering sea foods and fruits. They moved just a few kilometres inland to their dry-season base, obtaining hinterland resources at the beginning of the dry season by, for example, camping on earth mounds on the edges of swamps. Members of the group visited other communities for ceremonies, for which several hundred people camped together for a few days. At the end of the dry season, the coastal residence groups increased in size to about 100, then fell to about 30 or 40 people in the wet. Other, more mobile communities moved along the coast and to the islands. The pattern of settlement and movement would have been similar to that of Sandbeach people (see Figures 4.2 and 4.3).

Inland groups[40]

In the mid-1960s, Nicolas Peterson lived with people of Mirrngadja, on the south-eastern margins of the Arafura Swamp. There, during the summer wet season, people lived on high ground in somewhat sedentary residence groups of 20–50 people, their movement severely restricted by the amount of water as well as the high grass and understorey. People built wet-season houses of several kinds, depending on the material available. The mosquito platform (*gathawurdu*) of stringybark poles and bark had a smoky fire underneath, with a structure of poles and roof on top. A large paperbark dome (*liya-damala*, 'head of an eagle') provided an alternative type of dwelling.

In the late wet season, people of Mirrngadja moved down from their wet-season camping place, with its seasonal water supply, to the drier savannah woodland or wetter areas where they built *liya-damala* huts on earth mounds, raised above the flooded ground. As the country began to dry out, people became more mobile, following the retreat of the waters. They remained in residence groups next to permanent water sources and continued to use wet-season houses. Elsewhere, people used wind-breaks and in cold weather semi-circular huts of paperbark (*dhudi djerrakitj*, 'quail tails'). The wet-season residence group split into smaller, more mobile groups. But home bases were less mobile than individuals, who ranged further afield to forage for resources such as the eggs of magpie geese.

At the end of the dry season, individuals became less mobile, and congregated by permanent waters, especially for large-scale ceremonies. People camped in the open, using structures only for shade. Those in semi-permanent camps used open-ended tent-like or tunnel-shaped bark houses (*dhurrwarra marrma'*, 'two doors'). People at Mirrngadja lived by the streams and swamps during this season until late November or December, when they moved back to higher ground in the open forest.

As the rains set in, the larger groups broke up and people moved back to higher ground to establish wet-season camps (situated in the same general location every year), building substantial timber and bark structures. As in the northwest Kimberley, members of some inland communities would visit relatives on the coast regularly to hunt and gather coastal foods, taking foods of the hinterland as gifts.

One group in Peterson's study moved their home base four or five times during the year, over a total distance of between 15 and 40 kilometres. A second group, based in an adjacent patri-group country that incorporated more forest, moved up to seven times in the year, over a total distance of between 30 and 100 kilometres.[41]

Peterson shows that the foraging 'range' of each residence group (or 'band') near Mirrngadja was centred on one patri-group country, the location of its wet-season

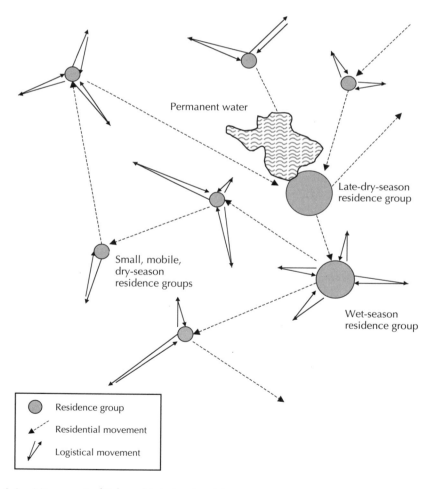

Figure 4.4   Movement of Yolngu hinterland residence groups

home bases. Their range of movement and foraging often extended into the country of neighbouring patri-groups, however, especially in the dry season. One residence group moved its home base from one patri-group's country into that of the adjacent patri-group over the course of two years. A second residence group moved between the countries of three patri-groups. Another residence group moved its home base within a single patri-group's country, but people from the group made short foraging trips into adjacent patri-group countries. Individuals ranged further afield to forage, visit relatives, attend ceremonies, and visit mission settlements and distant towns. Young bachelors travelled the most often and the most widely. Figure 4.4 provides a schematic representation of the inland Yolngu pattern of mobility.

The studies indicate rather varying patterns of settlement and movement among Yolngu people, especially between coast people and hinterland people, although the historical period of each piece of research needs to be taken into account. In the later period of Peterson's and Meehan's studies most people lived on missions, with just a few groups remaining in the bush. This was before the outstation movement, which began in the 1970s.

Comparisons and conclusions

In conclusion I will draw some contrasts between the population densities, mobility patterns and residence-group sizes of Western Desert people and people of areas richer in resources.

Population densities

The estimated population densities in the seven regions varied from about one person per 80–200 square kilometres in the Western Desert to about one person per two square kilometres or less on the coasts of eastern Cape York Peninsula and northeast Arnhem Land—an order of variation of about 100. Population densities varied roughly in accordance with aridity, but the high densities on the coast depended not only on resources that bred or grew locally but also on those brought from outside the region by major rivers and the sea. The Darling/Barwon River no doubt had an influence on Yuwaaliyaay densities (see Table 13.1).

Sedentism/mobility

The regions differed in their degree of sedentism and mobility, the seasonality of their resources, and the size of their residence groups (see Table 13.4).

Like the coastal Yolngu people and their Anbarra neighbours, Sandbeach people formed large residence groups on the beach, from which individuals and groups made logistical forays. In the dry season, they established smaller, inland home bases along the rivers, and continued to make logistical forays. The Yolngu groups on the periphery of the Arafura Swamp followed a somewhat similar strategy, but formed large residence groups at the end of the dry season. Western Desert people were more mobile, lived in small residence groups, and constantly shifted the location of their home bases. People occasionally congregated in larger camps when conditions allowed, but they seem not to have established large base camps to which they regularly returned.

The range of movement varied greatly. Gould reports a range of about 3000 square kilometres among Ngaatjatjarra people and their neighbours, and Myers shows that one Pintupi young man had lived and travelled with groups over an area whose longest axis was about 150 kilometres. Inland Arnhem Land groups moved their home base over a total of 15 to 100 kilometres through the year, but within a quite restricted area, with a longest axis of less than 10 kilometres. The mobility of individuals, especially unmarried young men, would have been much greater.

Seasonality

The case studies demonstrate the following contrasts in the seasonality of movement:
- a broad seasonal pattern in Gippsland (Kŭnai), with its strong temperature contrasts but year-round rainfall
- weaker seasonality in the Western Desert (Pitjantjatjara and their neighbours) and the Darling/Barwon River region (Yuwaaliyaay and their neighbours), where variable and unpredictable rainfall (and river 'flushes' in the case of the Darling/Barwon) dictated movement
- highly seasonal aggregation and mobility in the tropical north (Ngarinyin and Yolngu), with its summer monsoon, and the southwest (Wiil/Mi_nong), with its winter rains.

The Darling/Barwon River region had more irregular and less predictable resources than the coastal waters and estuaries of eastern Cape York Peninsula, and its resources depended more on rains further afield in the vast river catchment than on local rains. Local rains thus imposed an alternative (and sometimes competing) pressure to move away from the main river to take advantage of the growth of resources following rains. Of course, the permanent waters of the rivers and their pools attracted large numbers in times of drought, but localised rains led people to be more mobile.

A similar pattern prevailed in the Western Desert, but on a broader scale. The permanent waters there were not chains of riverine pools but scattered wells and soaks. Nevertheless, people gathered at these places in some numbers in times of drought, moving on when rains replenished the more ephemeral waters. The movement was long-distance, following lines of waters. The larger resources that resulted from the rains also attracted larger, temporary aggregations.

A beach location gave a group access to a constantly renewed resource base—the sea. Groups in this situation with the conditions and technology to exploit marine resources were the least mobile. Examples include the Sandbeach and Yolngu (together with Anbarra) groups, who lived by shallow coastal waters, and perhaps the Mi_nong groups on King George Sound. Kŭnai people of the coastal barrier and lakes may have formed similarly stable residence groups.

Sandbeach people balanced the availability (and desirability) of marine resources and those vegetable foods accessible behind the beach against the availability of resources further inland. One of the constraints leading people to live in large wet-season residence groups was the difficulty of travel caused by the rains and the growth of the understorey. In the dry season, people could mix beach residence with inland foraging.

Size of residence groups

The difference in the average size of residence groups of the Western Desert and the Arnhem Land mainland (and, going by estimates, of eastern Cape York Peninsula) makes sense in terms of the balance between three forces. One is the need to have sufficient producers in a group to hedge against variation in individual productivity. (Of course, except for in defence, a large group is of no use unless the food is going to be shared.) Another is the pressure to reduce the size of a group to reduce the cost of foraging further afield. A third is the need to balance this cost against that of moving and/or splitting up. The case studies presented a range of environmental conditions that led to a variety of solutions.

Further reading

The size and distribution of the pre-colonial Aboriginal population have been much argued over, but it is impossible to resolve these matters with any degree of certainty. Len Smith reviews the early population estimates in *The Aboriginal Population of Australia* (1980). In his much-cited paper 'Some environmental and cultural factors influencing the structuring of Australian aboriginal populations' (1953), Jo Birdsell attempted to model the relation of population density to rainfall with mathematical precision. The foundations are rather shaky, however, for he assumes that clearly bounded territorial 'tribes' existed all across Australia, with an average population of about 500.

In his *Our Original Aggression* (1983), Noel Butlin challenged the early population estimates on the ground that smallpox has already affected the Aboriginal population of Victoria before any censuses were taken. Judy Campbell confirmed the widespread effects of smallpox in her *Invisible Invaders* (2002), but concluded that the spread of the disease began on the north coast, and that it was not initially introduced by the British.

Robert Kelly provides an overview of the literature on settlement, mobility, and foraging strategies among hunters and gatherers in his book *The Foraging Spectrum* (1995).

Nicolas Peterson and Jeremy Long's *Australian Territorial Organisation: A Band Perspective* reviews the Australian evidence for band size, structure and movement.

Notes

1   See Sahlins (1972: 33) on the constraints on group size and settlement.

2   Typologies of degrees and patterns or mobility/sedentism have been proposed by Beardsley et al. (1956), Murdock (1967), and Binford (1980). On the spacing of resources see Kelly's discussion (1995: 132, 214–4) of Horn's model and its applications.

3   The forces determining the structure of hunter–gatherer residence groups are discussed by Binford (1983), Kelly (1995: 220), Myers (1986: 76–7), Smith (1988), and Winterhalder (1986).

4   On Aboriginal residence groups see Peterson and Long (1986: 135). For comparative figures worldwide see Kelly (1995: 211).

5   For discussions of territoriality and social boundary defence see Cashdan (1983), Dyson-Hudson and Smith (1978), Heinz (1972), Kelly (1995: 184–95, 203), and Smith (1988).

6   See Birdsell (1953).

7   The estimates of the Gippsland population by Fison and Howitt (1880: 181), Thomas (1860), and Tyers (1857) are of the same order (1000–1800), while the very high estimate was that of de Villiers (1847, cited in Cuthill n.d.). See also Bulmer (in Curr 1887 Book 3: 544), Gardner (1988), and McBryde (1983: 140). On the effects of smallpox see Butlin (1983: 25), Campbell (2002), and Hotchin (1990).

8   I have computed these areas by dividing the area of Gippsland (up to 1000 metres elevation) by the estimated number of country groups (about thirty), and the region around Lake Victoria, Lake King, and Lake Tyers by nine. The inferred boundary of this region is between the central locations of the lakes groups and those of adjacent country groups, as reported by Howitt and other sources; see Howitt (1880; 1904) on 'divisions' and Wesson (2000) for a reconstruction of the locations of groups and countries.

9   On encounters with groups of Kŭnai see Coutts (1967: 238).

10   On rights to Metung see Howitt (Papers, MV B4 F7 xm527).

11   The sources on Kŭnai seasonal movement are Bulmer (1994: 51; in Smyth 1878 vol. I: 141–2, 249), Howitt (Papers, SLV 1053/3b), and Hotchin (1990: 136).

12   The quotation is from Bulmer (1994: 49).

13   On seasonal movement and occupation in the west of the Lakes region see anon. (in Cuthill n.d., cited in Hotchin 1990: 137), Hotchin (1990: 237), and Hotchin (1990: 137, who cites Warman in the *Port Phillip Herald*, 1847).

14   On the coastal archaeology of the region see Coutts et al. (n.d.: 46), Coutts (1967), and Hotchin (1990: 117). The Robinson quotation is from Mackaness (1941: 11).

15   On Kŭnai participation in the gathering of bogong moths see Flood (1980: 72). On Omeo bogong hunters see Lambie (1840).

16   See Hotchin (1990: 88), Fison and Howitt (1880: 261), and Smyth (1878: 143).

17   Estimates of Western Desert population densities vary from the very high estimate by Berndt of one person per 36 square kilometres which he revised to one person per 143 square kilometres (1972: 180), through Gould's estimate (1969b: 64; 1980: 69) of one person per 80–100 square kilometres, to the lower estimates of Cane (1990) and Long (1970) of one person per 150–200 square kilometres.

18   On Western Desert residence groups see Hayden (1981: 174) and Layton (1986: 58, 60). The plan of a Western Desert camp is in Tindale (1972: 243). See Gould (1967: 56) for reports by Giles and Forrest in 1873–4.

19   For more recent census results and estimates see Cane (1990: 153) and Peterson and Long (1986: 135).

20   I have drawn on Gould (1967), Hamilton (1980: 11–12), Oliver (1989: 160), Myers (1986), Tindale (1972), and Tonkinson (1991) to construct this account of seasonal movement in the Western Desert. Information on finer-grained strategies is from Hamilton (1980).

21   Allen's estimate per mile of river translates into 250–500 in the summer along the river between Yuwaaliyaay/Yuwaalaraay country and the country of Gamilaraay and Wayilwan people on the opposite bank. I have divided half that number into the area of Yuwaaliyaay country (about 15000 square kilometres) to yield a density of about one person per 60–120 square kilometres, and doubled it to take account of the effects of smallpox and the presence of explorers. See Bonney (1883: 123; cited in Allen 1972: 98), Butlin (1983: 145–6), and Sullivan (1970: 44).

22   On residence groups in the Darling/Barwon River region see Allen (1972: 59–61, 64), who draws on Mitchell (1839 Vol. I), Sturt (1833 Vol. I), and Barker (1977).

23   Allen (1972: 59) calculates the spring–summer mean as 45 ± 23, and the autumn–winter mean as 13 ± 13.

24   On Wangaaybuwan camps see Sturt (1833 vol. I: 89).

25   The sources on seasonal movement in the Darling/Barwon River region include Allen (1972), Appleton (1995), Bonney (ms c1881, cited in Allen 1972: 84), and Sturt (1849 vol. I: 298).

26   For Wiil/Miṉong population estimates see Bird (1985: 126), Clark (1842), Ferguson (1985: 112), and Le Souëf (1980: 77–9).

27   On Miṉong residence groups see Le Souëf (1993: 9) and Nind (1831: 28). Le Souëf's sources include observations by Barker, Browne, Durville, Eyre (1845), Menzies, and Nind (1831).

28   See Bird (1985: 145–7, 176) and Le Souëf (1993) on seasonal movement.

29   See Ferguson (1987: 125) on Aboriginal pathways.

30   On Mokaré's range see Ferguson (1987: 134).

31   Chase (1980b: 157) bases his estimate of the pre-colonial population density on an average size of 25 for the land-owning patrilineal groups. I make the same assumption for inland groups, whose 'estates' he also mapped.

32   On Sandbeach residence groups see Chase (1980b) and Chase and Sutton (1987).

33   See Chase (1978: 163; 1980b: 157–8, 160; 1984) , Chase and Sutton (1987: 76–7, 92–3), and Thomson (1933: 458) on Sandbeach seasonal movement. The location and movement of camps on the Stewart River estuary are described and analysed by Hale (1927), Rigsby (1999: 110), and Thomson (1934: 241, Photographic collection MV 3296–7).

34   A map in Chase and Sutton (1987: 76) shows seven wet-season camps in the countries of seven Umpila patri-groups, but two of the countries have no wet season camp indicated, while two have two each. Presumably these camping places were not all occupied at the same time.

35   For estimates of the pre-colonial Aboriginal population of the Kimberley region see Shaw (1978: 9), Elkin (1932: 297), and Kaberry (1939).

36   On Ngarinyin and Worrorra residence groups see Blundell (1975 vol. 1: 118–9), Herndandez (1941), and O'Connor (1989).

37   On the seasonal movement of Ngarinyin people and their neighbours see Crawford (1982).

38 Warner's (1937: 157) estimate of 3000 for 1926–29 in northeast Arnhem Land included Burarra people of Cape Stewart. Thomson's (1937–38: 11) estimate for 1937–38 of 1500 covered eastern Arnhem Land and Groote Eylandt. For coastal and hinterland densities see Meehan (1982), Hiatt (1965: 17), Jones (1985: 291), Peterson and Long (1986: 41–2), Warner (1958: 16), and White et al. 1990. On Macassan visitors see MacKnight (1969; 1976).

39 On the seasonal movement of Yolngu coastal groups see Warner (1937: 139), and on the movement of the neighbouring Anbarra people see Meehan (1982: 41).

40 On the seasonal movement of inland Yolngu groups see Peterson (1973) and Shapiro (1973: 379). On house structures see Peterson (1976a) and Thomson (1948b: plate facing pp. 24–5).

41 See Peterson (1971: 255, maps 8–15) on the movement of inland Yolngu groups.

PART II

Institutions

5

Identities

Introduction

The chapters of Part I have built up a picture of the habitats and resources of the seven regions, and of the movement of residence groups and individuals. But how did people identify themselves and others, and what kinds of community did they form? This chapter looks at social identities in the seven regions—how people shared broad identities in terms of the country they lived in, the languages they spoke, and totemic identities.

These modes of identity are among the 'institutional fields' described in Part II of the book. Chapter 1 defined these as 'domains of coordinated ideas, actions, events, organisation, and roles'. Each institutional field centres on a particular array of concepts, modes of expression, rules, and conventions that define its character and govern activities and social relations. Some of the institutional categories fit Aboriginal concepts better than others. In Aboriginal societies kinship relations (*gurruṯu* in Yolngu languages) were based on the obvious facts of maternity, doctrines about paternity and conception, marriage, the definition of kin terms, and rules and conventions about how people in certain relations ought to behave towards one another. The domain of totemic ancestors and ancestral things (*maḏayin* in Yolngu languages) had stories and doctrines about those beings, and ceremonies reenacting their actions, at its heart. I bring these doctrines together with sorcery, magic, and medicine under the category of 'cosmology'. 'Identity' roughly equates to aspects of 'naming' (*ya:ku* is 'name' in Yolngu languages).

Social anthropologists have commonly made a simple distinction between a social 'category' and a social 'group'. The first simply classifies people in a certain way, such as 'cyclists' or 'white people'; the number of such people is unrestricted. Aboriginal moieties are examples of social categories. 'Group' implies some kind of organisation, which may be temporary, and a more restricted 'membership'. Anthropologists refer to a group with an identity that can survive the departure of any particular member and with members who hold some kind of common property as a 'corporate group'. Aboriginal 'clans' have often been described in this way. I shall use the term 'group' in a more informal way to cover looser collections of people as well as groups with a more defined identity and membership. I shall refer to the latter by more specific terms, such as 'patri-group' and 'matri-group'. In many cases a social category such as a semi-moiety provided the identity of land-holding groups.[1]

But rigid schemes cause problems. For example, I have been unsure whether to describe the matrilineal totemic 'clans' of the Yuwaaliyaay as matri-categories or matri-groups; I suspect that these identities linked an indefinite number of people across a wide region, such that a person of a given identity did not know all the others of the same identity. People of the same identity never cooperated as a whole, nor were they linked by a common administrative hierarchy (as, for example, all Australians are). But in a particular locality people of a given matri-category did coordinate their activities—in the organisation of ceremonies, for example.

Language and locality

A language-variety often provided a key to the identity of groups and individuals. I use the expression 'language-variety' to denote a way of speaking recognised by the people themselves, regardless of whether it had the linguistic status of a discrete language or dialect.

In several of the regions discussed in this book people regarded language-varieties as properties of groups of people and of broad areas of country, reflecting the attachment of people to places. It is for this reason that the tribe model of Aboriginal society and territory retained its currency for so many decades. Many early ethnographers assumed that Aborigines were divided into relatively large and discrete 'tribes', each of which shared a common language, culture, and territory. This model survived through the first two-thirds of the twentieth century, adhered to, with variations, by Radcliffe-Brown, Elkin, Tindale, and Birdsell. According to Tindale, for example, a tribe had a proper name, a discrete territory, a common language, and a shared kinship system. Its members met periodically, developed ideas in common, and shared initiation rites and ceremonies. They tended to marry each other rather than outsiders (i.e. the tribe tended to be endogamous). Members of a tribe lived in a number of smaller 'hordes', sometimes splitting up into family units.[2]

The tribe model had begun to unravel more than a decade before Tindale published his book and maps of Aboriginal tribes in 1974. Ronald Berndt questioned its applicability to the Western Desert in 1959. During the 1970s and early 1980s, a number of Queensland researchers demonstrated that the relationship between language, social identity, and community in Cape York Peninsula was far more complex than the concept of tribe allowed. These researchers found that individuals tended to be multilingual. Language-varieties tended to be distributed discontinuously across communities rather than coinciding with community boundaries, which, in any case, were largely absent. Many marriages took place between speakers of different dialects or languages. Patri-groups with common totemic links often spoke a variety of languages, and in some areas a patri-group held several discontinuous areas of country. Sharing a common language did not entail an ideology of unity, nor were there any clearly bounded linguistic units (a group identified by speaking or possessing a language) or language communities (a group whose members communicate with one another using one or more languages).[3]

In the seven case studies of this book, language-variety takes its place as one among a number of ways in which people identified themselves. But people did not use the criteria employed by linguists to differentiate dialects and languages. Some socially significant differences were minor ones from a linguistic point of view, such as the use or omission of a final syllable (as in the Yolngu dialects of *dhuwal-mirr* and *dhuwala-mirri*). Other names for language-varieties invoked isoglosses—contrasting words with the same meaning, such as words meaning 'yes', 'no', 'come' and 'this' in different language-varieties.

Modes of identity included reference to locality—the name of a place, the type of country (such as coast or hinterland, salt-pan or rocky country), or direction (such as 'northerners'). We shall see that in two of the case studies (Kǔnai and Wiil/Minong) broad regional identities with proper names were used in place of the language identities of the other regions. Also, people frequently referred to residence groups by the name of a leader or prominent resident.

Totemic identities and naming systems

We shall see in Chapter 7 that Aboriginal cosmologies centred around person-like ancestors who created the features of the landscape, instituted forms of social order, established the existing social groups, and left creative and dangerous powers that people could tap. These ancestors were linked to 'totemic' classification schemes: many possessed the identity of a species (such as kangaroo or echidna) or a celestial object or phenomenon (such as the moon), and many myths recount how an ancestor acquired the characteristics of its eponymous species or celestial object. The names of species and other phenomena also functioned as badges or insignia of groups or categories of people (such as males and females) or as individual identities. It is in this wide sense that I use the word 'totemic'. Nineteenth and early twentieth century social theorists thought of totemism as a mode of social organisation in which an exogamous group was identified by a natural species or other phenomenon from which members of the group believed they were descended, and which they worshipped. Some saw totemism as a stage in the evolution of religion and society. However, Claude Lévi-Strauss argued in 1962 that totemism was not a unitary phenomenon; all its elements could occur alone or in various combinations. People framed the identity of, differences between, and relations among social groups very widely in terms of natural phenomena.[4]

Social categories and groups included what are referred to in the anthropological literature as clans, moieties, sections, subsections, and semi-moieties. I shall divide these into *unrestricted* and *restricted* identities. Identities are 'unrestricted' if the number of possible related identities is indeterminate, although practical considerations will limit their number. 'Restricted' identities occur as pairs, fours, or eights, or sometimes as a group of five or six. Anthropologist have referred to these as 'marriage classes', or just 'classes':[5]

Unrestricted totemic identities
Individual totemic identity
'Clans', 'sibs', 'descent groups':
- patrifilial groups (patri-groups)
- matrifilial groups (matri-groups)
- groups with multiple bases

Restricted totemic identities
Gender totems (paired identities)
Moieties (paired identities)
Sections (four identities, eight with gender variants)
Semi-moieties (four identities)
Subsections (eight identities, sixteen with gender variants)

Unrestricted totemic identities

Totemic identities divided people into 'kinds' identified by one or more species or other phenomenon (such as the sun, moon, fire, or water). In Australia, patrifilial (or patrilineal) identities, in which a person takes his or her father's and father's father's identity, often had an association with the ownership of land and waters, as well as with totemic ancestors. Such groups also owned sacra—including songs, dances, designs, and sacred objects—associated with their ancestors. They were often, though not always, exogamous: that is, a person could not marry someone of their own totemic group or identity.

Writers such as A. R. Radcliffe-Brown and W. E. H. Stanner thought patrifilial land-holding groups (patri-groups) were universal in Australia, but recent research has shown that they were not, although it is not clear how widely they were distributed. Among the case studies in this book, Pitjantjatjara and Yuwaaliyaay groups were not patrifilial, and Kŭnai groups may not have been. Although textbooks present land-holding groups as having a similar structure in different regions, and call them 'clans', 'sibs' or 'local descent groups', they varied greatly in form. We shall encounter a few variants in this chapter and in Chapter 9. Patri-groups could coexist with other types of organisation, including moieties (patrifilial and matrifilial), sections, and subsections.[6]

Matrifilial totemic groups (or matri-groups, usually called 'clans' by anthropologists) of the kind found among the Yuwaaliyaay people and their neighbours were probably not associated with land-holding, but they seem often to have been exogamous; indeed, they were one of the means of regulating marriage and defining marriage rights. A person gained their identity at birth and had the same totemic identity as their mother, mother's mother, and mother's mother's mother. People of the same matrifilial identity would be found dispersed among several residence groups, but were together to the extent that siblings, mothers, and children resided together. Since they were not tied to particular localities, matri-groups enabled people of different regions to form social relationships on the basis of having the same or a similar totemic identity. People invoked these matrifilial totemic identities when organising marriage and ceremonies.

Matri-groups coexisted with other kinds of identity. In the Darling/Barwon River region they existed in conjunction with a 'section' system and with attachments to country based on place of birth.

Restricted totemic categories

Sections, subsections, and semi-moieties, which are 'naming systems', provided a way for people to form relationships beyond everyday kinship ties.[7] In moiety systems, which were widely distributed in Australia, everyone in the community took one of two identities on the basis of filiation (the relation of parent to child). In patrifilial moieties (or patri-moieties) a person took their father's identity (or, as a default, the opposite moiety to that of their mother). In matrifilial moieties (or matri-moieties), a person took their mother's and mother's mother's identity. Species of plants, animals, birds, and fish often denoted the contrast between the moieties—for example, 'Eaglehawk' and 'Crow' in areas of the southeast. According to a rule of exogamy, a person was supposed to marry someone of the opposite moiety, although the rigour with which people enforced this rule varied. Matri-moieties existed in such places as the Lake Eyre region, the Channel Country, the Darling River basin, part of the southwest region of Western Australia, and western Arnhem Land and the adjacent islands. Where matri-groups and matri-moieties coexisted, they sometime intersected, so that each matri-group included people of both moieties; in other cases, the matri-groups were divided between the moieties. Patri-moieties were common across the north of Australia and in isolated pockets on the southwest and southeast coasts.

Generation moieties grouped people of alternate generations together: a person's own generation with his or her grandparents' and grandchildren's generations, in opposition to the moiety consisting of his or her parents' and children's generations. They were endogamous—a person was supposed to marry someone of the same or alternate generation, not of his or her parents' or children's (or sibling's children's) generation. These moieties occurred across the Western Desert and into the hinterland of the southwest.

In general, moiety identities reinforced rules prescribing marriage between certain categories of kin by restricting the range of violations. Participants in ceremonies also invoked moieties, with people of different moieties taking contrasting roles. People classified land and waters by patrifilial moiety.

It is probably not correct to call gender categories (male and female) 'moieties', but in some areas each gender had its own totem, invoked as a guardian and in ceremonies. Kǔnai people associated each gender with a small bird, as we shall see. These have been called 'sex totems' by anthropologists.

Early anthropologists called section, subsection, and semi-moiety systems 'marriage classes' and assumed that their main function was the organisation of marriage. But anthropologists later came to the conclusion that kinship relations took precedence over section or subsection identity in marriage arrangements. Sections, subsections, and semi-moieties are best understood as naming systems.

Sections

In a region with a section system, everyone bears one of a set of four names, or four pairs of gender-related names, in addition to their personal names. The section names form pairs or 'matri-couples', notionally in reciprocal mother–child relations, which determine the section name acquired at birth. To use English names, the child of a female Jean must be Jo or Joe, and the child of Jo (female) must be Jean or Gene; the child of a female Petah must be Robyn or Robin, and Robyn's child must be Petah or Peter (see the diagonal arrows in Figure 5.1). Other rules specify ideal marriages between the matri-couples—any woman called Jean should marry a Peter and any man called Gene should marry a Petah; Joe should marry a Robyn and Jo a Robin. These marriages create two patri-couples (the vertical arrows in Figure 5.1) in addition to the matri-couples. The equals signs in the diagram denote ideal marriages.

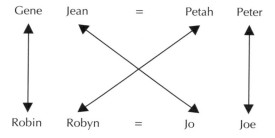

Figure 5.1 A section system

Section systems of this kind were (and are) prevalent in two parts of Australia: in the east of the continent, across much of what are now Queensland and New South Wales, and in the west. Sections were still in the process of spreading into the Western Desert at the time of colonisation. People used section names to generalise about kin relations, in the organisation of regional ceremonies, and to relate to people of distant communities in quasi-kin relations.

Subsections

Subsection systems have a similar form to section systems, but with eight pairs of names instead of four. The ideal marriages between subsections can be varied to produce alternative patterns of indirect 'descent' between them. In the classic study of the Arrernte system by T. G. H. Strehlow, subsections related as 'mother' to 'child' formed two 'cycles', each of four subsections (the diagonal arrows in Figure 5.2). Relations among subsections through links of 'father' to 'child' formed four patri-couples (the vertical arrows in the diagram), as opposed to the two patri-couples of section systems. Subsection systems also assigned precedence to either mother–child or father–child relations to determine a person's subsection in the event of a marriage that did not fit the subsection rules.

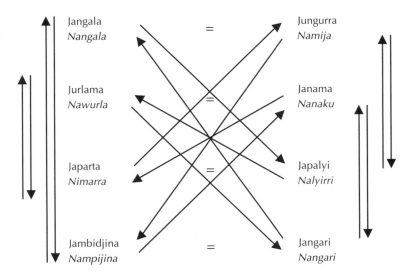

Figure 5.2   A subsection system (Gurindji language)

The main function of subsections seems to have been as a mode of inter-regional relationship, for, amongst other things, the organisation of regional ceremonies. People also used them as handy names when (as was usual) the uttering of personal names was impolite and dangerous, and to teach children the fundamentals of kinship. They do not need to have an association with totemic identities, but each category did in fact have a conventional relation with species, at least in some regions. Subsection systems appear to have been formed through the merger of two separate section systems, and spread from a centre in the vicinity of the upper Daly River in the Northern Territory; ethnographic records show that subsections were continuing to spread in the twentieth century, partly to facilitate relations among former strangers who were travelling more extensively.[8]

In some regions, subsections became integrated with the identity of groups holding land and waters. The conventional marriages linking subsections were arranged in such a way that they formed four pairs reciprocally related as father to son (i.e. four patri-couples). Each area of land and the people 'holding' it had the identity of a particular patri-couple. This form of subsection system was homologous with a patrifilial semi-moiety system.

Semi-moieties

Like sections, semi-moieties consist of four names, but a person belongs to the same semi-moiety as their father (in the case of patrifilial semi-moieties) or mother (in the case of matrifilial ones). Semi-moieties form pairs that are implicit moieties, or that coincide with named moieties. The preferred marriage is to someone of the semi-moiety of the opposite moiety, which should not be the mother's semi-moiety (in patrifilial semi-moiety systems) or father's semi-moiety (in matrifilial semi-moiety systems). As Kenneth Maddock points out (following Spencer and Gillen), the alternative marriage preference divides each semi-moiety into two categories—those who marry into one semi-moiety of the opposite moiety, and those those who marry into the other. But Maddock also represents marriage as a choice: for people with patrifilial semi-moieties a second preference is to marry someone of their mother's semi-moiety. Figure 5.3 depicts the first-preference marriage, and the resulting pattern of parent–child relations between semi-moieties. The letters P, Q, R, and S stand for the semi-moiety names; the arrows show mother–child relations. For example, if P(b)'s mother is R(a), then he should marry S(b), and his children will become P(a), like his father.

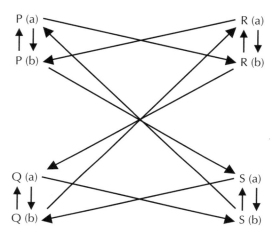

Figure 5.3   A semi-moiety system

Subsection systems with patri-couples are similar in form to semi-moiety systems, for the marriage relations between subsection patri-couples are like those between semi-moieties. Patri-semi-moieties were also linked to the holding of land and resources (along the south coast of the Gulf of Carpentaria, for example) and the organisation of rituals. Minong people seemed to have divided country between four patrifilial semi-moieties, while people in other areas of the southwest had matrifilial semi-moieties.

Putting totemic identities and naming systems together

A system of sections, subsections, or semi-moieties can overlap matrifilial, patrifilial, or generation moieties, or any combination of these. Land-holding patri-groups and their countries can be divided between patri-moieties or patrifilial semi-moieties or both. Section systems articulate neatly with Kariera-like kin terminologies and associated marriage rules, while subsection systems relate neatly to certain Aranda-like modes of kin classification. However, formally incompatible systems sometimes coexisted. Yuwaaliyaay people and their neighbours treated matrifilial totemic groups as strictly exogamous, but they did not all worry about marrying outside their section in a four-section system. In a similar way, Yolngu kin classification is logically incompatible with the more usual form of subsection system, and they had to modify the subsection rules to allow alternative marriages. Some peoples have modified their kinship system to better fit with their naming systems.[9]

Personal names

In many regions, an individual's personal name or names linked them to their place of birth, or to the totemic ancestors or the species, places, and ceremonies associated with them. Personal names also linked a person to the relative whose name they took, such as their father's father, mother's mother, or mother's brother. To address a person by their name was a breach of etiquette, because Aboriginal people believed in an intrinsic relation between a person and his or her name and its object, such that in some circumstances one could affect the person by uttering the name—one mode of sorcery attack. By the same token, some names of totemic ancestors had intrinsic power that could be tapped by invoking the name. (See also Chapter 7).

Kŭnai people

Of the peoples studied in this book, Kŭnai people had the simplest totemic systems—gender and patrifilial totems, combined with regional identities.

Kŭnai as an identity

In his published writing, A. W. Howitt depicted Kŭnai ('Kŭrnai') people as a single 'tribe' divided into five patrifilial 'clans', each of which was made up in turn of lesser groups that he called 'divisions'. Each division took its name from, or gave its name to, a locality. Tribal unity, Howitt thought, derived from a common language, common descent from the gender totems, kin relations, performance of the same songs and dances, and (except in the case of the Krauatŭn.golung people in the east) a shared initiation ceremony for males. However, Howitt's scheme is inconsistent with details of his own ethnography, published and unpublished, and with other evidence.[10]

'*Kŭnai*' was the word for 'man' or 'person'. It may indeed have be used as a proper name to mark the broad regional identity and commonality of language, in contrast with people of other regions who had a different word, such as '*murring*'. However, Howitt appears to have exaggerated Kŭnai unity; people of the region were not altogether united in their customs or wholly distinct as a group from their neighbours. As Howitt points out, people of the east of the region (Krauatŭn.golung or *krauatŭn kŭnai*), included as Kŭnai by Howitt, did not regularly participate in the Jerra-eil initiation ceremony with other people of the region; some went north to the Monaro to be initiated. Bidawal people, immediately to the northeast, apparently joined in Kŭnai initiation ceremonies, and also subscribed to Kŭnai gender totemism.[11]

Brajerak (male) and *lowajerak* (female) denoted 'stranger', thought of as dangerous, contrasting with *kŭnai*, 'people'. The status of *brajerak* was marked, it seems, by fighters eating pieces of skin from the thigh of a brajerak who had been killed, but not that of a fellow Kŭnai. However, some thought of Yuin people of coastal southern New South Wales as Krauatŭn.golung and not as *brajerak* (strangers), and of Bidawal people to the northeast as half Kŭnai and half *brajerak*. Distantly related people within Gippsland could be classified as *brajerak* or *lowajerak* as well. Moreover, people of different regions within Gippsland feared and distrusted each other. Thus, status as *Kŭnai* or *brajerak* had more to do with relatedness than language or local identity, and while *Kŭnai* denoted one's 'countrymen', it did not, in my view, constitute a unified group or tribe.[12]

Kŭnai dialects

According to one Kŭnai perspective, recorded by Howitt, people of Gippsland spoke three dialects—Nulit in the west, Mŭk-thang ('excellent speech') in the centre, and Thangquai ('broad speech') in the east—while the people of Wilsons Promontory spoke Nangai (see Map 5.1). The Kŭnai dialects, mutually intelligible according to

Map 5.1   Kŭnai and neighbouring dialects

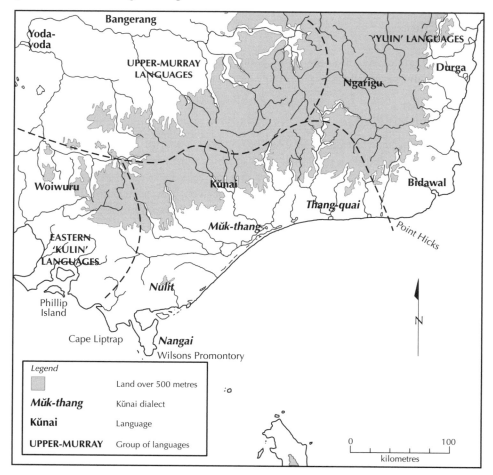

Sources: Hercus (1986) and Howitt (Papers)

linguists, made up the 'Kurnic' or Gippsland group within the Pama-Nyungan language family. Howitt records some minor variation between dialects in several lexical items. The size of the region in which they were spoken is approximately 30 000 square kilometres.[13]

Strong differences from neighbouring languages, especially those to the west and north, reflected the relative isolation of the Kŭnai people (Map 5.1). Some features of Kŭnai dialects, such as the frequency of the initial consonant cluster 'Br', marked them out from neighbouring languages. Hercus detected only weak links between Kŭnai dialects and languages to the west and northwest, with stronger, possibly recent, connections with the languages of peoples to the north (around Omeo and the Murray River region); they had substantial links with languages to the east. These linguistic similarities and differences reinforce the view that Kunai people were quite isolated from the people to the west. As in other parts of Australia, at least some Kŭnai people were multilingual.[14]

Map 5.2   Kŭnai regional identities

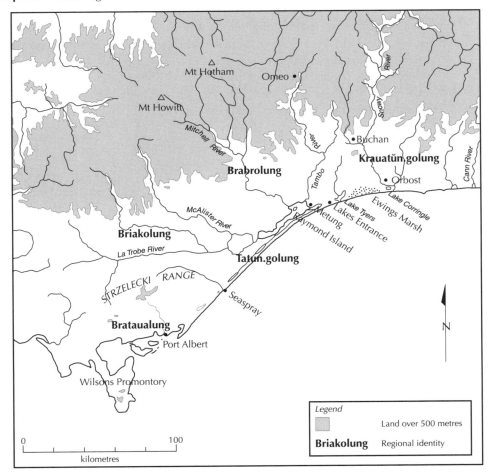

Source: Howitt (1980)

Regional identities

It is likely that what Howitt describes as the five 'clans' were broad regional identities somewhat similar in structure to the 'communities' of the Anbarra and their neighbours in north-central Arnhem Land, as described by Hiatt. Broad locality rather than descent or common language defined these loosely bounded populations. They cannot have been patrilineal groups, which is how Howitt depicts them, because marriages occurred between people of the same regional identity (as well as between people of different ones). Offspring of these unions would have had links to the region through both parents. Furthermore, the people living within each region came from several different regions (see Map 5.2).[15]

Three of the names may have included directional or broad locational terms: 'people of the west' (Briakolung or *bra-yak-golung* from *yak*, 'west'; alternatively *yak-thŭn Kŭnai*, 'western people'), 'people of the east' (Krauatŭn.golung), and 'people of the lakes' (Tatun.golung). The name Brabrolung may have incorporated a reduplication of *bra*, 'man'. These identities overlapped or were ambiguous on the margins; Bunjil Baul people of Raymond Island claimed to be, as one man told Howitt, 'partly Tatun.golung, and partly Brabrolung, but mostly Tatun.golung'. Furthermore, the designations may have been relative to particular perspectives—who counted as a 'westerner' may have depended on one's point of view. Taking Howitt's map at face value, each identity applied on average to a region of about 6000 square kilometres and some 300–500 people. If Howitt's mapping was generally correct, each regional identity except one included a broad drainage basin.[16]

Local identities

Howitt's 'divisions' were small territorial groups, each with a focal place. The names on his list of divisions are heterogeneous, however. Some are proper names of focal places. Others refer to the character of the country (such as 'island' or 'mud'), the name of a leader, or entities such as 'fire' and 'widgeon'. The latter may have been totemic or perhaps indicated expertise on the leader's part. This heterogeneity suggests that Howitt's division names were not all of the same status: some were names of places, perhaps extended to a wider area; others denoted the group of people living in an area, with reference to the name of a prominent man or to the name of the country. Recent reconstructions suggest that Kŭnai people recognised at least 30 focal places and corresponding groups among the five regional identities.[17]

Gender totems: Yiirŭng and djiitgŭn

The most pervasive totemic classification among Kŭnai people marked gender identity. The totemic bird *yiirŭng* (emu-wren, *Stipiturus malachurus*), a bird of heathlands and tea-tree scrub, represented men, while *djiitgŭn* (superb-wren, *Molurus cyaneus*), a bird of the open forests, represented women. The emu-wren was the 'elder brother' (*tŭndŭng*) of men, and the superb-wren was presumably 'elder sister' to women. Women and men invoked the names of their birds during the Jerra-eil initiation ceremony, and indeed male initiates danced as the birds. People were not supposed to injure their own gender totem, but young men and women teased each other by killing a bird of the other gender, a practice associated with elopement. These gender categories cut across regional identities of course.[18]

Je-ak patrifilial totems

The general term for a patrifilial totem was *je-ak*, meaning 'flesh' or 'meat'. Each person received the name of an animal, bird, reptile, or fish from his or her father at about the age of ten, or, in the case of boys, at initiation time. The person and the totemic animal were each the protector of the other, so that a person was not supposed to harm his or her totemic species. According to Kŭnai doctrines, the *je-ak* protected its human younger sibling by warning him or her in dreams of approaching danger; it also relieved sickness when appealed to in song, and assisted in other ways. Healers performed songs related to their *je-ak*, and, along with the gender categories, *je-ak* totems provided a basis of organisation in the Jerra-eil initiation ceremonies. In order to marry or for an elopement to be accepted, two individuals had to be of different *je-ak* and not closely related. The names of some country groups' 'bosses', such as Bunjil Tambun (*tambun*, Gippsland perch) incorporated their *je-ak* totems, reinforcing the relationship between a *je-ak* and a place. Some personal totems were, however, acquired in other ways—for example, through a dream indicating that the person has power over a totemic animal or a totemic phenomenon, such as the west wind.[19]

The names of species often served as personal names, given by the father's or mother's parents. A boy frequently took his mother's brother's or mother's father's name. Such inherited names provided a guide to how closely people were related. (A person was not to be addressed by their personal name but by a nickname, which often referred to some idiosyncracy or physical characteristic.)[20]

Countries included sites related to totemic ancestors (*mŭk je-ak*) and stories about them. Coral Dow has brought together the evidence of totemic associations, including the following examples:
- Tiddaluk the Frog—Gippsland lakes
- Borŭn the Pelican—Port Albert, Seaspray, Lower Tambo River
- Two Old Women—Turt-willan, Nicholson River
- Dingo—rocks at Metung
- Kangaroo Ribs—Walmajeri.

Kŭnai people may have linked their patrifilial guardian totems with places, but none of the *mŭk je-ak* associated with places appear as inherited patrifilial totems in the records, although the records are very incomplete. This mode of identity, then, linked individuals with totemic ancestors, but not in a direct way with country. Howitt and Bulmer both thought that *je-ak* were somewhat localised, in the sense that each was particularly prevalent in a given region. But a residence group must have included people of several *je-ak*, for one had to marry a person of a different *je-ak*, and from a different locality.[21]

To sum up, Kŭnai identities included regional identities, gender totems, and patrifilial guardian totems.

Pitjantjatjara people and their neighbours

Pitjantjatjara people and their neighbours lived in the arid Western Desert at very low population densities. How did this affect their modes of identity?

Language and locality

Pitjantjatjara people and their neighbours spoke a language that linguists refer to as the Western Desert language. It belongs to the Southwestern group of the Pama-Nyungan family of languages; the Southwestern group also includes the Nyungar languages of the southwest. The Western Desert language comprised a dialect chain across a very broad region, between Ooldea in South Australia and the Kimberley, and from Oodnadatta in South Australia to Meekatharra in Western Australia.[22]

Early accounts interpreted the names of Western Desert dialects as those of 'tribes', each with its own language and occupying a discrete territory. But as early as 1959 R. M. Berndt reported usages of names that were inconsistent with this model. A paper by Wick Miller cast Western Desert language and identity in an entirely different light. Western Desert people had no discrete political or social units, he argued. The use of language names depended on context, and they overlapped. Linguistic variation did not display clear boundaries but was continuous across the population. Moreover, variants of particular linguistic features overlapped, and each speaker would use a different variant of a feature (such as the word for 'come') on different occasions, making it difficult to map boundaries even of these.[23]

With some exceptions, such as Pintupi and Ngalia, most of the names for language-varieties in the Western Desert signal linguistic features. People picked out particular words to mark more or less localised variants and to classify and differentiate their speakers. But they did not use words of the same meaning to distinguish all language-varieties. For example, some are named according to the words meaning 'this':
- Ngaanyatjarra(nya), 'people who say "*ngaanya*"'
- Ngaatjatjarra(nya), 'people who say "*ngaatja*"'.
- others are named according to the word for 'come/go'—for example, Pitjantjatjara(nya), 'people who say "*pitja*"'.

People used these variants to pick out and differentiate people of broad localities and to distinguish themselves from others. But individuals differed markedly in the locations they attributed to particular language names. Moreover, people with different words for 'this' might share the word for 'come/go', which could be used as a more inclusive name. Pitjantjatjara speakers varied, however, in the way they used *pitja*—some used it to mean either come or go, others for only one of these senses—and in the past tense form they gave the verb.[24]

These language differences related to country to some degree, because people lived somewhat localised lives, and people who grew up and lived together tended to speak alike (Map 5.3). However, Western Desert people still travelled widely and far, and close relatives did not marry, which suggests there was a rather loose connection between ways of speaking and local populations; this is supported by the fact that residents in many residence groups spoke several dialects. Both Berndt and

Map 5.3   Pitjantjatjara people and their neighbours: Approximate location of language identities

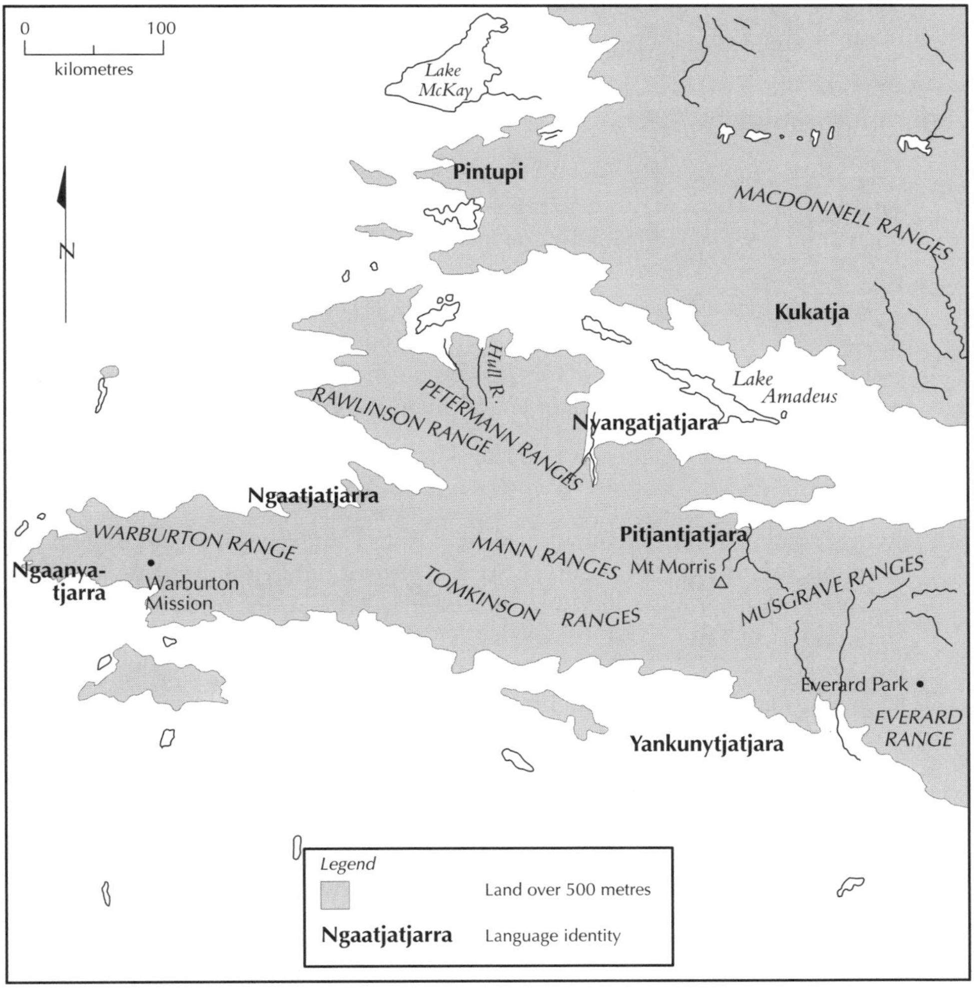

Sources: Dousset (1999) and Miller (1971)

Miller recorded people stringing together two or three names of language-varieties in identifying themselves, perhaps reflecting their parents' distinct identities, or picking out different linguistic features.[25]

The number of people identified in such ways is not recorded, and the context-dependent and overlapping character of these identities makes it difficult to estimate numbers. Maps of 'tribes' or languages suggest that each language-variety was associated with approximately 50 000 square kilometres of land. Given the range of population estimates (one person per 80 to 200 square kilometres), the number of people identified as Pitjantjatjara was perhaps between 250 and 600.

I have discussed language identity in this region at some length to bring out its contextual, shifting, and overlapping nature. The language identities were not the names of political communities or in-marrying groups, but reflected the mobility and interdependence of Western Desert people. People invoked distinct identities in different contexts, reflecting their relations both with the people they were with at the time and with others.

Generation moieties

Like other people of the Western Desert, Pitjantjatjara people and their neighbours sorted people according to generation, people of alternate generations each forming one of the two sets. Pitjantjatjara people referred to these by relative terms: *nganantarka* were people of one's own, one's grandparents', and one's grandchildren's generations; *tjanamilytjan* consisted of people of one's parents' and one's children's generations. Ngaatjatjarra people gave them proper names: *tjuntultukultul* ('sun-side') and *ngumpaluru* ('shade-side'). The generation moieties were endogamous: a person was not supposed to marry someone of their parents' or children's generation.[26]

Sections

According to Tindale, Pitjantjatjara people first encountered a section system at the beginning of the twentieth century. Section systems diffused into the Western Desert in a kind of pincer movement from the west and the northeast. People of the Great Victorian Desert moved west towards Laverton and Kalgoorlie and took on the section systems of the groups affected most by white settlement, whom they displaced. People in some regions adjusted their kin terminology to fit section systems.[27]

Among Pitjantjatjara people and their neighbours the section names were (and are) as shown in Figure 5.4. The vertical arrows show the patri-couples, the diagonal ones the matri-couples.

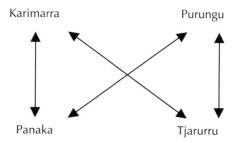

Figure 5.4 Pitjantjatjara section names

In the regions where the section systems originated, modes of kin classification corresponded to section names, but in the southern and southwestern Western Desert they did not. The kin terminology classified *father's mother* and *mother's mother* in the same way, but ideally they were of different sections. The kin terminology did not distinguish siblings from close cross cousins, but section names did. In the children's generation, however, the section of a man's own children and his sister's children differed, and so did the kin terms he applied to them. As mentioned, section names served primarily as modes of address, as ways of forming kin relationships with people of distant communities, and as aids in the organisation of ceremonies attended by people from a broad region.

Personal totems

Hamilton stresses the importance of the waterhole nearest to a person's birthplace in providing the primary grounds for a connection between a person and a totemic being, and in determining a person's totemic identity. Others, such as R. M. Berndt and Bob Tonkinson, give spirit conception or 'finding' the greater significance in the west of the region. A child's totemic identity would be revealed in markings in the skin or other physical peculiarities, sought for by the mother. Chapter 9 discusses in some depth how this relates to 'ownership' of country.[28]

Yuwaaliyaay people and their neighbours

Language identities among the Yuwaaliyaay and their neighbours, of the semi-arid savannah grasslands and woodland of the Darling/Barwon River region, appear to have overlapped rather less than those in the Western Desert, but they were still context-dependent 'shifters'. People of the region shared doctrines about Byamee (or Baiami, an ancestral being), spoke similar languages, and had related institutions. Ecology divided them, however, into riverine and back-country peoples.[29]

Language identities

Yuwaaliyaay was the name of a language-variety named after the word for 'no', which contrasted with 'no' in other language-varieties of the region. Other 'no-having' language-varieties of the region are shown (underlined) in Map 5.4.

Linguists place Yuwaaliyaay and Yuwaalaraay within the Wiradjuric group of languages of the Pama-Nyungan language family. The Wiradjuric group includes Wiriyaraay, Gamilaraay, Wayilwan, Wangaaybuwan, Gawambaraay, Guyinbaraay, and Wiradjuri. To the southwest of this group there lived peoples who spoke rather different languages and whose language names *reduplicated* their word for 'no' (Yitha-yitha, Yoda-yoda, etc.). Other language names had different meanings: Paakantji, for example, signified 'Darling River people'.[30]

A language name served as the identity of people of a loosely defined region, and people evidently thought of a language-variety as having a broad relationship to an area of country. However, language identities were not discrete—'Wangaaybuwan' and 'Wayilwan', each associated with a different area, denoted distinct ways of speaking a common tongue called 'Ngiyampaa'. Moreover, the country associated with a language was not very precisely defined. Drawing on informants' reports, Howitt writes of 'mixed' Gamilaraay and Yuwalaraay ('Wollaroi') areas north of the Gwydir River between Walgett and Bourke, and mixed Gamilaraay and Wiradjuri country on the Castlereagh River. Boundaries away from rivers appear to have been indeterminate.

Map 5.4 Yuwaaliyaay people and their neighbours: Approximate location of language identities

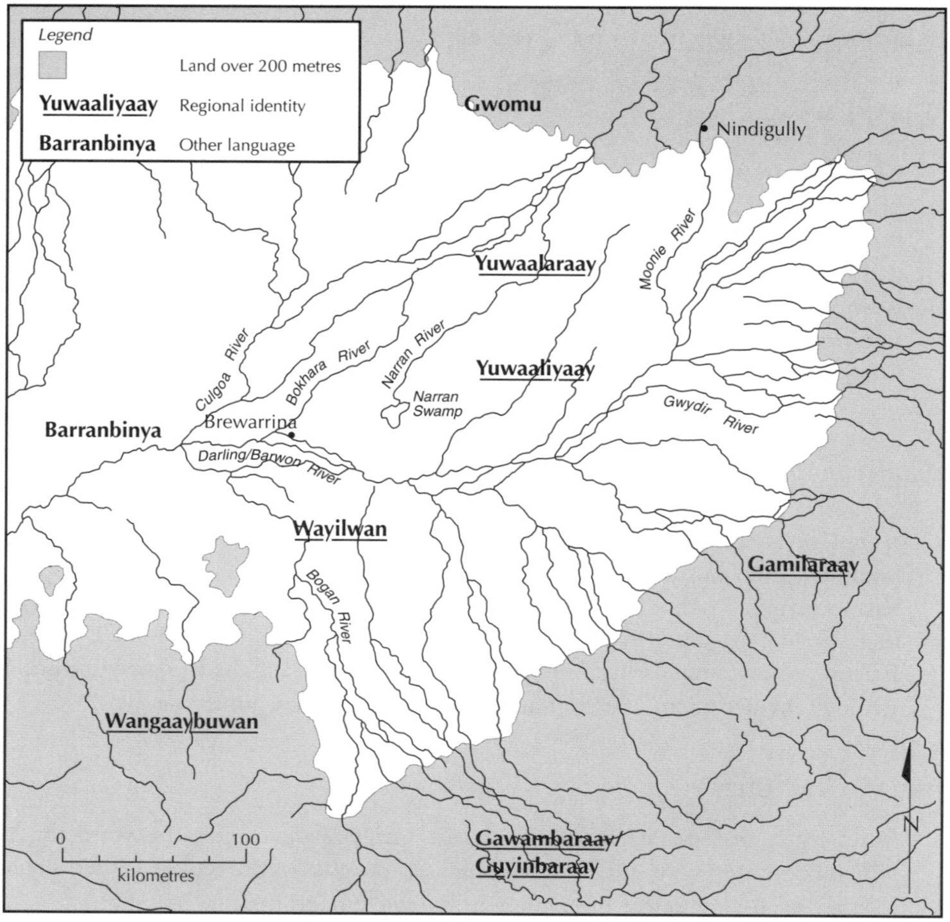

Sources: Austin (1993), Donaldson (1980), Ridley (1875), Howitt (1904), Tindale (1974), and Williams (1976)

Some marriages took place between people of different language-varieties; presumably their offspring were of mixed language identity. In any case, camps might contain people who spoke different languages as their first language. People probably did not inherit their relation to locality, but belonged to their place of birth.[31]

The Yuwaalaraay dialect seems to have been spoken by people living to the north or northeast of the Yuwaaliyaay people. The Yuwaaliyaay and Yuwaalaraay languages had 80% of their vocabularies in common; indeed, linguists regard these languages, together with Gamilaraay, as dialects of a single language. Neighbouring languages had a more distant relationship with Yuwaaliyaay (Wangaaybuwan, for example, had 36% of its vocabulary in common with the Yuwaaliyaay vocabulary).[32]

According to recent maps, Yuwaaliyaay country covered about 15 000 square kilometres, Gamilaraay country about 50,000 square kilometres, and Wiradjuri country some 90,000 square kilometres. Those living in drier country away from the major rivers had the bigger areas.

Locality

Later chapters (7 and 9) will outline the totemic and other associations of Yuwaaliyaay places. Suffice it to say here that people named discrete countries, often after a dominant plant species of the area, and interpreted many local sites (or parts of them) as the traces of the activities of the ancestral being called Byamee and his family. Ancestral and totemic associations, few of which had any connection with the matri-group totems, differentiated localities:[33]
- fish-traps at Brewarrina—made by Byamee's sons
- Narran Swamp—imprints of Byamee's hand and foot
- Narran Swamp—Crocodile, Byamee's wives
- rocks—impressions of Byamee's hair where he rested
- springs—Eaglehawk's victims
- springs—Yanta spirits
- Mildool—Byamee's dingo
- rock outcrop—cannibal woman and her dogs.

People belonged primarily to the countries of their birth. Each language identity included about half-a-dozen such countries.

Matrifilial moieties

Yuwaaliyaay people and their neighbours divided people into two kinds: 'light-blooded' people (*gwaigulleeah*) and 'dark-blooded' people (*gwaimudthen*), associated with the west wind and the 'spring wind' respectively. Parker referred to these paired identities as 'phratries'. In Yuwaaliyaay doctrine, light-blooded people originated from a red people who came from the west, while dark-blooded people came from the east. Again, a person took his or her mother's moiety identity. Strict exogamy applied, so that one's spouse had to be of the opposite moiety. People regarded a sexual and domestic relationship between two people of the same moiety as a grave offence. Other people of the broad region, such as Wangaaybuwan, combined these 'blood' moieties with named matri-moieties, in some cases sub-divided by the blood-moieties.[34]

Some matri-group subtotems were divided on the basis of moiety, so that there were 'light-blooded' and 'dark-blooded' people of the same matri-group. Wangaaybuwan people also divided matri-groups in this way, whereases Wiradjuri people assigned each 'clan' to one or other of the moieties. Matri-moieties and matri-groups cut right across language and local identity, linking people across broad regions. Sections had a similar effect.

Matri-groups

Unlike Kŭnai people, Yuwaaliyaay people and their neighbours practised what appears at first sight to have been a rather complicated system of matrifilial totemism, which they called '*dhé*' or '*mah*'. Wangaaybuwan people referred to the totemic species as 'meat' (*thingaa*)—one should not marry one's own 'meat'.[35]

Yuwaaliyaay people and their neighbours divided themselves into about 20 matri-filial totemic groups (matri-groups), each of which took the name of a particular species and was exogamous—that is, a person had to marry someone of a matri-group other than their own. A matri-group can most readily be understood as a cluster of lineages (relatives traced from a common ancestor) sharing the same name (an animal or bird), passed down through women. Not all people of the same matri-group identity could trace genealogical relationships to one another, but they did think of them-selves as like close 'brothers' and 'sisters' in that they could not marry one another. People with the same matri-group identity were not confined to a single residence group or language—they lived in many residence groups, across quite a wide region. Furthermore, matri-groups engaged in reciprocal marriage exchanges (see Chapter 6).

Jeremy Beckett believes that, though dispersed, two or three matri-groups had an association with each locality. Those most strongly represented in the Narran and Bangate districts where Katie Parker lived included Emu, Kangaroo, Goanna, and Bandicoot. These were major totems to which other species, as well as the winds, belonged as subtotem (or 'multiplex totems' in Parker's terminology). For example, the subtotems of Emu and Kangaroo included the following:

Emu	**Kangaroo**
Codfish	Topknot Pigeon
Silver Bream	Green Parrot
Crayfish	Ant-bed
Water Emu Spirit	Sandalwood
Magpie	Northeast Wind
Acacia	
Ironbark	
Northwest Wind	

Stars and other celestial phenomena were also subtotems of the matri-groups. For example, the Coalsack, known as Featherless Emu, belonged to the major totem Rat, and the Southern Cross, known as Eaglehawk, belonged to Emu.

These assignations had distinct patterns; Parker writes that all clouds, lightning, thunder, and rain 'not blown up by the wind of another totem' belonged to *Bohrah* (Kangaroo). Some matri-groups had the same winds, and so counted as relatives; for example, Kangaroo, Emu and Goanna all had Northeast Wind and so did not marry each other. Some totems had a protective value: a Paddymelon person supposedly never drowned. Totems were also important in the organisation of the Bora initiation rite. A person's subtotem had significance in other ways—for example, as familiars invoked in healing.

Sections

As outlined in the introduction to the chapter, a section system has four names, or four pairs of names distinguished by gender. The sections that existed in the

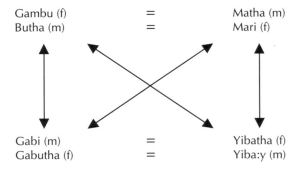

Figure 5.5   Section names in the Darling/Barwon region

Darling/Barwon region are shown in Figure 5.5.[36] Thus, a *gambu* woman was ideally supposed to marry a *matha* man, a *gabi* man should marry a *yibatha* woman, and so on.

To the extent that people married according to section rules, a person would find, at least among close relatives, certain kinds of kin in each section. Sections related as mother to child are diagonally opposite one another in Figure 5.6. See pages 179–80 for a key to the abbreviations (MMB, FZC, etc.) used in Figure 5.6. The figure shows that one's potential spouses include first and second cross cousins and people in one's grandparents' and grandchildren's generations. Ego is Gambu or Butha in Figure 5.6, but individuals of different sections would find their relatives distributed in different ways; this figure represents one of four ideal possibilities.

Ego Siblings (B, Z) Parallel cousins (MZC, FBC) MM, MMB FF, FFZ, FFB woman's DC, ZDC Man's son's children	First cross cousins (MBC, FZC) Second cross cousins (MMBDC, etc.) FM, FMZ MF, MFB Man's DC Woman's SC
Father Father's brother Father's sister Man's children Brother's children FFF, FFB, FFZ	Mother Mother's brother Mother's sister Woman's children Sister's children MMM, MMZ, MMB

Figure 5.6   Varieties of kin found in each section

Ideally, each totemic matri-group belonged to one of the section matri-couples (two sections related as 'mother' to 'child'); for example:

Gambu/butha–yiba:y/yibatha
Emu
Kangaroo

Bilby
Black Snake
Carpet Snake

Mari/matha–gabi/gabutha
Yellow-brown Goanna
Bandicoot
Possum
Paddymelon

These couples are in effect matri-moieties. (Other people of the region had named matri-moieties as well as the 'blood' moieties.) If people married according to the ideals of the section system, each nuclear family would have contained people of at least three sections (unless people of the same section-identity married, in which case it was two).

There is reason to believe that the system of four sections had been superimposed on the system of matri-groups and moieties, which took priority in the arrangement of marriages. Fison and Howitt reported 'anomalous' marriages among some Gamilaraay speakers; some marriages occurred between people who were members of different matri-groups but the same section, so called 'half-sister marriages'. Wangaaybuwan reconciled marriages regulated by exogamous matri-groups and blood-moieties with the section system by allowing alternative marriages between sections and by applying special kin terms to distinguish kin marriageable according to section but not according to kin relations.[37] All this suggests that the section system did not fit the pattern of marriage according to kin relations and totemic exogamy very well, and people disregarded relations between sections in arranging marriages, except if they wanted to justify a marriage regarded as wrong in other ways. Most Pakaantji people to the southwest had no sections, although some had adopted them from Ngiyampaa neighbours.

People used section identities as personal names and, along with matri-groups, in organising the Bora initiation ceremony. Because people of a region far larger than the Yuwaaliyaay region had section identities and related matri-groups, anyone could slot into a role in the ceremony, or even negotiate for a spouse. People could extend the range of 'kin' relations by computing a kin relationship from their section identities as well as totemic connections.

Personal totems

Wirreenun (magicians) and some lay people possessed *yunbeai* (personal totems), such as a snake or lizard. A wirreenun supposedly had the power to assume a *yunbeai*'s shape, and to send it into a patient. *Yunbeai* seem not to have been acquired through descent or indirect descent, but one person could bequeath their *yunbeai* to another before they died. An injury to the *yunbeai* affected the possessor, and, unlike the matrifilial totem, a person was not supposed to eat their *yunbeai* animal.[38]

Yuwaaliyaay people and their neighbours, then, possessed matri-moiety, matri-group, section, and personal totemic identities. Wiil and Minong people, considered next, combined semi-moieties and matri-moieties with patrifilial connections to country.

Wiil and Mi<u>n</u>ong people

Regional and language identities

People of the southwest identified themselves and others in a variety of ways: as coastal people (*waddarn-di*) as opposed to inland people, or according to the character of their country—for example, as riverine people (*bilgur*), estuarine people (*darbalung*), or people of the rocky hills (*buyung-gur*).

The early sources tend to be consistent regarding the broad, regional identities in the southern part of the southwest. Names such as Mi<u>n</u>ong, Mirram, Wiil, and Kaninyang turn up in several sources (with various spellings), and there is a fair amount of agreement about their general location relative to one another. However, at least some of these identities were relative to the speaker's location, such as Wil/Wiil,

Map 5.5   Regional identities in the southwest from a Mi<u>n</u>ong perspective

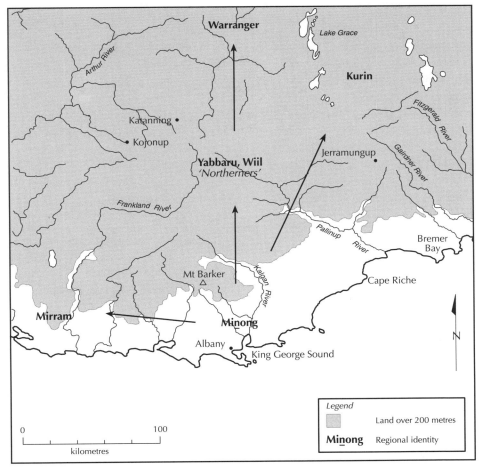

Sources: Barker (1992), Bates (1985), Browne (1856), Clark (1842), Le Souëf (1993), Nind (1831), Graham (in Curr 1886), and Spencer, Hossell and Knight (in Curr 1886)

Map 5.6   Regional identities in the southwest from a Kikkar perspective

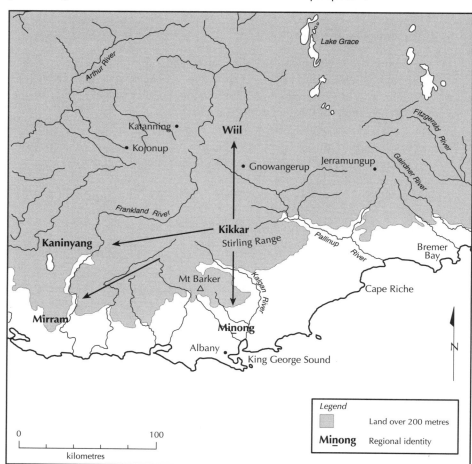

Sources: Barker (1992), Browne (1856), Clark (1842), Le Souëf (1993), Nind (1831), Graham (in Curr 1886),
and Spencer, Hossell and Knight (in Curr 1886)

meaning 'people to the north (of us)'. This usage contrasts with names such as Kurin
Wonga, which means 'those whose word for "east" is "*kurin*"'. The relative nature
of the former identities makes it difficult to map their location in an objective
way—the best one can do is to map relative perspectives (see Maps 5.5 and 5.6).
Nevertheless, there is general agreement in the sources that the Minong were people of the region between the coast and the ranges, and from Albany east to perhaps
Bremer Bay. Ethel Hassell did name the people of the uplands north of the ranges
'Wiil', suggesting that local people used that term to refer to themselves, or at least
acknowledged it.[39]

These were not the names of clearly defined territorial groups or 'tribes', but
referred, I think, more loosely to people belonging to a certain general region—
hence the relativity of some of the names. Minong people were people of the coastal

region south of the ranges, Kikkar belonged to the Stirling Range, Wiil were uplanders, and so on. They were not endogamous groups, especially given the preference for marriage to a distant cousin (see Chapter 6); consequently, many people probably had parents of different regional identities and their own regional identities would have been ambiguous (as with Kŭnai regional identities and Western Desert language identities).

People of the southwest spoke a cluster of related language-varieties, collectively referred to by linguists as Nyungar. They were part of the broader Southwestern group of Pama-Nyungan languages, which included the Western Desert language. Douglas names the southern dialects by the regional names mentioned above: Kaninyang in the southwest and Minong in the Albany–Bremer Bay region and its hinterland. He adds Kwetjman, meaning 'sharp talk', for the easterly region between Bremer Bay and Esperance and its hinterland. But the early sources do not support the view that Minong and complementary identities, such as Mirram and Kaninyang, were the names of languages, though they may have been. In my opinion the more inclusive identities in this region bore more resemblance to Kŭnai regional identities than to language identities, and had a similar scope.[40]

The area associated with the Minong people covered 4500 square kilometres, with perhaps 200–300 people living in the area. Wiil people would have occupied a more extensive, more thinly populated area.

Totemic identities: Patri-groups

According to Bates, the general term for totem in the southwest was *borungur*, meaning 'elder brother', an idiom similar to that used by Kŭnai people, but Hassell reports the word *coburne* (*kobong*) for Wiil totems. Many of the subjects of Wiil and Minong stories, especially the animals, birds, and celestial phenomena, were associated with totems, especially localised ones. This region enjoyed a rich array of totemic identities of various sorts and of different kinds of significance. They included moieties, semi-moieties, totems acquired by gift or exchange, and the traces of local totemic ancestors.[41] People of the southwest appear to have organised themselves into patri-filial groups, each associated with one or more local totems.[42]

But we do not know in any detail how a group's country was defined in relation to ancestral traces—whether one group's country incorporated places associated with one totemic place, a few, or many different ones. Recorded myths associate places in the King George Sound–Jerramungup region with totemic beings as follows:

Jerramungup

Yonger-pertin-girup rock	Kangaroo

King George Sound

Green Island	Woman
Oyster Harbour	Dingo
Yangenmere mountain	Avenging son

Cape Riche

| Reef at Cape Riche | Black Snake |
| Rocks on a hillside | Mopoke |

Cooma Nintup hill

| 'Possum's tail' hill | Emu and Possum |

Balbarup, near Albany

| White rocks | Men regurgitated by dingoes |
| Springs dug by dingoes | Dingoes |

Men and women of the inter-marrying Ballaruk and Tondarup semi-moieties took names related to Dingo.

Moieties

People of many regions in the southwest divided themselves into exogamous moieties called *manitchmat* (White Cockatoo people) and *wordungmat* (Crow people); or *nanitch* and *wording* among Wiil people at Jerramungup.[43] In some regions of the southwest the moieties were matrifilial, in others patrifilial, as among Sandbeach people. Bates asserts that they were patrifilial all across the southern part of the area, but the evidence is strong that Minong people of King George Sound had matri-moieties. (Hassell does not say if Wiil moieties were patrifilial or matrifilial.) Manitchmat people were supposedly shorter and more thickset than Wordungmat people, and had darker skins, while the Wordungmat were hairier. No rule forbade the eating of the moiety totems, although 'crow' (Australian raven) was not a preferred food.

Nind describes what seem to have been named matri-moieties at King George Sound. Everyone was divided into two 'classes': *Erniung* and *Tem* (or *Taaman*). A person took his or her mother's class, and the classes were exogamous—a person of one class married a person of the other; people who breached this rule were severely punished. It is possible, however, that Erniung and Tem were not proper names of moieties but terms for, respectively, 'my own family' and 'father's father'.[44]

Except in so far as they belonged to matri-moieties, matrifilial totems in this region do not seem to have signified exogamous categories, as they did among Yuwaaliyaay people. Hassell tells us that each person had one or more totems. He or she was not allowed to eat or destroy them, and they were ranked according to the following order (from most to least important): flying things (e.g. mopoke, 'blue crane', duck), running and jumping things (e.g. dingo), flying insects, creeping insects (e.g. ant), lizards and monitors (goanna), snakes, trees (e.g. native cherry, or '*chuck*'), and grasses.[45]

Semi-moieties

Some areas of the southwest had a system of four categories that Bates calls 'classes'; these were semi-moieties. Unlike with sections, a person acquired the semi-moiety identity of one of their parents, rather than acquiring an identity by indirect descent. Each semi-moiety was associated with a totem:

- Nagarnook—Emu
- Tondarup—Rain
- Didarruk—Rain
- Ballaruk—Manna.

Tondarup and Didarruk appear to have shared Rain as a totem, although they may have been associated with different kinds of rain. Again, in some areas these semi-moieties were matrifilial, in others patrifilial. Where semi-moieties were matrifilial (that is, a person was of the same semi-moiety as his or her mother), children were affiliated with the father's totem 'half and half,' as Bates's informants expressed it, and did not transmit it to their children.[46]

At King George Sound the semi-moieties appear to have been patrifilial, a situation not envisaged for that region by Bates. According to Nind, a son belonged to his mother's moiety but his father's semi-moiety (*Torndirrup* or *Moncalon*). Putting the accounts of Nind and Grey together, the semi-moieties at King George Sound seem to have been as follows:

Toondarup	Mongalon
Nyotungur	Noyan-nook

They may have been localised, for Mongalon people were more prevalent to the east of King George Sound, and Toondarup people to the west. But a country and its holders would have shared a semi-moiety identity with many other groups and countries in the region (see Chapter 9). Half-siblings and more distant 'siblings' could be of different semi-moieties, as Nind noted.

Personal totems transferred by bestowal, adoption, or gift

A senior relative, such as a grandparent, father, or parent's sibling, could bestow a personal totem on a child following some incident at his or her birth. Bates gives the sea, land, moon, stars, wind, and clouds as examples of personal totems, and a Minong woman of Bremer Bay had daylight as her totem. There was no ban on a person with a certain personal totem marrying someone with the same species or thing as their semi-moiety totem.[47]

Totems conferred by gift (*babbin*) had a strong association with marriage in the southwest. A baby born while his or her parents were visiting the country of distant relatives would sometimes be given the totem of one of those relatives, such as a 'mother's brother', if it was different to the child's own totem. A young man could stay with that relative during the initiation sojourn, and marry a woman of that country. The totemic connection allowed him to hunt there, and to eat animals of that totem without the owner's permission (which implies that restrictions did apply to others).

Bates reports that a person could bestow his or her patri-totem on a sister's son or other relative for life. Alternatively, following a bestowal or marriage, brothers-in-law sometimes exchanged their 'hereditary' totems (local totems presumably) and became *babbingur* ('friends'). The recipient did not pass on the totem acquired in this way to his children.

Wiil and Minong people combined regional identities, moieties, semi-moieties, patri-groups, and bestowed totems. Sandbeach people, considered next, combined patri-moiety and patri-group totems with language identities.

Sandbeach people

Sandbeach people lived in a coastal region on the other side of the continent with even richer resources and very high rainfall. They had surprisingly similar institutions to those of Wiil and Minong people, but language for them had greater salience as an identity.

Language identity

The languages of Sandbeach people and their inland neighbours are suffixing languages of the northeastern Pama subgroup of the Pama-Maric group, which many linguists place at one end of the widespread Pama-Nyungan family of languages. (Wiil and Minong were at the other end.) Umpila and Kuuku Ya'u shared 87% of their vocabularies, while Kaanchu—the language of upland ('on-top') people—was quite close to Umpila; they were related like dialects rather than distinct languages.[48]

Each language-variety had an association with a broad region, its 'country' or 'home', including the country of several patri-groups (see Map 5.7). A person of one of those patri-groups would identify himself or herself as an Umpila person (or whatever the language-variety of the group and country was) regardless of what language-variety they habitually spoke. The language identities belonged to the patri-groups and country, gained through the father. Some recorded names were those used by outsiders rather than by speakers of the language in question.

To the south, near Princess Charlotte Bay, lay country associated with the Lamalama, Umpithamu, Umbuygamu (or Morra-balama), and coastal Ayapathu languages. There, differences in ways of speaking all but coincided with differences in patri-group identity and country. Each individual in Cape York Peninsula could speak several language-varieties; more than one language would often be represented in a family camp, and several in the wider residence group.[49]

People grouped and named the northern Sandbeach language-varieties in several cross-cutting ways: directionally ('northside', 'middle', and 'southside'; 'leeward' and 'windward') and by reference to the verbs 'look' (e.g. Uutalnganu) and 'eat' (Map 5.7). At the time of Thompson's research, the 'windward people'—Uutaalnganu, Umpila, and Kuuku Yani—regarded themselves as a grouping separate from Kuuku Ya'u, who looked northward to Wuthathi for ceremony and marriage. The mythology related to initiation reflected this orientation. More recently, Kuuku Ya'u people saw themselves as divided into two sub-groups, Kungkay and Kanthanampu, which means nypa palm (*Nypa fruticans*). Among the coastal languages, Kuuku Ya'u,

Map 5.7 Sandbeach and neighbouring language identities

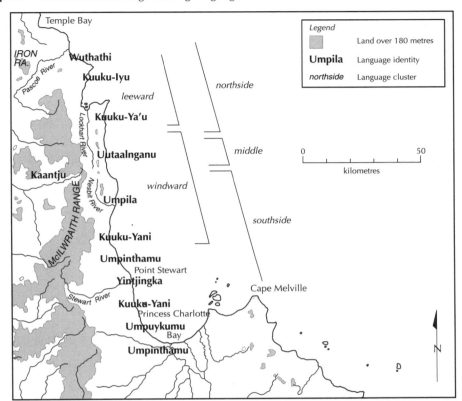

Sources: Thompson (1988)

Uutalnganu, and Umpila were associated with the largest areas, averaging about 3000 square kilometres of land each.[50]

We shall see that these language identities and other identities coexisted with patri-moieties and totemic patri-groups. By contrast with Kŭnai regional identities and Yuwaaliyaay and Pitjantjatjara language identities, Sandbeach languages related to quite clear-cut tracts of country—those of their constituent patri-groups.

Locality

The category 'Sandbeach people' (*pama malngkana* in Umpila, *ama-yaandhimunu* in Uuku-Umpithamu) contrasted with 'On-top people' or 'Inside people' (*pama kanichi*), who occupied the inland region from the coastal ranges westward.[51] Sandbeach people married On-top people of the immediate hinterland, traded with them, and participated in ceremonies that linked some of the neighbouring inland and coastal groups. However, they regarded coastal peoples from further south, and especially remote inland peoples, as *wapa* (potentially dangerous)—as only partly human cannibals who periodically raided the coast.

Patri-groups

In this region, totemic patri-groups owned countries that bore the traces of totemic ancestors. People gave countries and groups the names of animals, plants, and other entities (such as the moon) associated with ancestors, or a deceased man's name, or a topynym (such as *maangkal*, meaning 'river mouth'). The addition of the suffix *–tham-panyu* indicated the group's country. Totemic affiliations of patri-groups strongly differentiated them and appear to have created few links. Each group seems to have had totems linked to half-a-dozen 'story places' (including 'increase' sites) as well subsidiary totems. For example, Thomson lists the following totems of an Umpila patri-group: a flower species, Leichardt Tree, a beetle, Carpet Snake, a tree species, Green Python (shared with a Night Island group), and Flat Ant-bed.[52]

Patri-moieties

Countries, patri-groups, associated ancestors, and the related species at named sites belonged to one or other of the patrifilial moieties, *kaapay* and *kuyan*. Myths about conflicts between dugong and wallaby, emu and cassowary, represent relations between the moieties. According to Sandbeach doctrine, the details of a person's physiology and a country's vegetation and topography reflected their moiety association. Myths of the origin of moieties recounted battles of wits in which the cassowary stole the horny head-covering from the emu and the wallaby tricked the dugong into swapping tails and habitats.[53]

Personal totems: Relations with one's mother's country

Chapters 7 and 9 will describe Sandbeach doctrines that link an individual to his or her mother's country through the *nguunthal* ('spirit' or 'vital force') residing in an infant's fontanelle. When the fontanelle closed the spirit left the person and travelled to the mother's country, where it remained, as did the *mitpi* spirit at the person's death. An individual thus had strong links to their mother's as well as their father's country.[54]

Ngarinyin people and their neighbours

The Ngarinyin people and their neighbours also combined patri-moieties, patri-groups and language identities, but ancestral doctrines created extensive links among the patri-groups.

Language identity

The languages of the northwest Kimberley region are non-Pama-Nyungan prefixing languages, in contrast with the languages spoken by people from all the other regions studied, which are suffixing languages classified by many linguists as part of the large Pama-Nyungan family of languages. The languages of the Worrorran family bear quite a close relationship to each other. Ngarinyin was not a uniform language, and people had names for several local dialects. Worrorra, Ngarinyin, and Wunambal were definitely markers of identity as well as names of languages, but some of the names for language-varieties in the northern subgroup (such as Miwa, Kwini, and Yiiji) were not accepted by everyone, suggesting a less determinate relation of language to identity in the north. These language-varieties constituted a single language in linguistic terms (see Map 5.8).[55]

Each of these names—Ngarinyin, Worrorra, and Wunambal—refers to a language, a distinct area of land, more or less clearly bounded, and a set of people; in this way each language has an intrinsic link to a region, like Sandbeach languages. Ngarinyin mythology tells how Andarri (Possum) began to speak the language at a place called Guleman (Beverley Springs), and took it to other places from there, so establishing Ngarinyin country. A person became Ngarinyin (or Worrorra, etc.) through their father or mother; consequently, some people had a dual identity because their parents were of different language affiliations. As with Sandbeach languages, the language a person usually spoke could differ from their language identity. Moreover, people were multilingual: for example, Love thought that all Worrorra people could

Map 5.8   Western Kimberley languages of the Worrorran family

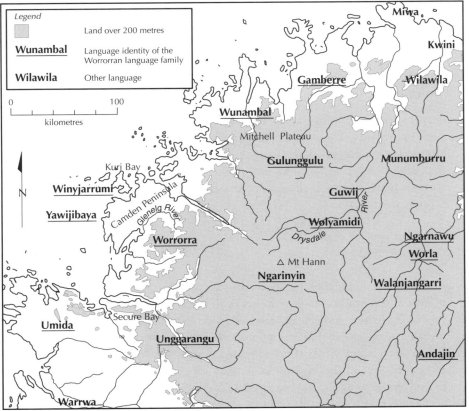

Source: Capell and Coates (1984) and McGregor (1988a)

speak Ngarinyin as well.[56] The territory associated with each language was divided into named 'countries' (*dambun*), each held by people of a patri-group or 'clan'. Topographical categories also had currency: the Ngarinyin regarded themselves as people of 'stony' country. On average, a language corresponded to an area of about 5800 square kilometres.

Patri-groups

Like Sandbeach patri-groups, totemic affiliations distinguished one patri-group from another. The principal totems of several patri-groups are shown in Table 5.1.

Table 5.1   Some Ngarinyin patri-groups and totems

Patri-group	Totem	Moiety
Agulangongo	Rock Devil	Wodoy
Balalangarri	Seven Sisters	Jun.gun
Brrejirad	Pink Hibiscus	Wodoy
Galiyamba	White Gum	Jun.gun
Gubungarri	Brains of Snake	Wodoy
Jibilingarri	Whistling Duck	Jun.gun
Wayangarri	Kangaroo Skin	Wodoy

Only 'top' and 'bottom' groups with the same *dambun* name possessed the same principle totem.[57]

Patri-moieties

Transcending and cutting across language identities, the two patri-moieties or 'skins' (*waya*) provided the 'most all-embracing form of social classification' among western Kimberley peoples, as Alan Rumsey put it. In principle everything in the world, including people, belonged to one of the two categories. Several different pairs of names, for the most part those of natural species, referred to the moieties. The commonest were these:

wodoy (spotted nightjar)	—	*jun.gun* (owlet nightjar)
walamba (red kangaroo)	—	*yarra* (hill kangaroo)

Children belonged to the opposite moiety to their mother and normally the same moiety as their father, and the moieties were exogamous. People thought of Wodoy people and their moiety ancestor as more intelligent, better looking, and more morally upright than Jun.gun people. And, similar to the contrast between Kŭnai gender totems, the Wodoy bird pertained to open places, while the Jun.gun bird was more secretive, inhabiting hollows in trees and rocks. Wodoy had an association with the colour red, and Jun.gun with white.

Each patri-group and its country (*dambun*) belonged to one of the patri-moieties as well, but patri-group countries of the same moiety tended to be contiguous, so that the country of each moiety formed great swathes (*mamalarr*) across the land and waters. Indeed, patri-groups formed same-moiety alliances, and disputes tended to be argued along moiety lines.[58]

Personal totems

Each individual had a link called *maanggarra* to his or her mother's patri-group, similar to that of the Sandbeach people. According to Petri, the totems of a person's mother's patri-group were his 'dream totems'—special friends and helpers who represented him to others in dreams. In some cases, spirit conception linked a person with a patri-group and country different from his or her own but of the same patri-moiety. A namesake relationship linked him or her to a 'father's father' or 'father's father's sister' of another patri-group.[59]

Yolngu people

The basic identities of the Yolngu region bore some similarities to those of the Sandbeach and Ngarinyin regions, but Yolngu people merged language identities with patri-group identities.

Language identity

The Yolngu area constitutes a fairly discrete cultural bloc, as Warner recognised, within which people spoke (and speak) related Yolngu dialects of the Pama-Nyungan language family, while neighbouring peoples to the west and south all spoke prefixing non-Pama-Nyungan languages. To the north and east lay the ocean. Linguistic diffusion has brought languages on the outer edges of the Yolngu region closer to neighbouring languages.

Like Howitt and Tindale, Warner sought names for the 'tribes' of the region, and thought that he found eight. But they include names for language-varieties, a regional name, and an outsider's name for a neighbouring group. All eight, he thought, were of the 'Murngin type' of social organisation. Other proposals for general names include 'Wulamba' and 'Miwuyt'. *Yolngu*, which means 'person' and 'man' in the local languages, is now generally accepted as a name for the Aboriginal people of the region, although this usage is of recent coinage. Not all speakers of what linguists call Yolngu languages agree that they are 'Yolngu'—some Djinang people, for example, assert that they are not (Djinang is a dialect group).[60]

Language-variety provided a much-used mode of shared identity, but Yolngu people identified ways of speaking primarily by patri-group names, each patri-group notionally having its own 'tongue' (*matha*), as well as countries and sacra. But Yolngu people grouped these 'tongues' together and named them according to the demonstrative pronoun 'this/here' (*dhuwal, dhuwala, djangu, dhangu*, etc.) plus the suffix 'having' (hence *dhuwalmirr, djangu'mi*, etc.). These nine language-varieties (or 'dialect groups', as Bernard Schebeck calls them) do not map onto the land and groups in the same way as with other regions in this study, for three (*dhuwal*, *dhuwala*, and *dhangu*) were moiety-specific and their distribution overlapped with that of dialects of the opposite moiety (see Map 5.9). Speakers of Djinang languages in the west of the region did identify themselves and their country as Djinang, like their westerly neighbours. Linguists have tentatively grouped these language-varieties into sub-groups on the basis of grammatical morphemes. The average area associated with each 'dialect group' was about 4000 square kilometres.[61]

People of each patri-group thought of their own *matha*, to which one of the group's names referred, as unique, and it was represented in some cases by a bird.[62]

Map 5.9   Yolngu dialect groups (underlined) and their neighbours

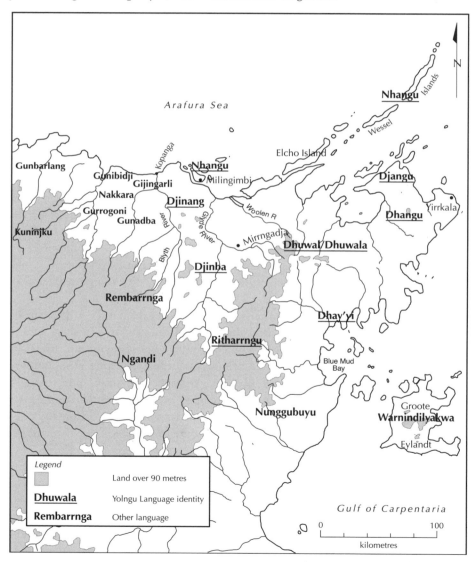

Sources: Hiatt (1965) and F. Morphy (1983)

Patri-group tongues of the same 'dialect group' differed primarily in details of vocabulary, and people often extended the name of their own *matha* to identify others of the same dialect group. Djambarrpuyngu people, for example, would say that Djapu people, who also spoke a *dhuwalmirr* language, spoke the Djambarrpuyngu tongue. Djapu people no doubt saw things differently.

Since dialect groups intermarried, a community was likely to include people who spoke different dialects, and it was normal for a Yolngu person to be multilingual. Some Yolngu people married speakers of suffixing languages, such as Gidjingarli (in the west) and Nunggubuyu (in the southeast).

Locality

People also identified themselves as individuals and groups on the basis of broad locality, the character of their country, proximity to the sea (saltwater versus inland people), and position on a river ('top' versus 'bottom'); there were also contrasts between mainlanders and islanders and between peninsular and river people. Other names applied to broad regions.[63]

Patri-groups

In contrast with those of the Sandbeach people, Yolngu patri-groups were linked by multiple, cross-cutting totemic affiliations. Sites on each patri-group's country belonged to several *wangarr* (totemic ancestors) and other beings, and each *wangarr* linked that country to a somewhat distinct cluster of countries belonging to other patri-groups of the same moiety. The links took the form of ancestral journeys, or simply relations of similarity between ancestral identities.[64]

Totemic associations formed two broad classes: those to do with secret *rangga* (sacred objects and revelatory ceremonies, including Nga:rra, Djungguwan, Ngulmarrk, and Gunapipi) and those to do with *garma* (public) ceremonies. The major totemic ancestors tended to be associated with resource-rich areas, such as swamps and estuaries. Each major *wangarr* (ancestor) associated with men's secret *rangga* linked several groups through its creative journey, and particular ancestral attributes distinguished one group from another. For example, Warner's list of 'clan' attributes shows that several Dhuwa moiety groups possessed sacred objects associated with a mature woman (*gongman*) and a young girl (*wirrkul*), but they represented different aspects (especially body parts). Patri-groups with Shark as ancestor possessed distinct parts of the ancestor's body, left in their country. Furthermore, the particular mix of totems differentiated even those groups that shared many; for example, Crab, Shark, and Sun differentiated three patri-groups in Warner's list possessing totems to do with women.

Patri-group identity did not come solely through patrifiliation. A person could be 'partially' of the patri-group of their genitor, if this was a different person from their mother's husband. If a widow remarried, her young children by her previous husband would take the patri-group identity of the new husband, who 'grew them up', in addition to their natal identity.

Patri-moieties

As with Sandbeach and Ngarinyin people, Yolngu people divided everything—people and places, species of plant and animal, other phenomena such as the sun and moon, ancestors and other spirit beings—into two kinds, Dhuwa and Yirritja. As a default (in the rare case of a same-moiety union), a person took the moiety identity opposite to that of their mother, normally their father's. And the moieties were exogamous. Patri-groups and their countries, totemic ancestors, myths, and ceremonies were thus divided between the moieties. Land and waters formed a rough mosaic of Dhuwa and Yirritja areas; in some places countries of opposite moieties alternated, while in other places countries of the same moiety were contiguous. Patri-groups of opposite moieties had separate ancestors and distinct mythologies (see Chapter 7). As among the Ngarinyin and their neighbours, colour symbolism, manifested in painted designs, was used to distinguish the moieties: Dhuwa had an association with red ochre, the rather purple haematite, with its distinctive sheen, and the orange breast-feathers of the red-collared lorikeet; Yirritja was associated with white clay, yellow ochre, and grey-white possum fur.[65]

Subsections

The spread of a subsection naming system into northeast Arnhem Land continued through the first half of the twentieth century; perhaps it accompanied the Gunapipi ceremony and other desert-style ceremonies as they moved across the region, for men applied body decorations in the ceremonies according to subsection affiliation as well as patri-group. The Yolngu subsections were as shown in figure 5.7.

Because of the incompatibility between subsections and the Yolngu system of kin classification, Yolngu had modified the subsection system by allowing alternative marriages in order to maximise the fit with kinship, in effect converting it into a four-section system. But the subsections do fit the patri-moieties. People used the subsection names as modes of address (together with kin terms and nicknames), in the organisation of certain ceremonies, and to form relationships with strangers.

Subsection names had male and female variants, and had conventional associations, enacted in Arnhem Land regional ceremonies, with certain species:[66]

Yirritja moiety

Ngarritj (m)/Ngarritjan (f)	antilopine wallaroo (*garrtjambal*), raw
Gadjak/Gutjan	chickenhawk, skink (*gudutjurrk*)
Bangadi/Bangaditjan	emu (*wurrpan*)
Bulany/Bulanydjan	antilopine wallaroo (*garrtjambal*), cooked

Dhuwa moiety

Balang/Bilinydjan	white-breasted sea eagle
Wa:mut/Wa:mutjan	black-breasted buzzard, 'black-nosed' kangaroo
Burralang/Galiyan	agile wallaby, rock wallaby
Gamarrang/Gamandjan	wedge-tailed eagle

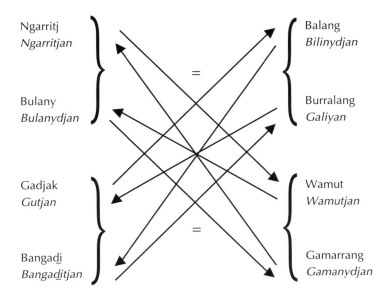

Figure 5.7   Yolngu subsection system (showing alternative marriages)

Personal totems

A Yolngu person certainly had strong rights in and responsibilities for their mother's group, but this did not involve the personal spiritual connection of Sandbeach doctrines. However, spirit conception linked a person to an ancestral place of a country of the same patri-moiety—his or her 'country of the water'—but, as among Ngarinyin people and their neighbours, not necessarily of his or her patri-group.

Comparisons and conclusions

This chapter has found a diverse mix of language, local, and totemic identities and of naming systems in the seven regions. They are summed up in Table 13.5.

The case studies reveal a mix of identities in terms of language-varieties with proper names (Sandbeach), isoglossically named language-varieties (Yuwaaliyaay and their neighbours, Pitjantjatjara and their neighbours, Yolngu), outsider names (Pintubi in the Western Desert), regional names (Kŭnai, Wiil, Minong), and language-varieties named by patri-group identity (Yolngu). The relations between language-variety, people, and country varied from very close ones (Sandbeach, Ngarinyin and their neighbours), to much looser, contextual connections (Pitjantjatjara and their neighbours). A person's public identity could be based on region and locality (Kŭnai, Wiil, and Minong), language-variety (Pitjantjatjara, Yuwaaliyaay, Sandbeach, Ngarinyin, Yolngu), or patri-group identity expressed as a way of speaking (Yolngu). Among Yolngu people the relationship between named 'dialect groups' and country varied.

The estimated areas encompassed by regional and language identities show some consistency in relation to population density, depending on the kind of environment and population. Among people of well-watered environments the areas associated with such identities ranged from 3000 to 6000 square kilometres of land. Yuwaaliyaay people, in a semi-arid zone but adjacent to the Darling/Barwon River, were associated with about 15,000 square kilometres, while their neighbours away from major rivers had much larger tracts. Western Desert languages were associated with larger areas—of the order of 50 000 to 60 000 square kilometres.

Patterns of totemic identity and differentiation also varied greatly. Peoples in regions of relatively high rainfall and rich resources tended to be organised by patri-group, patri-moiety, or semi-moiety, giving rise to greater differentiation between localities and groups (Sandbeach, Wiil/Minong, Ngarinyin, Yolngu). People of more arid regions organised themselves by matri-moiety, matri-group, and generation moiety, cutting across relations to localities (Yuwaaliyaay, Pitjantjatjara). This separation has partly to do with the selection of case studies—had other peoples of the arid and semi-arid zones been included (such as Arrernte people, from the better-watered hills of the arid zone, or Warlpiri people, from semi-arid country) we would have found patri-groups and patri-moieties associated with these regions as well, although more recent research emphasises the spread of links to country, linking them to the Western Desert.[67]

Where people used section and subsection naming systems (Yuwaaliyaay and their neighbours, Yolngu), they had not been fully reconciled with other forms of organisation. The semi-moiety system of Minong people appears to have been linked to the patri-group relations to country.

Identities and economy

What were these identities about? Language and regional identities defined who a person or group essentially was, in contrast with others. But identity depended on context—in some contexts what counted was one's language and country, in other contexts one's broader region, and so on. Often a person could choose an identity depending on what connections he or she wished to express. And language and regional identities were often partial or mixed, reflecting intermarriage, mobility, and networks of relations. This shifting character of identity reflected and indeed fostered the openness and mobility of residence groups and the web of marriage connections between localities and regions. The most clearly defined identities belonged to the resource-rich zones, such as Sandbeach country, while the most open identities were those of the Western Desert.

What bearing do these modes of identity have on the organisation of the economy? Part III of the book is about the implications of institutions for the economy, but I shall make a few remarks here.

Totemic identities had to do with the control of marriage and the ownership of land and sacra. Naming systems provided personal names and categories for the organisation of regional ceremonies, and they helped people to form relationships with people outside their normal range of kin relations.

We have already seen, in relation to settlement and mobility, that residence groups were important elements in the organisation of economy. The area associated with a regional or language identity would have included people of several residence groups, the number depending on the season. But because of intermarriage and visiting, many residence groups would have included people of more than one language or regional identity. Each camp and residence group would normally have had both moieties (patrifilial or matrifilial) represented, for husband and wife were of different moieties and a child's moiety differed from that of one parent. Except in temporary foraging camps and some bachelors' camps, it would have been unusual for only one of the generation moieties to have been present in a residence group. In the southwest, people of at least two semi-moieties would have been present in a camp or residence group. The section and subsection identities of spouses, parents, and children differed, so that a residence group would have contained a variety of these.

Ethnographers often report people's desire to live on their own patri-group country. But patri-groups tended to be dispersed because people often lived on their mother's country or with a husband's or wife's family on their country, and also because of patterns of movement related to resources and ceremonies. Not being strongly related to places, matri-groups were usually dispersed, except to the extent that mothers lived with children and daughters' children, and mothers' brothers with their sisters' children and sisters' daughters' children. Among Yuwaaliyaay people and their neighbours, it is likely that many people of the same matri-group identity came together for the Bora initiation ceremony, which celebrated their totems.

The next chapter turns to another mode of social identity, kinship, as well as associated marriage practices.

Further Reading

This chapter has touched on a number of issues about the nature of Aboriginal identities. A. P. Elkin's *Australian Aborigines: How to Understand Them* (1938; 1954) describes varieties of Aboriginal totemism. Lévi-Strauss drew on this work to deconstruct the concept in his *Totemism* (*La Totemisme Aujourd'hui*, 1962). The many approaches to Aboriginal totemism include Durkheim's social-psychology theory of the emotional force of Aboriginal totemic rites (in *Elementary Forms of the Religious Life*, 1915) and the psychoanalytical studies of Géza Roheim. Nicolas Peterson's 'Totemism Yesterday' (1972) makes an argument about the ecological functions of attachment to totemic places, while John Morton (1997) seeks, in analysing Arrernte ritual, to revive Émile Durkheim's emphasis on the emotional aspects of totemism.

A key work in the critique of the 'tribe' model is 'People with "politicks": Management of land and personnel on Australia's Cape York Peninsula', by Peter Sutton and Bruce Rigsby. Francesca Merlan and Alan Rumsey have both reviewed the relations of language to identity in Australia (see the endnotes to this chapter), and their jointly authored *Ku Waru* (1991) analyses social groups in a society of Papua New Guinea using the concept of 'identities' in a way that is relevant to Australia.

In 'Metaphor and the metalanguage: Groups in northeast Arnhem Land' (1995), I drew on Roy Wagner's article 'Are there social groups in the New Guinea Highlands?' (1974) to question the applicability of the term 'clan' to Yolngu social identities. This occasioned some debate, summed up in my article 'A bundle of sticks' (2000).

The *Macquarie Atlas of Indigenous Australia* edited by Bill Arthur and Frances Morphy (in press) includes maps of the distribution of naming systems and languages.

Notes

1   See Keesing (1975) on the concepts of *social category* and *social group*.

2   On the concept of *dialectal tribe* see Birdsell (1953) and Tindale (1974: 30–32); and see Peterson (1976b) for an overview.

3   For critiques of the dialectal tribe model see Berndt (1959), Merlan (1981), Rumsey (1993), and Sutton (1978).

4   See Lévi-Strauss (1962).

5   See Maddock (1972) on marriage 'classes'.

6   For discussion of patrilineal and matrilineal 'clans' see R. M. and C. H. Berndt (1981: 41–3) and Elkin (1954).

7   On sections, subsections, moieties, and semi-moieties see R. M. and C. H. Berndt (1981: 46–52), Maddock (1972), and Shapiro (1979). See Beckett (1959) on the uses of section terms.

8   See McConvell (1985) on the spread of subsection systems.

9   Fox (1967: 193) constructs formal models of integrated naming and kinship systems. On modifying subsection systems and kinship systems to fit one another, see Shapiro (1979).

10 On Kŭnai as a 'tribe' see Bulmer (Papers, letter to Howitt, MV B1 F4 sm77, 11 January 1878) and Howitt (1880: 232; 1904: 44, 73; Papers, MV B5 F1 ms672).

11 On Bidawal participation in Kŭnai initiation ceremonies see Howitt (Papers, SLV Box 8 ms1053/3(b): 24). There may have been a difference in meaning between *Krauatŭn.golung*, a proper name, and *krauatŭn kunai*, meaning 'person/people of the east'.

12 On *kŭnai* and *brajerak* see Bulmer (1994: 8; Papers, MV B10 F5 xm923: 73) and Howitt (1880: 214; 1904: 752). On enmities within Gippsland see Howitt (Papers, MV B10 F5 xm931: 9). On Bidawal identity see Howitt (Papers, MV B6 F1 ms672).

13 On Kŭnai dialects see Howitt (Papers, MV B4 F7 ms527; MV B6 F5 ms683; Papers, SLV B8 ms1053/3(b), ms1053/4(a): 48, 59) and Mathews (1907). Hercus (1986) takes Howitt's 'clan' identities as the names of dialects, but this does not seem to have ethnographic support in the older writings.

14 On links between languages in the southeast see Hercus (1986: 2, 164), Blake (1982: Map 3), and Wesson (1994). On multilingualism see Howitt (Papers, SLV Box 8 ms1053/3(a) 12 April 1899).

15 See Hiatt (1962, 1965) on Gijingarli communities.

16 On Kŭnai regional identities see Howitt (1904: 73–74; Papers, MV B6 F5 ms690: 6, SLV Box 8 ms1053/4(a): 65), Bulmer (Papers, letter to Howitt MV BI F4 xm88, 26 October 1881, B1 F4 xm77), Dow (n.d. a, ch.1), Dawson and Pettit (n.d.), and Dow (n.d. b).

17 See Wesson (2000) for a reconstruction of Kŭnai country groups.

18 See Howitt (1904: 148) and Bulmer (1994: 7) on gender totems.

19 On *je-ak* totems see Bulmer (1994: 7–8, 23; Papers, MV B1, F2 xm92 11.3.84) and Howitt (1904: 135). Bulmer records six examples of their inheritance from father to child, and of the difference between a husband's and wife's *je-ak*. On Kŭnai personal names see Bulmer (Papers, MV B1 F4 xm90 25.3.1882; MV B1 F4, xm96 21.11.84; letter to Howitt 11 March 1904).

20 See Howitt (1880: 191, 226; 1904: 491) on personal names. The name Gliŭn-kong ('curlew sandpiper beak') seems to have been inherited by Bunjil-baul men of Raymond Island.

21 On *mŭk je-ak* and *mŭk-kŭnai* see Bulmer (1994: 7; Papers, letter to Howitt 11 March 1904), Howitt (1904: 146; Papers, ms 1053/4(a)), and Frazer (1939: 22).

22 On the classification of Western Desert languages and the concept of a dialect chain see Yallop (1982) and Merlan (1981).

23 On the Western Desert 'tribe' see Berndt (1959: 93), Miller (1971), Thieberger (1993: 193), Tindale (1974: 30–31, 360), and Tonkinson (1991: 66).

24 Miller (1971) discusses variation among Pitjantjatjara dialects.

25 On multiple language-identity in the Western Desert see R. M. Berndt (1959: 93).

26 On generation moiety names see Tindale (1972: 256). I am grateful to Laurent Dousset (pers. com.) for correcting Tindale's information.

27 Elkin (1939–40: 302–5) and Tindale (1972: 254) describe the diffusion of sections into Pitjantjatjara country.

28 For accounts of personal totems see R. M. Berndt (1972: 191), Hamilton (1982: 99), Layton (1986: 46), Tonkinson (1991: 68), and Viesner (2000: 7).

29 On the riverine–back country distinction see Beckett et al. (2003).

30 See Yallop (1982) on the classification of Darling/Barwon River languages.

31 On mixed language areas see Howitt (1904: 57); on indeterminate boundaries see Teulon (in Curr 1886, vol. 2: 205), and on Ngiyampaa see Donaldson (1984), Beckett et al. (2003).

32 On the location of Yuwaaliyaay and Yuwaalaraay languages see Austin (1993), Donaldson (1980), Ridley (1875), Howitt (1904), and Williams (1976). The locations of events in myths recorded by Parker (1905, 1953) include Narran Lake and Brewarrina, implying that Yuwaaliyaay was spoken in the southwest of the region and Yuwaalaraay in the northeast. See Williams (1976) for an account of Yuwaaliyaay and Yuwaalaraay languages; on relations between languages see Austin, Williams, and Wurm (1980) and Donaldson (1980: 2).

33 Jeremy Beckett (pers. com.) has taken me to task for using 'totemic' too broadly. As a figure that transcends divisions between matri-groups and localities, Byamee was not a totem, he suggests. However, ancestors in the cosmologies discussed here did for the most part have identities of non-human species and entities, and I do not want to make an arbitrary division between these and ancestors such as Byamee and Djang'kawu that had solely (or predominantly) human identities.

34 See Parker (1905: 12, 17) on matri-moieties ('phratries'); on Wangaaybuwan moieties see Beckett (1959) and Radcliffe-Brown (1923: 424).

35 On Yuwaaliyaay matri-groups and totems see Parker (1905: 16); on Wangaaybuwan totems and matri-groups see Beckett et al (2003).

36 See Parker (1905) on Yuwaaliyaay sections.

37 Fison (1880) and Howitt (1904: 203–4, 214) describe 'half-sister marriages'; see Beckett (1959) and Radcliffe-Brown (1931) on Wangaaybuwan sections and kinship.

38 See Parker (1905: 21, 29) on Yuwaaliyaay personal totems.

39 On regional and language identities in the Albany–Bremer Bay region see Barker (1992, cited in Le Souëf 1993), Bates (1985: 49, 53), Browne (1856), Clark (*Enquirer*, 21 February 1842, cited in Le Souëf 1993), Le Souëf (1993: 39), Nind (1831), Graham (in Curr 1886 vol 1: 349), and Spencer, Hossell and Knight (in Curr 1886 vol 1: 386). Tindale (1974) was forced by his tribe model to fix these relative identities as territorial divisions, and Ronald Berndt (1980) followed suit.

40 On the classification of languages of the southwest see Yallop (1982), Douglas (1968), and O'Grady and Fitzgerald (1997: 344).

41 See Bates (1985: 191–2) and Hassell (1936) on categories of totems.

42 On local totems, patri-groups, and places recorded in myths see Bates (1985: 193–6, 199–200). A group with the same local totem with a large area was not strictly exogamous, according to Bates.

43 On moieties in the southwest see Bates (1985: 75, 192–3), Hassell (1936: 684), and Nind (1831: 37–8). Bates glosses *mat* and *gur* as 'stock'.

44 Bates records words akin to *taaman* in various parts of the southwest as meaning 'father's father' (*demman, dimma*) or 'cross cousin' (*denmangur*). She interprets variants on *dem* as 'father's mother' (*tem*) or sibling's child (*dem, tem, demmat*). *Erniung* may be a version of the moiety name *Wornung*, recorded by Bates, or perhaps *ngunning*, meaning 'my own family' (Bates 1985: 78–81, 84).

45 See Hassell (1936: 684) on personal totems.

46 On semi-moieties see Bates (1985: 193–4, 196); oddly, her account of marriage rules in patrifilial semi-moieties entails endogamous moieties. For evidence of semi-moieties at King George Sound see Barker (1992: 3 July 1830, cited in Green 1989: 33), Green (1989: 6), Grey (1841), and Nind (1831: 42–4).

47 On the transferral of personal totems by bestowal or gift see Bates (1985: 194, 196–7, 199).

48 See Chase (1980b: 142–3), Chase and Sutton (1987: 75), Laycock (1969), Rigsby (1992), Rigsby and Chase (1998: 202), and Thompson (1988: 2–3) on Sandbeach languages. See Rigsby (1980) on multilingualism.

49 Chase emphasises the correlation of language boundaries with patri-group boundaries, but Thompson reports some divergence (Thompson 1975: 2).

50 On recent divisions among Kuuku Ya'u see Queensland (1999: 29).

51 On the 'Sandbeach' category in contrast to strangers, see Chase (1980: 136–7, 144), Chase and Sutton (1987: 74–5), and Rigsby and Chase (1998).

52 On Sandbeach patri-groups and totems see Chase (1980: 135). The Green Python is *Chondropython viridis*.

53 See Chase (1980: 140–41) on patri-moieties.

54 See Thomson (1933: 493, 497, 499), Rigsby and Chase (1998: 197) on Sandbeach personal totems.

55 See Capell (1939a), Capell and Coate (1984: 2–5) and McGregor (1988a: 81–2, 1988b) on northwest Kimberley languages, and Rumsey (1996: 5) on the relation of language to country. On current relations among languages see Rumsey and Redmond (1999); they point out that nowadays people say that Worla/Walajangarri and Ngarnawu are 'kinds of' Ngarinyin, and that Guwij and Wurla are alternative names for the same thing.

56 On Worrorra multi-lingualism see Love (1936).

57 See Blundell (1975 vol. 1: 82–6) and Redmond (2001: 141–2) on Ngarinyin and Worrorra patri-group identities.

58 See Love (Paper: 30), Redmond (2001: 123–4), and Rumsey (1996: 6-7) on Ngarinyin moieties.

59 On personal totems see Blundell (1975 vol. 1: 72 citing Petri 1954: 177–83); on *maangarra* see Redmond (2001: 139).

60 See Warner (1937: 36) on Yolngu 'tribes'. On the classification of the languages of the regions see Capell (1940), Schebeck (1968), F. Morphy (1983), Oates and Oates (1970), and Zorc (1978). On 'Wulamba' as a name see Berndt (1958), and on 'Miwuyt' see Shapiro (1981). On Djinang identity see Elliott (1991).

61 See Schebeck (1968) and Zorc (1986) on Yolngu 'dialect groups'. 'Dhiyakuy' was an outsider's name for the dialect of Ritharrngu people, who referred to their language as 'Ritharrngu'. On groupings of Yolngu dialects see F. Morphy (1983: 3–4), Zorc (1978), and Waters 1989: xiv–xv), and on linguistic diffusion see Heath (1978).

62 See Warner (1937: 45) for an example of a language represented by a bird.

63 See Williams (1986: 59–60) on regional and local names.

64 On Yolngu totemic attributes and connections see Warner (1937: 39–51) and Keen (1978: 87).

65 On Yolngu patri-moieties and colour see Morphy (1991).

66 See Keen (1994: 161) on species associated with Yolngu subsections.

67 Personal communication from Diane Austin-Broos.

6

Kinship and Marriage

Introduction

Kinship took a central place in the organisation of Aboriginal economies because it was, and continues to be, the chief mode of organising people and their social relationships. Kinship bore a strong relationship to marriage, not only because marriages brought new families into being, but because Aboriginal people organised marriages on the basis of kin relations. Marriage also had an economic character: people exchanged access to persons as spouses in return for goods and services, or exchanged persons as spouses directly. As well as being a mode of organising reproduction, marriage reproduced social networks, which formed the basis of economic cooperation. To explain these aspects further, this chapter will first introduce some general features of Aboriginal kinship and marriage, and then turn to the seven case studies.

Kinship and society were co-extensive

In what Lévi-Strauss called the 'elementary structures' of kinship, everyone in a person's social universe is a relative of one kind or another, from very close to very distant. One consequence is that a person always marries a relative; marriage rules prescribe which category or categories of relative can be married and which can not. In the Aboriginal societies of this book, the social universe was indeed a universe of relatives. 'Strangers', regarded with suspicion and fear, were those with whom a person could not trace a kin relationship. In order to know how to behave towards each other—and even to just have a social relationship—two people had to know or discover their kin relationship.[1]

A system of kin relations is based on genealogical relations of maternity and usually (but not always) paternity. Aboriginal doctrines about procreation varied. People of some regions denied the link between sexual relations and procreation; a person's 'father' was the mother's husband, who 'found' a child in spirit form when it entered the mother. Others acknowledged the role of sex in procreation, and combined this with doctrines about other causes of pregnancy. In the Aboriginal societies covered in this book, people extended kinship relations to those to whom they could not trace an unbroken chain of genealogical links. This extension of genealogical links, together with the variation in conception doctrines, has led some to argue that the use of the word 'kinship' is inappropriate for Aboriginal modes of relatedness. I agree with Harold Scheffler that Aboriginal notions of relatedness had their *basis* in genealogical relations—that is, relations between parents and children.[2]

Aboriginal cultures seem to have been quite similar in the broad ways in which they defined relations. In the first, genealogical mode, two people are linked by an unbroken chain of (presumed) parent–child links; a person is one's 'sister' (to illustrate the point with an English term) if that person is female and one's parents' child, a person is one's 'grandparent' if that person is one's parent's parent, and so on.

But the relative of one's relative is also a relative in these systems. In cultures of European origin, two people are only regarded as genuine relatives if they are linked by an unbroken chain of genealogical links. In Aboriginal modes of reckoning, however, two people may have a kinship relationship regardless of whether all the genealogical links between them can be specified. Nevertheless, they express the relationship in the idiom of kinship and the relationship forms a basis to which known genealogical links can be added, so that their children can inherit a kin relationship through that link.

This feature of Aboriginal kinship systems means that two strangers can, in what Laurent Dousset calls the 'relational triangle', discover a kin relationship if they can find a relative in common, regardless of whether either of them can trace a fully genealogical relationship with that mediating relative. In this way the field of kinship can be greatly extended. Naming systems such as sections and subsections served a similar purpose, as we saw in the last chapter.[3]

In what Esther Goody called 'performative kinship', two people can become related in a certain way because of what happens to them—a man who 'grows up' a child becomes regarded as their real 'father'; people of the Western Desert who live, hunt, forage, and go to ceremonies together become 'siblings' rather than 'cousins', and hence become too close to marry. A person may deny that a person who fails to live up to expectations in a relationship is their 'real' relative.[4]

The classification of relatives

The classification of relatives varied (and varies) markedly among Aboriginal cultures. These differences had profound implications for the organisation of marriage and the resulting structures of social networks and groups dynamics.

Aboriginal modes of kin reckoning extend terms equivalent to those for close lineal relatives in English—'mother', 'father', 'brother', 'sister', 'grandmother', 'grandfather', and so on—to the siblings of these relatives. Thus, one's mother's sister (an 'aunt' in English) is also one's 'mother', one's father's brother is one's 'father', and so on. This had the practical implication that a person's father's brother or mother's sister, called 'father' and 'mother' respectively, could take the role of a father or mother.

These extensions have the important consequence of extending the terms applied to close kin to more distant kin. If one's mother's sister is also one's 'mother', then her children are one's 'brothers' and 'sisters'. By the same token, if one's mother's mother's sister is also one's 'granny', then her children are one's 'mothers' and 'mothers' brothers'. The same logic applies to one's father's brothers and one's father's father's brothers and their children, as well as other relations. Given the extension of kin relations to people with whom a genealogical connection cannot be traced (or not completely), all the nuclear family terms may be extended to distant relations— a person may have very distant 'fathers', 'mothers', 'brothers', and 'sisters', and not just distant 'cousins', as in English. Anthropologists usually refer to these extended usages as 'classificatory' relatives. Where the case studies below refer to 'distant' mothers or brothers, these kinds of extension are implied. We shall see that people reckoned degrees of proximity and distance, from very close to distant. Beyond the range of people to whom kin terms applied were 'strangers', likely to be dangerous. However, degrees of closeness were open to manipulation and relative to context.

There were other ways in which a kinship relation could be found far beyond the range of known genealogical connections. If two people had a connection to the same totemic entity then they could claim a kin relationship on that basis. Another way was through the sections, subsections, and semi-moieties described in Chapter 5.

Types of kin classification

Aboriginal kin terminologies varied in complex ways and several schemes have been proposed to analyse this variation. The most common way of classifying terminologies is by the names of societies, each of which exhibits a certain type of terminology, associated descent rules, etc. In Australia, the type cases were described by Radcliffe-Brown and Elkin—'Aranda', 'Kariera', 'Karadjeri' and so on—although the type cases do not fit all known variants. I shall use some of these type names to pick out certain features of the systems of kin classification.[5]

But Aboriginal kin terminologies had some common features. First was the 'equivalence of siblings' mentioned earlier: one's mother's sister is one's 'mother', and so on. A corrolary is that parallel cousins (the children of two brothers or two sisters) counted as each other's 'siblings'. The exceptions are where a distinct term applies to a relative's older or younger sibling, or where a distinct term applies to the children of a parent's older or younger sibling.

In a second general feature, kin terms in the parents' generation are 'bifurcate merging'. This means that a parent's same-sex sibling is referred to by the same term as the parent, so one's father's brother is one's 'father', and mother's sister is 'mother'. But each parent's opposite-sex siblings are in a distinct category: one's mother's brother is not a kind of 'father', and one's father's sister is not one's 'mother'.

Terminologies vary a great deal in how many kinds of kin they distinguish in each generation, how they group these within and across generations, and what bases of distinction (such as relative age) they use. The case studies focus primarily on the classification of relatives in a person's own generation, because marriage was usually to some kind of 'cousin'; the rules governing marriage specified which kinds of cousin could be married. The patterns of kin classification in the case studies fall into five main varieties (I retain the original spelling of the type cases):

- 'Hawaiian' (generational) terminology, in which a person referred to and addressed everyone in his or her own generation as a 'brother' or 'sister', but differentiated them by relative age and distance
- 'Aluridja' terminology, which distinguishes distant cross cousins from 'siblings' in one's own generation. (Cross cousins are the children of two people related as 'brother' and 'sister'.)
- 'Kariera-like' terminology, which distinguishes cross cousins from siblings in one's own generation, and differentiate between parallel grandkin (mother's mother, father's father) and cross-grandkin (mother's father, father's mother); the Sandbeach terminology combines these features with 'Omaha' skewing (see below)
- 'Aranda-like' terminology, which distinguishes second from first cross cousins, and distinguishes four kinds of grandkin; the Ngarinyin terminology combines this with 'Omaha' skewing
- 'Karadjeri-like' terminology, which distinguishes cousins on the mother's side from cousins on the father's side, and merges first and second cross cousins.

A set of moral rules, rights, and obligations quite explicitly defined and often capable of formal statement governed many kinds of relationship. This led functionalist anthropologists such as W. Lloyd Warner and Donald Thomson to describe kin relations primarily in terms of rules governing rights and obligations. More recently, anthropologists have emphasised the ways in which relatedness depends on social interaction—being someone's 'father' in more than a superficial way depended on acting in the appropriate way as well as being genealogically (or partly genealogically) related. Fred Myers has explored the emotional content of kin relatedness in some depth.[6]

A number of modes of behaviour can be summarised here rather than spelled out in every case study. In one, both close and distant brothers and sisters avoided all forms of intercourse; the rule would come into effect at about the time of male initiation. In another, a wife's mother and a daughter's husband, and those in the same category of relations, avoided one another. This meant passing messages, food, and other goods through an intermediary, and camping at a distance. This avoidance might be extended to other relations, such as the wife's mother's mother and (in a weaker form) the wife's mother's brother. Sexual relations among certain relatives were forbidden, although the categories varied with the kinship system. In the case of exogamous moieties, people regarded sexual relations between people of the same moiety as wrong, although the strength of the prohibition varied; it was very strong among Ngarinyin and Yolngu people.[7]

Some customary relations among kin have puzzled anthropologists. One is the Yolngu custom of *mirrirri*: if someone makes sexual allusions within a man's hearing and in the presence of that man's sister, the brother will be strongly motivated to attack his sister but not the person who makes the allusions. The sexual allusions violate the avoidance rule, but why such strong action must be taken, and against the sister and not the perpetrator, is hard to explain.[8]

Marriage

Studies of Aboriginal marriage systems have depicted them in three main ways. First, they were contracts (often referred to as 'promise marriages') in which men or women bestowed a daughter, niece, or other relative on a man. Kin relationships primarily governed who the parties to contracts were. We shall see that bestowal was a feature of marriage in all seven case studies, but was less dominant in one of them (Kŭnai).

Second, marriages involved relations between exogamous (out-marrying) groups or categories, often related to totemism. A person had to marry out of their own group or category, and in some systems into a specified category (such as a section), restricting the choice of partner (see the discussion of sections and subsections in Chapter 5). In several regions people of the same general locality were not supposed to marry.

Third, marriages were forms of exchange in which a person was given as a spouse in exchange for valued items (especially meat) or another person. People usually expressed this exchange as the gift of a woman rather than a man. This reflects power relations between men and women generally and also the fact that a girl's bestowal as a wife (or even as a mother of a potential wife) often took place in her infancy or even before her birth.

Several peoples among the case studies represented marriage as an exchange between categories or groups, or the places associated with those groups, or the ancestors of the groups. But groups as such did not arrange or control marriage; rather, small networks of kin arranged or agreed to a marriage.

Other ways of acquiring a spouse included elopement by an unmarried couple, the marriage of a widow to her husband's older or younger brother (leviratic marriage), and the marriage of a man to two or more sisters (sororatic marriage). In probably all the regions, some men acquired wives by raiding the camps of enemies and taking women by force. Elopement by a married woman sometimes resulted in the dissolution of the existing marriage and the recognition of the new union.

Marriage reproduced domestic groups (camps), which were units of consumption and were involved to a degree in production, and marriage gave children their status. They gained some identities through their father and some through their mother—the mix varying between regions, as we have seen.

Polygyny

Polygynous marriage—the marriage of a man to two or more wives concurrently—was practised by all the peoples studied in this book, although the number of wives a man could accumulate varied greatly. A man might acquire an additional wife by, for example, inheriting a brother's widow. In theory, some of the men of a population can marry more than one wife if the sex ratio is heavily skewed towards females. Alternatively, some men can marry polygynously if other men do not marry at all, or if women marry earlier than men and then remarry when widowed. This third condition seems to have been most relevant to Aboriginal marriage; a polygynous man married one or more younger women, as well as other men's widows. The greater the average age difference between husbands and wives, the higher the level of polygyny overall.[9]

My assessments of 'levels' of polygyny are simplifications, however. One would want to know not just the maximum number of wives a man may have concurrently, but how marriages were distributed across men of different age groups. That most men of a population had one or two wives concurrently but one had half a dozen may be less significant in its social and demographic effects than if several men of the same group each acquired four wives. But the information is too incomplete to make this kind of assessment.

Furthermore, the distinction between a man having several wives concurrently and serially is not so very important where what counted was engendering sons who would take their father's patri-group identity and ideally support him in disputes, and engendering daughters who would attract potential husbands and their economic contribution. The concurrent marriages of men to several women implies that women tended to marry several men, but serially (serial polyandry). Generally speaking, young women married older men and then remarried when they became widows. If a very young woman married an old man she could be widowed quite quickly, and such a woman could have several husbands through her life, as well as lovers. We shall see that there were high levels of polygyny, with profound economic and political consequences, in the northwest Kimberley and on the coasts and large islands of Arnhem Land.

Polygyny has effects on the size and structure of groups. In the case of patrilineal groups, a polygynously married man would (if his wives had many children) give rise to a larger lineage than a monogamous man. And if his sons married many wives the growth would continue. Since marriage was an exchange, highly polygynous men occupied a key place in exchange networks. The rules specifying which kin should and should not marry gave rise to social networks of varying form and extent.

Kin categories

The tables in this chapter use conventional anthropological abbreviations for kin categories:

Ego	The propositus, relative to whom a kin term applies
M	Mother
F	Father
S	Son
D	Daughter
C	Child
B	Brother
Z	Sister
Sb	Sibling
W	Wife
H	Husband
Sp	Spouse

eB	Elder brother
yZ	Younger sister
w, w.s.	Woman speaking (i.e. relative to a female Ego)
m, m.s.	Man speaking (i.e. relative to a male Ego)

Combinations of these symbols denote 'relative products' of these terms—for example:

MB	Mother's brother
FZ	Father's sister
FFB	Father's father's brother

Kŭnai people

The classification of kin

Kŭnai people referred to close kin as their 'countrymen' (*wŭrŭktun Kŭnai*). We do not have details about the calculation of kinship distance among Kŭnai people, although we have seen that the category of 'stranger' could be applied to speakers of Kŭnai dialects within Gippsland as well as beyond. [10]

Kŭnai people had a 'generational' or 'Hawaiian' terminology in Ego's generation (see Table 6.1). It classified grandkin into three kinds (two further distinguished by gender), but did not distinguish between siblings and cousins as classes of relative. Also, the only restriction on the choice of marriage partner was that the person had to be a distant relative of the opposite sex and perhaps the same generation. Kŭnai people classified everyone of a person's own generation as a close or more distant 'brother' or 'sister' (senior or junior according to the known or assumed age difference). A term applied by

Table 6.1 Kŭnai kin classification

					Generation
wehntjun FFZ, ?FMBW	*wehntwin* FF/FFB	*nallŭng* FM/FMZ/ FMB, ?FFZH	*nakŭn* MF/MFB/ MFZ, ?MMBW	*kukŭn* MM/MMZ/ MMB, ?MFZH	PP
	mŭmmŭng FZ, MBW	*munga* F/FB, MZH	*yŭkan* M/MZ, FBW	*babŭk* MB, FZH	P
	bauŭng eZ, PSbeD, SpBW (older than Ego)	*lundŭk* yZ, PSbyD, SpSbW (younger than Ego)	*tŭndŭng* eB, PSbeS, SpZH (older than Ego)	*bramung* yB, PSbyS, SpZH (younger than Ego)	Own
	leethi jutti ZC (?ms)	*bengŭn* wC	*lit leethi* C, BC, ZC		C
wehntjun mSD, BSD	*wehntwin* mSS, BSS	*nallŭng* wSC/ZSC	*nakŭn* mDC/BDC	*kukŭn* wDC	CC

Table 6.2 Kŭnai affinal terms

bendŭk HF, HM		ngaribil WF, ?BWF	queabŭn ?WM	
bra H/HB		maian worcak W/WZ, HZ	preppa worcak BW	bennŭng, jambi WB, ?BWB
ngaribil DH (ms)	gueabŭn, guiaban DH	bendŭk SW		

a woman to her child (*bengŭn*) complemented the general term for 'child' and 'sibling's child' (*lit*). Affinal terms differed from kin terms, with distinct terms for one's spouse, spouse's brother and sister, sibling's spouse, spouse's parents, and child's spouse.[11]

Marriage

Kŭnai people did not pick out narrowly defined classes of relatives as potential spouses. Nor did they organise marriages between exogamous totemic categories, except to the extent that one should not marry a person of one's own patrifilial guardian totem (*je-ak*). Most important was that a spouse be a distant relative, which in practice probably meant someone not related by a known genealogical link. Since genealogical memory probably did not extend further back than the great-grandparents' generation, it was likely that third cousins and closer could not marry. But we do not know whether a person could marry a distant 'parent', 'child', 'grandparent' or 'grandchild', or just a distant 'sibling'.[12]

A young man could marry after he became a *brewit* (bachelor) at a Jerra-eil initiation ceremony, while some girls went to their husband's camp when they were as young as 13. Kŭnai people discouraged marriage between geographically close people, expressing the ideal that people of the same local group and country ('division') should not marry. Some groups apparently prohibited the marriage of a man to a woman of his mother's locality, and others even rejected as partners those of the same broad regional identity ('clan' in Howitt's scheme), even if they were not closely related. But the pattern of marriages between named localities as recorded by Howitt shows that people with the same regional identity often did marry. People responded with strong sanctions against sexual relationships between close relatives, often beating up an offending young man and spearing the offending young woman in the legs or feet.

The many ways of acquiring a spouse in Gippsland included bestowal, leviratic and sororatic marriage, elopement, and raiding. Men exchanged 'sisters': a man bestowed his 'sister' (e.g. his father's brother's daughter) in exchange for a wife for himself. Alternatively, a man might negotiate directly with the intended spouse rather than her brother. Sometimes, however, the woman's or the girl's father and father's brother bestowed her as a wife. A woman might put on at least a show of resistance to a bestowed marriage, or indeed to a leviratic marriage.

The ethnographers do not depict only men as agents in marriage arrangements. A group of young women would provoke young men to fight them by killing a bird representing the male totem, then couples formed from among the fighting group; these couples might 'elope' to a place in the bush remote from the main residence group. A young woman might use stratagems based on beliefs in magic to induce her family to accept a relationship—for example, the gift of a lock of hair to a young man put her in apparent danger of sorcery from the young man and his family, leading the girl's parents to give her to the young man to prevent her death.

Another variety of reciprocal exchange occurred after marriage: the temporary exchange of partners by married couples, a practice called *beamu*. They did this after one couple had quarrelled, or at a major ceremony, or to avert a disaster heralded by the Southern Lights (Aurora Australis) or some other danger.

Bulmer writes that a man with no sisters to exchange would have to 'win the heart' of a woman and elope, but Howitt took elopement to have been the norm, except among Brabrolung and Krauatŭn.golung people.

Would-be partners typically chose a ceremony (especially the Jerra-eil initiation) as the occasion to run away together, and the girl's parents would supposedly be unaware of the proposal. As mentioned, young men and women would provoke each other by killing the totemic bird of the opposite gender, and after the ensuing fights some couples would pair off. If two young men both had an unmarried sister they could arrange to abscond with each other's sisters. Howitt reports (in Latin) the occurrence of group sex on some such occasions between a girl and a group of co-initiates (*brogan*, or 'mates'). A young man could call on a singer of love-magic songs (*bunjil-yenjin*), in return for gifts, to induce a woman to run off without her parents' consent. The parents would perform or commission magic in order to find them. An elopement provoked the animosity of the girl's family—the man would have to fight her brothers and the girl would have to endure a beating or spearing in the feet. In some cases, a couple would have to elope two or three times, or the girl would have to become pregnant, before the woman's family would finally consent to the marriage.

After the death of a husband, the senior brother had the first claim on the widow. If there were several widows, brothers claimed them according to the order of their seniority. However, a widow might refuse to go with her husband's brother and might choose someone else, at the risk of retaliation by sorcery. It seems that in some parts of Gippsland people practised sororatic marriage (i.e. of a man to two or more sisters), either subsequent to a wife's death or concurrently. The wives' parents would supposedly obtain a double supply of food because of the son-in-law's obligation to provide for them.

Kŭnai men also obtained wives in raids against *brajerak* (strangers), abducting the younger women. In return, men of other regions, such as the Monaro tableland to the northeast, sporadically raided Kŭnai country for wives.

The resulting level of polygyny appears to have been comparatively low in Gippsland. Early censuses suggest that about 17% of married men (mainly older men) had two wives and 3% had three wives. However, the social disruption resulting from two decades of colonisation may well have had an effect.[13]

Because of the prohibition on marriage between close relatives, the network of relations between localities (and kin groups) shifted from generation to generation—it had the form of a 'shifting web' or 'dispersed affinal alliance'. Howitt recorded

patterns of marriage between countries ('divisions'), as remembered by Kŭnai people in the 1870s. His list reveals a network of marriages linking localities for the most
part in reciprocal relations (in part reflecting sibling exchange), between neighbouring communities as often as distant ones, and both within and across regional
identities (or 'clans'). Each locality had links to between one and eight others in
Howitt's account. A few links extended outside the Kŭnai region—to the people of
Omeo in the north, and to the Bidawal and Yuin people in the east and northeast.[14]

Pitjantjatjara people and their neighbours

Pitjantjatjara kin classification has a similar form to Kŭnai kin classification, except
that, among other things, it distinguishes distant cross cousins from 'siblings'.
Marriage bestowal had links to circumcision initiation.

The classification of kin

Western Desert ethnography shows that through residing together people became
classified as close kin even if they were only distantly related genealogically—they
became 'countrymen'.[15]

In the kinship terminology (see Table 6.3), the grandparents' generation contained
only two categories, which distinguished male from female grandkin. But in a similar
way to Kŭnai kinship classification, a person referred to most relatives of their own
generation as 'brother' or 'sister', differentiated according to relative age as well as gen-

Table 6.3 Pitjantjatjara kin classification

tjamu		kami		
FF, FFB, MF, MFB, MMB, FMB, all other males of this generation		MM, MMZ, FM, FMZ, FFZ, MFZ, all other females of this generation		**Opposite moiety**
kuntili	mama	nguntju	kamaru	**Own moiety**
FZ, F's female cousin, MBW	F, FB, F's male cousin, MZH	M, MZ. M's female cousin, FBW?	MB, M's male cousin, FZH	
kangkuru	kuta	malanypa	watjira	**Opposite moiety**
Z, parent's sibling's daughter, parent's cousin's daughter, older than Ego	B, parent's sibling's son, parent's cousin's son, older than Ego	B, Z, parent's sibling's child, parent's cousin's child, younger than Ego	Distant 'sibling', child of 'MB' or 'FZ' (beyond second cousin)	
katja	yuntalpa	ukari		**Own moiety**
S, mBS, wZS	D, mBD, wZD	mZC, wBC, m"Z"C, w"B"C		
tjamu, pakali		kami, paliri		**Opposite moiety**
SS, DS, all other males of this generation		SD, DD, all other females of this generation		

Table 6.4 Pitjantjatjara affinal terms

minkayi HF, HM, SW, HFZ, HMB (Elkin adds ZSW)	umari WM, wDH (Elkin adds katja- umari as ZDH)	waputju WF, WFB, WMB, mDH	inkilyi Co-parent-in-law, CSpP, SpCSpP, SbCSpPSb
kuri Spouse, H, W	tjuwari Parallel sibling-in-law, female: wBW, HZ	marutju Parallel sibling-in-law, male: mZH, WB	inkani Cross sibling-in-law: mBW, WZ, wZH, HB

der. Unlike in Kŭnai terminology, however, the children of one's distant mother's brothers or father's sisters were not siblings but *watjira* (cross cousins), the category of preferred spouses. Cross cousins who associated closely with each other—who had the same conception site, or lived in the same community—were reclassified as 'siblings' and so could not marry.

Certain kin terms had a hierarchical component. A person would address their father and mother's brother with the respectful 'old man', and would address their mother and father's sister as 'old woman'. As those who provided one with meat, one's father, older brother, and mother's brother were all one's 'boss'.[16]

After marriage, Pitjantjatjara people applied distinct terms to relatives who became affines (see Table 6.4).[17]

Marriage

As among Kŭnai people, marriage ideally took place between people who were not closely related (preferable beyond the degree of second cousins) and who were from somewhat distant countries. Distantly related people of the same generation or alternating generations (the same generation moiety) could marry, but not people of adjacent generations. A boy's potential wife's father was likely to have been a distant 'mother's brother' (*kamuru*) of his, while his wife's mother would have been a 'father's sister' (*kurntili*) of his. According to Elkin, however, people in other kin relationships (such as distant 'brothers' and 'sisters') sometimes married, usually as the man's second marriage. Laurent Dousset believes this to be incorrect: the apparent sibling relationship derived from the practice of referring to a person of the same generation as a sibling in some contexts, because they were of the same generation moiety.[18]

Marriage in this region had links with male initiation. Circumcision resulted in a contract between the man who carried out the operation and the young man on whom he operated. As compensation for the injury, by which the circumciser symbolically 'killed' the initiate, the circumciser promised to give the young man his daughter or brother's daughter as a wife. The circumciser's helper might do the same. After the operation the circumciser became the young man's *waputju* ('wife's father') and they had to avoid one another, as did the circumciser and the boy's father. The bestowal initiated a prolonged series of gifts between the families of the circumciser and the young man, as well as relations of restraint and avoidance. The young man gave food to his wife's mother and gifts to his wife's mother's brother, who played a part in arranging the marriage. As the men had to avoid one another, the young man gave his wife's father food through the wife.

Elkin reports a bestowal ceremony. After the circumcision operation, the potential wife's mother made a fire for the young man's use while his wound was healing, and he was excluded from the camp. In such ceremonies, the wife's mother might give the young man a firebrand before his circumcision as a mark of the arrangement, or she may even have done so before the future wife was born.

As an alternative to bestowal, in the west of the Western Desert region at least, a suitor would simply make an indirect request to a girl's parents by sending them meat and other gifts through intermediaries over a number of years. An older man could marry his wife's younger sister as a second wife, and 'grow her up' with gifts. And young men sometimes married widows as their first wives. Dousset and the Berndts report the exchange of sisters and daughters as spouses between men. A significant proportion of wives also left their husbands for other men.

According to most studies of the Western Desert, the level of polygyny was low, with men usually having one or two wives concurrently but only exceptionally three or four. Age difference between spouses were concomitantly lower than in the high-polygyny areas. Because of the preference for marriage to a genealogically distant relative, the resulting network was a shifting web of connections, as among Kŭnai people. As Myers remarks, marriage maintained a regional network but with no long-term, continuous alliances between groups although some repetition of marriage patterns occurred after a few generations. The diversity of connections was important in ensuring mutual assistance in this difficult environment.[19]

Yuwaaliyaay people and their neighbours

Yuwaaliyaay kin classification had a more complex structure in which the sibling/cross cousin distinction was reflected in terms applied to each generation. Marriage involved exchanges between matri-groups.

The classification of kin

Like Kŭnai people, Yuwaaliyaay people distinguished familiar people from strangers, whom they regarded as potentially dangerous.[20] While incomplete, the record of Yuwaaliyaay kin classification is consistent with that of their Wangaaybuwan neighbours to the south, whose kinship terminology has been quite fully described and was 'Kariera-like' in form. The terminology distinguished 'parallel' grandkin (FF/FFB/MMB, MM/MMZ/FFZ) from 'cross' grandkin (MF/MFB/FMB, FM/FMZ/MFZ) and probably grouped first cross cousins (MBC, FZC, etc.) together and distinguished them from parallel cousins (MZC, FBC, etc.), who were a person's 'siblings'. Certain second cousins were classified with the first cross cousins—so that, for example, MMBDD and FMBSD were 'MBD'—while others, such as MFZSC, were classed with parallel cousins as 'siblings'.[21]

Table 6.5 Yuwaaliyaay kin classification[22]

Own (mother's) matri-moiety		Opposite (father's) matri-moiety			Distant cross cousin, spouse	Generation
taladi (?) FMF	?					PPP
[thilaa] FF/FFB/?MMB	ba:gi: MM/MMZ/?FFZ	nga:gi, nga:nga: FM/FMZ/?MFZ	da:da: MF/MFB/?FMB			PP
garugi: MB, [FZH, 'uncle'	gunidjar, ngamba (fam.) M, MZ	gamiyan FZ walgan MBW	bialahdee, buwadjar F/FB, MZH	walgandi HM, ?WM/WMB, WMZ		P
daga:n galuma:y eB yB [FBS, FZS, MZS, MBS, etc.]	bawa dawuran eZ yZ [FBD, FZD, MZD, MBD, etc.]	?nganga MBD, FZD BW	? MBS, FZS	? W/WZ WB		Own
? gunugaynga C(ws) ('nephew') ZC	? gunugaynga C(ws) ('niece') ZC	biraling mD, BD	biraling mS, BS			C
galumay, garimay 'ysB', mSS	galumay, garimay 'ySb, mSD	nanuwaydji wSC, mDC	?gamdil dangay mSS mSD			CC

An important feature of Wangaaybuwan kin classification, one that the Yuwaaliyaay system seems to have shared, was that that the term for one's father's father was 'elder brother', and the term for a man's son's child was 'younger sibling'. Similarly, one's 'cross cousin' was a 'cross grandparent' (MF/FMZ or FM/MFZ). (A similar feature is found in Ngarinyin kin classification.) The terminology also marks relative age, not just of siblings but of mother's sisters and father's brothers as well.

This form of terminology fits nicely with exogamous categories, such as moieties and sections. Ideally, categories of relative traced through women from one's mother's mother would be found in one's own matri-moiety, and those traced through women from one's father's mother (or MFZ) would be found in the opposite moiety. Ideally, kin would also be distributed between the different sections—for example, a person of Gambu section would have cross cousins in the Matha section. But since marriages did not strictly follow section principles, this did not always occur.

Marriage

Distant cross cousins—probably those beyond the range of second cousins—could marry. However, Parker writes that there was no bar on people of the same locality marrying, as there was for Kŭnai people. People of the same or closely related matri-totems and of the same 'blood' matri-moiety were not supposed to marry. However, it seems probable that in some cases Yuwaaliyaay people (like their Wangaaybuwan and Gamilaraay neighbours) allowed marriages between people of different matri-groups but incompatible sections, which supports the view that the section system had been incompletely integrated with older institutions.[23]

In infant betrothal (*bahnmul*), a baby girl would be 'given' to a man, possibly as recompense for services done for the mother or in an exchange transaction in which the girl's kin 'owed' her to the potential husband's kin, perhaps as a result of an earlier bestowal. When the child was about one month old her 'granny' (probably the mother's mother) decorated her and showed her to her prospective husband, typically saying to the child words to the effect of 'Look at him, and remember him, because you are promised to him'. People arranged some marriages at ceremonies, where other exchanges were also arranged and where people discussed illicit marriages. Yuwaalaraay men (close neighbours of Yuwaaliyaay) sometimes exchanged sisters in marriage, and it is likely that Yuwaaliyaay men did the same; men related as distant cross cousins could have exchanged sisters. Illicit marriages and wife 'stealing' could be settled by a marriage exchange as recompense.

Certain ceremonies led up to the time when a girl moved to her husband's camp. After a period of seclusion and dietary restrictions while living with an older female relative, such as a grandmother, she was adorned and led to the husband in the camp, then secluded again, then introduced to his hearth, where they slept apart; finally they slept on the same side of the hearth.

Not only did Yuwaaliyaay matri-groups exchange girls as spouses but, as elsewhere, the prospective husband gave gifts to the wife's mother or, if she were deceased, to the wife's nearest kin. However, as Parker remarks in a telling phrase, 'sometimes a man gives no presents and yet gets a wife'. It seems that if the husband did not like his bestowed wife, he could send her back to her kin. If, however, he mistreated his wife, her relations had the power to take her away from him.

Howitt reports that, in this region, a widow might marry one of her late husband's 'brothers'. Among Pakaantji people it was usually a younger 'brother'. Where a young man married an older woman, she would have been the widow of an older husband; Parker comments that a woman 'never seems to be too old to marry'.

Most Yuwaaliyaay men had only one wife, according to Parker, though some had two and she had heard of one man with three wives. So the level of polygyny was low, as it was among the Pakaantji neighbours, although population decline may have had an effect by then. Teulon assessed the average age difference between Pakaantji spouses as six years, with girls moving to their husband's camp at about the age of 13. This figure is consistent with low levels of polygyny.

The reciprocal exchange of spouses between matri-groups helped to shape Yuwaaliyaay social networks. Each totemic group exchanged spouses with several others, creating a continuous web of reciprocal ties; a marriage between second cross cousins could be repeated between two kin groups in every second generation.

Wiil and Mi̱nong people

Wiil and Mi̱nong people also had a Kariera-like terminology, allied again with marriage between distant cross cousins; exchanges, however, were between patri-groups and semi-moieties rather than matri-groups and sections.

The classification of kin

Wiil and Mi̱nong people distinguished strangers from known relatives, and marked them as potentially dangerous; ravens were seen as a sign of the proximity of dangerous strangers. In a counter tendency, semi-moiety identity extended the possibility of relatedness to other communities, and a boy's initiation journey created links between local areas and kin groups (see Chapter 8). Mi̱nong people at Albany referred to their relatives as *gen-ben* ('all the family').[24]

Wiil and Mi̱nong kin terminology (Table 6.6) had a somewhat similar form to Yuwaaliyaay terminology, in that it classified siblings and parallel cousins together (differentiated by gender and relative age), while cross cousins were distinct. Distant cross cousins were also differentiated from close cross cousins. Unlike in the Yuwaaliyaay terminology, age difference in one's parent's generation was carried down to one's own generation, so that one's father's younger brother's child was distinct from other siblings.[25]

In the grandparents' generation the terminology distinguishes four kinds of grand-kin, who appear to have been grouped into those of the 'father's side' and those of the 'mother's side', as indicated by similarities and differences in the terms. A person's relatives were also divided into those who could and could not be married, and sexual relations were prohibited between people of the same matri-moiety. A young man avoided the wives of his mother's brother, as well as the sisters of his *babbingur* (his guardians when he was an initiate).

Bates records terms applied to all the relatives in particular moieties and semi-moieties, relative to the speaker. *Ngunning*, 'my own family', were people of the two semi-moieties into which one did not marry. (These were people of one's own matri-moiety in matri-moiety areas). People of the opposing semi-moieties, into which one could marry, were *noyyung*.

Marriage

Mi̱nong people of King George Sound preferred to marry a distant relative, preferably one from a distant community: potential spouses probably included relatives in the 'distant cross cousin' category. A person found their cross cousins in the opposite matri-moiety, and in the two opposing semi-moieties (see Chapter 5). The ethnographic sources do not tell us whether alternative marriages were permitted, or if people of alternate generations could marry.[27]

An infant girl, or even an unborn baby girl, could be bestowed by her relatives on a young man. The bestowal of an unborn baby girl constituted, in effect, the bestowal of her mother on the young man as a future mother-in-law. (We shall see that this was explicit among Yolngu people.) According to Nind, girls 'appear to be at the disposal of their father'. The husband's gifts to the daughter included game or other foods, while the father might receive a cloak, spears, or other implements. Chapter 8 describes the *yardie* ceremony, in which betrothed couples stayed together for two or three days in one of the large huts between the bachelors' and girls' camps. (These huts were also where people arranged divorces.)

Table 6.6 Wiil/Miṉong kin classification[26]

	Own (father's) and mother's mother's semi-moieties		Mother's and father's mother's semi-moieties — 'Cross' kin cross-cousins		Distant cross	Generation
	moora, murran MM/MMZ/?FFZ	*demman* FF/FFB, ?MMB	*dem* FM, FMZ, ?MFZ	*moorr, dem* MF, MFB, ?FMB		**PP**
	? FZ	*maan, ma:m, mama mamon, maangur* F/FB	*ngangk, kaan eecher* MMZ	*kongk, konk, compere* MB		**P**
warinjob cousin's cousin "brother"	*tjuk, jook nguni* *jindam gnaiuk* *boorong kookan* eZ *koopetong* Z, yZ	*ngunt nguni* *ngoont ngammuk* *kojo maridal* *knondan knondan* EB B, yB		*dammap* MBC/FZC	*kordamun* 'MBC/ 'FZC'	**Own**
	korrurda kintercure *nooba caintecur* D BD (ms)	*nooba koolong* BC *beerdin* S	*moyer dem* *moyen deman* *curing demgur* ZC *demmat* ZD (ms) ZC (oder than EGO)			**C**
		moora, murran SC (ms) (Beverley dist.)	*dimma demman* DC (?ms) SS (ws) (Beverley dist.)			**CC**

The *barlee* ('armband') marriage among Wiil people involved a prolonged period in which the potential husband had to provide food to his potential wife's parents, notionally for the child whom he 'grew' (a similar conception to the Yuwaaliyaay one). He had to care for the girl if her parents died or the mother was captured, and she came under the protection of his female relatives. Just before consummation the man plucked hairs from his wife's head and bound them through his armband in the presence of witnesses, then his wife accompanied him to his hut. After a day or two they went off together for a 'bush walk'. (At King George Sound it was customary for a man to go on a long pre-nuptial walk.)

The potential husband had an obligation to marry the girl to whom he was promised; if he did not want to marry her he was supposed to find a substitute husband among his own kin. Conversely, if the wife absconded, men of the husband's kin group joined in seeking redress. This gives the transaction the appearance of a contract between the wife's kin and a group of men rather than an individual.

At King George Sound, as well as exchanging goods, kin groups exchanged women as wives, in a similar way to Yuwaaliyaay people. This is consistent with semi-moiety organisation and distant-cross-cousin marriage (see Chapter 5).

Both Wiil and Minong people practiced leviratic marriage; at King George Sound this usually involved the husband's younger brother and was sometimes conducted before the husband's death and in exchange for gifts. Infidelity was common among Minong people, according to Nind, and husbands often punished young wives, leading them to elope with younger men; gifts to a wronged husband might settle matters if such an elopement resulted in a pregnancy. Sometimes a man would abduct a woman without her consent.

Polygyny seems to have been of a low level among Wiil people at Jerramungup—Hassell remarks that most men had one wife, and only a few had two. Minong men at King George Sound enjoyed a moderate level of polygyny, with older men having up to four wives. (But the grandfather of a man living at King George Sound in 1830 was reputed to have had ten wives). The old men not only had several wives, Nind remarks, but wives of all ages.

Polygyny occasioned a great deal of conflict among men: many of the disputes recorded in observers' accounts arose from young wives running away with young men, leading to retaliation in the form of attempted spearing.[28]

As among Yuwaaliyaay people, second-cross-cousin marriages between groups could be repeated in alternate generations, and indeed ethnographers report marriage exchanges between kin groups. Initiation journeys also fostered ties between distant groups. So reciprocal exchanges modified a shifting web generated by marriages between distant cousins.

Sandbeach people

Sandbeach people combined a Kariera-like kin terminology with 'Omaha' skewing, and once more marriage was ideally between distant cross cousins.

The classification of kin

Sandbeach people distinguished four degrees of distance—from 'relations of my own heart', who were closest, to 'lower-leg' relations, who were most distant. Close relationships entailed obligations of respect and support; distant relatives could marry; even more distantly related people were potential enemies.[29]

The Sandbeach terminology (Table 6.7) classified grandkin and cousins in a similar way to the Yuwaaliyaay terminology, distinguishing cross cousins from siblings/ parallel cousins. But, as with Wiil and Minong terminologies, the relative age differences marked in one's parents' generation carried down to one's own. Thus, the children of one's father's elder brother were all one's 'elder brother' or 'elder sister', while the children of one's father's younger brother were all one's 'younger brother' or 'younger sister'. This feature may have structured seniority within a patri-group, but the senior–junior distinction also applied to cross cousins (who were in different patri-groups and of opposite moieties) as well as parallel cousins, who were classed as siblings. Ideally, the various kinds of relatives could be sorted into those of one's own (and one's father's) patri-moiety, and those of the opposite moiety—that of one's mother and father's mother.[30]

In a feature of kin terminologies known as 'skewing', the terms applied in one generation are carried down to the next on the mother's or father's side. Unlike Yuwaaliyaay and Wiil/Minong people, Sandbeach people regarded a person's close female cross cousin—*ngami* (senior) or *thaatha* (junior)—as 'like a mother', and consequently not someone who could be married. Conversely, one's closely related father's sister's child was classified as 'woman's child'. This did not apply to more distant (or 'outside') cross cousins, the children of distant 'fathers's sisters', who were potential spouses. These 'Omaha' skewing features appear to have been secondary in that their application was limited and their potential consequences for other kin relations were not followed through.[31]

A separate set of terms applied to relatives by marriage (see Table 6.8). Before marriage a man had to avoid his *wulumu* (intended wife), and relations with other potential affines required the use of the in-law respect vocabulary (*nguunki*, talking 'one side'), as well as an obligation to look after them and supply them with food. Only after a man's wife's mother (*yaami*) symbolically placed a spear-thrower on the man's head could he talk to his wife.[32]

Marriage

Though a somewhat distant cousin, one's spouse ideally came from a patri-group whose country was geographically close, ideally of the same dialect. However, some marriages did occur between close cross cousins, but any two people were related in different ways through different relatives, so a close relationship could be represented as more distant in order to justify a marriage. The wife's father would normally have been the daughter's husband's distant 'mother's brother'. But he could be another kind of relative (such as MFF/FMF) provided that the potential wife's mother was the husband's distant 'father's younger sister' (*piima tali*). A man would solicit another man's niece (ZD) not by asking directly but through gifts.[33]

Table 6.7 Sandbeach (Umpila/Kuuku Ya'u language) kin classification

Generation	Mother's patri-moiety: distant cross-cousins	Mother's patri-moiety	Own (father's) patri-moiety
PPP	—	*maampu* MFF/B FMF/B *maampu* MMM/Z FFM/Z	*pii'athu* FFF/B MMF
PP	—	*ngatyimu* MF/B FMB SpFF *pa'i* FM/FMZ MFZ SpMM	*puula* FF/B, MMB WMF, HMF *pii'atju* MFM FMM *miimi* MM/MMZ FFZ WFM HFM
P	MyB	*kaala* MeB mFFZS mMMZS *muka* M/MyZ *muka* mFFZS mMMZS *paapa* MeZ	*piipi* F/FyB *piinya* FeB *piinya* FeZ mMFeZS knondan *piima* FyZ
Own	*pilupa* "MyB"S "FyZ"S *mayu* "MeB"S "FeZ"S wH *wwulumu* "MB"D "FZ"D	*thaatha* MyBC FyZC mFFZSS *ngami* MeBC FeZC mFMBSS *maampa* mMBSS mMZDS	*yapu* eB, FeBS MeZS mMFZSS *ya'a* eZ FeBD MeZD *ya'athu* yZ FyBD MyZD *ya'athu* yB, FyBS MyZS mFMBDS
C	—	*maampa* wC./eZC mMBSC mFZSC *mukathu* yZC ?meBSC mFyZSD	*pii'athu* mC, eBC ?mMeBC *piinyathu* yBC myBDS ?myBDD *kamichu* wDC/ZDC wBSC
CC	—	*ngachichu* mDC/BDC mZSC *pa'yichu* wSC/ZSC w BDC	*puulathu* mSC/BSC mZDC
CCC	—	*kaala* wSSS wDDS mSDS mDSS *paapa* wDDD wSSD mSDD mDSD	*piipi* mSSS, mDDS wSDS, wDSS *piima* mSSD mDDD wSDD wDSD

Table 6.8 Sandbeach (Umpila/Kuuku Ya'u language) affinal terms

	ngatyichu mSDH mSSW	*pa'ichu* wDDH wDSW	*uungu* wDDH / *pa'ichu* wDDH		*kamichu* wSSW / *puulathu* meBSSW mDSW	*kamicha* wSDH	*thalichi* mDDH / *puulathu* mDDH		
maampa WeBC HeBC	*mukathu* HyBC WyBC MeBSC mFZySD	*ngacha-mangu* mSW	*ngacha-mangu* mDH		*uutanganu* wSW HF	*yaami* wDH	*piinyathu* HyZC	*pii'athu* WeZC HeZC	
	pilupa WB	*kulnta* W/WZ BW	*mayu* H ZH	**Ego**	*kal'i* MBSW FZDW WMBD WFZD HMBD HFZD	*kal'i* MBDH FZDH (DT has *onkaminya* as Hxcous)			
paapa FyBW	*kaala* FyZH	*muka* FeBW FeZH	*ampayi* WF HF		*yaami uuku* WM HM	*yaanu* WMB	*piipl* myZH *kal'i* MH		
		uungu WMM	*ngaachimu* WFF HFF			*thalichi* WMF		*piima* myBW	*piinya* MeZH MeBW

Bestowal often took place before the intended wife was born or even before the intended wife's mother was pregnant. This in effect constituted the bestowal of a woman as a man's wife's mother. The relatives of the prospective husband and wife with the greatest interest in the proceedings included the wife's mother, the wife's father, and the wife's mother's father. Others involved in bestowal ceremonies included the intended husband's mother or sister.

Three rituals, conducted in no particular order, formalised betrothal. In the first (of the Umpila versions) the prospective wife's mother placed a net-bag over her future daughter's husband's head; in the second the prospective wife's father placed his spear-thrower on the head of the young man; and in the third the prospective wife's mother's mother smeared a stripe of red ochre across the man's chest and a second down his sternum. Another ceremony, similar to one conducted by the Yuwaaliyaay people, marked the occasion when a girl moved to her husband's camp; before the ceremony the husband would have lived in the bachelors' camp. The girl's mother led her by the wrist, while carrying a firebrand, the girl's dilly-bag, and other gear. These ceremonies expressed the spouses' roles rather clearly in the symbolism of the net-bag, dilly-bag, fire, and spear-thrower. It was the sharing of the hearth by a man and woman that marked the currency of a marriage.

Bestowal and marriage involved obligations of gift exchange and service, in the main from the prospective son-in-law to his potential affines, coming into effect after formalisation of the betrothal. The man had to feed his prospective wife's father and mother regularly, or there was a danger that they might give their daughter to another man. (See Chapter 12 on exchanges following a marriage.) A younger brother would be expected to marry his older brother's widow.

Umpila and Kuuku-Ya'u people practised polygyny at a low to moderate level. Most marriages in Thomson's genealogies were monogamous, but he recorded two men with two wives (one had married two sisters), two with three wives, and one with four—the first by the levirate and the fourth also a widow. A corollary of polygyny was that women often married more than one man, but serially (serial polyandry). As in other regions, the age difference between husbands and wives provided the main condition for polygyny: Thomson remarked that 'so many young girls are married to old men' among the Kuuku Ya'u people, presumably at Lockhart River Mission; a girl would join her husband's camp before her first menses. Thomson also noted that a promiscuous woman ran the risk of spearing, but a promiscuous man went unpunished (unless an irate husband attacked him).[34]

The more polygynous men would have engendered somewhat larger lineages than the others, contributing to the growth of their own patri-group. Because marriage between close cousins was discouraged, the marriage partners of people of a given patri-group came from a number of neighbouring as well as more distant groups, creating a shifting web of connections between groups along the coast and in the hinterland, as among Kŭnai and Pitjantjatjara people. Multiple, cross-cutting links connected each group to several others, the network having relatively short filaments, as it were. Each person had close relatives in several different patri-groups. The neighbouring Ayapathu people currently refer to the web of genealogical links beyond living memory as the 'background' that structures current relations.[35]

Ngarinyin people and their neighbours

Ngarinyin kinship and marriage systems had a very different form from those of the preceding groups, for exchanges between sequences of patri-groups had an asymmetrical structure.

The classification of kin

Like Yuwaaliyaay, Wiil/Mi<u>n</u>ong, and Sandbeach kinship terminologies, Ngarinyin kin classification merged parallel cousins with siblings and distinguished them from cross cousins (see Table 6.9). However, it marked off several other varieties of cousin as well, so that the terminology resembles the 'Aranda' type of Radcliffe-Brown's and Elkin's typologies. Unlike the Yuwaaliyaay and Sandbeach terminologies, it divided the parallel and cross grandkin, distinguishing MM and MMB from FFZ and FF, MF from FMB, and MFZ from FM. Furthermore, first and certain second cross cousins (e.g. MBD and MMBDD) were distinct. 'Omaha' skewing transformed the terminology into an asymmetrical one.[36]

One way to represent the system of kin classification is as 'lines' of kin terms traced through men. From the individual's point of view, other patri-groups contained relatives belonging to each of these 'lines'. But each line would have been repeated in a number of groups, and some patri-groups would have contained relatives of more than one line, especially where it consisted of more than one lineage. The lines were as follows:

Mother's mothers, etc.
MM, MMZ, MMB *(gayangi)*, WM, WMB *(wolmingi/rambarr)*, WFM *(wolmingi)*

Father's mothers, etc.
FM, FMZ, WFZ, FMBSD 'wife' *(marringi)*, FMB, WF *(wayingi)*

Mothers, mother's fathers, etc.
MF, MFB, MFZ *(mamingi)*, M *(ngadji)*, MB *(garndingi)*

Own and father's fathers, etc.
FF, FFB *(ngolingi)*, FFZ *(lalingi)*, F, FB *(idja)*, FZ *(amalngi)*

Woman's and sister's children's, etc.
wC/ZC, FFZC *(marlangi)*, H, ZH, FFZH, etc. *(wuningi)*

Man's daughter's children, etc.
mDC *(mamingi, baba)*, FZC *(marlangi)*, FZSC (DH) *(wuningi)*

Woman's/sister's daughter's children, etc.
wDC/ZDC *(gayingi)*, wDH *(rambarr, wolmingi)*

Table 6.9 Ngarinyin kin and affinal terms

Generation	1 MM's line, gayingi etc. F	2 FM's line, marringi etc. M	3 M's line, ngadji etc. M	4 own, FF's line, ngolingi etc. F	5 wC line, marlangi etc. M	6 mDC line, mamingi (baba) etc. M	7 wDC line, gayingi etc. moiety: F
PP	gayingi MM/MMB	wayingi FMB marringi FM	mamingi maming garndingi garnding MF/MFB ngadji MFZ	ngolingi FF/FFB lalingi amalngi FFZ			
P	rambarr, wolmingi MMBD MMBS WM WMB	wayingi FMBS WF marringi FMBD WFZ	garndingi MB ngadji M/MZ	idja F/FB amalngi FZ	marlangi FFZD FFZSS	marlangi FZD FZS	gayingi MBW
Own	MMBD MMBS WM WMB	wayingi MMBDS FMBSS WB marringi MMBDD FMBSD MMBDD W/BW	garndingi MBS ngadji MBD	ngolingi eB margingi yB lalingi Z/yZ	wuningi FFZSD HZ/ZHZ H/HB/Z	wuningi FZSD FZSS mDH	gayingi FFZDD/S MBSW
C		wayingi FMBSSS marringi FMBSSD WBD	garndingi MBSS ngadji MBSD	idja mS amalngi mD	marlangi wD wS ZD ZS	mamingi, baba, marlangi mDD mDS	gayingi FFZDSD/S rambarr, wolmingi wDH
CC				mSS margingi mSD lalingi	wSD wSS ZSD ZSS wuningi		wDC/ZDC gayingi

The way that Ngarinyin kin classification marked relative age differed from the way other systems marked it. For example, if one's father's brother married before one's birth, then all his children were one's 'elder brothers' and 'elder sisters'.

As A. P. Elkin reported, the Ngarinyin terminology was unusual in that it extended kin terms applied in one generation to all the members of a patrilineal group—so that the members of a person's mother's group were the person's 'mothers' and 'mother's brothers', the members of a person's father's mother's group were their 'father's mothers' and 'father's mother's brothers', and so on. Alan Rumsey has shown more recently that the extension of kin terms in this way depended on context—on whether a person was referring to relations to and between patri-groups or to and between individuals.

When they were talking about group relations, people extended the terms for 'mother' (*ngadji*) and 'mother's brother' (*garndingi*) to denote people in all generations in the group. Conversely, one's FZC and FFZC became one's 'child' (woman speaking) or 'sister's child' (*marlangi*). However, when people discussed relations between *individuals*, they distinguished MF and MFZ from mother and mother's brother as *mamingi*. The same applied to the mother's mother's group—in some contexts people distinguished *rambarr* or *wolmingi* (MMBS and MMBD) from *gayingi* (MM/MMB). However, all patrilineal descendants of one's father's mother's brother (*wayingi*) were *wayingi* or *marringi* (FM) regardless of context. The implication of this 'skewed' terminology for marriage seems to be that men could marry a woman of an adjacent generation as well as of their own generation and the alternate generation in the opposite moiety, increasing the range of potential spouses.

Consistent with the extension of kin terms, Ngarinyin people and their neighbours projected kinship and marriage relations onto patri-groups as wholes. From the point of view of a person in a particular patri-group, other patri-groups were classified as 'mother's mothers', 'mother's fathers', 'father's mothers', 'father's fathers', 'women's children', and 'women's daughters' children'. People of a given patri-group regarded some groups as wife-yielders, some as daughter-receivers, some as wives' mothers (*wolmingi*). A man's 'wives' mothers' were in a 'mother's mother's' patri-group designated as wife-yielders.

Marriage

As among Sandbeach people, a person had to marry someone of a different patri-group to their own, and of the opposite patri-moiety. The ideal marriage took place between a man and a woman whom he classified as 'father's mother' (*marringi*), but not his own father's mother of course: The category included people of his own, adjacent, and alternating generations, preferably from a group classified as a wives' group. As a consequence of the skewing rules, potential partners included people of genealogical generations other than one's own. A man's FMBD, FMBSD, FMBSSD, and so on, close and distant, were all his *marringi*. A man could also claim the daughter of his wife's brother as a second wife—she too was his 'father's mother'. People seem to have had a degree of choice as to how close a relative to marry, at least in the case of a man marrying his 'father's mother'. Elkin recorded no marriages between a man and his close FMBSD, whereas Blundell recorded two.[37]

A marriage between a man and a woman of his father's mother's group repeated the marriage link between the two patri-groups two generations on. Because of the skewed terminology, this link occurred in alternating generations in the husband's group, but could be in adjacent generations, or after a two- or three-generation gap, in the wive's group. In an alternative type of marriage, a man married a second cross cousin on his mother's side ('MMBDD') who was not his FMBSD. A man was not supposed to marry a person of his own mother's patri-group, although marriage to a distant 'mother' (*ngadji*) attracted only mild sanctions, as did marriage between first cross cousins (FZS and MBD) and between a distantly related 'mother's brother' and 'sister's daughter'. Ngarinyin people and their neighbours discouraged men from exchanging sisters.

According to Love and Elkin, it was a girl's father, the potential husband's *waiingi* (FMB), who bestowed her on a young man, in cooperation with the young man's father, but women would certainly have played a role in marriage arrangements. Love writes that an important old man was likely to be favoured as a daughter's husband over a young man.

The man chosen to be the husband entered 'upon a long period, even a life-long period, of indebtedness to his future father-in-law'.[38] Love describes the kinds of gifts the man would give: for his wife's father, kangaroo fat, new spears, belts and ornaments, honey gathered by his mother, and possibly (in the colonial era) a new billycan bought in Broome; for his wife's mother, kangaroo meat and other gifts. She made gifts of hair string in return. A man also owed services to his wife's brother, who would have looked after him during his initiation. In Love's judgement, the girl went to her husband's camp at about the age of ten, and there the older wives instructed her.

Sometimes a younger brother inherited an elder brother's widow much older than himself. A man could also inherit his father's father's (or father's father's brother's) widow, but not of course his actual father's mother. In many cases a young man's first marriage was to an older man's widow.

In the early decades of the twentieth century, most older men had two wives, but one had four wives, and another had seven (most of whom were young, some acquired through leviratic marriage). Comparatively, then, the level of polygyny was high, and this implies a considerable average age difference between spouses, which anecdotal evidence bears out.[39]

Men often quarrelled and fought over women, and women over men. Frequent love affairs, as well as elopements, took place between young men and the wives of older men. Some older men treated their young wives violently, according to Love, although Lommel and Redmond stress the supportive relations that developed between spouses.

As Blundell and Layton point out, the net result of men generally marrying their 'father's mother', and of the prohibition of a man's marriage to a woman of his mother's patri-group, was that men of each patri-group had to get wives from at least two other patri-groups, and women of each patri-group married men of at least two others. In practice, each patri-group had most of its marriage links to between two and five other patri-groups.[40]

Two important features of the resulting network stand out. One is the asymmetry of the marriage exchanges between patri-groups: women's marriages 'flowed' in one direction between patri-groups, linking them in chains and circles. (Eighty per cent of marriages in Blundell's genealogies conformed to ideal relations between patri-groups.) Alternative and 'wrong' marriages led to some reciprocal marriage relations between patri-groups, however. So did the fact that some groups consisted of more than one lineage and a person applied different terms to people in each lineage. (For example, a person's 'mother's mother's' patri-group might include people who were their 'father's fathers' and 'fathers' and the sisters of these men.) The other important feature is that patri-group countries of the same moiety clustered together to form intersecting swathes of country. People of each group married people of groups in the opposite moiety, whose countries were usually close (although the country of other patri-groups often came in between). Ngarinyin people also expressed marriage as an inter-moiety exchange, represented in myths.

The high level of polygyny among Ngarinyin people and their neighbours would have led to the fast growth of some patri-groups, while others, less successful, would have quickly declined. Patri-groups in the first decades of the twentieth century had up to 35 members, although introduced disease may already have affected fertility.[41]

'Father's mother' marriage was one of the conditions for the high level of polygyny recorded in the region. Marriage between a man and his FMBSD tended to reproduce the average age difference between potential spouses down the generations (this also happens with matrilateral cross-cousin marriage, as we shall see in the next case study). I surmise that the prior claims of the older brother of a set of siblings with rights in women as *marringi* ('father's mothers'), in conjunction with leviratic and other modes of marriage, resulted in some such men being able to marry many wives. It may be that a highly polygynous man's sons' sons were themselves potentially more polygynous than others. A grandson could look to the patri-groups of his several 'father's mothers' for wives, as well as inheriting his father's father's widow. If so, polygyny tended to be reproduced down the generations, as among Yolngu people.[42]

Yolngu people

Yolngu kinship and marriage systems resembled those of the Ngarinyin people and their neighbours in several ways—notably in the polygyny and asymmetrical exchange—but with an even higher level of polygyny.

The classification of kin

The Yolngu social universe consisted wholly of people related in the idiom of kinship (*gurruṯu*), by contrast with 'strangers' (*mulkuru*). Like the people from the other regions, Yolngu people distinguished between 'full' (*dhangang*), 'partial' (*marr-gangga*), and 'distant' (*barrku*) kin, and assessed the quality of relatedness along a dimension of distance.[43]

Table 6.10 Yolngu kin terms

Generation	Mother's 1	Own 2	Mother's 3	Own 4	Mother's 5	Own (father's) 6	Mother's 7	Patri-moiety Line
PPP								
PP	waku MMM/MMMB	ga:thu MMF/MMFZ FFM/FFMB			dhuway FFZH/FFZHB	gurrung FFFZDC		
P	mumalkur ngathiwalkur MMMBD MMMBS WMM WMMB MMBW	ma:ri MMB MM WMF WMFZ	waku MFF/MFFZ FMF/FMFZ	ga:thu FFF/FFFB/FFFZ	waku FFZC FZHZ/ FZHB/FZH dhuway FZC/MFZDC H/HB/HZ	gutharra FFZDC FZDH gurrung FZDC wDH	dhuway FFZDDH	
Own	nga:ndi ngapipi 'M' 'MB' MMBSW galay 'MBC' 'WWZ/WB'	mukul maralkur rumaru MMBS MMBD WMB WM	mumu ngathi FW/FMZ MF/MFB MFZ FMB nga:ndi ngapipi M/MZ MB WF galay MBC/MMBDC W/WZ/WB	ma:ri'mu FF/FFB/FFZ mukul ba:pa ba:pa F/FB FZ yapa wa:wa Z Ego eB yukuyuku ySb	waku wC/ZC/FZSC mDH gaminyarr wSC/mDC mSDH mSDHB	gutharra wDC/ZDC FZDSC mukul ba:pa ba:pa wDSS 'FZ' 'F/FB' wDSD	waku FZDDH dhumun.gur FZDDC wDDH/ZDDH 'WMM/WMMB' nga:ndi ngapipi FZDDSD/S 'M' 'MB'	
C		ma:ri ngapipi MMBSD MMBSS WMFZ WMF	nga:ndi ngapipi MBSD MBSS mSW WF mSWB galay MBSSC W/WB mSSW/WB	ga:thu mC/BC MBDC/FZSC marratja mSC/BSC MBSDC	waku wSSC/mSDC/ mDSC			
CC		mukul maralkur rumaru MMBSSS MMBSSD WMB WM						
CCC								mukul maralkur rumaru FZDDDD/S 'WM' 'WMB'

The 'Karadjeri-like' form of the Yolngu terminology combined some features of both Kariera and Aranda terminologies (Table 6.10).[44] Like the Kariera terminologies, the Yolngu kinship terminology classified FM and MFZ together, and MF and FMB together, but it distinguished MM/MMB from FF/FFZ. And it made more distinctions among cousins than the previous terminologies. Parallel cousins were still merged with siblings, but—importantly for marriage—cross cousins on the mother's side (matrilateral cross cousins, or *galay*) differed from those on the father's side (*dhuway*). The matrilateral cross cousins of one's matrilateral cross cousins, 'siblings' in the other terminologies (except those of the Ngarinyin and their neighbours), were 'mother's mothers' and MMBs (*ma:ri*). A man could only legitimately marry his *galay*, and a woman had to marry her *dhuway*. Certain other kin were appropriate as lovers but not spouses.

With the addition of certain other kinds of kin, Yolngu kin classification arranges the kin terms into five 'lines' traced through men, or, with additional terms in some regions, seven lines. Taking just the terms in the grandparent and grandchild generations the lines are as follows:

1 MMMBD (*mumalkur*) and MMMBS (*ngathiwalkur*); not distinguished from relatives in line 3 in some regions
2 MM/MMB (*ma:ri*) and descendants through males
3 FM/MFZ (*mumu*), MF/FMB (*ngathi*), and descendants through males
4 FF/FFZ (*ma:ri'mu*) and descendants through males
5 wSC, ZSC (*gaminyarr*), and his or her fathers (*waku*) and father's fathers
6 wDC, ZDC (*gutharra*), and his or her fathers (*gurrung*) and father's fathers
7 FZDDC (*dhumun.gur*); not distinguished from relatives in line 1 in some regions.

The women to whom the terms in line 1 are applied (on the right in Table 6.10) were ideally the wives of males of the same generation, to whom Ego applied terms from line 2; the women in line 2 were ideally the wives of males of line 3; and so on. Each woman's 'husband' in the diagram was her patrilateral cross cousin (FZS, MFZDS) and each man's 'wife' was his matrilateral cross cousin (MBD, MMBDD, to his right in Table 6.10). People also traced three sequences of terms through women, cutting across the patrilineal 'lines' of terms. These named the relatives involved in marriage negotiations and exchanges. In a distinct feature of Yolngu kin classification, linked to potential marriage claims, certain kin terms were repeated in alternate generations in the male line—the 'alternate generations agnates' (AGA) feature. This widens the field of a man's potential marriage partners to include cross cousins two generations down. For example, a man's *galay* includes MBSSD as well as MBD.[45]

Strict patri-moiety exogamy ensured that a person would find certain kin only in his own patri-moiety (the even-numbered lines above) and others only in the opposite moiety. A man and his potential wife's mother were of the same patri-moiety, while spouses belonged to opposite patri-moieties, as in some other regions. As elsewhere, brother and sister avoided contact, as did people in a daughter's husband–wife's parent relationship. A distantly related 'mother's mother's brother' (*ma:ri*) and 'sister's daughter's son' (*gutharra*) were in a 'joking' relation, obliged to exchange obscene jokes about each other. Like Western Desert people, Yolngu people addressed older relatives (such as their father or mother's brother) with the respect term *mori* (Yirritja moiety) or *malu* (Dhuwa moiety).

As with Ngarinyin people and their neighbours, patri-groups, their countries, and their sacra lay in kin relations to each other as wholes—one group was the 'mother' and 'wife' group of certain other groups of the opposite moiety, the mother's mother's group of groups of the same moiety, and so on. Furthermore, groups as a whole were related to individuals, so that some patri-groups were a person's 'mother' groups (ngandi-pulu), some his 'mother's mother' groups (ma:ri-pulu), and so on. Conversely, a person was the waku (woman's child) of his mother groups, the gutharra of his MM groups, and so on.[46]

Marriage

Unlike most of the other peoples, Yolngu people preferred marriage between genealogically *close* cross cousins.[47] Such cousins belonged, by implication, to patri-groups whose countries were geographically close and of opposite patri-moieties. A marriage contract (wawun.guma, meaning 'promise a wife') could involve negotiations among relatives across several generations and between several lineages, so that there would be a long span of time between the making of the contract and its fulfilment. Exchange obligations, particularly on the part of the potential husband, lasted many years.

A young man and the people who helped arrange his marriage, such as his father and his mother's mother's brother (ma:ri), had a choice of strategies. He had a strong claim to galay of his mother's patri-group—the daughters of his mother's brothers. So the man could negotiate with his mother's close brother (ngapipi, gawal) and mother's brother's wife (mukul rumaru) for their daughter as a wife. He also had a strong claim to his close mukul rumaru (MMBD, MMMBDD) as wives' mothers. They were the daughters of his mother's mother's brothers (ma:ri), but not necessarily wives of his actual or even close mother's brothers. If the man followed this strategy, his MMB (ma:ri), as the 'father' of the man's potential wives' mothers, was a key mediator between him and his potential in-laws.

As Warner points out, a young man's father and brothers might have taken part in the negotiations on his behalf, and indeed sometimes a father took the young man's promised wife first, then handed her on. A short ceremony sealed the marriage contract: the future husband marked the future mother-in-law on her belly with nasal sebum. In return for the promise of a wife, the future husband had to provide gifts and services to his future affines, both before and after the wife had matured and they had begun to share a hearth (see Chapter 11 on distribution).

The system was capable of even greater elaboration. By a neat trick, a man could arrange for the bestowal of a sister's daughter's daughter on his ngathiwalkur (MMMBS), whose sister's daughter's daughter he had married, closing the circle between the two groups.[48]

Yolngu people grounded marriage in ancestral law in a particularly vivid way. The ideal kin relations between patri-groups came about because of repeated marriages between such groups down the generations. In Yolngu doctrine, marriages 'followed' the kin relations between patri-groups, their countries, and their sacred objects— 'marriage follows the rangga' (sacred objects). Men looked to people of their 'mother' country and sacred object for wives, and looked to people of their *ma:ri* ('mother's mother') country and sacred objects for wives' mothers.

Other ways of marrying included elopement, the levirate, and raiding. But elopement seems not to have been anything like as common or accepted as among Kǔnai people. Sometimes a young widow went to her former husband's son if they were not too closely related.

In all this, a potential wife, because of her youth, had little control of her destiny. Women gained more power in marriage negotiations as older widows, however, and as potential wives' mothers.

Yolngu people had one of the highest levels of polygyny recorded for Australian Aborigines—up to 26 concurrent wives (Warner recorded 17, Thomson 26). As with the Ngarinyin people and their neighbours, the oldest of a group of brothers with the same matrilateral connections had prior claims on their *galay* (MBD, MMBDD) as wives, and indeed older brothers tended to be the most polygynous. Sons of polygynous men were helped by having many 'mothers' (father's wives), to whose groups they could look for wives, although they had the strongest claims in their actual mothers' groups.

Warfare undoubtedly had an effect on the male population, but it was the average age difference between husbands and wives that made polygyny possible; it was about 13 years in the mid-1970s. As with Ngarinyin people and their neighbours, the demographic properties of the Yolngu system tended to ensure that the women to whom a group of brothers had the strongest marriage claims tended to be of an appropriate age, so that the average age difference tended to be reproduced down the generations.[49]

Men tended to marry into the same groups as their fathers (for they married their mother's 'brother's' daughter), and many marriages linked one patri-group to only one or two other patri-groups in the main, forming strong alliances. But many patri-groups consisted of more than one distinct lineage (tracing descent from a common ancestor). In practice, women of a particular lineage tended to marry men of more than one lineage and of more than one patri-group, so the resulting pattern was complex.

When mapped onto patri-groups, the affinal network included circles among some groups, long open chains, and reciprocal links between larger patri-groups with several lineages, between which the marriage network zig-zagged back and forth. But the affinal network did not have a uniform density. People of two inland Yolngu groups studied by Neville White married each other in 75% of cases. Only 2% of recorded marriages linked them to 'coastal' groups; the remaining 23% of marriages were presumably to people of other inland groups.[50]

The high level of Yolngu polygyny had implications for local exchange networks (see Chapter 12) and the dynamics of patri-groups. Very high polygyny combined with the patrifilial recruitment of groups tended to result in some patri-groups growing very quickly—especially if highly polygynous sons followed highly polygynous fathers—while others declined. Yolngu patri-groups at and around Milingimbi in the 1920s had up to 70 members according to Warner (although identifying discrete Yolngu patri-groups consistently is not straightforward).[51]

The result was the existence of marked military and political inequalities among patri-groups. Since a powerful group could press its marriage claims more effectively than a lesser one, this difference in turn implied the ability to reproduce those inequalities, at least for a while. Yolngu history includes some accounts of expansionist individuals, fighting for the country of other groups, and their women. This kind of aggression was linked to competition between men for wives; the high level of polygyny among some men increased this competition.

Comparisons and conclusions

I will now sum up some of the similarities and differences between these modes of kinship and marriage. Marriage took the form of an exchange—either the exchange of goods and support in return for a spouse or the direct exchange of persons as spouses. Commentators on Aboriginal marriage have viewed such exchanges as a relationship between individuals and small groups of kin, as well as a relationship between larger groups and categories.

In some regions at least, people described marriage as an exchange between groups and categories such as moieties, sections, and patri-groups, or even between countries, one country 'giving' women to another. However, ethnographies such as L.R. Hiatt's *Kinship and Conflict*, which describes negotiations, make it clear that the arrangement of marriages involved individuals and their close kin. Nevertheless, to the extent that it was enforced, the exogamy of moieties and groups placed constraints on individual choice, and channelled particular marriages. Table 6.11 summarises exchange relations in the seven regions.

Table 6.11 Marriage exchange between groups and categories

People	Patri-moiety reciprocity	Matri-moiety reciprocity	Generation-moiety endogamy	Semi-moiety reciprocity	Matri-group reciprocity	Patri-group reciprocity	Patri-group asymmetry	Cross-generation exchange
Kŭnai								
Pitjantjatjara			✓					✓
Yuwaaliyaay		✓			✓			
Sandbeach	✓							
Wiil/Minong		✓		✓		✓		
Ngarinyin	✓						✓	✓
Yolngu	✓					✓ (Larger groups)	✓	✓ (ZDD)

Looking at individual transactions, sister exchange occurred among Kŭnai, Pitjantjatjara, and Yuwaaliyaay people, and it may have occurred among Sandbeach and Wiil/Mịnong people. Sister exchange contravened marriage norms in the asymmetric systems of the Ngarinyin and Yolngu, but in the Yolngu system the exchange of sisters' daughters' daughters sometimes occurred.

Infant bestowal is commonly reported—among Pitjantjatjara, Yuwaaliyaay, Wiil and Mịnong, Sandbeach, Ngarinyin, and Yolngu people. Pre-natal bestowal occurred in all these societies except the Yuwaaliyaay (where it may have gone unreported).

Because of ethnographer bias and over-generalisation, in most of the cases it is hard to judge just who was usually involved in making marriage arrangements. Many ethnographers simply assert that a woman's father bestowed her on a man. The kin categories involved certainly differed. In at least five of the case studies, the wife's father was 'mother's brother' of the daughter's husband, and the wife's mother was his 'father's sister' (Yuwaaliyaay, Pitjantjatjara, Wiil/Mịnong, Sandbeach, and Yolngu). Pitjantjatjara marriage stands out in that a young man's circumciser bestowed a wife on him (or arranged for the bestowal to be made)—a common Western Desert pattern. In the case of the Ngarinyin and their neighbours, bestowal also had links to ceremony, for a male initiate's future wife's brother looked after him in the ceremony. The wife's father was usually the husband's 'father's mother's brother's son'. These men were somewhat distant relatives among Kŭnai, Pitjantjatjara, Yuwaaliyaay, Sandbeach, and probably Mịnong people, but could be close among Ngarinyin and Yolngu people. Certain kin had an important mediating role in marriage arrangements—a man's father's mother's brother among Ngarinyin people and a man's mother's mother's brother (*ma:ri*) among Yolngu people.

The planning of marriage among Kŭnai people was often an immediate affair, in the case of elopement, or short-term, in sister bestowal and exchange, but it was a longer-term affair in daughter bestowal. A singular feature of Yolngu marriage arrangments was the involvement of long chains of relatives in bestowal: a wife's mother might be bestowed on her potential daughter's husband. Over an even longer period, a marriage might complete the exchange of sisters' daughters' daughters between two men.

Marriage and social networks

The distinct forms of kin classification and marriage gave rise to very different social networks. *Shifting webs* resulted from marriages to distant relatives, precluding the repetition of a marriage tie in the next generation. In the resulting network a patri-group had links to many other groups, shifting at each generation. Kŭnai localities, Pitjantjatjara cognatic kin groups and Sandbeach patri-groups were embedded in this kind of web, complicated by reciprocal marriages between them.

Reciprocal exchanges occurred between Yuwaaliyaay matri-groups, between Wiil and Mịnong patri-groups (with their associated semi-moieties), and between the larger Yolngu patri-groups. Lévi-Strauss referred to this form as 'restricted exchange'.[52]

In the marriage networks of Ngarinyin people and their neighbours, *asymmetrical marriages* linked patri-groups in chains and loops, with a small percentage of reciprocal marriages. This is 'generalised exchange' in Lévi-Strauss's scheme. The Yolngu marriage network consisted of asymmetric links between lineages and small patri-groups, as well as reciprocal marriage ties between larger groups. The links formed long, open chains, loops, and circles among six lineages (closed by ZDD exchange). We saw that large patri-groups, joined by many marriages down the generations, formed powerful alliances.

These differences in marriage patterns had important consequences for the dynamics of groups and exchange networks.

Kinship, marriage, and social dynamics

The dynamics of groups with a high level of polygyny probably were very different from those of groups with low polygyny. A high level of polygyny among some men (three or four wives) would have enhanced patri-group growth somewhat. Kǔnai people had a rather low level of polygyny, and may not have had land-holding patri-groups. Pitjantjatjara people and their neighbours did not have patri-groups or matri-groups, although polygyny, in conjunction with men's attempts to affiliate sons to country to which they were strongly attached, would have had an effect. Yuwaaliyaay people and their neighbours also seem to have been attached to country on a number of bases, including place of birth, and were organised into totemic matri-groups. The kind of competition and group dynamics associated with a high level of polygyny were not a feature of Yuwaaliyaay politics and economy. I am incline to suggest that polygyny did nothing to increase the resources of matrilineal groups, explaining their low level of polygyny. Tiwi people, however, with their matrilineal 'clans', are famous for their very high levels of polygyny.[53]

An association between high to very high polygyny and asymmetric marriage results from the relatively predictable age difference between potential spouses in these systems, the restriction of marriage claims to a rather narrowly defined category or categories, and the primary rights of older brothers in relation to women who a group of brothers had a claim on as wives. The high polygyny of Ngarinyin patri-groups gave rise to groups with a wide range of sizes (anything up to 35 in the 1920s, but the Kimberley had suffered population decline by then), though not apparently reaching Yolngu levels. A very high level of polygyny among Yolngu people resulted in very fast growth and decline of patri-groups; some groups grew very large (up to 70 in the late 1920s) and competed with each other for wives and for land. As (generally speaking) the oldest of a set of male uterine siblings, a highly polygynous man was also usually a patri-group leader with control over the group's sacra. Such men occupied key positions in exchange networks.

Environmental conditions for polygyny

High and very high polygyny occurred in the rich tropical environments of the north, with their relatively high population densities, especially on large habitable islands. Levels of polygyny comparable to Yolngu levels occurred among Warnindilyakwa people of Groote Eylandt and Tiwi people of Melville and Bathurst Islands. While a rich environment and a relatively high population density appear to have been pre-requisites for these high levels of polygyny (and the resulting demographic, social, and economic dynamics), they are obviously not sufficient conditions. This is shown by the case of marriage among Gijingarli people, western neighbours of Yolngu people living in a very similar environment but with an Aranda-like kinship terminology. They had only a low level of polygyny (up to three wives concurrently) and their patri-groups were clusters of small lineages. The environment and resources enjoyed by Kŭnai people were similarly fruitful and diverse but polygyny appears to have been low. All of this suggests that a relatively high population density and comparative sedentism were preconditions of high and very high levels of polygyny, but that particular institutional systems were also required—including an asymmetical marriage system in conjunction with marriage bestowal and the levirate. Chapter 8 outlines other institutional conditions for polygyny, namely age-related authority based on the control of religious knowledge.

I have already alluded to the importance of kinship in organising economic relations and practices; Part III of the book explores this aspect in more detail. We shall see that the networks and dynamics associated with marriage are reflected in exchange relations more generally.

Further reading

Anthropological debates about Aboriginal kinship and marriage have revolved around, among other things, the nature of 'descent' in Aboriginal systems, the structure of exchange relations, the relationship between age and polygyny, the politics of bestowal, the functions of 'marriage classes', and the emotional tone of relatedness. For an overview of issues and approaches, see my chapter in *Social Anthropology and Australian Aboriginal Studies*, edited by R. M. Berndt and Bob Tonkinson (1988).

Claude Lévi-Strauss's *The Elementary Structure of Kinship* (1969), on marriage as exchange, generated a great deal of discussion and debate. Works with a specific focus on Aboriginal kinship systems include Warren Shapiro's *Social Organization in Aboriginal Australia* (1979) and David Turner's *Australian Aboriginal Social Organization* (1980). Harold Scheffler's *Australian Kin Classification* (1978) offers a structural-semantic analysis. The variety of Aboriginal kinship systems are outlined in textbooks by Kenneth Maddock (*Australian Aborigines: A Portrait of their Society*, 1982) and the Berndts (*The World of the First Australians*, 1981, reprinted by Aboriginal Studies Press in 1996). Among recent ethnographies, *Pintupi Country: Pintupi Self,* by Fred Myers (1986), explores how kinship relates to the more general field of social relatedness and its cultural content among Pintupi people.

The classic works on 'gerontocratic polygyny' in Australia are Hart and Pilling's *The Tiwi of North Australia* (1960) and Frederic Rose's *Classification of Kin, Age Structure and Marriage amongst the Groote Eylandt Aborigines* (1960). Les Hiatt reviews the topic in his article 'Maidens, males and Marx' (1985).

Notes

1. On the extension of the kin universe see Dousset (2002a), Lévi-Strauss (1969), Radcliffe-Brown (1931: 44), and Maddock (1982: 56).

2. See Scheffler (1978) and Schneider (1984) on the applicability of the term 'kinship'.

3. See Dousset (2002a) on the 'relational triangle'.

4. On 'performative kinship' see Goody (1982) and Sansom (1988).

5. See Elkin (1938–40) and Radcliffe-Brown (1931) on the types of kinship system.

6. See Myers (1986) on the emotional content of Pintupi kin relations.

7. On avoidance rules see, for example, Bulmer (1994: 10–11; Papers, MV B10 F5 xm933: 10), Hiatt (1982), Howitt (1904: 279), Love (1936: 127–8), Lucich (1968: 34), and Warner (1937: 65, 101–2, 116).

8. On *mirrirri* see Burbank (1985), who refers to other contributors to a lengthy debate, including Makarius and Hiatt.

9. See Meggitt (1965) on polygyny and age differences.

10. On Kŭnai 'strangers' see Bulmer (Papers, letter to Howitt, MV B1 F4 sm77 11 January 1878).

11. See Howitt (1904: 169) on Kŭnai kin terms.

12. On Kŭnai marriage see Bulmer (in Curr 1887: 546; 1994: 8–10, 15, 19–20; Papers, MV B1 F4 xm77, 78 10 October 1878; letter to Howitt, xm98 undated; MV B10 F5 xm922: 46), Howitt (1880: 199–204, 220; 1904: 214, 272, 275–7), and Smyth (1878: 46).

13. The sources on Kŭnai polygyny are Thomas (Thomas papers, Box 14); blanket distribution records of the Tyers district 1852; Bulmer (Papers, MV B10 F5 xm922, 931: 18; 1994: 10, 17; letter to Howitt, MV B1 F4 xm82 20 April 1880); and Coral Dow (pers. com.).

14. See Howitt (1904: 214, 272) on marriage networks. On 'dispersed affinal alliances' see McKinley (1971: 411).

15. For accounts of the Pitjantjatjara kin universe see Dousset (2002b), Elkin (1938–40: 217), and Scheffler (1978: 89); and see Myers (1986: 88–101) on 'one countrymen'.

16. On the hierarchical component of Western Desert kin terms see Myers (1986: 223).

17. On the Pitjantjatjara kin terminology and other Western Desert terminologies see Dousset (2002a; 2002b), Elkin (1938–40), Myers (1986), and Tonkinson (1991).

18. The sources on Pitjantjatjara marriage include R. M. and C. H. Berndt (1945: 113), Dousset (2002a; 2000b), Elkin (1938–40: 216–9, 341–3), and Tonkinson (1991: 64–5). On Western Desert sister exchange see Tonkinson (1991: 64), Elkin (1938–40: 217), and Dousset (pers. com.).

19. See R. M. and C. H. Berndt (1945: 50), Long (1970), Munn (1965), and Yengoyan (1967) on Western Desert polygyny; see Myers (1986: 175–6) and Sackett (1976) on networks.

20. On Yuwaaliyaay concepts of strangers see Parker (1905: 33).

21. Radcliffe-Brown (1931: 231) classified the system of the Gamilaraay ('Kamilaroi') and their neighbours, including the Yuwaalaraay ('Yualarai'), as of the 'Aranda type', on the grounds that Gamilaraay prescribed marriage between a man and his MMBDD and that the kinship system articulated with a four-section system. But the Wangaaybuwan system fits Radcliffe-Brown's 'Kumbaingeri type', which in Scheffler's view (1978) differs little from the 'Kariera type'; see Beckett (1959). Yuwaaliyaay kin terminology is incorrectly designated as a 'generational' system in Keen (2002), which relied too heavily on incomplete records.

22. The sources on Yuwaaliyaay kin classification include Laves (1929–32), Parker (1905), Ridley (1875; 1886), and Williams (1976).

23. On Yuwaaliyaay marriage see Howitt (1904: 217), Parker (1905: 55–6, 58, 79, 81), on Pakaantji see Teulon (in Curr 1886, vol. 2: 196–7).

24. On the extent of the Wiil/Miṉong kin universe see Bates (1985: 193,197).

25. See Barker (1992: 25 April, 13 July, 15 July 1830, cited in Green 1989: 20, 22, 47), Bates (1985: 84, 87), and Hassell (1936: 683) on Wiil/Miṉong kin classification. On avoidance see Bates (1985: 153–4).

26. See Barker (1992: 2 August, 30 November 1830, cited in Green 1989), Bates (1985: 84–5), and Nind (1831). Bates records many secondary terms current in other districts, and age-related terms such as 'father's elder brother' and 'mother's sister's older sons'.

27. For sources on Wiil/Miṉong marriage see Barker (1992: 1 January, 23, 25 April 1830, cited in Green 1989: 20, 48), Barker (1992: 31 January 1831, cited in Le Souëf 1993: 11), Bates (1985: 83), Goldsworthy (in Curr 1886, vol. 1: 338), Hassell (1936: 682–4), Le Souëf (1993: 16–21), and Nind (1831: 37–9, 44). On marriage exchange see Nind (1831: 38).

28. On Wiil and Miṉong polygyny see Barker (1992: 26 January, 3 February 1830); Clark (1842); Collie (1979 [1834]); Green (1989: 31, 71), Hassell (1936: 682), Le Souëf (1993: 9, 19–20), and Nind (1831: 38–9).

29. See Chase (1980b: 169–70, 175–6) on the Sandbeach kin universe.

30. On Sandbeach kin classification see Chase (1980), Scheffler (in Thomson 1972; 1978: 150–1, 169), and Thomson (1972).

31. A woman's senior cross cousin's child was her 'younger sibling' (*ya'athu*) and her junior cross cousin's child was her 'sister's daughter's child' (*kamichu*). Another extension rule applied to the children of male cross cousins, reclassified two generations up as 'mother's younger sister' or 'mother's younger brother'.

32. On avoidance and the respect vocabulary see Chase (1980: 177, 179).

33. Sandbeach marriage is described by Chase (1980: 175–7), Scheffler (in Thomson 1972: 9), Thomson (Papers, MV File 175, 206, 213 undated, 1935; 1972: 6–8); on polygyny see Thomson (Papers, MV File 213 undated, File 213, 1935, File 215; 1972: 7).

34. The quotation is from Thomson (Papers, MV file 213 n.d.).

35. In genealogies collected by Athol Chase (1980: 176), nearly a third of all marriages (nine) were between coastal and inland patri-groups and just over two thirds (21) were between coastal groups. Thomson's records of individuals, their patri-

groups, and their totems reveal some of these multiple affiliations (Thomson Papers, MV File 215). Ben Smith informed me about the Ayapathu concept of 'background' (pers. com.).

36 On kin classification among Ngarinyin and their neighbours see Elkin (1932: 315; 1954: 70), Love (1936: 94), Lucich (1968: 99–100, 102–3), and Rumsey (1981). On the application of kin terms to patri-groups see Blundell and Layton (1978: 234) and Rumsey (1981).

37 On Ngarinyin and Worrorra marriage see Blundell and Layton (1978: 234), Elkin (1932: 314; unpublished field report, cited in Scheffler 1978: 406), Love (1936: 95–6, 99, 129), Lucich (1968: 48), and Redmond (2001b: 90–123).

38 The quotation is from Love (1936: 99).

39 On the effects of polygyny see Love (1936: 31–6, 95, 100).

40 See Blundell and Layton (1978: 231–2, 235, 237), Lucich (1968: 46), and Scheffler (1978: 407) on marriage networks.

41 On patri-group size see Blundell (1980: 107).

42 If the average age difference between a father and child was 40 years, and the average age difference between a mother and child was 25 years, so that wives were 15 years younger than their husbands on average, then the average age difference between a man and his FMBSD can be computed as follows: Ego – F (+ 40 years), F – FM (+ 25), FMB – FMBS (– 40), FMBS – FMBSD (– 40), with a total of –15 years, reproducing the average age difference between father and mother. My speculation about the claims of older brothers is extrapolated from Yolngu marriage practices.

43 On the Yolngu kin universe see Keen (1994: 80).

44 See Keen (1978: 102–6), Shapiro (1981: 52), and Warner (1937: 59) on Yolngu kin classification.

45 See Scheffler (1978) on extension rules in Aboriginal kin terminologies.

46 On kin relations among patri-groups and their countries see Keen (1994: 107–11).

47 On Yolngu marriage see Berndt (1965b), Shapiro (1981), and Warner (1937).

48 On the exchange of sisters' daughters' daughters see Shapiro (1968), Keen (1978: 113–6), and Morphy (1978).

49 For a model of the demographic properties of the Yolngu marriage system see Keen (1982). On the effects of warfare see Warner (1937: 157–8, 166–7).

50 See Keen (1978: 130), Shapiro (1981), Warner (1937: 28–9), White (1976), and White et al. (1990: 178) on Yolngu marriage networks.

51 See Warner (1958: 66) on polygyny. See Keen (1982) and Warner (1937: 17) on the size of Yolngu patri-groups.

52 On forms of marriage exchange see Lévi-Strauss (1969).

53 See Hart and Pilling (1960) on polygyny.

7

Cosmology and Quasi-technology

Introduction

Many of the totemic identities outlined in Chapter 5 had intimate connections with broader bodies of beliefs and doctrines—the cosmologies and cosmogonies that are the topic of this chapter. These are relevant to the organisation of economy in a variety of ways. First, they framed regional orders of 'law' that provided the foundations of social order. Second, they were implicated in the ownership of and control of access to land and waters and their resources. Third, people believed, on the basis of these doctrines, that they could tap ancestral and magical powers to enhance the supply of resources and their power to acquire resources. And fourth, many economic rights, obligations, prerogatives, and prohibitions were framed explicitly in terms of ancestral law.

'Cosmology' means the body of concepts and doctrines about the origins and properties of the world and its inhabitants. 'Cosmogony' refers specifically to doctrines about the origins of things. I shall refer to people's 'doctrines' as well as 'beliefs'. The anthropological use of the term 'beliefs' (or 'belief system') for propositions and facts generally accepted by a group raises the problem of whether people always believed their 'beliefs'. The word 'belief' connotes 'mental acceptance' of a proposition, statement, or fact as true; the word 'doctrine' implies a body of dogma and tenets that are taught and that have authoritative standing. Recent anthropological discussions of the relationship between the domain of explicit ideologies and the domain of tacit, taken-for-granted (or 'doxic') propositions are relevant here. This distinction mirrors that between doctrine, which may be deliberately manipulated and inculcated, and belief, which implies acceptance. The subtle inculcation of belief is a hegemonic practice underpinning relations of power.[1]

Features of Aboriginal cosmogonies and cosmologies

We shall see that ancestral doctrines across the seven regions share a number of features. Fundamental doctrines concerned creators who brought the present order of the world into being; they did not create the world out of nothing, but they did give it its present shape. These beings had the character of 'ancestors' and were referred to as the senior kin of living people. Their creative actions occurred in what John Rudder calls the 'temporal space' of long, long ago.

According to a very widespread conception, ancestors left traces of their actions, being, and powers in the land, waters, and sky, creating consubstantial links between people, country, and the sacred objects and ceremonies, which followed ancestral precedents. W. E. H. Stanner writes of the 'corporeal connection' between a person, totem and 'spirit home', a connection in which body, spirit, name, shadow, ancestral track, and totem all imply one another. Because of these consubstantial links, damage to a person's country could make the person sick, a country and its ancestors could recognise a person by their smell, and a person could have intuitive insight into the state of a country and its resources.[2]

People gained some of their connections to ancestors and country from a parent or grandparent, often through the male line, while others had a more individual cause, such as place of conception. According to a common stereotype, Aborigines were ignorant of physiological paternity, attributing conception to the entry into the mother of a 'spirit' or some such entity, who would be revealed to the father in a dream or other experience. But theories about procreation varied greatly: the widespread doctrines of 'spirit conception' were combined in various ways with views about the contribution of sexual relations to procreation.[3]

It is difficult to avoid the English word 'spirit' when translating Aboriginal concepts, but in some ways it is inappropriate. The pervasive contrast in Western thought between the 'material' and 'spiritual' is not shared by Aboriginal cosmologies. Aboriginal people have used metaphors such as 'shade', 'shadow', and 'image' to describe presences sensed and sometimes glimpsed. Such beings had a presence 'inside' or 'beneath' the water, soil, or rocks; they also dwelt inside the body and its substances, vivifying the individual. They were thought of as hidden rather than lacking material substance. Dangerous beings of the forest and caves, such as the Nargŭns of Gippsland, did not lack bodies. Furthermore, many objects and substances thought of as material in Western thought had some of the attributes of persons in Aboriginal cosmologies and ontologies, especially if regarded as ancestral substance.

The power to transform outward appearance is a ubiquitous feature of Aboriginal cosmologies. Ancestors possessed multiple identities, and turned from persons into animals, or transformed into the substance of the landscape. A ghost could change into a small beetle, or a sorcerer–magician turn into the form of his familiar.[4]

Law

As a very general feature of cosmologies and cosmogonies, the ancestors bestowed 'law'—the precepts and practices that shaped human social life—on the humans that followed them. Aboriginal languages did not have words that could be translated simply as 'law', for Aboriginal people did not have specialised legal systems. But something like this meaning is embedded in concepts such as the Western Desert word *tjukurrpa* and the Yolngu word *rom*, which means (among other things) 'the proper way'. Certainly many Aboriginal people now refer to their ancestral doctrines, precepts, and practices with the English word 'law'.

As instantiations of law, ceremonies—and their components of song, dance, designs, and objects—'followed' ancestral journeys and ancestral precedents. People of some regions literally followed the course of ancestral journeys across the country in their rituals. While people did speak to creator ancestors as well as other beings during rituals or when visiting an ancestral place, Aboriginal people did not 'worship' creator ancestors, and anything like 'prayer' is rarely described. (For an exception see the Yuwaaliyaay section below.) Rather, people identified with ancestors in mimetic dances, as well as in songs and narratives, following their actions and journeys. In doing so, they believed that they could tap into ancestral power, channelling it for their own purposes. It is these aspects that led some early commentators to deny to Aboriginal doctrines and rituals the status of 'religion'.[5]

Ancestors and the living (and one might include the dead) did form a 'moral community' akin to the 'church' of Émile Durkheim's universal theory of religion. However, Aboriginal cosmologies did not divide the world into absolute good and evil. As W. E. H. Stanner has shown, ancestors performed both good and bad, benign and dangerous acts. While the creator ancestors would punish wrong behaviour by causing some misfortune, they did not judge individuals and punish or reward them in an afterlife. Certainly some cosmologies warned of the risk of bringing a cataclysm about by violating dangerous ancestral places, but this was not the occasion for the judgement of souls. At death, a person's 'spirit' simply returned to the country whence it came, travelled to a land of the dead, or (in some doctrines) was reincarnated.[6] Indeed, Heather McDonald suggests that such concepts as sin and redemption belong to hierarchical societies rather than relatively egalitarian societies like Aboriginal ones. The living were related to the creator ancestors not as subjects of rulers but as junior to senior kin. A person asked their ancestors for help (e.g. to make hunting successful) and propitiated them with gifts.[7]

As Stanner has also pointed out, Aboriginal cosmologies were about origins rather than the future. Doctrines explained how the world had come to be as it was, with its principles for living according to ancestral precedent, and with powers bestowed on people for good or ill. As a result, people continually revised ancestral doctrines to account for existing realities and new relations.

Except for very brief descriptions of male initiation, a major gap in this book will be the complex body of ceremonies and religious symbolism of each region. The main reason for this omission is their complexity, and the fact that the ethnography is so uneven—very rich for northeast Arnhem Land; very skimpy for Gippsland and the southwest. R. M. Berndt has written a comparison of Aboriginal forms of religion across Australia.[8]

The connection with 'magic' and 'sorcery'

Aboriginal cosmologies modelled ancestral powers, as well as those to do with sorcery and magic, on what people believed to be the inherent qualities of bodily substances, especially blood, fat, and flesh; 'spirits' inhered in these substances and gave them their potency. In Aboriginal cosmologies and ontologies these substances had inherent qualities of potency that survived an individual's death, so that they were sources of power to be harnessed by the living. Aboriginal people also had doctrines about the intrinsic connections between a person and things thought to be a part of the person. These things included, first, objects and substances shed or excreted by the person, such as hair, faeces, urine, and sweat. Second were images and traces of the person, such as shadows, footprints, and iconic representations. Third were names; Aboriginal people did not (and many do not) consider the connection between a name and a person, object or place to be arbitrary and a matter of convention, but considered it to be intrinsic, something to be found or discovered if unknown. By the same token, people thought speaking and singing to be efficacious not only through people's understanding of the meaning of words but in a more direct, instrumental way. A sung spell, for example, supposedly worked whether the victim heard it or not. These are among the principles of magic that Sir James Frazer inferred from a global comparative study.[9]

Doctrines about the intrinsic connections between persons and their excuviae, images, and names, as well as doctrines about the power of words, formed the basis for practices referred to in the literature as 'magic' and 'sorcery' (or 'witchcraft'). But they also formed the basis of doctrines and beliefs about ancestral powers. According to such doctrines, a person could act on the traces left by someone, or on that person's name, in order to affect the person—to attract him or her as a lover or to make the person sick. Causality in relation to ancestors worked in the opposite direction. Ancestors created species and places by uttering their names as well as leaving traces, substances, and powers, and by giving birth. A person or group could act on the traces, substance, or images of an ancestor, or on an associated object, in order to tap ancestral power for themselves or direct it towards some other object or person. Individuals thought to have special connections with ancestors and other powerful beings, such as ghosts of the dead, could acquire extraordinary power themselves—power to travel far and wide when asleep, to journey to the realm of the dead in the sky, and to change shape. Others, too, might encounter recent or remote ancestors in dreams and visions. People also believed that they could gain power from the dead by, for example, taking in their soul or spirit.

While people certainly distinguished between the domain of shared ancestors and the domain of personal 'magical' powers, these were not unconnected. For example, some Kŭnai spirit familiars, which people believed capable of doing harm, were the users' inherited ancestral totems. Objects and totemic songs used in rituals could also be employed in healing, and threats of sorcery guarded the boundaries of religious secrecy. Aspects of religious practice, magic, and sorcery were, therefore, a kind of technology. People believed that through their use they could change people and things; the effects, however, differed from what was intended.

Sorcery and healing

The case studies will not contain details of sorcery beliefs or healing practices, so I will generalise here.

In all seven regions, experts of various kinds claimed to have magical powers. Sorcerers supposedly harmed their victims in a number of ways. They could insert stones or other objects into a victim, or extract a vital part or essence, such as the heart-blood (and the spirit along with it) or kidney fat. The sorcerer could act on a detached part of the victim, such as faeces, urine, or sweat, with heat, songs, and invocations of the person's name. Or the sorcerer could act on an image of the person, such as a painting or the person's footprint. Poisons included the ground-up bones of a dead person (among Yuwaaliyaay and Yolngu people). A sorcerer could remove the spirit of a person (Yuwaaliyaay sorcerers removed a person's 'dream-spirit', which travelled during sleep), or the spirit could become the sorcerer's familiar in the form of an animal or fish (Yolngu). In a common technique, a sorcerer pointed a stick or bone towards the victim while intoning and saying the victim's name. Ngarinyin magicians purportedly directed lightning at a victim, and invoked lighting to detect a killer. Yolngu sorcerers supposedly made a victim unconscious and then removed or damaged internal organs, replaced them with grass, and sutured the wound.

Healing techniques included blowing on the body, sucking out objects (such as pebbles, pieces of bone, and shell) that had been placed in the patient's body by a sorcerer, and expelling malevolent spirits—by, for example, chanting over the person (Kŭnai, Yuwaaliyaay, Pitjantjatjara). A healer would swing a powerful object such as a bullroarer over the person; use a powerful possum-fur string to remove pain (Kŭnai); or send a spirit familiar into the body (Yuwaaliyaay). Other techniques included massage and manipulation to restore the patient's 'life-force' (Pitjantjatjara) and the application of urine or under-arm sweat to the patient's body (Wiil and Mi̱nong). Everyday medicines that could be used by anyone included poultices, unguents, infusions, and inhalants made from herbs and fruits.

These are some of the very general features of Aboriginal cosmologies and beliefs; let us now turn to the case studies for some of the details and variations.

Kŭnai people

The major emphasis in Kŭnai cosmology and cosmogony was on the sky and the clouds, the home of the 'father' of Kŭnai people and of the ghosts of the dead.

Ancestors

According to recorded Kŭnai doctrines, Mungan-ngaua ('our father') taught people everything, gave them names, and instituted the Jerra-eil initiation ceremony for males. (The son of an ancestor called Tŭndun made paraphernalia for the ceremony.) When women 'betrayed' its secrets long ago, Mungan-ngaua sent the fire of Aurora Australis (the Southern Lights) and the sea inundated the land. The survivors among the people became *mŭk-Kŭnai* (eminent men) and Mungan–ngaua went up to the sky. A being named Bullum-baukan stole fire from Kŭnai people, but Crow and Swamp-hawk recovered it, then Bullum-baukan climbed up a cord of wallaby sinews into the sky.[10]

Mŭk-kŭnai and *mŭk-rukŭt* (eminent women) lived long ago in the form of animals, birds, and reptiles. Kŭnai people referred to them as their 'grandfathers' (*wehntwin*), whose living equivalents were *mŭk je-ak* (excellent flesh) in the shape of animals and birds. The more immediate predecessors of humans were the *ngulembra kŭnai* (literally 'front people'), who were intermediate between the ancestors and the living.

Myths about the ancestors had to do with origins, and with the establishment of the social order. For example, stories recounted the beginnings of marriage in a fight between Superb Warbler and Emu Wren (the gender totems). A myth about a quarrel between Eagle and Mopoke explained why mopokes lived in holes in trees, and why eagles sat in the treetops. Some stories told of a great flood: Frog drank all the water, which was then released when an eel made him laugh by dancing on his tail.

Ancestral traces

A few of the recorded Kŭnai stories describe events that resulted in a being's metamorphosis into stones or rocks. Stories about Pelican (Borŭn) follow on from the flood story, recounting how he rescued people from the flood but tried to keep a woman for himself. The woman escaped by a ruse, then Pelican became angry, painted himself with white clay ready to fight, and (in some versions) turned to stone. Rocks at Yerŭk (Wilsons Promontory) were once two bullroarers, left there by *mŭk-kŭnai*, and were said to be in a relationship of older to younger brother. When Dingo rebuked people for not giving him some of the fish they had caught, they turned to stone because they had heard the Dingo speak; the rocks stand in the water at Metung on Lake King (although one has been destroyed).[11]

Some stars bore the names of living people, which were also the names of totemic beings. For example, Alpha Centauri was the spirit Brewin, who caused the moon to rise and set each day. According to some Kŭnai men, the earth floated on the sea, and below it was another country inhabited by people. The sun travelled back to the east under the sea to the south, while the moon walked round after setting, to rise on the other side.

Other beings

Other beings, often dangerous but sometimes benign, were ever present in the forests and caves. *Nargŭn* were females believed to live in caves and to drag in unsuspecting people. *Nyol* were 'little people' who supposedly lurked in the caves around Murrindal, grasping the feet of passers-by and dragging them underground. Bullum-dut (also known as Baukan or Bullum-baukan) caused various afflictions, and Brewin, who was 'like the wind', caused common ailments. According to Kŭnai doctrines, the man Lohan lived with his wife Lohan-tuka in the hills at Wilsons Promontory (Yerŭk) in the southwest of Gippsland; like Joto-wara-wara he took care of people and made their country dangerous to strangers. Kŭnai people took the behaviour of many animals and birds, such as ravens (and including *je-ak*), as portents of danger.[12]

Conception and personal spirits

According to recent records, Kŭnai people attached particular value to the place where they were conceived. At death the soul left the body, as it did in sleep, and followed the path to the sky, or travelled to a place in the east where food was plentiful. Ghosts of the dead (*mrart*), dangerous when among the living, wandered in the country that they formerly inhabited. The dead had more benign aspects also: they communicated with the living in dreams and they revealed songs, dances, and other forms of knowledge to the living during sleep. Tulaba Billy McLeod told Howitt that his 'other father', Bruthen Mŭnji, visited him from time to time in his sleep, teaching him songs to guard against sickness and other dangers. Ghosts of the dead inhabited the sky, where they initiated certain men into secret rites and conducted *birraark* (shamans) up a path or rope to the clouds.[13]

Healers and other experts

Kŭnai healing, magic, and sorcery were the province of experts of many kinds. *Mŭlla-mullŭng* (sorcerers/healers), dangerous men believed to practice *kulut* (sorcery), possessed specific powers relating to their familiars. *Birraark* (shamans) dreamed new songs, helped conduct Jerra-eil initiation ceremonies, and conducted séances in which they invoked the spirits of the dead. Men claimed to become *birraark* in a number of ways—through encounters with ghosts of the dead while hunting, for example. In one case ghosts carried a person off after he dreamt of being a kangaroo participating in a dance.[14]

Apparently only men could become *mŭlla-mullŭng*, although women also practised healing techniques, and could become very influential. The healing techniques of a *mŭlla-mullŭng* included extracting objects from a patient's body and expelling malevolent spirits. Healers claimed to have gained their powers in dreams in which the ghost of an ancestor visited them, communicated harmful or protective songs and knowledge, and perhaps carried them to another place to impart techniques and give them powerful objects. A healer sang of his *je-ak* (personal totem), which was attributed with the power to heal particular ailments; for example, the curlew sandpiper song was appropriate for straightening sinews in diseases of the limbs. Healers could see a person's spirit, and could fly. They possessed both benign and destructive powers—to attack people and to counter attacks by others. Several kinds of object were thought to be powerful aids to the healer, including quartz crystals (*groggin*), round pebbles (*bulk*), and possum-fur string.

The many other kinds of expert included the *makeega* (seer), who protected dancers from dangerous objects, and the *bunjil-yenjin* (singers of love-magic songs). Individuals deployed objects and animals with supposed magical powers (such as ironbark spear-throwers, lace monitors, and snakes) in order to impress and intimidate others. One man claimed to command the west wind.

While Kŭnai people blamed the spirit Brewin for some illnesses, they generally attributed other kinds of sickness (perhaps more lingering, serious ones), as well as accidents, acts of violence, and death, to the influence of sorcery (*kulut*). (The supposed techniques of sorcery included the ones outlined in the introduction.) The relatives of a dead person might seek revenge, either by 'counter plotting' or secret murder.

Kŭnai people accorded power to the remains of the dead. Individuals carried with them the desiccated hands of deceased relatives suspended on a possum-fur string. The hands were believed to have the power to avert danger by warning of the approach of enemies, and to ward off dangers such as the Aurora Australis.[15]

The most direct link between magic and economy lay in rainmaking, which could also be used as a weapon. Rainmakers (*bunjil-willŭng*) of the various regions had responsibility for rains from the various quarters. People also credited them with the ability to bring thunder, and songs were revealed to them in dreams.[16]

Pitjantjatjara people

The doctrines of the Pitjantjatjara people and their neighbours in the Western Desert put less emphasis on the sky and more on ancestral traces in the country, as well as long ancestral journeys.

Ancestors

Closely related to 'dream', the word *tjukurrpa* denoted the creative time of the ancestors, a 'story', and 'ancestral law' in Western Desert languages.[17] In Munn's interpretation, Pitjantjatjara people and their neighbours divided time into two broad zones: *tjukurrpa*, the time of the ancestors, and *mularrpa*, the present and recent past of humans (*anangu*). However, ancestral transformations linked or transcended the two.

In the doctrines of Pitjantjatjara people and their neighbours, some ancestors (*tjukurritja*) were wholly human but most had both human and non-human attributes. The ancestors, indefinite in number, some female and some male, moved continually from place to place or travelled around a single locale. Some travelled on to places far away, while others died and went inside the country.

Some stories recount very localised events, although similar events may have occurred in other places, while others describe very long journeys, connecting many countries. The Seven Sisters (Pleiades) story, for example, describes a long journey through the Warburton, Rowlinson, Petermann, Mann, and Musgrave Ranges to Arrernte country. The women came down from the sky, were chased by Nirunja, and escaped. As in other regions, some stories about ancestors were 'just-so' stories—about how Perentie Lizard got his spots, for example. Some incorporated moral points—about the consequences of jealousy between co-wives, or of the failure to make an adequate gift of meat.

Men and women had (and have) distinct ceremonies and sacred objects, dangerous to each other. Some women's ceremonies were 'travelling rituals', performed widely across the Western Desert and handed over from one group to another during major assemblies. Each genre of ceremony had its own particular ancestors and myths; *inma* (song cycles) followed the ancestral journeys from place to place, and each group possessed and performed its own section of the songs and stories.

The word *tjukurrpa* has also been translated into the English word 'law', the foundations of which were country and sacred objects. Ancestors 'created the constraining moral imperatives, the "lawful" behaviour patterns and norms, of the traditional society', as Nancy Munn puts it.[18]

Ancestral traces

As in the doctrines of other regions, ancestors left traces (*tjina*, 'footprints') in the land and sky and 'spirit essence' (*kurarnpa*) in the land, and gave places their names. Nancy Munn writes of consubstantial relations between an ancestor and the objects and country that he or she created, which contain something of the ancestor within them. (Only the transformations of ancestors remained visible.) The term *walga* means ancestral designs, typically concentric circles, as well as places that are conceived of as ancestral marks. Many places became 'increase' sites, where the *kurunitja* ('essences') could be released to encourage the reproduction of species, including people. Ancestors left stores of sacred objects, which were the prototypes of the objects made by men and women.[19]

People interpreted stars and constellations in the same way as features of the ground—as traces of ancestors. For example, footprints and the nest of Wedge-tailed Eagle appear in the Southern Cross, the Coalsack, and Alpha and Beta Centauri, while the Seven Sisters were the Pleiades.

The landscape included artefacts such as rock carvings, paintings in rock shelters, and stone arrangements that were said to have been made by ancestors, as well as the natural features interpreted as ancestral traces. Ancestors made waterholes by digging for water and left creek-beds where they crawled; depressions remained where they had slept. Their bodies and bodily substances changed into rocks and markings. Accoutrements such as clubs changed into living beings such as snakes (which in turn changed into rocks). Ancestors became sacred objects of wood or stone, identified with their bodies and related places. Pitjantjatjara people conceived of these objects as the 'progeny' (*kurunitja*) of the ancestors, like the people to whom the ancestors gave birth or pulled out of their bodies and left at various places. And the transformation of the ancestors, places, and sacred objects contained their power or 'strength'.

People identified living kin (such as one's father) with sacred objects and the related ancestors and places. At death, a person 'became' country and ancestors. Hence, successive generations were born of the ancestors, died, and became identified again with their totemic ancestors.

Unlike *tjukurritja*, the rather distinctive 'Rainbow Serpents' (*wanambi*) remained alive in the permanent waterholes and underground channels, and were dangerous if offended. A visitor would announce his or her presence by throwing stones in the water, or frighten the *wanambi* off with fire. Some were credited with stealing the *kurarnpa* (life essence) of the living.

Other beings

Other beings in the cosmologies of Pitjantjatjara people and their neighbours included the incestuous and cannibalistic *tjangara* (ogres). According to some doctrines, *mamu* spirits, thought of as hybrid dog–people, lived in hollow trees and under rocks. In some stories the *mamu* appear as ordinary people but make insidious cannibalistic attacks or cause accidents to happen. In others, they attack, mainly at night, by ripping open the belly of their victim with their teeth. They would penetrate the body (as in a sorcery attack) and lodge in the belly or the back, stealing a person's *kurarnpa* (life essence) and leaving it in the bush or eating it. The *ngankari* (healer/sorcerer), who had the ability to see *mamu*, would try to retrieve and replace the *kurarnpa*.[20]

Conception and personal spirits

In Pitjantjatjara doctrines, an ancestral woman created conception places on her long journey, during which she also gave birth to many children. Her sites were also places where one could increase sexual desire (as well as resources, such as some fruits) and ensure the supply of children. 'Spirit children' (*kunti*) awaited passing women and then entered their uteruses. The totemic ancestor of a child's birthplace or of the place where the stump of the child's umbilical cord fell off left its mark on the child's body.

People of the western region of the Western Desert denied any connection between sexual intercourse and conception; a child's 'father' was simply the mother's husband. The father would see the spirit child approach in a dream or hunt it in the form of an animal. Some unusual characteristic or activity on the part of an animal or object—for example, a wallaby apparently allowing itself to be speared with ease—indicated the presence of the spirit child. The sign of the spirit child became the child's personal totem. This designation entailed no special bond to or prohibition on eating the totemic animal (if it was an animal), and no particular relationship with people having the same conception totem.[21]

Spirits of the dead (*kuran*, *kurarnpa*) would hang around the grave of a recently deceased person and try to steal the spirit from the grave. The healer/sorcerer would hunt them away or, according to Charles Mountford, try to capture the spirit of the dead at the end of the burial rites and place it in the body of a living person, giving him or her extra vitality. (See also Yolngu below.) The spirit dissipated at the end of that person's life. An escaped soul might become a *mamu* spirit.[22]

Ancestral powers: 'Increase' sites

In Pitjantjatjara doctrine, *kurunitja* (spirit essences), which were responsible for the life and abundance of all resources, including rain, inhered in those rocks, caves, and waterholes that were the traces of ancestors. These ancestral sites (*pitilyiri*) were 'increase centres', which people could tap in order to increase the supply of rain and food species and also to ensure the supply of children. Hundreds of increase centres were scattered throughout the country. Some sites were the source of healing power—used to treat dysentery, for example.[23] Increase procedures (*paluni*) caused *kurunitja* to 'spurt out'; initiated men with spiritual ties to the ancestor and site would clean the site, rub the rock, and anoint it, while chanting and speaking requests and exhortations to the ancestor.

Those responsible for an increase site were duty-bound to perform increase rites each year at the site, to provide food and other resources for everyone in the region. According to Mountford, Pitjantjatjara doctrines did not allow increase sites to be used for aggression; an attempt to do so would not only kill the person trying to use the site in this way, but everyone else as well.

Both men and women, alone and in groups, practiced so-called 'love magic' in the form of songs to attract members of the opposite sex.[24]

Sorcerer–healers

The *ngankari* of the Pitjantjatjara people and their neighbours combined the roles of healer, sorcerer, and rainmaker. A person with aptitude usually inherited the role from his or her father, father's brother, father's sister, or mother's brother, who would transfer a stone and spirit familiar to the novice. The novice would also have a powerful dream, of such things as encounters with spirit beings. The *ngankari* treated patients with suction, massage, and manipulation—to, for example, reposition the patient's life-force. He or she might also cure backache with kurrajong, expel sickness with a stone, or intone a chant to remove a dangerous *mamu* spirit, taking it into his or her own belly.[25]

Instead of the overwhelming emphasis on magic shown by Kŭnai people, among Pitjantjatjara people ancestral sites and rites were dominant. With the doctrines of Yuwaaliyaay people and their neighbours we return to a region with a strong emphasis on the sky, but they also had sorcerer–healers similar to the *ngankari*.

Yuwaaliyaay people and their neighbours

Ancestors

Like Kŭnai people, Yuwaaliyaay people and their neighbours recognised a 'father of all'. The creator, the 'Great One', came from afar according to Yuwaaliyaay doctrines, accompanied by his two wives. As Parker recounts:

> There was an age … when only birds and beasts were on earth; but a colossal man and two women came from the remote north-east, changed birds and beasts into men and women, made other folk of clay or stone, taught them everything, left laws for their guidance, then returned whence they came.[26]

There was some ambiguity about the identity of these creators: women referred to the man simply as 'father' (*boyerh*), whereas men learned that his name was Byamee (in Parker's spelling). Totem names covered Birrahgnooloo—the 'mother of all' and the elder of the two wives—one for each part of her body, including fingers and toes, and she was a source of rain. When she acceded to a request for rain, a flood from her menstrual blood rolled down the mountain. Cunnumbeilee, the younger wife, bore children and attended to domestic duties. As the family moved on their journey they gave totems to each of the matrilineal totemic categories. The ancestors thus literally 'embodied' the source of unity and diversity of groups of the region.

Yuwaaliyaay people shared affiliation to Byamee (or Baiami) with other speakers of languages belonging to the Wiradjuri group, as well as other peoples. Pakaantji people to the southwest had a different name, Kurlawirra, for their creator, and had a distinct male initiation ceremony. People understood Byamee to be a giver of laws and the origin of customs.[27]

Ancestral traces

Byamee and other ancestors left traces of their actions and presence in the land.[28] Certain trees had particular significance, including one tree from which Byamee cut the first bullroarer and others that he marked as sources of honey. Spirits of various kinds resided in trees, while others belonged to *wirreenun*, people who combined the roles of healer, medium, sorcerer, and ritual leader.

Yuwaaliyaay doctrines linked named places primarily to Byamee and his wives and sons, although other totemic associations and details of myths differentiated them. For example, people interpreted several rocky and stony places as traces of Byamee and his family: Byamee's sons made the fish-traps at Brewarrina; the imprints of Byamee's hand and foot at Narran Swamp left scoops in certain rocks; and the impressions of Byamee's hair remained in a rock where he rested. Like Birahgnooloo, a number of totemic beings, including relatives of the victims of Eaglehawk and spirits called Yanta, were credited with having created springs. A site at Narran Lake was associated with Crocodile, who was said to have swallowed Byamee's wives; they were restored by Byamee. At a place near Mildool, Byamee scooped out a rock to hold water for himself, and a smaller one for his dingo. An outcrop of rocks was the remains of a cannibal woman and her dingoes.

Byamee and his wives could be seen in the camp in the sky. Indeed, heavenly bodies in general were accorded elaborate mythological significance. For example, the Coalsack in the Milky Way was Gowargay, the featherless Emu woman; Venus was 'the laughing star', a man who laughed at his own obscene jokes; the Clouds of Magellan were Brolga mother and daughter; and two dark spots in Scorpio were *Wurrawilberoo* ('devils'), who would try to catch spirits of the dead, and came to earth in the form of whirlwinds. Many celestial phenomena, as well as the winds, were associated with the matrilineal totems. Emu was particularly important in cosmology and ritual.

Other beings

Parker describes a wide variety of dangerous spirits. One removed and ate the bodies of the dead; a 'red devil' of the scrub killed and ate anyone he met; *Marahgoo* spirits, who wore red capes and white swansdown caps, gave people a drink that engendered visions and led them into their world, which lay beneath a certain water-hole in the scrub. Like *kurdaitji* in the Western Desert, invisible men armed with poison sticks or bones carried out expeditions to punish law-breakers. Other beings in Yuwaaliyaay cosmology included men possessed by dangerous *Euloowayi* spirits; they had long nails and came from beyond the sun at sunset. A red-painted pole adorned with red-ochred strings kept them at bay. Dangerous beings of a kind usually called 'Rainbow Serpents' in English (*Waaway* in the Ngiyampaa language) guarded waterholes and Bora grounds, while others inhered in trees and whirlwinds. People had to take ritual precautions when approaching places associated with *Waaway*; Mount Grenfell in Wangaaybuwan country was such a place.[29]

Conception and personal spirits

Yuwaaliyaay people subscribed to a number of doctrines about conception. Their doctrines contrast with those of other regions in not tying a person to a particular country. As recounted by Parker, the spirits of girls came from Bahloo's spirit stone on the Culgoa River, where they lay in a hole in the creek-bed. Another being sent baby-spirits to hang on trees; they seized and impregnated a woman passing underneath, or tree spirits and spirits of whirlwinds impregnated women with twins.

An individual possessed a number of 'spirits'. A person's *yowee* (soul) grew with the body and at death it could be reincarnated in another form—but, except for infants who died young, people were not reincarnated as people. A person's *doowee* (dream-spirit) wandered while they were asleep, and their dream experiences reflected those of the spirit. An enemy might try to capture the dream-spirit, killing the person. The *mulloowil* (shadow-spirit) could be stolen or reduced in size, leading the victim to sicken and die. At death, a person's spirit might visit the camp in the form of a bird, then follow his deceased relatives to a sacred mountain, to be pulled up by spirits into Byamee's camp, accompanied by the sound of thunder. The sky, then, was a home of the dead. Signs of sickness and death included the crying of a passing galah or magpie—a child had to be lain on its side in such a case, or on its stomach if it was a passing crow.[30]

Sorcerer–healers

Judging by Parker's account, Yuwaaliyaay people mostly used their magic in acts of aggression or healing.[31] To make rain, a *wirreenun* (sorcerer–healer) could send a tutelary spirit to ask Birrahgnooloo or could feed the clouds from a creek using songs and special sticks; and a child could make rain when the sky was cloudy. The ancestor Birrahgnooloo made rain by throwing a handful of crystal pebbles into a stone 'basin' on top of the sacred mountain; the water splashed up into the clouds and fell as rain. Unlike with Kŭnai people, stopping much-needed rain could be an act of aggression.[32]

Wirreenun combined the roles of healer, sorcerer, shaman, rainmaker, and male ritual leader. (People considered Byamee to be the most powerful of all *wirreenun*.)

In the conventional account of initiation into the role, a practising *wirreenun* chose an adept, who underwent a period of seclusion at a burial ground, and later at a bower-bird's bower, where spirits of the dead and totemic beings appeared, one of whom would insert a translucent pebble (*gubberah*) into the adept's head. A woman of Parker's acquaintance called Bootha became a *wirreenun* after a period of strange and asocial behaviour following the death of a grandchild; she worked as a healer and rainmaker.

Every *wirreenun* possessed one or two *yunbeai* (personal totems), such as a snake or lizard that resided in a 'spirit stone' (*goomarh*), as well as a special tree, called *minggah*, where the *wirreenun* could consult the spirits and discover the identity of sorcerers. In his or her basket (*boondoorr*), a *wirreenun* carried a variety of sticks, stones, herbs, down, and hair-strings for healing, far-sight, and sorcery.

A *wirreenun* claimed a variety of powers: to send their dream-spirit to consult the spirits; to see past, distant, and future events with the aid of their pebbles; to send the spirits of the crystals to kill victims at a distance; and to get their dream-spirit (*mullee-mullee*) to do their bidding—for example, to capture someone else's dream-spirit or to intercede with Birrahgnooloo. Any perceived lack of success might be blamed on the intervention of a more powerful *wirreenun*.

Healing techniques included the familiar ones, but, in addition, a *wirreenun* might exorcise a troublesome spirit. *Wirreenun* were also self-confessed sorcerers, claiming to be able to cause injury and death using a variety of techniques, which included not only the familiar ones of pointing a bone or stick, heating the victim's hair, or using poison, but also calling dangerous spirits from the *minggah* tree or spirit stone.

The only direct 'economic' application of Yuwaaliyaay doctrines was rainmaking. As a part of mortuary practice, people ingested body fluids and small pieces of flesh to impart strength; perhaps they believed that they could tap this power for economic activities. More significantly, ancestral doctrines have important implications for rights in and connections to land and waters (Chapter 9).

Wiil and Mi_nong people

Less is recorded of Wiil and Mi_nong cosmological doctrines than Yuwaaliyaay doctrines. Totemic ancestral connections to country are apparent, but the sky does not figure as prominently as it does in Kŭnai and Yuwaaliyaay cosmologies.

Ancestors

Wiil and Mi_nong people had a cosmology similar to those already described, in that events 'long ago' involving people, animals, and celestial phenomena determined the present shape of the landscape, the characteristics of animals, and social customs. According to Bates, ancestors were *demma goomber* ('grandparents—great/large').[33] There does not appear to have been such an emphasis on particular beings as originators of law, but many Wiil and Mi_nong myths have moral implications. Barker and others recorded (very briefly) origin myths among Minong people at King George Sound. The following is my summary of the story:

> A long time ago the only person living was an old woman named Annapan. She was delivered of a daughter called Noemang, who had several children (boys and girls), who were the mothers and fathers of the black people.

Stories of a great flood explain how the present landscape came into being. To summarise the story (or Hassell's version of it):

> As the rains fell and fell the country flooded. People collected rocks to form hills, dropping some as they went. They and the animals were confined to the pile of rocks. As the waters receded the rocks formed the mountains, and the sea had made the rivers brackish, as they are today. Many people drowned, the babies died, and there were no marriageable girls.

> The people of that time were huge. One of the men lost his wives to drowning and became a gigantic cannibal spirit called Coombar *jannock* (Coombar spirit), who wandered in the mallee forest where men went to get spear sticks.

Minong versions refer to peaks to the north of Albany. But many Wiil myths, as recorded by Hassell, are 'just-so' stories that explain how species and other phenomena acquired their physical and behavioural characteristics. Some myths are also moral tales, recounting the consequences of not behaving in an appropriate way towards relatives.

Ancestral traces

As in the previous case studies, stories trace the journeys of ancestral beings and interpret places as the results of ancestral activities and as the transformed bodily substance of ancestors. Barker records a moral tale that also explains the origin of Oyster Harbour at King George Sound, and in which the dingo's journey links at least two places. The following is my summary of Barker's account:

> A long time ago a woman found a quiet snake in the bush, and ate it all without giving any to her husband. He struck her and broke her leg. She managed to walk to Green Island, where she died. The island is called 'Narrecoolyup', 'female walk place'. A dingo called Whatemia smelled her putrifying body from some 60 kilometres away, came to the island and scratched the ground to form Oyster Harbour. The man and woman's son came to kill his father near a mountain, now called 'man spear' (*yangenmere*).

Hassell records three such stories among Wiil and Minong people. One is the long story of Black Snake and Mopoke, which explains how a reef at Cape Riche and a rock on a hillside came into being.[34]

Will and Minong people interpreted the stars and other heavenly bodies as humans, and their movements as people visiting one another. For example, the stars of the Southern Cross were traces of girls blown into the sky by the wind, and Orion's Belt and the Pleiades were a family blown into the sky after a dispute.

Other beings

There were many dangerous spirits in Wiil and Mi̱nong doctrines, as in Kŭnai doctrines. I have already mentioned Coombar Jannock. Others included spirits who assumed the form of a whirlwind to blind or choke a person with dust; they caused great dust-storms and water-spouts at sea. Some spirits caused insomnia, made children cry at night, stole the warmth of the fire, and made food disappear at night. People lit a second fire at the hearth and left food for the *jannock* spirits.[35]

Noatch the shape-changer lived in the mists covering Bluff Knoll in the Stirling Ranges. *Marghet*, large-headed many-toothed males, lived deep in freshwater lakes, ponds, and springs, causing bubbles to rise and dragging down the unwary. They made the permanent springs found in muddy mounds away from the margins of rivers in the dry, rocky country. Giant snakes appear to have been creatures of distant places, although they appear as *wakal* in the cosmologies of other parts of the southwest.

People took the call of the 'night-cuckoo' (koël) to be a portent of death, and took a dream of a totemic animal to be an ill omen. Ravens signified misfortune and the presence of strangers. Finding a dead animal or plant was taken as a sign that a person of that totem had died.[36]

Conception and personal spirits

According to Bates, the doctrines of the region stated that the spirits of children resided in stones or trees. An unborn child's mother's brother would dream that the child's spirit sat on his thigh, then went to its mother. This event had implications for exchange relations and access to country and resources. Wiil doctrines linked the spirits of the dead with the sun, which was the land of the dead. But ghosts of the dead stayed around their country for a while, where they could be dangerous. Mokaré told Barker that his father had seen ghosts dancing in the air at night.[37]

'Increase'

According to Bates, older men performed songs for the 'increase' of species. Each 'district' had its own distinct totemic species, including Black Swan, Salmon, Banksia, and Possum. She describes a variety of procedures used to increase species: a cooperative winter rite for banksia honey; songs performed by an older man about the eponymous totem when lizards began to appear in late spring, or about swans preparing a nest; and the imitation of possums climbing trees. But it is possible that Mi̱nong people at King George Sound did not perform increase rites: Mokaré told Barker that they did not ask any beings to give them success in hunting and fishing (a slightly different thing).[38]

Sorcery, magic, and healing

Magic in the region centred on the possession of special stones (*booliah*). Men reserved some kinds of stone for their own use, while women possessed others, as well as objects of human hair and fur. Both men and women practiced magic, but the term *mulgar* (magician) seems to have been reserved for men; *mulgar* were graded according to the kind and strength of their powers. Both *mulgar* and women magicians interpreted people's dreams of the dead and of totemic animals. A *mulgar* supposedly had the power to travel at night in the form of his familiar and fly into the sky; doing so allowed him to obtain information about other groups, identify a sorcerer, or kill an enemy.[39]

Using certain stones and techniques, magicians were supposed to be able to curse individuals, cure illness, make game more plentiful, and make and stop rain. They could apparently cause whirlwinds, thunderstorms, and eclipses, stop the wind, make the sun shine and the grass grow, and bring about the birth of a child of the desired sex. *Mulgar* could see and commune with the spirits of the long dead. They directed their magical powers towards economic production—not only could they purportedly control the elements, including rain, but they assisted hunters by working on spears and dogs after an unsuccessful hunt, taking the 'magic' out of them with a smoky fire.[40]

Sandbeach people

Sandbeach cosmologies contrasted with Wiil and Miṉong ones in a number of ways. Increase sites were a marked feature, and they did not have a sorcerer–healer role.

Ancestors

According to Sandbeach doctrines, long ago (*wuulamu*), in the beginning (*yilamu*), animals (except the dingo), birds, and fish were people, although they retained some non-human characteristics.[41] Indeed, like Kŭnai people, Sandbeach people referred to them as *minya*, meaning 'flesh' or 'meat'. Among these, the creator ancestors ('big men'—a concept similar to the Kŭnai people's 'eminent men') went on journeys and established the ceremonies that people inherited. They shaped the country and all its features, gave places their names, established 'law', and later assumed the form of animals. The ancestors passed on the traditions to the 'middle people' (*yi'achiku*), who in turn passed on the stock of knowledge to recent generations. Sandbeach people recounted and reenacted ancestral events in stories, songs, and ceremonies.

Sandbeach ancestors were divided among patri-groups and patri-moieties. A patri-group's ancestors were its *puula*, 'fathers' fathers' and 'father's fathers' sisters', or *puulaway*, 'important father's fathers' (similar to Wiil/Miṉong conceptions); all the members of the group shared the same *puula*, and inherited them patrilineally. The ancestors were also 'like brothers'. Members of the group could kill and eat the associated animal (except the Crocodile). Each patri-group owned a corpus of knowledge, songs, and designs for body decoration related to their *puula*, and dances in the initiation ceremonies dramatised the actions of the *puula*.

Ancestral traces

The ancestors left various kinds of trace in the land and waters: a single rock or rock formation, a sunken reef, a clump of trees or bushes, a small hollow, or a small area of land or sea-bed. Each patri-group's country included some ten to 20 named places of this kind, of which six to 12 or more were 'story places', also referred to as *puula*, or 'fathers' fathers'.[42]

Some sites, such as the cyclone story place, were self-contained. Narratives such as that of Diamond Mullet's movement into the sea recount brief journeys of a hundred metres or so. Saltwater Crocodile, associated with male initiation, made a long journey by Sandbeach standards. He married, created sexual relations between men and women, then traversed the country of Kuuku-Ya'u speakers from southwest to northeast and entered the country of Wuthathi speakers. On his journey he encountered other beings, transforming them into rocks, and left powerful forces behind. Story places and ancestors could appear in dreams, signifying, for example, a person's imminent return or a child's sickness.

Conception and personal spirits

Unlike many other Aboriginal peoples, Sandbeach people did not subscribe to a doctrine of spirit conception from a conception site. A child's spirit (*mitpi*) was like a shadow and came from afar, perhaps from the west. Men and women both contributed to the child's body through repeated intercourse—bone from the semen, flesh from the woman's blood. A person gained his or her 'navel name' from a 'father's father' or 'father's father's sister' during the severing of the umbilical cord, and the child and the original bearer of the name entered an avoidance relationship. A 'mother's brother' carried the umbilical cord, encased in beeswax, for life.[43]

Thomson describes *ngachimu nguunthachi* ('mother's father having the vital force') as an individual's personal totem. It belonged to the person's mother's moiety, the opposite to his or her own moiety, and was not passed by a man to his own children. The mother's relatives determined what the totem was when, at puberty or a little later, they avulsed the person's upper incisor (usually the right-hand one); they called out a series of totemic names, and the one called as the tooth came out became the person's totem. This took place after initiation and before marriage in the case of a young man.

According to Sandbeach doctrine, a *nguunthal* ('spirit' or 'vital force') resided in an infant's fontanelle, where it could be seen pulsating. When the fontanelle finally closed the spirit left the person and travelled to the mother's country, where it remained. The *mitpi* spirit, or '*kobi*' (in Thomson's spelling), remained in the person's body till death, when it too travelled to the mother's country, appearing as a shooting star, to be received by *Wo'odi Mukkän*, the being who presided over the land of the dead. Mortuary rites included the placing of a lighted torch in the hand of the corpse, who was told to take it to his or her *ngachimu nguunthachi*. Two to three years after the death, relatives buried the person's remains with the head towards the mother's country. These doctrines indicate the strong connections to and rights in the mother's country (see Chapter 9).

Ancestral powers

Like Pitjantjatjara people and their neighbours, Sandbeach people practiced 'increase' rites at certain ancestral sites. If people noticed a decline in the number of dugong, for example, then old men of the group with Dugong as their totemic ancestor carried out a ceremony at the Dugong site to increase the numbers of animals. Men who owned a story place associated with women performed rituals there to attract women. The powerful songs and dances of initiation rites could also arouse people sexually, according to Sandbeach doctrine, and could give the sick new vitality.

People believed that they could direct powers associated with ancestral sites at their enemies. 'Big men' with the appropriate identity, knowledge, and power knew how to manipulate a site associated with a powerful force, such as a cyclone or the death adder, using the appropriate body painting and ceremony. This contrasts with the cooperative nature of Pitjantjatjara increase rites. Sandbeach people conceived of rainmaking as an act of aggression, as Kŭnai people did, in contrast with Western Desert people, who saw it as a service to all. (Among Yuwaaliyaay people, *stopping* the rain constituted an aggressive act.)[44]

Sorcery, magic, and healing

Sandbeach people attributed much of the success of a hunter to his knowledge and use of magic, directed towards the capture of the animal, as well as his avoidance of circumstances that would nullify the magic's efficacy. Thomson records a number of ways in which men could enhance their hunting success.[45]

Men carried a 'magic bundle', a lump of beeswax regarded as powerful, which was best obtained from people of the hinterland (such as Kaantju and Ayapathu) in exchange for other goods. To make a dugong or turtle sluggish and easier to kill a harpooner pressed the warmed beeswax against his abdomen several times. Eating nearly raw dugong meat also conferred power, and Kuuku Ya'u people nibbled, or rubbed on their equipment, pieces of what was supposedly human flesh (some traded from Kaantju people) in order to make them fearless and confer prowess in hunting. First-stage male initiation included a rite to make a young man 'good for turtle'. Men would also chant a spell to make a dugong easier to catch and kill—'singing' the dugong—and hunters were supposed to avoid sex for a few days before a hunt; women could not go near or touch a man's hunting equipment. Men smeared animal blood onto spear shafts, and applied underarm sweat as well as saliva to spear shafts and heads 'to make them strong'. As in many Aboriginal societies, underarm sweat ('smell', *wuuyiinyu*) was incorporated into rituals and other procedures.

Sandbeach people explained deaths, except those of the very young and very old, as the result of sorcery attacks. But it was people outside the everyday circle of social relationships whom people feared most as potential sorcerers—for Sandbeach people this was Kaantju and Ayapathu people of the hinterland. Apparently there was no sorcerer/magician role, but as in other regions healing techniques involved ritual action on a person's name, excuviae, or other traces. A healer (*maparanga*) treated supposed victims of sorcery by giving them bush medicines, by appearing to suck out the object, by blood-letting, or by passing underarm sweat under the patient's nostrils.

The significance of the paucity of ancestral tracks, and of the strength of ties to one's mother's country, will be explored in Chapter 9.

Ngarinyin people

The sorcerer–healer role reappears in the cosmology and practices of Ngarinyin people and their neighbours, as do the multiple connections through ancestral journeys. Doctrines about increase sites link them to Pitjantjatjara and Sandbeach doctrines.

Ancestors

The *wanjina* (ancestors) and the associated *wunggurr* (pythons), which appear in extensive galleries of paintings in rock shelters and caves, were (and are) a very distinctive feature of the doctrines of the Ngarinyin people and their neighbours. In Andreas Lommel's interpretation of Wunambal cosmology, *wunggurr* denoted a generalised creative being or power associated with the Milky Way (Walanganda) who 'dreamed' the individual *wanjina* into existence, 'finding' them under the waters and giving them names.

Wanjina were persons, depicted in the form of clouds and identified with rain. They also had the identity of plants, animals, reptiles, and insects (such as Kangaroo, King Brown Snake, and Wild Honey) as well as celestial objects, taking on some of the characteristics of the totemic species or object. They had particular associations with the rain-bearing cumulo-nimbus clouds of the wet season. *Wanjina* are depicted in rock art as androgynous, cloudlike, and mouthless, often taking the form of a head or a head and shoulders, sometimes with rain falling from the underside, their feathered head-dresses the lightning.[46]

In *lalan*, the creative era, the long, eventful journeys of some *wanjina*, such as the Dingoes, criss-crossed the west Kimberley and linked it to other regions. They encountered other beings and became the ancestors of particular patri-groups. *Wanjina* dwelt below permanent waters, in the land of the dead, making some waters dangerous to bathe in, and people credited some *wanjina* with creating fresh and salt waters. Some supposed subterranean connections were very long. As elsewhere, people attributed to *wanjina* the creation of 'law', including initiation ceremonies, items of technology, and practices such as fighting and wife-stealing. Stories about the moiety ancestors Wodoy and Jun.gun concern the creation of correct marriage and exogamy. (On 'law' see Chapter 8.)

Each patri-group was associated with several totemic species, many of which appeared in rock paintings and one of which was its principle totem. Its main *wanjina* was associated with a rock shelter and a waterhole on the patri-group's country. Events recounted in stories linked a particular *wanjina* with other associated totemic beings—the 'fathers', 'father's sisters' and 'siblings' of the *wanjina* and the people of the patri-group. For example, a story about a great fight concerned owls, lizards, and the root of a native plum that were depicted in rock paintings.

The totemic identity of *wanjina* and the associated clusters of totems differentiated the patri-groups. However, *wanjina* and *wunggurr* as categories linked them all, and each particular ancestral journey, above or below ground, long or short, connected two or more groups through the traces of the ancestors' activities. *Wanjina*, together with related patri-groups, country, and species, were divided into two patri-moieties, which were established, according to Wunambal doctrines, by two *wunggurr* named Kurangali and Banar. According to Crawford, the doctrines of coastal people differed somewhat from those of the hinterland people, in that the ancestors took the form of cyclones.

As in other regions, some myths accounted for the characteristics of species—for example, how herons gained their cloacas, and how humans came to have anuses. A particular feature of western Kimberley mythology was the dispersal of ancestral beings out from a centre, as well as the short and long journeys familiar from the Western Desert. Another is the coexistence of, and antagonism between, *wanjina* and people long ago. In what Crawford describes as the 'most important' *wanjina* myth, they dispersed from a place called Wanalirri after fighting humans in revenge for the killing of Owl by two children (though versions of the fight story varied). In a similar way, Honeybees spread out from Secure Bay.

Images in paintings often combine *wunggurr* (the ancestral rock-pythons) with *wanjina*—indeed, the categories were not altogether discrete. *Wunggurr*, also associated with rain, lived beneath permanent waters, and were associated particularly with conception. They could transform themselves into rainbows, and into dangerous logs floating in the waters that might swallow or drown people. Like *wanjina*, the *wunggurr* travelled, sometime long distances.

Like the Sandbeach ancestors, the *wanjina* were referred to by members of each patri-group as their 'fathers' or 'father's fathers', and older men identified with their *wanjina* by referring to them in the first person. Consistent with their association with the *wanjina*, patri-groups had a cloudlike structure, in that patri-group countries of the same moiety were clustered together in long, interlocking swathes across the region.

Dreams linked an individual to the *wanjina*, as well as to child spirits. For example, a dream might predict the dangerous action of a *wanjina*, such as the creation of a great storm. People were also connected to *wunggurr* through dreams; but to dream of a *wunggurr* was dangerous—it meant, according to one man, that the python would kill someone.

Ancestral traces

Myths relate how the *wanjina* settled or 'lay down' to establish focal places in patri-group countries (*dambun*). Each country contained the traces of several *wanjina*, one of which was the principal *wanjina* of the group. The *wanjina* travelled across the land, made rain fall, shaped the earth, made the rivers, piled up mountains, and shaped the plains. One caused a great flood and created saltwater fish. Some rock formations were ancestral traces—the traces of, among other things, transformed spearheads, the backbones of the *wanjina*, the cloudlike form of *wanjina*, and the bodies of *wanjina* killed in fights. Tony Redmond brings out the malleable, soft, and 'greasy' quality of rocks in Ngarinyin cosmology, capable of becoming soft again in the hands of healers. Other ancestral traces were stone arrangements, which were the ancestors' tracks, and stone fish-traps on the coast.[47]

Ancestral traces also took the form of paintings on the surfaces of large sandstone boulders and in the many caves and rock shelters of the region (and their eggs took the form of stones). These were the home of groups of male and female *wanjina*, and of *wunggurr*. Each patri-group's country contained one or more of these painted galleries. Ngarinyin people and their neighbours thought of the paintings as impressions left on the soft rock by the *wanjina* at the end of their creative journeys, or as paintings made by them. People addressed the *wanjina* and other beings at painting sites, introducing themselves, perhaps pleading with them not to get angry and cause a flood. In Wunambal interpretations, an older rock art tradition, the 'Bradshaw figures', were 'very old' and had no connection with *wanjina*.[48]

The boab tree, or 'bottle tree', with its huge girth, had a particular connection with the *wanjina*. Often the focus of a camp where the nuts were processed, boabs were regarded as tranformations of *wanjina* or *wunggurr* (such as two snake sisters) and their bark provided a ground for carvings.

The heavens also contained traces of *wanjina*. The Milky Way was seen as the body of, and was named after, Walanganda; people also conceptualised it as a coolamon, and as *wunggurr* in Wunambal doctrines. The Southern Cross was Emu's footprint, or the black plum that is Emu's food. Bodies of water in the sky had their equivalents in the land.

The ethnography of this region emphasises the traces on the human body of totemic species, and the process of spirit conception. Men's cicatrices were said to follow the patterns on Crocodile or King Brown Snake, while a man's 'finding' of his child, by spearing an animal for example, might leave a mark on the child's body. Ancestral doctrines were also related to dreams—a new song might be revealed in a dream, for example.[49]

Other beings

Several other categories of spirit being appear in the doctrines of Ngarinyin people and their neighbours. Yam spirits sang and danced, and their faeces became yams. Dangerous *agula* (rock spirits) carried souls to the land of the dead, haunted the bereaved, stole babies and goods, and turned people's heads to make them lost. *Jilinya* were dangerous, cannibalistic, shape-changing females who inhabited dense scrub and swamps, preyed on men as lovers, and fed their desire for tasty food.[50]

Conception and personal spirits

Ethnographers have recorded several Ngarinyin and Worrorra doctrines about conception. Spirit children (*anguma*) resided in waters associated with *wunggurr* and *wanjina*, especially in grassy water-weed. The father would 'find' the child by eating fish or reptiles from the pool, or it might attach itself to his hair-bun, or a man might capture a spirit child in a lightning flash. The father would dream about the spirit child and its name; his own deceased father might bring the spirit child, which then entered the mother (but conception could occur much later than the 'finding'). Parents had discussions about how and where the conception event took place, often some time after the child's birth. Such doctrines clearly allowed a father much scope in attaching a child to a conception place, which could in any case be altered later. Some Wunambal people denied any connection between sex and conception. The strong identification between incipient people and the *wanjina* led people to identify with the *wanjina* by speaking in the first person when narrating ancestral stories, as among Pitjantjatjara people.[51]

According to Ngarinyin doctrines, refractions of *anguma* (shadow spirits) lurked near the grave and worried the living, or became part of the *wunggurr* at the time of reinterrment. The spirits of the dead went on a long journey before returning to the world of the dead (*dulugun*) beneath the waters in their own country, or (in Worrorra doctrines) on an island across the sea, to become identified with the *wanjina* once more or to rejoin the body of a *wunggurr*. A spirit then attached itself to a man of the next generation as a child spirit, to be reincarnated as a grandchild.

Ancestral powers

Ngarinyin people and their neighbours had doctrines about 'increase' similar to those of Pitjantjatjara, Sandbeach, and (perhaps) Wiil people.[52] *Wanjina* were responsible for the fertility of other species as well as humans. Retouching of a *wanjina* image took place when it had faded: the senior men of a patri-group, their sisters' sons, or men whose conception country it was, 'brightened' the image and were recompensed for their work with gifts of kangaroo meat or honey. Retouching took place during ceremonies in which large numbers of people came together to sing and dance, organised by a senior custodian of the *wanjina* paintings. Retouching *wanjina* and *wunggurr* images and spraying them with water caused the rain to fall, replenished the animals and plants, and caused an increase in human births. Carrying out the retouching at the wrong time would cause the monsoon rains to come in the wrong season, while failure to retouch them altogether would cause the *wanjina* to leave and the country to wither.[53]

Senior men and women could make rain, according to Ngarinyin doctrine, for example by entering a pool inhabited by certain snake sisters and pounding its surface. Songs were thought to be efficacious in a number of other ways, such as in making the ground near a *wanjina* cave muddy.

Rituals conferred powers. As one of a number of ritual responses to colonisation, in the 1930s Ngarinyin people were in the process of teaching Wunambal people the Djanba ceremony. According to Wunambal doctrines, people stole carved sacred objects from Djanba, a white-skinned man who lived in a corrugated-iron house in the desert surrounded by grass imbued with new diseases. Djanba disseminated the ceremony by boat, aeroplane, car, and train. It was replacing the older Mayangari ceremony, said to have come from the north, associated with Djanba's father, Nangai. In that ceremony, men displayed sacred objects said to have been made by Nangai and distributed them through the *wurnan* exchange network. Doctrines predicted that the world would end if the Djanba sacred objects reached Nangai, and that there would be a revolution in the social order if women gained access to them.

Magic, sorcery, and healing

Barnman (sorcerer–healers), dominant figures among Ngarinyin people and their neighbours, gained their powers from *wunggurr* in a dream, or by being struck by lightning. In one doctrine, *wunggurr* deposited stones or crystals within the healer's body and resided curled up in his (or her?) belly, where they bred; in others, the *wunggurr* placed child spirits in his body. These gave the *barnman* clear sight and the ability to fly while asleep on the body of *wunggurr*, connected by a cord along which a singer travelled when dreaming songs (*buyu*). *Barnman* could supposedly enter the world of the dead and the *wanjina* beneath the waters by making a hole in the ground.

Healers applied techniques familiar from other regions, including the sucking out of intrusive objects such as shell fragments, and the transfer of stones from his belly to the patient. *Barnman* could supposedly control snakes, make thunder and lighting (a power associated with subincision), and kill enemies. Lightning could also be deployed to detect killers. *Barnman* assisted hunters using magic. Wunambal women sang to help smoke rise when they were burning the grassland, and they practiced love magic.[54]

As among Yuwaaliyaay people, mourners used to ingest small parts of the flesh of the dead in order, according to information given to Love, to obtain (in the case of men) greater skill in spearing kangaroo. Doctrines about the powers of totemic ancestral substances are clearly related to beliefs about the powers of the body.[55]

The *wanjina/wunggurr* complex of doctrines and practices had its own particular character, whereby the beings link clouds and rain, conception, increase, and human powers. Yolngu doctrines, considered next, created a stronger division between the ancestors and the giant snakes and pythons, and the latter did not have such an intimate connection to conception. Increase places and rites did not feature, but people did tap the powers of ancestral places.

Yolngu people

Ancestors

In this region, stories about totemic ancestors (*wangarr*) recount events from long, long ago (*baman'*). Ancestors took the form of animals, fish, plants, rocks, and other entities, as well as of humans, and certain key creator ancestors, especially those of the Dhuwa patri-moiety, were women. Some stories tell of how groups came to be created, others of how they gained their sacra and land. Yolngu stories of ancestral journeys create a complex web of cross-cutting connections between countries of the same moiety, for the *wangarr* and their stories, designs, and rituals were divided between the moieties. These links implied and expressed patterns of ownership of ritual elements, and cooperation in the performance of ceremonies.[56]

For example, stories about Djang'kawu, two sisters (and in some versions a brother) of the Dhuwa patri-moiety, recount their journey by canoe and on foot from the land of the dead in the east across the sea, 'following the sun' westward along the coast. They gave birth to the first people of the Dhuwa moiety groups, and gave them their languages, songs, ceremonies, and sacred objects—all aspects of their 'law' (*rom*). Myths of the Yirritja moiety also recount long journeys, such as the travels of Barramundi and Mangrove Log along the north coast. Among ancestors of the Yirritja moiety were Macassan men who came from what is now Sulawesi.

Wangarr had both aggressive and benign aspects. Among the most dangerous *wangarr* were the giant pythons and snakes (*motj*, *malagatj*) of the two patri-moieties, believed to lie beneath the deep waters of permanent waterholes, and believed to create lightning and monsoon rains (not unlike the *wunggurr* of Ngarinyin people and their neighbours). The giant snakes took the form of thunder clouds in the wet season, and were one of the sources of the monsoon rains. Conception spirits fell with the rains. To pollute the snakes' waters with blood or disturb them in other ways was thought to bring about extreme danger of storms and cyclones.

By Western standards, the ancestral times were relatively close. In some stories, human ancestors interacted with *wangarr*, and the recently dead returned to the domain of *wangarr* in the waters or across the sea.

Ancestral traces

As in other regions, the activities of ancestors left signs in the country, and their bodies, bodily substances, and belongings transformed into rocks, ochres, and trees. Rivers, lines of trees, and sandbanks marked the lines of ancestors' journeys, and mounds marked their camps. Springs bubbled up where they dug. Their digging sticks changed into living trees and their canoes into rocks. *Wangarr* brought living things, places, and groups into being by naming them, as well as through other creative acts. Manifestations of *wangarr*, as well as of spirits of the dead, could still be encountered by the living. [57]

Some *wangarr* belonged to the sky. The Sun ancestor (associated with the Djang'kawu) belonged to certain Dhuwa moiety groups, the Moon had his own myths, and an exchange ceremony celebrated the Morning Star. Certain stars represent Brolga, Possum, and Crocodile, associated with a mortuary ceremony.[58]

People spoke of traces of *wangarr* and other beings as their 'feet/footprints' (*luku, djalkiri*). They took the form of places, sacred designs and objects, songs, and dances.[59] Geometric designs 'of the elbow' (*likanbuy*) differentiated the patri-groups, and depicted sacred objects, which were the 'bones' (*ngaraka*) of the ancestors whose traces lay in a patri-group's 'bone country'. 'Elbow names' (*likan ya:ku*), called out at key points in ceremonies, connoted the connection between a patri-group, its land, and its ancestors.

Each patri-group had on each of its several countries a cluster of places associated with a variety of beings, each linked to a different set of other places and groups through ancestral journeys (or through similarity of their totemic ancestors). The sites and ancestors were associated with a variety of genres of ceremony, secret and public. A dominant theme in the relationship between ancestors and country is the mixing of salty and fresh water—in tidal rivers, on flood plains, and where rivers expel their water into the sea. It connotes both the cooperation of the patri-moieties and fertility through relations between opposite moiety groups, inland and coastal.

Individuals could gain knowledge of ancestral things through dreams or 'visions' (*mabuga*); for example, following an experience in a dream, a singer could compose a new song that, if accepted by other members of the group, would be added to his patri-group's corpus of songs.[60]

Other beings

Yolngu doctrines did not include a wide variety of dangerous beings of the forest; ghosts of the dead filled this role. *Mokuy* denotes both corpse and ghost of the dead in Yolngu languages. The word also referred to dangerous tricksters who were libidinous and cannibalistic and lived in the forests. Intermediaries between the living and the *wangarr*, they were the subject of public (*garma*) songs and dances, and interacted with *wangarr* in stories. Other beings with a similar role in public songs and dances were the honey-hunter Wurray, Bol'ngu the 'thunder-man', and Wandjuk the stick-insect.

In some myths the first people, coevals of the *wangarr*, had unique patrifilial group identities. Their personal names were 'big names', adopted recently as family surnames. In the 1970s, some Liyagawumirr people located human ancestors at the 'root' (*luku*) of their genealogies, only five or six generations before living adults.[61]

Conception and personal spirits

According to Yolngu doctrine, pregnancy occurred when a child spirit (*mali*, 'image') entered a woman from a waterhole or a place in the sea associated with *wangarr*. A man would 'find' (*malng'marama*) a child in a dream, reverie, or strange experience (such as catching an unusually large animal or fish or seeing a water-spout), and the mother would announce her pregnancy. The parents would consult with members of the patri-group in whose country the event occurred, and then the place would be deemed to be the child's place 'of the water', his or her 'very own country'. It was always of the same patri-moiety of the child but not necessarily the same patri-group. Men 'found' children, especially sons, strategically, in order to create new connections to country, especially the areas of dying patri-groups. Marks on the child's body indicated an aspect of the conception event, and water linked the baby's head, especially the soft fontanelle, to the waterhole of conception.[62]

Unlike Ngarinyin people and their neighbours, Yolngu people did not subscribe to an explicit doctrine of reincarnation. At death, a refraction of a person's spirit (*mokuy*) hung around the camp, dangerous to the living. The *birrimbirr* (soul) returned to a waterhole on his or her country, and/or to a land of the dead across the sea. One Yirritja-moiety land of the dead was Macassar ('Yumaynga') in what is now Sulawesi, from whence visitors sailed annually on the monsoon, until the beginning of the twentieth century, to collect and smoke trepang. The main land of the dead for the Dhuwa moiety was Burralku, a mythical island off the east coast, from whence the Djang'kawu sisters journeyed.

Ancestral powers

Yolngu people did not practice increase rites—indeed, one man told me in the 1970s that they were not necessary, for the *wangarr* gave them everything as a gift. Nevertheless, Yolngu people, like Sandbeach people, did believe that they could tap ancestral power in order to harm their enemies, for example by painting an image of a victim at an ancestral place or smearing ancestral substance (in the form of ochre) on a spearhead to render it more effective. There were also more benign uses of ancestral power: at regional ceremonies, for example participating groups were required to make peace, and the ceremony released ancestral power (*ma:rr*) for the benefit of participants. And people credited ancestral places, particularly waterholes and springs reserved for older men, with the power to turn one's hair grey.[63]

Sorcery, magic, and healing

Yolngu people distinguished the role of healer (*marrngitj*) from those of ritual leader and sorcerer. Other experts included rainmakers and clairvoyants. Yolngu people did not usually identify themselves as sorcerers, and sorcery was not part of the role of a healer (*marrngitj*). Rather, people accused outsiders, enemies, or the marginalised of sorcery in the event of a severe illness or death. However, some *marrngitj* and their families had reputations as sorcerers (*galka*); and one man of my acquaintance in the mid-1970s claimed to have caused many deaths in his region. It was the task of healers to combat the effects of sorcery by restoring bodily tissue and replacing essential organs. A sorcerer used heat and fire to enhance the effects of his or her actions while a healer used the cooling effects of water.[64]

Healers supposedly gained their powers through an encounter with a spirit or spirits, such as spirit children, a totemic animal or bird, or a spirit of the dead who adopted the person and conferred on him or her powers and magical objects. Or the person had an experience such as dying and coming to life again. A potential *marrngitj* also had to demonstrate an ability to treat illness. A child could also be a *marrngitj*. The various stones used by a *marrngitj* had a variety of healing powers, and healers were also believed to have familiars (*djamarrkuli*, 'children'), some with the identity of a totemic animal or bird. In Janice Reid's view, a community encouraged an individual who showed aptitude to take on the role of healer.

Yolngu hunters wore what were supposed to be packages of human blood and flesh on the forehead and behind the neck to impart keen sight and skill in hunting and fighting—the flesh, fat, bone, and blood of the dead supposedly enhanced an individual's power. According to a related doctrine, the spirit of a killer's victim supposedly entered his heart (via his leg), giving him greater strength, as if he had taken in the dead person's blood. The spirit might appear as a cockatoo or raven, or take the form of an animal that the killer could in turn kill. The meat, which was very fatty, was distributed to other men but kept from women.[65]

Comparisons and conclusions

The reader will have noticed similarities between the cosmologies of the seven regions. They include the creative events by ancestors long ago; their traces and powers in land, waters, and sky; the identity of totemic ancestors as game animals or 'meat'; the intermediate position of forerunners between the living and the ancestors; and the powers accorded to bodily substances. What were the implications of these cosmologies and of the differences between them for the organisation of economy? As I suggested earlier, the cosmologies were of particular importance in the framing of ancestral law (and relations of cooperation in its enactment), the constitution of country and connections to land, the direction of ancestral powers as well as 'magic' to economic ends, and resources of power available to individuals and groups. The case studies contrast strongly in the significance given to earth and sky, in the scale and scope of ancestral connections, and in the doctrines regarding ancestral and magical powers.

Earth and sky

Doctrines about traces of ancestors and ancestral events in the land, waters, and sky drew imaginary but unbreakable connections between places and persons, conceived of as the descendants and kin of the ancestors. So the location of ancestors above or below, their identity and distribution, and the connections between them through ancestral journeys or relations of identity had implications for the ways that people related to each other and to places.

Pitjantjatjara and Sandbeach people provide a telling contrast—between the rather localised totemic places of Sandbeach people, little connected by ancestral journeys, and the long and short cross-cutting ancestral journeys in Pitjantjatjara cosmology. The connections between places in Pitjantjatjara cosmology implied the sharing of songs, designs, and dances, and hence cooperation in performing them. What ancestral connections there were between Sandbeach countries were related to cooperation in male initiation ceremonies, in which local identity was also celebrated.

The cosmologies and cosmogonies of Wiil and Minong people, Ngarinyin people and their neighbours, and Yolngu people mixed shorter with longer ancestral connections. These had to do with the interplay between cooperation in major revelatory ceremonies (such as the Yolngu Nga:rra ceremony, which invoked the ancestral journeys of ancestors such as Djang'kawu) and the more local or restricted cooperation for mortuary ceremonies and some initiation ceremonies. In all these cases, the connections lay between clusters of patri-groups rather than the multi-based and overlapping groups of the Western Desert. The great snakes and pythons associated with lightning and the wet season provided another kind of diffuse, universal link among Ngarinyin and Yolngu groups, not through ancestral journeys but through their common identity and significance in spite of differences. The 'regional' ceremonies of the Yolngu, including Gunapipi, Mandayala, Djungguwan, and Ngulmarrk, reenacted their stories.[66] Common relations through Byamee had a similar quality among Yuwaaliyaay people and their neighbours.

The contrast between shared beings of the sky and local totemic identities echoes the one between long journeys and local ancestral traces. Common recognition of Byamee implies greater commonality of connection than the long ancestral journeys of the above regions (which were moiety-specific among Ngarinyin and Yolngu); this commonality was expressed in the cooperation between groups of a wide region in the performance of the Bora initiation. Similarly, the ancestors Mungan-ngaua and Tŭndun of the Kŭnai people were connected with the sacred objects at the heart of the Kŭnai Jerra-eil initiation. Local totemic places differentiated countries and country groups among both Kŭnai and Yuwaaliyaay people, although sites associated with Byamee also linked Yuwaaliyaay countries. Matri-group totems and matri-moieties further differentiated Yuwaaliyaay people, cutting across local identities, while gender totemism cross-cut Kŭnai communities.

The Kŭnai emphasis on ghosts of the dead in the sky from whom *birraark* (shamans) supposedly obtained their powers had a different significance. Kŭnai séances invoked the recently dead relatives of individuals or small overlapping kin groups, rather than remote ancestors of patri-groups or matri-groups. Yuwaaliyaay *wirreenun* played a similar role.

The cloud-beings of Ngarinyin people and their neighbours provide yet another contrast. The objectification of sky beings in the form of rock paintings linked them to patri-groups and patri-moieties. But connections to the sky both united groups, through the common categories of *wanjina* and *wunggurr*, and differentiated them, through their totemic identities and associations, just as clouds amass in the wet season and break up in the dry. Not that the sky was unimportant in Pitjantjatjara and Yolngu cosmologies; certain of the major creators were associated with the sun, and others with cloud formations and stars. But there were no doctrines of interaction between sorcerer–healers and ghosts of the dead in the clouds.

Conception doctrines linked individuals to places and groups in varying ways; from no definite location among Yuwaaliyaay people, apparently, to the doctrine of reincarnation among Ngarinyin people and their neighbours. These doctrines were linked to rights in land and waters (Chapter 9).

Ancestral powers and magic

I have tried to bring out some of the practical elements of Aboriginal cosmologies. Quasi-technologies with a central place in production rested on doctrines about ancestors and ancestral power and about the powers attributed to bodily substances, including those of the ancestors. In all the regions, people believed that people with the requisite powers could control the elements.

The 'increase' sites of Pitjantjatjara, Wiil and Minong, Sandbeach, and Ngarinyin people and their neighbours are cases in point. They were clearly related to ideas about the powers of human remains, especially the flesh and blood of the dead, which were central to magic and sorcery. A number of the case studies included doctrines about the power of places (when acted on with the proper rituals or procedures) to encourage the reproduction of food species and people, to attract lovers to a person, and to harm a person's enemies. Personally acquired magic of various kinds complemented these shared ancestral resources, but often included powers attributed to the remains of the human dead and 'spirits' of the dead.

Some notable features of the case studies were the variety of types of personal magic in the southeast (Kŭnai) and the contrast between, on the one hand, the regional economy of 'increase' sites in the Western Desert and west Kimberley, and, on the other hand, the competitive and aggressive use of ancestral powers among Sandbeach and Yolngu people. Western Desert people were indeed dependent on each other for access to resources in an unpredictable environment. In their resource-rich environment, Sandbeach people were economically dependent only on close neighbours; they tended to fight members of the groups into which they married and to accuse those just beyond that range of sorcery. While similar in many ways, Yolngu and Ngarinyin people differed in that Ngarinyin held 'increase' rites at ancestral sites while Yolngu did not.

Healers, sorcerers, and leaders

The ways in which people of the seven regions defined roles associated with their cosmologies varied. Kŭnai differentiated between healers, shamans (*birraark*), magician–sorcerers (*mŭlla-mullŭng*), who were local bosses with a wide array of imputed magical powers, and others such as seers. The shamans stand out as particularly important, being conductors of both séances and (along with the *mŭlla-mullŭng*) regional ceremonies. Yuwaaliyaay people combined the healer, shaman, and rainmaker roles into that of *wirreenun*, and acknowledged these as dangerous sorcerers as well. It seems likely that it was the matri-group elders, in control of their particular totemic representations, who organised Bora initiations and other rituals, along with the *wirreenun*. Some men may have been both a *wirreenun* and a matri-group elder.

Pitjantjatjara healer–sorcerers do not seem to have performed the role of shaman in the same way as their Kŭnai and Yuwaaliyaay equivalents, and increase rituals and other rituals were in the hands of elders with affiliations to the sites and ancestors in question. Sorcery takes on particular significance in the activities imputed to *kurdaitji*, especially in enforcing the secrecy of male rituals (see Chapter 8). The theme of corporeal interchange in the cosmology of Pitjantjatjara people and their neighbours is shared with Yolngu people—the 'life essence' of a person could be acquired and internalised by a sorcerer–healer to accrue power.

Sorcerer–healers re-emerge as dominant figures in the ethnography of Wiil and Minong people; they have both benign and aggressive powers, including the ability to commune with the dead and to give aid in hunting and gathering. Among Sandbeach people, by contrast, healers do not stand out as especially important figures. Indeed, Chase comments that people avoided hierarchical relations, except on the basis of kinship seniority. The display of local totemic representations in initiation ceremonies involved elders of local patri-groups.

Ngarinyin people and their neighbours attributed significance to *barnman* (healer–sorcerers), while patri-group elders were responsible for the totemic and increase rituals associated with the *wanjina* (ancestors). Yolngu people attributed sorcery largely to strangers, and differentiated the role of *marrngitj* (healer) from that of a patri-group elders, who led rituals, and from that of a moiety-specific ritual expert.

Cosmologies varied in other ways as well—for example, in their doctrines of conception and reincarnation. The doctrines of Ngarinyin people and their neighbours specified the most direct form of reincarnation, which was only implicit in Yolngu cosmologies. Others, such as Kŭnai and Yuwaaliyaay people, proposed a distant land of the dead.

Cosmologies and the economy

The organisation of the economy drew upon the totemic–ancestral domain in a variety of ways. First, ancestral doctrines (together with regional cooperation in rituals that reenacted ancestral events) underpinned ancestral 'law' and relations of authority. Second, as an aspect of 'law' people held and controlled land and waters (and in some regions items of equipment) in an idiom of ancestral connections and consubstantiality.

Third, people appealed to ancestral law to legitimate obligations among kin, as well as gender and age roles and consumption restrictions. Fourth, ancestral things—such as sacred objects, ceremonies and elements of ceremonies, and religious knowledge and experience—constituted items of exchange, and exchange lay at the heart of the Aboriginal economies of this book, as we shall see in Chapter 12.

The significance of the differences in the cosmologies and quasi-technologies are taken up in later chapters on exchange and the control of access to land and waters. Cosmological doctrines are also deeply implicated in governance, as the next chapter shows.

Further reading

For overviews of approaches to Aboriginal religions see Howard Morphy's chapter in *Social Anthropology and Australian Aboriginal Studies*, edited by R. M. Berndt and Bob Tonkinson (1988), and Tony Swain's *Interpreting Aboriginal Religion: An Historical Account* (1985). This chapter touched on the old debate about the status of Aboriginal doctrines and practices as 'religion'. Both Émile Durkheim, in his *Elementary Forms of the Religious Life* (1965 [1915]), and W. E. H. Stanner, in *On Aboriginal Religion* (1964) interpreted Aboriginal rituals as akin to 'sacrifice', one of their criteria for doctrines and practices counting as a religion.

The early debate over the supposed Christian origins of beliefs in sky beings in the southeast has recently been resurrected in a different form by Tony Swain in his *A Place for Strangers* (1993). L. R. Hiatt reviews the debate in *Arguments about Aborigines* (1996).[67]

The expressions 'the Dreaming' and 'the Dreamtime' have been the subject of a heated debate between Patrick Wolfe, who argues that the expressions were imposed as an aspect of the colonial gaze, and Howard Morphy, who insists that Arrernte people were active in explaining their view of the world to Baldwin Spencer and F. J. Gillen. See Wolfe's *Settler Colonialism and the Transformation of Anthropology* (1999) and Morphy's 'Empiricism to metaphysics' (1996).

Notes

1   See Needham (1972) on 'belief' in anthropology; see Rose (1988) on concepts of cosmogony and cosmology. The sense given to 'doctrine' here is from the *Oxford English Dictionary*. On 'doxa' see Bourdieu (1990).

2   On 'temporal space' see Rudder (1993). On consubstantial links see Stanner (1965b) and Munn (1970).

3   See Merlan's review of conception doctrines (1986).

4   See Munn (1970) on transformations in Warlpiri and Pitjantjatjara cosmologies.

5   On the concept of 'following' ancestral precedent see, for example, Tamisari (1998: 253).

6   See Stanner (1965b) on Aboriginal religion and totemism.

7   See McDonald (2002) for a comparison between Aboriginal and Christian cosmologies.

8   On Aboriginal religions see Berndt (1974).

9   On universal principles of magic see Frazer (1923–27).

10 Accounts of Kŭnai myths appear in Bulmer (1994, Papers: *passim*), Howitt (Papers, SLV Box 8: ms1053/3(b), MV B4 F7 xm527; MEB Howitt 'Legends and Folklore' cited in Howitt 1904), and Frazer (1939). On *mŭk-kŭnai* and *mŭk-rukŭt* see Howitt (1904: 487). On 'old time people' or 'front people' see Bulmer (Papers, MV B10 F5 xm931).

11 See Bulmer (in Curr 1887: 547), Dow (n.d.) and Howitt (Papers, MV B4 F7 xm527; SLV Box 8 ms 1053/4(a): 68) on Kŭnai ancestral traces.

12 For doctrines of other beings in Kŭnai cosmology see Buchan Sesquicentenary Committee (1989: 1), Howitt (in Fison and Howitt 1880: 250, 254–5; 1904: 355–6, 485; Papers, MV B4 F7 xm527; Papers, SLV B8 ms1053/4(a): 50), Smyth (1878: 472), and Walker (1971: 200).

13 On Kŭnai beliefs about the soul and about ghosts of the dead see Howitt (1880; 1904: 437–8, 439, 461; Papers, SLV Box 8 ms1053/3(b): 24; 1904: 390, 437), Bulmer (Papers, MV B10 F5 xm922: 49). *Yambo* may have had the meaning 'image', as in *yamboginni*, 'image magic'. The information on conception is from Coral Dow (pers. com.)

14 On Kŭnai healers and other experts see Bulmer (1994: 21–4), Frazer (1939: 24), Howitt (in Fison & Howitt 1880: 252; 1904: 274, 355–6, 376–9, 389–90, 397, 408–10).

15 See Howitt (Papers, SLV Box 8 ms 1053/4(a): 58) on the imputed powers of the hand.

16 Howitt (1904: 397, 397n) describes Kŭnai rainmaking.

17 On Pitjantjatjara and other Western Desert doctrines about ancestors see Douglas (1977), Layton (1979: 17–32), Munn (1970: 143–4), Mountford (1976: 221, 462), Tonkinson (1991: 109–11), and Viesner (2000: 3).

18 The quotation is from Munn (1970: 151).

19 Sources on ancestral transformations and sites include Mountford (1976: 222–8, 259, 458–9, 558), Munn (1970: 144–51), and Tonkinson (1991: 110–11, 126–7).

20 See Viesner (2000) and R. M. and C. H. Berndt (1945) on other beings.

21 Western Desert conception doctrines are described by Mountford (1976: 546, 553), Tonkinson (1991: 80–2), and Viesner (2000: 7).

22 See Mountford (1976: 558) on spirits of the dead.

23 On increase and healing sites see Mountford (1976: 53, 134, 139, 557), Tonkinson (1991: 79, 113, 118), and Viesner (2000: 3–5); on regional responsibility for increase rites see Mountford (1976: 133) and Tonkinson (1991: 117).

24 See R. M. and C. H. Berndt (1945: 183–6) on love magic at Ooldea.

25 See Mountford (1976: 560) and Viesner (2000: II 1g) on Pitjantjatjara *ngankari*.

26 The quotation is from Parker (1905: 6).

27 On Yuwaaliyaay ancestral doctrines see Parker (1905: 4, 7–8), and on others of the region see Beckett et al. (2002). See Berndt (1947) for similar conceptions among Wiradjiri and Wangaaybuwan people. I infer the menstrual source of rain from Parker's reference to a 'ball of blood' rolling down the mountain from Birrahgnooloo.

28 See Parker (1905: 95–104) on Yuwaaliyaay ancestral traces in the land and sky. On the importance of Emu, see Blows (1975).

29 On other beings in Yuwaaliyaay cosmology see Parker (1905: 47, 59, 135ff).

30 See Parker (1905: 27–8, 35, 50–1, 53) on conception spirits, dream-spirits, spirits of the dead, and portents. On the ingestion of bodily fluids see Parker (1905: 38).

31 See Parker (1905: 25–30, 35–8, 40) on *wirreenun*, healers, and other experts. On Byamee as the most powerful *wirreenun* see Parker (1896).

32 On Yuwaaliyaay rain-making see Parker (1905: 8, 47–9).

33 On Wiil/Miṉong ancestral doctrines see Barker (Journals, 14 May 1830, 19 June 1830, quoted in Le Souëf 1993: 27), Green (1989: 20, 21, 24), Hassell (1934; 1935; 1936), and von Brandenstein (1977: 172).

34 Wiil/Miṉong ancestral stories and sites are described by Barker (Journals, 25 November 1830 quoted in Le Souëf 1993: 27), Bignell (1977: 19), and Hassell (1935: 124–5); see also Le Souëf (1993: 26). On the sky see Hassell (1934: 235–8) and Barker (1830–31 cited in Le Souëf 1993: 26).

35 See Barker (1992: 4 March 1830, cited in Le Souëf 1993: 25), Bates (1985: 192–3,197, 219), and Hassell (1936: 702–3) on other beings in Wiil/Miṉong doctrines.

36 On portents see Bates (1985: 197).

37 See Barker (1992: 25 April, 14 October 1830, cited in Green 1989: 20, 53), Bates (1985: 133–4, 232) on conception doctrines, personal spirits, and ghosts of the dead.

38 On 'increase' in the southwest see Barker (1992: 7 November 1830, cited in Green 1989: 23) and Bates (1985: 199–200).

39 For doctrines on magic and magicians in the southwest see Bates (1985: 230), Hassell (1936: 706–8), Nind (1831: 41).

40 On rainmaking see Bates (1985: 231, 237) and Hassell (1975: 97), and on other powers see Bates (1985: 231–2) and Barker (1992: 5 May 1830, cited in Green 1989: 7, 20).

41 Sandbeach ancestral doctrines are described by Laade (1964: 12), Rigsby and Chase (1998: 196, 200), and Thomson (1933: 460–1, 500–1).

42 For Sandbeach doctrines on ancestral sites and 'story places' see Chase (1978: 166; 1980b: 134, 139–41, 147–9; 1984) and Thomson (1933: 463–7).

43 See Chase (1980: 182–3), Rigsby and Chase (1998: 197), and Thomson (1933: 493–7, 499) on conception beliefs and *ngachimu nguunthachi*.

44 On increase rites and rainmaking see Chase (1980: 148) and Thomson (1933: 501; 1934: 25l; Papers, MV File 164, 168, 189; Photographic collection 3070–78).

45 See Chase (1980: 194) and Thomson (1934: 240, 250–2; Papers, MV Files 189, 196 undated, p.6) on magical techniques.

46 For reports on the ancestral doctrines of Ngarinyin people and their neighbours see Blundell (1975: 69–70), Blundell and Layton (1978), Capell (1972: 26, 57–8), Crawford (1968: *passim*), Lommel (1949; 1997 [1952]), Lommel and Mowaljarlai (1994: 283–7), Love (1936: 21–2, 181), Mowaljarlai and Malnic (1993), Pentony (1938 #34), and Redmond (2001a: 206–64, 284–311).

47 For doctrines of ancestral traces among Ngarinyin people and their neighbours see Crawford (1968: *passim*), Lommel (1997: 17, 43), Redmond (2001a: 122–3; 2001b: 206–64, 284–311), and Lommel and Mowaljarlai (1994: 283–7); and see Crawford (1968: 119, 121) on cicatrices and Redmond (2001a: 295–7) on conception marks.

48 On 'gwion' ('Bradshaw') figures see Doring (2000) and Lommel (1997: 17).

49 See Redmond (2001b: 121) on the dreaming of new *balga* songs.

50 On doctrines of other beings see Crawford (1968: 91, 94), Lommel (1997: 66), Redmond (2001b: 265–9, 301–4), and Pentony (1938 #38).

51 On northwest Kimberley conception doctrines see Crawford (1968: 34), Lommel (1997: 35), Love (1936: 181), and Redmond (2001b: 151–6). On doctrines of death and reincarnation see Blundell (1975: 73), Crawford (1968: 33, 46, 105), Lommel (1997: 33), Love (1936: 23, 184), and Redmond (2001b: 265–71).

52 On increase sites and beliefs see Blundell (1975 vol. 1: 69, 72–3), Crawford (1968: 24–6, 34, 37), Lommel (1997: 19), Love (1936: 22, 64), and Redmond (2001b: 209). On rainmaking see Redmond (2001b: 284–5).

53 Some writers assert that retouching took place every year, while others say that it took place only when necessary—see Capell (1939b: 390), Crawford (1968: 137), Lommel (1997: 19), and Love (Papers: 7). Tony Redmond (pers. com.) believes the latter view to be better supported.

54 See Crawford (1968: 96, 111), Lommel (1997: 50–61), Lommel and Mowaljarlai (1994: 283–7), Love (1936: 202–4), and Redmond (2001b: 286–9) on *barnman*.

55 On necrophagy see Love (1930: 134).

56 Sources on Yolngu ancestral doctrines include Keen (1994), Morphy (1984: 17; 1990), Rudder (1993), Tamisari (1998), Warner (1937: 10, 250–9), and Williams (1986: 28).

57 On the creative acts of the ancestors see Tamisari (1998: 253–5).

58 On the creation of stars see Groger-Wurm (1973: 121).

59 On Yolngu ancestral traces and places see R. M. Berndt (1976), Keen (1994: 106, 135, 204), Morphy (1989; 1991). On the concept of *gaṉma* see Creighton (2003) and Marika-Munungguritj et al. (1990).

60 See Tamisari (1998: 258) and Toner (2000; 2001) on new songs.

61 See Rudder (1993: 271–2) on intermediary ancestors, and Warner (1937: 554–7) on the *mokuy* Wurray ('Ure').

62 See Rudder (1993: 91), Tamisari (1998: 255), and Warner (1937: 21–5) on Yolngu conception doctrines. The information on links through water is from Sophie Creighton (pers. com.).

63 On Yolngu ancestral powers see Morphy (1991: 133, 194; 1992) and Thomson (1975).

64 See Reid (1983), Warner (1937: 198–206, 210–18, 226–7), and Webb (1935) on Yolngu sorcerers and healers.

65 On packages of flesh see Thomson (1948b: 414); on a dead person's spirit see Warner (1937: 165).

66 Warner (1937: 259–311) describes these ceremonies and the associated mythology.

67 For a critical review of Swain (1993) see Keen (1994b).

8

Governance

Introduction

A comparative study of Aboriginal economy and society must provide an understanding of the ways in which social orders and the power relations embedded in
them were maintained and reproduced. This chapter is about general features of
social control and relations of power, but it will pay special attention to the place of
ancestral 'law' in the social order.

It is useful to separate out a number of aspects of governance.[1] The first is the
framing of principles, norms, and rules of behaviour, to which people attempt to
hold one another in the governing of social life. Second is socialisation, through
which people attempt to shape others, especially young people, more permanently.
This is governance in the long term, as people work to inculcate in others dispositions to behave in desired ways—what Pierre Bourdieu calls their *habitus*.

Third is action through which people try to control people and exert power in a
more direct way. Such action varies from subtle attempts to influence others, through
persuasion, manipulation, and command, to coercion involving force. One form of
direct control is closely related to socialisation: it is the ritual allocation of roles
through *rites de passage* in which a person undergoes certain formal procedures in
order to acquire a certain status. More obviously to do with law and governance are
processes to do with the enforcement of norms, processes of adjudication and redress
for wrongs. Certain forms of action were characteristic of Aboriginal disputes and
dispute resolution, especially talion, or 'payback', as well as mediation.

Fourth are the kinds of relations and structures involved in governance and the
exercise of power. In Aboriginal contexts, these relations include kinship, age, and
gender. The ethnographies reveal very specific concepts and values of individual
autonomy and relatedness. It is also necessary to look at the resources that people
drew upon in establishing and maintaining power differences.

Ancestral law

Shared norms do not require specialised law-making bodies. We shall see that people of several of the regions, perhaps all of them, shared a concept that can be translated as 'ancestral law' or the 'proper way', having its origin in the intentions and actions of totemic creator ancestors. People of broad regions agreed about the fundamentals and the legitimacy of 'law', though specific doctrines varied from group to group. A body of law consisted of both explicit rules and implicit principles about obligations related to kinship and about connections to and rights in land, waters, and their resources. It also included the proper way to do things not so easily thought of as following rules, such as performing ceremonies, making designs, and manufacturing equipment. As Myers points out, the concept of ancestral law places the making of rules and norms outside the realm of human action, representing them as nonarbitrary and transcending immediate relations.[2]

The genius of ancestral law was that people of a wide region could agree to a body of legitimate law without there being legislators, and in spite of the autonomy of individuals and kin groups. However, because they were contained and transmitted in oral tradition and in the absence of centralised legislative and judicial institutions, the rules and principles of ancestral law had a large discretionary component. People even of adjacent areas adhered to somewhat different doctrines and principles , and the principles were multivalent enough to allow a good deal of latitude in their interpretation.[3] The extent to which a person could gain acceptance of their interpretation of law in order to justify their actions depended on the social resources he or she could bring to bear on the matter.

Networks of regional cooperation underpinned the sharing of ancestral law. People of a wide region, often including people of several regional or language identities, cooperated in the performance of ceremonies that reenacted ancestral events and made ancestral beings visible and tangible. These networks of cooperation also provided the framework for structures of authority that were moulded around relations of age and gender, imbued with authority, and that transcended local relationships. Male initiation ceremonies combined socialisation practices with these features.

Socialisation through initiation

Socialisation techniques inculcate values, beliefs, attitudes, knowledge, and skills, changing people's dispositions and hence the ways in which they behave generally. Anthropologists and educationists have described the particular quality of Aboriginal socialisation techniques, with their stress on imitation and trial and error rather than pedagogy.[4] Male initiation combined socialisation techniques with dramatisations of ancestral action. And it was these dramatisations that reinforced the ancestral basis of law, by making ancestral events seem, in Clifford Geertz's words, 'uniquely realistic'. Importantly, people across a wide region, usually speakers of a variety of languages, cooperated in the performance of these ceremonies.[5]

As several anthropologists have remarked, certain ritual practices tended to induce in young people a disposition to conform to shared values and norms, and to defer to people in authority. These dramatic interventions in people's lives imposed varying degrees of privation, pain, mutilation, and other harsh treatment. We shall see that the most physically rigorous modes of male initiation occurred in the Western Desert, while the Jerra-eil ceremony performed by Kŭnai people and the Bora ceremony of the Yuwaaliyaay did not centrally involve the infliction of pain and mutilation.

The initiation and revelatory ceremonies also served as 'gateways' to formalised social statuses and social powers related to the life-cycle. Several of the ethnographies document these statuses, as well as the prerogatives and constraints attached to each.

Direct action

Direct and immediate forms of control include such actions as influence, persuasion, manipulation, command, and coercion. I cannot consider here all the ways in which people controlled one another, in all kinds of context, but I will describe the general character of control, some of the ways in which people applied 'law' to settle disputes and to pursue their interests, and the structures involved in these.

The Berndts remark that informal meetings of older people were often used to discuss problems and help settle disputes, and Nancy Williams has described the role of elders in the resolution of Yolngu disputes. In a more unusual practice, described by George Taplin, among Ngarinyerri people of South Australia the leaders of neighbouring groups would come together to hear evidence from defenders, accusers, and other witnesses, and to mete out punishment. In a similar vein, Ken Maddock finds a resemblance between the procedures used to discover the identity of a sorcerer after a death and the inquests of Western law.[6]

In the absence of overarching governmental bodies with the power to make and enforce laws and to adjudicate disputes, it was up to individuals and their kin to take measures to enforce their interpretations of law, both to guide behaviour (such as contracting a marriage) and to deal with perceived breaches. R. M. Berndt called this kind of practice 'self-help'. People of a wide region agreed about the general principles of proper behaviour, such as the right relationships for marriage and the binding nature of bestowal contracts. When a law was breached, or allegedly breached, it was up to the aggrieved party to gain the support of kin and take redressive action; no specialised political or legal bodies existed to which they could appeal.[7]

In the conduct of affairs, what Basil Sansom calls 'jurisdictions' and 'orders of business' tended to be discrete. Once children joined a peer group, their activities were their own affair, and adults seldom intervened unless the children were putting themselves in some danger. Marrying was the business of the kin groups involved, although a wider community became involved if incest prohibitions were broken. The regulation of fertility and childbirth was strictly women's business, while the enforcement of religious secrecy fell to senior men in charge of the secret ceremonies, objects, and knowledge.

One disadvantage of this kind of governmental structure was that things could, and did, get out of hand. Application of the principle of reciprocity to redress for wrongs in the form of talion, or 'payback', resulted in endless feuds, such as those described by W. Lloyd Warner. (People conceptualised payback as equivalent to reciprocity in exchange—it achieved balance.) Furthermore, those with the greatest resources were able to enforce their interpretations of law, and hence further their interests. But there were checks and balances. The intricate web of kinship meant that some individuals who had conflicting loyalties played the role of mediator. Ancestral law provided means for settling disputes, such as the Yolngu Makarrata ceremony; alternatively, a dispute might be settled through some kind of reparation (see Plate 8.1).

These forms of redressive action bring out Aboriginal concepts of agency, responsibility, and blame. David Martin writes of the way in which Wik people displace responsibility from the individual onto other agents, and are taught to do so from an early age. A person who injures or kills another may claim that sorcery caused them to act in that way. Conversely, retribution may legitimately fall on the kinsman or kinswoman of an offender, or a person of the same shared identity, rather than the offender.[8]

Relations and resources of power

If Aboriginal societies did not have specialised governmental and judicial bodies, then how did governance take place, and upon what resources did people draw?[9]

The anthropologist Lauriston Sharp strongly emphasised the networks and dyads of kin relations, the norms governing them, and the roles associated with them. These roles entailed relations of deference, respect, intimacy, subordination, and superordination. While the ethnographic case studies bear out this view, other factors, such as age and gender, also came into play. An important feature of these categories is their pervasiveness, cutting across local affiliations and kin networks. The case studies will reveal some variation in the effect of these relations, especially gender, among the seven regions.

A number of writers on Aboriginal social relations highlight the interplay between the assertion of individual autonomy and embeddedness in networks of obligation, support, and authority (see Athol Chase on Sandbeach people below). In Myers's account of Pintupi politics, people expressed relations between senior and junior people in the age hierarchy in terms of nurturance or 'looking after' (*kanyiny-inpa*). Autonomy, in terms of the ability to make choices, increased with age and ritual status. But Pintupi people also valued the field of relations (*walytja*) for the support it gave them.

European observers of Aboriginal social life have looked for positions akin to those of the holders of chiefly office—some thought that they found them while others denied their existence. While unique positions of command were not a feature of Aboriginal governance, individuals achieved or were assigned prominence in a number of ways. One was through birth order: a younger sibling generally deferred to an older sibling, and the firstborn was generally the leader of a group. In another, individuals gained prominence through their knowledge and skills—ritual knowledge, singing and fighting skills, magical powers, sorcery ability, etc. But the ability to gain control of localised material resources, as well as social resources, was central to relations between (in English terms) a 'boss' and their 'followers' or 'helpers'. These resources included resource-rich places, localised spiritual and magical resources associated with ancestors, the ability to perform ancestral ceremonies, and the social capital associated with marriage. To be a 'boss' one had to control a resource (such as a ceremony or a place rich in swan eggs) that required the work of helpers and entailed the responsibility to provide for them generously.

Gender relations in Aboriginal societies have been the subject of continuing discussion. Early professional anthropology certainly suffered from a male bias, although this cannot be said of the ethnography of Ethel Hassell and Katie Parker. Writing in early 1930s, W. Lloyd Warner depicted Yolngu ('Murngin') women as less than complete social beings and as ritually inferior. Phyllis Kaberry very swiftly attempted to restore the balance—her book on Kimberley women appeared two years after Warner's. Female anthropologists working later in the mid-twentieth century, notably Catherine Berndt and Isobel White, depicted gender relations as complementary rather than unequal. Writing from the point of view of neo-Marxist theory, John Bern saw women as exploited by men. The feminist anthropologist Diane Bell depicted Kayteje women as having lost their former independence through the colonial process, while Annette Hamilton depicts men's and women's domains in the east of the Western Desert as separate spheres of 'homosociality', both more separate and more equal than in northern Australia.

In her review of the anthropology of gender in Aboriginal societies, Francesca Merlan takes a measured position. Marriage practices defined women, not men, as bestowable. Although not mere objects, women were mainly reactive to marriage arrangements made by others, though they gained control with age. Men tended to deploy women's sexuality in wider relations, and women occupied a structurally disadvantaged position in ritual life, 'more excluded than excluding' and subject to the threat of violent sanctions.[10]

Governance and economy

What has all this to do with the economy? The neo-Marxist program related power to the economy in a direct way: relations of dominance were the political corollary of economic exploitation, and religion provided the ideology justifying male dominance. While I do not find it helpful to take domination as primary, nevertheless the economic bases and consequences of power differences remain an important concern and a significant aspect of variation between the regions. Weiner and Godelier propose a different kind of link in which inalienable possessions and 'the sacred' underpin relations of authority and hierarchy in the constitution of social order, and give value to 'inalienable gifts' in exchange networks (see Chapter 12).

One link between governance and economy is in the direct organisation of economic activities, considered in Chapter 11. Other chapters of this book also touch on matters of governance—the control of access to land, waters, and their resources, for example, and marriage bestowal. Rules governing production and consumption are another aspect. The case studies in this chapter concern broader, more general effects—ancestral law; the socialisation aspects of initiation; direct action, such as fights and feuds; and relations of power, including age, gender, and leadership. I have selected these aspects of governance in order to bring out similarities and differences, and to reflect the kinds of ethnographic evidence available. At the end of the chapter I will draw some inferences from the cases studies for the organisation of economy.

Kŭnai people

Ancestral law

It is not certain whether Kŭnai people conceived of a system of law with its origins in the ancestors. Nevertheless, Howitt writes of the 'old ancestral virtues', which older men hoped to restore through a revival of male initiation, and 'ancient customs', of which the older people were the 'repositories'.[11] There is evidence that the more senior people had the authority to interpret and enforce rules governing, for example, marriage. And people of the region cooperated in performing large-scale rituals that celebrated ancestral creation and invoked regional principles of identity and relationships. Furthermore, control of magic, access to ghosts of the dead (and their world in the sky), and control of highly valued secret rituals were central to relations of power and authority.

Socialisation through initiation

Male initiation through the Jerra-eil ('leaf') ceremony turned 'boys' into 'bachelors' and separated them from women; it created bonds among co-initiates and revealed to them the religious secrets of adult men. People from a wide region participated in Jerra-eil and it was a major public event. But it was quite distinct from the equivalent rituals of the regions to the east, north, and west; it did not, for example, involve bodily mutilation (such as tooth avulsion or circumcision), although piercing of the nasal septum was an adjunct.[12]

When the Jerra-eil ceremony's organisers decided that a sufficient number of youths were ready for initiation, they summoned people from the region through messengers. The ceremony had a number of distinct phases: a camp phase, which involved both men and women and in which initiates underwent disciplines; a secluded phase, in which they came under dietary restrictions and the older men revealed sacred objects; and a water ceremony, through which the initiates returned to life in the residence group. Senior men and women and the *mŭlla-mŭllŭng* (sorcerer–magicians) oversaw the organisation of the ceremony.

Boys moved from the status of *wot-woti* (uninitiated boy) to *tutnŭrrŭng* (novice) at the end of the camp phase, then to *brewit* (bachelor), conferred with the male apparel of belt, apron, armlets, forehead-band, nose-peg, and necklace. As adepts of the ceremony, they were now *jerra-eil*. Co-initiates became 'brothers' and 'mates' (*brogan*). They joined the bachelors' camp, sleeping away from their parent's hearth. Girls of the same age remained with their parents in the camp.

At the time of Howitt's research, Kŭnai people were explicit about the socialisation effects of the Jerra-eil—youths had been 'growing wild' as a result of spending too much time with white people. *Mŭlla-mŭllŭng* performed magical action on initiates to engender in them an inclination to share, and not be selfish and greedy. During the seclusion phase, the youths were enjoined to adhere to certain moral precepts; as Howitt translated them they were to:

- listen to and obey the old men
- share everything they had with their 'friends'
- live peaceably with their friends
- not interfere with girls or married women
- obey the food restrictions until released from them by the old men.

Initiates had to avoid contact with women for a period.

Kŭnai youths did not have cicatrices, except for those who gained the marks (on the arms, for example) from their Monaro neighbours in the colonial period. However, some time before a boy was initiated, a friend would pierce his nasal septum with a bone point, and insert a bone into the hole. But this was not a formal process of initiation. Girls wore scars across the back and arms, said to be merely for decoration.

Direct action

The principle of 'self-help' certainly applied in Gippsland. John Bulmer remarks that after a murder it was up to the victim's 'friends' to avenge the death.[13] Bulmer thought that fights at Lake Tyers Mission (using boomerangs or clubs) occurred about four times a week, occasioned by disputes over magic, sorcery, and relations between men and women. Disputes about marriage or the treatment of women led to fights and feuds between men. Kŭnai people blamed strangers (*brajerak*) for homicides committed by strangulation in silent sneak attacks.

Networks of alliances in disputes followed kin lines, and reflected marriage networks that cross-cut regional and local identity. In his account of a revenge killing in about 1865, Howitt shows that those who cooperated were related to the dead man through patrilateral and matrilateral connections. Indeed, the first man to spear the killer in one feud was the murdered man's sister's son, reflecting the importance of this relationship.

Howitt describes a form of 'ordeal', similar to the Yolngu Makarrata ceremony described later in the chapter, in which an alleged offender submitted to spears and throwing sticks thrown by the alleged victim's kin.

Relations of power[14]

Body mutilation—piercing of the nasal septum for boys, scarification for girls—marked the passage from one age grade to another, and differentiated the genders. As well as kinship relations, totemic and gender identity, age, and ritual status governed the place of males in the social world, while age and reproductive status primarily governed that of females, although details of Kŭnai age grades have not been recorded. Kin terms differentiating the generations, as well as younger and older siblings, marked seniority in kin relations.

Howitt comments that a man's influence increased with age, until he was regarded as 'one of the elders'. Being the son of an influential man also conferred advantage.

Influential older men played a particularly central role in the organisation of initiation rites, and had the last word in matters of moment. Prominent men and women were active in dealing with breaches of law and custom.

Older men taught young men fighting techniques, and punished offences by young men, although it is not altogether clear which offences were punished, or how. People grumbled about old men committing offences with impunity, but the possibility of collective retaliation placed limitations on the abuse of power by senior men.

Bulmer remarks that Kŭnai people seldom spoke about the activities of men and women in the same breath, suggesting that there were rather distinct male and female domains of social relations and activities. As elsewhere, men excluded women from the secret spheres of ceremonies, and though some women may have known male secrets, they could not admit to that fact. Women supposedly knew the sky-being only as 'our father' (*mungan-ngaua*), while males had access to more detailed knowledge of cosmology. Men excluded women from secret aspects of male initiation; however, women took a prominent role in the public phases of initiation. Moreover, the ethnography conveys an impression of greater gender equality than in some other regions. Certainly Bulmer and Howitt report violent punishment, including pack rape and spearing, against women deemed to be unfaithful. However, it could happen that a wife attacked her husband with an axe; and an adulterous man was supposed to undergo communal punishment from women using yam sticks.[15] Howitt comments on the willingness of men to carry their aged and infirm wives about the country.

Decision-making processes appear to have included discussions in which senior women enjoyed authority as well as the men; Howitt writes:

> In affairs of moment the women have a voice, and it is not without weight. They consulted with the men about the ceremonies of initiation. They kept alive the stringent marriage laws. They are also, with the men, repositories of the ancient customs, and strongly influence public opinion.[16]

There were no hereditary positions of authority or leadership in Gippsland. The control of magic provided a significant instrument of influence; Bulmer remarks that the *mŭlla-mullŭng* took full advantage of their position by keeping people 'in dread of their powers', although they 'had no other authority in the direction of affairs'. Some prominent men had reputations as 'great men' (*gweraeil-kŭnai*, 'old man') on the basis of fighting skill or skill in magic; there were also young men who achieved prominence, through their ability to fight well or talk well. It seems likely that some older men had considerable authority among close kin—Bulmer recalled an older man taking to two troublesome young men with a club. And one man claimed to Howitt that he 'carried' or 'held' his people, former leaders having died.[17]

Initiation ceremonies provided a means for influential men from different communities across the region to cooperate and exercise their power. *Mŭlla-mullŭng* (magicians) evidently had prominent positions as leaders of rituals and *birraark* (shamans) as conductors of séances, but the prohibition of homicide must have limited the role of the latter as fighters. Hagenauer describes a woman accredited with powers to heal and notes that she had considerable influence in the community.[18]

Governance among Pitjantjatjara people and their neighbours had a similar structure to Kǔnai governance, but authority relations between generations were particularly significant.

Pitjantjatjara people and their neighbours

Rather little has been published on the character of governance among Pitjantjatjara people and their immediate neighbours. I supplement writings specifically about Pitjantjatjara and their close neighbours with Fred Myer's writings about Pintupi people to the north.

Ancestral law

The Western Desert concept of *tjukurrpa*, often translated as 'the Dreaming', incorporates the notion of ancestral law. The word refers both to particular myths and to the creative epoch as opposed to *yuti* (the visible) or *mularrpa* ('what really happened').[19] As Myers explains it, *tjukurrpa* 'constitutes the ground or foundation of the visible, present-day world' and objectifies social norms. Nancy Munn argues that, by becoming identified with ancestors and places through the succession of generations and by being put in contact with sacred objects and designs in rituals, an individual was socialised into a totemic landscape imbued with ancestral authority.

Socialisation through initiation

Myths about the long journeys of certain ancestors explained how male initiation rites came into being.[20]

Fully initiated men, including old men, organised the initiation of two or three novices, mediated by the novices' mothers' brothers rather than their fathers. The boys were taken away to experience a secret male rite, had the nasal septum pierced and an upper incisor avulsed, and were then prohibited from any social relations with women. After a period of seclusion in the camp, the boys were beaten and tossed into the air by men and women. Women's dances were followed by a fire ceremony, in which the throwing of firebrands expressed hostility between the gender moieties.

Men organised their ceremonies by totemic 'lodge' (a group with common relations to ancestral sites and ceremonies) as well as generation moiety. Novices attended secret men's songs and dances, and then were circumcised with a stone knife. The man or men who carried out the operation, each a 'mother's brother' of the initiate, became obligated to bestow a wife on him. The boy's status changed to that of 'man', and he was given sacred objects. After the wound had healed, he undertook a journey from waterhole to waterhole, the exact path being determined by his totemic connections. He could then attend male totemic ceremonies and hunt for his own meat, which would be cooked by his mother or another female relative.

After a year or two the young man was subincised, and his hair was cut. He could then marry, be introduced to other esoteric totemic ceremonies, and have sacred objects revealed to him. About a year after subincision, his 'brothers' would cut cicatrices on his back, after which he was fully initiated.

By comparison with the other regions, the notable feature of male initiation in this region is the number of physical ordeals a young man had to undergo—piercing of the nasal septum, tooth avulsion, circumcision and subincision of the penis, and scarification. Men punished infringements of ritual secrecy with death.

Direct action

Fights, revenge expeditions, and feuds were commonplace in the Western Desert, as elsewhere in Australia. Myers comments on both men's and women's pride in their fighting prowess, and on their acceptance of violence as way of expressing feelings. Conflict and attempts at intimidation occurred regularly; people threatened those who declined to share food, for example. However, people resolved conflict less often by collective action and subordination of individual autonomy than by moving away from conflict situations.[21]

Revenge expeditions were commonplace in the Western Desert, occasioned by accusations of sorcery as well as acts of violence. One violent act gave rise to others as people attacked those they blamed for failing to protect a victim. The institution of *kurdaitji* ('feather-foot men') constituted both a means of secret attack and of explanation. Men carried out such attacks as punishment for ritual offences (such as breaches of secrecy) or as revenge for alleged wrongs. But people also explained strange events, especially at night, as the actions of *kurdaitji*.[22]

It was important for an individual's security and support that they have an extensive network of relatives—people stressed that they were not alone. But people also lived with their enemies.

Disputes were sometimes settled at the times when people gathered in large numbers for ceremonies. Individuals and groups had the opportunity to air grievances or seek redress for wrongs, with a minimum of violence. Ideally, the ceremony would then proceed peacefully and fruitfully.[23]

Relations of power

Dyadic kin relations—such as father to son, mother's brother to sister's son, and mother to daughter—had a hierarchical component. The senior could tell the junior what to do, at least in somes contexts; for example, a mother had a say in her daughter's bestowal. Their ability to tell others what to do manifested itself mainly in relation to rituals, ancestral sites, and marriage.[24]

Myers's view of Pintubi political relations is that they were gerontocratic but without 'true leaders'. Age-related hierarchy showed itself in the deference of juniors to elders, which Pintubi people expressed in a particular idiom: older and more knowledgeable people 'looked after' (*kanyinyinpa*) younger people. In particular, older men had the ability to transmit valued ritual knowledge to younger men. People had little interest in domination; rather, hierarchy carried a 'tone of support'. And this allowed age-related hierarchy to be sustained within an essentially egalitarian framework.

Pintubi people accorded value to seniority, but believed that the source of hierarchy and personal autonomy was outside individual will, grounded in ancestral law.

In Hamilton's analysis of gender relations among neighbours of Pitjantjatjara people, what she calls 'homosociality' provided the institutional basis of the relative autonomy of the women. Women's secret ceremonies were the foundation of this rather separate social sphere, complementing men's secret rituals. She contrasts this with sociality in north-central and northeast Arnhem Land, where women did not have separate rituals, but conducted distinct aspects of rituals in areas adjacent to exclusive men's grounds, where men sang and danced. While men and young initiated men were excluded from women's rituals, uninitiated boys were not. Bob Tonkinson takes the view that cross-cutting ties provided checks on the potential for gender inequalities, in domestic relation as well as in the sphere of rituals.[25]

No formal governing body of elders existed among Pintupi people, and people showed little interest in dominating others. Rather, young people tended to defer to older people, allowing them priority in discussion, and respecting the right of 'old men' (*tjirlpi tjurta*), to whom they attributed deeper knowledge, to speak on communal affairs. The Berndts report the influence of the group of 'old men' at Ooldea, a category that included middle-aged men. The group included men of several totemic groups ('cult clans'), and one particular Ngalia man was regarded as 'boss' of the camp, making decisions about such matters as where the camp should be located. Myers comments that a 'boss' was one who 'helped' and 'looked after' subordinates.

Yuwaaliyaay people and their neighbours

Ancestral law

We have very clear evidence of a concept of religious 'law' among Yuwaaliyaay people and their neighbours. Byamee and his wives and sons were the law-givers. At the Bora ceremony, men proclaimed that Byamee was father of all, 'whose laws the tribes are now obeying', in Parker's words. Byamee's laws covered, among other things, the proper performance of the Bora and other rites, and the need to care for the old and sick. Men impressed three strict rules on initiates: do not commit unprovoked homicide, do not lie to elders, and do not have relations with a woman of the same matrifilial totem.[26]

Socialisation through initiation

The local form of male initiation was a regional rite called Bora (or Pura) by Yuwaaliyaay and Gamilaraay speakers and Burba (or Purrpa) by their Wangaaybuwan neighbours. In recorded performances, about 200 people attended from neighbouring localities connected by creeks and rivers. *Wirreenun* (sorcerer–magicians) from a wide region cooperated in putting on performances. The Bora initiation connected people of a large part of northern New South Wales and southern Queensland. Pakaantji people to the southwest practised a different type of ceremony, called Milya.[27]

The phases of the Bora bore some similarity to those of the Kŭnai Jerra-eil ceremony. In the first camp phase, men danced out of the secluded ground into the public ring each evening. Women responded to the voice of Bora with their '*brumboorah*' call, and boys as well as men had wrestling matches and sham fights. Men and women sang and performed public songs and dances ('corroborees').

In the first seclusion phase, the initiates underwent various ordeals in the men's secluded ground, and older men revealed sacred objects and rituals to them, the number and kind depending on how many Bora ceremonies they had undergone. Boys from some neighbouring groups had a front incisor avulsed. Some distance away from the men's secret ground at a 'little Bora' ground (*Durramunga*), older women greeted the initiates, who now had the status of *boorabayyi*, and danced round them. The boys were secluded again for about two months and instructed about the powers of *wirreenun* (sorcerer–healers), among other things.

In the final phase, one of reincorporation, the initiates were smoked at a fire under a *dheal* (acacia tree), after which they camped near the main camp. After about two months, painted white and decorated with a man's *yunbean* (belt), forehead band, kangaroo teeth, and feathers, the initiates were again smoked, after which their mothers rubbed the paint off their bodies and they reentered the camp. They were not supposed to speak to women for a year. Each initiate was given a small sacred stone during the Bora, and he had to keep it for life. He could now make fire, and marry.

With each successive Bora, the older men revealed more to the initiates, and gradually lifted food prohibitions. At his fifth Bora, a young man joined the *dorrunmai* category of hunters and warriors. Mature men who had been through five or so Bora performances were *dorrunmai*, who held 'councils of war', and were the accepted authorities in matters of war and hunting, according to Parker. They had few privileges beyond these, Parker thought.

Although the Bora ceremony differed from the Kŭnai Jerra-eil ceremony in that it centred on the making and revelation of very large ground-sculptures and carvings, it was similar as an instrument of socialisation. It dramatised Yuwaaliyaay doctrines and inspired awe and terror in young initiates. Stories told to Mathews and Parker about cannibalism and the killing of recalcitrant initiates in the Bora were undoubtedly means of inducing awe rather than descriptions of real events. Men drew initiates into complicity in the subtle manipulation of fiction and reality in these rites.

Gender categories, matrilineal totems, and section identities came into play as organising principles of the Bora. They enabled people from an extensive region to cooperate in a performance. In the Bora ceremonies organised by Yuwaaliyaay people (which Parker describes) and in the performances organised by Gamilaraay people (described by Mathews) ground-sculptures and carved trees represented four major matrilineal totems of the Yuwaaliyaay, sub-totems of these, four other major totems, and Byamee. Not only did neighbouring peoples share matri-categories and totems, but the main matrilineal totems of one area appeared as sub-totems in another. In this way, the totems represented in the ceremony belonged to people of a wide region, who were able to make the sculptures and perform the dances together. People unrelated by kinship could find a relationship through section identity or matri-group identity.[28]

Direct action

The published ethnography records little about how Yuwaaliyaay people and their neighbours sought redress for offences, or how they conducted and settled disputes.[29] Parker does explain how attempts at sorcery could lead to a vendetta. People would give an enemy's lock of hair to a *wirreenun* to perform sorcery on their behalf. Sometimes the *wirreenun* would bring feelings of enmity into the open, perhaps in an attempt to settle simmering disputes, or perhaps to provoke a feud.

Relations of power

Relations of authority between age grades are implicit in the descriptions of initiation; older men and women gradually admitted younger people to adult status and knowledge. It is difficult from the ethnographic material to come to any conclusions about the general character of Yuwaaliyaay gender relations. Parker does note the double standard according to which women but not men were punished for promiscuity and infidelity. Brothers and other male relatives reportedly punished a habitually promiscuous woman by binding her and tossing her between themselves, and then pack-raping and often killing her. How often such an event might have occurred is not recorded. Men did not always dominate in the domestic sphere, however; Parker remarks that she had encountered 'henpecked husbands'.[30]

The most powerful Yuwaaliyaay men were the *wirreenun*, 'by reason of their skill in magic'.[31] The Bora provided a major arena for them, and for senior women. It would be interesting to know whether each Yuwaaliyaay matri-group had its own *wirreenun*, and to what extent the sons or sister's sons of *wirreenun* became *wirreenun* in turn. Parker tells us that adepts were chosen by *wirreenun* but not why certain people were chosen. However, we can say that Yuwaaliyaay male leaders combined roles that in some other regions were divided.

Wiil and Minong people

In a significant variation, governance in the southwest lacked formal male-initiation rites; nevertheless, Wiil and Minong people evidently had similar male leadership roles as Yuwaaliyaay people.

Ancestral law

While writing on this topic is scarce, it is clear that Wiil and Minong people shared a conception of moral law; Hassell remarks on the existence of 'certain fixed laws which it was everyone's duty to see enforced'. Initiation journeys included instruction on the proper ways to behave in relation to various categories of relative, and they engendered a healthy respect for the powers of *mulgar* ('doctors'). The 'principal moral laws' (for men) inculcated during initiation were obedience to elders, conformity to food prohibitions, and the avoidance of women who belonged to other men or who were in the wrong relationship to be married. What is not recorded is whether people understood the totemic ancestors to be the originators of law. However, many of the myths about totemic beings transcribed by Hassell have the character of moral tales, as we have seen.[32]

Socialisation through initiation

People of the southwest differed from those of the other regions in not practising elaborate male initiation ceremonies involving ordeals such as circumcision and tooth avulsion. Rather, piercing of the nasal septum preceded a long journey to other communities, during which the initiate received instruction and during which he formed relationships of importance for his later marriage. (Journeys were a feature of initiation rituals in other regions as well, but they seem to have been given special prominence in this region.) Rites of exclusion and the revelation of secret paraphernalia do not appear to have been a feature of initiation either; instead, a sexual exchange ceremony marked the beginning of the process, and an exchange ceremony marked its end.[33]

In the first stage of Wiil male initiation, in a procedure called 'nose-bone' (*noilyet*), a *mulgar* pierced each boy's nasal septum while he was being held by his father or another kinsman.

Initiation journeys were arranged at a ceremony called *yardie* by Wiil people, and what Bates called 'a feast of licence'. Groups of people came together from a number of communities, and camped separately. Bachelors (*ngarnock*) occupied a separate group of huts, under the eye of several older men. Older women guarded marriageable girls (*grane*) at another camp. As Hassell describes it, betrothed couples stayed together for two or three days in larger huts between the bachelors' and girls' camps. Sometimes a young man was allocated to an older woman but later married a younger wife. Divorces were also arranged for those who were not satisfied with their marriages. People sang songs and danced each night. Bates describes how, at the *yardee kaangur* at Albany, a man would ask a woman to have sex, and in response she would sing a song of rejection or acceptance. If she accepted, the two would retire to a secluded place singing another song. Apparently people applied food prohibitions more rigorously after a *yardie*.

After the ceremony each initiate left with the group to which he had been allocated, and remained away for a year or more. (Hassell does not describe the initiate's journey; the following draws on Daisy Bates's writing.) A boy began his journey from group to group at about the age of nine, remaining for a month or two at the camps that lay along his 'proper road'. The boy's mother's brother or an older brother-in-law took the boy to the camp of some of the boy's affines, where he was placed in the care of 'brothers-in-law', his 'husband people' (*ngooljarma*), reckoned according to semi-moiety: they were his 'friends' or 'mates' (*babbingur* or *kobungur*). He was placed under food prohibitions (see Chapter 11) and prohibited from contact with girls or women, especially his 'sisters'. His hosts taught him songs and taught him how to use weapons and how to hunt; they also engendered in him a fear of the *mulgar*.

On their journeys initiates formed a number of 'blood-brother' relations, and these acted as a safeguard against conflict between neighbours—indeed, the cementing of ties between people of somewhat distant communities was an explicit purpose of the journeys. Bates writes of the exchange of names between guardian and initiate, and 'pledged friendship'.

On an initiate's return the *mulgar* publicly removed his nose-bone and the young man was able to marry. Representatives from each of the communities the initiate had visited attended a ceremony marking his return to his own community, timed to coincide with the plentiful availability of resources such as fish. People of the two moieties danced and exchanged gifts. In a similar way to Yuwaaliyaay initiates, the initiate was decorated with a man's apparel of hair belt and possum-fur strings on the arms, with emu or eaglehawk feathers attached. He wore a bone through his nasal septum and had his hair tied up with fur string and decorated with feathers, perhaps with a bandicoot-fur tassel over each ear and dingo-fur tassels over the forehead.

According to Bates, a boy moved from the category of *moolyeet* (initiate) to *wee-abindee* (marriageable man) and stayed thus until he was married, when he became *mammarup* or *moorrgurt*—'a man'. However, Mokaré's reported account of initiation suggests several stages over a number of years.[34]

Direct action

Wiil people administered punishment collectively, Hassell asserts, but she does not say what kinds of offences existed or what the forms of punishment were.[35] The most likely offences seem to have been breaches of incest prohibitions. The *mulgar* and 'wise women' had considerable influence, she remarks, and made decisions about whether laws had been broken. But it was up to the offended parties to take action. For minor offences, such as encroachment on one's country, a person was content to inflict a minor injury in redress, such as spearing the offender in the calf or thigh, a frequent form of punishment. Graver wrongs, such as homicide or imputed homicide through sorcery, elicited stronger redressive action, such as a revenge killing, which could lead to a continuing feud. But revenge, which was supposed to be delayed until some months after the death, was a moral obligation; Mokaré told Barker how dead men's spirits stole spears from their relatives until their deaths were avenged.

Minong people at King George Sound and Wiil people to the north joined in constant fights and feuds. Combatants fought most in spring, as the scarcity of food led to greater friction. Hassell attributes most fights to conflict between men over women, particularly in relation to elopements. She distinguishes between conflicts limited to a few kinsman and 'tribal' fights, involving wider communities.

It is evident that Wiil and Minong people attempted to minimise injuries in fights; reports show them being satisfied with the injury of only one person in one large-scale fight, with the use of hunting spears instead of fighting spears on another occasion, and with a fight without injury on another. Moreover, a person might act as a 'peacemaker' (*atur*), and try to settle a dispute. On the other hand, some individuals had reputations as habitual killers (*moyen*).[36]

Relations of power

The oldest man of a group seems to have been a figure of authority in his local community (as was the eldest of a group of siblings among his family). An example was Nakina, a man of 40 to 50 years in 1830, who was the older brother of Mokaré and the owner of land on which the European settlement was established. Adult men exercised authority over boys and young men: sending or threatening to send boys and young men 'into the bush' seems to have been a regular aspect of social control; another was the prohibition of a young man joining others in a hunt.[37]

It is evident that Wiil and Minong men tended to be very violent towards women, as well towards each other. Early white observers reported signs of regular spearing of women in the legs, and myths tell the same story. Infant bestowal and early marriage meant a young girl had little influence in marriage arrangements, although young men were equally bound by marriage contracts. And men evidently had the power to dispose of a wife in an exchange. Women did gain independence with age, and some older women were attributed with magical powers. Some practiced as healers, and some women achieved high status and were called *maintyn*. Moreover, young women frequently asserted their independence by absconding with other men, even though it was a risky business. Women do not seem to have been excluded from secret phases of ceremonies.

Early observers at King George Sound expressed puzzlement over leadership, seeking chiefs and finding none. Most puzzling was the demeanour of some younger bachelors, whose flamboyant style (the wearing of feathers and other body decoration) led the white visitors to think at first that they possessed authority. Hassell asserts, convincingly enough, that Wiil people possessed no headmen or chiefs. She stresses the communal nature of life and the independence of each family group; a husband and wife might together visit other communities for extended periods, and each man governed 'his own home and family' (this perhaps underestimates the growing independence of women as they got older).[38]

The most powerful and influential individuals among Wiil and Minong people are said to have been the *mulgar* (magicians), who had a similar role and powers to Kŭnai *mŭlla-mullŭng*, Pitjantjatjara *ngankaṟi*, and Yuwaaliyaay *wirreenun*. Hassell describes a *mulgar* as 'a very capable person as well as powerful because of his profession'.[39] She thought them to be greatly feared, although a man at King George Sound named Tallumund speared 'Doctor' Uredale in the leg, in retaliation for a death. In spite of being feared and respected, the *mulgar* were not general-purpose leaders, and Nind remarks that they varied in their reputed powers. Wiil people made decisions in important matters collectively, according to Hassell, and leadership in matters of fighting was *ad hoc*, depending on the transient reputations of individual men.

Sandbeach people

Sandbeach people resisted any person's attempts to assert dominance, and had no influential sorcerer–healers. However, their processes of governance did include secret male initiation.

Ancestral law

While I have found no direct evidence of a concept of 'ancestral law' among Sandbeach people and their neighbours, people conceptualised basic identities and relationships to country in terms of ancestors, their actions, and their traces. Regional ceremonies, with their songs and designs and masked dances, reenacted ancestral events and dramatised and made real the ancestors and their powers. Thomson writes that old men were the guardians of traditional knowledge, which they passed on to the next generation at initiation, in the form of songs and stories.[40]

Socialisation through initiation

Sandbeach people shared two ceremonies of male initiation and revelation with their neighbours. The first ceremony was associated with different ancestral beings among Kuuku Ya'u people and people of the Stewart River, and the second with another being, one of universal significance. The first ceremony had to do with revelation for males, while the second had a more disciplinary character, especially in relation to diet. The ceremonies had an underlying similarity in their ritual items, but there were variations in the designs used.[41]

The ceremonies included both secret and public phases, each with a distinct spatial domain. In an early phase, male dancers emerged from the men's ground in the forest to take the initiates from the women. The initiates resisted, then followed the male dancers towards the men's ground, but were sent back by the men. Finally, in the men's secret ground, the male initiates were put under various behavioural and dietary prohibitions while older men performed dances and made and revealed paraphernalia to them, all depicting various totemic ancestors of the patri-groups. In the public phases, male initiates danced to the accompaniment of drums, while women also danced. Throughout the ritual men performed songs associated with its main myth, but they incorporated their own distinct patri-group designs into ritual paraphernalia, implying the assertion of difference as well as relations of cooperation. Dietary restrictions for male initiates included bans on many animals, large birds, reptiles, and fish (but not the green turtle, the most valued species for food).

People of rather distinct social networks participated in local variants of the ceremony in which each participating group expressed its own totems and identity. Each version of the first ceremony, as reported by Thomson, drew on a region with several hundred adult residents.

Direct action

Chase emphasises Sandbeach people's individualism—the assertion of being 'one person' distinct from the group. (This seems different from the autonomy asserted by Pintupi people.) Lockhart people remembered their forebears as assertively independent; a man was quick to respond to a challenge by putting a spear to his spear-thrower. Some individuals were aggressive, devious, and immune to attack by sorcery, and might spear a man to take his wife. Although people tolerated periods of anti-social behaviour in others, persistently dangerous and anti-social individuals might be secretly killed. People also dealt with breaches of incest prohibitions secretly.[42]

Offences such as physical violence, imputed sorcery, eloping with someone else's husband or wife, and reneging on a marriage contract could lead to an ambush or fight. In fights, or at least in men's fights, relatives of the offender and the aggrieved would support them and intermediary kin would try to calm the dispute. Some disputes were settled by making the offender face his accusers and fend off spears with his spear-thrower, ending in his injury or his acceptance of a spear in the thigh. But an ordeal of this kind might escalate into a battle between the two groups of kin. Chase recorded a number of fighting places along the coast used for the settlement by formal spear combat of disputes between people of different communities, usually of different languages. Mothers and sisters supported the men in spear fights, supplying them with spears. (See also below on Kimberley women's support of men.)

Relations of power

In Thomson's view, the old men were the guardians of traditional knowledge, passing it on to the next generation at initiation ceremonies. Age conferred status, but this probably depended in part on control of religious and magical knowledge. Cape York people held age and grey hair in the highest regard, and according to Thomson no-one who was not an elder (*chilpu*) 'would think of raising his voice during a discussion on tribal affairs'. Kin relations had hierarchical aspects, reflected in the marking of kin terms for relative age and the inheritance of sibling seniority.[43]

With some exceptions, Thomson thought that women had little to say about 'social' affairs, except matters such as childbirth. (Presumably he was generalising about public discourse.) However, he writes, 'I have met with more than one woman who freely expressed her opinion in the discussions that took place from fireside to fireside in the camp at night, and whose words always carried weight'.[44] (This recalls Howitt's remarks about Kŭnai women.) Chase gives a rather negative assessment of the status of women. Although they had their own dances in initiation and mortuary ceremonies, women had no secret rituals or separate totemic sites of their own. Men excluded women from secret initiation grounds, the punishment for disobeying this rule being pack rape and death by strangling. Old women, however, became 'like men' and gained in status. Conversely, Thomson reports that old men helped women gather and process vegetable foods.

Certain Sandbeach men were 'big men' (*pama mukkana*), and some were renowned for their skill at dugong hunting (*pama watayichi*). Such a reputation required both physical skills and knowledge of dugong behaviour, as well as knowledge of charms and 'medicines'. Nevertheless, Chase reports a lack of conspicuous leaders at Lockhart in the 1970s and early 1980s: 'the ethos is that to set oneself up as a spokesperson or leader of people against others is an act of foolhardiness, and one which will lead to public humiliation'.[45]

Ngarinyin people and their neighbours

Governance among Ngarinyin people and their neighbours appears to have been similar in a number of ways to governance in the Western Desert.

Ancestral law

As mentioned in Chapter 7, people credited *wanjina* (ancestors) with the institution of 'law'. According to Lommel, Wunambal people attributed the founding of each practice and technology to specific *wanjina*. One ancestor instituted exogamy and the avoidance relation between wife's mother and daughter's husband; others invented fish dams and stone axes.[46]

Socialisation through initiation

A Worrorra boy had to kill a kangaroo before initiation. Lommel reports from his research in 1938 that boys used to be circumcised 'at an early age' in a ceremony involving songs and dances; a boy was later subincised when his beard began to grow. An 'elder brother' of the boy performed the subincision with a stone knife, as other men sang and danced in a 'great festival'. Wunambal men attributed greater importance to subincision than circumcision according to Lommel, the opposite of the Western Desert, although Love reports that subincision was voluntary. Before subincision, a young man was not allowed to make a complete spear; he was expected to acquire the necessary skill by working on parts of spears. After the operation he could marry. Cicatrisation of the buttocks followed subincision, copying the precedent set by two Crocodile *wanjina*.[47]

Direct action

Love recorded a dispute between a young man who received a girl as a wife and the older man to whom she had been promised. The two men fought with clubs and shields without others intervening; the older man won with a severe blow to the young man's head. A husband's brothers would intervene to stop an elopement: they would punish or kill the runaway wife and perhaps attack the man. It seems that a wrongful union (one in which the parties were in an unacceptable kin relation for marriage) attracted action on the part of a wider circle of people than a dispute between two men with competing claims. Love reports how several older men threatened to kill the brother of a young man who had eloped with his father's wife, the young man's distant 'mother'. (Love intervened, and when the young man returned he received only verbal abuse.)[48]

Among the causes of fights among Worrorra people were quarrels over the sharing of food, sexual jealousy, and elopement. Love reports that one man killed a woman for failing to give him some yam, and a man broke another man's arms for failing to share kangaroo meat with him. Thus, disputes sometimes resulted in violent injury or death. People commonly explained other deaths and illnesses as resulting from sorcery. Kinsmen of the victim avenged a death by violence or sorcery by killing the supposed perpetrator or a relative of that person, in all probability provoking a further attack in return. However, the wider network of kin of the two parties could step in to settle a dispute, agreeing to administer formal punishment to the perpetrator, typically a spear in the thigh. (See also the Yolngu Makarrata ceremony below.) But a greatly feared man was largely immune from revenge attacks, even if he had committed repeated homicides.

It seems that people of the region expressed antipathies and alliances in terms of language identity. At least some Wunambal people regarded Worrorra as friends but Ngarinyin as enemies.

Relations of power

As in other regions, age was an important basis for deference. For example, the ranking (by age) of siblings structured the receipt of gifts, an older sibling taking precedence over a younger one. Wunambal people appear to have associated age with proximity to the ancestors, as did Yolngu people. Lommel reports that the oldest people of a patri-group were considered to be the 'incarnation' of the *wanjina* (ancestors), and they were in the habit of speaking of *wanjina* in the first person: 'When I came here in primeval times and left my image on the stone …'[49]

If the level of polygyny can be taken as an index of gender relations, then the high polygyny among Worrorra speakers indicates considerable gender inequality. Love reports rather violent behaviour on the part of the most polygynous men towards their wives, although he may have selected the most sensational incidents. Not all men's wives did their husband's bidding, however: Love describes how one old man with an older wife and two younger wives protested ineffectively when they would not give him food. In a more positive aspect of gender relations, young sons looked after ageing mothers by providing them with food.

Relations of power and authority have not been very fully described for this region. Lommel attributes considerable influence to *barnman*, the healers, rainmakers, magicians, and sorcerers; much of their dangerous power resulted from their knowledge of people's *wunggurr* names and supposed control of lightning. Love describes how a Worrorra *barnman* organised a revenge killing: he interpreted stones that identified two strangers as the killers, and ordered the punishment (by spearing in the arm) of those unwilling to participate in the revenge expedition. Members of the avenging party were summoned with a lock of the dead man's hair.

A patri-group's senior men played a prominent part in the exchange network, the performance of 'increase' rites to do with *wanjina*, the organisation of rituals, and the imparting of religious knowledge. Prominent men among Worrorra people included those with a reputation as singers.

Yolngu people

Patri-group elders, rather than sorcerer–healers, appear to have been dominant in Yolngu governance.

Ancestral law

Speakers of Yolngu languages more or less agreed on a shared body of religious 'law' (*rom*) governing social relations—land-holding, relations of production, the control of technology, marriage, exchange, dispute settlement, and so on. *Rom* (translated by Yolngu people as 'law' or 'culture') included explicit rules that the *wangarr* (ancestors) had established. For example, they granted rights to land and waters, and specified proper behaviour towards kin. But *rom* also covered such practices as the subsection system and the proper performance of ceremonies. Yolngu spoke of ancestors 'setting down the law' (*rom nhirrpan*).[50]

Socialisation through initiation

Unlike initiation among peoples further to the west, Yolngu male initiation (*dhapi*, meaning 'foreskin') included circumcision. The relatives of an initiate could choose from a variety of ritual genres.[51] People could use their patri-group songs and dances in the camp or they could commission a Mandayala or Djungguwan cere-mony from a Dhuwa-moiety owner of these rituals, available to Dhuwa and Yirritja initiates. Relatives often sent an initiate on a journey to distant communities before the circumcision rite.

A *dhapi* ceremony using patri-group *garma* ('public') songs, designs, and dances had a number of phases. In the first, men painted the boy with the ancestral designs of his patri-group or a closely related one (such as his mother's mother's) while singing and dancing in the camp. This phase might occur more than once. In the second phase, women circled the men's group as the men again painted the boy, and threatened the men with toy spears. They had licence to 'snatch' food and tobacco (available from the time of Macassan visits). Then, young men surrounded the boy and held him down on the back of another as a specialist circumciser carried out the operation with a stone knife (or, more recently, a razor blade). Bachelors looked after the boy in seclu-sion while the injury healed, and he came under certain restrictions—he could not drink water, directly touch the ground, or touch food (he had to eat using sticks). After a 'water' ceremony lifted the prohibitions, he joined the bachelors' camp. The *dhapi* ceremony involved members of the initiate's patri-group and other relatives; alternatively, groups of both moieties would coordinate their *dhapi* ceremonies.

The Mandayala and Djungguwan ceremonies had a more regional character. Mandayala reenacted elements of the Wagilak and related mythology but in a public context—only the preparation of men's body decorations occurred in a secluded place. Djungguwan also belonged to the Wagilak mythology, but included a secret phase of men's songs and dances, followed by the circumcision operation. This cere-mony drew on a wider region of participants of both moieties.[52]

Yolngu people also possessed mortuary ceremonies and an elaborate body of rev-elatory rites. The revelatory rites included (as well as Djungguwan) the Nga:rra ceremonies of both moieties, the Ngulmarrk ceremony (derived from the Ubarr cer-emony of western Arnhem Land), and the Gunapipi ceremony, related to the Warlpiri Gadjari. All these included public phases, as well as the performance of secret men's dances (and songs in some cases) and the revelation of sacred objects to initiates. In a related aspect of governance, older men gradually revealed the esoteric meanings of designs and songs to young men.[53]

Direct action

As in the other regions, it was up to each party in a dispute to try to enforce their interpretation of 'law' by recruiting kin for support. Those who were able to garner the most support were more able to press their case.

Warner recorded a number of stories of what he called 'warfare' and feuds, including a protracted feud that involved a number of patri-groups in a cycle of killing and revenge killing. The causes of fights included adultery and quarrels over the distribution of food. Fighters goaded each other with obscene insults, often implying incestuous relations. Women fought with digging sticks or men's clubs, usually over adultery; sisters would aid each other. Men killed or threatened to kill women and uninitiated young men for seeing men's sacred objects, and attacked other men for infringements of rights over the making of totemic objects.[54]

The main reasons for armed conflict between men were revenge for a homicide or alleged sorcery killing, and rivalry between men of the same moiety over women of the opposite moiety. In order to instigate revenge for a death, relatives of the dead person gave young male relatives either a piece of the spear that caused the death or finger bones from the corpse, wrapped in string, wax, and feathers, which would be carried perhaps for years in a dillybag. People believed that the spirit of the dead person inhered in the object; if it was thrown in a fire it supposedly had the power to make the intended victim sleep, or if a fighter carried it in his mouth it would make his opponent heavy-footed.

Warner describes several types of men's fights: fights over adultery involving swearing, spear-throwing, and parrying; nocturnal revenge killings by stealth; and all-in fights involving members of several patri-groups—the worst of this kind was the *ganygarr* ('spear fight to end all spear fights'). Warner thought the patri-group ('clan') was the main war-making group; most hostilities occurred between patri-groups of the same moiety, because of rivalry among men over women. I think it is unlikely that men of a patri-group as a whole combined in a fight; rather, men called on brothers, sons, and sisters' sons to assist them, and identified themselves and their enemies by patri-group identity. As a result, some groups had the advantage of numbers. The cross-cutting loyalties of individuals, all of whom had ties to more than one group, somewhat modified a group's strength through sheer numbers.

Warner describes one young man as a 'natural fighter', always keen to organise a fight, and he notes that some notorious killers raided camps and took women by force. Such men would be killed by members of their own group to put an end to the constant trouble they caused.

Attempts might be made to settle a conflict with an offer of cycad-palm bread or tobacco, and Yolngu people also possessed a formal institution for settling up after an injury or homice—the Makarrata ceremony (from *makarr*, 'thigh'), shown in Plate

Plate 8.1   Yolngu Makarrata dispute-resolution ceremony at Milingimbi in the 1930s (photograph by Harold Sheperdson)

8.1. According to Warner's account, after an injury or death men of the victim's group would send a message to their enemies proposing a Makarrata to settle matters, often during a large ceremony when people of many groups were gathered. Men of the two sides performed their totemic dances, then those who instigated the original attack—the 'pushers'—would run the gauntlet between the groups while the aggrieved men threw spears with spearheads removed at them, and cursed the other group in order to work off their anger. The killers then ran the gauntlet again as the aggrieved threw their spears, this time with spearheads attached. Older men of the aggrieved group urged the throwers to avoid injuring or killing the men, and older men of the offending group urged their young men not to retaliate. The ceremony ended with one of the aggrieved group dancing up to an offender and spearing him in the thigh. Warner comments that this was the ideal form of the process, and that treachery might occur or things could get out of hand and another fight ensue.[55]

Relations of power

Warner depicted women (*miyalk*) as a 'profane' category in contrast with the 'sacred' category of men (*ḏirramu*). This represents a misreading of Yolngu conceptions, although it did reflect men's regular assertions (reflected in practice) that women lacked control of *rangga* (sacred objects). If we take the level of polygyny as an index of gender relations, then Yolngu women enjoyed much less equality with men than Kŭnai women did. However, some wives dominated their husbands; many women's knowledge, independence, and influence increased with age; and senior wives had considerable status, as did leaders of women's rituals. Franca Tamisari shows that women's religious knowledge was as profound as the men's, although they were unable to publicly demonstrate expertise in male concerns (just as men deferred to women in matters of procreation).[56]

A Yolngu patri-group leader had a particular responsibility to 'hold' and 'look after' the group, its country, and its sacra. Patri-group leaders were 'firstborn' (*ngurru-dawalangu*), in practice the oldest of a group of brothers or, if the oldest was not deemed competent, the next oldest. In some cases two brothers shared the leadership.[57] If a group's oldest male was a young man, he was likely to defer to the leader of a related group, especially in the context of rituals. People did acknowledge a sister as firstborn where appropriate, but her gender precluded her from taking the same kind of role as a man in ceremonies. Not all groups had a ritual specialist (*ḏalka-rramirri, djirrikaymirr*) whose particular task was to call out the names of ancestors, and whose authority extended across a wide region.

The main tasks of a male leader lay in the enactment of ceremonies, the conduct of feuds, and dispute resolution. But as the oldest of a group of brothers, he was likely to be the most polygynous man, and hence the most influential in terms of social connections. With the death of his older brother or brothers (of the same patri-group), a younger brother would become the oldest male of the group and its leader, but there would be some tension between him and the former leader's eldest son, who would also want to be recognised as leader; in other words, there was conflict over fraternal succession versus primogeniture. As a result of rivalry between the oldest males of a lineage, a group might split up.[58]

Very high levels of polygyny resulted in marked military and political inequalities between patri-groups. Since a more powerful group could press its marriage claims more effectively than a weaker one, these inequalities could be reproduced in successive generations, at least for a while. Yolngu oral history includes some accounts of expansionist individuals who fought for the country and the women of other groups. This kind of aggression was linked to competition between men for marriage to the same women, and hence to polygyny.[59]

A number of factors limited the ability of patri-groups to establish hegemony. People could evade the political control of particular groups simply by moving, which was made possible by an individual's rights in and connections to many countries through different kin links, and by the fact that they were not tethered to cultivated resources. Internal dynamics limited the growth of a patri-group: groups growing to a certain size tended to split along lineage lines, making continued unity under a leader problematic.

Comparisons and conclusions

As might be expected, a number of common features as well as variations show up in the case studies, in spite of the uneven quality of the ethnography.

Ancestral law

A conception of totemic ancestors as law-givers is apparent in most if not all of the case studies. Parker writes of the 'commands' of Byamee. The Western Desert concept of *tjukurrpa* links stories, ancestral events, and moral precepts, along with the experience of dreaming. Bates and Hassell write respectively of 'fixed laws' and 'principal moral laws' inculcated at initiation among Wiil and Mi̱nong people. But conceptions of ancestral periods and ancestral law varied. The Yolngu concept of *rom* lacks connotations of 'dreaming' and has a more general sense of 'the proper way', with a wide range of applications. Everywhere, ceremonies in which people of intersecting regions cooperated expressed bodies of doctrine shared by people of these regions, albeit with local variants and disagreements. Especially important among these were male initiation rites and revelatory ceremonies, which brought together people of a broad region.

But the regions whose people cooperated in this way were not discrete. Imagine a social network stretching from one coast to the other, with some fissures and sparse patches to be sure, but more or less continuous. In any one area, people identified themselves and others using the multiple, overlapping identities that were reviewed in Chapter 4. The most clearly bounded identities in terms of membership were the patrifilial groups, but even these joined with others in more extended and overlapping associations. The case studies have revealed one apparent major discontinuity in the social networks, and that is the relative isolation of Kŭnai people from those to the north and west of them.

Table 8.1   Forms of initiation

People	Categories of initiation ceremony and forms of mutilation	Degree of gender exclusivity
Kŭnai	Jerra-eil male initiation, no circumcision or subincision, informal piercing of nasal septum	Joint-gender and male-exclusive domains
Pitjantjatjara and neighbours	Circumcision and subincision rites, tooth avulsion	Joint-gender and male-exclusive domains
Yuwaaliyaay and their neighbours	Bora male initiation, no circumcision or subincision, some tooth avulsion	Joint-gender and male-exclusive domains
Wiil/Mi̱nong	Piercing of nasal septum, yardie ceremony of sexual licence, initiate's journey and exchange ceremony, no circumcision or subincision	Public ceremonies
Sandbeach	Two-phase initiation, no circumcision or subincision	Joint-gender and male-exclusive domains
Ngarinyin and neighbours	Circumcision and subincision, informal scarification	Joint-gender and male-exclusive domains
Yolngu	Dhapi male initiation in several genres, several revelatory rites, circumcision and informal scarification	Joint-gender and male-exclusive domains in some circumcision and all revelatory ceremonies

Region-wide cooperation in the performance of major ceremonies, as well as agreement over the outlines of ancestral law, involved intersecting social networks rather than territorial groups. Looked at in another way, social affairs generally involved *focussed networks*; a person's death mobilised people related to that person. By the same token, a male initiation ceremony drew in relatives of the initiates. A major ceremony performed in one area would involve some of the same people who attended a ceremony some distance away.

In a similar way, those who cooperated in a major celebration of ancestral law set aside their doctrinal differences; the same dances and to some extent the same songs could accommodate a wide range of mythologies. People could cooperate with those having a certain mythological tradition at one ceremony, and with those espousing a rather different tradition at another. But people also reenacted ancestral events in ceremonies of more local scope.[60]

Initiation as socialisation

Initiation and revelatory ceremonies served as modes of socialisation as well as reenactments of ancestral events. Initiation journeys widened the social field of an inititate. But they varied in form, rigour, and degree of elaboration. Wiil and Minong people and their neighbours appear not to have practised a specific rite of male initiation but mixed exchange ceremonies with initiation journeys. Male initiation among Kŭnai, Yuwaaliyaay, and Sandbeach people lacked bodily mutilation, except as an informal adjunct. Yolngu people circumcised their young men, and required them to undergo one or more of an elaborate corpus of revelatory rites. People of the Western Desert practised the most rigorous forms of initiation, combining male circumcision and subincision with other forms of mutilation in an elaborate series of rites.

Circumcision as an aspect of male initiation appears to have spread outwards from the arid zone, but people of certain areas, including the southeast, the southwest, Cape York Peninsula, and western to central Arnhem Land, did not practice it. Subincision had also diffused from the arid zone, but less far than circumcision.

This chapter has brought out the importance of the structural dimensions of governance, by which I mean admission through formal procedures to statuses and their powers and prerogatives. The admission procedures primarily took the form of initiation and other life-crisis rituals, and, especially in the case of women, stages in the reproductive cycle. They conferred the right to use certain items of equipment, to forage for certain resources, to marry, to gain admission to certain phases of ceremonies, to learn esoteric knowledge, and so forth. The organisation and control of rituals involved local networks of kin, kin groups, and the loose coalitions already mentioned.

Gender relations

The pervasiveness of social identities based on gender, age, and ritual and reproductive status comes through in all the case studies. The distinctiveness and separation of the genders is also a general feature, but the degree both of the separateness of men's and women's lives and of gender inequality appears to have varied considerably.

Given the uneven quality of the ethnography, assessment of these matters has to be tentative and impressionistic.

Kŭnai gender relations seem to have been the most egalitarian. This is evident in the predominance of elopement as a mode of marriage, the low level of polygyny, the complementary and pervasive gender totems, the formal right of women to punish male adulterers, and the centrality of women's participation in the Jerra-eil initiation in all but the most secret men's phase. Pitjantjatjara and neighbouring men and women lived in rather separate spheres, according to Hamilton's analysis. Wiil and Minong women were victims of a good deal of violence inflicted by men, but they do not appear to have been excluded from rituals in the same way as elsewhere. Indeed, sexual exchange ceremonies in which older women initiated liaisons accompanied male initiation ceremonies. I suggested that gender relations among Sandbeach people contrasted with the more egalitarian relations among Kŭnai people and among Pitjantjatjara people and their neighbours. If levels of polygyny provide some indication of the degree of gender inequality, then Yolngu gender relations lay firmly at the unequal end of the continuum, with Ngarinyin and their neighbours not far behind.

Age and birth-order

We saw that certain kin relations entailed formal prerogatives. Limited in scope as it was, kinship seniority allowed a person to tell others what to do; this applied especially in the relations of older to younger sibling, parent to child, and parent's sibling to sibling's child. One mode of 'leadership' extended this principle to the oldest of a kin group, especially the oldest male. Thus, a Yolngu patri-group leader was ideally *ngurrudawalangu*, or 'firstborn'.

This position of firstborn took on particular importance where, as in the Yolngu case, a patrifilial or matrifilial group held a body of sacra, such as ancestral designs, songs, dances, sacred objects, the exegetical traditions that accompanied these things, and procedures such as increase rites. However, older men in general had the right to teach their sons their group's traditions. Kin-group leaders are evident in several of the case studies, and rituals that involved the cooperation of several kin groups gave rise to coalitions of such leaders, perhaps with the chief organiser taking the most prominent position. Thus, authority tended to be diffused among the older, more experienced people—'all the old people', as Pintupi put it. Indeed, Howitt reports that, among Kŭnai people, just as the original creator was referred to as 'our father', so any elder in an initiation ceremony was the 'father' of a junior. On such occasions there was no overall leader, but rather a loose coalition of 'fathers' and 'older siblings' who acted as leaders.[61]

Resources of power

Individuals could draw on rather different resources of power in the seven regions (see Table 13.8). A recurrent role in the case studies has been the sorcerer–healer, a role that was combined with magician and rainmaker in some regions. This was not a position in a hierarchy of command, but rather a specialist role that engendered respect and sometimes fear. It carried varying weight in the seven regions, each of which had a somewhat different mix of leadership roles.

Most regions had both leaders of patrifilial or matrifilial totemic groups and distinct sorcerer–healer roles (Pitjantjatjara and their neighbours, Yuwaaliyaay and their neighbours, Wiil and Minong, Ngarinyin and their neighbours). Kŭnai people appear to have been distinctive in the wide range of magical powers claimed by individuals, and in having the role of shaman (*birraark*). Sandbeach people appear to have discouraged attempts to dominate, but recognised healers (*maparanga*) as specialists. Participation in the *wurnan* exchange network seems to have been a source of male power among Ngarinyin people and their neighbours. Yolngu people recognised healers (*marrngitj*) as important counters to the actions of hidden sorcerers, but had no public sorcerer–healer figure; patri-group leaders and fighting men dominated public affairs in this region. As a key strategy, both Ngarinyin and Yolngu men combined the attainment of a high level of polygyny with the status of patri-group elder and a strong position in the exchange network.

Implications for the economy

These features of governance have implications for the conduct of the economy. First, the concept of ancestral law underpinned many aspects of economy. Elements of cosmologies, enacted in ceremonies, provided the framework for the control of access to land and waters and their resources, and some items of equipment (see Chapter 9). People invoked ancestral law to validate principles of generosity, norms governing specific relationships, and the right way to behave more generally.

As instruments of socialisation and the reproduction of authority relations, male initiation and revelatory rites were crucial to the reproduction of the social order. They also provided a context for regional cooperation and the reproduction of social relations across wide regions; these relations were important for the economy. The resulting patterns of authority, including age and gender relations, underpinned many aspects of economic practice, not least marriage exchange.

Status conferred through initiation governed access to equipment (see Chapter 9), and involved various production and consumption restrictions, while wider age, gender, and reproductive statuses entailed other restrictions and prerogatives. Initiation and revelation constituted arenas for and components of the exchange of valued items (see Chapter 12).

We should also note the scale of governance. Events such as male initiation required the largest-scale cooperation in Aboriginal economic and social life (albeit involving only a few hundred people on any one occasion), and involved loose coalitions of local leaders and ritual specialists. Most productive activities, however, required only small-scale cooperation and coordination at most (see Chapter 10). In larger-scale productive activities, perhaps hundreds of people converged on a resource and worked in parallel groups, in simple or extended cooperation. As later chapters show, distribution and exchange networks largely involved hand-to-hand transactions between individuals. This is all consistent with the very fluid size and composition of residence groups, and the local and kin-based nature of leadership.

The chapters of Part III examine the implications of kinship, marriage, and other institutional fields for the organisation of economic relations and practices.

Further reading

Long-standing debates about governance and power in Aboriginal social life have concerned the relative power of men and women, the question of whether Aboriginal societies had 'chiefs' and 'councils of elders', and the relationship between authority in the realm of ritual and 'secular' authority. For an overview, see Les Hiatt's *Aboriginal Political Life* (1986) or R. M. Berndt's *Law and Order in Aboriginal Australia* (1965a), which retains its value. Nancy Williams makes a close study of recent Yolngu dispute resolution in *Two Laws: Managing Disputes in a Contemporary Aboriginal Community* (1987).

Francesca Merlan reviews and assesses the literature on gender relations in her chapter in *Social Anthropology and Australian Aboriginal Studies*, edited by R. M. Berndt and Bob Tonkinson (1988). Two important papers on gender relations are Annette Hamilton's 'Dual social systems' (1980) and 'A complex strategical situation' (1981). In these papers she qualifies John Bern's assessment of gender relations as fundamentally exploitative. See Bern's article 'Ideology and domination' (1979). Fred Myer's analysis of Pintubi age relations in terms of 'nurturance' and 'autonomy' has been influential; see his *Pintupi Country: Pintupi Self* (1986).

The control of religious knowledge is a central aspect of Aboriginal governance; see Howard Morphy's *Ancestral Connections* (1991) and my *Knowledge and Secrecy in an Aboriginal Religion* (1997).

Notes

1   See Hiatt (1986) and Keen (1989) for reviews of approaches to Aboriginal governance.

2   See Myers (1986: 154–6, 224) on ancestral law and regional cooperation.

3   Keen (1994) explores this aspect of Yolngu mythology and ritual.

4   On Aboriginal socialisation see Hamilton (1981b) and Harris (1984). On the effects of initiation see Keen (1994: 189–90), Myers (1980; 1986), and Stanner (1963: 150).

5   On this effect of religion as a cultural system see Geertz (1966: 8–12).

6   See R. M. and C. H. Berndt (1981: 348), Maddock (1982: 146–7), and Taplin (1873) on quasi-legal procedures.

7   See Berndt (1965a) on 'self-help', and Sansom (1980 *passim*) on 'jurisdictions'.

8   See Martin (1993) on the displacement of responsibility.

9   On relations and resources of power, see Sharp (1958) on kin hierarchy, Myers (1986: 221–3) on 'looking after', Keen (1994: 93) on leaders as firstborn, Myers (1986: 223) and Anderson (1988) on 'bosses', and on gender relations, Merlan (1988).

10 On Aboriginal gender relations see Bern (1979), C. H. Berndt (1970), Hamilton (1980; 1981a), Kaberry (1939), Merlan (1988), Warner (1937), and White (1970).

11 See Howitt (1880: 212; 1904: 626) on Kŭnai ancestral law.

12 On Kŭnai male initiation see Howitt (1880: 194–9; 1904: 617–8, 626, 633; Papers, SLV Box 8 ms1053/3 (a)). On the piercing of the nasal septum see Howitt (1880: 191–2), and on girls' scarification see Howitt (1880: 192).

13 See Bulmer (1994: 16–17, 25; Papers, MV B10 F5 xm931: 19), Howitt (1880: 217) on Kŭnai fights and feuds and Howitt (1904: 344–7) on the ordeal.

14 Sources on Kŭnai power relations include the following: on age, Bulmer (Papers, MV B10 F5 xm931: 19; 1994: 14) and Howitt (1904: 317–18, 325); on gender relations, Bulmer (1994: 7, 10, 14–15; letter to Howitt, Papers, MV B1 F4 xm79 16 October 1879) and Howitt (1880: 205–6; 1904: 766); on decision making, Howitt (1880: 212); on leaders, Bulmer (1994: 13–14) and Howitt (1880: 211–13); and on *mŭlla-mullŭng*, Bulmer (Papers, MV B10 F5 xm922: 14, 21) and Howitt (1880: 211–12; 1904: 301; Papers, SLV Box 8 ms1053/3(b): 16, 18).

15   Basil Sansom (1980: 92–8) calls the kind of punishment in which the victim offers no resistance 'moral violence'.

16   The quotation is from Howitt (1880: 212).

17   See Howitt (1880: 231n). On the authority of an old man among his kin see Bulmer (Papers, MV B10 F5 xm922: 46).

18   See Hagenauer (in Curr 1886, vol 3: 539–57).

19   On the concept of *tjukurrpa* see Munn (1970) and Myers (1986: 48–9, 118–19).

20   This section draws on the account of initiation at Ooldea by R. M. and C. H. Berndt (1945: 95–106, 117).

21   On fights and feuds see Myers (1986: 160, 161, 167–70, 259).

22   See Viesner (2000 IV) on *kurdaitji*.

23   See Tonkinson (1991: 145) on dispute settlement at ceremonies.

24   On kinship hierarchy see R. M. and C. H. Berndt (1945: 61) and Myers (1986: 219–20, 223); on gender relations see Hamilton (1980; 1981a); on leaders see R. M. and C. H. Berndt (1945: 61) and Myers (1986: 219–21, 223).

25   See Hamilton (1980) on homosociality in Aboriginal gender relations, and Tonkinson (n.d.) on cross-cutting ties.

26   See Parker (1905: 4, 7–8) on Yuwaaliyaay ancestral law.

27   On initiation among Yuwaaliyaay people and their neighbours see Berndt (1947), Mathews (1895–96), and Parker (1905: 70–82). On Pakaantji initiation see Beckett et al. (2003: 9).

28   I compared the subjects of carvings and sculptures as described by Parker (1905) and Mathews (1895–96; 1898) with Parker's list of totems and sub-totems (1905: 16).

29   On direct political action see Parker (1905: 33).

30   On Yuwaaliyaay gender relations see Parker (1905: 58–60); on leaders see Parker (1905: 81).

31   The quotation is from Parker (1905: 81).

32   See Bates (1985: 218) and Hassell (1934; 1936: 681) on Wiil and Minong 'law'.

33   For accounts of initiation in the southwest see Bates (1985: 151–8), Ferguson (1987: 136–7), and Hassell 1936: 684–6); on piercing the nasal septum see Bates (1985: 153).

34   On Mokaré's initiation stages see Barker (1992; 22 November 1830, cited in Green 1989: 24, 43).

35   On direct political action in the southwest see Hassell (1936: 681, 700), Barker (1992: 31 January, 1 February, 5 April, 16 April, 13 July 1830, cited in Green 1989: 19, 22, 27, 46), Goldsworthy (in Curr 1886, vol. 1: 339), and Nind (1831: 45–6).

36   On aspects of fighting and mediation see Barker (1992: 19 June, 22 July, 12 December 1830, cited in Green 1989: 47, 68–9) and Nind (1831: 45–6).

37   On Wiil and Minong relations of power see the following: on kin-based authority, Barker (1992: 1829–31, 13 October, 30 October, 24 December 1830, 22 January 1831, cited in Green 1989: 31–6, 43, 51, 64, 68–9); on gender relations, Browne (1856: 34, cited in Le Souëf 1993: 14), Collie (1979: 12 July 1834), and Nind (1831: 37).

38   On leaders see Barker (1992: 23 April 1830, cited in Green 1989: 7), Hassell (1936: 681, 706–7), and Nind (1831: 40–1).

39   The quotation is from Hassell (1936: 706).

40   See Rigsby and Chase (1998: 201) and Thomson (1933: 459, 462) on Sandbeach ancestral law.

41   On Sandbeach initiation ceremonies see Laade (1964), Rigsby and Chase (1998: 202), and Thomson (1933). In the mid-twentieth century a version associated with Night Island, in Uutaalnganu country, was current.

42   See Chase (1980b: 189–93) and Thomson (1933: 461; Papers, MV File 196 undated) on Sandbeach fighting.

43   For references to Sandbeach gender relations and other power relations see Chase (1980b: 195; 1984; 1989: 173) and Thomson (1933: 459, 462). On old men taking women's roles see Thomson (Papers, MV File 170, 1.7.29).

44   The quotation is from Thomson (1933: 459).

45   The quotation is from Chase (1984: 117).

46   See Crawford (1968: 35, 40, 55–6) and Lommel (1949: 160; 1997: 20, 25) on concepts of ancestral law among Ngarinyin people and their neighbours.

47   On Worrorra initiation see Love (Papers). On Wunambal initiation see Lommel (1949: 159–60; 1997: 42–4).

48   See Love (1936: 37–8, 50, 73, 100, 107–111; Papers: 76) on direct political action.

49   On power relations among Ngarinyin people and their neighbours see Love (1936: 31–5, 96, 166–9).

50   See Keen (1994: 137), Morphy (1991) and Tamisari (1998: 262) on Yolngu concepts of ancestral law.

51   See Warner (1937: 285–90) and Keen (1994: 171–3, 189–90) on Yolngu male initiation.

52   On the Mandayala and Djungguwan ceremonies see Warner (1937: 259–90, 329–34).

53   See Keen (1994) and Morphy (1991) on secret knowledge.

54   On Yolngu fighting and feuds see Warner (1937: 155–90).

55   See Warner (1937: 174–6) on the *makarrata* ceremony.

56   For one view of Yolngu gender relations see Warner (1937: 387, 394); for a contrasting view see Tamisari (1998).

57   See Williams (1987) and Keen (1994: 91–100) on Yolngu leaders.

58   The term 'succession' may not be appropriate: I have argued (Keen 1994: 93) that Yolngu leadership is not a unique 'office' with only one incumbent at a time.

59   On polygyny see Warner (1937: 77–8) and Keen (1982).

60   See Keen (1994) on cooperation between people with distinct doctrines in multivalent ceremonies.

61   See Bern (1979) on coalitions of leaders.

PART III
Economy

9

Control of the Means
of Production

Introduction

Part II outlined institutional fields in the seven regions. The chapters of Part III examine resources, relations, and practices according to economic categories: the control of the means of production, the organisation of production, distribution, consumption, exchange and trade. And they will relate these to the environmental conditions, resources, and institutions described in the first two parts of the book. We begin with the control of access to the means of production.

The control of access to land and waters and their resources is one dimension of the control by members of a community of the means of producing the necessities of life; the control of access to items of equipment is another. This chapter examines variation in the forms of control of country and resources in the seven regions, and more briefly the control of technology.

The shape of Aboriginal 'local organisation' or 'land tenure' has been the subject of much debate, and has been described with competing models. The earliest studies of Aboriginal societies were made decades after people from Britain had appropriated their land and waters, and had begun to farm, while other immigrants mined for gold and other metals. Anthropologists such as A. W. Howitt based their models of land ownership and residence not on observations but on *a priori* assumptions, in light of which they interpreted information from their informants about pre-colonial life.

In the most influential early anthropological analyses of Aboriginal relations to land, such as those of A. W. Howitt and A. R. Radcliffe-Brown, the land-owning group was a patrilineal descent group—a group of people tracing descent through the male line from an apical ancestor or a group of ancestors. These models did not distinguish a descent group that owned land from a group of people living together on the land. The 'horde' (as Radcliffe-Brown called the residence group) was supposedly patrilineal but included men's wives. In his later writings, Radcliffe-Brown did distinguish between a descent group that owned land and its sacred sites and a residence group living together and using the descent group's land. He believed that the landowning descent group was everywhere patrilineal. A 'horde' (residence group) consisted of men of the descent group, their wives, unmarried young women of the group, and the men's children. Thus residence was patrilocal, and it was women who moved at marriage. However, where the horde was not strictly exogamous, more than one 'line of descent' might be found among members.[1]

Challenges to this academic orthodoxy began in the 1950s. One or two anthropologists who had lived for extended periods in the bush early in the twentieth century had already found difficulties in reconciling their observations with Radcliffe-Brown's model. A. P. Elkin thought that relations to land in the southeast of the continent and in western Arnhem Land were probably not based on patrilineal descent groups. (He was wrong about western Arnhem Land but probably right about at least parts of the southeast.) Other serious challenges to the model came from those who carried out fieldwork from the 1950s onward. L. R. Hiatt pointed out in 1962 that many field reports of the first part of the century were inconsistent with the 'orthodox model'. In the Kimberley region, for example, men of more than one patrilineal group lived in the same residence group. On the Daly River, individuals moved between their own and neighbouring countries with great freedom, and bands ('hordes'), which were aggregates of contiguous totemic clans, interacted quite a lot to organise food-gathering and ceremonies. Several ethnographers had described how men lived with their wives' people for at least part of their lives. Like Mervyn Meggitt, Hiatt proposed that residence groups were not patrilineal, patrilocal groups, but that, in some cases at least, they were (or had been) larger 'communities' consisting of members of several inter-marrying groups. However, Jo Birdsell presented evidence to show that residence groups were smaller than the community model implies.[2]

In his defence of Radcliffe-Brown, W. E. H. Stanner made the very influential distinction between, on the one hand, the patrilineal group or clan with its 'estate' of land, and, on the other the band (equivalent to the 'horde'), a residence group living together and occupying a 'range'. The term 'range' meant the area of land (and waters on some parts of the coast) exploited by the band; a range usually included the land of a number of contiguous 'clan' estates.

Land-claim research in the Northern Territory, which proliferated during the 1970s and 1980s, brought to light a wide variety of arrangements. These included many different kinds and degrees of connection between a patri-group and its country, and between an individual and their mother's patri-group's country. Other research published in the 1970s and 1980s showed that attachment to country in the Western Desert had multiple bases, including place of birth, place of initiation, and place of parent's initiation. Nurit Bird-David points out that the general switch in hunter–gatherer studies from the patrilocal-band model to a picture of more fluid organisation coincided with the shift in the focus of research from male hunting to gathering by women.[3]

The lesson of this story—very briefly outlined here—is that we should be open to considerable variety in relations to country and in the structure of groups. But how should the groups be described? And what is the nature of the connections between individuals, groups, and country? Modes of attachment by individuals and groups have been expressed in a legalistic language of 'rights' and 'corporations'; this can be explained by the fact that British social anthropology had its origin in part in legal history. More recently, influenced by cultural anthropology, anthropologists have sought to capture the quality of indigenous conceptions of connection in terms of ancestral substance, the body, and concepts of the person.[4] For the purposes of this study, it is necessary to use more than one frame of reference. The language of 'rights', judiciously applied, helps us to describe the powers people claimed and accorded to others—powers they justified in terms of ancestral law—and this kind of description complements descriptions in terms of cosmology and subjectivity.

For a group of people who are deemed to have intrinsic connections to country and who 'own' or 'hold' it, I use the expression 'country-group' (coined by Peter Sutton). Others have called them 'local descent groups', 'estate groups', or 'clans'. In five of the case studies, the country-group was some kind of patrifilial group; a person gained their identity from and held the country of their father and father's father. They were not all 'descent groups', strictly speaking, for membership was not constituted in terms of descent from a common human ancestor or ancestors, although people often traced their origin back to a totemic ancestor.[5]

Elsewhere I have argued that anthropologists should attend closely to the language and metaphors that people use to frame their identities and delineate groups. Concepts such as 'clan' and 'corporate group', together with taxonomies of tribe, phratry, clan, and clan sub-group, may distort indigenous conceptions. Most ethnographies drawn on in this work do not explore such subtleties but simply substitute terms such as 'division' and 'clan' for indigenous conceptions. Furthermore, I do need general terms. The expression 'patrifilial group', or 'patri-group' for short, denotes a shared identity that each person takes from their father and father's father. It picks out two key features of identity and leaves the subtleties and complexities open for exploration. Some subtleties do emerge in the cases studies on Ngarinyin people and their neighbours and Yolngu people. The expression 'complementary filiation' is useful in a similar way, and applies to a situation in which an individual has special ties to their mother's group and country in conjunction with patrifilial identity; the mother–child relation 'complements' the father–child link through which identity is transmitted. We shall see that this is a widespread pattern.[6]

The ways in which people defined and gave significance to land and waters cannot be divorced from the forces shaping patterns of movement, which were discussed in Chapter 4. In that chapter I suggested that the control of access to country in all seven regions took the form of a 'social boundary defence', which was a response to variance in the productivity of individuals and to the unpredictable, rather dispersed resources. The degree of exclusivity/reciprocity varied between the regions and with the resources.

The case studies in the first part of this chapter look at the definition and constitution of 'countries' and the associated groups, and the ways in which people gained their identity and relations to country. A particular issue is 'succession'. Kin groups, or descent groups, especially unilineal ones, are subject to demographic processes.

If a patrifilial group has the misfortune to give rise to a generation without males, normal succession through the male line cannot take place. Many Aboriginal societies had means to deal with such contingencies. Polygynous marriage had a bearing on succession because it affected the rate of growth or decline of a kin group. In looking at use rights, each case study includes a discussion of links between individuals and places, such as complementary rights in one's mother's country. We shall see, however, that the distinction between group and individual connections does not always hold up.[7]

Each case study then turns to the exercise of control over access to country and resources: concepts of permission, rites of entry to another group's country, and the control of specific resources. The kin relations outlined in Chapter 6 and the cosmologies described in Chapter 7 are, as I said earlier, deeply implicated in the significance given to country and technology and people's relations to them.

Kŭnai people

Countries and country-groups

The Kŭnai word for 'country' was *wŭrŭk* (or *wŭrk*). We saw that, like Aboriginal people elsewhere, Kŭnai people appear to have named broad localities after a focal place (such as Dura, near the present town of Orbost). Reconstructions of their localities show about 30 focal places, situated along the coastal barrier, around the lakes, in the middle and upper reaches of rivers, on estuaries, and around Corner Inlet. There is little evidence indicating how firm the boundaries between countries were. Moreover, rather than drawing clear 'boundaries' around whole areas, people may have drawn 'divisions' of limited extent between some places in the landscape (especially those with rich resources), leaving the identity of other places indeterminate. People named many small localities within each country, some associated with totemic ancestors and mythical events. Some countries may have extended out to sea, especially into the shallow coastal waters around Port Albert and Corner Inlet and the associated islands.[8]

Kŭnai countries clustered into the five loosely bounded regional identities that Howitt inappropriately referred to as 'clans' (Map 5.2). We saw in Chapter 4 that in this region no localised moieties, sections, or semi-moieties were to be found.[9]

Bulmer reports that the expression *bunjil wŭrŭk Kŭnai* ('owner-place-person') signified an inhabitant of a particular place. According to Howitt, the people of each country-group ('division') had their own tract of land for foraging, and claimed property rights over the country and its resources. People looked after the country in a number of ways: they protected birds' nests, sank wells, protected waterholes against the encroachment of animals, covered springs with stones and branches, and burnt off the country. But this picture is too simple; as Chapter 4 showed, people of each residence group foraged across several countries during the seasonal round of movement.

Country-groups took their name from the proper name of a focal place, the character of the country (such as 'island' or 'mud'), the name of a prominent man (such as Bunjil Kraura, 'he who controls the west wind'), or some other entity (such as 'fire' or 'widgeon') that may have been totemic or perhaps have indicated expertise on the leader's part. A person's identity usually derived at least in part from his or her country-group, so that a man of Binnajerra (a place) would be referred to as *Binnajerra kŭnai*, or 'Binnajerra man'. Conversely, a place could be named after the group—for example, Kŭtbŭntaura-wŭrŭk, or 'Fire-holders' country'. But people of this group might also be known by the name of their leader, Bunjil Nŭlŭng.

Names of different kinds may have had different scope—some applied perhaps to a larger range of people than others. Some evidence suggests that some identities were context-dependent and could merge, so that country groups did not form uniform segments of regional identities; for example, Howitt reports that people of Jimmy's Point (Brt-britta) were also known as Ngrŭngit, or 'Lakes Entrance' people. These considerations lead me to be a little sceptical about the way in which Howitt and subsequent writers have identified 'divisions'; we do not know what the status of each recorded name was, and so what kind of entity each one referred to. My earlier figure of 30 country-groups should therefore be treated as tentative.

Howitt took patrilineal inheritance of country to have been the rule, but provides rather little direct evidence to support this assertion. He records three cases of men inheriting rights to country from their fathers, and one case of a 'brother' inheriting such rights. A man claimed Raymond Island through his father, but was also able to hunt at Lake Tyers, the country of his father's birth. In another case, a son had the same country-group identity as his father but was of a different regional identity, perhaps because of a difference in residence.

Kŭnai people may have linked their patrifilial guardian totems with their father's country. However, none of the *mŭk je-ak* (totems) associated with places appear as inherited patrifilial guardian totems in the records, although this may be due to chance, as the records are very incomplete. Totemic affiliations both distinguished localities and created connections, as we saw in Chapters 5 and 7. Port Arthur, Seaspray, and the lower Tambo River shared stories about Pelican, while Frog, Scarlet Robin, Swamp Hawk, Moon, and Dolphin each had an association with a different place. I have found no information about succession to the ownership of country where links of patrifiliation failed, but connections by birth are suggestive of a possible means.

Use rights

As well as patrifilial connections, birth seems to have been an important basis of relations to country, as it was among Yaitmathang people of Omeo in north Gippsland. Given the practice of residing with the wife's parents (see Chapter 11), it is likely that some people were born on their mother's country. Because distantly related people of different residence groups married, people moved between communities—both in order to marry and after marriage—and this gave groups an open quality. Whatever the nature of the difference between 'owners' and visitors, we do have evidence for a range of bases of use rights (although the evidence is biased towards males). These supported use rights to:

- a man's father's country
- a man's place of birth
- a man's father's place of birth
- a person's spouse's country.

The inheritance of personal names from one's mother's people may have been indicative of rights in one's mother's country as well. As mentioned earlier, seasonal movement, from wetlands to forest and back, took people across several countries.[10]

Control of access

Howitt's own evidence shows that people did not enforce exclusive use of their own land. Nevertheless, people clearly asserted control over access to particularly valuable scarce resources. This indicates that there was a practical distinction between 'owners' (denoted by the expression *bunjil wŭrŭk*) and visitors. Thus, Bunjil-baul people of Raymond Island claimed exclusive rights to the swan's eggs found there, and such claims may have been commonplace. With permission, visitors to Raymond Island could take food or game; Howitt reports that anyone who foraged without permission would be attacked. I have found one reference in the ethnographic record to a senior man claiming an exclusive right to a particular waterhole, but this may have been related to his particular magical powers and not have been a normal prerogative of age. Strangers visiting a place had to take precautions against the hostility of the spirit beings of the country; for example, visitors to Wilsons Promontory (Yerŭk) who spoke a different tongue from the locals had to drink water from a vessel stirred by a man of the country in order to avert danger.[11]

Connections and rights to country in the Western Desert had a more open character, reflecting the greater mobility of people and greater unpredictability of resources.

Pitjantjatjara people and their neighbours

Countries and country-groups

In the Western Desert, the polysemous term *ngurra* ('camp', 'place', 'country') applied to places at various levels of inclusion—from the place where one sat or slept, to a camp, to a person's or group's totemic country. Places, especially water sources, had ancestral significance, as Chapter 7 showed. Ancestral stories and songs traced long and short intersecting journeys across the land. In some areas, places formed associations with different ancestors but events described in narratives linked them. Stories and songs linked each site to others through the narratives of long ancestral journeys from place to place across the desert, as did the intersecting and overlapping routes taken when foraging.[12]

Some anthropologists, however, have interpreted site-clusters as 'estates' linked to patrifilial groups.[13] According to Munn, people conceived of a cluster of sites as 'one country', ideally owned by a group of agnates. The cluster comprised the bodily remains of several ancestors, one of which was dominant. Mardu people tended to emphasise the unity of a cluster of places such as Giinyu, leading Tonkinson to call the cluster an 'estate', owned by an 'estate group'. He links variation in the integrity of estates to the richness of resources: the west of the region tended to have more integrated countries. Robert Layton identified site-clusters in the vicinity of Uluru and the Musgrave Ranges, each with an area of between 2500 and 3000 square kilometres.

Myers writes of socio-centrically defined 'ranges' or resource areas around permanent or semi-permanent waterholes. Emotional ties linked individuals to their home resource-areas, to which they tended to return regularly. (The waterholes were important totemic sites as well.) The group of 'holders' consisted of a 'descending kindred' with a patrifilial core, but including the children of women of that group, as well as others.

Myers reports that particular ancestral events and totemic associations distinguished places. A person with responsibility for a particular site joined with people of other locations on an ancestral track to sing and enact the ceremonies of their common ancestor. Pintupi people conceived of places linked by a totemic ancestral journey as 'one country', implying that a person associated with a particular place could claim rights to a country related to his or her own country through one or more ancestral journeys.

Land had no moiety or semi-moiety identity, and, like Yuwaaliyaay people, Western Desert people projected language identities and differences onto country in a rather loose, context-dependent way (see Chapter 6). The multiple bases of attachment to places, as well as people's great mobility, meant that these identities overlapped greatly when related to space.

The early ethnographers of this region, such as Tindale and the Berndts, followed Radcliffe-Brownian orthodoxy, and they thought they found patrilineal descent groups in the Western Desert. Yet reports on Pitjantjatjara people and their neighbours, including Ronald Berndt's reports, tend to pick out birth as the primary connection.[14] Ethnographers have listed a number of grounds on which people could claim a connection to a site in the Western Desert: birth, spirit conception, conception at a place associated with the same or a related ancestor, place of circumcision, one's parent's or grandparent's links to a place by one or more of those grounds, living in the area, and the death of a close relative at or near the place. (Munn says that the place of birth might differ from a person's father's country.) The coincidence of a number of grounds strengthened a person's claim.

Conception appears to have been the basis for an individual totemic relation between a person and the sign of the spirit child revealed to the father. A person bore marks such as moles and warts on their body that were identified with ancestral traces (*tjukurritja*) in the country of their birth. A person also referred to their birthplace in the first person singular, and identified in this way with the place.

Myers emphasises the processual aspect of becoming an 'owner' or 'holder'. A person had to convert a 'claim' into an 'interest' by negotiating with owners to be included in activities and to gain access to knowledge. A place became a person's 'own country' (expressed using the term *walytja* in Pintupi) as a result of prolonged association; failure to maintain a regular association lessened the force of one's claim. Existing owners tended to favour close kin as new owners, especially (among men) sons and sisters' sons, so constituting what Myers calls a 'descending kindred'. Indeed, men tried to arrange for sons to be born where they had the strongest ties, and passed on knowledge to sons and sisters' sons, giving rise to a de facto descent group. Pintupi people referred to the group with primary responsibility for a place as 'the group of sons' (*katjapirti*). To be an 'owner' meant to have control over the stories, rituals, and sacred objects associated with the place. To hold this degree of responsibility one had to be knowledgeable about the country and its ancestral traditions. Pintupi people talked about a person coming to 'hold' country when their father and father's father had died—it was a case of responsibility being handed on, rather than an essential identity conferred at birth.

Some 'countrymen', then, had a primary claim to 'hold' country, control the related rituals, make decisions about the claims of others, and teach people about the country. Initiated men of the group collectively owned and organised the related rit- uals and cared for the sacred objects. Ownership implied control over secret knowledge related to the stories, sacred objects, and ceremonies associated with a place and its totemic ancestors. People performed important ceremonies at some sites, and instructed people at others.

The group with connections to a place were known as the people of that place— for example, the 'Giinyu mob'—or were identified by one of its ancestors. But each individual had ancestral ties to more than one place, so that groups of 'owners' over- lapped. Moreover, it may be that individuals clustered ancestral places together in different (but overlapping) ways, and a person could choose one of a number of sites to refer to the same broad region. (At Ooldea, according to R. M. Berndt, some peo- ple picked out a single site as their country, others a cluster of sites.)

In contrast with Yolngu patri-groups, people of the Western Desert did not construct deep genealogical connections. In general, adults traced links back only to their grand- parents' generation, and even then the simple kin terminology in that generation, as well as inhibitions on uttering the names of the dead, generalised those connections.[15]

The ethnography of the region gives a male-centred view of country-groups, and it seems likely that they were most salient in the context of male rituals.

Use rights

A strong formal difference between 'owners' of country and others with subsidiary rights does not emerge from the Western Desert ethnography. Even distantly related non-residents could claim a connection to a place. People had different degrees and kinds of rights and responsibilities: some were simply able to camp at and use the resources of the place; others had full responsibility for looking after its ancestral sites and objects and for performing its ceremonies. According to Myers, rights to exploit country followed from joining a residence group that was already exploiting it. People conceived of the links between an individual and the people he or she lived with as those of 'one countrymen' (*ngurra kutjungurrara*).

Several writers have linked the flexibility of group membership to ecological constraints. The general argument goes that extensive and varied (rather than exclusive) rights to areas of land were a response to the unpredictability and variability of rainfall (and hence water) and of vegetable and animal foods. Individuals had a broad range of options as to where they could travel, reside, and exploit resources, drawing on their many connections.[16]

Control of access

Holders of country had at least some control over access to land and waters and their resources. They also had preferential access—it was thought to be hazardous for a person to enter and use land of which they had scant knowledge, because of the risk of violating sacred and dangerous sites.

The essence of 'ownership' of country in the Western Desert, Myers remarks, was 'the right to be asked'. People always liked to be consulted, but the norms of kinship and reciprocity led them to grant requests. It was above all secret entry that upset people. Rites of entry similar to those reported by Peterson in northeast Arnhem Land governed camp boundaries: a visitor announced his or her presence by lighting a fire some distance from a camp, waited to be identified, and was then conducted into the camp. People tended to be restrained in an unfamiliar camp, and announced their intentions to visit an area tentatively. Residents guided strangers through distant country to avert danger. Residents of an area expected people from another group's range to make their presence known, and could monitor the presence of others through observation of smoke. A number of cultural conventions gave people more unfettered access to countries other than their own, as Tonkinson points out; these included attendance at the frequent initiation rites.[17]

Yuwaaliyaay people and their neighbours

The rather more clearly differentiated language identities of Yuwaaliyaay people and their neighbours suggests a somewhat more defined relationship to country, but with a wide range of individual connections and a similar emphasis on birthplace.

Countries and country-groups

We saw in Chapter 4 that Yuwaaliyaay people and their neighbours projected language identities onto people and country, but that they were diffuse at the margins, and people could have mixed identities.

The six or seven discrete Yuwaaliyaay countries or 'homelands' (*nguremba, ngurrampaa*) got their name from a local resource, usually a plant or tree, combined with the suffix *–bara* (*burrah* in Parker's orthography). The average area of the countries was about 2000 square kilometres. Local place names were legion. Gamilaraay place names were derived from dominant species of plant and animal (for example, 'place of the Australian ash' and 'abounding in echidnas') and from topographical features, such as bare ground, the presence of pipe clay, expansive water, or the shape of a river. Some Wayilwan *ngurrampaa* took their names from focal places within the area. People saw boundaries as meeting places rather than borders.[18]

People of the same country were 'relations' (or 'countrymen' in more recent Aboriginal English). Parker writes that a person belonged to the 'country or hunting ground' (*nguremba*) where they were born, and their mother named them after the country. A person born in Noonga (Kurrajong) country took the name 'Noongahburrah', for example. This identity was not a 'blood relationship' and did not imply prohibition of marriage to someone of the same identity. Confusingly, Parker writes elsewhere that a person's country was 'hereditary'. On the basis of later research, A. R. Radcliffe-Brown insisted that patrilineal groups owned land in the region. However, a number of other ethnographies of the region stipulate birth as the basis of connections to country.

Wangaaybuwan people to the south held country through their relationship to their father, mother, and wife's father, so that an individual might have rights in a series of swamps; other people had to ask permission to hunt and gather in these places. Taken together, this evidence suggests there were multiple bases of rights to land, including birthplace, patrifilial links, matrifilial links, and spouse's country.[19]

Many traces of ancestral action in the land had associations with Byamee, his wives and his sons, although other totemic associations distinguished countries, as we saw in Chapter 7. But sites were probably not associated with descent groups or descent-based identities. The strongly differentiated totemic identities were those of dispersed matri-categories, roughly articulated with the four-section naming systems. Only three sites recorded by Parker had an association with matrilineal totems: the tree of Millyan (Eaglehawk), a place connected to a subtotem of Maira (Paddymelon), and a hole in the Culgoa river that was the source of spirit children from Bahloo the Moon.

In the absence of patrifilial country groups, and with people having connections on several bases, succession to the country of a dying group may have been irrelevant.

Use rights

The variability of rainfall and the unpredictability of the river and its resources forced people to hedge their bets by being able to exploit alternative resources in different places, as people did in the Western Desert. There is no direct evidence about use rights, but the Wangaaybuwan evidence suggests a range of rights, and the dispersed matri-categories and the section system may have formed the basis for relationships between people of different communities. The Bora and initiation journeys were likely to have fostered personal links between individuals, who subsequently would have visited one another. Neighbouring groups had common rights to camping areas along the river, where they also owned stone fish-traps said to have been made by Byamee and his giant sons (Plate 3.6). At the river 'during the fishing festival, peace should be strictly kept, all meeting to enjoy the fish, and do their share towards preserving the fisheries'.[20]

Control of access

I have found no evidence regarding how people controlled access to country directly. Men did assert individual property rights in resources, at least temporarily. A man would mark a tree in which he had found a bees' nest and honey, if he was unable to chop it out at the time. For anyone else to take the honey from the marked tree was considered 'theft'. A certain tree on Yuwaaliyaay country had been marked by Byamee for this purpose, according to Yuwaaliyaay doctrine.[21]

Wiil and Mi̱nong people

Land-holding in the southwest contrasted with Yuwaaliyaay land-holding in that it centred on patri-groups.

Countries and country-groups

Individuals and groups among Mi̱nong people owned countries ('districts' in Bates's terminology), access to which they guarded 'jealously'. Countries appear to have been identified and strongly differentiated by totemic affiliations, as we saw in Chapter 7, and some myths (such as the Dingo story) connected distant places. Smaller localities took their names from, among other things, recent events—for example, 'Mirilyan asked mother for water'. Several prominent names of places have been recorded, such as Balbarup, near Albany. The country belonging to Mokaré, around the west of Princess Royal Harbour, had an area of about 40 square kilometres, more if we include shallow waters. This is comparable with the size of Sandbeach and Yolngu coastal countries.[22]

People of the same country were *bidkal* (literally 'one sinew/vein', glossed by Bates as 'one stock'), or *kal-ip-gur*, 'one hearth/home'. Country-groups seem to have been known by the name of their country—for example, Mongup people, Corackerup people, Quaalup people, and people of Kincannup at Albany. It seems from Barker's 1830 journal that ownership of land passed in the male line, sons taking on responsibilities as they became adults. But, as in the previous case studies, place of birth was important among Wiil people. Hassell asserts that birth 'always took place, if possible, in the country of the tribe'. If a pregnant woman visited another country, 'every effort was made to return home before the child was born'.[23]

Semi-moieties at King George Sound seem to have been localised, at least to the extent that Tondarup people tended to be 'more prevalent' on the west side of the Sound, and the people they married were more prevalent on the east side.[24] Thus, as I suggested in Chapter 5, it may be that people identified country by semi-moiety; this is consistent (if semi-moieties were patrifilial) with the evidence for the patrilineal inheritance of land at King George Sound. According to Collie, if patrilineal succession failed, a neighbouring group succeeded to the country; it may have been of the same semi-moiety. Polygyny would have enhanced this process, as some groups grew while others declined.

Use rights

Nind seems to describe a situation not unlike that of the larger Sandbeach residence groups, in which owners of neighbouring countries, who intermarried, lived in a common home base. Consistent with this, people had rights of access to several countries. We saw in Chapter 7 that a mother's brother dreamed of a future child for his sister, suggesting a strong relationship with the mother's country and group. Furthermore, children had special affiliations with the country of their birth, and 'brothers' of that country looked after boys at their initiation. Totemic identity conferred by a distant relative or close mother's brother gave the recipient the right to hunt in that country, and the conferring of a totem by a brother-in-law perhaps linked up with access to one's spouse's country.[25] Men acquired rights of access to more distant countries through initiation journeys, and marriages between people of widely separated communities also extended connections.

Control of access

Nind lists the actions that could be taken with and without the permission of the owner of a country: 'Thus all of [those who live together] have a right to break down grass-trees, kill bandicoots, lizards, and other animals, and dig up roots; but the presence of the owner of the ground is considered necessary when they fire the country for game.'[26]

Nind construed the exercise of certain rights as individual property in country. But I think (as does Bill Ferguson) that this was more likely the action of patri-group members within a residence group that included people belonging to other countries. Non-owners required a senior owner's permission to burn the country to hunt wallaby and kangaroo. Disputes over burning off seem to have been commonplace—one man was speared in the leg during such a dispute. Access to an area was prohibited for a period following the death of an important person associated with it, during which time people also could not utter the person's name (a pattern found also among Yolngu people).[27]

Owners guarded certain resources, such as zamia nuts and birds' nests, rather jealously. Minong people tried to assert individual rights over grass trees (*pāāluck*, *Xanthorrheoa* sp.) in which grubs were found, but not overly successfully:

> Of their *pāālucks* they are extremely tenacious; the person who breaks down the tree being entitled to its produce. And if robberies of this nature are detected, the thief is always punished. They believe also that stolen *pāālucks* occasion sickness and eruptions. Yet when hungry, a friend will not scruple to have recourse to the grass-tree of another who is not present, but in this case he peels a small branch or twig, and sticks in the ground, near the tree. This is called *keit a borringerra*, and is intended to prevent anger or other ill consequences.[28]

Sandbeach people

Relations to country among Sandbeach people were quite similar to those of Wiil and Minong people, but with complementary filiation a strong feature.

Countries and country-groups

Among Sandbeach people each coastal patri-group's country or 'estate' consisted of a strip extending from the crest of the range in the west out to sea, including islands, reefs, cays, sandbanks, and patches of seagrass between the reefs and the beach. Their size was about 80 square kilometres on average (or 200 square kilometres if coastal waters were included).[29] The name of a country was that of an animal or plant or other entity (such as the moon) associated with an ancestor, or a deceased man, or it was a topynym (such as *maangkal*, meaning 'river mouth') plus the suffix *–ngaachi*. Divisions between countries showed most clearly along the beach, marked by the ownership of specific sites, each associated with a totemic ancestor. Divisions were much fuzzier in the hinterland— here few sites delineated the patri-group identity of country and areas belonged to neighbouring groups as 'half and half' in Aboriginal English, or two groups might share a fighting ground or initiation ground ('box-up'). A series of named places also marked the patri-group identity of coastal waters. Among sacred or forbidden places (*ngaachi kincha*) were men's secret initiation grounds, prohibited to women, girls, and uninitiated males. People had a strong sense of a cared-for landscape—since its abandonment the country had 'gone wild', with camping grounds overgrown and graves neglected.

Each country, inland or coastal, had an association with one of the two exoga- mous patri-moieties, *kaapay* and *kuyan*. The patri-moieties did not strictly alternate, however, as two or three distinct countries of the same moiety often clustered together. Most animal and some plant species had an associated story place, and took the moiety affiliation of that place.

In this region, as we have seen, country groups were exogamous patri-groups with proper names. These names and the totemic affiliations differentiated them strongly, with only one name, the generic 'river mouth' people, duplicated among 53 patri-groups. Other names, often distinct in different dialects, included 'ti-tree', 'cyclone', 'wattle', and a woman's name. An individual described their patri-group country as the place of their 'heart' or 'life', the 'place from my father', or 'the place from my father's father'. Patri-group members traced descent from a single, apical human ancestor, according to Chase.

A number of usually adjacent patri-groups spoke one of a series of closely related dialects. And two or three adjacent patri-groups, ideally of the same language and with some inter-married members, shared a main wet-season camp. Towards the south of the region, some patri-groups held two or more non-contiguous countries. Moiety identity was discontinuously distributed across the landscape, forming some- thing of a chequerboard pattern.

If patrifilial inheritance of country failed, it was possible, in order to ensure con- tinuity, for a man to succeed to his mother's country or for a group as a whole to succeed to the mother's country of one of its members, crossing moiety boundaries. Chase reports that people at Lockhart River sometimes argued heatedly about the inheritance of particular countries, and also about the precise location of boundaries. How the moiety identity of individuals was adjusted to that of the country, its sites, and its ancestors is unclear. Polygynous men were likely to have engendered larger groups than their monogamous neighbours, enhancing the succession process. [30]

Use rights

A person not only identified with the country of their own patri-group, but also had a connection to their mother's country.[31] Except in the very south of the Sandbeach region, people apparently did not subscribe to a doctrine of connection to country through conception or personal spirit. Rather, the doctrine of the *nguunthal* (spirit) residing at the mother's country, together with the carrying of the umbilical cord by the mother's brother, and burial of the umbilical cord and the avulsed tooth at the mother's country, attest to a strong corporeal and essential connection between the individual and their mother's country and group. However, there are strong differences between the two modes: a man's children inherited his identity and consequently a connection to his father's and father's father's country, but not to his mother's country.

A person also had rights to reside in and use the country of his or her spouse. Additional attachments could arise out of a number of contingencies, such as being raised by adults other than one's own parents and of a different patri-group, or having as one's mother's husband a different man from the one whose semen contributed to one's conception and (according to Sandbeach beliefs) one's growth. Bruce Risgby records a recent expression of kinship between people and country among Stewart River people: the land (or what they call 'ground'), trees, and animals were 'our family'. Presumably other residents joined those with core connections through various links of kinship and marriage.

Control of access

We may infer that these two modes of connection to country—through one's father and father's father and through 'complementary filiation'—gave a person their strongest formal claims to possess, use, and control of country. What rights did these connections confer? According to Rigsby and Chase, residents regularly monitored their country to see who was, or had been, on it. Outsiders were expected to make their presence and intentions known. Presumably patri-group members, if present and if sufficiently senior, had the most say over control of access. A person living away from their mother's country who was seeking to visit it and use its resources 'should seek permission and advise their intentions'.[32]

Ngarinyin people and their neighbours

Relations to country among Ngarinyin people and their neighbours bore several similarities to Sandbeach ones, but with more links between patri-groups and distinctive individual connections.

Countries and country-groups

Chapter 7 showed that each named patri-group country (*dambun* in Ngarinyin) contained one or more rock-art galleries associated with the group's *wanjina* (ancestors) and other totemic beings. A country also included 'child-spirit' centres associated with *wunggurr* (pythons associated also with rain), and often with *wanjina* conflated with *wunggurr*. Countries of the same patri-moiety formed two interlocking, curvilinear swathes (*mamalarr*), rather than a chequerboard pattern. Each language area included countries of both moieties.

A named patrifilial group (also *dambun*) held each country. However, a person could be linked to a 'father' of another patri-group through a namesake relation or through adoption, either of which conferred dual membership—a person would be 'partly A, partly B' patri-group. These relationships provided modes of succession.

Blundell's survey of patri-groups and their countries ('estates') reveals some of the complexities of patri-group structure. One named country was associated with a 'top' and 'bottom' group. Three Worrorra groups shared a common *dambun* name, two of them distinguished by their own names; one was said to have been Wunambal originally, but migrated south. The groups had different affinal relations with a third group. One patri-group had its principle *wanjina* site within another group's country, affiliated to a different language. A Worrorra patri-group comprised three lineages each associated with a distinct part of the *dambun*, although they shared a *wanjina* site; the *wanjina* site too had shifted language identity. Tony Redmond identifies three *dambun* with distinct 'top' (up-river) and 'bottom' (down-river) groups.[33]

Totemic affiliations strongly differentiated the patri-groups. Each group had one or more *wanjina* regarded as the 'father' or 'father's father' of the group. Patri-groups took their names from topographical features, trees and other plants, snakes, rain, honeybees, birds, etc., and a group's name was derived from its principle totem; for example:
- Biyarrngongo—Red Gravel
- Brrewarrgu—Eagle-hawk's Nest
- Galarungarri—Rain
- Gurungongo—Cypress Pine
- Mandangarri—Gum.

None of the principle totems recorded by Blundell and Redmond were shared among patri-groups.

In spite of this totemic differentiation between patri-groups, there were, as Lommel emphasises, important connections between groups. For example, people of two patri-groups of the same moiety received most of their conception spirits from the waters of one of them, and some child-spirit centres were said to have moved from one country to another.[34]

One feature of relations among patri-groups that was not recorded in the previous cases, but that appears in both Ngarinyin and Yolngu cultures, is the projection of kin relations between groups as wholes, and by individuals onto groups as wholes (see Chapter 6). Some adjoining Ngarinyin patri-groups of the same moiety were 'brothers'. People of one might succeed to the country of the other, and they shared similar relations with other patri-groups, such as 'mother' groups. Other adjacent groups of the same patri-moiety were in a 'mother's mother'–'woman's daughter's child' relation, and people applied the reciprocal kin terms to the group and its country and ancestors. Tony Redmond remarks that people's experience of country reflected the emotional tone of the kin relationships associated with a place. These group-level relations derived from the repeated asymmetric marriages between the same groups down the generations.[35]

Succession

Two of the main modes of succession to the country of an extinct patri-group, or one reduced only to women members, were through the namesake relation and through adoption by a man of another group. Both conferred dual patri-group membership. Blundell records a case in which one patri-group was dying out through lack of males, and people of another group of the same moiety were calling themselves by that patri-group name. Succession through a namesake or adoptive relationship may account for the fact that one 'sub-group' was originally of a different language than others of the same group.[36]

The complexity of Ngarinyin and Worrorra patri-groups may have derived in part from the demographic consequences of polygyny, together with the several modes of succession. The high level of polygyny recorded among Worrorra people would have given rise to both fast-growing and fast-declining lineages, so that some regularly died out while others split to take over the country and sacra of the dying groups; this sometimes resulted in a changed language identity, either for the original group or the incoming successors.

Use rights

Apart from in one's own patri-group's country, a person had use rights in the countries of their mother, father's mother, spouse, daughter's husband, and place of conception. A person had the right of access to their mother's country and could 'walk around' it, because they were 'born from that place'. A person's connection to country through place of conception (*wunggurr*) was independent of patrifilial connections, although there was plenty of room for manipulation to locate a child's conception place on the father's *dambun*; sometimes this was done long after a birth. As in the Western Desert, individuals also had connections with patri-group countries other than their own through ancestral journeys that connected their own country to others.[37]

Control of access

Certain principles of etiquette governed access to countries other than one's own patri-group's country. A person was not supposed to enter someone's country if no one was living there at the time. A group wanting to visit another group's country first sent a messenger carrying a message stick, announcing his coming with smoke. (An unannounced visitor might be regarded as a 'spy' from another group.) In principle at least, visitors would only be received if they could demonstrate a close kin relationship to the host group and country—that it was one's mother's or father's mother's country, for example. However, Hernandez reports relations of hospitality between neighbouring residence groups (see Chapter 10), and we saw that Lommel highlights connections between patri-groups (Chapter 7), which may have had implications for access. Blundell reports that people needed permission to collect chert from the site at 'Yinindja', and owners placed restrictions on the activities of non-owners.[38]

People who accompanied visitors to *wanjina* paintings would address the spirits to warn them of the visitors' approach, and to assure them that their own spirits came from the place and that they would do no harm. People had to behave decorously at the site; if they offended the *wanjina* they might be struck by lightning.

Control of specific resources

I have not come across evidence of individual control of or exclusive rights to resources, but, as elsewhere, particular ancestral sites (and in this case paintings) came under the exclusive control of patri-group members. Responsibility for maintaining *wanjina* paintings followed from patri-group identity (including adoptive identity), and was handed on from father to son. Woolagoodja told Blundell that his father said this to him: 'This is our painting and this is our country. *Wandjina* put it here for us. If I finish … this is your business.'[39] The painting was at the site of another patri-group that Woolagoodja's group had taken over.

Yolngu people

A similar pairing of patri-group with complementary connections is found in Yolngu relations to country, but with more complex patri-groups and a different range of individual rights.

Countries and country-groups

The Yolngu word *wa:nga* had a similar range of senses as the Western Desert term *ngurra*, from sleeping place to wider country. People divided land and waters into countries named after an important focal place, usually a source of fresh water, and each country was replete with 'small names'. I calculated the average area of named countries at about 36 square kilometres on the coastal plains, and about 80 square kilometres in the forested hinterland, but larger further inland. Each of the many named locales in each country was associated with a particular totemic being, so that a country as a whole had a wide variety of totemic associations. These linked the place with other countries of the same moiety through ancestral journeys and related songs, designs, dances, and sacred objects. In this way, each country had cross-cutting links with many others of the same moiety.[40]

Certain names, ancestral designs, and sacred objects denoted the unique identity of each country. Resource-rich countries had connections with the major *wangarr* ancestors and associated ceremonies, designs, and so on, while others were associated with lesser beings, such as the named 'ghosts' (*mokuy*) celebrated in public songs and dances. A small enclave within another group's country gave a group permanent access to it and the surrounding area.

Patri-moiety and patri-group identity also extended out into the shallow coastal waters, marked too by ancestral sites, including rocks, reefs, sandbars, and mud-banks, and by the flow of fresh water (*gapu raypiny*) and brackish water from the estuaries, mixing with the salt water (*gapu monuk*). Patri-group countries also included exposed seabed. Geoff Bagshaw has shown, however, that the identity of salt waters themselves around the Crocodile Islands and Cape Stewart differed somewhat from that of land. Yan-nhangu speakers of the islands and Burarra people of Cape Stewart divided the waters into two separate bodies—*gapu dhulway*, which flows over mud (Yirritja moiety), and *gapu maramba*, which flows over rocks (Dhuwa moiety). Jointly owned by patri-groups whose country abutted them and possessed the related songs (*manikay*), these waters were linked to the waters around the islands to the east and were associated with marine *wangarr*.[41]

Each named patrifilial group (*mala*, *matha*, or *ba:purru*) held two or three usually non-contiguous countries, and several smaller places as enclaves within other groups' countries (or as pockets on the coast). Between 40 and 50 patri-group names have been recorded. However, because of the complexity of patri-group structure and the fact that each group had many names, often shared with others, it is difficult to give a precise number. The term *mala* ('group') denoted the collectivity. *Matha* ('tongue') refers to the way of speaking thought to be co-extensive with patri-group identity, while *ba:purru* denoted the group's ancestral connections. People often characterised their patri-group identity as the name of a 'tongue' (*matha*), reflecting the ideology that each group had its own way of speaking. This 'tongue' name could be extended to identify the dialects of other patri-groups of the same dialect group. The pairing of names—*matha* and *mala*, or *mala* and *ba:purru*—was a common way of identifying a patri-group. Consistent with the extension of patri-group identity to ways of speaking, a group's language came from its waters according to Yolngu doctrines, or from a related *wangarr*, such as Threadfin Salmon. A person was *wa:nga-watangu* ('country-holder') in relation to their own patri-group country. They were said to 'hold' (*ngayathama*) and 'look after' (*dja:ga*) the country and its sacra.[42]

Patri-groups varied greatly in their structure. Many consisted of more than one lineage, the descent links between which were unknown or the subject of a variety of opinions. These lineages were sometimes identified and differentiated with reference to proper names inherited from human ancestors. Yolngu people traced deeper genealogical connections than Western Desert peoples, back (or 'down') to the great-grandparents of the older members of a group, who were at its 'roots'.

In some cases, a patri-group's main countries were distributed between its several lineages. Some patri-group identities were shared by rather independent 'top' (upriver) and 'bottom' (downriver) groups with distinct countries (as among Ngarinyin people and their neighbours), but in at least one case the two groups shared a focal ancestral site.[43]

Probably all patri-groups shared *ba:purru* identities with open-ended 'strings' of other groups of the same moiety, through shared sacra, while other *ba:purru* names distinguished the groups. Places called *ringgitj* signified the connections between patri-groups through ancestral and other links. In some cases, the shared identity formed a salient public identity of the kind that Warner called a 'phratry' (for example, the many Djambarrpuyngu and Mandjikay groups, and the two main Gupapuyngu patri-groups). In one case, people regularly paired the names of two patri-groups with separate names (Ngaymil and D̲atiwuy), nearby countries, and very similar totemic design, and referred to them as one group. People classified countries and patri-groups according to patri-moiety (Dhuwa or Yirritja), forming a loose and in places fuzzy mosaic. Patri-groups also belonged to dialect groups, three of which were moiety-specific (see Chaper 5).

As with Ngarinyin people and their neighbours, Yolngu patri-group identities were related to each other in terms of kin relations—a group was the 'mother' (and 'wife') group, the 'mother's mother' group, or the 'sister' group of other groups, and so on. Groups also had a relationship as a whole to individuals—for example, *ngandi-pulu*, a person's mother's group and country; *ma:ri-pulu*, a person's mother's mother's group; and *yapa-pulu*, a person's 'sister' group. Conversely, an individual was one group's *waku* (wC/ZC), another group's *gutharra* (wDC/ZDC), and so on. Of particular importance was the *ma:ri–gutharra* (mother's mother–daughter's child) relation between patri-groups, which often implied a relation between inland and coastal, freshwater and saltwater (or 'top' and 'bottom'), countries and groups.

The main principle governing succession to the country of a group without male heirs was that women's daughter's children succeeded to their mother's mother's (*ma:ri*) country and sacra. These were people with the closest matrilineal connections to the group in question but of the same patri-moiety. The country of one's spirit conception, one's country 'of the water', provided a somewhat weaker basis of claim. Given the fact that people of several groups might be the *gutharra* (wDC) of the dying group, and that there were several varieties of *ma:ri–gutharra* (MM–wDC) relations, from very close to distant, the way was open for competition and conflict over succession. The very high level of polygyny, which led to fast growth and decline of and large size differences between patri-groups, may have increased the frequency at which groups died out, and hence increased the incidence of succession claims.[44]

Use rights

As noted in Chapter 4, a person's patri-group identity could be dual—that of both their genitor and their mother's husband, where these differed. As 'mother-holder' (*ngandi-watangu*), an adult had strong connections to their mother's patri-group, and a duty to look after its sacra. A person also had the right to perform the public songs of their mother's mother's (*ma:ri*) patri-group, and according to Williams such people (the *gutharra*, women's daughter's children) had to be consulted by the owners (*wa:nga-watangu*) in matters related to country. These close connections through ritual translated into strong claims to the resources of one's mother's and mother's mother's patri-group countries, although in theory people required permission from 'country-holders' for access. A person had access to their spouse's country (often the husband's mother's country). Links between patri-groups based on the journey of a major *wangarr* (ancestor) with whom *rangga* (sacred objects) were associated provided weaker grounds for claiming use rights. In practice, residence reflected a wider range of connections (see Chapter 10).[45]

Control of access

How were these rather formal connections manifested in residence and the control of country and resources? The people with the greatest control over the day-to-day use of a country and its resources were the senior residents of a camp, rather than members of a patri-group as such. They often included senior members of the owning patri-group, as we have seen, and/or people living on their mother's and mother's mother's patri-group country. But control was as much a matter of politics as of rights; the dominant man of one outstation in the mid-to-late 1970s lived on the country of one of his many wives, a country that was not his mother's country. He justified his presence by saying that the river connected the country to his mother's country.[46]

Patri-group members enjoyed at least the notional right to deny access to people of other patri-groups (other than co-residents), and in theory people were supposed to gain permission even to use their mother's country and its resources. Nancy Williams describes the gaining of permission by close relatives as informal and often *post hoc*. It was more a matter of letting the *wa:nga-watangu* know that one intended to visit their country and take resources. Close relatives had, as it were, 'standing' permission to enter a patri-group's country (including seas), and knew enough about the country to avoid the dangerous places. (The danger came from *wangarr* and other spirit beings.) Moreover, the possession of an enclave within another group's country gave members of a group and their close kin access to the surrounding area (apart from restricted ancestral sites). Since residence groups included people of several groups, whose countries were often contiguous, permission to use each other's country was presumably tacit. Less closely related people who lived further away would, it seems, ask for permission to exploit particular resources by sending an emissary with a carved message stick. Those using another group's country were expected to make a gift of part of the yield.

Where a small residence group was focused on a particular country it could monitor the country's use by others, for example by seeing smoke from fires and from burning off. In the formalised rites of entry, the visiting person or group stopped at the periphery of the residence group's camps and waited to be approached; the group's children usually approached first and then conveyed the visitors' intentions to the older people, who would eventually approach the visitors or beckon them.[47]

As in other regions, a person visiting an area for the first time was supposed to be reserved and cautious, because he or she was not recognised by the land, and the spirits could be hostile. Such a person had to be introduced to the country by an owner, who would anoint them with underarm sweat so that the country and the ancestors would recognise their scent; otherwise there was danger for both owner and visitor from the ancestors.[48]

As among Ngarinyin people and their neighbours, certain scarce resources were subject to very specific controls. These resources included raw materials such as softwoods suitable for the manufacture of dugout canoes, and stone for spearheads, interpreted as ancestral substance.[49] The gathering or hunting of foods was forbidden at or near certain ancestral places, such as the standing stones at Baringura on the Woolen River. Senior men of each group reserved certain wells and springs for their own use, forbidding women, children, and younger men to use them. Altman records restrictions that were placed on the hunting of certain reptiles and large fish at certain times of year in order to allow them to breed and fatten (this was among eastern Kunwinjku people). A more temporary restriction applied to access to the land surrounding a camp for a period after a person's death at that camp.

Comparisons and conclusions

The case studies have sampled a wide variety of relations to country, but some similarities have emerged (see Table 9.1).

Table 9.1 Modes of connection to country in the seven regions

People	Identity of countries	Totemic connections between countries	Country-groups	Use rights	Succession
Kŭnai	Focal place, topography, leader's name, group's name	Some recorded, but few links to patrifilial guardian totems	Identified by proper name, country, leader's name	Patrifiliation, birth, spouse's country	Not recorded
Pitjantjatjara and their neighbours	Ancestral sites and site clusters	Multiple and extensive between clusters of related totemic associations	Identified by site name	Birth and a variety of other bases	Not recorded
Yuwaaliyaay and their neighbours	Plant species	Common connections to Byamee, with local totemic associations	Identified by eponymous plant species, single country	Birth and other bases, perhaps matri-group and section	Not recorded
Wiil and Minong	Focal place, ?semi-moiety	Some short ancestral journeys recorded	Identified by country, ?semi-moiety	Patrifiliation, birth, mother's brother's country, spouse's country	Neighbouring country
Sandbeach	Ancestral name, deceased person, topography	Few—connected to male initiation	Single country, identified by name of country	Patrifiliation, mother's country, spouse's country	Mother's country
Ngarinyin and their neighbours	Principal totem	Multiple links through totemic connections, ancestral journeys	Some top and bottom groups of same identity	Patrifiliation, mother's country, father's mother's country	Namesake, adoption
Yolngu	Focal place	Multiple, cross-cutting links between clusters of totems	Complex patri-groups, each with several non-contiguous countries.	Patrifiliation, mother's country, mother's mother's country, conception country	Mother's mother's country, conception country

Countries

In all regions, people named places and grouped them into broader, named countries, often identified by a focal place (usually a source of water). All seven regions had some sort of country-group, although their structure varied, as did other identities associated with country. In all seven case studies a 'totemic geography' linked places to groups and individuals, although the proportion of places interpreted as ancestral traces probably varied—they seem to have been most prolific in the Western Desert.

The countries varied from fairly well-defined strips extending from hills out to the reefs (Sandbeach people) to clusters of sites and overlapping areas identified in a variety of ways by different individuals (Pitjantjatjara people and their neighbours). People identified countries in a variety of ways—for example, by the names of plants, topographical features, principal totems, and complex proper names. The sizes of countries varied with population density, as might be expected, from about 40 square kilometres (Yolngu coast) to about 2000 square kilometres (Yuwaaliyaay) and some 2500–3000 square kilometres in the case of the more dense site-clusters of the Pitjantjatjara people and their neighbours.

The totemic character of countries varied, as we saw in Chapters 5 and 7; those chapters described variation in the degree of differentiation among groups, the kind and number of links between them, and the scope of links such as ancestral journeys. One way in which totemic associations differentiated countries and groups was through the non-duplication of totemic identities. The most highly differentiated groups in terms of totemic identity appear to have been the Sandbeach ones, only some of which were connected by ancestral journeys associated with male initiation. The exclusive use of increase sites and their aggressive powers among Sandbeach people, by contrast with their cooperative use by Pitjantjatjara and Ngarinyin people, underscores the high differentiation of the former in a resource-rich environment with a marine orientation. As Athol Chase has remarked, it reflects the relative self-sufficiency of the residents of each cluster of patri-group countries sharing a main camp.

In the case of Pitjantjatjara and Yolngu countries, clusters of sites with multiple totemic identities connected with other places in a web of cross-cutting links, or what have been called 'songlines', so that places were at once differentiated and connected. But the ubiquitous snakes and pythons associated with rain and lightning connected places in a more diffuse way (moiety-specific among Yolngu people). Regional ceremonies celebrated these ancestors and these connections. Relations among the patri-groups of Ngarinyin people and their neighbours appear to have been similar to the Yolngu pattern, except that principal *wanjina* totems differentiated countries and groups to a greater extent than with Yolngu groups.

Diffuse links characterised relations between places among Yuwaaliyaay people and their neighbours, for, as well as some local totemic associations, all countries appear to have had sites belonging to Byamee and his family. These sites were connected with the regional Bora ceremony and related ceremonies.

Do the long ancestral journeys of the totemic ancestors of Pitjantjatjara people and their neighbours have an ecological explanation? They linked people in a desert-wide web that made a lot of sense in terms of access to resources in the uncertain environment of the arid zone. The extended ancestral journeys and other cross-cutting totemic affiliations of Ngarinyin and Yolngu patri-groups seem to have had less to do with ecological necessity than with exchange, cooperation in ceremonies, and processes of succession. Nevertheless, people may have valued such links because they allowed them to exploit a variety of resources in these ecologically heterogeneous regions.

Country-groups

Although detail is lacking in two of the case studies, the structure of country-groups evidently varied. In the Western Desert, individuals differed in how they identified their relations to country—whether to a single site or a site-cluster—and the multiple bases of claims gave groups an open and contested character. While Yuwaaliyaay people and their neighbours appear to have shared some of the Western Desert connections to country, with birth the dominant mode, they seem to have identified countries quite unambiguously, which is not to say that they drew clear boundaries. Wiil and Minong people named countries after a focal place, and may have identified them in terms of patrifilial semi-moieties—if so, each country would have been connected to others of the same semi-moiety.

Sandbeach patri-groups appear to have been relatively simple in form, with each named group holding a single named country, although Chase reports some arguments over succession and boundaries. Patri-groups among Ngarinyin people and their neighbours had quite a complex structure; some were divided into a 'top' and 'bottom' group, comprised more than one lineage, or included migrating groups originally of a different language. Patri-group countries of the same patri-moiety joined to form long swathes across the region. Yolngu patri-groups had even more complex and varied structures. Named patri-groups held a number of, often non-contiguous, countries, sometimes distributed between lineages, as well as enclaves within other groups' countries. Some comprised autonomous top and bottom groups, or took the identity of a cluster or extended string of groups with the same proper name and some shared ancestral connections. The complexity of patri-groups in these societies may have arisen in part from their high levels of polygyny and their processes of succession, as well as the exchange of ceremonies and names.

Use rights

People everywhere enjoyed a mix of rights in a number of countries, and less formal access to others through intermediaries. The Western Desert exhibited the most diverse range of grounds for use rights, including place of birth, long association, depth of knowledge, links to a parent's country, and so on. Regions with patri-groups combined these identities with complementary filiation—rights and connections to one's mother's country—as well as access rights on other grounds, such as rights to one's spouse's country. Ngarinyin people linked the latter to rights in the father's mother's country (that of a man's potential spouse), and Yolngu added strong connections to the mother's mother's country (and its sacra)—the country of a man's potential wives' mothers and country to which a person succeeded in the event of the group's demise. The structure of Kŭnai land-holding remains unclear, although people evidently enjoyed access on the grounds of patrifiliation and birth, as well as access to a spouse's country.

Concepts of permission ('the right to be asked') were probably universal. But, regardless of formal rights, who in practice had the ability to monitor and control access? I think the senior 'core' residents, who had the closest connection to the country, usually exercised control of access to the country. The ability to control access did not follow automatically from formal kin relations to country, however; it was subject to political processes in which a person with a more distant connection might gain control from a person who was more closely related.

Modes of land-holding overlapped a range of other identities (see Table 9.2). The strongest association is between patri-groups and patri-moieties (Sandbeach, Ngarinyin, Yolngu) or patrifilial semi-moieties (Minong). Those with weaker patrifilial connections (Kŭnai), or other bases of connection (Pitjantjatjara, Yuwaaliyaay), had other kinds of totemic identity, such as gender totemism, generation moieties, matri-groups, and matri-moieties.

Processes of succession had particular relevance for patri-groups, because the single dominant mode of inheritance could readily be interrupted. The records show that people had claims to succeed to country in the following ways in four of the regions:

- Wiil and Minong people—a country contiguous to their own
- Sandbeach people—their mother's country (or a patri-group member's mother's country), reflecting the strong spiritual link of the *nguunthal* spirit
- Ngarinyin people—a namesake's or adoptive father's country of same moiety, and their country of conception
- Yolngu people—their mother's mother's country, 'mother's mother's' country, or country of conception (same moiety).

Table 9.2 Association of the bases of land-holding with various identities

People	Bases of land-holding	Regional or language identities	Other patrifilial and matrifilial identities	Moieties and gender totems	Sections and subsections
Kŭnai	Patrifilation, birth	Regional identities	Patrifilial guardian totems	Gender totems	
Pitjantjatjara	Birth, other bases	Language identities		Generation moieties	Incoming sections
Yuwaaliyaay	Birth, other bases	Language identities	Matri-groups	Matri-moieties	Sections
Wiil and Minong	Patrifiliation, semi-moieties	Regional identities		Matri-moieties	
Sandbeach	Patrifiliation	Language identities		Patri-moieties	
Ngarinyin	Complex patri-groups	Language identities		Patri-moieties	
Yolngu	Complex patri-groups	Patri-group languages, dialect groups	Patri-moieties	Subsections	

The multiple connections to country among Pitjantjatjara people and Yuwaaliyaay people and their neighbours may have made formal processes of 'succession' unnecessary.

Patterns of rights and connections varied with gross differences in ecology. People had multiple and flexible connections to place in the Western Desert by virtue of the long ancestral tracks, and perhaps through matri-group identity in the uncertain environment of the Darling/Barwon River. Sandbeach people, in their rich coastal environment, had the most restricted connections, derived from patri-group identity and kin links—especially (but not only) to the mother's country and group. However, it may be that the shallow coastal waters constituted something of a commons when a group was chasing turtle or dugong.

Control of access to land, waters, and resources

It is evident that ancestral significance, as outlined in Chapter 7, grounded the control of access to countries and resources in ancestral law. People were able to exploit the resources of many countries, and ancestral connections as well as kin relations to ancestors and groups provided the structure that underpinned and ordered access and control. We might regard this simply as an extension of ancestral law into this domain, bringing country under a common order with other institutions and practices.

The ancestral significance of country was not simply a means of controlling access to food resources, however. Moreover, people asserted different degrees of exclusive rights in different resources. The most exclusive were ancestral sites (especially those to do with secret rituals), which were believed to be redolent with ancestral power. I suggest that the totemic/ancestral significance of country had much to do with ancestral powers as a resource, which people believed that they could tap for economic, aggressive, and erotic purposes. People did not benefit from mutual access to these resources, except in so far as they performed increase rites for the benefit of others as well as themselves. People did benefit from varying degrees of mutual access to food resources. But even here we have seen that individuals tried to assert exclusive claims over particular plants, although with no great success, and that groups tried to control access by others to their most valued foods (such as swan eggs in Gippsland), as well as the right to control burning off, which might yield a significant harvest.

As with land and waters and their resources, people used ancestral significance to structure control of access to technology.

Control of access to technology

Writers on hunting-and-gathering societies have treated items of equipment as personal property. 'In hunter–gatherer societies', Alan Barnard and James Woodburn write, 'simple movable property—weapons, tools, clothing, and so on—seems invariably to be personally owned, but in ways that are strongly constrained by custom'. People make their own tools and weapons, Barnard and Woodburn say, and are entitled to the yield from their own labour, unless this entitlement is overridden by some other principle, such as the obligation to share an item when it was not needed for immediate use. Elsewhere, James Woodburn distinguishes the property rights of hunters and gatherers with 'immediate return' economies from those with 'delayed return' systems. The former have little in the way of property, whereas the latter hold rights over valued assets that represent a return for labour applied over time, as well as other kinds of assets. The valued assets include technical facilities used in production, processed and stored foods and materials, and wild products that have been improved or increased by human labour. Aboriginal economies fit Woodburn's category of delayed return systems.

We shall see that people did not just control access to technical facilities but to smaller items of equipment as well. In the seven regions, restrictions on access to equipment had to do primarily with age, gender, and kin relations. Control of technology also had links with the possession of land and waters, for people of some regions gave ancestral significance to larger items of equipment, turning them into inalienable possessions like land, waters, and sacra.[50]

Annette Hamilton is one of the few anthropologists to have examined the social aspects of Aboriginal technologies. She argues that the system of inheritance and use of the heavy, rather immovable grindstones of the Western Desert inhibited the formation of patrifilial groups. Women cooperated in the production and processing of seed, and daughters inherited the grindstones from their mothers or other uterine relatives. As men relied on women's production in order to engage in ceremonies, they had to live at the location of productive forces owned by their wives, and groups of sisters often lived together with their parents and their husbands. The result was that brothers, fathers, and sons tended to be dispersed by comparison with sisters, mothers, and daughters, inhibiting the formation of 'local corporations of men'. However, small matrilineages are not obvious in Long's many censuses of Western Desert communities. Furthermore, in northeast Arnhem Land a man's residence at his wife's country, mother's country, or his mother's mother's country was perfectly compatible with the patrifilial inheritance of country and sacra. Nevertheless, the need to keep women together as a labour force does seem to have inhibited the level of polygyny in the Western Desert. Moreover, grindstones do not seem to have been as immovable as Hamilton suggests, for the transporting of heavy grindstones is reported for other areas.[51]

Information on the control of access to technology in each region is insufficient to do a meaningful comparison; I shall discuss some aspects of this control, giving examples from the case studies.

Restrictions based on gender and age

The case studies show that certain categories of people were allowed to use items of equipment forbidden to others. The granting of permission on the basis of gender, age, or ritual status sometimes involved formal procedures. In all regions, the genders had their appropriate items of equipment: Pintubi people referred to men as 'those with spear-throwers' (*lankurrutjarra*) and women as 'those with digging sticks' (*wanatjarra*). In at least some regions, social rules and sanctions applied—for example, among Pitjantjatjara people no female over the age of about two was permitted to touch a spear or even pretend to throw one.[52] The vines used for men's spears at Mimili were prohibited to women for religious reasons. Men and women tended to make their own implements, but women shared the use of some tools and techniques with men (unretouched stone tools, fire, grinding techniques). Among Sandbeach people, Chase reports, women were prohibited from touching men's spears and spearthrowers and from approaching the canoes, ropes, harpoons, and other equipment used for dugong hunting. Women used a small unbarbed spear for catching crabs and other small marine animals, but were forbidden from using a spearthrower.[53]

Age restrictions also applied. For example, a Yuwaaliyaay boy could not make fire with fire-sticks until he had attended his first Bora initiation, and a young man could only have 'war weapons' and become a 'warrior' and hunter after his first Bora.[54]

Borrowing

Although ancestral means were available to inhibit others from using one's own items, notably vesting an item with ancestral significance, individuals had the freedom to use certain items of relatives' equipment, such as spears. Older brothers among Minong people appear to have had the right to take a younger brother's weapons. Young Sandbeach men had the right to borrow spears and other items from their father's fathers, mother's fathers and mother's brothers without asking.[55]

Inheritance

Individuals and families owned key items, notably grindstones and perhaps nets. People applied sanctions against those who violated their rights. As in the case of land, waters, and sacra, some implements were passed down from generation to generation.[56] At a person's death, Kǔnai people usually rolled up weapons, implements, and garments with the deceased, although men told Howitt that a valuable axe would be inherited by a man's father, elder or younger brother, or father's father (in that order). After a Minong man's death, relatives broke his spears so that on awakening and finding them broken he would undertake the journey to the land of the dead and not haunt the camp. Others things were left nearby for the person to take with him.

Relatives in the female line inherited seed grindstones among Pitjantjatjara and perhaps Yuwaaliyaay people. Parker writes that if a member of any other family used a grindstone without permission a fight would ensue. Grindstones were also owned by and inherited within a group among Sandbeach people, as canoes may have been; grindstones remained on a group's country and were not moved. Thomson records what may have been the inheritance of a man's grindstone by a sister's son. The amount of labour invested in large nets makes it likely that they too were owned and inherited.

Ancestral and magical significance

One way of controlling the use of an item of equipment was to give it ancestral significance, permanently or temporarily. People did this by proclaiming ancestral names over the object or painting it with an ancestral design. As Bill Gammage points out, fire, a major technological instrument, had totemic significance in many regions, celebrated in songs, dances, designs, and sacred objects. The Arnhem Land literature is rich with other examples. *Ad hoc* prohibitions restricted consumption by investing equipment or country with temporary ancestral significance. Items of equipment classified as sacred objects both belonged to particular patri-groups as 'inalienable possessions' (see Chapter 12) and were governed by age- and gender-related authority. Large immobile facilities in particular had that kind of significance, and people conceived of some raw materials, especially ochres and rock, as ancestral substance or living beings.[57]

Some Kŭnai items of technology acquired power from the domain of rituals and ancestors, notably certain kinds of spear-thrower that were credited with magical properties. Women's yam sticks were important among the paraphernalia used in Jerra-eil initiation ceremonies.

According to the doctrines of Yuwaaliyaay people and their neighbours, Byamee and his sons made the stone fish-traps in the Darling/Barwon River. They seem to have been divided between groups with a common language, or perhaps between country-groups. Yuwaaliyaay people also believed that some stones were capable of speaking and moving, because of the presence of a spirit.

Sandbeach hunters abstained from sex for several days before using their dugong-hunting equipment, for fear that they would injure themselves while hunting or that the dugong would disappear.

Many items of technology among Ngarinyin people and their neighbours had ancestral significance, not only for having been created by specific ancestors but for being ancestral transformations (for example, the coolamon, discussed in Chapter 7).

Among the *ad hoc* restrictions applied by Yolngu people were those applied to foods killed with equipment sacralised through the calling of ancestral names. According to Thomson, no women were allowed to use a 'name-bearing' object, although a rite making the object *wakinngu* (wild, not sacred) enabled women to eat food it was used to obtain.

Certain Yolngu patri-groups and their close kin claimed exclusive rights to use certain sacralised items of productive technology. Ancestral significance restricted control of the particular item to those with authority over the groups' sacra, mainly older men of the group and their sisters' sons (*waku*). Thus, Yolngu patri-groups with the Shark (Bul'manydji) as ancestor claimed sole rights to the use of shark spines for fish-spears. Liyagalawumirr and related patri-groups owned the *gurrka gol* fish-trap; certain sacred objects represented components of the fish-trap. Ritual observances surrounded the use of this fish-trap (Plate 3.8): menstruating women were forbidden to eat fish from the trap, and men using the trap had to refrain from eating the major snakes and pythons related to the Gunapipi ceremony and other ceremonies owned by these groups, and also from eating bandicoot. Breaking these prohibitions would stop the fish from coming. Forked uprights and cross-pieces, and other components of stringybark houses and of fish-traps, featured as sacred objects and in the ancestral designs of these groups, and in the Wagilak myths of these groups (in which a giant python swallows the Wagilak sisters). By the same token, the decorated dilly-bags that feature in the Djang'kawu mythology were also sacred objects.[58]

Certain raw materials also had ancestral significance. People regarded ochres as the transformed bodily substance of ancestors, especially their blood or fat. People regarded the stone from the quarry at Ngilipidji, a powerful ancestral site associated with the Wagilak sisters in the country of the Wagilak patri-group, as living, powerful 'fat' (Plate 12.1). Immature stone that yielded small flakes would, if left in the ground, mature like a plant. Men traded stone spear-points manufactured at this site to other regions.

To sum up, ancestral cosmologies played a significant part in the conceptualisation and control of access to land and waters and their resources, and to technologies. The literature on other hunters and gatherers shows that people could use quite different means to achieve similar ends. However, ancestral significance integrated country, resources, and technologies into the all-encompassing framework of ancestral law, not only as a mode of control but as ways of being.

Further reading

In his introduction to *Aboriginal Landowners* (1984), L. R. Hiatt reviews the literature (up to the early 1980s) on 'local organisation'. For an approach to relations to country using a legal concept of 'rights', see Nancy Williams's *The Yolngu and their Land* (1986). Harold Scheffler discusses the applicability of the term 'descent' in Australia in his *Australian Kin Classification* (1978). Fred Myers's *Pintupi Country, Pintupi Self* (1986) constitutes a watershed in his rejection of the clan/band model for the Western Desert, and I criticised the 'clan' concept as applied to northeast Arnhem Land in my article 'Metaphor and the Metalanguage' (1995). For a recent approach, see Deborah Bird Rose's *Country of the Heart: An Indigenous Australian Homeland* (2002).

The debate over relations to country took on a new significance in relation to the *Aboriginal Land Rights (Northern Territory) Act* of 1976. *Aborigines, Land and Land Rights*, edited by Nicolas Peterson and Marcia Langton (1983), reviews the state of anthropological research and litigation at that time. More recently, the *Native Title Act*, following the High Court's findings in the Mabo and Wik cases, has provided a new context for anthropological understandings of Aboriginal relations to country; see *Anthropology in the Native Ttitle Era* (1995), edited by Jim Fingleton and Julie Finlayson, and *Connections in Native Title* (1999), edited by Finlayson, Rigsby, and Bek.

Descriptions and analyses of the control of items of equipment are for the most part embedded in more general ethnographic studies. This chapter mentions two of the exceptions: Donald Thomson's 'A new type of fish trap' (1938) and Annette Hamilton's 'Dual social systems' (1980).

Notes

1   On the patrilocal 'horde' see Elkin (1938: 40), Howitt (1880; 1904), Radcliffe-Brown (1913; 1918; 1931), and Stanner (1965a).

2   For critiques of the patrilocal band or horde model see Hiatt (1962). For challenges and revisions to the patrilocal horde model see Elkin (1950: 17–18), Hiatt (1962; 1984), and Stanner (1965a); for overviews see Hiatt (1984) and Peterson and Long (1986: 13–25). See Birdsell (1970) for his refutation of the community model.

3　On Western Desert relations to country see Hamilton (1982), Tonkinson (1991), and Myers (1986). For a comparison with Warlpiri and Warumungu land tenure see Keen (1997). On the switch in anthropological views more generally see Bird-David (1991: 19).

4　See Williams (1986) and Sutton (1996) for approaches based on 'rights' and see Munn (1970) on consubstantial links. See Pannell and Vachon (2001) for a critique of the 'rights' approach.

5　On the expression 'country group' see Sutton (1999). On the appropriateness of 'descent' see Scheffler (1978: 518–22) and on 'local descent group' see R. M. and C. H. Berndt (1981).

6　See Fortes (1953), Keesing (1975), and Sutton (1998) on 'complementary filiation'.

7　See Peterson et al. (1977) on succession in relation to land.

8　On the naming of Kŭnai countries see Dow (n.d.) and Howitt (in Fison and Howitt 1880: 225, 228–9; 1904: 73, 76–7).

9　See Howitt (in Fison and Howitt 1880: 215–16, 224–5, 232; 1904: 73, 270) on 'clans' (regional identities). On the concept of 'owner' and the activities of owners see Bulmer (in Smyth 1878: 143n; Papers, letter to Howitt MV B1 F4 xm82 20 April 1884). On the names of country-groups see Howitt (in Fison and Howitt 1880: 227–9). On the concept of 'divisions' (country-groups) see Howitt (in Fison and Howitt 1880: 215–16, 224–5; 1904: 73, 270), and on alternative place names for groups see Howitt (in Fison and Howitt 1880: 231). See Howitt (1904; Papers, SLV Box 8 ms 1053/4(a): 65) on fraternal and patrifilial succession to country, and see Howitt (in Fison and Howitt 1880: 203–4) on affiliation to one's country of birth.

10　See Helms (1896: 398) on the significance at Omeo of place of birth.

11　Howitt (Papers, MV B10 F5 xm923: 56) describes an old man's rights to a waterhole. On Bunjil-baul see Howitt (1904: 73–5), and on introducing a stranger to one's country see Howitt (Papers, MV B4 F7 xm527, 1904: 73–5).

12　On the concept of country in the Western Desert see Munn (1973: 146) and Myers (1982;1986: 54–7).

13　On 'estates' in the Western Desert see Layton (1986: 184–93), Munn (1973: 147, 150), Myers (1982; 1986), and Tonkinson (1991: 68–71).

14　See Berndt (1959: 97–8), Myers (1982), Munn (1973: 147, 150), and Tonkinson (1978: 51–3) on Western Desert affiliations to country.

15　On genealogical depth in the Western Desert see Tonkinson (1991: 69).

16　On the flexibility of Western Desert land tenure see, for example, Hamilton (1980), Myers (1986: 294–6), and Tonkinson (1986).

17　See Myers (1982) on concepts of permission in the Western Desert; see also Tindale (1974: 18). And see Tonkinson (1991: 96–7) on conventions regarding access to country.

18　References on Yuwaaliyaay countries include Parker (1905: 12, 46, 146). On the names of Gamilaraay groups see Greenway (1878: 238–9). I am inferring the number of Yuwaaliyaay countries from Gamilaraay countries as reported by Donaldson (1980: 1), and from Jimmy Barker's account of Murruwarri countries (1977). On boundaries see Cameron (1899, cited in Becket et al. 2002).

19　See Parker (1905: 12, 46, 146) on affiliation to country. On rights to country on the basis of birth elsewhere in the region see Mathews (1906: 153–5), Allen (1972: 105), and Beckett (1967: 457). Elkin (1953: 418) contended that there was no bias towards patrilineal groups in the southeast; for a contrary view see Radcliffe-Brown (1954: 106). See Ridley (1875: 26–30) and Howitt (1904: 57) on Gamilaraay country-groups; Donaldson (1980: 1) on Wangaaybuwan groups, and Teulon (in Curr 1886, vol. 2: 205) on Pakaantji groups.

20　On use rights see Allen (1972: 105) and Beckett (1959: 206). The quotation is from Parker (1905: 8).

21　See Parker (1905: 101) on individual rights in trees.

22　On Wiil and Minong countries see Ferguson (1987: 130), who draws on Collie's description (1979 [1834]) of Mokaré's 'natal ground', Nind (1831: 44), and Barker (1992: 1 December 1830, cited in Green 1989: 15).

23　On Wiil and Minong country-groups see Bates (1985: 48) and Browne (1856, cited in Le Souëf 1993: 39). On patrifilial succession see Barker (1992: 12 December 1830, cited in Green 1989: 8). On succession by a neighbouring group see Barker (1992: 12 January 1830) and Collie (1979 [1834]), both cited in Le Souëf (1993: 36). The quotation is from Hassell (1936: 682).

24　See Nind (1831: 42).

25　See (Nind 1831: 44) on conferred totems and use rights.

26　The quotation is from Nind (1831: 28).

27　On rights to control burning of country see Barker (1992: 13 January 1830, cited in Green 1989: 35), Collie (1979 [1834], cited in Le Souëf 1993: 36). On the closure of country after the death of Uredale, see Barker (1992: 13 January 1831, cited in Green 1989: 8).

28　See Le Souëf (1993: 37) on the assertion of individual property rights. The quotation is from Nind (1831: 34).

29　On Sandbeach countries and sites see Chase (1980b: 132, 135, 138); on moiety affiliation see Chase (1980b: 140–1); on names of countries and groups see Chase (1980: 135); on descent see Chase (1980b: 136) and Rigsby and Chase (1998: 196); and on the relation of patri-group countries to dialects see Chase (1980b) and Rigsby (1992: 358).

30　On succession among Sandbeach people see Rigsby (1980: 93) and Rigsby and Chase (1998).

31　See Rigsby and Chase (1998: 197, 205) on use rights. On rights to one's mother's mother's country among southern Sandbeach people see Rigsby (1980: 92), and on country as family see Rigsby (1998: 33).

32　The quotation is from Rigsby and Chase (1998: 205).

33　On countries and country-groups among Ngarinyin people and their neighbours see Blundell (1975 vol. 1: 87–8, 92, 99, 107, 109, 162) and Redmond (2001a: 139–47).

34　On shared child-spirit centres see Lommel (1997: 37–8).

35　See Redmond (2001a: 143) on the emotional tone of country.

36　See Blundell (1975 vol. 1: 92) on succession.

37 See Blundell (1975 vol. 1: 122, 161), Lommel (1997: 3–8), and Redmond (2001: 297) on use rights.

38 On the control of access to country see (Blundell 1975 vol. 1: 145); on visitors to *wanjina* sites see Crawford (1968: 32).

39 On inheritance of responsibility for *wanjina* sites see Blundell (1975 vol. 1: 141).

40 See Williams (1986) on the Yolngu concept of *wa:nga* (country); Keen (1977: 167) on connections between countries; and Keen (1978: 49) on the size of countries. On the relation of names, designs, and sacra to countries see Morphy (1991).

41 On the identity of coastal waters see Bagshaw (1998).

42 On Yolngu countries and country-groups see Berndt (1965), Keen (1995), Morphy (1997), Peterson (1972), Shapiro (1981), Warner (1937: 39–51), and Williams (1986). See Toner (2001) for an example of 'top' and 'bottom' groups sharing a focal ancestral site. The information on language and waters is from Sophie Creighton (pers. com.).

43 For examples of genealogies see Keen (1994: 69).

44 See Keen (1994: 126) and Williams (1986: 53–4) on succession. See Peterson (1983), Morphy (1997), and Keen (2000) on patri-group dynamics.

45 On Yolngu use rights see Williams (1986: 75–86).

46 On permission and the control of access see Peterson (1971) and Williams (1986: 84–6).

47 See Peterson and Long (1986: 24, 27–9) on rites of entry.

48 See Thomson (1938: 198) and Williams (1986: 85) on introducing visitors to land and ancestors; see also Tamisari (1998: 256) on smell. On dangerous places see Biernoff (1978) and McKenzie (1983).

49 On the control of specific resources see Altman (1982: 315–16), Thomson (1949), and Dunlop (1981). On waterholes reserved for older men see Keen (1994: 114). On hunting restrictions see Altman (1982: 315).

50 On property among hunters and gatherers see Barnard and Woodburn (1988: 16), quoted in the previous paragraph, and Woodburn (1988: 32).

51 See Hamilton (1980: 9–10) on technological constraints on male corporations. On the portability of grindstones between the Lachlan and Darling Rivers see Bennett (1887: 3, cited in Allen 1972: 79). On Kŭnai inheritance see Howitt (1880: 245).

52 On gendered ownership of implements in the Western Desert see Hamilton (1980: 5–7), Love (1942: 216), Myers (1986: 74), and Tindale (1972: 245). These reports are rather contradictory.

53 See Chase (1980b: 195) on restrictions relating to gender.

54 See Parker (1905: 61) on Yuwaaliyaay age restrictions on the use of fire-sticks.

55 On rights to borrow a relative's equipment see Barker (1992: 19 July 1830, cited in Green 1989: 33) and Thomson (1972: 11).

56 On the ownership and inheritance of grindstones see Parker (1905: 117) (Yuwaaliyaay), and Thomson (1933: 469; Papers, MV File 190 October 1932) (Sandbeach). The information about grindstones remaining on a group's country is from Bruce Rigsby (pers. com.).

57 On the sacralisation of equipment see Howitt (1880: 195n, 245; 1904: 620) (Kŭnai), Parker (1905: 109–10) (Yuwaaliyaay fish-traps), and Thomson (1938: 195–7; 1949: 57, 62) (Yolngu fish-traps and spears). See Keen (1978: 269) on the sacralisation of fire. On *ad hoc* restrictions see Thomson (1939; 1949: 47–8). On the ancestral significance of fish-trap and house components see Reser (1977: 211–12). On ochres see Morphy (1991: 148). On Ngilipidji see Jones and White (1988). See Gammage (2002: 2) on fire as a totem.

58 See Hamby (2001) on the ancestral significance of Yolngu dilly-bags.

10

The Organisation of Production

> The women of the Worora are pre-eminently the food providers, and the firewood providers.
>
> The men's share of food providing is to spear fish, turtle and dugong or other sea animals, and to hunt big game on land; but it falls to the women to provide the staple foods; roots, fruits, small game and wild honey.
>
> Soon after sunrise each morning the women will leave the camp, in groups of half a dozen or so, and scatter in different directions for the day, not usually returning till the evening sun is low in the sky. They are accompanied by their dogs, most of which are owned by the women, and most of the women owning three or four each. Each woman carries a large bark dish or trough, the *anggam*, which is made from an oblong sheet of the bark of the box gum tree, with the ends pinched up and bound with string holding about three gallons ... Inside the *anggam*, as she sets out on the day's hunt, are the yam stick, or *wondoon*, the two sticks for making fire—the *liruku*, and the stone tomahawk—*lembalja*, now fast being replace by the white man's steel tomahawk—called *ngadjura*.
>
> J. R. B. Love, *Stone Age Bushmen of Today*, p. 67

Introduction

The previous chapter looked at the control of the productive means; but how did people organise their productive activities? This chapter is concerned with such matters as the division of labour by age and gender, the size and constitution of work teams, the social relations involved, and the structure of residence groups. Ideally, it would cover all activities devoted to the production of the material means of life, including the preparation of raw materials, the manufacture of implements used in production (including tool-making tools), the collection of fuel and water, and the acquisition and processing of subsistence products. We should probably also include time spent discussing and planning a day's activities, as well as the preparation of magic and enactment of ceremonies that people regarded as essential for the reproduction of species or that were used to enhance productive success. And people put time and effort into managing land and resources—burning off the understorey, cleaning up wells and waterholes, and so forth. Also, since exchange involved the transmission of religious knowledge, ideally we should include religious production as well. Estimates of the proportion of time spent on such activities are few, so I have not included them in the discussion of work time.

Gender and the division of labour

Textbooks generalise about the division of labour by gender: men hunted large animals and fished, while women gathered plant foods. The outcome of men's hunting was more uncertain than that of women's food-collecting, so that women contributed the greater part, overall, to the food supply. Moreover, women worked more regularly than the men. The Berndts qualify these generalisations by saying that the division of labour was not fixed: a woman would catch a kangaroo with her dog if the opportunity arose, and women hunted small game; men would sometimes dig for yams or collect fruits when hungry or if the occasion arose. Even when foraging in a group, women collected food on an individual basis for husbands, children, and other close relatives. In his hunting, a man had wider responsibilities—he had to divide up the game he killed, which included large animals, among a larger number of people. The case studies bear out this general picture.[1]

The concept of 'band'

Most of the ethnographies report that a number of distinct family households or hearth groups, in addition to a bachelors' camp, made up the larger residence groups. But some studies show that the 'household' or its equivalent was not the main unit of cooperation in production, which often cut across such groups. We need to know more, therefore, about the structure of residence groups, whose members cooperated in productive work.

Residence groups among hunters and gatherers have often been described as 'bands' (or 'hordes' in the ealier terminology). This term, which owes much to Julian Steward's analyses, denotes a group of women, men, and children who live together and exploit a common area, the band's 'range'. A band comprises a number of family groups who cooperate in economic, social, and reproductive activities. It may split up in a certain season and then come together again later, and although the core of residents remains fairly stable, individuals may move between bands.[2]

Nicolas Peterson argues that people's aggregation into bands (as against being scattered in small family groups) was a result of the principle of optimum numbers. For people to monitor the relation of population to resources and to maintain the optimum population density, they had to cooperate in the food quest and share food. There also needed to be a degree of group closure, achieved by having rites of entry for outsiders, as well as links between residence and the ownership of land on the part of 'clans'. Peterson develops a processual model of clan and band demography to account for the maintenance of relations among bands, clans, and clan lands ('estates').[3]

But the concept of 'band' is problematic, at least when applied to some regions. It implies that relatively enduring groups of people lived together—so that a band had a fairly stable membership—or that people entertained notions of such enduring entities, or both. In many parts of Australia, residence groups split up at certain times of the year into smaller residence groups, then people again came together into larger residence groups in the next season. It is open to question whether the newly formed groups were the same 'bands' as the previous year's groups.

It may be that in some regions people did think of residence groups as having an enduring identity, related to particular places. Camping places or influential members provided metonyms for the group's identity. I think this was true of north-east Arnhem Land. However, in the Western Desert, where groups were much more fluid and movement more wide-ranging, there do not seem to have been any such enduring residence groups. Extended families tended to live together but individuals were very mobile, while families and aggregations of family groups had a transient existence. It is for these kinds of reasons that Fred Myers found the concept less than useful in writing about stories told by older Pintupi people about their early lives in the Western Desert.[4]

Rather than write in terms of 'bands', I will simply look at the evidence regarding the dynamics of residence groups (short-term and long-term, large and small) and regarding movement, aggregation, and dispersal.

Camps and residence groups

Most of the ethnographers of this study tell us that a 'household' or 'family' of some kind formed the basic unit of a residence group. A 'household' consisted of a monogamous or polygynous family, or a single men's camp. But applying the concept of 'household' or 'hearth group' to Aboriginal residence is tricky; camps had a more complex and fluid structure than these terms suggest. I shall refer to a group of people who resided together, forming a relatively discrete cluster in space, as a 'residence group', and the more or less discrete elements of which it was composed as 'camps'. A 'camp', often named after a senior or dominant resident, consisted of one or more shelters (if only wind-breaks) and one or more hearths. Very large groups living together temporarily for a ceremony or to exploit a major resource would be made up of people from several distinct residence groups and from a number of areas. It should not be assumed *a priori* that people always formed well-defined clusters of shelters—perhaps people sometimes formed straggly lines of camps along a beach or riverbank.

Aboriginal languages often included places of very different scope within the category of 'camp'. As we have seen, the word *wa:nga* in Yolngu dialects can refer to the precise place where one temporarily sits or sleeps, one's house or shelter, the residence group or township in which one lives, or one's patri-group country. The same is true of the term *ngurra* in the Western Desert language.

People formed camps and residence groups in such a way as to reduce risk—they evened out variance in production by ensuring there was a sufficient proportion of male and female producers. Distribution between camps in a large residence group further redressed imbalances between camps. The camp formed one possible arena of cooperation in hunting and gathering, and was a primary focus for the distribution of food. Altman's research shows that some eastern Kunwinjku work teams drew on people of a single camp or smaller group within a camp, while others drew on residents of more than one camp in a larger residence group. Men and women strongly differentiated their tasks, and men tended to cooperate in production with men of other camps, as did women with women from other camps.[5]

Families

According to Radcliffe-Brown, the 'family' constituted the primary unit of organisation, but each band ('horde') was autonomous in looking after its own affairs. However, like 'household', the term 'family' is difficult to apply to Aboriginal social arrangements. The expression 'nuclear family'—a married couple together with their child or children—can refer either to a conceptual entity whose members may or may not live together, or to the residents of a household or camp. An 'extended family' is a nuclear or polygynous family, or part of one, plus one or more other relatives, such as a spouse's parent, a child's spouse, or a grandchild. This expression refers to a group living together.[6]

The studies show that not all members of a monogamous or polygynous family necessarily lived together—young children often resided with a mother's sibling, mother's mother or other relative to be 'grown up'. Sometimes older wives resided separately from their husbands, who often spent periods away from their wives and children. Daughters usually remained in their natal or adoptive camp until marriage, which was generally at a young age, and helped their mothers by, for example, looking after younger siblings. Young boys tended to spend much of their time with their peer group (when living with a large residence group) rather than at the camps where they slept and were fed. After initiation, a young man joined a bachelors' camp within the wider residence group. A family's members often slept and ate together; as the family camp broke up with the initiation of sons, the marriage of daughters, and the death of a spouse, the remaining widow or widower joined others—through leviratic marriage of the wife, the remarriage of the husband, or the formation of an extended family camp or joint camp.[7]

Patrilineal, patrilocal bands?

The previous chapter discussed the earlier orthodoxy that hordes or bands had a patrilineal, patrilocal structure. Radcliffe-Brown explained these features according to their adaptive advantage in utilising the local knowledge of male hunters; he ignored the role of women. Two questions arise from the discussion of 'local organisation' in that chapter: (1) What were the relations among people living together in a residence group? (2) What was the relation of residents to the country or countries that they lived on and whose resources they used? In a patrilineal, patrilocal band, a core of residents would have belonged to the same patri-group, living on their own totemic country. The patri-group being exogamous, wives of men of the patri-group lived on their husband's country, while young women of the patri-group moved away to their husband's country at marriage. Radcliffe-Brown countenanced the possibility of a more complex structure, and Stanner elaborated the orthodox model to accommodate a variety of relations through inter-visiting and other activities. Not least, Stanner argues that a band's 'range', over which members habitually hunted and gathered, might include the country of several patri-groups. We saw that Hiatt depicted a much wider residence group, a 'community', with foraging rights over the country of several patri-groups, whereas Birdsell's review challenged this suggestion. This chapter will ask what the ethnographies of the seven regions tell us about internal relations among residents, and about relations of residents to the country on which they lived.

Work teams

The teams of people cooperating in productive activities often cut across camp boundaries, and for larger tasks they might include visitors from other groups. The following typology of work teams, adapted by Jon Altman from the work of Emmanuel Terray, distinguishes between several basic modes of cooperation:[8]

- *Individual activity:* a person worked alone.
- *Simple cooperation:* production was on an individual basis, but people worked alongside others and sometimes exchanged information.
- *Extended cooperation:* individuals had distinct tasks and cooperated in carrying out activities such as game drives, but they did not employ collective implements (such as fish-traps).
- *Complex cooperation:* individuals had distinct tasks and used a collective work implement (such as a dugout canoe, fish-trap, net, or firebrand) or used distinct but complementary implements.

In two of the case studies (Pitjantjatjara people and their neighbours, and Yolngu people), it is possible to say something about the time spent on different productive activities, the productivity of various activities and producers, and the relationship between producers and dependants. There is little information in any of the ethnographies about kin relations among members of work teams.

The dependency ratio

As we saw earlier in Chapter 4, Winterhalder's model predicts that in a residence group of 25 people only seven or eight will be producers (28–32%). Few of the ethnographic studies on which this book relies include censuses of residence groups, or data on the ratio of dependants to producers. But the application of Winterhalder's model to a range of residence groups is shown in Table 10.1.

A group of 30 adults and children would normally contain sufficient producers for the kind of extended cooperation required for working fish-traps, large nets, fish dams, and the like. A consideration that appears to be omitted from such calculations of the dependency ratio is the productive activities of children, which, as we shall see, were quite significant, especially in the Western Desert.

Table 10.1   The number of producers and dependants in relation to residence group size

Residence group size	Producers	Dependants
30	8–10	20–22
100	28–32	68–72
200	56–64	136–44

Just as relevant to the dependency ratio are the life-cycles of men and women. Men's productivity tended to fall off after the age of about 35 years, whereas women continued to be productive later in life. Older men devoted themselves more and more to the preparation and performance of rituals. However, while not all the ethnographies are complete enough for us to make a clear assessment, rituals seems to have been much more elaborate, and required a much greater input of time in some regions than others.

Kinship and the organisation of production

Although kin relations played a central role in the organisation of production, they were invoked in such a general way that the subtle differences between modes of kin classification seem not to have been particularly relevant to differences in the organisation of production. Although the ethnographies provide few details, the kin relations involved in the organisation of production, at least as reflected in the structure of residence groups, appear to have been rather similar in the seven regions. Still, the variation in forms of marriage and levels of polygyny must have had an impact on the structure of camps.

The Marxist anthropologist Frederick Rose has explained polygyny as an economic adaptation. Women 'tended to aggregate themselves' in polygynous households in order to share the burden of child-rearing and food-gathering. Because of his experience, the male in a polygynous household reached his productive peak at 40 to 50 years of age, at the time of his wives' greatest burden in terms of child-bearing. In order to provide the conditions for polygyny, older men delayed the marriages of young men at their sexual and physical peak through the control of initiation (see Chapter 8). Ethel Hassell reports friendship and cooperation between senior and junior co-wives, but there are problems with this argument. First, it implies that women chose to live in polygynous households, yet infants and girls had little discretion in the matter—apart from taking the risk of refusing to go to a promised husband, or of eloping later. It may have been in the society's interests to ensure that this kind of arrangement took place, however. Second, Jon Altman's research shows that eastern Kunwinjku men in their forties and fifties had generally passed their productive peak, so that Rose's theory does not apply to cases of high and very high polygyny, where older men had the most wives; his argument has greater force when applied to moderate levels of polygyny.[9]

Let us now compare the structure of residence groups in the seven regions. In several cases the comparison will require some creative interpretation of rather scanty information.

Residence groups

Kŭnai people

Chapter 4 indicated that Kŭnai camps varied in size from 30 to about 200 people in the early colonial era, according to the few reports available. Some were no doubt smaller. Howitt's inquiry into the spatial organisation of camps provides some clues about the relations among co-residents.[10] He generalises as follows, taking a husband and wife as the reference point:

- son and son's wife— 5 paces north
- father and mother—20 paces N 30° E
- brother and brother's wife—20 paces N 60° E
- wife's father and mother—100 paces or more E
- wife's brother and wife—near the last
- father's sister and husband, and mother's brother and wife—10 paces S 30° E
- mother's sister and husband—10 paces S 60° E
- mother's brother's son and wife—20 paces S.

When discussing the distribution of food, Howitt includes the hunter's brothers and sisters, mother's brother's children and daughter's husband as possible recipients, and hence as co-residents.

This list indicates something of the structure of camps; we should also add a bachelors' camp, and polygynous marriage would have had some effect on the size and composition of camps. The list shows that a brother and sister (for example, the F and FZ or W and WB of the reference male) as well as brothers would sometimes live in the same residence group, with their spouses. A man and his wife's parents could co-reside, as could a woman and her husband's parents. If children are added to the 20 adults in Howitt's list, the result is perhaps 40 individuals, depending on the structure of the population. Such a group could have split up into smaller camps. At other times, people of several residence groups would gather together into larger groups to exploit particular resources and to conduct ceremonies.

All of this suggests that the larger Kŭnai camps consisted of a network of cognates and affines, large enough to ensure an adequate number of able producers and to allow for cooperation when needed. Residents of camps were of mixed regional and local identity, for localities were exogamous, and people of distinct regional identities often married. People from time to time visited or lived for longer periods with those of a different local identity.[11]

As for relations to country, Howitt assumed that patrilocal residence was the norm: only women moved at marriage; men remained in their own country (their 'division'). While Howitt does provide some evidence of older men living on their own country (such as Bunjil Baul of Raymond Island), his account of the ideal structure of a camp suggests a range of possibilities. Assuming that the focal male of his ideal camp was living on his own (and his father's) country, then his wife's mother, wife's father, wife's brother, father's sister's husband, mother's brother, mother's brother's wife, mother's brother's son, mother's sister, and mother's sister's husband were all therefore living non-patrilocally. If the mother's brother was living on his own country then the focal male, his parents and various other relatives were residing non-patrilocally. This mix fits the picture of residence groups, marriage networks, and seasonal mobility from earlier chapters.

Pitjantjatjara people and their neighbours

While information is available on the demographic structure of groups living in the desert, especially in the 1950s and 1960s, much less has been written about their internal structure, either in terms of kin relations among members of the group or people's relations to the country on which they were living. Nevertheless, some of this can be gleaned from the survey by Nicolas Peterson and Jeremy Long.[12] Although they describe few of the kin relations among families, these can be inferred to some degree from section and subsection affiliations, which Long did record during his field surveys.

We saw in Chapter 4 that residence groups in Peterson and Long's study varied in size from four to 28; occasional larger aggregations have been recorded by others. Residence groups consisted of the camps of monogamous or polygynous family groups (with seldom more than two wives), plus single men's and single women's camps. Long recorded a few definite wife's parent–daughter's husband relations, and I have inferred 14 possible ones on the basis of subsection affiliation, including possible promised husbands. Six camps included co-wives of the same section or subsection, who were therefore 'sisters'; and six camps were those of polygynous families. Out of 31 residence groups (numbers 1 to 31 of Peterson and Long's cases), the following links between adults of different camps can be tentatively inferred (the number in brackets indicates the number of residence groups in which such links occurred, and the terms in quotation marks are kin relations inferred from section or subsection relations):

- 'father'–'son' (5 out of 31)
- 'brothers'–'sisters' in different hearth groups (19)
- mother–son (3)
- 'mother'–'daughter' (7)
- 'mother's brother'–'sister's son' (5)
- wife's parents–daughter's husband (14)
- 'brother's wife'–'husband's sister' (or 'wife's brother'–'sister's husband') (4)
- wife's mother's brother–sister's daughter's husband (1)
- 'husband's mother'–'son's wife' (1).

Clearly, affinal links were important in the composition of residence groups. The structure of residence groups was thus consistent with the presence of the husband or promised husband before or in the early years of marriage, at the very least. (Some of the 'mother's brother–sister's son' relationships between males may have been those of wife's father–daughter's husband.)

Annette Hamilton's study of an Everard Ranges residence group shows that the group included:

- the two oldest men of alternating generation moieties, who occupied adjacent shelters
- a camp with two shelters comprising a man, his son, and his son's wife
- a women's camp, with camps nearby of daughters of the women and their husbands
- adjacent shelters belonging to two sisters and their husbands
- a bachelors' camp.

Uterine connections and matrilocal residence are very evident in this residence group.[13]

Peterson's assessment of Western Desert dependency ratios is a demographic one, and rather low according to Winterhalder's model; the proportion of actual producers is likely to have been greater but there appears to have been a shortage of mature men:

- Females $1:2.4 - 1:3.9 = 20\% - 29\%$
- Males $\quad 1:4.1 - 1:5 \quad = 16.7\% - 19.6\%$

There is not sufficient information for us to infer the relationship of residents to the country on which they were living.

Yuwaaliyaay people

Explorers observed residence groups of between about 10 and 100 people on the Darling/Barwon River. It seems safe to say that Yuwaaliyaay residence groups included a mix of cognates and affines, but we do not know in any detail how they were structured, or how people changed residence at marriage. Mathews conveys a picture of patrilocal residence among Wiradjuri people; however, Fred Biggs and D. Harris stated that men of the region tended to live with their wives' people.[14]

Wiil and Minong people

Ethnographers have recorded little about the social relationships among residents in this region, although there is some information about the size and location of groups. We saw that residence groups varied in size up to a maximum of 26 huts, with a camp of six to eight huts being most common. This implies a modal size of 20 or so people, though smaller at times, reaching a maximum of 90 or so people. Even more people may have come together for major ceremonies.

The basic Minong camp comprised a monogamous or polygynous family (or part of one). Bachelors again slept in a separate camp. Several people slept in a hut with the dingoes, covering themselves with their skin cloaks. According to some accounts, a married man usually slept in a hut with one wife, while his other wives and children slept in larger huts nearby. In other camps, a man, his wives, and their children slept together in one hut. No doubt widowed men and women had their own dwellings, perhaps attached to others in a single camp. Women gave birth in a maternity hut on the outskirts of the camp area. Young bachelors spent long periods away from their natal group on initiation journeys and visits.

Observers inferred a pattern (almost certainly too simple) of patrilocal residence, and anecdotes imply that the relatives living with a man might include his 'brothers', a wife and wife's sister, his mother, and his married daughter.[15]

Sandbeach people

Donald Thomson did not record the size or structure of Sandbeach residence groups, either at Point Stewart or Lockhart River Mission. In Chapter 4, I inferred from the estimated population density and the number of recorded camps a range from about nine people in the small dry-season camps to about 70 on average in the wet-season residence groups, which presumably consisted of several camps.[16]

According to Bruce Rigsby and Athol Chase, Sandbeach camps ('households') included married couples who maintained a common hearth together with their dependants. A camp's space was distinct from the public space of a residence group, and was not generally open to non-members unless they were invited in. Guests were provided with their own camping areas. A residence group also normally included a bachelor's camp, to which a boy had to move when prohibitions on interacting with his sisters came into force at initiation; he would leave the camp when he first married. Donald Thomson's field notes include strong suggestions of virilocal residence at the level of camp if not residence group; a promised wife went to live in her future husband's camp even as a child, in order to be raised in his camp before they cohabited.[17]

In his reconstruction, based on the memories of the older people at Lockhart, Chase proposes that the 'core' residents of Sandbeach residence groups came from a cluster of several contiguous estates of opposite moieties, usually within the same dialect area, plus visitors from inland and more distant coastal places. Residents included affines from neighbouring countries who were not close kin. (The clustering of countries of the same moiety would spread the geographical range of affinal links, however.) Chains of kinship and affinal relations linked individual residents and families, who also had ties and attachments of various kinds to country, although we do not know the details. The limited polygyny probably gave rise to complex camps with several shelters and hearths.

Ngarinyin people and their neighbours

The Ngarinyin residence group, Blundell writes, was 'highly flexible in terms of its size and composition', from a single family unit to a larger group.[18] Each Worrorra residence group consisted of several 'family groups', each centred on a fire in front of a hut, according to Love. Most camps consisted of a man, his wife or wives, and their children. There were also bachelors' camps, but no single women's camps it seems. Some camps that moved around the country consisted of male initiates with a 'teacher'.

Blundell presents patrilocal residence as the Worrorra and Ngarinyin ideal, although, because of inter-visiting, each residence group included male members of two or more patri-groups. Hernandez reported, however, that the residence groups (djog, 'mobs') of Wunambal people and their northerly neighbours did not consist of 'totemic groups', had little unity or cohesion, and were not clear divisions of a 'tribe'. Each group more or less permanently inhabited a certain part of the country, but neighbours frequently visited each other. Each group provided food to visitors, who were permitted to hunt and gather. As with Minong people, neighbours had to get permisson to burn off a group's woodland to hunt kangaroos; doing so without permission might lead to a fight. Neighbouring groups ('hordes') would cooperate to mount a large-scale hunt, the occasion of a big *malga* dance. Love reports that when people from different countries came together they camped separately, some 100 metres apart.

Assuming that a few men and women of a patrifilial group were living on their own country, the pattern of use rights reported in the last chapter suggests that other residents might include their wives, wives' fathers and mothers, husbands, children, and women's sons' sons (the last category would be living on their father's mother's country—that of potential wives). This collection of people alone would include members of several patri-groups, related by a wide range of cognatic and affinal links.

Yolngu people

The basic unit of a Yolngu camp was a hut owned by a husband and wife, who both contributed to its making, according to Warner. Unlike men, women tended to be restricted to the camp at night. There was also a bachelors' camp. Many of Thomson's photographs from the 1930s appear to depict residents of individual camps—typically a man with several women; some groups of women included a few young women, some included an older woman, and some included children. A bachelors' camp had half a dozen or more young unmarried men, and a larger group of men gathered for a ceremony.

Based on his study of groups living on the southeastern edge of the Arafura swamp in the 1960s, Nicolas Peterson proposed a developmental cycle of residence groups in which older men, who tended to be attached to their own patri-group country, could either retain control of daughters for as long as possible, maintaining access to their labour and that of sons-in-law, or procure a young wife. One might add to these two factors the demography of patri-groups: if a group had few or no mature men, then there was more room for residents of other patri-groups on its country. Warren Shapiro, who studied a number of mission camps and outstations in the 1960s, argued that residence groups were based primarily on affinal ties, but that people preferred to live on the father's or the mother's country of at least one of the residents.

Genealogies and censuses of the residence groups studied by Shapiro and Peterson show the following range of relations among the camps forming residence groups:[19]

- same-sex siblings (brothers or sisters, 'brothers' or 'sisters') and their spouses and children (n = 4)
- opposite-sex siblings and their spouses and children (2)
- more distant patri-group members of the same and opposite sex, plus their spouses and children (3)
- parents, their child or children, and daughter's husband (in one case the WF was the MB of the DH) (5)
- co-wives of a polygynous family (2)
- nuclear families connected by the marriage of the daughter in one to the son in another, with the parents, sibling, and sibling's spouse of one of these families (2)
- a 'chain' of in-laws (opposite-sex siblings, the woman's husband, his sister and her husband, his brother and wife or wives, etc.) (2)

As well as these links, matrilateral kin in a potential bestowal relation—such as *maralkur–gurrung* (MMBS–FZDS) and *mumalkur–dhumun.gur* (MMMBD–FZDDS)—tended to live close to one another at Milingimbi Township in the 1970s. Once more, we find a mix of cognatic and affinal connections.

How were Yolngu people related to the country on which they were living?[20] Warner thought that residence was patrilocal after the first few years of marriage, so that all sisters and daughters went to their husband's patri-group country to live and raise their families. Thomson followed Radcliffe-Brownian orthodoxy in proposing that Yolngu local groups were patrilineal, patrilocal groups. We have seen that Peterson thought that there was a tendency for older men to remain on or return to their own patri-group country, whereas Shapiro included the mother's country.

Information from Peterson's and Shapiro's censuses, as well as my own of Milingimbi and its outstations in the mid-1970s, shows that on average a quarter (but up to half) of the adults of a residence group lived on their own patri-group land. About 10% on average (but up to 40%) lived on their mother's patri-group country. Spouses of these people formed the largest category of residents after patri-group members. A man's wife's country was likely to be that of his mother's and father's mother's patri-group as well, or that of another close 'mother'; and individuals quite often lived on their mother's mother's (*ma:ri*) country. Thus many residence groups formed around a core of people living on their father's or mother's country. Where a patri-group had died out, the core residents would have been on their mother's mother's country, their place of conception, or a place they were connected to through some other link, such as an ancestral track.

Peterson calculated the proportion of productive members in the Mirrngadja residence groups to be 59% on average.[21] This figure is considerably higher than Winterhalder's model predicts, apparently because of the contribution of some younger men and older women. The dependency ratio in the eastern Kunwinjku outstations analysed in Altman's research (to the west of the Yolngu region) ranged from 30% to 37%. This was in a population with a relatively high proportion of children, following a period of high population growth in Arnhem Land, and in which women did not need to be as production as in former times.

Altman's findings show the returns of senior men to have been generally small. Men were at their productive peak in their late twenties and early thirties, and spent less time in production activities after their late thirties to early forties, while women were most productive in their mid-fifties. Thus, the young people and senior men spent the least time in production activities.

Summary

To sum up, the most comprehensive surveys among these case studies are from northeast Arnhem Land, while the ethnography of other regions provides only a few clues. Residence groups in all seven regions had bachelors' camps, and Western Desert groups included women's camps. Larger Yolngu residence groups included people related by a wide variety of cognatic and affinal ties. People in all seven regions appear to have drawn on the same kinds of links, and chains of links, in making decisions about who to live with and where. But differences would no doubt emerge were comprehensive data available. In terms of camps, Sandbeach residence at marriage seems to have been virilocal, whereas Yolngu people had an expectation of uxorilocal residence at marriage. As for relations to country, the Yolngu cases show that patrilocal residence was not the norm, although the evidence demonstrated a strong bias in this direction.

The estimates of the dependency ratio among Western Desert and Yolngu people show that a simple demographic model has limitations. The number of substantial producers depends on the make-up of the group, and the productivity of children may have been underestimated. Studies do agree, however, on the fact that women generally remained productive for longer than men.

Gender, age, and the division of labour

Do the ethnographies support the textbook accounts of the division of labour by gender? Table 10.2 summarises information about the size and gender composition of work teams in the seven regions; I summarise gender roles from that table.

Women[22]

Generally speaking, women seem to have made tools and implements, such as digging sticks, for their own use. Ngaatatjarra women, for example, fashioned digging sticks out of mulga wood using the sharp edge of a stone or stone core, and by burning and scraping. They also made fighting sticks and dishes.

Women made string as well as string artefacts, such as net-bags and items of apparel. Kŭnai men made nets from the string made by women; a woman working alone produced up to 100 metres per day. Yolngu women made string bags on a simple loom. In the southeast, women made twined baskets of sedge and grass, while in the tropical north (Sandbeach and Yolngu) they made them of pandanus and other materials. Sandbeach women also made children's toys. Yuwaaliyaay women made possum-skin bags and cloaks, while Minong women made kangaroo-skin cloaks for themselves and the men, and built huts. During the men's fights, Wiil women made stone flakes for the men's spear-heads; Worrorra women flaked spear-points during fights.

Women collected vegetable foods, grubs, insects (such as honey ants), shellfish, and crustacea, and hunted small animals and reptiles. The digging stick was the universal tool; it was used in combination with containers such as wooden dishes, bark containers, twined baskets, and net-bags. The digging stick was essential for getting at the many root foods, as well as grubs and burrowing animals, while hatchets were required for cutting echidnas out of hollow logs, bees' nests from hollow trees, and cassid-moth larvae out of wood. Ngarinyin and Worrorra women killed lizards with the aid of dingoes.

Women in several of the case studies (e.g. Kŭnai, Yuwaaliyaay, and Sandbeach) engaged in fishing. Like Yolngu people, Ngarinyin women and children gathered shellfish (using bark containers), and felt with their feet for freshwater mussels or dived for them. They caught crabs with digging sticks and fished with the poison from bark.

Women prepared foods, some of which required considerable labour and skill. In the 'grain belt', women gathered, winnowed, stored, ground, and cooked seeds and grains, using grindstones and mullers, and cooked dampers. Wiil and Minong women also pounded and ground seeds. In the southwest and tropical north, women processed irritant or toxic food plants—such as *Macrozamia*, mangrove pods (Sandbeach but not northern Kimberley), certain roots and tubers, and cycad palm nuts—which required pounding, leaching, or multiple cooking to render them edible.

As a significant component of their work, women collected firewood and water; women in the Western Desert used wooden dishes for this task. Most younger women performed all their tasks while carrying an infant on their hip or straddled on their neck.

Children[23]

Rather in contrast with reports for northeast Arnhem Land, in the Western Desert children were active foragers according to several observers. They gathered vegetable foods while women dug for grubs, and they gathered eggs, collected hawk moth caterpillars, snared small birds, dug for *Cyperus* nuts, and gathered small animals and reptiles burnt by grass fires. In a recent study, Douglas and Rebecca Bird have shown that Western Desert children used different strategies than adults when hunting— children tended to forage at a shorter range and targetted rocky outcrops and low-lying ranges, whereas adults preferred sand-dunes and plains.

Men[24]

Men prepared raw materials and made tool-making tools as well as items of equipment. Their work included stone-knapping and edge-grinding; hafting hatchets and adzes; and the manufacture of string and, among Sandbeach people, three-ply turtle rope (requiring at least four men). Ngarinyin and Worrorra men spent much of the day making spear-points by pressure flaking, working sometimes alone and sometimes in the company of others. Love remarks on the amount of time men spent in this activity. Depending on the region and the tool kit available, men made weapons (including spears, spear-throwers, and harpoons), nets for fishing and birding, containers such as wooden dishes (Pitjantjatjara) and twined baskets (Yolngu men as well as women), canoes and rafts, fish-traps, and ritual objects.

Groups of men would burn off the understorey, often in conjunction with game drives. The cooperation of several men in drives for kangaroos, wallabies, and emus is widely reported. A Minong man would be given the responsibility of using the fire-stick, in complex cooperation with others. A party of Worrorra men would cooperate in a communal fire-drive for kangaroos, wallabies, and emu, in which some men carried firebrands while others waited ahead of the fire with spears; Love describes their dance with spears before the game drive.

Men hunted large as well as small game, alone or in groups. In the Western Desert at least, the hunting of large game was the prerogative of the younger, more active men. Men in most regions used the spear in conjunction with a spear-thrower, but not Yuwaaliyaay or Pitjantjatjara men. Yuwaaliyaay men carried boomerangs.

Hunting strategies included using lures and snares, as well as nets and brush fences, to catch birds and small game as well as larger animals (Kŭnai, Yuwaaliyaay); surrounding animals and trapping them in undergrowth (Minong); communal fire-drives in which small game such as quail as well as large animals like kangaroos would be killed (Ngarinyin and their neighbours); and drives in which boys would bark like dogs to drive kangaroos through a patch of vine forest towards the spears of waiting men (Yolngu).[25]

Small parties of Sandbeach men hunted dugong and turtles from outrigger canoes, prepared stingray flesh, and butchered and cooked dugong and turtle. Coastal Ngarinyin and Worrorra men hunted these animals from double-layer rafts and reef platforms at low tide. Yolngu men on the coast and islands used dugouts without outriggers to hunt dugong and turtle; three or four men cooperated, with one man, the leader and harpooner, looking out for turtles near the beaches, and assisting the others from time to time with the paddling.

Men climbed trees to catch koalas (Kŭnai), possums (Minong), or flying foxes (Yolngu), or to collect coconuts (Sandbeach); and they dug for burrowing game such as wombats (Kŭnai). Ngarinyin and Worrorra men caught freshwater turtles by swimming underneath them and grabbing them. They caught waterbirds in a similar way, as did Yolngu men.

Except in the arid zone, men caught fish; they used spears, traps, and framed scoop nets and larger nets. Kŭnai men (and women) dived for mussels. Sandbeach men fished with small framed nets as well as fish-spears. In some seasons, large numbers of Minong men fished with spears from the beach (Plate 10.1). Using the three-pronged fish-spear, Worrorra men caught fish from reef platforms and rafts, and caught crabs. Men collected marine turtles from reefs at low tide, or caught them on the beach when they were copulating or laying eggs. A Johnston's crocodile was killed by swimming underneath it and attacking it with a stone knife. The complex Yolngu fish-traps, such as the *gurrka gol*, required the cooperation of several men, and Yolngu men skimmed across the reeds of the Arafura swamp in bark canoes in expeditions for goose eggs.

Plate 10.1   Minong fishing party returning from the beach at King George Sound (Robert Havell, *Panorama of King George's Sound*, published 1834, Rex Nan Kivell collection 759; courtesy of the National Library of Australia)

Pitjantjatjara men, and probably men of other regions, would gather fruits, other vegetable foods, and grubs for their own consumption, and communicate the location of such foods to women. In all regions, men as well as women collected honey and the eggs of birds and reptiles. Minong men would sometimes dig up roots, but usually left that task to women.

Men and women[26]

Women's and men's activities overlapped to some extent. For example, Ngarinyin and Worrorra men and women both made string (though they tended to use different materials). They spun fibre on the thigh or, in the case of hair string, used a spindle. Both men and women built shelters. Both also found and chopped bees' nests out of trees with stone axes, and tracked and hunted for small game and eggs.

Some activities required the cooperation of the sexes. Yuwaaliyaay grass-seed processing, especially the threshing of the seed in pits, may have involved both men and women. At the height of the grass-seed season, winnowing and storing of grass-seed was followed by a 'great hunt', feast, and 'corroboree' lasting several nights. Both men and women ground seed with muller and grindstone. Mixed Yuwaaliyaay teams may have engaged in fishing using stone fish-traps, and hunting and fishing using nets, with women driving fish or ducks into the net, as is reported for the lower Darling River.[27] A Sandbeach man and wife cooperated in building huts, and joined together

Plate 10.2   A group of Yolngu men and women of the Djinang language and Mildjingi patri-group collecting fish (photograph by D. F. Thomson, TPH801, courtesy of Mrs D. M. Thomson and Museum Victoria)

for foraging trips, with children in tow. Minong men and women joined to burn off the grass and heath to hunt lizards, snakes, and bandicoots, which they would cook and eat together. Men, women, and children certainly congregated together on the beach for large-scale fish-spearing (conducted by the men). Communal fish drives with grass dams, and the use of some types of fish-trap among Yolngu (and perhaps Ngarinyin) people, involved the cooperation of the sexes (Plate 10.2). Thomson reports that old Sandbeach men helped women gather and process vegetable foods.

Regional differences

The ethnographies do suggest some differences in the gender division of labour in the seven regions. Among Pitjantjatjara people and their neighbours, men's and women's work appears to have been more separate than among Yuwaaliyaay people. As we have seen, Hamilton goes so far as to suggest that Pitjantjatjara people and their neighbours had a 'dual social system' that governed such things as the kinds of tools uses, tool-making, techniques and work organisation, and distribution. Pitjantjatjara men and women did not conduct entirely separate productive activities, however. For example, both gathered spinifex (*Triodia*), from which they beat out and winnowed the resin dust for hafting men's equipment.

Other peculiarities in gendered tasks arose from the particular resources and technologies of the different regions. Kŭnai women, for example, fished from canoes on the lakes, sometimes in large numbers, 'creeping along the shore' at night, fishing with lights.[28] Teams of Sandbeach men hunted marine turtles and dugong from outrigger canoes.

To sum up, there was some overlap in men's and women's tasks (such as string-making and seed grinding), but direct cooperation between men and women seems to have varied, with considerable cooperation among Yolngu people and perhaps Yuwaaliyaay and Ngarinyin people, but strong separation reported for Pitjantjatjara people and their neighbours. If the reports are correct, the greatest separation occurred where gender relations were most equal, and cooperation occurred where they were least equal. The contribution of children's labour appears to have varied—it was important in maximising returns in the marginal environment of the Western Desert, less so in the rich environments of the tropical north.

Work teams

We turn now to the organisation of work teams. Table 10.2 summarises the size and composition of teams engaged in various kinds of tasks in the seven regions.

Table 10.2 shows that many of the women's tasks required only one person, using a spindle, loom, or grindstone or just their hands or feet. However, women often worked in parallel in small or large teams. As well as providing company and security, this was a useful means of sharing information about the location of resources, the presence of danger, and so on. Louise Hamby shows that in current Yolngu basket production one woman, such as a daughter, will often help another woman to make a basket.[36]

Table 10.2 Work teams in the seven regions (activities in square brackets are likely, but without direct supporting evidence)

People	Working solo		Small teams (2–4)	
	Women	Men	Women	Men
Kŭnai[29]	Make string for nets.	[Manufacture artefacts.]	Make net bags (simple cooperation).	Manufacture canoes (two or three men).
	Fish from canoes.	Climb trees for koalas, dive for mussels, hunt with spear and spear-thrower or throwing stick, dig out wombats.	[Collect and prepare vegetable foods, hunt small game.]	[Hunt in small teams]
Pitjantjatjara and their neighbours[30]	Make artefacts, spin hair, fur, and vegetable fibre into string.	Make artefacts.		Make fire with a spear-thrower used as a fire-saw (two men).
	Forage occasionally.	Hunt large game.	Forage, share information (simple cooperation).	Hunt, often in groups of two or three, up to six, often at night (simple cooperation). Conduct game drives for common wallaroo (euro); drive game down hills (extended cooperation); trap emus; conduct fire-drives (complex cooperation).
	Prepare food.			
Yuwaaliyaay and their neighbours[31]		[Make artefacts.]		
	Cut echidnas out of hollow logs.	Hunt large game with spear and spear-thrower, kangaroo snare, and emu lure.	Dig yams, forage for other foods (simple cooperation).	Net game, waterfowl, and fish.
	Grind seed with muller and grindstone.	Grind seed with muller and grindstone.	Thresh seed in pits (two people, complex cooperation).	
Wiil and Minong[32]	Spin possum fur into string using wooden spindle.	Spin possum fur into string using wooden spindle.		
		Fish with spear, hunt kangaroo.	Collect and prepare seed, 'ant eggs' and other food; burn off country to catch small game; catch fish by hand.	Spear fish (three to six men, simple cooperation), catch fish by hand.
	Grind and pound seed with hammer-stone or muller and grindstone.	Grind and pound seed with hammer-stone or muller and grindstone (possibly women as well as men).	Prepare food, eat together (possibly large team).	

Table 10.2   Continued

People	Working solo		Small teams (2–4)	
	Women	*Men*	*Women*	*Men*
Sand beach[33]	Make string, women's pubic coverings, net-bags, baskets, and children's toys.	Make and repair rope, spears, harpoons, bark containers, and canoes; haft axes and adzes.	Construct houses (extended cooperation).	
	Fish, dig roots, gather vegetable foods.	Hunt large game, climb trees for coconuts, spear and net fish with framed scoop nets.	Gather vegetable foods, including nonda plum and mangrove pods (simple cooperation).	Fish with small framed nets (simple cooperation), hunt turtle using a canoe (two men, complex cooperation).
	Prepare and cook foods (e.g. cook wallaby and prepare mangrove pods and yams).		Prepare and cook foods (simple and possibly extended and complex cooperation).	Prepare stingray flesh and turtle.
Ngarinyin and their neighbours[34]	Make string and baskets.	Manufacture spear-points.		Make rafts.
	Dig for yams and other roots and tubers; track and kill small game; gather marine and freshwater shellfish, grubs, turtle eggs; poison fish.	Fish with spears, hunt large game, spear dugong (alone or possibly in a small team), catch and kill tortoises and waterbirds.	Conduct many of the single-person activities using simple cooperation; possibly conduct fire-drives.	Fish with grass dams; hunt small animals in fire-drives, often using dingoes; spear dugong from reef platform or raft (solo or small team possibly); kill Johnston's crocodiles (extended cooperation); possibly collect marine turtles.
	Prepare food.			Butcher and cook kangaroo (extended or complex cooperation).
Yolngu[35]	Make string, baskets, and net-bags.	[Make artefacts.]	Collect and prepare pandanus and other raw materials, make baskets (simple cooperation).	Manufacture dugout canoes, manufacture three-ply turtle rope (four men or more).
		Hunt wallaby, kangaroo, and flying fox; fish with fish-spear or hand-net; collect honey and beetle larvae.	Forage for vegetable foods, dig *ra:kay* (rush-corms), collect cycad-palm nuts (simple cooperation).	Operate the *gurrka gol* fish-trap, hunt turtles from dugout canoes (three to four men, complex cooperation).
	Prepare and cook foods, including the leaching of cycad-palm nuts (also done in small and large teams).		Prepare food, including cooking *djitama* in hot ashes, pounding cycad-palm nuts with pounding stone and anvil (two or three women, simple cooperation).	

Table 10.2   Continued

People	Larger teams (5+)		Mixed-gender teams
	Women	*Men*	
Kŭnai	[Large teams in simple cooperation likely for main staples.] Fish from canoes on lakes (simple cooperation).	Make nets, use set-nets. Fish from canoes (complex cooperation). Hunt kangaroo by encircling the animal.	None reported.
Pitjantjatjara and their neighbours	Forage (groups of five to nine women), make coolamons (six women).	Hunt, often in groups of two or three, up to six, often at night (simple cooperation). Conduct cooperative drives for macropods (usually five to six, but up to 11 men) using fire, or drive animals over a cliff (extended or complex cooperation).	None reported.
Yuwaaliyaay and their neighbours	[Forage for vegetable foods and small game (simple cooperation).]	Stalk kangaroos, using portable hides, kill emus using large nets or brush fences (complex. cooperation).	Possibly hunt with nets for fish or ducks; use stone fish-traps on the Darling/Barwon River; gather, winnow, and store grass seed at height of season (possibly in mixed teams).
Wiil and Miṉong	[Forage for vegetable foods (simple cooperation).] Burn off and hunt, possibly in large teams (complex cooperation).	Burn off understorey. Surround and stalk or trap kangaroo in undergrowth (large number of men, extended cooperation). Spear fish (up to 60 men, simple cooperation).	Conduct game drives. Men, women, and children gathered together on the beach during large-scale fish-spearing. Men and women cooperated to make fish weirs.
Sandbeach	[Large teams in simple cooperation likely for main staples.]	Fish with nets (simple cooperation, up to seven men), hunt turtle and dugong using outrigger canoes (up to six men, complex cooperation), butcher and cook dugong (seven or eight men, extended cooperation).	Build houses (husband and wife, extended cooperation). Women and children were spectators when men netted fish.
Ngarinyin and their neighbours	[Forage for vegetable foods (simple cooperation).] Hunt small animals in fire-drives, often using dingoes (complex cooperation).	Conduct fire-drives for kangaroos, wallabies, and emus (complex cooperation).	Communal fish drives with grass dams may have involved both sexes (complex cooperation).
Yolngu	Gather lilies and wild taro (six women, simple cooperation); gather shellfish (simple cooperation); dig *ra:kay* (rush-corms) for major ceremonies (up to 30 women, simple cooperation); prepare pandanus (eight women, simple cooperation).	Conduct kangaroo drives from vine forest (extended cooperation); go on canoe expeditions in Arafura Swamp for magpie-goose eggs (ten men recorded, simple cooperation).	Build houses, use swamp fish-trap (small mixed team, complex cooperation), fish with grass dams and large fish-fences (large mixed team, complex cooperation).

Men carried out many of their activities alone. These activities included preparing raw materials, making artefacts, digging out wombats, and hunting with a spear and (perhaps) a spear-thrower or with a fish-spear and hand-net. Like women, men did some of these things in parallel (simple cooperation)—for example, sitting together while pressure-flaking or spear-fishing along a beach.

Some tasks required the cooperation of a small team of women or men. Among Sandbeach people, a mother and daughter-in-law cooperated in hunting (and exchanged gifts of food). Two Kŭnai men would combine in complex cooperation to hunt koalas, one climbing a tree (by using a band and/or cutting notches) and dislodging the animal, the other killing it on the ground. Howitt describes three Kŭnai men hunting and cooking a kangaroo together: one killed the animal and lit the fire, two cut up the animal, and all three cooked it and ate the entrails. Threshing seed in pits required two people in complex cooperation (Yuwaaliyaay)—one to trample the seed in a square pit, the other to thresh with a wooden paddle. Thomson says that a young man's main teachers in matters of hunting, fishing, and bushcraft were his father, father's elder brother, and father's father, which implies that people in these relations cooperated while the teaching was going on. The manufacture of turtle rope required three or four men and Louise Hamby reports that mothers and daughters, or sisters, often worked together when gathering materials for and making baskets. She records two teams of four women working in parallel preparing pandanus (Yolngu).

Most of the larger teams reported in the ethnographies consisted of people working in parallel (that is, in simple cooperation)—spear-fishing, digging rush corms, etc. Large quantities of food would have been gathered, perhaps to feed participants at a major ceremony. Chapter 3 recounted how Yankunytjatjara women would fan out along a creek-bed and call to their companions with information about the best trees.[37]

Men's hunting often required a large group in extended or complex cooperation. Satterthwait comments on the complex division of labour involved in hunts with large nets—there were scouts, beaters, net-holders, and administers of *coups-de-grace*. Men formed large groups to hunt turtle and dugong from a dugout canoe (Sandbeach), and in drives for kangaroos and other game, in which men surrounded and killed the animals or used fire to drive them towards the hunters or over a cliff (in the Western Desert, for example).

The only reliable reports (or other evidence such as photographs) of cooperation between men and women come from eastern Cape York Peninsula and northeast Arnhem Land. Thomson's photographs show men and women cooperating in building huts (Sandbeach), and larger teams working a movable grass dam (Yolngu). A mixed-gender team of about 11 Yolngu people cooperated to push a grass barrier through a reedy swamp to trap fish in June 1937 (Plate 10.2); the fish were picked up and put in a large basket. The use of large fish-fences in swamps and estuaries also required teams in complex cooperation. Grass-seed production and hunting with nets may have involved both genders working together (Yuwaaliyaay people and possibly others).

The available information, then, seems to show that the fundamentals of the organisation of work were very much the same in the seven regions, regardless of the specific resources garnered and the technology used. All seven regions exhibit a very similar mix of arrangements—from working alone to working in large groups in simple, extended, or complex cooperation—and a similar mix of single-gender and mixed-gender teams. The level of cooperation between the genders varied, from marked separation in the Western Desert to cooperation in the tropical north in such activities as fish drives, and perhaps, on the Darling/Barwon River, in the processing of seed.

The control of productive activities

The governance of work included controls over access to technology (reviewed in the previous chapter), as well as prohibitions on killing various species and more direct controls of the production process. Information on the latter, however, is very patchy.

Controls include production restrictions, by contrast with consumption restrictions (discussed in Chapter 11). A Yuwaaliyaay boy, for example, could only kill an emu after his first Bora ceremony. When he killed his first emu, he had to lie on the dead bird before it was cooked; later a *wirreenun* and the boy's father rubbed the emu's fat into the boy's joints, and he had to chew a piece of the flesh and express disgust. Parker says that Yuwaaliyaay men did not approve of female cooks; older men would not eat bread made by women, or fish or game that a woman had gutted, although they allowed women to cook food after men had prepared it.[38]

Various production restrictions applied to Yolngu young men. They had to become familiar with the major species in revelatory ceremonies before they could hunt game such as crocodiles. And if an initiated man killed a large game bird before the birth of his first child, he had to leave it for an older man to divide, and was unable to eat it. A ceremony removed these restrictions after the man 'found' his first child (that is, after his wife became pregnant).[39]

Jon Altman's analysis of the control of men's work among Kunwinjku people is instructive on more direct controls. For the most part, the governance of productive work had an informal character based on what Altman calls 'consensus'. The extended discussion about the day's activities with which the day began, and people's reluctance to leave the camp, meant that the day's work seldom got under way until mid-morning. If a senior man or woman wanted to organise an expedition, he or she usually floated the proposal the previous evening to gauge the response of prospective participants. Men tended to debate publicly, women more covertly, pressing men of their camp to act as spokesmen on their behalf. Overt or covert pressure rarely succeeded, and where expeditions were led, leadership was temporary.[40]

Altman points out that asymmetrical authority relations between kin came into play: older brothers were able to coerce younger brothers (especially unmarried ones), wives' fathers were able to coerce daughters' husbands, and ritual guardians their wards. However, the ability of individuals to move provided a check on exploitation. This is consistent with the picture of governance drawn in Chapter 8.

Where productive work formed an adjunct to the performance of a ceremony, or where a productive implement had ancestral associations (being next to a sacred site, for example), people accepted the authority of male leaders. At one ceremony, for example, the senior men of the participating groups conferred over the shortage of meat and organised a fire-drive with 17 hunters, killing 22 kangaroos, the young men being keen to impress the older men. During such fire-drives men split up by patri-moiety, as they did during the ceremony. Satterthwait reports that senior men tended to control the use of nets for duck and wallaby drives, and took responsibility for clubbing emus.[41]

Specialisation provided another way in which an activity could have a clear leader. Altman describes the use of a conical fish-trap in the early dry season among eastern Kunwinjku people. Only men with ritual seniority were permitted at the site of the trap, adjacent to a sacred site, and a senior man demonstrated the intricate use of the trap to younger men. The sacred character of Yolngu fish-traps implies similar controls.

Productivity and labour time

Sahlins based his generalisations about the very short working hours among hunters and gatherers on limited studies by McCarthy and Macarthur of two Arnhem Land groups living temporarily away from missions. These studies showed average adult working time of five hours per day where vegetable foods were plentiful, and close to four hours per day at a dry-season camp, where mammals were in good supply. Other research reveals longer hours spent on subsistence production, especially when corrected for biases and omissions. Estimates often omit the time women spent in gathering firewood and water, and the hours spent making artefacts and performing rituals, some of which were regarded as essential to the provision of resources.[42]

Information about labour time is very scanty. In relation to the seven regions of this book, the only systematic information is that of Richard Gould on the Western Desert, and it has its limitations. Betty Meehan and Jon Altman provide estimates for north-central Arnhem Land, close to the Yolngu region. People living at the Anbarra outstation studied by Meehan had replaced some of the vegetable foods formerly gathered by women with purchased flour, sugar, and rice, and the people of the eastern Kunwinjku outstation of Altman's study had replaced most vegetable foods in that way.

Kŭnai and Yuwaaliyaay people

No direct information on labour time is available for the southeast. However, Hotchin argues that Kŭnai set-nets required collective labour in production and maintenance, and that the use of nets for fishing allowed large groups to live together. Satterthwait brings anecdotal evidence to bear on the production of the types of nets made in the Darling/Barwon region. They required the gathering of fibrous mater-ial, the making of cord, and the making of the net. He estimates that a large fine-meshed net could have required 9000 metres of cord, and involved 100 person-days or more for its manufacture; each person worked for six to seven hours per day on the net. (This is consistent with Hotchin's estimate of Kŭnai women's production of string.) The nets also required maintenance and mending.[43]

Western Desert people

Nearly everyone in Richard Gould's study of Ngaatjatjarra groups foraged every day. Old people were an exception, but they still tried to forage when they could. Children also foraged, rather in contrast with reports for northeast Arnhem Land; Tindale estimates that children, by the age of ten, were capable of satisfying perhaps a quarter of their daily requirements.[44]

According to Gould, nine adults and 11 children averaged nearly five hours per person per day in foraging activities; men spent more hours hunting than women, but with poorer results. To these hours we should add time spent in the collection of firewood and water, and the making of artefacts. It seems that vegetable foods foraged by women and girls provided the bulk of the diet, for Pitjantjatjara and Yankunytjatjara people as well as Ngaatjatjarra people, although according to Hamilton the contribution of small game hunted by women of the Western Desert may have been underestimated by other researchers; women saw their foraging as going out for meat. The dependable efforts of the women freed the men for the less dependable hunting activities. Only on the rare occasions of sustained, heavy localised rainfall in areas dominated by mulga scrub would game become abundant enough for men's hunting to provide the bulk of the diet.[45]

It is not possible to estimate the average daily time men or women spent making hunting and gathering equipment, but the time required to make some individual objects has been recorded. It took about 50 minutes to make an adze shaft, and more than 11 hours to shape and finish a spear-thrower. A sacred board took four Pitjantjatjara men two days of continuous work.[46]

Yolngu people

Peterson shows that Yolngu women joined the work force at puberty (which was the age at which a girl joined the camp of her promised husband) and continued to be productive into old age, but girls were not very productive. The regular contributors to the food supply in the camp at Mirrngadja on the Arafura swamp in the mid-1960s were the adult women, two of the adult men, and two of the 15 boys of the group; none of the five girls contributed regularly. Men left the group for weeks at a time to attend ceremonies or visit other groups, leaving women as the main supporters of the very young and the old. Moreover, the productive life of men was shorter than that of women. (Worrorra women also remained active producers into their later years.)[47]

Altman recorded the time spent by eastern Kunwinjku men and women in subsistence production, although the use of vehicles and shotguns and the substitution of bought foods for bush foods mean that comparisons with the Western Desert data must be tentative. (Eastern Kunwinjku are western neighbours of Yolngu people.) Altman calculates that, in the absence of store-bought food, women would have to have foraged for more than nine hours per day during the wet season to meet a target of only 2000 kilocalories per person per day, so that even in conjunction with men's production it is likely that intake in these months fell below the optimum. In April and May about 5.5 hours per day would have been required to meet this target. Altman estimates that another half-hour per day should be added for the collection of firewood and water, mainly women's work. Men spent 2–4.6 hours per day in subsistence production, fishing with nets and traps and hunting with guns. Building houses took up 1% of people's work time, making equipment 0.9%, and mining pigment 0.2%.

The productivity of the eastern Kunwinjku men in Altman's study peaked at around 23 years and again at 35 years, declining in later years, while women's productivity was more stable over time. This lends some support to Rose's hypothesis that it was men at their productive peak who married younger women polygynously, at least for low to moderate polygyny. A highly polygynous hearth group probably enjoyed some economic benefits from recruiting young wives into the labour force, as Peterson suggests, and from attracting more sons-in-law to a camp.

On the relative contribution of different sectors of the community, Meehan's findings on shellfish gathering among Anbarra people are generally consistent with Peterson's findings. Women's productivity gradually rose until they reached the age of 45, when it started declining, although women in their sixties still made a significant contribution (equivalent to that of a 16-year-old in Meehan's sample).

As older men dropped out of major productive activity, they became increasingly involved in ritual performances, although they did not become full-time ritual specialists. This structural difference between the tasks of men and women tends to support the view that women's production in part 'financed' men's rituals. It is also reflected in the Yolngu story of the Djang'kawu (and similar myths), which gave a justification of women's place being at the hearth as 'workers' and of men having control of secret ceremonies and religious knowledge. It was not only older men who devoted time to the religious sphere, however; Thomson comments on the amount of time young men spent making symbolic artefacts for exchange.[48]

Comparisons and conclusions

This chapter has shown that the gender division of labour, though marked, was not absolute. Men and women shared certain tasks, such as spinning and seed-grinding, and women would occasionally hunt large game, while men would sometimes forage for vegetable foods and shellfish. They cooperated in undertaking certain tasks.

Some strong similarities in the organisation of production in the seven regions have become apparent—in the kinds of links that bound people into camps and residence groups, the size and composition of work teams, and the kinds of cooperation, from simple to complex. The complexity of organisation of hunts may have been greatest in the use of several large nets in density drives. The numbers of people working in parallel varied; in some regions very large numbers congregated to exploit a resource—the exploitation of fish, cycad-palm nuts, and rush-corms stood out in the case studies. Some Kŭnai people may have joined the very large gatherings of people who collected bogong moths in the mountains.

The evidence suggests that people of the seven regions drew on rather similar cognatic and affinal relations in organising co-residence, so that, as I suggested earlier, subtle differences in the classification of kin may not have had much of an impact on the organisation of production. What counted was having an adequate balance between producers and non-producers and between producers of different kinds. Camps and residence groups had a flexible constitution, based on ties of various kinds between spouses, parents and children, siblings, other cognatic kin, and affines.

This chapter has also brought out significant differences between the regions. One contrast was in the degree of cooperation between men and women. It seems that in the Western Desert women and men worked more separately than in the tropical north, where they cooperated in certain tasks, notably fishing with grass barriers. This pattern is consistent with the greater separation of women's from men's ceremonies in the Western Desert, and the more egalitarian relations (see Chapter 8). In northeast Arnhem Land women appear not to have had their own secret ceremonies, although they conducted secret aspects of a revelatory ceremony, and the high level of polygyny reflected greater domination by men.

Patterns of marriage had effects on social relations within camps, and on women's experiences (when they married). An obvious difference was between regions in which close kin married and those in which distant relatives did so. A Yolngu woman who married a man of her father's sister's extended family remained with people with whom she may have had close contact, whereas a Kŭnai man who married a distant 'sister' and resided with her parents was living with people who, if not strangers exactly, were less intimately known.

In regions of high polygyny, some camps or even residence groups would have consisted of, or been dominated by, a single polygynous family of a man and his many wives. Such an arrangement implies a lack of balance in the ratio between productive men and women; this was redressed by the presence of would-be and actual sons-in-law, as well as sons.

It is difficult to calculate differences between the regions in the time spent on productive work—the information is just too incomplete. What information there is suggests that Yolngu and neighbouring men may have spent less time in subsistence production than men of the Western Desert. Gould stresses the extensive hours spent in hunting, for little return; Altman's figures are much lower, even taking into account the use of guns, and he thinks that returns from hunting were reliable. The productivity of men's hunting appears to have been greater in the more fertile areas. Animal foods constituted a significantly higher proportion of the diet in north-central and northeast Arnhem Land (among Yolngu people and their neighbours) than in the Western Desert (among Pitjantjatjara people and their neighbours). All the coastal, lacustrine, and riverine peoples of this study in all likelihood enjoyed a high animal-food component in their diet; these groups included Kŭnai people, Yuwaaliyaay people and their neighbours, coastal Minong people, and coastal Worrorra people. This productivity may have been reflected in the hours that men spent working, and in the time available for other tasks and activities, such as ceremonies.

The most notable outcome of this aspect of the study is the broad similarity in the organisation of production in the seven regions, in spite of the differences in ecology and technology.

Further reading

L. R. Hiatt began the debate over the orthodox model of patrilineal clans and patrilocal bands in his article 'Local organisation among the Australian Aborigines' (1962). This provoked a defence and revision of Radcliffe-Brownian concepts by W. E. H. Stanner, in his 'Aboriginal territorial organisation' (1965). For a 'band' perspective see *Aboriginal Territorial Organization* by Nicolas Peterson and Jeremy Long (1986). Fred Myers analyses Pintubi relations to country from the perspective of individual life-histories in *Pintupi Country, Pintupi Self* (1986)

Some of the key works on the the relative production of animal and vegetable foods are Mervyn Meggitt's 'Aboriginal food gatherers of tropical Australia' (1964), Richard Gould's 'Subsistence behaviour among the Western Desert aborigines of Australia' (1969a), and Betty Meehan's *Shell Bed to Shell Midden* (1982).

Marshall Sahlins's article 'The original affluent society', reprinted in his book *Stone Age Economics* (1972) set the agenda for a debate about the time spent by hunters and gatherers in productive work; his key Australian sources were articles by McCarthy (1960) and McArthur (1960). The more extended studies drawn on in this chapter include Richard Gould's *Living Archaeology* (1980), Betty Meehan's *Shell Bed to Shell Midden* (1982), and Jon Altman's *Hunter-Gatherers Today* (1987). James O'Connell and Kristen Hawkes have studied foraging practices among Alyawarre people in terms of optimal foraging theory; see, for example, 'Alyawara plant use and optimal foraging theory' (1981). Robert Kelly reviews this approach in *The Foraging Spectrum* (1995). The Birds are conducting ongoing research on Mardu hunting and gathering; see 'Mardu children's hunting strategies in the Western Desert, Australia' (2002) and see Douglas Bird's website at http://www.ume.maine.edu/iceage/ IQCSDir/people/bird.html.

Notes

1   On the division of labour by gender in Aboriginal economies see R. M. and C. H. Berndt (1981: 119–20) and Maddock (1974: 25, 188).

2   See Kelly (1995: 10–14), Peterson and Long (1986: 1–12), and Steward (1936) on the concept of a patrilocal band.

3   For a processual model of Aboriginal bands see Peterson and Long (1986: 144–51).

4   See Myers (1986: 71–91) on the band concept; Myers's attitude to the band concept is more positive in an earlier article (1982).

5   See Altman (1987: 102–4, 118–20) on cooperation in eastern Kunwinjku bands, and Musharbash (n.d.) on Warlpiri camps.

6   On concepts of family and horde see Radcliffe-Brown (1931: 34–43); see also C. C. Harris (1990: 70) and Keesing (1975: 35).

7   See Hamilton (1981b) on the role of peer groups in child socialisation.

8   See Altman (1987: 119) and Terray (1972) on modes of cooperation. I have changed Altman's 'restricted simple cooperation' to 'simple cooperation' and included the exchange of information; I have also changed 'extended simple cooperation' to 'extended cooperation' and revised 'complex cooperation' to include several implements.

9   See Hassell (1936: 682), Hiatt (1985), and Rose (1968: 208) on polygyny and women's interests.

10   See Howitt (1880: 218–20; 1904: 774) on Kŭnai residence groups.

11   Howitt's narrative of a feud (1880: 218–20), albeit in the early colonial period (1856 or 1857), shows people of a variety of 'clans' (regional identities) camping together. On patrilocal residence as a norm see Howitt (1880: 230; cf. 1904: 271).

12   On Western Desert residence groups see Peterson and Long (1986).

13   See Hamilton (1979: 25–7) on an Everard Range camp.

14   See Mathews (1906: 941–2, cited in Allen 1972: 105) on patrilocal residence; see Beckett et al. (2002), Biggs (1957), and Harris (1964) on uxorilocal residence.

15 On Wiil and Minong residence groups see Barker (1992: 10 May 1830, 17 June 1830, 31 January 1831, cited in Le Souëf 1993), Clark (1842), Collie (1979: 12 July 1834, cited in Le Souëf 1993: 8), Ferguson (1987: 121), Green (1989: 40, 66), and Nind (1831: 28). For anecdotes containing information about co-residents, see Barker (1992: 31 January, 24 April 1830, cited in Le Souëf 1993) and Green (1989: 40, 48).

16 Sources on Sandbeach residence groups include Chase (1980b: 157, 160), Rigsby and Chase (1998: 199, 206), and Thomson (1932: 162–3).

17 See Thomson (Papers) on virilocal residence.

18 On residence groups among Ngarinyin people and their neighbours see Blundell (1975 vol. 1: 80, 112, 114), Love (1936: 93), and Hernandez (1941: 221, 224).

19 See Peterson (1978), Shapiro (1973: 379), Thomson (Photographic collection MV 1157–1209A), and Warner (1937: 129–30), on Yolngu residence groups.

20 On relations of Yolngu residents to country see Peterson (1971), Shapiro (1973), Thomson (1949), and Warner (1937: 19, 138–40).

21 See Peterson (1973: 184) on the Yolngu productivity and dependency ratio; Altman (1987: 79–95) on eastern Kunwinjku; and Meehan (1982) on Anbarra.

22 On the Kŭnai gender division of labour see Bulmer (in Smyth 1878: 143; 1994: 50–1; Papers, MV B4 F7 xm527, B10 F4 xm924: 5), Haydon (1846, cited in Coutts 1967: 236), Hotchin (1990: 132), and Howitt (1880: 261). On Western Desert women see Hamilton (1980: 7, 10–11), Myers (1986: 74–5), Gould (1969b: 262), and on the separation of the genders see Hamilton (1980: 7, 12–13), Hayden (1981), Myers (1986: 75), and Tindale (1972: 245–9). On Yuwaaliyaay women's production see Parker (1905: 107). On Wiil and Minong women see Collie (1979 [1834] cited in Le Souëf 1993: 38), Hassell (1936: 688–90, 701), and Nind (1831: 36–7). On Sandbeach women's activities see Thomson (Photographic collection MV 2970–1, 3546, 3026, 3038, 3041, 3553–6, 3557–9b, 3566–9, 3582; 3028, 3368–70, 3371–81). On women among Ngarinyin and neighbours see Blundell (1975 vol. 2: 503, 529, 543) and Love (1936: 66, 76–7). On Yolngu women see Hamby (2001), Thomson (Photographic collection MV 889, 960–2, 964, 977, 1000–10, 1020,1041–3, 1208A, 2970–1, 3026, 3028, 3038, 3041, 3368–70, 3371–81, 3546, 3553–59b, 3582, 3566–9), and Warner (1937: 478). Hamilton (1980) comments on the continued use of a chopper/chopping-tool technology among Western Desert women, who were excluded from more recent innovations; see also Hayden (1977).

23 On Western Desert children's production see Hamilton (1980: 10), Tindale (1972: 249), and Bird and Bird (2002).

24 On men's production among Kŭnai people see Bulmer (in Curr 1887, vol. 3: 548; 1994: 50; Papers, MV B10 F4 xm924: 5; Papers, MV B10 F5 xm931: 47); among Pitjantjatjara people and their neighbours see Tindale (1972: 247–8) and Myers (1986: 74); among Wiil and Minong people see Barker (1992), Collie (1979 [1834] cited in Le Souëf 1993: 3), Lockyer (1827: 485, cited in Le Souëf 1980: 77), and Nind (1831: 29, 30, 33, 36–7); among Sandbeach people see Thomson (1934; Photographic collection MV 2813, 2843–60, 3299, 3322–5, 3460–76, 3480–2, 3545–5h, 3549–51, 3560–5a, 3583–99b, 3612–6) and Chase (1980: 196); among Ngarinyin people and their neighbours see Blundell (1975 vol. 2: 467, 474–5, 483, 497, photo on 498, 524–5), Love (1936: photo facing 4, 7, photo facing 72, 74–5, 85, 137, 139, 141); among Yolngu see Thomson (Photographic collection MV 720–50, 779–94, 1022, 1051, 1080, 1090, 1093–4, 2813, 3545–5h, 3549–51, 3560–65a, 3583–99b, 3606–10, 3612–6, 2843–60, 3299, 3322–5, 3383–90, 3399–404; 3460–76, 3480–2) and Warner (1937: 140–1, 493). See Love (1936: 74) on the amount of time Worrorra men spent making spearheads.

25 Dingoes do not usually bark, so these were either post-colonial dingo–dog hybrids or dog strains introduced by Macassans—or else ethnographers misinterpreted Yolngu concepts.

26 On shared tasks and cooperation among men and women: for Pitjantjatjara see Gould (1980: 80); for Yuwaaliyaay see Parker (1905: 105–10, 118–19); for Wiil and Minong see Hassell (1936: 693–4) and Nind (1831: 36–7); for Ngarinyin and their neighbours see Blundell (1975 vol. 2: 470–2, 483, 485, 497, 524, 529) and Love (1936: 70–1, 140); for Yolngu see Warner (1937: 477) and Thomson (Photographic collection MV 796–804, 829–32, 1030–7).

27 See Satterthwait (1987: 622) on gender cooperation in net hunting.

28 See Bulmer (in Smyth 1878: 143).

29 On Kŭnai work teams see Bulmer (1994: 50–1; in Curr 1887: 548, 1994: 50; in Smyth 1878: 143; Papers, MV B10 F4 xm924: 5, B10 F5 xm931: 47), Haydon (1846, cited in Coutts 1967: 236), Hotchin (1990: 133), Howitt (1880: 261), Halstead (1977), and Hotchin (1990: 132). Family expeditions are implied in the story of Eagle and Mopoke (Smyth 1878: 451).

30 On work teams among Pitjantjatjara people and their neighbours see Brokensha (1975: 25), Gould (1980: 75, 77, 80), Hamilton (1980: 11–12), Love (1942: 26, cited in Hamilton 1980: 7), and Myers (1986: 74–5).

31 On Yuwaaliyaay work teams see Parker (1905: 105–10, 118–19) and Allen (1972). On the organisation of net hunting (including gender cooperation) see Satterthwait (1987: 622–3).

32 On Wiil and Minong works teams, see Barker (1992, cited in Le Souëf 1980: 35), Hassell (1936: 688, 693–4, 688–90), Le Souëf (1993: 33–4, 38), Lockyer (1827: 485), and Nind (1831: 29–30, 35–7).

33 The evidence regarding the organisation of Sandbeach work teams is taken from Thomson's descriptions of ideal kin relationship and his photographs and field notes from the late 1920s. There is no direct evidence of how teams were constituted in terms of kin relationships, but we can infer gender and age relationships from the photographic evidence. See Thomson (Photographic collection 3383–90, 3399–404, 3606–10). On dugong hunts see Thomson (Papers, MV DT File 190, October 1932; Photographic collection 2939, 2958–61, 3421, 3510, 3530–40). On cooperation among Sandbeach people between a mother and son's daughter see Thomson (1972: 10–14).

34 On work teams among Ngarinyin people and their neighbours see Blundell (1975 vol. 2: 467, 525) and Love (1936: 85).

35 On Yolngu work teams see Hamby (2001: 160–1, 182), Thomson (Photographic collection 720–50, 779–94, 796–804, 829–32, 889, 960–2, 964, 977, 978–9, 996, 1000, 1020, 1022, 1041–3, 1051, 1080, 1090, 1093–4, 1208A), and Warner (1937: 140–1, 477–8).

36 On cooperation in Yolngu basket-making see Hamby (2001: 161).

37 On Yankunytjatjara women's cooperation see Hamilton (1980: 11–12).

38 On Yuwaaliyaay production restrictions see Parker (1905: 24). On attitudes to female cooks see Parker (1905: 111).

39 The information on Yolngu production restrictions is from Nicolas Peterson (pers. com.) and Warner (1937: 130, 287); cf. Altman (1982: 179, 183) on eastern Kunwinjku.

40 On decision-making among eastern Kunwinjku see Altman (1987: 122–6) On fire-drives and sacred fish-traps see Altman (1987: 123–4).

41 See Satterthwait (1987: 623) on older men's control of nets.

42 On the Arnhem Land studies see McCarthy (1960), McArthur (1960), and Sahlins (1972: 14–18).

43 On the labour involved in net-making see Hotchin (1990: 133) and Satterthwait (1987: 615).

44 On productivity in the Western Desert see Gould (1980: 62, 64, 78–9, Table 7), Hamilton (1980: 10–11), and Tindale (1972: 249).

45 In contrast, on the basis of kilocalorie requirements, labour requirements, and returns from various plant foods, O'Connell and Hawkes estimate that Alyawarra foragers worked at least four or five and sometimes as many as 10 hours per day simply to feed themselves (O'Connell and Hawkes 1981: 118–19, 123–5).

46 On Western Desert artefact production see Brokensha (1975: 20, 23), Gould et al. (1971a: 152), Hamilton (1979; 1980), Hayden (1981), Mountford (1941: 316), and Thomson (1964: 411).

47 On Yolngu productivity see Peterson (1973: 184); on eastern Kunwinjku see Altman (1987: 78, 81, 84, 91, 109–10); and on Anbarra see Meehan (1982: 124, 132, 150). See Love (Papers: 71) on Worrorra producers.

48 On the Djang'kawu myth see Keen (1994: 296); on the manufacture of symbolic objects see Thomson (1949: 26–7).

11

Distribution and Consumption

Introduction

Distribution and exchange are two aspects of the allocation of valued items. 'Distribution' refers to the track particular items follow in going from producer to consumer; 'exchange' refers to transactions and processes in which valued items are transferred from one person or group to another, usually reciprocally. Together they comprise the 'circulation' of valued items. 'Consumption' refers to the ways in which valued items are used and 'used up' in particular social contexts. It thus brings together a rather diverse set of processes—eating food, burning firewood, and being the beneficiary of a ritual service (such as the cleaning of the bones of the dead) or of a spouse's activities and powers.[1]

This chapter will describe and analyse patterns of distribution and consumption in the seven regions, while exchange and trade will be examined in the following chapter. I am including consumption in this chapter for two reasons. First, the ethnographies do not include enough information on consumption for it to merit a separate chapter. Second, what information there is describes consumption restrictions and prohibitions (usually related to gender, age, ritual, and reproductive status), which affected distribution.

Distribution in Aboriginal economies has been described in four main ways by anthropologists:

• as the consequences of obligations based on kin relations
• as a system of reciprocity
• as a set of strategies of risk reduction
• as demand sharing.

Anthropological concepts of *gift economies* and *inalienable possessions* are also important, but I am going to delay discussion of these concepts until the next chapter.

According to the first of the four approaches to distribution, kinship obligations structured all aspects of social relationships and each kind of relationship had its own particular obligations.[2] The Berndts express this view as follows: 'there is in every community an arrangement of obligations which every growing child has to learn. In this network of duties and debts, rights and credits, all adults have commitments of one kind or another. Mostly, not invariably, these are based on kin relationships.'

The early functionalist ethnographies, such as Warner's and Thomson's, list kin relationships and attach to each a statement of rights and obligations. The social theory behind this model is the jural one of rights and duties entailed by social statuses. Several of the ethnographies that form the basis for the seven case studies conform to this general model. But a report of formal obligations only goes so far in explaining particular patterns of distribution. Altman and Peterson have shown that formal sharing rules accounted for only 50% of the allocation of meat on an eastern Kunwinjku outstation, and came into play mainly in times of shortage. Furthermore, people often quarrelled over distribution.[3]

Obligations have a reciprocal character according to the second approach—each gift or service demands a return.[4] The Berndts write: 'All gifts and services are viewed as reciprocal. This is basic to their economy—and not only to theirs, although they are more direct and explicit about it. Everything must be repaid, in kind or equivalent, within a certain period.'

'Reciprocity' is a concept that owes much to the sociology of Marcel Mauss, who developed a theory of the gift as a mode of exchange, an exchange that involved the obligation to repay. Reciprocity appears in Karl Polanyi's threefold classification of kinds of economic relations, along with redistribution and house-holding; he links these three modes to types of social organisation. Sahlins developed Polanyi's concept of reciprocity, relating each form of reciprocity to a general pattern of social relations. *Generalised reciprocity* refers to 'transactions that are putatively altruistic, transactions on the lines of assistance given and, if possible and necessary, assistance returned'. The mid-point is *balanced reciprocity*, which is 'less personal' and 'more economic' than generalised reciprocity. Examples include marital exchange, pledges of brotherhood, and affirmations of alliances in the form of feasts. *Negative reciprocity* is 'the attempt to get something for nothing with impunity'; it is at the 'impersonal' extreme of the continuum. Generalised reciprocity was characteristic of the closest relationships in 'primitive societies'—those of the household. As one moves through relations of increasing distance—the lineage sector, the village sector, tribal and inter-tribal sectors—so one approaches the pole of negative reciprocity.[5] Tim Ingold has pointed out, however, that balanced reciprocity can occur between strangers in the form of bartering, while negative reciprocity in the form of 'demand sharing' is found (alongside positive reciprocity) in the closest of relationships. We will return to demand sharing shortly.[6]

Eric Smith argues that the advantages of sharing arise from the risk experienced by each producer: the harvest of each producer varies from day to day and the harvest of different producers can differ in the same period. Truly generalised reciprocity—altruistic or indiscriminate sharing—is unstable, and prone to be undermined by freeloaders. The costs of sharing include enforcement costs incurred to reduce cheating.

Peterson addresses the problem of controlling freeloaders in his model of 'demand sharing'. What he calls 'inertial generosity' is the tendency to respond to demands rather than make unsolicited gifts. In a small community, the accumulation of mutual obligations would make it difficult for a person with a surplus to decide who to share it with—should he or she rank debts, meet the largest or oldest debts, or recompense only close kin? Peterson sees demand sharing as a solution to this problem:

> An alternative to this bookkeeping approach is simply to respond to demands as they are made. This has at least four advantages: difficult decisions are avoided; the onus is placed on others; discrepancies in the evaluation of relationships are not laid bare; and an excellent excuse is provided for not meeting some obligations within the context of behaving generously. Further, it fully recognizes the inherent difficulty in delayed reciprocity: time alters the value of objects and the perception of relationships, compounding the difficulties of calculating the correct return.[7]

It also makes it possible to avoid complying with requests. Potential receivers may also hide what they have, to magnify their apparent neediness.

While Peterson does not say how 'demands' are expressed, I take them to be requests in the imperative mode ('Give me some fish!') or tacit requests of the kind reported by Annette Hamilton.[8] Peterson reports that in northeast Arnhem Land spontaneous giving was infrequent outside the camp (or 'household'). The reason is very interesting: giving placed the receiver under an obligation to receive (it was very difficult to refuse) and to make some kind of return. A person might praise another, for their fine dancing perhaps, as a way of demanding something. Men made frequent demands for spears and other items of material culture. A person could evade a request by hiding items that were likely to be asked for, by lying, or by vesting ownership of an item in a close relative. Peterson also reports various means of blocking the too-frequent requests of a persistent bludger.

Bringing these approaches together, I suggest that the constitution of kin relationships entailed a pattern of rights and obligations among close kin, such that a party to a relationship could ask for something and the requestee ought to comply. Degrees of familiarity and constraint entailed by different kin relationships also affected the ability to make demands. However, particular individuals would be disposed to evade or refuse requests as a rule or on some occasions. In any relationship of obligation, a requestee or potential requestee could take steps to avoid complying with a request—by, for example, hiding, lying, making the desired items sacred, or vesting ownership of the items in another relative. But few of the ethnographies on which the case studies draw cover such subtleties; for the most part they record normative statements of obligations among relatives.

Certain kinds of relationships required particular kinds of gifts. Such was the case with the wife's mother–daughter's husband relationship, for example, where the content of requests (or of unsolicited gifts), typically meat, followed from the gift of a daughter as a wife. Ancestral law specified how people should conduct such relationships; it did so in the form of myths that usually recounted the consequences of breaches of obligations to relatives. Again, some individuals were more likely than others to comply.

Consistent with the kin-obligation model, it is clear from Peterson's survey that particular kin relationships channelled requests. In western Cape York Peninsula, he reports, girls were trained to serve older siblings, who could 'ask for anything from younger siblings'.[9] Merlan distinguishes between relationships of familiarity, in which it is possible to make demands (although not all will be satisfied), and those marked by distance or lack of familiarity (at its strongest in avoidance relations). In the latter case, an overriding sense of obligation is grounded in a gift or a promise (or the possibility of promise) of a spouse, along with an expectation of frequent return gifts and of attention. The dimension of distance in relationships should be added, for distance and lack of familiarity inhibited the making of demands. However, restraint marked some close relationships as well.[10]

Other short-term and long-term obligations arose from particular events and circumstances rather than formal, enduring relationships. What Sansom calls a 'signal service' placed the receiver under an enduring, diffuse obligation to the giver in return for some greatly valued help.[11]

Consumption and demand

In a market economy, it is in the interests of producers and middlemen to compete for market share (in order to increase profits) by trying to induce consumers to consume more. In Aboriginal economies, in the absence of a market for ever-new varieties, the overall demand for food was stable although individual demand varied. There was a demand for goods manufactured in other districts that were in short supply in one's own district. Among some men at least there was a demand for more wives. The domain of religious knowledge created a demand for secret information, access to which might be exchanged for subsistence products, wives, equivalent ritual knowledge, or services. (I have already suggested that Sahlins's picture of the Zen road to affluence does not fit Aboriginal economies—see Chapter 1.)

But the applicability of the concept of demand requires some discussion, for it belongs primarily to the analysis of market economies. Economists distinguish *demand*, which expresses the relationship between prices and the quantity of goods and services purchased, from *wants*. The 'quantity demanded' of a good or service is the amount that consumers plan to buy in a given period of time, whereas wants are, in the words of one textbook, 'the unlimited desires or wishes that people have for goods and services'. Demand reflects 'a decision about which wants to satisfy'. (The word 'demand' in the expression 'demand sharing' refers to something different, namely the *action* of asking, requesting, or making one's wants known.) In the absence of markets and price mechanisms, the economic concept of demand requires qualification. I use the term to mean the disposition to acquire a valued item, manifested in attempts to acquire it.[12]

The case studies describe consumption prohibitions and prerogatives. As mentioned earlier, however, some researchers have described food preferences, ranking species according to taste. In a common strong preference, hunters discarded animals lacking sufficient fat—perhaps an indicator of the general health of the animals—and myths recount the conflicts that arise when a hunter keeps all the fat to himself.

Mention should also be made of the commonly reported 'feast-or-famine' attitude to resources. Aboriginal people had the ability to go without food and even water for prolonged periods, but when both did become available they might feast on large quantities. For example, I once observed a party of Yolngu men pluck and eat a very large number of magpie geese after a hunt, before taking the remainder back to their community.[13]

Accumulation

In an economy in which there was no money and most food was consumed soon after its production, what were the opportunities for accumulation? Peterson suggests that demand sharing made accumulation difficult—anyone with a perceived surplus would probably be targeted with requests. In any case, there was little point in accumulating perishable foods; strategies to avoid sharing enhanced short-term consumption rather than accumulation.[14]

The literature points to three kinds of resources that might be accumulated incrementally over the long term: wives, religious knowledge, and sacred objects. Woodburn treats the accumulation of wives as a long-term investment yielding a 'delayed return'. There is some sense in this—a young man made a long-term investment by giving his labour and its products to a potential wife's parents and siblings. This investment yielded not only the wife's productive and reproductive power, but also the potential flow of gifts from daughters' husbands, as well as the daughters' labour and productive power. People were able to accumulate religious knowledge— 'symbolic capital' in Pierre Bourdieu's terms—by passing through successive initiations and gaining senior roles in rituals, and by attending other groups' ceremonies and being granted access to their secret places and objects. A reputation for being highly knowledgeable was an important aspect of age relations.[15]

Kŭnai people

Though idealised and generalised, Howitt's and Bulmer's notes on obligations among various categories of relatives provide some clues about Kŭnai distribution and consumption.[16]

Women distributed vegetable foods and small game within their camp, while meat produced by men had a wider distribution. After cooking an animal whole in the skin, men made cuts along each side of the spinal column, leaving the head on the spine. They then sent the meat 'round the camp first to those who had most right, then to the rest'.[17]

An unmarried man had obligations to distribute food, chiefly to his parents and other close relatives. A married man's primary obligations, on the other hand, were to his wife's parents; in particular he had to give them the portion of meat called *neb-orak* (or *nebrak*)—the head, neck, and upper back according to Howitt, the 'hind cut' according to Bulmer. Howitt remarks that 'a man with several daughters well married found himself provided for'.[18]

Table 11.1 Kŭnai distribution of game according to Howitt

Game	Recipients							
	Wife's parents	Self and wife	Hunter's parents	Helper	Brothers	Sisters	MB and MBW	Other relatives
Not specified	Head, back, shared with other kin	Some, if no other meat	Remainder	Leg, leg and tail, or leg and haunch	Leg			
Wombat	Whole animal, distributed by WF	Entrails; some meat given later by WF						
Emu	Leg	Intestines, liver, gizzard	Body					
Possums	One or more animals	One animal if sufficient	One animal					
Swans	One or more bird		One or more bird					
Goanna		Left leg	Upper half of body		Right hind leg	Lower half of body, tail		FF: foreleg FM: backbone
One eel	Whole fish							
Several eels		One large eel			Large eel	Large eel	Large eel	(MBC, D, DH) Small eel
One koala	Whole animal, or right side and legs	Head, liver, part of head to wife	Left side and legs					Ears to WZ
Two koalas	One animal	Liver	One animal					
Three koalas	Two animals	Liver	One animal					

Howitt describes two ideal distributions of meat within a residence group (Table 11.1); the first assumes that a married couple was camping with both the wife's and husband's parents and no one else, while the second includes a range of other relatives in the group. He gave these as examples only, and I suspect that they derive from hypothetical examples that he elicited, and not observations of actual distribution. I have merged them in the table.

The priority accorded to the wife's parents is striking: if one koala was killed it went to the wife's parents; if two, then one each went to the wife's and husband's parents; if three, then two went to the wife's parents and one to the husband's, the hunter keeping the livers for himself. The hunter's wife looked to her parents for a share if she had none—her husband's prior obligations lay elsewhere. Reciprocally, the wife's mother would give her daughter's husband fish, conveying it through her daughter, or meat if the daughter's husband had none, provided that he had given her meat the day before. The wife's mother would take him to task (again through her daughter) if he did not provide sufficient meat. Children, in Howitt's view, looked primarily to their grandparents for food.

If a man's other relatives (such as his brother, son, mother's brother, and mother's brother's wife) were in the camp, and if a number of prey such as eel were caught, each person would receive one. Once the food was distributed, each recipient would distribute their portion further—the wife's father to his daughter, the wife to her sister, and so on.

Even low-level polygyny may have afforded similar advantages to those found in northeast Arnhem land and elsewhere, for a man with more than one wife increased his chances of bearing daughters, and hence of receiving gifts from daughters' husbands. While the obligation of married sons to provide for their own parents was the lesser one, it did provide some insurance for a couple without daughters.

Consumption prohibitions shaped the distribution of food. Only old men were allowed to eat species related to the *je-ak* or *mŭk kŭnai* totems, such as dingos, pelicans, frogs, and 'robins'. Other restrictions that have been reported related to initiation and marital status:

- uninitiated boys—female animals except wombat, male echidna, sexual organs of any animal, black duck (unless cooked and given by father's brother), grubs from eucalypt trees
- unmarried girls—eaglehawk, hind part of emu
- boys during the seclusion phase of initiation—echidna, emu, eel
- permitted for boys during the seclusion phase of initiation—male possum, koala, kangaroo.

These prohibitions do not seem to have benefitted any particular category of person, such as older men, but perhaps followed from doctrines about the effects of foods on certain bodily conditions.

Pitjantjatjara people and their neighbours

As in other regions, women distributed their products mainly within the camp and among certain close kin—for example, a woman would share food with her mother, her husband's mother, infirm older women, and the woman who had looked after her children while she foraged. Women also provided food to their unmarried male relatives in the bachelors' camp, including brothers, sons, and brother's sons of varying degrees of relatedness, receiving meat in return. The unmarried men gave meat to their families in return for damper of *wangunu* seeds and for other vegetable foods, including fruits collected and prepared by women. Hamilton writes that a woman had strong obligations to feed her mother and children, expressed in explicit norms, but only a tacit requirement to provide food for her husband, although he expected her to do so. Women could withhold food to sanction their husbands, especially for infidelity.[19]

Hunters supported themselves while travelling, but their main obligation, Hamilton reports, was to support others of their residence group. Men distributed large game throughout the residence group, with the hunters themselves taking a poorer cut and being the last to receive a share. Complex rules governed the sharing of meat among the various categories of relative; each animal was divided into a fixed number of named portions and offered to the various kin of the hunter who were present. The hunter never himself cooked or distributed the meat of an animal he had killed.[20]

To give an example, Ngaatjatjarra men cooked and divided a kangaroo into nine portions near the kill site; the spear-man did not cook the animal, unless he was alone—the proper person for this job was one of his 'mother's brothers'. At the camp, the portions were laid out on a bed of mulga boughs or eucalypt leaves. The hunter's wife's father and his brother, and the wife's brothers, had first choice, followed by the hunter's older and younger brothers, and finally the hunter himself. Each recipient further distributed the meat, so that everyone in the residence group received a portion. When a group of men had cooperated in hunting a large animal, the killer was last to receive a share. A typical division was as follows:

- hunter—neck, head, and backbone (cf. Kŭnai)
- hunter's wife—part of hind leg, received from her mother and father
- old men—tail and innards
- children—meat from anyone they could get it from, tail not permitted.

Gould describes how a Ngaatjatjarra man cooked and divided a goanna into two halves and laid it on the ground; the hunter's wife's brother then selected the hindquarters portion, as was his right. As I have said, meat, once divided and distributed, would be distributed by the recipients to a further set of relatives. In Gould's study, between one and six people (mean of 4.7) received kangaroo or euro meat in the first phase of distribution, while between nine and 64 people (mean 42.7) received meat in the second phase.[21]

Women were comparatively advantaged by the rules of distribution of meat in Hamilton's view, as mothers and mothers-in-law more than as wives. The hunter had a primary duty to his wife's parents and brothers but not his own parents. A man made gifts to a second wife he was 'growing up'. In return for meat, a man received vegetable food from his wife's parents. I have been unable to find any reference to consumption restrictions related to initiation and the life-cycle.[22]

Certain consumption restrictions benefited older men: women at Everard Park were not allowed to eat kangaroo tail, while in the Tomkinson Ranges the tail and innards were the prerogative of older men, and forbidden to children.[23]

Yuwaaliyaay people and their neighbours

Unfortunately, Parker has very little to say about the distribution of food. She reports that rules governed the butchering of game and the distribution of portions according to kin relationships, but provides no details. She does note that an infant's mother's mother (*ba:gi*) would inculcate a spirit of generosity in the child with a song:[24]

> When a baby clutches hold of anything as if to give it to some one, the bargie—grandmother—or some elderly woman takes what the baby offers, and makes a muffled

clicking sort of noise with her tongue rolled over against the roof of her mouth, then croons the charm which is to make the child a free giver: so is generosity inculcated in extreme youth. I have often heard the grannies croon over the babies:

Oonahgnai Birrahlee,
Oonahgnoo Birrahlee,
Oonahgnoo Birrahlee,
Oonahmillagnoo Birrahlee,
Guhnnoognoo oonah Birrahlee.

Which translated is:

'Give to me, Baby,
'Give to her, Baby,
'Give to him, Baby,
'Give to one, Baby,
'Give to all, Baby.'

A person was not supposed to eat their *yunbeai* (personal totem), but they could eat their *dhe* (matrilineal totem). Other consumption prohibitions (*wunnarl*) applied to young boys and girls; those applying to a boy were gradually lifted at each successive Bora ceremony that he attended.

Male initiates
- Fish—restriction lifted after the third Bora
- Honey—the restriction lifted after the fourth Bora
- Bustard eggs, kangaroo, echidna—all restrictions lifted after the fifth Bora

Girls
- Fish—restriction applied for four months after a girl became a *wirreebeeun* ('woman girl'), presumably after the onset of menstruation

When the prohibition came off a particular meat, a *wirreenun* (sorcerer–healer) poured melted fat and blood of the animal over the boy or girl, and rubbed it in; the recipient had to express disgust when first chewing a piece of the meat, as with the first emu kill. It is not clear when these restrictions first applied, but, in contrast with Kŭnai prohibitions, they do seem to have benefitted adult men by making more of the prized foods (such as kangaroo meat) available to them. One other rule of consumption was that only the very old and very young were supposed to eat honey.

Reflecting the importance of Emu in the cosmology, people were supposed to cook an emu in a pit; supernatural punishment would follow from cooking the meat on a fire.[25]

Wiil and Minong distribution and consumption

Soon after hunting or gathering food, Nind reports, Minong women ate some themselves and then distributed part of their product to men and children at the camp.[26]

But property rights over some resources modified patterns of distribution. Among Wiil people, the black acacia seeds stored in skin bags and hung from the poles of huts were 'the common property of all the women'—which women, Hassell does not say.

Like people from other regions, Wiil people shared game widely among the people of a residence group, although Minong men reserved part of the kill for their wives, after eating some of it themselves. The owner of a dog was entitled to a larger proportion of the kill. Collie records a telling incident: 'Mokare and Dr Collie met Botup in the bush; he returned to Collie's camp with his wife and two young children, and were joined by Tallyen who contributed a possum bandicoot, kangaroo rat and frogs to "the communal meal".'[27]

Recipients of distributed food included dangerous spirits: people lit a fire for *jannock* (spirits) and left them a small portion of food (such as part of a kangaroo's paw) to appease them.

Some consumption at King George Sound took place soon after the food was garnered: women cooked and ate a portion of roots or other vegetable foods, but kept a portion for the children and men, to be eaten at the camp. The whole party involved in burning off and catching small game ate together. Men also cooked and ate part of their kills before returning to camp. Nind describes the style of consumption: 'They are extremely jealous of their food, concealing and eating it silently and secretly; yet if others are present they usually give a small portion: they tell me that one-half of what they procure they eat and divide with their companions, and the remainder they keep for the night'.[28]

Minong consumption restrictions, as outlined by Nind and Barker, related mainly to fertility and hunting success rather than ritual status. The recorded prohibitions were as follows:
- girls older than 11 or 12—bandicoot meat, as it inhibited fertility
- young men—'black eagle', as it inhibited growth of the beard and hindered success in hunting kangaroo
- reserved for older men—quail (*pourriock, pourrha*).

Kangaroo meat was believed to help Minong women's fertility; however, the converse was the case among Wiil people. Wiil prohibitions included the following:
- pregnant women—kangaroo, fish, and certain other meats
- male initiates during their initiation journey—bandicoot, emu, goanna, emu eggs, wallaby, the tail of 'brush kangaroo'.

Other Wiil consumption prohibitions were age-related:
- young people—dingo and eaglehawk
- all but old men and women—eggs of Gould's Monitor, which were highly prized
- all but older men—certain unspecified meats.

Taken as a whole, these restrictions reserved more highly prized meat for older people.[29] Consumption restrictions also applied to totemic animals in the southwest. Male relatives refrained from eating goanna, kangaroo, or the animal of a totem conferred as a gift (*babbin*) when a person with that totem died. A minor rite, such as smearing the face with charcoal or stirring the fire in which the animal was being cooked, marked the lifting of the prohibition. Another restriction on production mentioned in the literature is that kangaroos were not speared at night for fear of offending spirits of the dead.

Sandbeach people

While direct evidence about the distribution of Sandbeach women's products is unavailable, Thomson's descriptions of ideal kin relations among Umpila people suggests that certain relations were especially important in distribution. The evidence brings out obligations among a wide variety of kin and affines.[30]

Parents provided for their children (although a mother did not give her son food during initiation), and children provided for their aged or widowed parents. A senior brother provided for a junior sister, and the senior of the mother's brother–sister's son pair (mother's older brother or older sister's son) gave to the junior in a quasi parent–child relationship. In particular, an older sister's son gave dugong meat to his mother's younger brother. A younger sister's child provided food for his or her mother's elder brother when the latter became widowed. Brothers were supposed to provide for one another reciprocally.

I described marriage gifts in Chapter 6. A man's obligations towards his future wife's father came into play after formalisation of the betrothal. He also had to feed his prospective mother-in-law, who was his 'outside' father's younger sister (*piima tali*), or there was a danger that she might give her daughter to another man. After the marriage the obligations were as follows:

DH ──────▶ WF   Daughter's husband gave food to wife's father, but wife's father did not give to daughter's husband.

SW ◀═══════ HF   Son's wife gave food to husband's father, and husband's father could give to son's wife, although certain foods (perhaps with sexual connotations) were prohibited.

HM ◀═══════▶ SW   Husband's mother was under a strong obligation to look after and to feed her son's wife, and they might exchange gifts of food.

Thus, women in these relations had reciprocal obligations, but the daughter's husband–wife's father relationship was asymmetrical. A man's obligations to his wife's father increased if the latter was widowed, in which case the son-in-law was obliged to get food and water for him. These obligations seem likely to have been strongest in the early years of marriage, and were practicable only when parents and married children lived in the same camp. The division and distribution of dugong was strongly formalised and controlled. Donald Thomson writes of the obligation of a man to his mother's younger brother in relation to dugong:

> If a man harpoons a dugong his *pola* (FF) takes charge of the quarry and divides it, or his *ŋatjimo* (MF) may do this. If his *pola* or *ŋatjimo* are not in the camp, then his *mukka* [MeB] takes charge, or in *mukka*'s absence *kala* [MyB] does so, the seniority of these kin being in that order. Much restriction and many tabus surround the eating of dugong flesh. To illustrate the attitude towards *kala*, one informant said 'If *kala* sends me away from a dugong that I have killed, to look for fish, I must go without sulking'.[31]

These rules bring out the formal relations of seniority among kin. But a distant 'father's father' ('outside' *puula*) might secretly give dugong meat to his 'son's son' (*puulathu*), who was not normally permitted to eat it until he reached a certain status, when his father, father's brothers, and grandfathers gave him permission.

Consumption rules related to age and initiation status are not very fully recorded for this region, but prohibitions included the following:[32]

- children—dugong meat until 'long after he has been initiated', although a distant father's father might sneak some to a young 'grandson'
- male initiates during the first-stage initiation ceremony—kingfish, goanna (*Varanus* sp.), flying fox, echidna, possum, bandicoot, cuscus, emu, cassowary, species of python, stingaree, turtle, coconuts.

Dietary restrictions also no doubt applied to women at various stages of their reproductive lives.

Ngarinyin people and their neighbours

When out foraging, Love writes, women halted around midday to light a fire, cooked part of their catch, ate some of it perhaps, and then returned to the camp during the afternoon and gave food to their husbands and to other men, including bachelors. Children and other women were presumably also among the recipients.

Men would eat at least part of their kill away from the base camp. They distributed large game according to formal rules (as in other regions), the backbone going to certain relatives, the forelegs to others, and the hind legs to yet others. A Worrorra man was supposed to share food with his wife's parents, his own parents (as among Kŭnai people), and others of the residence group, in that order, and also with his children. After a collective hunt, men distributed meat according to their relative position in the *wurnan* exchange system—the head to the 'top' patri-group, the tail to the 'bottom' one, and the hind legs to both.[33] People particularly valued fat. Men removed a kangaroo's fat (concentrated in the intestines and the base of the tail) and wrapped it around a spear shaft: 'Most of it will be given, as a really worthwhile gift, to a relative who has a special claim on the hunter'.[34] Women removed the fur, to be spun into string for a belt or pubic covering.

As mentioned earlier, fights arose over a refusal to share or perceived neglect. People would hide their good fortune in hunting or fishing in order to avoid the demands of relatives, while others would complain that they had been given a poor cut or insufficient food. Men could restrict distribution by singing and dancing over the meat, especially kangaroo, or by declaring the hunting ground and all the game killed on it *mamaa* (taboo), so reserving the meat for themselves. Love reports that they did this when meat was in short supply. Men imposed short-term prohibitions on women and children if they considered that women were not bringing a sufficient proportion of plant foods to the camp, where men could have a share.[35]

Other consumption restrictions included the following prohibitions:

- boys until initiation and girls until first menses—kangaroo livers, in case they should bleed excessively (boys at initiation), bitter tubers
- pregnant women—kangaroo intestines, for fear of causing difficulties in childbirth; native cat, which caused bad labour pains; echidna, as the fat harmed the newborn child's eyes; crocodile meat, which caused the baby to get sores

- all except mature adults—*gunu* (*Dioscorea elongata*), meat of young wallabies, tail and hindquarter of male 'plains kangaroo' (antilopine wallaroo?).

In this region people avoided eating their totemic animals. One patri-group ate only goannas among the lizards, as their totems included other lizards and skinks. Prohibitions on the consumption of certain birds applied to everyone because of their totemic importance; these birds included the white-breasted sea eagle, the king-fishers, and the moiety totems, such as the nightjars.

Yolngu people

Both Warner and Thomson attest to the fact that a woman distributed the vegetable foods, small game, and shellfish that she gathered to members of her camp—her husband, who had first call, and her children if she had any. A short film shot by Nicolas Peterson, in 1966, shows that women did not share their product with each other during or after gathering in a group; even if they pooled the food for the purpose of transport, they divided it again later according to what they produced. Women would eat shellfish while gathering and before returning to camp. Young bachelors received food from their mothers, sisters, and other female relatives, although not from a sister when she was menstruating.[36] According to Thomson, men cooked and butchered large game on the spot, and divided it equally among themselves. Each took his portion, often wrapped in paperbark, to camp, dividing it in turn according to his kin obligations and subject to various restrictions. In the case of turtles, specific cuts were allocated to the owner of the boat, the harpooner, etc. Warner adds that large game animals were divided between and eaten by 'the whole group', meaning presumably the residence group. Ideally, men divided macropods according to kin obligations in the following way:
- mesenteric fat to hunter's male kin (WB, MF, MB)
- fat from the base of the tail and the lower back (*djimbitj'puy djukurr*) to the hunter's wife
- the head to the hunter
- the back to the hunter, unless there were a lot of people to share with
- the base of the tail and the lower back (*djimbitj*) to anyone except the hunter's sister, unless old men with several children cleared the taboo.

Much of a young man's product went to his potential wife's parents. A young bachelor could supply game to an older married brother, but not to his sister until he was married and had a child.

I have already mentioned the *ad hoc* consumption restrictions made by declaring an item of equipment sacred. Other prohibitions were associated with reproductive status and the life-cycle:
- brothers and certain other relatives of women who were menstruating—all food gathered by the woman
- mothers and sisters of an initiated but unmarried male—all game killed by him (designated *galng'puy*)

- initiated males before the birth of their first child—echidna, emu eggs, snake eggs, goanna eggs, turkey eggs, crayfish, large barramundi, crab (eating such foods would supposedly make the man sick and weak in a fight).

If a person of the last category killed a large game bird he had to leave it for an older man to divide, and was not allowed to eat it. A ceremony removed these restrictions after the man's wife became pregnant with their first child, the sign of his maturity. During the same period the man's female relatives were supposed to carry the bones of his first kills of large macropods, birds, and porcupines, to be buried in a hollow-log coffin after the birth of his first child. Those who had eaten such game had to place gifts into a sand sculpture at the ceremony.[37]

The elaborate mortuary ceremonies in this region included burial of the body or its exposure on a platform, mourning, exhumation and cleaning of the bones, the carrying of the bones by relatives of the dead, re-interrment in a hollow-log coffin left standing in the forest to decay, and purification of close relatives of the dead with water and smoke. All these phases involved elaborate songs, dances, body-painting, and ritual objects that identified a person with totemic ancestors, their eponymous animals and other species, and the places regarded as traces of ancestral activities, substance, and power. The carrying and burial of a man's first kill not only marked his change in status but expressed these totemic relations; the rites treated the animal as if it were a person. They also expressed the link between death (in this case of the animal) and the regeneration of life, a theme common to mortuary ceremonies and revelatory ceremonies.[38]

Other prohibitions applied to participants in ceremonies:
- circumcision initiates—large game, until the long grass appeared in the following wet season
- adepts in Djungguwan and Nga:rra ceremonies—all meat; the application of a body-painting removed the restrictions.

Men imposed *ad hoc* ritual restrictions on the food that been killed or collected using everyday items of technology that had been imbued with ancestral significance. Only senior men of the patri-group or senior male *waku* (sisters' sons) were able to divide game killed with spears 'dedicated' to the patri-group totem, and only initiated men could eat the game made sacred (*dhuyu*) in this way. Men also restricted distribution of game by painting the 'elbow design' (*likanbury minytji*) of the patri-group on a canoe paddle or other object used for production, or by giving it a totemic name. Men sometimes restricted the use of a tobacco pipe in the same way. Game killed through the use of a *dhuyu* object was itself *dhuyu* and 'name-bearing' (*ya:kumirri*), so that consumption was restricted to initiated men of that patri-group. Franca Tamisari's recent research at Milingimbi shows that women also have the power to impose restrictions on foods and objects by invoking ancestral names (what Tamisari refers to as 'cursing').[39]

Thomson records how a young man participating in a Madayin ceremony killed a turtle when he was covered in dust (*ganu*) from the ceremony ground. Older men declared the turtle *ya:kumirri* ('name-bearing') and the uninitiated were only permitted to eat the flesh after a ceremony. Even then they had to make reciprocal gifts. Nicolas Peterson recalls an occasion at Mirrngadja when, after blood had been accidentally shed in a canoe, the men restricted the right to eat game caught using the canoe until it was purified.[40] The implication of these prohibitions on distribution was that male elders had considerable control over most subsistence produce. Older men were also the main beneficiaries of religious dietary prohibitions, many of which they could impose or remove at will. Older women, too, could impose restrictions by declaiming sacred names. The people most disadvantaged by prohibitions were women, youths, unmarried men, and married men without children; those least disadvantaged were children and older men. Women during their reproductive lives and adult men before and in the early years of marriage bore the brunt of consumption restrictions, perhaps to balance their control over their own production and consumption.[41]

Comparisons and conclusions

Patterns of distribution, as well as the specific obligations, appear to have been rather similar across the seven regions. In all cases, a woman's product had a narrower distribution than a man's—namely to her camp and (recorded in some cases) certain other relatives, including unmarried sons and brothers. In all cases, men distributed large game throughout the residence group, the distribution being structured in part according to specific obligations. In all cases, a man provided meat to his (potential or actual) wife's parents, and in most cases to the wife's brother. It is widely reported that men and women consumed part of their yield before returning to the home base, at 'dinner camps'. The formal butchering of large game was also common.

The incompleteness of the records make it difficult to draw contrasts, but certain idiosyncrasies are apparent. Kŭnai and Worrorra men had obligations to provide meat to their parents and their wife's kin. Men among Yuwaaliyaay and Pitjantjatjara people and their neighbours provided food to a prospective wife, and 'grew her up'. Obligations on the part of a man to his mother's brother appear only in two cases (Kŭnai and Yolngu); among Sandbeach people it was the senior of a MB–ZS pair who did the giving (including senior sister's son to junior mother's brother). Kŭnai and Pitjantjatjara husbands gave food to their wives indirectly, through a parent. Since women distributed their yield mainly within the hearth group, the size and structure of hearth groups, as well as relations between them, had an impact on patterns of distribution. Again, it was polygyny that made the most difference—polygynous camps had the advantage of spreading risk among producers, and polygynous men had an advantage in their access to women's product.

Consumption prohibitions were based on age, reproductive status, life-cycle (especially in relation to initiation), and ritual status (especially for initiates and adepts during a ceremony). The justification of many restrictions was that eating the food in question would supposedly have ill effects on someone in a particular state, such as pregnancy or impending circumcision. Young men commonly had limited access to meat during initiation. Prohibitions affected consumption not only by the person in a given state or of a certain status, but by potential recipients of that person's production. In some regions, consumption restrictions benefitted older people, who had highly valued foods reserved for them—for example, quail (Minong), dugong (Sandbeach) and kangaroo tail (Yuwaaliyaay). And in at least some regions older men could use their religious authority to impose restrictions for their own benefit. Men divided the most valued game, such as turtle and dugong, with great formality; and it is worth noting that valued cuts (such as kangaroo tail), which combined flesh and fat, appeared as totemic designs (in Yolngu rituals, for example).[42] Patterns of primary distribution, then, were rather similar in the seven regions. Some forms of exchange varied more radically, as we shall see in the next chapter.

Further reading

For examples of explanations of distribution in terms of kin-based roles and obligations, see W. Lloyd Warner's *A Black Civilization* (1937; 1958) and Donald Thomson's *Kinship Behaviour in North Queensland* (1972). Jon Altman and Nicolas Peterson show the limitations of that approach in their 'Rights to game and rights to cash among contemporary Australian hunter gatherers' (1988).

On the key concepts of reciprocity see Karl Polanyi's *The Great Transformation* (1944) and Marshall Sahlins's 'On the sociology of primitive exchange', reprinted in his book *Stone Age Economics* (1972).

Nicolas Peterson introduced the very productive concept of 'demand sharing' in 'Demand sharing: Reciprocity and the pressure for generosity among foragers' (1993). This article was a response to analyses in terms of risk, such as Eric Smith's 'Risk and uncertainty in the 'original affluent society'' (1988).

Notes

1   On the definitions of 'circulation', 'distribution', 'exchange' and 'consumption' see Altman (1987: 175) and Narotzky (1997: 42, 71, 104–5).

2   The following quotation on kinship obligations is from R. M. and C. H. Berndt (1981: 122). See also Elkin (1954: 46).

3   See Altman and Peterson (1988) on the salience of sharing rules.

4   See Gregory (1994: 920–3), Polanyi (1944: 48), and Sahlins (1972: 193–5) on reciprocity; the quotation in the next sentence is from R. M. and C. H. Berndt (1981: 122).

5   The quotations in this paragraph are from Sahlins (1972: 193–5).

6   On reciprocity and distance see Ingold (1986) and Gregory (1994: 924).

7   On risk-reduction models of sharing see E. Smith (1988). See Peterson (1993) on demand sharing; the quotation is from Peterson (1993: 864).

8   On tacit demands among Western Desert women see Hamilton (1980: 12).

9   See Peterson (1993: 863), who cites Diane Smith (Von Sturmer 1980) on the obligations of younger siblings.

10   On kinship distance see Merlan (1997: 113–14).

11   On 'signal services' see Sansom (1988: 168).

12   The quotations are from McTaggart, Findlay, and Parkin (1992: 66–7). See also Samuelson (1970: 61) on demand. Narotzky (1997: 112) prefers to reserve the concept of demand for commodities acquired in a market.

13   See Rudder (1977) on Yolngu food preferences, and Oliver (1989: 161) on the feast-or-famine attitude.

14   On accumulation in Aboriginal economies see Sansom (1988) and Peterson (1993: 867–8).

15   See Bern (1979) and Morton (1997) on the accumulation of religious knowledge and sacred objects, and Woodburn (1988) on delayed return. On symbolic capital see Bourdieu (1990).

16   On Kũnai distribution and consumption see Howitt (1880: 207, 261, 263, 295) and Bulmer (1994: 55–6; Papers, letter to Howitt, MV B1 F4 xm98 undated). I am grateful to Coral Dow for clarifying several points.

17   The quotation is from Bulmer (1994: 55).

18 See Howitt (1880: 207, 261–3).

19 See Gould (1967: 55; 1969b: 16–17), Hamilton (1980: 12), Myers (1986: 75–6), and Tonkinson (1991: 53) on distribution in the Western Desert.

20 See Hamilton (1980: 10) on meat distribution. Myers (1986: 75) points out that since meat went bad quickly, it was in any case uneconomical for a hunter to keep a lot of meat for himself—wide distribution, on the other hand, led to future returns in kind.

21 On Ngaatjatjarra meat distribution see Gould (1967).

22 On marriage gifts see R. M. and C. H. Berndt (1945: 54), Elkin (1938–40: 345), Gould (1969b: 16–17, 19; 1980: 86), Hamilton (1980: 13), and Tonkinson (1991: 53). The Berndts include the wife's brother as a recipient of gifts at Ooldea.

23 See Brokensha (1975: 29) and Hamilton (1980) on consumption restrictions.

24 On Yuwaaliyaay distribution and consumption see Parker (1905: 23–4, 52, 81, 117). The quotation is from Parker (1905: 52).

25 On the removal of prohibitions see Parker (1905: 23–4, 81). See Blows (1975) on restrictions on cooking emu.

26 See Bates (1985: 198–9), Hassell (1936: 681, 688, 690, 702), and Nind (1831: 29, 36–7) on Wiil and Minong distribution and consumption.

27 The quotation is from Collie (1979 [1834] cited in Green 1989: 46).

28 The quotation is from Nind (1831: 37).

29 On Wiil and Minong initiation see Bates (1985: 151–8) and Hassell (1936: 685–6).

30 On Sandbeach distribution and consumption see Chase (1980b: 196), Thomson (1972: 11–13, Papers, MV File 213 undated).

31 The quotation is from Thomson (1972: 12).

32 On Sandbeach consumption restrictions see Laade (1964) and Thomson (1933: 475); the following quotation is from Thomson (1933: 475).

33 On distribution and consumption among Ngarinyin people and their neighbours see Blundell (1975 vol. 2: 472, 485, 487, 518), Blundell and Layton (1978) (on distribution after collective hunts), Crawford (1982: 6), Love (1936: 73, 83, 86–7), Lucich (1968: 196), and Redmond (2001b).

34 The quotation is from Love (1936: 83).

35 On the imposition of restrictions see Crawford (1982: 6, 45) and Love (1936: 86–7).

36 On Yolngu distribution and consumption see Peterson (1967), Thomson (1949: 21, 25–6; Papers, MV File 33 n.d.), and Warner (1937: 66, 68, 140, 283, 287).

37 See Warner (1937: 130, 287) on consumption restrictions in ceremonies. Altman records an equivalent eastern Kunwinjku ceremony (1982: 313).

38 On the symbolism of death and the regeneration of life see Clunies Ross and Hiatt (1977) on north-central Arnhem Land, and see Bloch and Parry (1982) for comparative studies. On Yolngu mortuary rites see Morphy (1984).

39 See Tamisari (1995) on Yolngu women's invocation of ancestral names.

40 On *ad hoc* prohibitions I drew on Thomson (1949: 42) and Nicholas Peterson (pers. com.).

41 Altman (1987: 175–80) found that about 17% of the food men produced (a significant proportion in some months) was covered by taboos, to be consumed only by children and initiated men.

42 See Groger-Wurm (1973: 59) for an example of Yolngu totemic designs.

12

Exchange and Trade

Introduction

We move now from distribution and consumption to exchange and to what has been referred to as 'trade'. Again, the institutional fields outlined in Part II come together in the ways in which Aboriginal people defined valued items and organised networks of exchange. I shall draw on the writings of Chris Gregory, Annette Weiner, and Maurice Godelier for key concepts in the analysis of exchange. The concept of 'inalienable possessions' is of particular relevance. It relates to the 'sacred' character of some exchange items, which enhanced their value, and the immunity of some kinds of 'possessions', notably the most sacred objects, from exchange. The concept of inalienable gifts has been applied to items that, while passed from hand to hand as gifts, at the same time maintained their connection to the giver.

Another important concept is Gregory's 'gift economy', an ideal type that draws on the work of Marcel Mauss. Marilyn Strathern notes that Mauss had in mind a contrast between economies based on gift exchange and economies based on the principles of utilitarianism ('natural economies'). In Gregory's work, however, 'gifts' contrast with 'commodities'. In the gift economy, gifts are 'inalienable', meaning that they remain attached to the donor and so create a bond between donor and recipient. Commodities in a market economy, on the other hand, are 'alienable', and a commodity transaction does not create an enduring bond.[1]

Annette Weiner contrasts inalienable possessions with commodities. Inalienable possessions, 'imbued with the intrinsic and ineffable identities of their owners', are not easy to give away, and include rights in land, material objects, and religious knowledge. Control over the meaning and inheritance of inalienable possessions accords authority to their owners, and is the seed of differences between groups— they represent enduring social identities. Weiner intended her analysis to be a corrective to the view of Mauss and Malinowski that reciprocity, with its egalitarian implications, underlies exchange.[2]

For Godelier, society is constituted and sustained by the interdependence of the alienable and the inalienable. The social sphere rests on the combination of 'contractual exchange' and 'non-contractual transmission', which are equally necessary. No society or identity, he writes, 'can survive over time or provide a foundation for the individuals or groups that make up a society if there are no fixed points, realities that are exempted (provisionally but lastingly) from the exchange of gifts or from trade'.[3] The realm of the 'sacred' provides fixed points in a social order, to which inalienable possessions are connected, and it is also a source of political power. In Godelier's scheme, 'exchange valuables' are at once inalienable and alienable, caught between the inalienability of sacred objects and the alienability of commodities. The paradigmatic inalienable gifts are humans (as in sister exchange) and gifts that substitute for sacred objects.[4]

In spite of criticisms of both the gift/commodity dichotomy and the analysis of inalienable possessions, the concepts remain useful heuristically. Particularly helpful to this study is the movement through these works from the relatively undifferentiated gift economy in Gregory's work (and his sources) to the more complex mix of inalienable possessions, inalienable gifts, and alienable gifts in Godelier's book. Both Weiner and Godelier point to the heterogeneity of forms of exchange within gift economies, explore the sacred character of inalienable possessions, and draw links between the domain of inalienable possessions and authority.

There are many resonances with Australia. Aboriginal economies wove together inalienable possessions (such as land) connected with totemic ancestors, inalienable gifts, including sacred things as well as spouses, and alienable gifts, especially food, raw materials, and equipment. The ancestral domain provided (in Godelier's terms) relatively 'fixed points' on which the social order depended. The control of access to religious/magical knowledge and experience, itself one side of an exchange transaction, formed an important basis of authority.

Certain kinds of inalienable possessions, particularly land and waters and sacred objects, had intrinsic connections with totemic ancestors. They were not usually given, but kept and inherited. Some kinds of exchange items, including sacred objects, ceremonies, and parts of ceremonies, formed gifts whose value derived from their connections with inalienable objects and places and totemic ancestors. These exchange items had the character of inalienable gifts, for they maintained their connections to the giver and created new relationships (or renewed existing ones) through the giving. Other items used in exchange transactions, such as meat and yams, were not inalienable gifts unless deliberately imbued with ancestral significance through ritual action. Nevertheless, the donor may well have had a claim on the recipient by virtue of the gift.

Women and girls given in marriage had the quality of inalienable gifts, in that their relatives transferred their productive and reproductive powers to husbands (and, in some cases, the husband's kin as well), but women retained their inherited identity as well as their kin connections with the givers. Thus, a marriage created new relations between affines, or rather it converted existing kin relations into affinal ones.

Categories of goods and services

I have divided valued items into eight categories: provisioning, durable objects, services, compensation, spouses, rights of access to country and its resources, magical objects, religious knowledge and experience, ceremonies, and sacred objects. Items in each of these categories had their own distinctive properties in exchange.

People gave and exchanged food, water, and fuel, which would be more or less immediately consumed. Fuel had to be collected and supplied at least daily. With limited ability to store them, people consumed most foods quickly. In the relations and transactions of generalised reciprocity (demand sharing and kin obligations) people expected regular giving, for enduring exchange relations involving consumables required a continual series of gifts. While gifts of food were not inalienable, transactions involving food and other provisions were not the closed and often anonymous transactions of the market. People invested in the productivity of others through their own generosity, and expected recipients to be generous in return. Indeed, continuing relatedness required constant affirmation through giving.

Gifts of durable objects, whether body ornaments or implements such as spears or axe-heads, had the potential to form sequential relations by being passed from hand to hand in a series of transactions through time and social space. The continual renewal of such a series between individuals, groups, and localities created what people of at least some regions conceived of as 'paths' or 'roads' of exchange, paths shaped by marriage and kin networks.

Longer-distance 'trade' occurred both through barter and through the exchange of gifts following a journey—either solely for the purpose of exchange or to attend a ceremony at which people exchanged goods. It seems likely that a greater degree of secrecy surrounded the acquisition of magical objects and substances intended for aggressive use than the acquisition of more benign objects.

As an object of exchange, a 'service' consisted of the performance of an action for the benefit of a person or group. I include under this category such actions as the performance of a ritual, the circumcision of an initiate, giving support in a fight, and assisting an injured person. The first two required customary recompense, usually food, while the last two created a more diffuse obligation. The effects of a service on a relationship could be enduring, depending on the perceived value of the action.[5]

An exchange for compensation consisted of the transfer of goods in return for forgiveness, averting the exchange of one harmful act for another—'payback' in Aboriginal English. If all went well, the transfer of a benefit persuaded the aggrieved to refrain from taking revenge. The most common occasions for compensation in the ethnographies were wrongful marriage, injury, and homicide.

Metaphorically, Yolngu affines 'ate' each other, but persons as objects of exchange were, of course, more durable than food. People did not yield exclusive possession of the whole person in exchange for goods, but rather yielded access to, and a degree of control over, the person's productive and reproductive capacities. These capacities were relatively enduring, with productive capacity outlasting reproductive power in the case of women.

In most of the regions, the gift of access to a girl or woman as a wife required, in return, the long-term supply of provisions, especially meat. Regardless of the personal aspects of the relationship, the husband gained in return an enduring relationship, and in regions with patrifilial totemic groups the children of the marriage took his identity. The value of both sons and daughters lay in their economic productivity, while sons (it was to be hoped) also lent political support and daughters also attracted gifts from potential and actual husbands. In some regions, husbands had the power (and were willing) to grant other men temporary sexual access to their wives. Kŭnai couples sometimes swapped spouses in a mutual exchange.

The gift of access to a sister, daughter, or niece as a wife bore some similarity to the gift of an inalienable object, as we have seen. After the bestowal, the kin relationship between the donor (for example, the wife's mother) and the person bestowed endured, and the bestowal created a new relationship, or transformed an existing one, between the spouses and between the spouses' relatives.

As with spouses, it was *access* to land, waters, and their resources rather than exclusive possession that was given and exchanged. In probably all of the seven regions, people conceived of land and waters and their resources as the gifts of totemic ancestors. Primary possession and identity passed through inheritance from generation to generation; it passed from father to child in several of the case studies, and was based on birth, conception, and other links in other cases. Some evidence shows that a holder of country and ancestral sites passed on responsibility to descendants as a gift or grant.

Generally speaking, it seems that people living on adjacent countries had access to each other's land and waters. This was, therefore, an indirect form of exchange, but it was not a matter of reciprocal exchange between groups as such. Instead, people of an owning group granted access to individuals by virtue of their relationships to the group and its country. The groups to which those individuals belonged granted access to other individuals in turn, according to their relationships to the group. In effect, the country-groups of a region agreed that each would grant access to a limited range of people from other groups for their mutual benefit. We found in Chapter 9 that there were varying degrees of exclusivity of access in the seven regions.

The exchange network provided means for enhancing personal powers—sexual, productive, and aggressive. These usually took the form of magical packages, often consisting of the flesh and fat of the dead (at least notionally), other magical items, such as stones, or participation in ancestral rituals.

The many distinct aspects of ancestral things entered exchange networks in a variety of ways: one group could transfer rights to perform ceremonies to another group; the right to perform a ceremony, use a design, or make an object could be given as a permanent gift; a person could give an object to another person without granting the right to make it; men could grant access to ancestral knowledge—to see a design or object, participate in a ceremony, or hear stories and exegeses. (The gift of an object such as feathered string did not of itself confer a right to make it.) The temporary handing on of paraphernalia linked to a ceremony conferred the power to organise a performance, which would be handed on in turn to others.[6]

In some societies, such as Kŭnai and Ngarinyin and their neighbours, individuals 'found' and owned songs, and had the right to give them to other people. In others, such as Yolngu, groups owned ceremonies or aspects of them, even those 'found' in dreams, as common property and as part of their ancestral heritage. If the giver of a song, ceremony, or design did not relinquish ownership, the gift created an enduring relationship between donor and recipient, who became co-owners. The similarity between this and the gift of a wife comes from their mutual connections to kinship. Common possession of a ceremony or sacred object, a manifestation of a totemic ancestor, implied common totemic ancestry. Such a relationship could pre-exist the gift or be 'found' by inferring a relationship of identity between two groups' totemic ancestors.

It goes without saying that valued items of one kind could be exchanged for those of another, although not everything could be exchanged for everything else. People also exchanged items of the same general kind: food, spouses, durable goods, and so on. In the conclusions to the chapter I will draw out some general patterns in the exchange of one kind of item for another, linking these to differences in social position and movement through the life-cycle.

Trade

Drawing together a wide range of ethnographic materials, F. D. McCarthy wrote the pioneering study of what has been referred to as 'trade' in Aboriginal Australia. 'Trade' linked production within regional systems of specialisation. But the term confuses three rather different phenomena: the diffusion of durable goods across long distances through hand-to-hand transfers within the normal course of day-to-day interaction, exchanges between exchange partners, and the exchange of goods between people of different regions who came together for that purpose, perhaps bartering goods. Similarly, by trade 'routes' McCarthy refers to two rather different processes. In one, goods passed hand to hand, and in time diffused across wide distances. In the other, people travelled along well-established paths beyond the country in which they carried out their everyday activities, in order to acquire or exchange goods such as native tobacco (*pituri*).[7]

Johannes Falkenberg's description of the *kulu* exchanges of Murinh-patha people brings out the fact that exchange was not simply about giving people access to items for consumption—it also maintained social relations. Exchange partners in the early 1950s handed on collections of valued items from one to the next in the series; at least one collection passed through more than 100 hands.[8]

The very extensive network associated with *pituri*, linking the Gulf of Carpentaria to western Victoria, involved both hand-to-hand transactions and travel. Dieri men made annual expeditions to gather *pituri* hundreds of kilometres away from their homelands, expeditions made possible by links through ancestral journeys and shared ceremonies. Some groups had a monopoly on the distribution and ownership of secret preparation techniques. Participants in the *pituri* exchange network met at 'markets' to barter, exchanging such items as red ochre, axe-heads, boomerangs, and softwood for shields and grindstones as well as *pituri* (which had great exchange value because of its addictive properties). Pearl-shell from the west Kimberley found its way across most of the western two-thirds of the continent—as far as Yalata in South Australia.[9]

McCarthy and his sources describe the exchange of goods during major ceremonies, in conjunction with the exploitation of concentrated food resources, for which people travelled long distances. Special exchange ceremonies, such as Morning Star in northeast Arnhem Land, also provided occasions for the exchange of goods.[10] At what Howitt described as 'trade centres', people from several regions met regularly. Sites for the manufacture of highly desired and scarce goods constituted another kind of node in exchange networks. Typical of these were quarries where men extracted stone and made stone tools (Plate 12.1). As we shall see, in some regions two people established a special relationship as exchange partners.[11]

Let us now turn to the information on exchange in the ethnography of the seven regions.

Kŭnai people

The main recorded exchanges in Gippsland included provisioning in exchange for marriage rights and as payments for ritual services. Marriage involved exchanges, especially between the husband and his wife's parents, as we have seen. It is not clear whether Kŭnai people practised long-term bestowal involving gifts, but a man certainly hunted for his wife's parents after marriage as a primary obligation. Sister exchange comprised the exchange of like for like.

In an exchange of durable objects for services, young lovers gave singers of love-magic songs presents of weapons, skin rugs, and other items. Presumably Jerra-eil initiation performances depended on women's production to support the male ritual specialists, and the product of young men's hunting may have gone to the secret men's camp, for animals prohibited to initiates were reserved for older men.[12]

Networks of exchange probably extended across the region, allowing goods from one area to reach other areas; one known example is the use on the coast of stone from hinterland quarries. As Isabel McBryde has shown, Kŭnai people did not participate in the extensive networks facilitating exchange of greenstone quarried in central Victoria among speakers of several different languages to the west of Kŭnai country. The difficult terrain, as well as hostility between Kŭnai people and people to the west and north, restricted interaction. Kŭnai people interacted most with the peoples to the east and northeast.[13]

Pitjantjatjara people and their neighbours

According to Tonkinson, gift exchange in the Western Desert took place in three main contexts: as a part of obligations between kin and affines; when small residence groups met; and at large-scale meetings for rituals. The Berndts mention a fourth context at Ooldea, namely the differential distribution of skills. Among specialised services were those of healers, paid for with food, tobacco, or artefacts. Performers of mortuary rites received payment in the form of spears, spear-throwers, hair-bands, pearl-shell, and other objects.[14]

Marriage was a kind of exchange. In the normal process, a man arranged a bestowal as compensation for the injury of circumcision and in return for gifts following the bestowal. In a secondary mode, a suitor solicited a bestowal through gifts of meat and other goods. In at least some parts of the Western Desert, men could arrange reciprocal exchanges of their sisters or daughters (see Chapter 6).

While the makers of most objects manufactured them for their own use, some particularly skilled people at Ooldea spent much of their time making artefacts to be exchanged by barter. Among scarce and valued objects that travelled over long distances, hand to hand, were red ochre, white clay, and stones for tool-making. Pearl-shell, used in ceremonies and love magic, came into the region from the north-west; native tobacco moved from north to south; and wombat fur, used to make string, moved into the region from the south, in return for ochre. Tindale writes of the exchange by Pitjantjatjara people of pearl-shell, which they obtained from the northwest, for manganese-dioxide pigment, which came from the southeast.

Pintubi people expected exchange relations to be reciprocal (*ngaparrku*) or 'level', whether they involved marriage, revenge, or material items. Unfulfilled expectations led to conflict. At rituals, men exchanged sacred objects—the gift of one would be reciprocated later by a return gift. What counted as reciprocation, however, depended on status: less would be expected from a junior than a senior person, and initiation transformed that status. A young man gave gifts of spears and hair-string to the man who circumcised him, and then the circumciser's marriage obligations to the young man took effect and he would bestow a wife on the young man. Dussart records women's exchanges of *yawulyu* ceremonies among Warlpiri people to the north, and exchanges of designs between men and women, a practice not recorded by Munn in mid-century.[15]

Certain objects had a particularly high value, reflected in exchange. The Berndts report that specimens of pearl-shell were rare in the Western Desert, 'and always cost a bundle of good spears, a hair belt or other objects'. Some men kept such objects, and handed them on to a son or grandson.[16]

Yuwaaliyaay people and their neighbours

Marriage was the main context for Yuwaaliyaay exchange. Reciprocal exchanges connected the totemic matri-categories, each of which 'exchanged' spouses with several others. Like Kŭnai men, Yuwaalaraay men (close neighbours of Yuwaaliyaay) sometimes exchanged sisters in marriage. Wrong marriages or wife 'stealing' could be compensated for with a marriage exchange. All these were exchanges of like for like, but marriage also involved the exchange of different kinds of valued items—for example, a bestowal in return for services to the mother and gifts from a daughter's potential husband. But, as I noted in Chapter 6, Parker observed that a man could give few gifts yet still get a wife.

Male initiation also involved exchange relations—between initiators and initiates, men and women. As part of their role, young men hunted and gathered foods to support those most busily engaged in preparing the Bora initiation ritual and to support those who performed in it. A few days after the end of a Bora ceremony, men collected yams, honey, fruit, and other foods as gifts for women. These gifts were supposedly left by the uninitiated men's spirit-wives (referred to by women as *kumbuy*, 'sisters-in-law'), who seemed to bark like dogs (or rather, in precolonial times, howl like dingoes). Parker describes the gifts of food as compensation to the women for the temporary loss of their male relatives. This interpretation contrasts with the more recent anthropological view that men exploited women's labour in putting on the ceremonies. (See later in this chapter on exchange and exploitation.)[17]

Parker briefly describes *boodther* (giving) meetings, in which each person gave or received presents, sang and danced. She remarks: 'A person who went to a boodther without a goolay [netbag, hammock] full of presents would be thought a very poor thing indeed'.[18] Parker does not say whether or not people of distant communities met; nevertheless, Yuwaaliyaay people did exchange goods over an extensive region. Axe-heads of dark-green stone moved into the area from outside. Both grass-tree gum, which came from the Narrabri mountains to the south, and the flat, light shields that came from the north were exchanged for boomerangs of *gidya* wood.

Wiil and Minong people

In Minong communities, the owner of a dingo would lend it out to another person for hunting, in return for a share of the kill.[19] We have seen that a prospective husband made gifts to his young prospective wife and her parents to 'grow her up'. In another form of exchange related to marriage, a man would compensate the husband of a woman with whom he eloped, following her pregnancy.

Gifts could be given as compensation for an injury. Barker recorded 'peace-offerings' on three occasions. Wiil people held a dance and a kangaroo feast for King George Sound groups after two weeks of conflict. On another occasion, two men of King George Sound were to undergo a spearing ordeal after killing a Wiil man, then make offerings of spears, skins, and other goods. On a third occasion, a man planned to make a gift of spears, skins, and knives to two men as reparation for an attack.

During exchange 'meetings', Wiil people obtained unburnt ochre (*wilgie*) from further inland and honey from Minong people on the coast. In return, they traded spear shafts (from the mulga country), stone flakes, throwing sticks, and various foods. Hassell comments that items 'were often traded for hundreds of miles'.[20]

As we saw in Chapter 8, a boy's initiation began with a sexual exchange ceremony. The end of his initiation journey provided an occasion for large-scale gift-giving; the boy's kin payed his guardians, who had accompanied the initiate on his return journey to his own people, and the guardians gave gifts in return. According to Bates, in the Vasse (or Bunbury) district, at the end of the ceremony in which the initiate was formally received, the *babbingur* (guardians) placed their gifts on a kangaroo rug near the boy, each local group making its own heap. The gifts included war spears, hunting and fishing spears, clubs, boomerangs, human hair, kangaroo-skin cloaks, axes, and other products specific to each region. The boy's people made return gifts of pearl-shell, ochre, spear-throwers, and shields. Some of these had been gained through barter from further north. Donors placed the gifts in separate bundles, and they also supplied food, such as fish, for the guardians. Having set some aside for himself, his brothers, and his son, the boy's father distributed the gifts from the guardians, calling up the senior person of each country (Bates's 'district group') among the boy's close relations to choose for themselves. The guardians shared their gifts among themselves in a similar way.

Sandbeach people

We have seen that a person was supposed to exchange gifts with the one who had avulsed his (or her?) incisor before speaking to them again. Gift exchange also had a central place in potential and actual affinal relationships. Bestowal and marriage involved obligations of gift exchange and service, in particular from the prospective son-in-law to his potential affines, especially the wife's father and mother. In the Sandbeach region, the husband's mother was expected to look after and feed her son's wife, and they might exchange gifts of food. Also, Thomson reports that a man's 'older brother' (*yapu*) would 'lend' him his wife when the younger man visited visited him alone.[21]

Sandbeach exchanges attest to a degree of regional specialisation in relation to raw materials and material culture. Men exchanged certain items (such as bailer shells, bailer-shell blanks for woomera weights, and stingray-barbed spears) with their exchange partners inland. Kuuku Ayapathu people of the hinterland supplied magical charms for dugong hunting, red ochre, flat grindstones, and reed spears to coastal Ayapathu people of the Stewart River (referred to by Thomson as 'Yintjingga tribe'), who were close southern neighbours of nothern Sandbeach groups. In return, they obtained bailer shells to be used as water containers and for the manufacture of spear-thrower handles, stingray spines for fighting spears, and mother-of-pearl pendants. According to Sandbeach traditions, Torres Strait Islanders came south down the coast in canoes to get stone (for axes and magic) and *orla* gum, in return for shell called *pitiwiti*. Exchange by barter followed initial fights.[22]

Kuuku Ya'u people valued certain items of technology very highly; these included a spear with some 35 stingray barbs. Thomson tried to induce the possessor of such a spear to part with it for a great quantity of tobacco, but he had no success.[23]

Ngarinyin people and their neighbours

As we saw in Chapter 6, among Ngarinyin people and their neighbours a man made gifts of food, implements, and apparel to his potential wife's father. He gave meat and other gifts to his wife's mother, in return for hair string. Certain exchanges took place at initiation—for example, a youth was supposed to kill a kangaroo at the end of the initiation ceremony to provide meat to the older men. Love vividly describes the pride of a young man who succeeded in killing a kangaroo and was praised by the older men who ate the meat. During mortuary ceremonies, visitors made gifts to the dead (such as spears, honey, and meat), later distributed to relatives of the dead. Brothers of the deceased person gave food to those who had handled the bones.[24]

Male visitors to *wanjina* painting sites would brings gifts of food, native tobacco (which might be burned for the spirits), and other goods for the *wanjina* (ancestors), assuring them that they had obeyed ancestral law. People would leave fish for the *wanjina* who created the stone fish-trap.

The *wurnan* system of exchange of Ngarinyin people and their neighbours is of particular interest because of its formal integration across the region, and its relationship to marriage. People represented *wurnan* as a system of 'paths' of exchange homologous with marriage relations, linking individuals and patri-groups and connecting adjacent regions. The goods exchanged included foods such as meat and honey, ochres, stone spear-points wrapped in paperbark, bamboo spears, songs, and sacred objects. We saw in the last chapter that after a collective hunt men distributed meat according to their relative position in the *wurnan* system. People sometimes imbued exchange goods with magical properties, such as a spear point for use in a revenge killing, or tobacco (after colonisation) to attract the recipient to the donor sexually.

Along the *wurnan* 'paths' went sacred objects, food, and goods, among them gifts sent back to initiates' communities by their hosts from distant communities, as compensation for the 'loss' of their children. Initiation ceremonies themselves provided occasions for exchanges: not only did hosts make gifts of durable objects to visiting performers, but visitors brought goods such as ochres with them to exchange for other goods. Visitors would perform a ceremony for a host community in return for gifts, and recognised ceremony grounds provided sites for exchanges. Some grounds formed major nodes in the network, points where the paths of different kinds of goods intersected.

A person received goods of a certain kind (such as pearl-shell) from an exchange partner in a particular direction, and returned goods of a different variety (such as red ochre). Sacred objects moved from north to south, and from east to west; quartz spearheads moved into Mirriwung country to the east. Exchange in *wurnan* was delayed: etiquette required that a recipient wait before requesting a return gift, but not for too long, for the person came under pressure from others to share what he or she would receive in turn.

As Tony Redmond describes it, *wurnan* ordered patri-groups into a sequence or ranking from 'top' to 'bottom' groups, each under the control of a senior man of a particular patri-group and country. The ranking (by age) of siblings also structured the receipt of gifts, an older sibling taking precedence over a younger one. To violate the patri-group rank order was to invite trouble, but the sanction of expulsion enforced conformity with the system. Conversely, a man with a grudge could threaten to close his section of the exchange network, bringing all exchanges to a halt. Nevertheless, with the permission of other partners, individuals could bypass them in order to carry out a 'private' exchange (for example, of ochre for meat).

The everyday distribution of food, and of gifts between close relatives, was also thought of as part of *wurnan*, but my impression is that senior patri-group members primarily controlled the exchange of items with religious significance, including ochres and sacred objects. Men of the same patri-moiety in 'brother' patri-groups formed ritual partnerships when performing ceremonies associated with a particular ground. They 'held' the sacred objects and country, and stored ritual objects at the ground before handing them on to exchange partners in neighbouring residence groups.

Wurnan formed part of a more extensive exchange network that spanned from the northwest Kimberley east to Port Keats (and the Murinh-patha *kulu* exchange), southeast towards the desert region, and southwest to the Dampier Peninsula and along the coast.[25]

Ngarinyin people and their neighbours exchanged ceremonies as well as sacred objects. At the time of the Frobenius expedition in 1938, Ngarinyin people were introducing a ceremony called Kuranggarra to Wunambal people. (Kuranggara may have derived from a segment of the Gunapipi ceremony of Arnhem Land). It was said to have replaced an earlier ceremony; men exchanged sacred boards in that earlier ceremony, following their relationships in the *wurnan* exchange network. But other Ngarinyin people and neighbours exchanged other ceremonies as well, and men admitted men of other languages and groups to their secret ceremonies and taught them songs, in exchange, perhaps, for a gift of kangaroo. Men believed that they received 'power' from the sacred objects.[26]

Yolngu people, considered next, had a similar but less formalised exchange network.

Yolngu people

Very important point made by Raiwala: when he listed *mindjalpi* [man's dilly-bag] in the *gerri* [goods] he receives from *Gurrutai Miwait* [relations to the northeast] and from *Buku larrnggai* [inland] I asked him if he did not make *mindjalpi* [dilly-bags] himself. He replied 'I mak'em but different country; he must give me *wetj* [in return], like this (holding his hand out)—you give me, I can't say "no want'im" because this one arm belong him go his way—him point'm along me[,] me *marr* [therefore] go this way, I must take it'.

Extract from Donald Thomson's field notes[27]

Items such as dilly-bags, spears, lumps of wax, and ochre were the personal possessions of Yolngu individuals. If relatives cooperated in making an item such as a boat, it was jointly or collectively owned. What Thomson describes as 'violent abuse', leading to a general fight in camp, often resulted from minor theft—for example, bachelors taking vegetable food belonging to women. Close relatives of the offenders would make large expiatory payments 'to avert more serious consequences'. Personal-property rights were waived between a man and his distant *ma:ri* (MMB), however, the *gutharra* (zDC) could take or borrow his *ma:ri*'s possessions. Thomson describes this as a 'joking relationship' marked by the exchange of obscene jokes.[28] Personal possessions could be made inalienable by saying ancestral *likan* ('elbow') names over them, or by painting an ancestral 'elbow' design on them. In this way, individuals protected objects such as smoking pipes (*longiny*, introduced by Macassan trepangers).

Nevertheless, all categories of kin were involved in gift exchange, although different individuals stressed different kin as being of particular importance as exchange partners.[29] Some Yolngu categories of exchange were as follows:

- *mundhurr*—a gift made with no formal expectation of a return, or, in other words, one that was 'just given' (*ya:na gurrupan*)
- *djili, dha:dutj*—a gift in exchange for a service or privilege, given as 'payback' (*ba:ka-bakmarama*)
- *marangguma*—the making of a gift in repayment of a debt
- *buku-djaw'yun*—to exchange gifts or wives reciprocally
- *bala-lili*—'back and forth', relations of reciprocal interdependence
- *mali'yun*—to purchase with money (beginning in the Macassan era).

Yolngu discourse defined women as objects of exchange in marriage: a girl's mother, father, and brother 'gave' her to a man as a future wife. A man owed particular obligations to his potential or actual wife's kin, his *milmarra*. A young man, helped by his father and brothers, made gifts to these relatives for many years before he and his wife cohabited, and thereafter for as long as the relationship endured. The wife or potential wife and her kin made reciprocal gifts to the husband or potential husband's kin. A girl would make gifts to her 'father's sister' (*mukul ba:pa*) as the mother of her future husband. These exchange relations were transmitted to the next generation: a man's wife's mother and wife's mother's brother become his son's mother's mother and mother's mother's brother (*ma:ri*), with whom the son was in a reciprocal exchange relationship. The man's wife's brother became his son's mother's brother, and a potential wife's father.

Various kinds of transactions took place during ceremonies.[30] Women prepared cycad-palm-nut bread (*ngathu*) for men on the inside ground at the Nga:rra revelatory ceremony. Senior men cooked the cakes and called ancestral names over them to make them sacred (*dhuyu, madayin*); the ancestral spirit then supposedly entered the bread. Women's production supported the large group who assembled for major rituals at the end of the dry season. Men hunted and fished in what Warner calls a 'casual way' at these times, although Altman shows hunting to have been carefully organised during eastern Kunwinjku rituals. A similar provisioning by women occurred in the Ngulmarrk ceremony. The value accorded to the cycad-nut bread is revealed by the fact that some Yolngu men contended that more distant relatives should be given only 'ordinary' (*wakinngu*) food, over which ancestral names had not been proclaimed.

During the Dhuwa-moiety Nga:rra ceremony, men danced as the Djang'kawu sisters through the camps, soliciting food and other gifts; at night women, on hearing sounds supposedly made by ghosts of the dead, provided gifts to men 'for the *wangarr* ancestors and the dead'.[31] Neophytes made gifts to the leaders, and men collected food and other goods from women in the camp 'to feed the *wangarr* and the spirits' at the men's ground.

The Dhuwa-moiety 'owners' of the Gunapipi ceremony made gifts to the Yirritja 'workers' for their services, and men made gifts to the women they would later have sexual intercourse with on the last night of the ceremony. Participants from Dhuwa and Yirritja moieties exchanged food at the end of the proceedings.

In the Hollow-log mortuary ceremony, women gave food classified as sacred (*madayin*) to the leader, supposedly for the spirits of deceased ancestors; it was placed at the foot of the erect coffin and consumed by the old men. In the Macassan grave-post ceremony, described by Warner, men begged for food from people in the camp. Sharing cycad-palm-nut bread after a man's death was supposed to encourage the ghost to leave the camp and stop frightening away the game.

Howard Morphy describes gifts made to the dead in mortuary ceremonies. The deceased's mother's mother's patri-group performed songs and dances as a gift, and as part of its role of looking after the dead. Groups of both moieties placed feather strings and pigments into the grave; the contributors included the mother's brother's patri-group, who were giving to their senior sister's son (*waku*). Various participants made gifts of cloth to wrap the body in (reflecting the history of Macassan contact), as well as food and tobacco to placate the spirit (cf. Wiil and Minong food for the dead). The body in turn gave 'gifts' to the living. Hair of the dead went to the mother's group to make into hair string, which would be returned and incorporated into the feather string attached to the dead person's son's dilly-bag. Flesh from the buttocks aided relatives in hunting. Finger bones and pieces of the deceased's spears (if male), marking obligations to take revenge, were distributed to close matrilateral relatives. Larger items of the deceased's property, such as a dugout canoe, went to the dead person's mother's mother's group; spears went to the *waku* and his relatives.[32]

Payments for ritual services included gifts of vegetable foods for the senior singers in the purification ceremonies after a death, given by the close kin of the deceased. Relatives of the dead gave the person referred to as *gong wukindi* ('hand taboo') presents for cleaning the bones in the *bukubut* ceremony.

A circumcision initiate collected gifts on the long pre-circumcision journey, later to be distributed to his father, father's brothers, older brothers, mother's brothers and mother's mother's brothers in a procedure similar to those described earlier.[33] Female relatives of the initiates could 'snatch' food (and in recent times tobacco and money) from people's camps during the initiation ceremony. This recalls the 'compensation' given to female relatives of Yuwaaliyaay initiates.

According to Warner, a man who eloped with another man's wife would give the husband food and a 'totemic emblem' (he does not say what kind) as compensation. Acceptance of these gifts by the husband signified that the two men were friends, and that the husband recognised the rights of the new husband. However, Warner thought that such a happy reconciliation was rare, and that revenge was a more common response. A group could compensate another for a wrong with gifts of bread made from cycad-palm nuts (*ngathu*). One man bestowed a woman on a man as a wife as recompense for killing an enemy.[34]

Sacred objects were items of exchange. Men gave feather strings taken from *rangga* (sacred objects) to their sisters' sons (*waku*), not expecting any immediate return, and to close mother's mother's brothers (*ma:ri*) or sister's daughter's sons (*gutharra*); these were relationships of mutual support and exchange. The gift of *rangga* might be made to a person for cleaning the bones of the dead. According to Yolngu doctrine, the

Plate 12.1   Yolngu man at Ngilipidji with a finished spear fitted with a long *ngambi ḻirra* blade; note the paperbark wrappers (photograph by D. F. Thomson, TPH1792 courtesy of Mrs D. M. Thomson and Museum Victoria)

power (*ma:rr*) of such objects imparted skill (*djambatj*) and clear sight in hunting. Arm-rings (made of bamboo, wound with string, and adorned with lorikeet feathers or possum fur) and *waṉa* (cords) were supposed to help break the spears of enemies.[35]

At the end of the Nga:rra ceremony, a man could make gifts of string from the windings of the *rangga* to relatively close relatives, especially to his mother's brother (his potential wife's father). Warner comments that 'this is the finest gift one man could make to another, unless it were the ranga [*rangga*] itself or a hair belt made from a dead clansman's hair'.[36] The mother's brother should reciprocate with a return gift. Making too many 'totemic emblems' (presumably *rangga*) to exchange as gifts was given as a reason for one man's baldness. (By the same token, people explained their greying hair as the result of visits to important ancestral waterholes.)

Yolngu men sometimes explained the sharing of songs, dances, and designs between two patri-groups as being the result of a gift from one of the patri-groups to the other. Here the gift was not simply an object, such as a bark painting or a sacred object, but a right to perform a ceremony or make an item of inalienable property. The granting of this right connected the donor with the recipient through co-performance.[37]

Through networks of interpersonal links of these kinds, goods of different provenance moved along 'paths' (*dhukarr*) of exchange. Particular craft techniques were localised, and articles moved from hand to hand over very long distances. Boomerangs from the southwest moved north along the Katherine River and others from the south moved north along the Wilton River. Iron-bladed spears came from the east and northeast, and stone spearheads moved west and northwest. Certain places, such as Gaṯṯji, just south of Cape Stewart, were renowned centres both of ceremonies and exchange. Thomson shows the provenance of various items of exchange from the point of view of a person of the Glyde River estuary (see Figure 12.1). Thomson's friend Rraywala explained that he made a 'path' of exchange in a certain direction, for he passed certain items along the beach, and received others in return from inland, which he had to accept. [38]

Men and women established exchange relationships (*djukarrŋgu* or *gumurr-maṉda*) with people of distant countries, and they regularly exchanged gifts with these people. Various kin relations were involved, including half-siblings whose mothers were sisters but whose fathers were of widely separated patri-groups; a distant mother's mother's brother and sister's daughter's child (*ma:ri–gutharra*); a distant mother's brother and sister's child (*ngapipi–waku*); and a relationship inherited from women who were exchange partners. (The ethnography is very male-centred, so that exchange relations among women are hardly described.)[39]

These long-range exchange relations were associated with the Marradjirri exchange ceremonies, in which one group made and presented a semi-sacred decorated pole and a string to another group. People regarded these ceremonies as a means of establishing and maintaining social relationships with socially and geographically distant peoples. (The related Rom ceremony of Burarra people has been described as a 'ritual of diplomacy'). People of Djambarrpuyngu patri-group regularly presented their Marradjirri ceremony, named after the Morning Star (*Baṉumbirr*), to Rembarrnga people of southern Arnhem Land, and joined with Djinang groups, who owned the ceremony.[40]

Any of a number of circumstances could trigger the performance of a ceremony. One was the occasion when a child made their first 'gift'—that is, picked up an object such as a pebble and gave it to a parent or other close relative. The object was tied into a bundle and sent to a socially and geographically distant male relative, who incorporated the object into his own group's *marradjirri* (string and pole), which he and his group presented to the child's parents in a large public ceremony. An exchange of goods accompanied the presentation. At the end of the ceremony, the recipients removed the string from the core around which it was bound and incorporated it into arm-rings or men's dilly-bags (*bathi minydjalpi*). The psychosocial basis of the gift was here acknowledged in its most ritualised form. The process echoes the inculcation of generosity in the young through rituals and exhortations to be generous. A person or group could commission a performance of a Maradjirri ceremony by giving a gift of hair from a dead person, or it could be performed as a post-mortuary rite in which the hair of the deceased was incorporated into the string. Some *marradjirri* strings were used for love-magic following such a ceremony. A man looped the string over the hands of a sweetheart or errant wife, who was then supposed to be impelled to follow him.

Figure 12.1 indicates that items of Macassan origin entered the exchange network. I mentioned earlier that from the early eighteenth century Macassarese and Bugis sailors voyaged every wet season from Makassar in Sulawesi (as it is now) to the north coast, in order to collect and process trepang, which they traded on the

Figure 12.1 Provenances in Yolngu exchange relations

North
Gumurr muwadhak
('facing calico')
Calico, tobacco, blankets, glass
for scrapers and spears, steel
axes, knives, belts, smoking
pipes, other goods of Macassan
origin

West to northwest
Gumurr gaṯṯjirrk
('facing west')
Gaḻamba (forehead bands),
marwat ('hair') or *djanawu*
(bibs), *matjinydji* (biting bags),
baḻatha (fighting clubs)

East to northeast
Gumurr miwatj
('facing east')
Gayit (iron-headed shovel
spears), *buypuru* (pounding
stones for cycad-palm nuts),
ngambi ḻirra (stone spear-points),
minydjaḻpi (baskets)

South to southwest
Gumurr ga:rri
('facing in')
Galikaḻi (boomerangs), hooked
spears with bamboo shafts,
human-hair belts, *lama* (iron-
headed spears), *djimindi*
(fencing wire for fish spears),
iron bars for digging sticks,
gaḻamba (forehead bands for
the Maṉḏayala ceremony)

Southeast to east
Gumurr djalk
('facing spear-point wrappers')
Ngambi ḻirra (stone spear-
points), galikaḻi (boomerangs),
chain-mesh bags, buḻnyin
(possum fur), ngatjin (aprons)

Source: Thomson (1949)

Chinese market. The Macassans camped and built their smoke-houses on a number of beaches around the northeast Arnhem Land coast, and they formed strong social and economic relationships with Yolngu people.

Yolngu and other Aboriginal people of the north coast obtained food, tobacco, alchohol (gin), cloth, nails, fish-hooks, metal axes and knives, dugout canoes (*lipalipa*), and other items from the Macassans, and even incorporated a number of Macassan words into their languages. In return, they permitted the Macassans to camp and work on the beaches, supplied labour, and provided some exchange goods, such as turtle shell and pearl-shell. The Macassans conferred the title of 'king' on older Yolngu male leaders, and some Yolngu men travelled to Makassar and other places in southeast Asia; indeed, a number settled in Sulawesi. Relations occasionally turned violent.

Yolngu people adopted a number of items of Macassan material culture, notably the long smoking-pipe, the dugout canoe with its mast and sail (but without the out-rigger), and iron, used to make weapons and implements. They also incorporated elements of Macassan rituals into their own, and many Yolngu ceremonies came to refer to practices and objects of Macassan origin, such as prahus, knives, tobacco, cloth, and alcohol (*nga:nitji*). The domain of the *wangarr* came to include ancestors of Macassan identity, with their own particular song cycles, sacred objects, and cere-monies. Some ceremonies seem to have referred to diseases introduced by the Macassans, such as smallpox and venereal diseases.

The relationship with Macassan trepangers may have had an effect on longer-range exchange. Chris Clarkson's archaeological recent research suggests that from about 400 years ago, long *ngambi-ḻirra* (stone points) from northeast Arnhem Land found their way as far south as the country of Wardaman people, near what is now Katherine in the Northern Territory. It may be that the iron brought by the Macassans into Arnhem Land, hammered into leaf-shaped 'shovel-head' spear-points by Yolngu men, partly replaced the stone spearheads, which were instead traded south. If so, it supports Donald Thomson's view that trade with the Macassans stimulated trade networks more widely.[41]

Comparisons and conclusions

The institutions of exchange in the seven regions bore some similarities. Yuwaaliyaay and Wiil people held meetings for the purpose of exchanging goods, while ceremonies of various kinds, such as the Wiil/Miṉong and Ngarinyin initiation ceremonies and the Yolngu Marradjirri ceremony, also provided occasions for the exchange of goods. The evidence suggests a similar general shape of exchange in the seven regions, both in the exchange of like for like and of items of different kinds.

The exchange of similar valued items

Producers distributed foods in accordance with generalised reciprocity, through its modalities of demand sharing and kin obligations, as we saw in the last chapter. What an individual was able to contribute depended on their age, gender, ritual status, and stage in the life-cycle.

The exchange of raw materials, tools, weapons, items of apparel, and so on formed the bulk of wider exchange networks and 'trade'. Food and sacra also entered into these networks. 'Trade' linked regions producing rather different materials and objects. It allowed people to obtain scarce raw materials, implements, and weapons, but it was not an isolated sphere of exchange, for such goods entered other exchanges. The Berndts have shown that in the Western Desert certain highly valued items, notably pearl-shell, attracted a comparatively large quantity of other goods in exchange. At Port Keats in 1950, Johannes Falkenberg recorded equivalent values in the Murinh-patha people's *kulu* exchange system, similar to the *wurnan* of Ngarinyin people and their neighbours. For example, a four-kilogram lump of red ochre was equivalent to five spearheads, and a hair-belt equivalent to one. The exchange value of an item depended on the season, however, which affected its utility.[42]

While not explicitly described in many of the ethnographies, the obligation to provide mutual aid characterised many relationships, such as sibling relationships. Indeed, among Yolngu people mutual help was the mark of positive social relationships. It was commonplace at the end of a major ceremony for a leader to stand and say 'Dhuwa and Yirritja people help one another', expressing the interdependence of the patri-moieties; his statement would be received approvingly by the listeners.[43] It goes without saying that services were not confined to an exclusive sphere; people exchanged services for goods.

The direct exchange of girls or women as spouses featured in five case studies (Kŭnai, Yuwaaliyaay, Pitjantjatjara, Wiil/Minong, and Yolngu), if we include the temporary exchange of sexual access among Kŭnai people. The asymmetry of Ngarinyin marriage precluded direct exchange, unless, as in Yolngu marriage, delayed reciprocity was possible. In the Yolngu case, this took place through the exchange between two men of their sisters' daughters' daughters—delayed reciprocity spanning six genealogical generations (see Chapter 6). Even where reciprocal exchanges could be made, they were not a substitute for the exchange of wives for goods and services (in particular provisioning).

The reciprocal exchange of sacra, such as sacred strings (Yolngu), is found in the case studies. Although not well documented for the case studies, the exchange of knowledge and of more important sacred objects also occurred; it was a matter for more senior men and women.

In some regions, certain ceremonies (or rights to organise them) were objects of exchange, passed from group to group: Gunapipi is an example among Yolngu people and their neighbours. Furthermore, Yolngu people explained certain relations among patri-groups as having arisen from the exchange of rights to perform songs and dances or to make sacra. This is the quintessential inalienable gift, for it results in both groups possessing a song or ceremony, and being able to perform together.

I suggested earlier that we can think of the control of access to land, waters, and resources as a form of reciprocal exchange: for their mutual benefit, all the country-groups of a region granted access to a limited range of people from other groups. Of all the valued items, access to country came closest to being an exclusive sphere of exchange.

Exchange between categories

Turning to exchange across categories, perhaps the most common and important form of exchange in the case studies was the exchange of provisioning for access to women as spouses. The case studies demonstrate some variation in this area, as we saw in Chapter 6. Provisioning was also the main way to pay for ritual services and the main form of compensation. Foodstuffs could be exchanged for durable objects, and could be given as payment for the manufacture of implements. We have seen that people who foraged on country belonging to another group were expected to give part of the catch to the owners as 'rent' and as an acknowledgement of ownership. Novices in initiation and revelation ceremonies, especially young men, supplied food to those who gave them access to religious knowledge and experience.

Durable objects were mentioned as being part of marriage payments in two of the case studies (Wiil and Ngarinyin), and were among payments for ritual services (Western Desert) and other services, such as love–magic (Kŭnai). Gifts given as compensation for injury or death (Minong), or for women's loss of their sons in initiation (Yuwaaliyaay), included durable objects.

Services could be exchanged for provisioning, as we have seen, and, in one case (Yuwaaliyaay), for wives. Could access to spouses be exchanged for goods and services apart from those already mentioned? Though this is not exactly an exchange, marriage conferred the right of access to one's spouse's country in probably all seven regions (although a Yolngu man already had rights in his mother's country, which could also be his wife's country). There is some evidence that a senior Yolngu man could obtain a wife in return for granting access to ceremonies and sacred objects. Men in some regions could exchange religious knowledge for sex, and Warner records a man being promised a wife in exchange for killing someone.

Many kinds of sacred things could be exchanged for other goods and services, but the most profound sacred things remained outside the realm of exchange. In north-east Arnhem Land, men sent small copies of 'inside' sacred objects as 'messengers' to invite others to major ceremonies, so 'keeping while giving'. As I stated earlier, spouses can be thought of as inalienable gifts because both wives and husbands retained their natal identity after bestowal, and the marriage created a new relationship with the spouse's relatives, or transformed an existing one. Now we will return to the matter of sacra as inalienable possessions, and the question of what could *not* be exchanged.

Objects that could not be exchanged

Holders could grant *access* to inalienable possessions to varying degrees. The possession of land and waters and their resources, together with consubstantial identity, was transmitted from generation to generation through inheritance and other means. Holders granted access to others on various grounds. In the case of sacred things, such as secret ceremonies, sacred objects, 'inside' stories, and exegeses, holders could grant *knowledge* of them to others, usually in exchange for goods and services. People did tell me at Milingimbi in the 1970s that people of other Manydjikay groups (a string of patri-groups with the same *wangarr*) had given a Milingimbi patri-group its *rangga*. And some groups held parcels of land 'on top' of the land of another group that had granted them this right.

Inalienable gifts—strings taken from sacred objects, small copies of 'inside' objects, painted equivalents of sacred objects, performances, tokens of minor totems, and so on—all had connections to the more inalienable of sacred objects and places. The most powerful inalienable gifts were grants of rights to perform elements of ceremonies or make sacred items, such that the donor and recipient became co-owners of related forms. We could think of the imparting of religious knowledge as a kind of inalienable gift, because through it the recipient joined the company of the knowledgeable.

Variation in exchange

The similarities in production technologies, ways of organising production, and patterns of distribution limited the possibilities for elaboration and radical difference in exchange between the regions. Marriage provides the strongest contrast, as we have seen. To recapitulate, the main dimensions of variation were as follows:
- shifting webs (Kŭnai, Pitjantjatjara, and Sandbeach), with sister exchanges between families and localities among the first two of these

- reciprocal exchanges between matri-groups and patri-groups (Yuwaaliyaay, and Wiil/Minong)
- asymmetrical exchanges between lineages and patri-groups (Ngarinyin and Yolngu), with some reciprocal exchanges between large patri-groups (notably Yolngu).

Differences in the exchange value of spouses appeared, with at one extreme the possibility of escaping the obligation to make gifts to affines (among Yuwaaliyaay people, with their matrilineal totemic categories), and at the other extreme a long period of marriage payments (among the highly polygynous Yolngu people).[44]

Ngarinyin people and their neighbours had a much more integrated exchange 'system' than did people in other regions. They organised exchanges as flows from patri-group to patri-group, ideally in a set order, and assimilated all exchanges to *wurnan*. Yolngu people shared similar conceptions of serial and circular relations among patri-groups of the same moiety, but these did not make up an integrated regional system. Rather, 'paths' of exchange reflected the generalised directional flows of various goods. A key difference was that the larger Yolngu patri-groups had reciprocal marriage relations with others of the opposite moiety, although relations among lineages were more consistently asymmetrical.

The relative isolation of Kŭnai people contrasts with the embeddedness in extensive networks of people of the other regions. Nevertheless, the population would have been large enough to allow for flows of goods within Gippsland, as well between Kŭnai people and those to the northeast.

The ability to control inalienable possessions, and the production of inalienable gifts, tended to increase with seniority. But these powers were also conditional on personal qualities of assertiveness and ability. In a converse movement, productive powers, especially those of men, declined with seniority.

Movement through the system of exchange relations

As people moved through different positions in the field of exchange relations they gained control of the production of particular resources, and had distinct 'wants' associated with each social position that gave rise to demand for particular goods and services. In Aboriginal economies, demand varied between the genders, changed with age and social status, and was related to people's changing needs as well as their ability to satisfy them. Many kinds of desires, social relations, and events underlay demand. For example, the demand among Yolngu men for several wives derived from sexual desire, economic considerations, strategies for reinforcing useful social networks, and pressure from others. However, demand did not operate as in a market, and 'supply' did not respond through a market mechanism.

As Narotzky points out, access to resources is conditioned by and conditions the position of individuals and groups 'within the political and economic field of forces'.[45] The goods and services that people demanded and commanded differed according to gender and age. To take provisioning first, children as well as old and infirm people were largely dependent on others, without being able to reciprocate in kind. All active older children and adults who engaged in hunting, fishing, and gathering, supplied

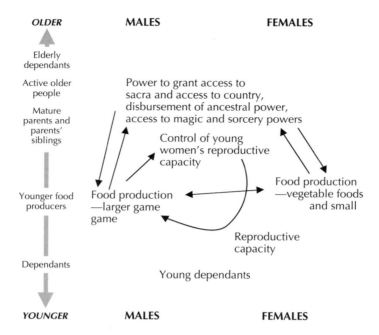

Figure 12.2   Movement through exchange relations

themselves as well as others. Near the bottom of Figure 12.2, above young dependants, are the producers of food and other consumables (fuel, water, etc.). Food production should be skewed from bottom–middle left to bottom–top right—as older men became less productive and more involved in ritual production. In the diagram the small arrows indicate exchanges related to gender and age.

Young men could exchange the yield that resulted from their productive power for items they desired or needed and did not yet control—religious knowledge and experience, wives, etc. Productive power was transferred through teaching and the formal conferring of rights to use implements and to kill certain game, in a continual exchange between the generations.

There was a demand among producers for a share in other people's yields when their own productivity fell short, and for complementary items produced by other people, especially of the opposite sex. As the productivity of an individual fell, with age or infirmity or for other reasons, so their demand for the products of others rose. The people who were able to meet this demand were younger men, and women into late middle age or even old age. Men's productivity as hunters declined sooner than women's productivity as foragers and hunters.

People's ability to make their own implements moderated the demand for durable objects, although people could obtain implements through demand sharing or by borrowing from certain kin. What drove 'trade' was a degree of local specialisation and the need for raw materials and implements unavailable locally but produced in surplus elsewhere. In a feature of the exchange of some durable objects, as well as of spouses and some ceremonies, a gift was received only to be handed on to another, creating in some circumstances a series of linked relationships.

Near the top of Figure 12.2 is the power to use or control access to ceremonies, sacred objects, exegetical knowledge, magic, and sorcery. It bore a strong relationship to gender, age, birth order, and personal ability. High levels of religious knowledge were scarce resources—made scarce by the control of access—for which initiates made recompense. Those in control of these resources exchanged them for other valued items, especially food; this contrasts with the disbursement of ancestral power by means of increase rituals and the release of generalised 'power' at other rituals. Control tended to be gender-exclusive. Knowledge and experience was graded, from just being at and seeing a ceremony, to participating in, leading, or organising a performance, to having the power to grant access to secret and public forms. The degree of exclusivity varied: access to the most secret, powerful, and 'heavy' things was restricted and was exchanged for gifts, while access to experience of public aspects tended to be reciprocal among co-residents of a community.

Aboriginal people's tendency to speak, in relation to marriage bestowals, of women being given rather than men partly reflects the relative age of spouses; females lacked power over their own bestowal, often being bestowed as infants or even before their birth, although they gained more control as they got older. Thus, in Figure 12.2 the control of women's reproductive power is in the hands of more senior men and women, as well as siblings.

The 'production' of daughters to be spouses required a long-term investment of productive and reproductive power by the parents, supported in part (in some areas) by the potential daughter's husband's gifts, given to 'grow up' his future wife. And each mother could be expected to produce only one daughter on average. As a woman's parents, especially her father, became less productive themselves, so they relied more on their daughter's husband's productive power.

The long-term potential return on a bestowed daughter took the form of provisioning by a future and actual son-in-law, following the betrothal and continuing after the marriage. A man thus made a long-term investment of labour to acquire his wife or wives, providing gifts especially of meat.

Institutions created and enhanced the scarcity of spouses by restricting the categories of marriageable relatives. Marriage gave individuals legitimate and perhaps more regular sexual access to one another, legitimate offspring, status, and access to the fruits of one another's production. But within the constraints of personal attraction, incest prohibitions, and opportunities, people also had access to one another as lovers outside marriage.

The main demand among men was for wives, because women bore the children needed by patrifilial groups who could not marry their own, and daughters attracted valued items. But where matrilineal groups prevailed (as among Yuwaaliyaay people) the demand for wives may have been lower, reflected in the reduced pressure to make gifts to wives' parents. It expanded in highly polygynous systems, for two reasons: the greater delay in the marriages of males and the perceived benefits (to men) of multiple marriages, which helped create a productive camp, an extensive exchange network, and a growing lineage or patri-group.

Polygynous marriage also resulted in women have access to more husbands, but serially, so that polygyny seems to have been in the interests both of older men and older women. Older men gained sexual access to young women, as well as access to their labour and reproductive power, and older widows could gain younger and more active and productive husbands through leviratic marriage (see Chapter 6).

Bestowal systems everywhere gave a girl's close relatives a scarce resource for which they could extract provisioning and other gifts in return. (If one lacked a daughter, one might have the power to bestow a deceased sibling's daughter.) With luck, men began to be beneficiaries at just about the time of their productive peak (around the age of 30), and continued to benefit as their own productivity fell. Women as bestowers benefitted from a supply of meat, which complemented their own production. As they were widowed and re-bestowed, sisters and daughters continued to yield a return for bestowers.

Variation in exchange relations

Variations in marriage systems affected the rate at which a person could move through different positions in the web of exchange relations and the resources that they could control. For women, the main variable seems to have been the potential for status in the domain of women's ritual, in which Western Desert women had greater autonomy than Arnhem Land women. In Kŭnai society, which had low polygyny and marriage at a quite early age, men could become parents and bestowers of daughters quite early. At the other extreme, Yolngu men married later on average, and the life chances of senior and junior brothers differed. Older brothers had a greater chance of marrying polygynously and gaining access to resources related to marriage. On the whole, Yolngu men also became fathers later, but the age of marriage of men did not affect the age at which a man would become a 'mother's brother' and take part in the bestowal of his sister's daughter. Overall, the chances and timing of access to resources varied both between societies and between individuals in different positions in the same society.

It is evident, then, that those in possession or control of items of great value, especially access to religious knowledge (connected to inalienable possessions), access to girls and women as spouses, and access to valued foods and raw materials, could command valued resources in return, in quantity or on an enduring basis. So the gift of a sister, daughter, or niece as a wife could yield many years of gifts of food and services in return.

Those older men and women (especially the men) who controlled access to religious knowledge could use this control to acquire what they needed and desired, especially what they could not provide for themselves. They could command deference on the part of younger and less experienced people, as well as gifts and services. As we saw in the last chapter, senior men were able to deploy their control of sacra and magic in a variety of ways to secure preferred foods that others were more capable than them of killing or gathering.

The availability of opportunities to gain religico-magical knowledge and experience was not demand-driven, as in a market economy; the initiation of the young simply followed the normal course of events. Nevertheless, the young did require this knowledge and experience to achieve normal adult status, and older people were able to withhold access, perhaps as a punishment (for attempting to marry too young, for example). Where certain other social and institutional conditions were present, this control also gave senior men the power to sustain a regime of high polygyny, at the expense of women and younger men.

I have put control of access to land and waters towards the top of Figure 12.2, for it was primarily in the hands of the mature and senior residents of a camp on the country in question. The fact that land and waters (and sky) were personified as the traces of totemic ancestors means that people were related to country as kin. It is a simple consequence of this that connections were nowhere exclusive, so that everyone in a region (of varying scope) had some sort of connection to and claim over most places in a region. People guarded some resources more closely than others—for example the most important ancestral places, ochres, stone from quarries, some waterholes in northeast Arnhem Land (reserved for older men), and swan eggs in Gippsland.

While particular groups (or group-centred networks) possessed and controlled inalienable possessions, they disbursed the benefit. Holders could grant varying degrees of access to inalienable possessions such as land, ancestral sacra, and the ancestral power inherent in places, objects, and ceremonies. People in some regions exchanged these powers (as in increase rites) in the mode of generalised reciprocity, rather than in direct exchange for other valued items.

People of both the Western Desert and the northwest Kimberley participated in a kind of regional economy of magic in which each group conducted increase rites at ancestral sites (maintaining *wanjina* paintings in the western Kimberley, anointing and rubbing certain rocks in the Western Desert) for the benefit of all in the region. The release of ancestral powers for the benefit of all participants was also a feature of regional ancestral ceremonies, such as Gunapipi and Djungguwan. Sandbeach people, however, exercised rather exclusive rights over ancestral sites, used for increase and for aggression against other groups.[46]

To sum up, each person's access to desired resources—food, durable objects, spouses, the religious experience needed for adult status, and so on—was governed by the resources that they could produce, and hence exchange, at a given time of life. The resources a person could produce and deploy changed with age, the acquisition of skill and knowledge, and reproductive status, and in light of opportunities as well as institutions that were shaped by particular interests. Children could contribute some labour, but in the main were the recipients of care. As a young man became more mature he gained access to the paraphernalia of hunting, and could contribute food in return for religious knowledge and access to women as wives. Women gained foraging skills, mothers could produce daughters, and brothers gained sisters whom they could bestow. Ageing men lost many of their hunting and fighting powers, but not skill in the use of the more complex technologies (such as fish-traps) or in ritual practice, and some older men and women held secret religious and magical knowledge as well as authority in ancestral law. All being well, older men and women could ensure the satisfaction of their basic needs through the bestowal of daughters, sisters, and nieces. Demand sharing and the obligations of relatives safeguarded the interests of the less competent and the infirm.

Key points in exchange relations

The least powerful in all this were the young girls given as wives; the most powerful were those who could control several linked resources. The control of ancestral rituals (which had implications for the control of access to country) and the control of access to girls and women as wives were key components of male power. However, older women could also exercise power in marriage arrangements, in the sphere of women's production, and in women's rituals.

Regions varied greatly in the kinds of opportunities available for the exercise of power, as we have seen. For Kŭnai and Yuwaaliyaay men the control of personal magic, shamanic powers, and rainmaking provided opportunities. In the northwest Kimberley and northeast Arnhem Land, polygynous males had the potential to benefit from their favoured position in exchange relations, as well as from (potentially) expanding patri-groups. As long as his wives bore daughters, such a man found himself at the centre of an extensive exchange network. Actual and prospective sons-in-law (his 'sisters' sons') were sources of a continual flow of provisions, other gifts, and military support to him, his wives, and his wives' brothers. He was obligated to direct part of this flow to his wives' relatives, or at least those of his younger wives. He was also likely to benefit from his sisters' marriages, the more so if he was the son of a polygynous man and had several sisters by more than one 'mother'. If, like the renowned Yolngu leader Wonggu, he had many sons, he would find himself at the head of a fast-growing lineage, and of a potentially independent patri-group.

To return to the topic of women's labour in male initiation ceremonies, John Bern has interpreted the channelling of women's product into the secret male sphere as an aspect of exploitation. According to his neo-Marxist view, religion constituted an ideology that underpinned essentially unequal gender relations. Anthropologists such as Catherine Berndt and Isobel White had earlier represented gender roles as complementary rather than unequal; similarly, Diane Bell posited a pre-colonial era in which women of central Australia had much greater autonomy than they came to have in the context of colonial authority and life on settlements. However, Annette Hamilton pointed out that there were differences between the eastern Western Desert where, as we have seen, women lived rather more separate and independent lives, with their own secret ceremonies, and the Yolngu region, where women's secret ceremonies were integrated with male ones.[47]

To interpret regional initiation and revelatory ceremonies fundamentally as instruments of male hegemony seems to me to be too narrow. They were as much about relations of authority between older and younger people of the same gender as they were about gender relations. Although myths and ceremonies certainly legitimated unequal gender relations in regions such as northeast Arnhem Land, the control of potentially violent and disruptive young men was in everyone's interests. Women's role in supplying food for the ceremonies could be seen as a contribution to that common interest rather than as an example of gender exploitation. It should be admitted, however, that these ceremonies, and the systems of ancestral law of which they were a part, sustained regimes of power that worked in the interests of certain categories and individuals.[48]

The sacred and exchange

The importance for this study of Weiner's and Godelier's discussions of inalienable possessions lies in the way they relate the sacred to exchange. In the Aboriginal societies of this study, ancestral and totemic doctrines underpinned regional orders of law, and formed one of the main bases of social identity, authority, and power relations. How did ancestral/totemic orders relate to exchange? Certain sacred things with ancestral significance, associated land and waters, and even some items of technology were tied to kin groups and country-groups of various kinds and rendered inalienable. Members of these groups and coalitions of groups controlled access to land (and waters) and to knowledge and experience of ancestral forms.

The ancestral order was also the source of the value of certain exchange items, notably sacred objects, ceremonies and their elements, and religious knowledge. The granting of access to ancestral knowledge was a valuable service for which those in control could demand other valued items in return. It was a source of power, especially in securing the deference of the young (a condition for polygyny), and it reinforced differences in gender-related power. Inalienable gifts with ancestral connections (such as feathered strings) often expressed relationships important in marriage, or formed a part of marriage gifts.

This concludes the analysis and comparison of the economies of the seven case studies. The final chapter will bring the comparisons of Parts I, II, and III together.

Further reading

Recent writers on gift exchange and 'inalienable possessions' trace their concerns back to Marcel Mauss's *The Gift* (1954). Key works drawn upon in this chapter include Chris Gregory's *Gifts and Commodities*, Annette Weiner's *Inalienable Possessions* (1992); and Maurice Godelier's *The Enigma of the Gift* (1999).

Chris Gregory's polarised typology of 'gifts' and 'commodities' has occasioned much debate; see, for example, Arjun Appadurai's *The Social Life of Things* (1986), Marilyn Strathern's *The Gender of the Gift* (1988), and Mark Mosko's 'Inalienable ethnography: 'Keeping-while-giving and the Trobriand case' (2000).

On the view that Aboriginal men's rituals involved the exploitation of women, see John Bern's 'Ideology and Domination' (1979).

Notes

1   See Mauss (1954). On gifts and commodities see Gregory (1982) and Strathern (1988: 19).
2   See Weiner's analysis (1992) of inalienable possessions.
3   The quotation is from Godelier (1999: 8).
4   See Godelier (1999) on inalienable possessions and the social order. On spouses as inalienable gifts see Godelier (1999) and Weiner (1992).
5   See Sansom (1988) on the 'signal service'.
6   Harrison (1992: 235) makes a similar distinction in defining intellectual property as 'the ownership, not of things but of classes of things, of their images or typifications'.

7   See McCarthy (1938, 1939) on trade.

8   See Akerman (1994: 17) on pearl-shell, Falkenberg (1962: 142–51) on *kulu* exchange.

9   See McCarthy (1938: 407, 415–16) on trade routes; and see Watson (1983) on *pituri*.

10 On ceremonies as occasions for trade see McCarthy (1938: 83–6).

11 See Howitt (1904: 714–6) and McCarthy (1938: 425) on 'trade centres'.

12 On Kũnai exchange see Bulmer (Papers, letter to Howitt, MV B1 F4 xm98 n.d.; 1994) and Howitt (1880; 1904: 274–5).

13 See Hotchin (1990: 200) on the exchange of stone in Gippsland, and McBryde (1984) on central Victoria.

14 For sources on exchange and trade in the Western Desert see R. M. and C. H. Berndt (1945: 70, 72–3), Tindale (1972: 256), and Tonkinson (1991: 53).

15 See Myers on Pintubi exchange (1986: 171–4, 239), and Dussart (2000: 133, 183–4, 198) on Warlpiri women's exchange.

16 On the rarity of pearl-shell see R. M. and C. H. Berndt (1945: 73). An image reproduced by Tonkinson (1978: 27) shows a *mabarn* (healer) with a pearl-shell pendant.

17 See Parker (1905: 59, 81, 124) on Yuwaaliyaay exchange. On the view of women's provisioning of male ceremonies as exploitative see Bern (1979).

18 The quotation is from Parker (1905: 81).

19 On Wiil and Miṉong exchange and trade see Barker (1992: 17 February, 22 November 1830), Bates (1985: 280), Green (1989: 4, 59), Hassell (1936: 685), and Le Souëf (1993: 3l, 42–43). On exchanges following male initiation journeys see Bates (1985: 157, 158). Miṉong people at King George Sound entered into complex exchange relations with the British garrison.

20 The quotation is from Hassell (1936: 685).

21 See Thomson (Papers, MV File 175, n.d.) on Sandbeach wife-lending.

22 Sources on Sandbeach exchange include Rowland and Franklin (1992: 16) and Sutton and Rigsby (1998).

23 See Thomson (1933: 468) on the highly valued spear.

24 On exchange among Ngarinyin people and their neighbours see Blundell and Layton (1979), Crawford (1968: 37, 40), Love (1936: 87), McCarthy (1938: 436), Redmond (2001b: 178–98), and Rumsey (1996: 6). On mortuary gifts see Love (Papers: 59, 72, 121, 123).

25 See Akerman (1994: 16) on this more extensive network.

26 On Kuranggara and Djanba see Swain (1993: 233–7) and Lommel (1997). See Love (Papers: 80–1) on the exchange of ceremonies.

27 The quotation is from Thomson (Papers, MV File 27, n.d.). I think what Thomson transcribed as '*marr* go', which implies that the man's 'power' (*marr*) travelled, may be a mistranscription of *marr ga*, 'because' or 'therefore'.

28 See Thomson (1949: 54–5) and Warner (1937: 147) on Yolngu personal possessions.

29 On Yolngu exchange partners and transactions see Thomson (1949: 50–2, 77, 79), Warner (1937: 145), and Zorc (1986).

30 On exchange in the context of rituals see Altman (1987: 196–202), Keen (1978), and Warner (1937: 33, 140, 306, 328–9, 341, 355–6, 370, 417, 442, 433, 508).

31 See Keen (1994: 202–4) on gifts in the Nga:rra ceremony. The *waku* (sisters' sons) of the Dhuwa-moiety owners of the ceremony did the collecting. The quotation is from Keen (1994: 202).

32 On gifts in mortuary ceremonies see Morphy (1997) and Peterson (1976: 101).

33 Warner writes that lack of generosity on the part of the donors could lead to retaliation (1937: 261–3).

34 See Creighton (2003, citing Wangambi) on *ngathu*. See Warner (1937: 88, 181) on the totemic emblem as compensation and the gift of a wife for a homicide.

35 On sacred objects as exchange items see Thomson (1949: 48) and Warner (1937: 93–4, 234, 341, 355, 508–9).

36 The quotation is from Warner (1937: 93).

37 On the gift of ceremonies see Keen (1994: 274).

38 See Thomson (Papers, MV File 27, n.d.; 1949: 71–4, 88) and Warner (1937: 95) on Yolngu exchange networks, and Altman (1982: 346ff) on eastern Kunwinjku networks.

39 On Yolngu exchange partners see Warner (1937: 95, 145) and Thomson (1949: 75).

40 See Borsboom (1978), La Mont West (1962), Peterson (1976), Warner (1937: 423–25), and Wild (1983) on Yolngu and Anbarra exchange ceremonies. The term *marradjirri* denotes a class of decorated strings and poles, each of which represents a clan ancestor or other totemic figure. On the use of strings in love-magic see Peterson (1975: 105) .

41 On Yolngu relations with Macassan trepangers see Macknight (1976), Thomson (1949), and Warner (1958). Warner thought the Macassan influence on Yolngu culture was minimal; Thomson thought it to be more profound. Information on stone spear-points of Yolngu origin in Wardaman country is from Chris Clarkson of the School of Archaeology and Anthropology, Australian National University, who is currently carrying out archaeological research in the region.

42 See Falkenberg (1962: 148) on relative values in *kulu* exchange.

43 Nowadays the homily has been extended to 'Yolngu and Balanda (white people)' (Sophie Creighton, pers. com.).

44 I may be drawing a long bow here – the inference of Yuwaaliyaay men's reluctance to make marriage gifts rests on a single remark by Parker (1905: 58).

45 On the position of individuals within exchange relations see Bohannan (1968), Malinowski (1935), Narotzky (1997: 72, 112), and Weiner (1976).

46 See Keen (1994: 268), Morphy (1991: 128), and Warner (1937: 236) on the release of ancestral power in Yolngu ceremonies and on the power of sacred objects.

47   On gender relations see Bell (1983), Bern (1979), C. H. Berndt (1970), Hamilton (1980; 1981a), and White (1970). See Merlan (1988) for an overview; she concludes that while men did appropriate women's labour for their ceremonies, they did not succeed in consolidating dominance over women (1988: 31).

48   See Keen (1994: 189–90) on the effects of initiation as a tool for socialisation of the young.

13

Conclusion

It remains to bring together the comparisons of the previous chapters, bring out the key points of similarity and difference, and suggest some explanations for the variations.

Similarities and differences

Ecology

The case studies have covered a very wide range of environments, from the tropical north, through the arid and semi-arid zones, to the temperate southeast and the Mediterranean climate of the southwest (see Table 13.1). Local economies varied according to subtle variations in the environment from the coast and islands to rocky hinterland and desert.

Population densities in the seven regions varied from about one person per 80–200 square kilometres in the Western Desert to about 100 times more on the coasts of eastern Cape York Peninsula and northeast Arnhem Land, where there was about one person or more per 2 square kilometres (Table 13.1). This variation must have affected 'social density', as measured by the number of interactions one might expect to have within a given area. It was correlated to rainfall to some degree, but the high densities on the coast and major rivers also depended on resources brought from outside the region.

The range of resources available varied according to the environment (see Table 13.2). We saw in Chapter 2 that the case studies fit into four broad resource regions: the southeast, the 'grain belt', the southwest, and the tropical zone. While many broad classes of resources were found in all regions (though, of course, marine and riverine resources were not found in the arid zone), rather different clusters of species provided key staples. Some examples of staples are grass seeds and other seeds in the grain belt, *Macrozamia* in the southwest, and cycad-palm nuts, 'cheeky yams', and mangrove pods in the tropical zone. Several of these important food species required intensive processing.

Many basic similarities in technologies are to be found in the seven regions (see Table 13.3). All groups used fire as the main mode of conversion of energy. The only transport technologies were simple watercraft in marine, riverine, and lacustrine areas, some drawing on wind power and others taking advantage of the movement of water. Each group's set of technologies included tools and equipment using human power, 'hand-tools', and simple machines such as fire-drills and spears with spear-throwers. The main tool-making technologies consisted of objects made of bone, stone, fibre, and wood, techniques for working these materials, and techniques involving the use of fire. Digging-sticks, spears and clubs took a variety of forms. I argued in Chapter 3 that these were the technologies of 'hunter-gatherer-cultivators'. Aboriginal people intervened in the reproduction of plants and animals in a more radical way than earlier recognised—through the propagation of plants, small scale irrigation in some areas, seed planting in others, and above all through the use of fire.

Technological variation reflected differences in key resources and differences in the environment (see Table 13.3). To give some examples, Yuwaaliyaay and Pitjantjatjara people of the Aboriginal grain belt used seed-grinding technology; skin cloaks were used in the cold winters of the southeast and southwest; people of the west Kimberley coast, which had huge tidal currents, used double-layer rafts; leaching techniques were

Table 13.1 Environments and estimated population densities

People	Environment	Population density
Kŭnai	Temperate forests, plains, lakes, and coast; moderate year-round rainfall	Medium to very high: one person per 2.5–20 km²
Pitjantjatjara and their neighbours	Arid zone, sandy, montane and shield desert, tussock grassland, and scrub; very low, very variable rainfall	Very low: one person per 80–200 km²
Yuwaaliyaay and their neighbours	Semi-arid grassland and woodland, perennial and intermittent rivers; low, variable rainfall, droughts and floods	Medium-low to low: one person per 30–60 km²
Wiil and Minong	Coast, estuaries, forests and heath; 'Mediterranean' climate, moderate winter rainfall	Medium to high: one person per 5–25 km²
Sandbeach	Forested foothills, coast, coastal waters, reefs, and islands; tropical monsoon climate, very high rainfall	Medium to very high: one person per 2.5–14 km²
Ngarinyin and their neighbours	Woodland on rocky plateau, rivers, broken coast, and islands; tropical monsoon climate, high seasonal rainfall, cyclones	Medium-low to high: one person per 10–25 km², perhaps higher on coast
Yolngu	Open forest hinterland, swamps, rivers, coast, and islands; tropical monsoon climate, high seasonal rainfall	Medium to very high: one person per 2–20 km²

used to process the toxic plants of the tropical north; and Yolngu people used specially designed canoes in their region's swamps. Some differences reflected the availability of particular resources, such as skins for containers in the southwest and pandanus fibre in the north.

In a common feature of Aboriginal settlement and mobility patterns, people formed home bases (residence groups) from which they made logistical forays and within which they shared their produce (Chapter 4). Differences emerged in the average size of residence groups—they were larger on the coast, smaller in the arid zone—and in patterns of mobility. The movement of some groups was markedly seasonal (Kŭnai, Wiil/Miṉong, Sandbeach, Ngarinyin, Yolngu), while that of others was less predictable (Yuwaaliyaay, Pitjantjatjara). The degree and range of mobility varied from very great in the Western Desert (Pitjantjatjara and their neighbours) to rather sedentary on the tropical coasts (Sandbeach, coastal Yolngu and their neighbours).

Patterns of residence and mobility, as well as exploitation strategies, depended again on certain differences in the environment and in the nature and location of

Table 13.2   Broad resource zones

Zone/people	Resources
Southeast	
Kŭnai	Southeast flora and fauna—wide array of food plants, especially 'roots', with lacustrine, estuarine, and coastal resources
'Aboriginal grain belt'	
Pitjantjatjara and their neighbours	Arid zone; grass and other seeds important as well as fruits and small game; larger mammals and birds more rare; reliance on reptiles and small mammals for meat
Yuwaaliyaay and their neighbours	Semi-arid zone; grass and other seeds, plus other resources of grassland, woodland, floodplain, rivers, and swamps
Southwest	
Wiil/Miṉong	Heath and mulga, with forest to west; broad array of resources; little emphasis on marine resources; 'root' foods, fish of basins, estuaries, and rivers; complex processing of *Macrozamia* and other plant foods
Tropical north	
Sandbeach	*Dioscorea* yams featured as staples, as well as toxic cycad-palm nuts and tropical fruits; resources of shallow coastal waters, reefs, and islands, dugong and turtle in particular
Ngarinyin and their neighbours	*Dioscorea* yams, toxic cycad-palm nuts, tropical fruits; riverine resources in rocky interior; coastal and island resources on west coast; dugong and turtle from sea
Yolngu	*Dioscorea* yams, toxic cycad-palm nuts, tropical fruit trees; riverine and swamp resources in hinterland; coastal, estuarine, and island resources on north and east coasts

Table 13.3 Some contrasting features of technologies in the seven regions

Region/people	Technologies
Southeast	
Kŭnai	Canoes adapted to use on the lakes; spears of stone flakes hafted in resin; large nets; bone fish-hooks; skin cloaks
'Aboriginal grain belt'	
Yuwaaliyaay and their neighbours	Bark canoes; seed collection, storage, and grinding technology; wide variety of nets; complex stone fish-traps; skin cloaks.
Pitjantjatjara and their neighbours	Multi-functional implements; seed-grinding tools; no large facilities
Southwest	
Wiil/Minong	No canoes; *kodj* (hammer–hatchet) and *taap* (saw–knife); fish-traps, sewn kangaroo-skin cloaks; leaching of toxic and irritant plant foods.
Tropical north	
Sandbeach	Double-outrigger canoes; multiple spear types; pounding and leaching of toxic and irritant plant foods
Ngarinyin and their neighbours	Double-layered timber raft; fine pressure-flaked spearheads (used as trade items); pounding and leaching of toxic and irritant plant foods
Yolngu	Watercraft for use on grassy swamps and in coastal waters; multiple spear types; pounding and leaching of toxic and irritant plant foods; various fish-traps

resources (see Table 13.4). Regions differed markedly in the range of movement, and in the degree of mobility. The overall picture, then, is one of considerable variation in environments, ecologies, and some aspects of technology.

Identities

Turning now to institutional fields, the study has revealed some broad similarities in the use of ways of speaking (dialects and languages) for the construction of identities, but there are interesting differences. Language identities appear to have been context-dependent 'shifters'. This characteristic was at its most extreme in the Western Desert, but was also apparent in other regions, such as the Darling/Barwon River region (Yuwaaliyaay and their neighbours). The same goes for regional identities in the southeast and southwest (see Table 13.5).

In five of the seven regions, people mapped ways of speaking (identified by isoglosses or proper names) onto both people and countries. In at least three of these (Sandbeach, Ngarinyin, and Yolngu) a person's language identity followed from their totemic patri-group. Yolngu people identified languages by patri-group names. In two regions (Kŭnai and Wiil/Minong) the broadest geographical identities were 'regional' and relative to perspective (see Table 13.5). Relating these to estimates of population

Table 13.4   Patterns of movement in the seven regions

People	Summer	Late summer, early winter	Winter	Late winter, early summer
Kŭnai	Beaches, estuaries, and lake entrances for fish, in temporary camps	Greater mobility; move inland for forest foods, including mammals; congregate for ceremonies	Live in huts up-river for fishing and forest resources	Move down to wetlands for wildfowl, eels, and fish
Pitjantjatjara and their neighbours	Rather aseasonal, but tendency for:			
	Smaller, more mobile groups after summer rains		'Cold time'; greater mobility after winter rains; larger groups for ceremonies	'Hot time'; aggregation on permanent waters, or dispersal in drought
Yuwaaliyaay and their neighbours	Rather aseasonal; drought concentrated people on permanent waters; rains drew people to back-country, where they obtained aquatic resources; river flushes drew people to the rivers for fish. But tendency for:			
	Large numbers on riverbanks in groups of variable size, for fishing and grass-seed harvest		Small groups by river; others moved away from rivers	Spring fisheries after rises in river waters
Wiil/Miṉong	Dry season; larger residence groups on permanent waters; large groups for fishing on coast	Move inland from coast for fish and large mammals	Wet season; smaller groups on ephemeral waters; larger groups for fishing	Move to form large groups on permanent waters; move back to coast in spring
Sandbeach	Wet season; residence groups on beach; marine and coastal foods		Dry season; larger residence groups on river mouth or head-land; small camps in hinterland	Late dry season; aggregation for major ceremonies
Ngarinyin and their neigbours	Wet season; residence groups on higher ground in huts and caves; visits to coast	Move down to valleys and pools	Dry season; residence groups in valleys and by pools; burning off; aggregation for ceremonies	'Hot season'; concentration around permanent waters; move up-country as rains approached
Yolngu coast	Wet season; smaller residence groups		larger residence groups as home bases, inland foraging and visiting	large aggregations for major ceremonies
Yolngu hinterland	Wet season; residence groups in houses on high ground; visits to coast	Move down to waters; more mobile; smaller groups as water retreated	Small, mobile groups; fishing in retreating waters	Concentration around permanent waters; large aggregations for major ceremonies; move back to wet-season camps as rains set in

Table 13.5   Language, locality, and totemism in the seven regions

People	Language and regional identities	Local identities	Totemic identities and naming systems
Kŭnai	Five regional identities; three or four local dialects	Countries with totemic significance, identified by focal place, leader, character of country	Gender totems; patrifilial guardian totems; country-groups identified by locality or leader's name
Pitjantjatjara and their neighbours	Intersecting isoglossic language identities, loosely related to tracts of country	Ancestral sites and site clusters	Generation moieties; sections (recently introduced); personal totems by place of conception
Yuwaaliyaay and their neighbours	Isoglossic language identities related to tracts of country	Countries with totemic significance, identified by plant species	Matri-moieties; totemic matri-groups; sections; personal totems
Sandbeach	Named languages related to clusters of local patri-group countries; cross-cutting moieties	Countries with totemic significance, identified by name of principal totem and other names; patri-moieties	Patri-moieties; patri-groups; personal links to mother's country
Wiil and Mi<u>n</u>ong	Broad regional identities, perhaps related to language-variety	Countries with totemic significance, identified by focal place, and possibly patri-semi-moiety	Matri-moieties; patri-semi-moieties; patri-groups; personal totems by gift or exchange; links to mother's brother's country
Ngarinyin and their neighbours	Named languages related to broad tracts of country; patri-moieties; patri-groups	Countries with totemic significance, identified by principal totem, forming bands of same-moiety countries	Patri-moieties; patri-groups; conception site
Yolngu	Languages named by patri-group identity and clustered into 'dialect groups', named isoglossically, related to country and in two cases moiety	Countries with totemic significance, identified by focal site, moiety, and patri-group	Complex patri-groups; patri-moieties; subsections

densities suggests a similar order in the size of language/locality identities in the seven regions—a few hundred. However, as Jo Birdsell pointed out long ago, they varied greatly in the area to which a given identity related—smaller on the coast, huge in the arid zone (see Table 13.6). Totemic identities varied greatly in form as well (Table 13.5). Among the case studies, totemic patri-groups were restricted to the coasts and coastal hinterland. (It is unclear whether Kŭnai country-groups were patri-groups.) People living in less predictable envronments had more 'flexible' modes of attachment. Yuwaaliyaay people of the Darling/Barwon River region held country on the basis of birth, and possessed matri-moieties, matri-groups, and sections. In the Western Desert, multi-based groups held totemic sites, with birth as the dominant mode, and organised relations in terms of generation moieties. In the southwest, patri-groups probably clustered into patrifilial semi-moieties, while in the tropical north

Table 13.6 Population densities and areas of countries

People	Population density	Average area of language or regional identity	Average country-group area
Kŭnai	1 person per 2.5–20 km²	ca 6000 km²	ca 700 km² (lakes: 100 km²)
Pitjantjatjara	1 person per 80–200 km²	ca 50 000 km²	ca 2500–3000 km² (Uluru)
Yuwaaliyaay	1 person per 30–60 km²	ca 13 000 km²	ca 2 000 km²
Wiil and Miṉong	1 person 12–25 km²	ca 4500 km² (Miṉong)	Not known
Sandbeach	1 person per 2.5–14 km²	ca 3000 km²	80 km² (120+ km² including coastal waters)
Ngarinyin	1 person per 10–25 km², higher on coast	ca 5800 km²	Not known
Yolngu	1 person per 2–20 km²	ca 4000 km²	ca 80 km²

(Sandbeach, Ngarinyin and their neighbours, and Yolngu) patri-groups correlated with patri-moieties, and Yolngu people had subsections as well.

Kinship and marriage

Modes of kinship involved similar extensions of kin-like relations to the whole of the social universe, and common aspects of kin classification included same-sex sibling-merging and bifurcate-merging in the parents' generation (Chapter 6).

Differences in kin classification were strongly related to differences in forms of marriage; this is so because people framed marriage preferences and prescriptions in terms of kin categories. While common, bestowed or 'promise' marriage did not dominate everywhere; it was least common among Kŭnai people. The timing of bestowal (in relation to the potential wife's age) varied, as did relations involved in bestowal and exchange patterns.

Kŭnai people practised institutionalised elopement as well as father–daughter and brother–sister bestowal. Pitjantjatjara people and their neighbours saw bestowal as compensation for the injury of circumcision; the circumciser was the bestower. I suggested in Chapter 12 that, as the result of matri-group organisation, Yuwaaliyaay men may have valued marriage less than the more polygynous peoples did, and may have been more reluctant to make marriage gifts. At the other extreme, wife's-mother bestowal among Yolngu people involved a chain of matrilateral relations across at three or possibly four generations. The exchange of sisters' daughters' daughters by men comprised an even more long-term exchange.

The kinship terminologies were correlated to some degree with levels of polygyny. The generational Kŭnai terminology was associated with a low level of polygyny, and the asymmetrical Ngarinyin and Yolngu terminologies were related to high and very high levels of polygyny. The Aluridja and Kariera-like terminologies were associated with low to moderate levels (Table 13.7).

Table 13.7   The relationship between kinship terminologies and polygyny

Kinship terminology	Level of polygyny
Generational kin classification (Kŭnai)	Low (usually up to two wives, sometimes three)
Aluridja system (Pitjantjatjara and their neighbours)	Low to moderate (usually up to two wives, occasionally three or four)
Kariera-like systems (Yuwaaliyaay, Wiil/Mi<u>n</u>ong, Sandbeach)	Low to moderate (up to four wives)
Aranda-like terminology with Omaha skewing (Ngarinyin and their neighbours)	High (up to seven wives recorded)
Karadjeri-like terminology with AGA rule (Yolngu)	Very high (up to 26 wives recorded)

We saw that the different forms of marriage resulted in very different social net-works, exchange relations, and patri-group dynamics (Chapters 6 and 12). Marriage between distant kin—among Kŭnai, Pitjantjatjara, and Sandbeach people—created shifting webs (or 'dispersed affinal alliance') in which relations between kin groups changed each generation. Several regions practised sibling exchange, repeatable in alternate generations in the case of second-cross-cousin marriage. Yuwaaliyaay peo-ple and their neighbours, who prescribed marriage between distant cross-cousins, engaged in reciprocal exchanges between matri-groups, and Wiil and Mi<u>n</u>ong peo-ple did so between patri-groups and semi-moieties. The asymmetrical cross-cousin marriages among Ngarinyin people and their neighbours and among Yolngu people created 'paths' of exchange and alliance between patri-groups, repeated down the generations. Large Yolngu patri-groups were linked by reciprocal marriages, although marriages between constituent lineages were asymmetrical.

Chapter 6 showed that high to very high polygyny in regions with patri-groups generated dynamics of fast growth and fast decline of the patri-groups (especially if highly polygynous sons followed highly polygynous fathers), resulting in competition and enhanced processes of succession to country and sacra. These systems were also associated with exchange networks in which powerful men occupied key positions.

People married close kin or people from geographically close communities in some regions of rich resources, such as the northwest Kimberley, northeast Arnhem Land, and eastern Cape York Peninsula. Marriages to distant relatives created ties across a region, but so did the asymmetrical chains of bestowal relations evident in Ngarinyin–Worrorra and Yolngu marriage.

Cosmologies and quasi-technologies

People of all seven regions had doctrines about a creative era when human-like and totemic ancestors lived, and about intermediaries between the totemic ancestors and the living (and the recently dead). However, cosmologies and cosmogonies varied across the continent (see Table 13.8), ranging from the strong celestial emphasis in the southeast to the strong terrestrial emphasis in the Western Desert and some other

Table 13.8   Some contrasting features of cosmologies

People	Emphasis on sky	Isolated totemic sites, short ancestral journeys	Long ancestral journeys linking sites	'Increase' sites	Aggressive use of ancestral sites and powers
Kŭnai	✓ (ghosts of dead)				
Yuwaaliyaay	✓ (Byamee)				
Pitjantjatjara			✓	✓	
Wiil/Mi<u>n</u>ong					
Sandbeach		✓		✓	✓
Ngarinyin	✓ (wanjina)		✓	✓	
Yolngu			✓		✓

regions. Doctrines differed over the length of ancestral journeys—and hence connections among localities and their peoples—and in the character of totemic sites,
which could be used for anything from 'increase' rituals to aggressive acts.

Kŭnai cosmologies had a strong celestial emphasis. Shamans obtained their powers
from ghosts of the dead living in the sky, and were thought to be able to invoke these
ghosts during séances; Yuwaaliyaay sorcerer–magicians had some similar powers.
The universal affiliation to Byamee and his family, who resided in the sky, modified
the way countries were differentiated according to local totemic beings.

Ngarinyin people and their neighbours also placed a strong emphasis on the sky,
for they conceived of and depicted *wanjina* ancestors as clouds. But for them, the sky
and the realm beneath the terrestrial waters were mirror worlds, connected by *wunggurr* (pythons). In other regions, totemic ancestors left their marks mainly on and
under the surface of the earth and their traces became powerful, local totemic sites.

Another contrast is between long ancestral journeys connecting many places and
short (or absent) ones. I have suggested that the long journeys of the totemic ancestors of Pitjantjatjara people and their neighbours linked people in a desert-wide
web that made a lot of sense in terms of access to resources in the uncertain environment of the arid zone. The extended ancestral journeys and other cross-cutting
totemic affiliations of Yolngu patri-groups seem to have had less to do with economic necessity than with exchange and cooperation in ceremonies. However,
people may have valued such links because they allowed them to exploit a variety
of resources in this ecologically heterogeneous region. Marriages to distant relatives
may have accomplished a similar result among Kŭnai and Yuwaaliyaay people. These
long links contrast strongly with Sandbeach ancestral doctrines, according to which
few ancestral sites had links to others through ancestral journeys, and totemic identities strongly differentiated countries. This pattern may reflect the fact that the
region had very rich resources to which people claimed more exclusive access than
in other regions.

People cooperated to draw on the powers of places in regional increase rites; by
contrast, they also used these powers to strike at enemies. The aggressive use of totemic

sites, in attempts to harm enemies, and the *ad hoc* procedures for increasing species, belonged to the more exclusive groups in resource-rich countries (Sandbeach, Yolngu). The Western Desert peoples, who had a high degree of regional interdependence, had cooperative increase rites, but so did Ngarinyin people and their neighbours, fore-stalling any simple environmental determinism. The cultural construction of 'magical' powers and sorcery was very similar across the regions, but their importance as resources of power and dominance in local life varied considerably.

Governance

There were (at least) four common features of governance in the seven regions:
- Ancestral law was framed more or less through shared doctrines, enacted in regional ceremonies.
- Male initiation and revelatory rites constituted formal modes of socialisation.
- Autonomous but intersecting networks of kin enforced norms and took redressive action (known as 'self-help').
- Power relations lay primarily along age and gender lines.

Rituals of male initiation varied. Secret revelatory rites were practised in the eastern part of the continent, while people of the southwest combined piercing of the nasal sep-tum with a long initiatory journey followed by an exchange ceremony. Yolngu people had both public and secret circumcision rites, while Ngarinyin people and their neigh-bours and people of the Western Desert had secret circumcision and subincision ceremonies. No doubt a comprehensive study of rituals would reveal variation in the way religico-magical knowledge was controlled, but the very uneven ethnography of the seven regions makes comparisons problematic. Some contrasts are readily apparent. Esoteric knowledge in the southeast, mainly related to Jerra-eil male initiation, centred as much on forms of magic as on the ancestral realm. The apparent absence of formal male initiation in the southwest suggests that people there may not have had anything like the elaborately layered forms of religious knowledge characteristic of other regions, though the absence may just be due to the incompleteness of the ethnography.

Table 13.9   Roles related to ancestral and magical resources

People	Roles
Kŭnai	*Birraark* (shamans), magicians/local bosses, healers, and seers
Yuwaaliyaay and their neighbours	*Wirreenun* (healer/magician/rainmakers), matri-group elders
Pitjantjatjara and their neighbours	*Ngankaṟi* (healer–sorcerers), ritual elders
Sandbeach	Patri-group elders, rainmakers
Wiil and Miṉong	*Mulgar* (healer–sorcerers), patri-group elders?
Ngarinyin and their neighbours	*Barnman* (healer–sorcerers), patri-group elders
Yolngu	Patri-group leaders, specialist ritual leaders (*djirrikaymirr, ḏalkarramirri*), separate *marrngitj* healers

Resources of male power varied from the personal magic of local 'bosses' in Gippsland (Kŭnai people), to the control of ritual lodges and patri-group sacra in the Western Desert and the tropical north. Prominent sorcerer–healer roles combined in various ways with other resources (see Table 13.9). Athol Chase has contrasted the suppression of achieved status (as opposed to age-related seniority) among Sandbeach people with competition for key environmental resources on the west coast of Cape York Peninsula (analysed by John Von Sturmer). Chase relates the former to the relative self-sufficiency of patri-group countries, each of which had a broad array of microhabitats.[1]

Gender relations appear to have varied from relatively egalitarian (Kŭnai, Yuwaaliyaay), through very separate (Pitjantjatjara), to markedly unequal (Yolngu). Except for the 'homosociality' of the desert, this variation seems not to have had a very direct connection to production, but it was indirectly implicated through the level of polygyny and the resulting structure of camps. Gender relations also had an indirect link to exchange, for the highly polygynous systems involved asymmetical exchange networks.

Control of the means of production

People framed what has been called 'local organisation' or 'land tenure' according to kin relations combined with idioms of ancestral connections, totemic geography, and totemic identity (Chapter 9). While senior residents tried to control access to their country on a day-to-day basis, ideally those with the closest ancestral and kin connections had the most say; concepts of permission were widespread. Other controls included production restrictions related to age, gender, and initiation status.

It seems that (in the seven case studies) patri-group countries existed in the better-watered zones near the coast. Other connections—to one's mother's patri-group country and one's place of conception, for example—complemented patri-group identity. In the arid zone, people belonged to places by virtue of a variety of connections (with birth and spirit conception the most important), giving people a wide range of options. (In other parts of the arid zone, however, there are patri-groups.) The patri-group growth and decline associated with high levels of polygyny have implications for competition over access to land, waters, and resources, and for processes of succession.

As for the control of access to technologies, people governed access to equipment according to age and gender, through male initiation ceremonies and other means. People of at least some regions identified items of equipment and facilities with sacred objects and ancestral sites, and gave items *ad hoc* ancestral significance to restrict their use and to restrict the distribution of foods produced with them. Some raw materials, such as ochres and stone, were also thought to have been the transformed bodily substance of ancestors.

Organisation of production

In spite of ecological and institutional variation, the organisation of production appears to have been very similar in the seven regions, as far as we can tell from the ethnographic information. In all regions, women focused on vegetable foods and small game, using digging sticks and containers as their main items of equipment, while men concentrated on larger game (including fish and marine animals where they were available). Nevertheless, the boundaries between roles were not rigid, and the genders cooperated in some productive activities. Some work was done alone; other work was done in small single-gender or mixed-gender teams (up to four people) or in larger teams (five or more). The mix of solo work, small-team work, and large-team work was similar in the seven regions. People engaged in simple cooperation (working in parallel, perhaps exchanging information), in extended cooperation (which involved a division of tasks between members of the work team), and in complex cooperation (a division of tasks in relation to one or more items of equipment). Net hunting may have increased the scale of complex cooperation, while concentrated resources such as bogong moths increased the scale of simple cooperation.

Residence groups varied in size—they were small in the arid zone, large on beaches in resource-rich areas. They varied in structure according to forms of marriage. Where people married close cousins, residence groups tended not to incorporate strangers, but reproduced existing relations. Where people married distant relatives and non-relatives, residence groups constantly incorporated people who were strangers to some degree, and gave people access to distant countries. Residence groups formed around highly polygynous men would have had a distinctive structure, with men remaining bachelors longer and many of the women and young children being attached to the same camp.

Distribution and consumption

The fundamentals of distribution in the seven regions were also quite similar, especially in the contrast between the distribution of women's product to their immediate camp and to certain other relatives (such as sons and mothers) and the distribution of men's product to the wider residence group and to wives' and potential wives' parents (Chapter 11). I suggested that kin obligations, demand sharing, and generalised reciprocity combined to shape patterns of distribution.

Some differences in patterns of distribution came to light. Kŭnai and Ngarinyin men had specific obligations to provide meat to their parents and their wife's kin. Men among Yuwaaliyaay and Pitjantjatjara and their neighbours provided food to a prospective wife to 'grow her up'. Specific obligations on the part of sister's sons to mother's brothers appear to have been recorded in only two cases (Kŭnai and Yolngu); among Sandbeach people the senior of a MB–ZS pair did the giving (including senior sister's son to junior mother's brother). Kŭnai and Pitjantjatjara husbands gave food to their wives indirectly, through the wives' parents. Consumption prohibitions related to age, gender, and initiation and reproductive status were widespread, although the uneven reports make comparisons difficult. Senior Yolngu men could impose *ad hoc* prohibitions to make certain resources available only to them.

Exchange

Relying on the concept of 'inalienable possessions' and other concepts from the work of Gregory, Weiner, and Godelier, Chapter 12 traced the movement of individuals through exchange networks during the course of their lives. People were able to produce valued items of different kinds according to their gender, age, and structural position (such as birth order), and they exchanged them for other valued items. In all regions, inalienable possessions included land and waters and related sacra. In at least some regions, these were related to inalienable gifts in the form of sacred objects and ceremonies, linked to marriage exchange and the exchange of everyday objects. We also saw that movement through the field of exchange relations varied both between different societies and between different individuals in the same society. Older brothers in the highly polygynous societies had greater opportunities to accrue control of resources associated with marriage.

Marriage exchange, which articulated with both production and distribution through marriage gifts and the reproduction of kin networks, highlights the most obvious contrasts in exchange networks among the seven regions. In contrast to the shifting webs of Kŭnai, Pitjantjatjara, and Sandbeach people, and the reciprocal exchange of Yuwaaliyaay and Wiil/Minong people, the asymmetrical forms of marriage among Ngarinyin people and their neighbours (and to an extent Yolngu people) reproduced very structured regional systems of exchange. In the *wurnan* exchange system of the northwest Kimberley, marriage articulated with the exchange of foods, raw materials, and sacred objects along 'paths' linking patri-groups in established sequences. Yolngu people probably did not have quite such a neat and tidy system, but they did think in terms of paths of exchange, and items came from and went in customary directions.

The high and very high levels of polygyny among Yolngu people and Ngarinyin people and their neighbours placed certain men at the nodes of exchange networks—they received gifts from intending and actual daughters' and sisters' husbands, and made gifts to intended and actual wives' relatives. These same men (or some of them) led powerful and growing patri-groups, and controlled patri-group sacra.

Key commonalities

A number of basic similarities have become apparent in the case studies. The fundamentals of technology were similar, although some regional differences came to light, related to environmental features and resources as well as local preferences. Everywhere kin relations extended to the whole social universe, structured social roles, and incorporated certain common features of kin classification and avoidance relations. Cosmologies presupposed rather similar temporal relations between ancestors, the living, and the dead, and everywhere the landscape was imbued with totemic significance. Of particular importance was the centrality of ancestral law in governance and regional relations. In spite of differences in ecologies, technologies, and patterns of mobility, the basics of the organisation of production appear to have been quite similar in the seven regions—in the division of labour by gender as well as the size and composition of work teams. Common features of distribution included, first, the distinction between the distribution of women's product to the camp and certain other relatives and of men's product to the wider camp; and, second, the obligations of a man to his wife's parents.

In spite of the fact that population density varied by a factor of at least 100, the scale of social life was similar in many respects in the seven regions—in the organisation of work teams, the number of people sharing a language or regional identity, and the maximum number attending major ceremonies, for example.

Of what magnitude were the differences that emerged? The strongest contrast was between Kŭnai economy and society, with its low level of polygyny, and the highly polygynous Yolngu society. Men in the former drew mainly on personal magics, of which there were many, as resources of power, as well as the influential role of shaman. Gender relations appear to have been more egalitarian than in other regions. The main resources of power for Yolngu men, by contrast, lay in the control of patri-group sacra, in fighting skill, and in the marriage system. The marriage system resulted in a distinctive pattern of rapid patri-group growth and decline, competition between patri-groups, and strong, enduring, and reproduced alliances between groups of opposite moieties. Gender relations had a more exclusive and unequal quality than among Kŭnai people. The marriage systems of the two societies account for the marked differences in the structure of social networks and exchange—between the shifting web of the Kŭnai and the asymmetrical networks of the Yolngu. The asymmetrical networks of Ngarinyin people and their neighbours, which were similar to the Yolngu networks, were articulated with a distinctive exchange system.

Polygyny and associated dynamics are another aspect of scale. High and very high levels of polygyny gave rise to an increase in the size of patri-groups and kin networks centred on a single individual; women's serial polyandry also necessarily increased with polygyny. The degree of variation between groups increased, power became more concentrated, and, perhaps, ritual became more elaborate.

The limited productivity of these ecologies and economies imposed strict constraints on social differentiation. In particular, the limited, fluctuating, and vulnerable nature of resources meant that it was in people's interests to give one another access to the resources under their control. Brian Hayden proposes the hypothesis that, among hunters and gatherers, where there were conditions of greater abundance and less fluctuation (and assuming competition did not lead to over-exploitation), exclusive ownership of resources was likely to have arisen and enduring hierarchies are likely to have been established. These features did occur on the northwest coast of North America, but even the richest environments of Australia did not provide these conditions. It is for these reasons that the main sources of power—marriage, magic, and the control of ritual and ancestral knowledge—were somewhat (but not altogether) independent of the material resource base. Within these limitations, the case studies present strongly contrasting qualities that hinge on such symbolic resources.

Some of the major differences between the regions, such as those in population density and patterns of mobility, have to do with environmental conditions and ecological relations. Others, such as the existence of doctrines about sky-beings in the southeast, appear to have a more arbitrary, historical character. Certain features (such as high levels of polygyny, which had ramifying effects through the whole fabric of social life) depended on environmental conditions but were not wholly determined by them. A look at the way in which various features correlate will bring out some of those relationships.

Correlations

This chapter has shown that the economies and societies of the cases studies do not fall into clearly differentiated categories. Each exhibits a particular cluster of features, but these cut across the cases in a variety of ways. Nevertheless, certain features are strongly related, and some have a marked association with certain environmental conditions (see Table 13.10). How are we to explain the correlations?

To return to the topic of comparison, introduced in Chapter 1, comparative analyses have looked for two kinds of broadly 'causal' link. Two or more variables may be found to co-occur in several independent cases because of direct causal connections between them—one brings about or gives rise to the other. Or they may co-occur for historical reasons; each has causal links to antecedent conditions that happen to run in parallel, and one *could* occur without the other. Common links to historical antecedents explain their co-occurrence in the same society or region. Anthropologists have developed methods to distinguish between these two kinds of connections—choosing case studies from widely separated areas, for example. In order to identify causal connections more readily, 'controlled comparison' selects case studies that resemble each other in several ways but differ in others. One then looks for the causes or conditions of the differences.[2]

There are many kinds of links through which one trait is related to another. Two traits may be linked as means to ends (e.g. mass production of washing machines and a certain kind of factory organisation), as causes and consequences (e.g. a rising incidence of infectious disease brought about by urban overcrowding), as part–whole relations (e.g. production lines and industrial factories), or by semantic relations (e.g. the relation between money and arithmetic).

A number of hazards beset comparative analysis. People in different regions may employ distinct means to the same ends, obscuring the correlations. Because of the complexity of social arrangements and the multiplicity of causes, a similar practice or trait in two societies may have different consequences and correlates. In spite of these difficulties, I shall propose some explanations for certain associations among the case studies (Table 13.10).[3]

Some features reflect broader geographical distributions and historical links, as I have suggested. Cases in point inlcude the sky-oriented cosmologies of the southeast (Kŭnai and Yuwaaliyaay) and the distribution of Aluridja kin classification across the Western Desert (Pitjantjatjara and their neighbours). These tend to have been reproduced from generation to generation in the same region, and probably have a long history.

Certain institutional forms seem to have required certain others to be practicable. For example, Kariera-like kin terminologies and associated marriage patterns had an association with patrifilial or matrifilial totemic groups, moieties, and (in the case of

Table 13.10 Selected variables in the seven case studies

People	Environment and population	Kin classification	Polygyny	Networks	Country-groups	Moieties, sections, etc.	Cosmology	Resources of power
Kūnai	Temperate climate, high rainfall; coast, lakes, and forest; medium to high population density	Generational	Low	Shifting webs	Local, possibly patrifilial	Gender totems	Celestial orientation, some local totemic differentiation, ghosts of dead	Personal magic, shamanic powers, initiation
Pitjantjatjara and their neighbours	Arid zone; sandy desert and ranges; very low population density	Aluridja	Low to moderate	Shifting webs	Birth and other bases	Generation moieties	Terrestrial orientation, long ancestral tracks, increase sites and rites	Local sacra, sorcerer–healer–magican role
Yuwaaliyaay and their neighbours	Semi-arid zone; grass-land and woodland; low to medium-low population density	Kariera	Low	Reciprocal exchanges	Birth and other bases	Matri-groups, matri-moieties, sections	Celestial orientation, universal creator, local totemic differentiation	Matri-group sacra, sorcerer–healer–magican role
Wiil and Miŋong	Mediterranean climate; coast, estuaries, swamps, heath, and forest; medium to high population density	Kariera plus transmitted relative age	Low to moderate	Reciprocal exchanges	Patri-groups	Patri-semi-moieties, matri-moieties	Local totems, ancestral tracks	Patri-group sacra?, sorcerer–healer–magican role
Sandbeach	Tropical monsoon climate; forest, coast, and sea; very high population density	Kariera plus transmitted relative age and Omaha skewing	Low to moderate	Shifting webs	Patri-groups	Patri-moieties	Local totems, few ancestral tracks, increase/aggression sites and rites	Patri-group sacra, hunting powers
Ngarinyin and their neighbours	Tropical monsoon climate; plateaus, woodland, coast and sea; medium to high population density	Aranda with Omaha skewing	High	Asymmetrical alliances	Patri-groups	Patri-moieties	Regional and local totems, short and long ancestral tracks, increase sites and rites	Patri-group sacra, polygyny, exchange, sorcerer–healer–magican role
Yolngu	Tropical monsoon climate; forest, swamps, rivers, coast, coastal waters, and islands; high to very high population density	Karadjeri plus particular features	Very high	Asymmetrical alliances among lineages	Complex patri-groups	Patri-moieties, subsections	Regional and local totems, short and long ancestral tracks	Patri-group sacra, polygyny, exchange

Yuwaaliyaay people and their neighbours) sections. The Aranda-like and Karadjeri-like terminologies, associated with asymmetrical marriage, required patri-groups and patri-moieties or their equivalents. These kinds of association are well-documented in the anthropological literature.[4]

The environment appears on the face of it to be a poor predictor of kinship systems. The case studies show Kariera-like systems to have been very adaptable, occurring in a range of environments, including semi-arid grasslands, coast and heathland areas with a Mediterranean climate, tropical forests, and coastal waters. They are associated with a variety of population densities, as well as a variety of kinds of cosmology. Conversely, a given type of environment could support quite different systems: rich coastal environments were home to generational, Kariera-like, Aranda-like, and Karadjeri-like terminologies, and varying levels of polygyny.

However, the Aluridja terminology appears to have been restricted to the Western Desert. And the peoples in this book with high to very high polygyny lived in regions with roughly similar environmental conditions—namely the rich resources and relatively high population densities near and on the coast in the tropical zone. Indeed, the other recorded societies with very high levels of polygyny belong to the coast and large habitable islands of this region; they include Tiwi people of Melville and Bathurst Islands and Warnindiljakwa people of Groote Eylandt.

How then should we explain these associations? First, some can be explained in terms of means–ends relations. I have suggested that moiety and descent-group exogamy was associated with Kariera, Aranda, and Karadjeri types of terminologies; exogamy may have helped to regulate the cross-cousin marriage that reproduced these systems. The authority and deference engendered by older men's control of religious knowledge and magic provided a condition for substantial levels of polygyny; they worked in conjunction with other institutional and population conditions. Second, certain forms of practice had consequences, intended or not. The properties of social networks were in part consequences of forms of marriage, and had important implications for differences between regions in social and political dynamics.

While a relatively high population density appears to have been a prerequisite for high and very high polygyny, certain institutional conditions were also necessary. For example, Gijingarli-speaking neighbours of Yolngu, with their Aranda-like kin classification, reciprocal exchanges between mother-in-law groups, and alternative marriages, married at only low levels of polygyny, and their patri-group dynamics were of a much smaller scale than those of Yolngu people. One of the requisite institutional conditions for high and very high polygyny appears to have been asymmetrical marriages, made possible by modified Aranda or Karadjeri terminologies in association with marriage between men and their first or second matrilateral cross-cousins. (This includes FMBSD as a 'matrilateral cross-cousin', for the Yolngu category *galay* includes FMBSD as well as other relationships.) I have already noted the relations of the structure of social networks to modes of marriage.

The multi-based affiliations to country in the Western Desert have an ecological explanation, at least in part—they maximised a person's links to different areas in an uncertain environment. A similar argument might be proposed for Yuwaaliyaay people; their drought- and flood-prone region necessitated a large degree of flexibility in relations to country, precluding patrifiliation as the main mode of connection. Conversely, the more exclusive patri-groups of Sandbeach people belonged to the richest environment in terms of rainfall and the diversity of resources available to each country-group. But the cross-cutting totemic tracks of the Yolngu region do not have a ready ecological explanation. Although they did give people access to a diverse range of countries, they were perhaps related more strongly to marriage, ritual exchange, and patri-group dynamics.

The above scheme gives explanations in terms of human actions and interests, and of institutions as instruments. Environments provided resources and enabling conditions, and also constrained and modified action. Like technologies, social institutions provided instruments for acting in relation to people and the world, but instruments that, being social products, could not readily be modified. They were not available to all people in equal measure and so were resources of differential power.

Anthropology and history

This has been a 'synchronic' study of social and economic systems and their short-run dynamics, rather than a study of processes of historical change. An issue that arose in the Introduction was the validity of the synchronic analysis used here—does it do too much violence to the historical situatedness of social life? I used this type of analysis to make the comparisons practicable; the introduction of histories, whether colonial histories or reconstructions of pre-colonial history, would have made the task impossibly complex.

These were not, of course, static societies. The analysis has looked at some short-run and repeated social processes, such as the growth and decline of patri-groups through competition over marriage, and demographic processes. A number of inconsistencies and anomalies in social forms have also emerged, such as the lack of fit between the section system and marriage relations between matri-groups among Yuwaaliyaay people and their neighbours. This may be evidence of the relatively recent adoption of sections; indeed, the recent diffusion of section systems into the Western Desert and subsections further north has been well documented. The eclecticism of Yolngu religion, in which ceremonies have links with western Arnhem Land (the Ngulmarrk or Wubarr ceremony), the arid zone (Gunapipi), and the Gulf (Mandayala), is testimony to an ongoing exchange of ceremony types. Yolngu people have thoroughly integrated Macassan themes into their own rituals over a period of 300 years or less, and more recently have combined Christian doctrines and rituals with their own myths and rituals.

For those interested in how these differences emerged through the course of Australian prehistory, linguists and archaeologists have recently begun to collaborate in order to reconstruct temporal relations and movements in Australia. They base their inferences on relations among languages as well as the archaeological record. The topics they explore include the diffusion of Pama-Nyungan languages across vast regions of the continent, the spread of subsections, and the more local movement of languages and their speakers.[5] It is beyond the scope of this book to relate the similarities and differences in the seven case studies to these broad historical factors. However, ethnological studies of this kind play a role in the investigation of historical processes.[6]

The book may also be relevant to the history of colonial and postcolonial relations. It is possible that the particular character of Aboriginal economy and society in a given region helped to shape the course of relations on the frontier and beyond. Perhaps certain forms of social organisation and leadership made stronger resistance possible in some areas, or made it possible for Europeans and others to become incorporated into Aboriginal exchange systems. While this has been a study of variation in Aboriginal economy and society 'at the threshold of colonisation', it is also intended to be a contribution to the understanding of history.

Further reading

Examples of regional studies include A. L. Kroeber's *Cultural and Natural Areas of Native North America* (1939), Marshall Sahlins's *Social Stratification in Polynesia* (1958), Paula Rubel and Abraham Rosman's *Your Own Pigs You May Not Eat* (1978), on New Guinea, and Alan Barnard's *Hunters and Herders of Southern Africa* (1992).

For recent approaches to comparison in anthropology see *Anthropology, by Comparison*, edited by Richard Fox and André Gingrich (2002). Siegfried Nadel's *Witchcraft in Four African Societies* (1952) is a much-cited example of controlled comparison in anthropology.

Archaeology and Linguistics, edited by Patrick McConvell and Nicholas Evans (1997), brings together collaborations between archaeologists and linguists working in Australia, in order to infer the past, using archaeological research, from recorded linguistic variation. In *Hawaiki*, Patrick Kirch and Roger Green (2001) draw on archaeology, linguistic research, and ethnographic studies of variation to infer a Polynesian proto-society from which the variants have arisen; the book describes the history of the movement of Polynesian peoples from their homeland, named Hawaiki. The connections and cross-currents in Australia are likely to have been more complex and certainly much longer-term than in Polynesia, and therefore much harder to trace.

Notes

1 On the contrast between eastern and western Cape York Peninsula see Chase (1984).
2 For a classic example of controlled comparison see Nadel (1952).
3 See Holy (1987: 4).
4 For example, McKinley (1971) discusses the relationship between Omaha terminologies and patrilineal descent groups.
5 See McConvell and Evans (1997) on collaborations between archaeologists and linguists.
6 See Kirch and Green (2001) on the construction of histories of Australia and the Pacific.

References

Akerman, K., 'The double raft or kalwa of the West Kimberley', *Mankind*, vol. 10, no. 1, 1975, 20–3.
—— 'Flaking stone with wooden tools', *Artefact*, vol. 4, no. 3–4, 1979a, 79–80.
—— 'Heat and lithic technology in the Kimberleys, W.A.', *Archaeology and Physical Anthropology in Oceania*, vol. 14, no. 2, 1979b, 144–51.
Akerman, K. and J. Stanton, *Riji and Jakuli: Kimberley Pearl Shell in Aboriginal Australia*, Northern Territory Museum of Arts and Sciences, Darwin, 1994.
Allen, H., 'Where the crow flies backwards: Man and land in the Darling Basin', PhD diss., Australian National University, Canberra, 1972.
—— *Nineteenth-Century Faunal Change in Western New South Wales and North-West Victoria*, University of Auckland, Auckland, 1983.
Altman, J. C., 'Hunter-Gatherers and the state: The economic anthropology of the Gunwinggu of North Australia', PhD diss., Australian National University, Canberra, 1982.
—— *Hunter-Gatherers Today: An Aboriginal Economy in North Australia*, Australian Institute of Aboriginal Studies, Canberra, 1987.
Altman, J. C. and N. Peterson, 'Rights to game and rights to cash among contemporary Australian hunter gatherers', in T. Ingold, D. Riches and J. Woodburn (eds), *Hunters and Gatherers Vol. 2: Property, Power and Ideology*, Berg, Oxford, 1988, 75–94.
Anderson, C., 'The political and economic basis of Kuku-Yalanji social history', PhD diss., University of Queensland, St. Lucia, 1984.
—— 'Anthropology and Australian Aboriginal economy 1961–1986', in R. M. Berndt and R. Tonkinson (eds), *Social Anthropology and Australian Aboriginal Studies*, Australian Institute of Aboriginal Studies, Canberra, 1988, 125–88.
Appadurai, A. (ed), *The Social Life of Things*, Cambridge University Press, Cambridge, 1986.
Arthur, W. and F. Morphy (eds), *Macquarie Atlas of Indigenous Australia*, The Macquarie Library, Sydney, in press.
Attwood, B., 'Off the mission stations: Aborigines in Gippsland 1860–90', *Aboriginal History*, vol. 10, no. 2, 1986, 131–51.
—— *The Making of the Aborigines*, Allen and Unwin, Sydney, 1989.
Austin, P., C. Williams and S. Wurm, 'The linguistic situation in north central New South Wales', in B. Rigsby and P. Sutton (eds), *Papers in Australian Linguistics, No. 13: Contributions to Australian Linguistics*, Department of Linguistics, Research School of Pacific Studies, Australian National University, Canberra, 1980, 167–80.
Austin, P. K., *A Reference Dictionary of Gamilaraay, northern New South Wales*, Department of Linguistics, La Trobe University, Bundoora, 1993.
Bagshaw, G., 'Gapu dhulway, gapu maramba: Conceptualisation and ownership of saltwater among the Burarra and Yan-nhangu peoples of northeast Arnhemland', in N. Peterson and B. Rigsby (eds), *Customary Marine Tenure in Australia*, University of Sydney, Sydney, 1998, 154–77.

Bamforth, D. B. and P. Bleed, 'Technology, flaked stone technology and risk', in M. Barton and G. A. Clark (eds), *Rediscovering Darwin: Evolutionary Theory and Archeological Explanation*, American Anthropological Association, Arlington, VA, 1997, 109–39.

Barker, C., *Commandant of Solitude: The Journals of Captain Collet Barker, 1828–1831*, Melbourne University Press, Melbourne, 1992.

Barker, J., *The Two Worlds of Jimmie Barker: The Life of an Australian Aboriginal 1900–1972, as Told to Janet Mathews*, Australian Institute of Aboriginal Studies, Canberra, 1977.

Barnard, A., *Hunters and Herders of Southern Africa: A Comparative Ethnography of the Khoisan Peoples*, Cambridge University Press, Cambridge, 1992.

Barnard, A. and J. Woodburn, 'Introduction', in T. Ingold, D. Riches and J. Woodburn (eds), *Hunters and Gatherers Vol. 2: Property, Power and Ideology*, Berg, Oxford, 1988, 4–31.

Bates, D., *The Native Tribes of Western Australia*, National Library of Australia, Canberra, 1985.

Beard, J. S., *The Vegetation of the Albany and Mount Barker Areas, Western Australia*, Vegmap Publications, Perth, 1979.

—— *The Vegetation of the Kimberley Area, Western Australia*, University of Western Australia Press, Nedlands, 1978.

—— *The Vegetation of the Newdegate and Bremer Bay Areas, Western Australia*, 2nd edn, Vegmap Publications, Perth, 1976.

Beardsley, R., P. Holder, A. Krieger, M. Meggers, J. Rinaldo and P. Kusche, 'Functional and evolutionary implication of community patterning', *Seminars in Archaeology, 1955. Society for American Archaeology Memoir 11*, 1956, 129–57.

Beckett, J., 'Further notes on the social organisation of the Wongaibon of Western New South Wales', *Oceania*, vol. 29, no. 3, 1959, 200–7.

—— 'Marriage, circumcision and avoidance among the Maljangaba of north-west New South Wales', *Mankind*, vol. 6, no. 10, 1967, 456–64.

Beckett, J., T. Donaldson, B. Steadman and S. Meredith, *Yapapunakirri, Let's Track Back: The Aboriginal World Around Mount Grenfell*, Office of the Registrar, *Aboriginal Land Rights Act 1983*, Sydney, New South Wales, 2003.

Bell, D., *Daughters of the Dreaming*, McPhee Gribble, Melbourne, 1983.

Bennett, K. H., *Descriptive List of Australian Weapons, Implements, etc, from the Darling and Lachlan Rivers, in the Australian Museum*, William Gullick, Government Printer, Sydney, 1887.

Bern, J. E., 'Ideology and domination: Toward a reconstruction of Australian Aboriginal social formation', *Oceania*, vol. 50, no. 2, 1979, 118–32.

Berndt, C. H., 'Digging sticks and spears, or, the two-sex model', in F. Gale (ed.), *Woman's Role in Aboriginal Society*, Australian Institute of Aboriginal Studies, Canberra, 1970, 39–48.

Berndt, R. M., 'Wuradjeri magic and "clever men"', *Oceania*, vol. 17, no. 4, 1947, 327–65.

—— 'Murngin (Wulamba) social organization', *American Anthropologist*, vol. 57, no. 1, 1955, 84–106.

—— 'The concept of "the tribe" in the Western Desert of Australia', *Oceania*, vol. 30, no. 2, 1959, 81–107.

—— 'Law and order in Aboriginal Australia', in C. H. Berndt and R. M. Berndt (eds), *Aboriginal Man in Australia*, Angus & Robertson, Sydney, 1965, 167–206.

—— 'Marriage and the family in North-eastern Arnhem Land', in N. M. Nimkoff (ed.), *Comparative Family Systems*, Houghton Mifflin, Boston, 1965, 77–104.

—— 'The Walmadjeri and Gugadja', in M. G. Bicchieri (ed.), *Hunters and Gatherers Today*, Holt, Rinehart and Winston, New York, 1972, 177–216.

—— *Australian Aboriginal Religion*, E. J. Brill, Leiden, 1974.

—— 'Territoriality and the problem of defining socio-cultural space', in N. Peterson (ed.), *Tribes and Boundaries in Australia*, Australian Institute of Aboriginal Studies, Canberra, 1976, 50–71.

Berndt, R. M. and C. H. Berndt, *A Preliminary Report of Field Work in the Ooldea Region, Western South-Australia*, Australian Medical Publishing Co., Sydney, 1945.

—— *Arnhem Land: Its History and its People*, Cheshire, Melbourne, 1954.

—— *The World of the First Australians*, 2nd edn, Lansdowne Press, Sydney, 1981.

—— (eds), *Aborigines of the West: Their Past and Present*, University of Western Australia Press, Nedlands, 1980.

Beveridge, P., 'Of the Aborigines inhabiting the great lacustrina and riverina depression of the lower Murray, lower Murrumbidgee, lower Lachlan and lower Darling', *Royal Society of New South Wales: Journal and Proceedings*, vol. 17, no. 1, 1883, 19–74.

Biernoff, D., 'Safe and dangerous places', in L. R. Hiatt (ed.), *Australian Aboriginal Concepts*, Australian Institute of Aboriginal Studies, Canberra, 1978, 93–105.

Biggs, A. J. W. and S. R. Philip, *Soil Survey and Agricultural Suitability of Cape York Peninsula*, Office of the Coordinator General, Brisbane, 1995.

Biggs, F., Interviews with Jeremy Beckett, Beckett notebooks, author's collection, Sydney, 1957.

Bignell, M., *The Fruit of the Country: A History of the Shire of Gnowanderup, Western Australia*, University of Western Australia Press, Nedlands, 1977.

Binford, L. R., 'Willow smoke and dogs' tails: Hunter-gatherer settlement systems and archaeological site formation', *American Antiquity*, vol. 45, 1980, 4–20.

—— *In Pursuit of the Past*, Thames & Hudson, London, 1983.

Bird, C., 'Prehistoric lithic resource utilisation: A case study from the southwest of Western Australia', PhD diss., University of Western Australia, Nedlands, 1985.

Bird, C. and C. Beeck, 'Traditional plant foods in the southwest of Western Australia: The evidence from salvage ethnography', in B. Meehan and R. Jones (eds), *Archaeology with Ethnography: An Australian Perspective*, Australian National University, Canberra, 1988, 113–22.

Bird, D. W. and R. B. Bird, 'Mardu children's hunting strategies in the Western Desert, Australia', Ninth International Conference on Hunting and Gathering Societies, Website http://www.abdn.ac.uk/chags9/1bird.htm, 2002.

Bird-David, N. H., 'Hunters and gatherers and other people—a reexamination', in T. Ingold, D. Riches and J. Woodburn (eds), *Hunters and Gatherers Vol. 1: History, Evolution and Social Change*, Berg, Oxford, 1991, 17–30.

Birdsell, J. B., 'Some environmental and cultural factors influencing the structuring of Australian aboriginal populations', *American Naturalist*, vol. 87, no. 834, 1953, 171–207.

—— 'Local group composition among the Australian Aborigines: A critique of the evidence from fieldwork conducted since 1930', *Current Anthropology*, vol. 11, no. 2, 1970, 115–42.

Blake, B. J., 'Australian case systems: Some typological and historical observations', in S. A. Wurm (ed.), *Australian Linguistic Studies*, Australian National University, Canberra, 1979, 323–94.

Blanket distribution records of the Tyers district 1852–58, Tyers Squatters' Runs A842, Mitchell Library, Sydney.

Blows, M., 'Eaglehawk and Crow: Birds, myths and moieties in south-east Australia', in L. R. Hiatt (ed.), *Australian Aboriginal Mythology*, Australian Institute of Aboriginal Studies, Canberra, 1975, 24–45.

Blundell, V., 'Hunter-gatherer territoriality: Ideology and behavior in northwest Australia', *Ethnohistory,* vol. 27, no. 2, 1980, 103–17.

Blundell, V. and R. H. Layton, 'Marriage, myth and models of exchange in the West Kimberley', *Mankind*, vol. 11, no. 3, 1978, 231–45.

Blundell, V. J., 'Aboriginal adaptation in northwest Australia', PhD diss., University of Wisconsin, 1975.

Bohannan, P and L. Bohannan, *Tiv Economy*, Longman, London, 1968.

Bonney, F., 'On some customs of the Aborigines of the River Darling, New South Wales', *Journal of the Royal Anthropological Institute*, vol. 13, no. 2, 1883, 122–37.

—— unpublished manuscript, Mitchell Library, Sydney, c1881.

Borsboom, A. P., 'Maradjiri: A modern ritual complex in Arnhem Land, north Australia', PhD diss., Nijmegen Katholieke Universiteit, 1978.

Bourdieu, P., *Outline of a Theory of Practice*, Cambridge University Press, Cambridge, 1977.

—— *The Logic of Practice*, Polity Press, Cambridge, 1990.

—— *Distinction: A Social Critique of the Judgement of Taste*, Routledge, London, 1992.

Brokensha, P., *The Pitjantjatjara and their Crafts*, Aboriginal Arts Board, Sydney, 1975.

Browne, J., 'Statement for the Aborigines Protection Society respecting the natives of King Georges Sound', 26 June, 1838, State Library of New South Wales.

Buchan Sesquicentenary Committee, *Bukan-Mungie: 150 Years of Settlement in the Buchan District— 1839–1989*, E-Gee Printers, Bairnsdale, 1989.

Builth, H., 'New evidence supports claims that not all Aboriginals were nomads', Flinders University website: News, Events and Notices, http://www.flinders.edu.au/news/articles/?story=fj15v13s01, 2001.

Bulmer, J. M., Papers, Museum of Victoria, B1 F2, BI F4, B4 F7, B10 F5.

—— *Victorian Aborigines: John Bulmer's Recollections 1855–1908*, Museum of Victoria, Melbourne, 1994.

Burbank, 'The *mirrirri* as ritualised aggression', *Oceania*, vol. 56, no. 1, 1985, 47–55.

Burbidge, A. A., N. L. McKenzie, A. Chapman and P. M. Lambert, *The Wildlife of Some Existing and Proposed Reserves in the Great Victoria and Gibson Deserts, Western Australia*, Department of Fisheries and Wildlife, WA, Perth, 1976.

Burrows, N., B. Ward, A. Robinson and Y. Woods, *Gibson Desert Nature Reserve Field Trip, August 10–26, 1987*, Department of Conservation and Land Management, WA, Perth, 1987.

Butlin, N. G., *Our Original Aggression: Aboriginal Populations of Southeastern Australia 1788–1850*, Allen & Unwin, Sydney, 1983.

—— *Economics and the Dreamtime: A Hypothetical History*, Cambridge University Press, Cambridge, 1993.

Cameron, A. L. P., 'On some tribes of western New South Wales', *Science of Man (n.s.)*, vol. 2, no. 1, 217–8; no. 12, 221, 1899.

Camm, J.C.R. and J. McQuilton, *Australians: A Historical Atlas*, Fairfax, Syme & Weldon Associates, Sydney, 1987.

Campbell, A., 'Elementary food production by the Australian Aborigines', *Mankind*, vol. 6, no. 5, 1965, 206–11.

Campbell, J., *Invisible Invaders: Smallpox and Other Diseases in Aboriginal Australia 1780–1880*, Melbourne University Press, Melbourne, 2002.

Cane, S. B., 'Desert demography: A case study of pre-contact Aboriginal densities', in B. Meehan and N. White (eds), *Hunter-Gatherer Demography: Past and Present*, University of Sydney, Sydney, 1990, 149–59.

Capell, A., 'The languages of the Northern Kimberley Division, WA', *Mankind*, vol. 2, no. 6, 1939a, 169–75.

—— 'Mythology in northern Kimberley, northwest Australia', *Oceania*, vol. 9, no. 4, 1939b, 382–404.

—— 'The classification of languages in north and north-west Australia', *Oceania*, vol. 10, no. 3–4, 1940, 241–72, 404–33.

—— *Cave Painting Myths: Northern Kimberley* (Oceania Linguistics Monographs no. 18), University of Sydney, Sydney, vol. 18, 1972.

Capell, A. and H. H. J. Coate, *Comparative Studies in Northern Kimberley Languages*, Australian National University, Canberra, 1984.

Carnahan, J. and T. Deveson, *Atlas of Australian Resources: Vol. 6 Vegetation*, Australian Surveying and Land Information Group (AUSLIG), Department of Administrative Services, Canberra, 1990.

Cashdan, E., 'Territoriality among human foragers: Ecological models and an application to four Bushman groups', *Current Anthropology*, vol. 24, no. 1, 1983, 47–66.

Chase, A. K., 'Between land and sea: Aboriginal coastal groups in Cape York Peninsula', *Workshop on the Northern Sector of The Great Barrier Reef, Papers and Proceedings of a Workshop held in Townsville, Australia, 20 and 21 April 1978*, Townsville, 1978, 160–76.

—— 'Cultural continuity: Land and resources among East Cape York Aborigines', in N. C. Stevens and A. Bailey (eds), *Contemporary Cape York Peninsula*, Royal Society of Queensland, Brisbane, 1980a, 83–8.

—— 'Which way now? Tradition, continuity and change in a North Queensland Aboriginal community', PhD diss., University of Queensland, St Lucia, 1980b.

—— 'Belonging to country: Territory, identity and environment in Cape York Peninsula, Northern Australia', in L. R. Hiatt (ed.), *Aboriginal Landowners: Contemporary Issues in the Determination of Traditional Aboriginal Land Ownership*, University of Sydney, Sydney, 1984, 104–22.

—— 'Perceptions of the past among north Queensland Aboriginal people: The intrusion of Europeans and consequent social change', in R. Layton (ed.), *Who Needs the Past? Indigenous Values and Archaeology*, Unwin Hyman, London, 1989, 169–79.

Chase, A. K. and P. Sutton, 'Australian Aborigines in a rich environment', in W. H. Edwards (ed.), *Traditional Aboriginal Society: A Reader*, Macmillan, Melbourne, 1987, 68–95.

Chippendale, G. M., *Eucalypts of the Western Australian Goldfields*, Australian Government Publishing Service for the Minister for Primary Industry, Canberra, 1973.

Clark, W. N., 'An enquiry respecting the Aborigines of south-western Australia', *Enquirer*, Perth, 1842.

Clunies Ross, M. and L. R. Hiatt, 'Sand sculptures at a Gidjingali burial rite', in P. J. Ucko (ed.), *Form in Indigenous Art: Schematization in the Art of Aboriginal Australia and Prehistoric Europe*, Australian Institute of Aboriginal Studies, Canberra, 1977, 131–46.

Coate, H. H. J. and A. P. Elkin, *Ngarinjin-English Dictionary*, University of Sydney, Sydney, 1974.

Collie, A., 'Anecdotes and remarks relative to the Aborigines at King George's Sound, 1834', in N. Green (ed.), *Nyungar—The People: Aboriginal Customs in the Southwest of Australia*, Creative Research in association with Mt. Lawley College, 1979.

Commonwealth Bureau of Meteorology, website, http://www.bom.gov.au/climate, 2003.

Commonwealth of Australia, *Australian National Resources Atlas*, National Land and Water Resources Audit, National Heritage Trust, http://audit.ea.gov.au/website/latest/index.cfm, 2003.

Conservation Commission of the Northern Territory, *Vegetation Survey of the Northern Territory: Southern Sheet*, Conservation Commission of the Northern Territory, Darwin, 1991.

Coutts, P. J. F., 'The Archaeology of Wilson's Promontory', MA diss., Australian National University, Canberra, 1967.

Coutts, P., V. Witter, R. Cochrane, and J. Patrick, *Coastal Archaeology in Victoria*, Victorian Archaeological Survey, Melbourne, n.d.

Crawford, I. M., *The Art of the Wandjina: Aboriginal Cave Paintings in Kimberley, Western Australia*, Oxford University Press, Melbourne, 1968.

—— *Traditional Aboriginal Plant Resources in the Kalumburu Area: Aspects in Ethno-Economics*, Western Australian Museum, Perth, 1982.

Creighton, S., 'Teach me black: An ethnographic account of recent transformation in education at Yirrkala, Northeast Arnhem Land', PhD diss., Australian National University, Canberra, 2003.

Cundy, B., 'Australian spear and spearthrower technology', PhD diss., Australian National University, Canberra, 1980.

Curr, E. M., *The Australian Race, Vol. 1, 2*, John Ferres, Melbourne, 1886.

—— *The Australian Race, Vol. 3, 4*, John Ferres, Melbourne, 1887.

Cuthill, W. J., 'Documents referring to "wild" or captive white women in Gippsland, Victoria', MS10065, Cuthill Collection, n.d.

Danaher, K. F., *Marine Vegetation of Cape York Peninsula*, Australian Government Publishing Service, Brisbane, 1995.

Dargin, P., *Aboriginal Fisheries of the Darling-Barwon Rivers*, Brewarrina Historical Society, Brewarrina NSW, 1976.

Davey, K., *Australian Desert Life*, Periwinkle Books, Melbourne, 1969.

Davidson, D. S., 'Fire-making in Australia', *American Anthropologist*, vol. 49, no. 3, 1947, 426–37.

Dawson, W. T. and J. H. W. Pettit, 'Gippsland vocabularies and place names', State Library of Victoria, Howitt Papers, MS 9356, Box 1054/2(c).

Dingle, A. E., *Aboriginal Economy: Patterns of Experience*, McPhee Gribble, Melbourne, 1988.

Division of National Mapping and Department of National Development, *Atlas of Australian Resources*, 6 vols, Division of National Mapping, Canberra, 1986.

Donaldson, T., *Ngiyambaa, the Language of the Wangaaybuwan*, Cambridge University Press, Cambridge, 1980.

Doring, J., *Gwion Gwion: Secret and Sacred Pathways of the Ngarinyin Aboriginal People of Australia*, Konemann, Koln, 2000.

Douglas, W. H., *The Aboriginal Languages of South-West Australia*, Australian Institute of Aboriginal Studies, Canberra, 1968.

—— *Illustrated Topical Dictionary of the Western Desert Language Warburton Ranges Dialect, Western Australia*, Australian Institute of Aboriginal Studies, Canberra, 1977.

Dousset, L., 'Accounting for context and substance: The Australian Western Desert kinship system', *Anthropological Forum*, vol. 12, no. 2, 2002a, 193–204.

—— 'The global versus the local: Cognitive processes of kin-recognition in Australia', unpublished manuscript, Discipline of Anthropology, University of Western Australia, 2002b.

Dow, C., 'The totemic landscape', unpublished manuscript, author's collection, Canberra, n.d. (a).

—— 'Tatungalung plant use', unpublished manuscript, author's collection, Canberra, n.d. (b).

Dunbar, G. K., 'Notes on the Ngemba Tribe of the Central Darling River, Western New South Wales', *Mankind*, vol. 3, no. 5, 1943, 140–8; vol. 4, no. 5, 1944, 172–80.

Dunlop, I., *At the Canoe Camp*, (16mm film), Film Australia, Sydney, 1981.

Durkheim, É, *The Elementary Forms of the Religious Life*, Free Press, New York, 1965 (1915).

Dussart, F., *The Politics of Ritual in an Aboriginal Settlement: Kinship, Gender, and the Currency of Knowledge*, Smithsonian Institute Press, Washington, 2000.

Dyson-Smith, R. and E. A. Smith, 'Human territoriality: An ecological reassessment', *American Anthropologist*, vol. 80, no. 1, 1978, 21–41.

Elkin, A. P., 'The social organisation of South Australian tribes', *Oceania*, vol. 2, no. 1, 1931, 44–73.

—— 'Social Organisation in the Kimberley Division, north-western Australia', *Oceania*, vol. 2, no. 3, 1932, 296–333.

—— *The Australian Aborigines: How to Understand Them*, 1st edn, Angus & Robertson, Sydney, 1938.

—— 'Kinship in South Australia', *Oceania*, vol. 8, no. 4, 1938, 419–52; vol. 9 no. 1, 1939, 41–78; vol. 10, no. 2–4, 1940, 196–234, 295–349, 369–88.

—— 'The complexity of social organization in Arnhem Land', *Southwestern Journal of Anthropology*, vol. 6, no. 1, 1950, 1–20.

—— 'Murngin kinship re-examined, and remarks on some generalisations', *American Anthropologist*, vol. 55, no. 3, 1953, 412–19.

—— *The Australian Aborigines—How to Understand Them*, 3rd edn, Angus & Robertson, Sydney, 1954.

Ellen, R., *Environment, Subsistence, and System: The Ecology of Small-scale Social Formations*, Cambridge University Press, Cambridge, 1982.

Elliott, C., '"Mewal is Merri's name": Form and Ambiguity in Marrangu Cosmology, North Central Arnhem Land', MA diss., Australian National University, Canberra, 1991.

Eyre, E., *Journals of Expeditions of Discovery into Central Australia, and Overland from Adelaide to King George's Sound*, T. and W. Boone, London, 1845.

Falkenberg, J., *Kin and Totem: Group Relations of Australian Aborigines in the Port Keats District*, Humanities Press, New York, 1962.

Ferguson, W. C., 'Archaeological investigations at the Quininup Brook site complex, Western Australia', *Records of the Western Australian Museum*, vol. 8, no. 4, 1981, 609–37.

—— 'A mid-holocene depopulation of the Australian southwest', PhD diss., Australian National University, Canberra, 1985.

—— 'Mokaré's domain', in D. J. Mulvaney and J. P. White (eds), *Australians to 1788*, Fairfax, Syme & Weldon, Sydney, 1987, 120–45.

Fingleton, J. and J. Finlayson, *Anthropology in the Native Title era*, Australian Institute of Aboriginal and Torres Strait Islander Studies, Canberra, 1995.

Finlayson, J., B. Rigsby, and H. Bek, *Connections in Native Title: Genealogies, Kinship and Groups* (CAEPR Research Monograph No. 1), Centre for Aboriginal Economic Policy Research, Australian National University, Canberra, 1995.

Fison, L. and A. W. Howitt, *Kamilaroi and Kurnai: Group-Marriage and Relationship, and Marriage by Elopement*, George Robertson, Melbourne, 1880.

Flannery, T. F., *The Future Eaters: An Ecological History of the Australasian Lands and People*, New Holland Publishers, Sydney, 1997.

Flood, J., *The Moth Hunters: Aboriginal Prehistory of the Australian Alps*, Australian Institute of Aboriginal Studies, Canberra, 1980.

Fortes, M., 'The structure of unilineal descent groups', *American Anthropologist*, vol. 55, no. 1, 1953, 17–41.

Foster, M. L., 'Symbolism: The foundation of culture', in T. Ingold (ed.), *Companion Encyclopedia of Anthropology*, Routledge, London, 2002, 366–95.

Fox, R., *Kinship and Marriage: An Anthropological Perspective*, Penguin, Harmondsworth, 1967.

Fox, R. G. and A. Gingrich, 'Introduction', in A. Gingrich and R. G. Fox (eds), *Anthropology, by Comparison*, Routledge, London, 2002, 1–24.

Frazer, S. J. G., *The Golden Bough: A Study in Magic and Religion*, vol. 1, MacMillan, London, 1923–7.

—— *The Native Races of Australasia*. Arranged and edited by Robert Angus Downie, Humphries, London, 1939.

Frith, H. J., *Waterfowl in Australia*, Angus & Robertson, Sydney, 1967.

Frith, H. J. and J. H. Calaby, *Kangaroos*, Cheshire, Melbourne, 1969.

Gammage, B., 'Australia under Aboriginal management', The Barry Andrews Memorial Lecture, Australian Defence Force Academy, 2002.

Gardner, P. D., *Through Foreign Eyes: European Perceptions of the Kurnai Tribe of Gippsland*, Gippsland Institute of Advanced Education, Churchill, Vic, 1988.

Geertz, C., 'Religion as a cultural system', in M. Banton (ed.), *Anthropological Approaches to the Study of Religion*, Tavistock, London, 1966, 1–46.

Gentilli, J., *Physioclimatology of Western Australia*, Department of Geography, University of Western Australia, Perth, 1978.

Gibson, K. R., and T., Ingold (eds), *Tools, Language and Cognition in Human Evolution*, Cambridge University Press, Cambridge, 1993.

Giddens, A., *Central Problems in Social Theory: Action, Structure and Contradiction in Social Analysis*, Macmillan, London, 1979.

—— *The Constitution of Society*, University of California Press, Berkeley, 1984.

Godelier, M., *The Enigma of the Gift*, University of Chicago Press, Chicago, 1999.

Goodall, H., *Invasion to Embassy: Land in Aboriginal Politics in New South Wales, 1770–1972*, Allen & Unwin, St Leonards, NSW, 1996.

Goody, E., *Parenthood and Social Reproduction*, Cambridge University Press, Cambridge, 1982.

Gott, B., 'Ecology of root use by the Aborigines of southern Australia', *Archaeology in Oceania*, vol. 17, no. 1, 1982, 59–67.

—— 'Use of Victorian plants by Koories', in D. B. Foreman and N. G. Walsh (eds), *Flora of Victoria*, vol. 1, Inkata Press, Melbourne, 1993, 195–211.

—— 'Cumbungi, *Typha* species, a staple Aboriginal food in Southern Australia', *Australian Aboriginal Studies*, no. 1, 1999, 33–50.

—— 'Aboriginal fire management in south-eastern Australia: Aims and frequency', Native Solutions: Indigenous Knowledge and Today's Fire Management Conference, Hobart, 2000.

—— 'Notes on the file of plants of the Central Highlands and Gippsland utilised by Aborigines', unpublished manuscript, author's collection, 2001.

Gott, B. and J. Conran, *Victorian Koorie Plants: Some Plants used by Victorian Koories for Food, Fibre, Medicines and Implements*, Yanennanock Women's Group, Aboriginal Keeping Place, Hamilton, Vic, 1998.

Gould, R. A., 'Notes on hunting, butchering, and sharing of game among the Ngatatjara and their neighbours in the West Australian desert', *Kroeber Anthropological Society–Papers*, vol. 36, 1967, 41–66.

—— 'Subsistence behaviour among the Western Desert aborigines of Australia', *Oceania*, vol. 39, no. 4, 1969a, 253–74.

—— *Yiwara: Foragers of the Australian Desert*, Charles Scribner's Sons, New York, 1969b.

—— 'Uses and effects of fire among the Western Desert Aborigines of Australia', *Mankind*, vol. 8, no. 1, 1971, 14–24.

—— *Living Archaeology*, Cambridge University Press, Cambridge, 1980.

Gould, R. A., D. A. Koster and A. H. L. Sontz, 'Lithic assemblages of the Western Desert Aborigines of Australia', *American Antiquity*, vol. 36, no. 2, 1971, 149–69.

Green, N., *Aborigines of the Albany Region 1821–1898*, University of Western Australia Press, Nedlands, 1989.

Greenway, C. C., 'Kamilaroi language and traditions', *Journal of the Royal Anthropological Institute*, vol. 7, 1877–78, 233–46

Gregory, C. A., *Gifts and Commodities*, Academic Press, London, 1982.

—— 'Exchange and Reciprocity', in T. Ingold (ed.), *Companion Encyclopedia of Anthropology: Humanity, Culture and Social Life*, Routledge, London, 1994, 911–39.

Gregory, C. A. and J. C. Altman, *Observing the Economy*, Routledge, London, 1989.

Grey, G., *Journals of Two Expeditions of Discovery in North-west and Western Australia, During the Years 1837, 38 and 39*, 2 vols, T. W. Boone, London, 1841.

Groger-Wurm, H., *Australian Aboriginal Bark Paintings and their Mythological Interpretation: Vol. 1 Eastern Arnhem Land*, Australian Institute of Aboriginal Studies, Canberra, 1973.

Haebich, A., ' "A Bunch of Cast-Offs": Aborigines of the southwest of Western Australia, 1900–1936', Ph.D diss., Murdoch University, 1985.

Hale, H. M. and N. B. Tindale, 'Aborigines of Princess Charlotte Bay, North Queensland', *Records of the South Australian Museum*, vol. 5, no. 1, 1933, 63–116

Hall, J. 'Fishing with dolphins: Affirming a traditional Aboriginal fishing story in Moreton Bay, S.E. Queensland', *Royal Society of Queensland Symposium: Focus on Stradbroke—New Information on North Stradbroke Island and Surrounding Areas, 1974–84*, Boolarong Publications, Brisbane, and Stradbroke Island Management Organisation, Amity Point, 1984, 16–22.

Hallam, S., *Fire and Hearth: A Study of Aboriginal Usage and European Usurpation in South-western Australia*, Australian Institute of Aboriginal Studies, Canberra, 1975.

Halperin, R. H., *Cultural Economies, Past and Present*, University of Texas Press, Austin, 1994.

Halstead, G., *The Story of Metung and its First Inhabitants*, Gay Halstead Publishing, Sydney, 1977.

Hamby, L., 'Containers of power: Fibre forms from Northeast Arnhem Land', PhD diss., Australian National University, Canberra, 2001.

Hamilton, A., 'Timeless Transformation: Women, Men and History in the Australian Western Desert', PhD diss., University of Sydney, 1979.

—— 'Dual social systems: Technology, labour and women's secret rites in the eastern Western Desert of Australia', *Oceania*, vol. 51, no. 1, 1980, 4–19.

—— 'A complex strategical situation: Gender and power in Aboriginal Australia', in N. Grieve and P. Grimshaw (eds), *Australian Women: Feminist Perspectives*, Oxford University Press, Melbourne, 1981a, 69–85.

—— *Nature and Nurture: Aboriginal Child-Rearing in North-Central Arnhem Land*, Australian Institute of Aboriginal Studies, Canberra, 1981b.

—— 'Descended from father, belonging to country: Rights to land in the Australian Western Desert', in E. B. Leacock and R. B. Lee (eds), *Politics and History in Band Societies*, Cambridge University Press, Cambridge, 1982, 85–108.

Harris, C. C., *Kinship*, Open University Press, Milton Keynes, 1990.

Harris, D., 'Interview with Jeremy Beckett at Murrin Bridge', Australian Institute of Aboriginal Studies, 1964.

Harris, D. R., 'Subsistence strategies across Torres Strait', in J. Allen, J. Golson and R. Jones (eds), *Sunda and Sahul: Prehistoric Studies in Southeast Asia, Melanesia and Australia*, Academic Press, London, 1977, 421–63.

—— 'Introduction: Themes and concepts in the study of early agriculture', in D. R. Harris (ed.), *The Origins and Spread of Agriculture and Pastoralism in Eurasia*, Smithsonian Institute Press, Washington D.C., 1996, 1–9.

Harris, M., 'A "New Deal" for Victorian Aborigines 1957–1968', MA diss., Monash University, Melbourne, 1988.

Harris, S., *Culture and Learning: Tradition and Education in North-east Arnhem land*, Australian Institute of Aboriginal Studies, Canberra, 1984.

Harrison, S., 'Ritual as intellectual property', *Man (n.s.)*, vol. 27, no. 2, 1992, 225–44.

Hart, C. M. W. and A. R. Pilling, *The Tiwi of North Australia*, Holt, Rinehart & Winston, New York, 1960.

Hassell, E., 'Myths and folk-tales of the Wheelman tribe of South-Western Australia', *Folklore*, vol. 45, no. 3, 4, 1934, 232–48, 317–41.

—— 'Myths and Folk-tales of the Wheelman tribe of South-Western Australia—III–IV', *Folk-Lore*, vol. 46, no. 2, 1935, 122–47; no. 3, 1935, 268–81.

—— 'Notes on the ethnology of the Wheelman tribe of south Western Australia', *Anthropos*, vol. 31, 1936, 679–711.

—— *My Dusky Friends: Aboriginal Life, Customs and Legends and Glimpses of Station Life at Jarramungup in the 1880s*, C.W. Hassell, East Fremantle, 1975.

Hayden, B. D., 'Stone tool functions in the Western Desert', in R. V. S. Wright (ed.), *Stone Tools as Cultural Markers: Change, Evolution and Complexity*, Australian Institute of Aboriginal Studies, Canberra, 1977, 178–88.

—— 'Subsistence and ecological adaptations of modern hunter/gatherers', in S. O. Harding and D. Teleki (eds), *Omnivorous Primates: Gathering and Hunting in Human Evolution*, Columbia University Press, New York, 1981, 344–421.

Heath, J., *Linguistic Diffusion in Arnhem Land*, Australian Institute of Aboriginal Studies, Canberra, 1978.

Heathcote, R. L., *Australia*, Longman Scientific & Technical, Burnt Mill, Harlow, 1994.

Heinz, H., 'Territoriality among the Bushmen in general and the Ko in particular', *Anthropos*, vol. 67, 1972, 405–16.

Helman, P., *The Darling River: A National Estate Study of the Natural Environment*, National Trust of Australia, New South Wales, 1986.

Helms, R., 'Anthropological notes', *The Proceedings of the Linnean Society of New South Wales*, vol. 20, no. 3, 1896, 387–408.

Hercus, L. A., *Victorian Languages: A Late Survey*, Department of Linguistics, Research School of Pacific Studies, Australian National University, Canberra, 1986.

Hernandez, T., 'Social organisation of the Drysdale River tribes, Northwest Australia', *Oceania*, vol. 11, no. 3, 1941, 122–33.

Hiatt, B., 'The food quest and economy of the Tasmanian Aborigines', *Oceania*, vol. 38, no. 3, 1967, 190–219.

—— 'Woman the gatherer', in F. Gale (ed.), *Women's Role in Aboriginal Society*, Australian Institute of Aboriginal Studies, Canberra, 1970, 4–15.

Hiatt, L. R., 'Local organisation among the Australian Aborigines', *Oceania*, vol. 32, no. 4, 1962, 267–86.

—— *Kinship and Conflict: A Study of an Aboriginal Community in Northern Arnhem Land*, Australian National University, Canberra, 1965.

—— 'Your mother in law is poison', *Man (n.s.)*, vol. 19, no. 2, 1982, 184–98.

—— (ed.), *Aboriginal Landowners: Contemporary Issues in the Determination of Traditional Aboriginal Land Ownership*, (Oceania Monographs No. 27), University of Sydney, Sydney, 1984.

—— 'Maidens, males and Marx: Some contrasts in the work of Frederick Rose and Claude Meillassoux', *Oceania*, vol. 56, no. 1, 1985, 34–46.

—— *Aboriginal Political Life (The Wentworth Lecture 1984)*, Australian Institute of Aboriginal Studies, Canberra, 1986.

—— *Arguments about Aborigines: Australia and the Evolution of Social Anthropology*, Cambridge University Press, Cambridge, 1996.

Hiscock, P., 'A cache of tulas from the Boulia district, western Queensland', *Archaeology in Oceania*, vol. 23, no. 2, 1988, 60–70.

—— 'Blunt and to the point: Changing technological strategies in Holocene Australia', in I. Lilley (ed.), *Archaeology in Oceania: Australia and the Pacific Islands*, Blackwell, Oxford, in press.

Holy, L., 'Introduction—description, generalization and comparison: Two paradigms', in L. Holy (ed.), *Comparative Anthropology*, Basil Blackwell, Oxford, 1987, 1–21.

Horn, A. M., *Surface Water Resources of Cape York Peninsula*, Office of the Coordinator General, Brisbane, 1995.

Horton, D. R., 'The burning question: Aborigines, fire and Australian ecosystems', *Mankind*, vol. 13, no. 3, 1982, 237–51.

Horton, R., *The Pure State of Nature: Sacred Cows, Destructive Myths and the Environment*, Allen & Unwin, St. Leonards NSW, 2000.

Hotchin, K. L., 'Environmental and cultural change in the Gippsland Lakes region, Victoria, Australia', PhD diss., Australian National University, Canberra, 1990.

Howitt, A. W., 'The Kŭrnai tribe: Their customs in peace and war', in L. Fison and A. W. Howitt (eds), *Kamilaroi and Kurnai: Group-Marriage and Relationship, and Marriage by Elopement*, George Robertson, Melbourne, 1880, 177–260.

—— *The Native Tribes of South-East Australia*, Macmillan, London, 1904.

—— Papers (AIATSIS), Australian Institute of Aboriginal and Torres Strait Islander Studies, Canberra.

—— Papers (MV), Museum Victoria, B4 F7, B5 F1, B6 F1, B6 F5, B10 F5,

—— Papers (SLV), State Library of Victoria, B8 ms1053/3a, 3b, 4a,

Hugill, P., *World Trade Since 1431; Geography, Technology and Capitalism*, Johns Hopkins University Press, Baltimore, 1993.

Hutton, G., *Australia's Natural Heritage*, Australian Conservation Foundation, Hawthorn, Vic, 1981.

Ingold, T., *The Appropriation of Nature: Essays on Human Ecology and Social Relations*, Manchester University Press, Manchester, 1986.

—— 'Growing plants and raising animals: An anthropological perspective on domestication', in D. R. Harris (ed.), *The Origins and Spread of Agriculture and Pastoralism in Eurasia*, Smithsonian Institute Press, Washington D.C., 1996, 12–24.

Isbell, R. F., 'Climate, rocks, soils', in J. Wright, N. Mitchell and P. Watling (eds), *Reef, Rainforest, Mangroves, Man*, Wildlife Preservation Society of Queensland, Brisbane, 1980a, 24–5.

—— 'Soil landscapes of Cape York Peninsula', in N. C. Stevens and A. Bailey (eds), *Contemporary Cape York Peninsula*, Royal Society of Queensland, Brisbane, 1980b, 5–57.

Jones, R., 'Fire-stick farming', *Australian Natural History*, vol. 16, no. 7, 1969, 224–8.

—— 'The neolithic, palaeolithic and the hunting gardeners: Man and land in the Antipodes', in R. P. Suggate and M. M. Cresswell (eds), *Quaternary Studies: Selected Papers from IX INQUA Congress*, Royal Society of New Zealand, Wellington, 1975, 21–34.

—— *Archaeological Research in Kakadu National Park*, Australian Parks and Wildlife Service, Canberra, 1985.

Jones, R. and J. Bowler, 'Struggle for the savanna: Northern Australia in ecological and prehistoric perspective', in R. Jones (ed.), *Northern Australia: Options and Implications*, Research School of Pacific Studies, Australian National University, Canberra, 1980, 3–31.

Jones, R. and N. White, 'Point Blank: Stone tool manufacture at the Ngilipitji quarry, Arnhem Land, 1981', in B. Meehan and R. Jones (eds), *Archaeology with Ethnography: An Australian Perspective*, Dept. of Prehistory, Australian National University, Canberra, 1988.

Kaberry, P. M., *Aboriginal Woman: Sacred and Profane*, Routledge, London, 1939.

Keast, A. (ed.), *Ecological Biogeography of Australia, Vol. 3*, W. Junk, The Hague, 1981.

Keen, I., 'Yolngu sand sculptures in context', in P. J. Ucko (ed.), *Form in Indigenous Art: Schematisation in the Art of Aboriginal Australia and Prehistoric Europe*, Australian Institute of Aboriginal Studies, Canberra, 1977, 165–83.

—— 'One ceremony, one song: An economy of religious knowledge among the Yolngu of northeast Arnhem Land', PhD diss., Australian National University, Canberra, 1978.

—— 'How some Murngin men marry ten wives: The marital implications of matrilateral cross-cousin structures', *Man*, vol. 17, no. 4, 1982, 620–42.

—— 'Aboriginal governance', in J. C. Altman and F. Merlan (eds), *Emergent Inequalities in Aboriginal Australia*, (Oceania Monographs no. 38), Sydney, 1989, 5–57.

—— *Knowledge and Secrecy in an Aboriginal Religion: Yolngu of Northeast Arnhem Land*, Clarendon Press, Oxford, 1994.

—— 'Metaphor and the metalanguage: Groups in northeast Arnhem Land', *American Ethnologist*, vol. 22, no. 3, 1995, 502–27.

—— 'The Western Desert vs the rest: Rethinking the contrast', in F. Merlan, J. Morton and A. Rumsey (eds), *Scholar and Sceptic: Australian Aboriginal Studies in Honour of L. R. Hiatt*, Aboriginal Studies Press, Canberra, 1997, 65–93.

—— 'A bundle of sticks: The debate over Yolngu clans', *Journal of the Royal Anthropological Institute*, vol. 6, no. 3, 2000, 419–36.

—— 'Seven Aboriginal marriage systems and their correlates', *Anthropological Forum*, vol. 12, no. 2, 2002, 145–57.

Keesing, R. M., *Kin Groups and Social Structure*, Holt, Rinehart & Winston, Fort Worth, 1975.

Kelly, R. L., *The Foraging Spectrum: Diversity in Hunter-Gatherer Lifeways*, Smithsonian Institution Press, Washington, 1995.

Kendon, A., *Sign Languages of Aboriginal Australia: Cultural, Semiotic and Communicative Perspectives*, Cambridge University Press, Cambridge, 1988.

Kirch, P. V. and R. C. Green, *Hawaiki, Ancestral Polynesia: An Essay in Historical Anthropology*, Cambridge University Press, Cambridge, 2001.

Klappa, S., 'Gathering cultivated resources, cultivating wild resources', Poster presented at the Ninth International Conference on Hunting and Gathering Societies, Edinburgh, October 2002.

Kroeber, A. L., *Cultural and Natural Areas of Native North America*, University of California Press, Berkeley, 1939.

Laade, W., 'Catalogue of Field Tape Recordings 1963–64. Part I: Cape York Peninsula', Australian Institute of Aboriginal Studies, Canberra, 1964.

Lake, J. S., *Freshwater Fish of the Murray-Darling River System: the Native and Introduced Fish Species*, Government Printer, Sydney, 1975.

—— *Australian Freshwater Fishes*, Thomas Nelson, Melbourne, 1978.

Lambie, J., 'Letter to Secretary of State for the Colonies', 14 January 1840, Mitchell Library, MLms 1227, 1840.

Land Conservation Council of Victoria, *Final Recommendations: North-eastern Study Area District 2*, Land Conservation Council of Victoria, Melbourne, 1974.

—— *Report on the Gippsland Lakes Hinterland Area*, Land Conservation Council of Victoria, Melbourne, 1982.

—— *Report on the East Gippsland Area Review, August 1985*, Land Conservation Council of Victoria, Melbourne, 1985.

Langton, M., 'The Aboriginal use of fire at Princess Charlotte Bay', Paper presented at the Donald Thomson Centenary Symposium, Prince Philip Theatre, University of Melbourne, 13 July 2001.

Latz, P. K. and G. F. Griffin, 'Changes in Aboriginal land management in relation to fire and to food plants in Central Australia', in B. S. Hetzel and H. J. Frith (eds), *The Nutrition of Aborigines in Relation to the Ecosystem of Central Australia*, CSIRO, Melbourne, 1978, 77–85.

Lavarack, P. S. and M. Godwin, 'Rainforests of northern Cape York Peninsula', in G. L. Werren and A. P. Kershaw (eds), *The Rainforest Legacy. Vol 1*, Australian Government Publishing Service, Canberra, 1987, 201–22.

Laves, G., 'Papers', Australian Institute of Aboriginal and Torres Strait Islander Studies, 1929.

Lawrence, R. J., *Aboriginal Habitat and Economy*, Department of Geography, School of General Studies, Australian National University, Canberra, 1968.

Laycock, D. C., 'Three Lamalamic languages of North Queensland', *Pacific Linguistics*, 1969, 71–97.

Layton, R. H., *Uluru: An Aboriginal History of Ayers Rock*, Australian Institute of Aboriginal Studies, Canberra, 1986.

Layton, R. H. and M. Rowell, *Ayers Rock–Mount Olga National Park and Lake Amadeus Traditional Land Claim*, Central Land Council, Alice Springs, 1979.

Le Souëf, S., 'The Aborigines of King George Sound at the time of early European contact: An ethnohistorical study of social organisation and territoriality', in B. K. de Garis (ed.), *Portraits of the South West: Aborigines, Women and the Environment*, University of Western Australia Press, Nedlands, 1993, 1–56.

Lee, P. C., 'Effects of ecological opportunities and constraints on social structure among primates', in J. E. Fa and C. H. Southwick (eds), *Ecology and Behaviour of Food-enhanced Primate Groups*, A.R. Liss, New York, 1988, 297–311.

Leeper, G. W., *The Australian Environment*, CSIRO in association with Melbourne University Press, Melbourne, 1970.

Lemmonier, P., *Elements for an anthropology of technology*, Museum of Anthropology, University of Michigan, Ann Arbor, Michigan, 1992.

Lévi-Strauss, C., *La Totemisme Aujourd'hui*, Presses Universitaires de France, Paris, 1962.

Lévi-Strauss, C., *The Elementary Structures of Kinship*, Eyre & Spottiswoode, London, 1969.

Lewis, H. T., 'Fire technology and resource management in Aboriginal North America and Australia', in N. M. Williams and E. S. Hunn (eds), *Resource Managers: North American and Australian Hunter-Gatherers*, Westview Press, Boulder, Colorado, 1982, 45–67.

Lockyer, E., 'Journal of Major Lockyer', *Historical Records of Australia*, vol. 4, 1827, 461–505.

Lommel, A., 'Notes on sexual behaviour and initiation, Wunambal tribe, North-Western Australia', *Oceania*, vol. 20, no. 2, 1949, 158–64.

—— *The Unambal: A Tribe in Northwest Australia*, Takarakka Nowan Kas Publications, Carnarvon Gorge, Qld, 1997.

Lommel, A. and D. Mowaljarlai, 'Shamanism in Northwest Australia', *Oceania*, vol. 64, no. 4, 1994, 277–87.

Long, J., 'Polygyny, acculturation and contact: Aspects of Aboriginal marriage in Central Australia', in R. M. Berndt (ed.), *Australian Aboriginal Anthropology: Modern Studies in the Social Anthropology of the Australian Aborigines*, University of Western Australia Press, Nedlands, 1970, 292–304.

Lourandos, H., 'Intensification: A late Pleistocene-Holocene archaeological sequence from southwestern Victoria', *Archaeology in Oceania*, vol. 18, no. 2, 1983, 81–94.

Love, J. R. B., 'Papers by J. R. B. Love: Prepared by Kim Akerman', South Australian Archives, 1927–40.

—— *Stone Age Bushmen of Today*, Blackie & Sons, Glasgow, 1936.

—— 'A primitive method of making a wooden dish by native women of the Musgrave Ranges, South Australia', *Royal Society of South Australia: Transactions*, vol. 66, no. 2, 1942, 215–7.

Lucich, P., *The Development of Omaha Kinship Terminologies in Three Australian Tribes of the Kimberley Division, Western Australia*, Australian Institute of Aboriginal Studies, Canberra, 1968.

McArthur, M., 'Food consumption and dietary levels of groups of Aborigines living on naturally occurring foods', in C. P. Mountford (ed.), *Records of the Australian-American Scientific Expedition to Arnhem Land, Vol. 2: Anthropology and Nutrition*, Melbourne University Press, Melbourne, 1960, 90–135.

McBryde, I., 'Exchange in south Eastern Australia: An ethnohistorical perspective', *Aboriginal History*, vol. 8, nos. 1–2, 1984, 132–53.

McCarthy, F. D., ' "Trade" in Aboriginal Australia, and "trade" relationships with Torres Strait, New Guinea and Malaya', *Oceania*, vol. 9, no. 4, 1938, 405–38; vol. 10, nos. 1–2, 1939, 80–104, 171–95.

McCarthy, F. D. and M. McArthur, 'The food quest and the time factor in Aboriginal economic life', in C. P. Mountford (ed.), *Records of the Australian-American Scientific Expedition to Arnhem Land, Vol. 2: Anthropology and Nutrition*, Melbourne University Press, Melbourne, 1960, 145–94.

McCarthy, W. J., 'Tools', in *The New Encyclopaedia Britannica*, Encyclopaedia Brittanica Inc., Chicago, 1982.

McConnel, U., *Myths of the Munkan*, Melbourne University Press, Melbourne, 1957.

McConvell, P., 'Time perspective in Aboriginal Australian culture: Two approaches to the origin of subsections', *Aboriginal History*, vol. 9, no. 1, 1985, 53–80.

McConvell, P., and N. Evans, *Archaeology and Linguistics: Aboriginal Australia in Global Perspective*, Oxford University Press, Melbourne, 1997.

McDonald, H., *Blood, Bones and Spirit: Aboriginal Christianity in Halls Creek, Western Australia*, Melbourne University Press, Melbourne, 2002.

McGregor, W., *Handbook of Kimberley Languages, Vol. 1*, Dept. of Linguistics, Research School of Pacific Studies, Australian National University, Canberra, 1988a.

—— 'A survey of the languages of the Kimberley region: Report from the Kimberley Language Resource Centre', *Australian Aboriginal Studies*, vol. 2, 1988b, 90–102.

McKinley, R., 'Why do Crow and Omaha kinship terminologies exist? A sociology of knowledge interpretation', *Man (n.s.)*, vol. 6, no. 1971, 408–26.

McTaggart, D., C. Findlay and M. Parkin, *Economics*, Addison-Wesley, Sydney, 1992.

Mackaness, G., *George Augustus Robinson's Journey into South-Eastern Australia, 1844 with George Henry Haydon's Narrative of Part of the Same Journey*, D. S. Ford, Sydney, 1941.

MacKnight, C. C., 'The Macassans: A study of the early Trepang industry along the Northern Territory coast', PhD diss., Australian National University, Canberra, 1969.

—— *The Voyage to Marege': Macassan Trepangers in Northern Australia*, Melbourne University Press, Melbourne, 1976.

Maddock, K., *The Australian Aborigines: A Portrait of their Society*, 1st edn, Penguin, London, 1972.

—— *The Australian Aborigines: A Portrait of their Society*, 2nd edn, Penguin, Ringwood, Vic, 1982.

Malinowski, B., *Coral Gardens and their Magic: Soil-tilling and Agricultural Rites in the Trobriand Islands*, Allen & Unwin, London, 1935.

Marika-Mununggiritj, R., B. Maymuru, M. Munungurr, B. Munyarryun, G. Ngurruwutthun, and Y. Yunupingu, 'The history of the Yirrkala Community School: Yolngu thinking about education in the Laynha and Yirrkala area', Paper presented at the Remote Aboriginal and Torres Strait Islander Community Futures Conference, Townsville, Qld, 1990.

Martin, D. F., 'Autonomy and Relatedness: An Ethnography of Wik People of Aurukun, Western Cape York Peninsula', PhD diss., Australian National University, Canberra, 1993.

Mathews, R. H., 'The bora, or initiation ceremonies of the Kamilaroi tribe', *Journal of the Royal Anthropological Institute*, vol. 24, no. 2, 1895, 411–27; vol. 25, no. 2, 1896, 318–39.

—— 'Aboriginal initiation ceremonies', *Science of Man*, vol. 1, no. 4, no. 9, 1898, 79–80, 202–6.

—— 'Ethnological notes on the Aboriginal tribes of New South Wales and Victoria', *Man*, vol. 6, no. 99, 1906, 153–5.

—— 'Ethnological notes on the Aboriginal tribes of New South Wales and Victoria', *Nature*, vol. 76, 9 May 1907, 31–2.

Mauss, M., *The Gift: Forms and Functions of Exchange in Archaic Societies*, The Free Press, Glencoe, IL, 1954.

Meagher, S. J., 'The food resources of the Aborigines of the south-west of Western Australia', *Records of the Western Australian Museum*, vol. 3, no. 1, 1974, 14–65.

Meagher, S. J. and W. D. L. Ride, 'Use of natural resources by the Aborigines of south-western Australia', in R. M. Berndt and C. H. Berndt (eds), *Aborigines of the West: Their Past and Their Present*, University of Western Australia Press, Nedlands, 1979, 66–80.

Meehan, B., 'Changes in Aboriginal exploitation of wetlands in Northern Australia', in D. Wade Marshall and P. Loveday (eds), *Northern Australia: Progress and Prospects*, North Australia Research Unit, Australian National University, Darwin, 1980, 1–23.

—— *Shell Bed to Shell Midden*, Australian Institute of Aboriginal Studies, Canberra, 1982.

Meggitt, M. J., 'Aboriginal food gatherers of tropical Australia', in *The Ecology of Man in the Tropical Environment. Ninth Technical Meeting of the International Union for the Conservation of Nature and Natural Resources: Proceedings and Papers, Published Series 4*, Morges, Switzerland, 1964, 30–7.

—— *Desert People: A Study of the Walbiri Aborigines of Central Australia*, 2nd edn, University of Chicago Press, Chicago, 1965.

Merlan, F., 'Land, language and social identity in Aboriginal Australia', *Mankind*, vol. 13, no. 2, 1981, 133–48.

—— 'Australian Aboriginal conception beliefs revisited', *Man (n.s.)*, vol. 21, no. 3, 1986, 474–93.

—— 'Gender in Aboriginal social life: A review', in R. M. Berndt and R. Tonkinson (eds), *Social Anthropology and Australian Aboriginal Studies*, Australian Institute of Aboriginal Studies, Canberra, 1988, 15–76.

—— 'The mother-in-law taboo: Avoidance and obligation in Aboriginal Australian society', in F. Merlan, J. Morton and A. Rumsey (eds), *Scholar and Sceptic: Australian Aboriginal Studies in Honour of L. R. Hiatt*, Aboriginal Studies Press, Canberra, 1997, 95–122.

Merlan, F. and A. Rumsey, *Ku Waru: Language and Segmentary Politics in the Western Nebilyer Valley, Papua New Guinea*, Cambridge University Press, Cambridge, 1991.

Miller, W. R., 'Dialect differentiation in the Western Desert language', *Anthropological Forum*, vol. 3, no. 1, 1971, 61–78.

Mitchell, T. L., *Three Expeditions into the Interior of Eastern Australia*, 2 vols, Boone, London, 1839.

—— *Journal of an Expedition into the Interior of Tropical Australia in Search of a Route from Sydney to the Gulf of Carpentaria*, Greenwood Press, New York, 1969 [1848].

Moore, G. F., 'Vocabulary of the south west Aborigines, 1884', in N. Green (ed.), *Nyungar—The People: Aboriginal Customs in the Southwest of Australia*, Creative Research in association with Mt. Lawley College, North Perth, 1979, 102–10.

Morphy, F., 'Djapu, a Yolngu dialect', in R. M. W. Dixon and B. J. Blake (eds), *Handbook of Australian Languages, Vol. 3*, Australian National University Press, Canberra, 1983, 1–188.

Morphy, H., 'Rights in paintings and rights in women: A consideration of some of the basic problems posed by the asymmetry of the "Murngin" system', in J. Specht and P. White (eds), *Trade and Exchange in Oceania and Australia (Mankind 11, Special Issue)*, 1978, 208–19.

—— *Journey to the Crocodile's Nest: An Accompanying Monograph to the Film Madarrpa Funeral at Gurka'wuy*, Australian Institute of Aboriginal Studies, Canberra, 1984.

—— 'From dull to brilliant: The aesthetics of spiritual power among the Yolngu', *Man (n.s.)*, vol. 24, no. 1, 1989, 21–40.

—— 'Myth, totemism and the creation of clans', *Oceania*, vol. 60, no. 4, 1990, 312–29.

—— *Ancestral Connections: Art and an Aboriginal System of Knowledge*, University of Chicago Press, Chicago, 1991.

—— 'Empiricism to metaphysics: In defence of the concept of the Dreamtime', in T. Bonyhady and T. Griffiths (eds), *Prehistory to Politics: John Mulvaney, the Humanities and the Public Intellectual*, Melbourne University Press, Melbourne, 1996, 163–89.

—— 'Death, exchange and the reproduction of Yolngu society.' in F. Merlan, J. Morton and A. Rumsey (eds), *Australian Aborigines and Contemporary Social Enquiry: Essays to Honour L.R. Hiatt*, Aboriginal Studies Press, Canberra, 1997, 123–50.

Morton, J., 'Totemism now and then: A natural science of society?' in F. Merlan, J. Morton and A. Rumsey (eds), *Scholar and Sceptic: Australian Aboriginal Studies in Honour of LR Hiatt*, Aboriginal Studies Press, Canberra, 1997, 151–70.

Mosko, M., 'Inalienable ethnography: Keeping-while-giving and the Trobriand case', *Journal of the Royal Anthropological Institute*, vol. 6, no. 3, 2000, 377–96.

Mountford, C. P., 'An unrecorded method for manufacturing wooden implements by simple stone tools', *Transactions of the Royal Society of South Australia*, vol. 65, no. 2, 1941, 312–16.

—— *Nomads of the Australian Desert,* Rigby, Adelaide, 1976.

Mowaljarlai, D. and J. Malnic, *Yorro Yorro = Everything Standing up Alive: Spirit of the Kimberley*, Magabala Books, Broome, WA, 1993.

Mulvaney, D. J., 'The end of the beginning: 6000 years ago to 1788', in D. J. Mulvaney and J. P. White (eds), *Australians to 1788*, Fairfax, Syme & Weldon Associates, Sydney, 1987, 75–117.

Mulvaney, J. and J. Kamminga, *Prehistory of Australia*, Allen & Unwin, St. Leonards NSW, 1999.

Mumford, L., *Technics and Civilization*, Routledge, London, 1947.

Munn, N., 'A report on field research at Areyonga, 1964–5', PMS 1104/5, Australian Institute of Aboriginal Studies, Canberra, 1965.

—— 'The transformation of subjects into objects in Walbiri and Pitjantjatjara myth', in R. M. Berndt (ed.), *Australian Aboriginal Anthropology*, University of Western Australia Press, Nedlands, 1970, 141–63.

—— *Walbiri Iconography: Graphic Representation and Cultural Symbolism in a Central Australian Society*, Cornell University Press, Ithaca, 1973.

Murdock, G. P., 'The Ethnographic Atlas: A summary', *Ethnology*, vol. 6, no. 2, 1967, 109–236.

Musharbash, Y., 'Ngurra-kurlu—about camps: the household, the hearth group and the domestic cycle revisited', unpublished paper, School of Archaeology and Anthropology, Australian National University, Canberra, n.d.

Myers, F. R., 'The cultural basis of politics in Pintubi life', *Mankind*, vol. 12, no. 3, 1980, 197–214.

—— 'Always ask: Resource use and land ownership among Pintupi Aborigines of the Australian Western Desert', in N. M. Williams (ed.), *Resource Managers: North American and Australian Hunter-Gatherers*, Australian Institute of Aboriginal Studies, Canberra, 1982, 173–96.

—— *Pintupi Country, Pintupi Self: Sentiment, Place and Politics among Western Desert Aborigines*, Australian Institute of Aboriginal Studies and Smithsonian Institution Press, Canberra and Washington, 1986.

Nadel, S., 'Witchcraft in four African societies: An essay in comparison', *American Anthropologist*, vol. 54, no. 1, 1952, 18–29.

Narotzky, S., *New Directions in Economic Anthropology*, Pluto Press, London, 1997.

Needham, R., *Belief, Language and Experience*, Blackwell, Oxford, 1972.

Nind, S., 'Description of the natives of King George's sound (Swan River Colony) and adjoining country', *Journal of the Royal Geographical Society of London*, vol. 1, 1831, 21–51.

O'Connell, J. F. and K. Hawkes, 'Alyawara plant use and optimal foraging theory', in B. Winterhalder and E. A. Smith (eds), *Hunter-gatherer Foraging Strategy: Ethnographic and Archaeological Analyses*, University of Chicago Press, Chicago, 1981, 99–125.

O'Connor, R., G. Quartermaine and C. Bodney, *Report on an Investigation into Aboriginal Significance of Wetlands and Rivers in the Perth-Bunbury Region*, Western Australian Water Resources Council, Perth, 1989.

O'Connor, S., 'The stone house structures of High Cliffy Island, north west Kimberley, WA', *Australian Archaeology*, vol. 25, no. 1, 1987, 30–9.

—— 'Saltwater people of the southwest Kimberley coast', in G. Burenhalt (ed.), *People of the Stone Age: Hunter-gatherers and Early Farmers*, Harper, San Francisco, 1993, 226–7.

O'Grady, G. and S. Fitzgerald, 'Cognate search in the Pama-Nyungan language family', in P. McConvell and N. Evans (eds), *Archaeology and Linguistics: Aboriginal Australian in Global Perspective*, Oxford University Press, Melbourne, 1997, 341–56.

Oates, W. J. and L. F. Oates, *A Revised Linguistic Survey of Australia*, Australian Institute of Aboriginal Studies, Canberra, 1970.

Oliver, D. L., *Oceania: The Native Cultures of Australia and the Pacific Islands*, University of Hawaii Press, Honolulu, 1989.

Pannell, S. and D. Vachon, 'Notes and queries in the Native Title era', *The Australian Journal of Anthroplogy*, vol. 12, no. 2, 2001, 238–44.

Parker, K. L., *Australian Legendary Tales: Folk-lore of the Noongahburrahs as Told to the Piccaninnies*, Melville, Mullen & Slade, Melbourne, 1896.

—— *The Euahlayi Tribe: A Study of Aboriginal Life in Australia*, A. Constable, London, 1905.

—— *Australian Legendary Tales*, Angus & Robertson, Sydney, 1953.

Pentony, B., 'The Dream in Australian Culture', BA Honours diss., University of Western Australia, Perth, 1938.

Pepper, P. and T. De Araugo, *The Kurnai of Gippsland: What Did Happen to the Aborigines of Victoria*, vol. 1, Hyland House, Melbourne, 1985.

Peterson, N., *Nomads in Clover: Contemporary Murngin Hunters*, (16mm film), Australian Institution of Aboriginal Studies, Canberra, 1967.

—— 'The Structure of Two Australian Aboriginal Ecosystems', PhD diss., University of Sydney, 1971.

—— 'Totemism yesterday: Sentiment and local organisation among the Australian Aborigines', *Man*, vol. 7, no. 1, 1972, 12–32.

—— 'Camp site location amongst Australian hunter-gatherers: Archaeological and ethnographic evidence for a key determinant', *Archaeology and Physical Anthropology in Oceania*, vol. 8, no. 3, 1973, 173–93.

—— 'Ethno-archaeology in the Australian Iron Age', in G. de G. Sieveking, I. H. Longworth and K. E. Wilson (eds), *Problems in Economic and Social Archaeology*, Duckworth, London, 1976a, 265–75.

—— 'Mortuary customs of Northeast Arnhem Land: An account compiled from Donald Thomson's fieldnotes', *Memoirs of the National Museum of Victoria*, no. 37, 1976b, 97–108.

—— 'The importance of women in determining the composition of residential groups in Aboriginal Australia', in F. Gale (ed.), *Women's Role in Aboriginal Society*, Australian Institute of Aboriginal Studies, Canberra, 1978, 9–16.

—— 'Rights, residence and process in Australia territorial organisation', in N. Peterson and M. Langton (eds), *Aborigines, Land and Land Rights*, Australian Institute of Aboriginal Studies, Canberra, 1983, 134–45.

—— 'Demand sharing: Reciprocity and the pressure for generosity among foragers', *American Anthropologist*, vol. 95, no. 4, 1993, 860–74.

Peterson, N., I. Keen and B. Sansom, 'Succession to land: Primary and secondary rights to Aboriginal estates', in *Hansard of Joint Select Committee on Land Rights in the Northern Territory*, Government Printer, Canberra, 1977, 1002–14.

Peterson, N. and M. Langton (eds), *Aborigines, Land and Land Rights*, Australian Institute of Aboriginal Studies, Canberra, 1983.

Peterson, N. and J. Long, *Australian Territorial Organization: A Band Perspective*, (Oceania Monograph no. 30), University of Sydney, Sydney, 1986.

Petri, H., *Sterbende Welt in Nordwest-Australien*, A. Limbach, Braunschweig, 1954.

Pfaffenberger, B., 'Social anthropology of technology', *Annual Review of Anthropology*, vol. 21, 1992, 491–516.

Polanyi, K., *The Great Transformation*, Rinehart, New York, 1944.

Powell, A., *Far Country: A Short History of the Northern Territory*, Melbourne University Press, Melbourne, 1982.

Queensland Land Tribunal, *Aboriginal Land Claim to Iron Range National Park by the Kuuku Ya'u People. Report of the Land Tribunal to the Hon the Minister for Natural Resources under the Aboriginal Land Act 1991*, Department of Natural Resources, Brisbane, 1999.

Radcliffe-Brown, A. R., 'Three tribes of Western Australia', *Journal of the Royal Anthropological Institute*, vol. 43, no. 1, 1913, 143–94.

—— 'Notes on the social organisation of Australian tribes', *Journal of the Royal Anthropological Institute*, vol. 48, no. 2, 1918, 222–53.

—— 'Notes on the social organisation of Australian tribes', *Journal of the Royal Anthropological Institute*, vol. 53, no.2, 1923, 424–47.

—— *The Social Organization of Australian Tribes (Oceania Monographs No. 1)*, University of Sydney, Sydney, 1931.

—— '[Letter in Reply to A.P. Elkin]', *American Anthropologist*, vol. 56, no. 1, 1954, 105–6.

Redmond, A., 'Places that move', in A. Rumsey and J. F. Weiner (eds), *Emplaced Myth: Space, Narrative, and Knowledge in Aboriginal Australasia and Papua New Guinea*, University of Hawaii Press, Honolulu, 2001a, 120–38.

—— '*Rulug Wayirri*: Moving Kin and Country in the Northern Kimberley', PhD diss., University of Sydney, 2001b.

Reid, J., *Sorcerers and Healing Spirits*, Australian National University Press, Canberra, 1983.

Reser, J. P., 'The dwelling as motif in Aboriginal bark painting', in P. J. Ucko (ed.), *Form in Indigenous Art: Schematisation in the Art of Aboriginal Australia and Prehistoric Europe*, Australian Institute of Aboriginal Studies, Canberra, 1977, 210–19.

Ridley, R. W., *Kamilaroi and Other Australian Languages*, 2nd edn, Thomas Richards, Government Printer, Sydney, 1875.

Ridley, R. W., J. Moseley and F. Bucknell, 'The Kamilaroi language', in E. M. Curr (ed.), *The Australian Race. Book 14*, John Ferres, Melbourne, 1886, 304–7.

Rigsby, B., 'Land, language and people in the Princess Charlotte Bay area', in N. C. Stevens and A. Bailey (eds), *Contemporary Cape York Peninsula*, Royal Society of Queensland, Brisbane, 1980, 89–94.

—— 'The language of the Princess Charlotte Bay region', in T. Dutton, M. Ross and D. T. Tryon (eds), *The Language Game: Papers in Memory of Donald C. Laycock*, Department of Linguistics, Research School of Pacific Studies, Australian National University, Canberra, 1992, 353–60.

—— 'A survey of property theory and tenure types', in N. Peterson and B. Rigsby (eds), *Customary Marine Tenure in Australia*, University of Sydney, Sydney, 1998, 22–46.

—— 'Genealogies, kinship and local group organisations: Old Yintjingga (Port Stewart) in the late 1920s', in J. Finlayson, B. Rigsby and H. J. Bek (eds), *Connections in Native Title: Genealogies, Kinship and Groups*, Centre for Aboriginal Economic Policy Research, Australian National University, Canberra, 1999, 107–23.

Rigsby, B. and A. Chase, 'The Sandbeach people and dugong hunters of eastern Cape York Peninsula: Property in land and sea country', in N. Peterson and B. Rigsby (eds), *Customary Marine Tenure in Australia*, University of Sydney, Sydney, 1998, 192–218.

Roberts, S., 'Law and dispute process', in T. Ingold (ed.), *Companion Encyclopedia of Anthropology*, Routledge, London, 2002, 962–82.

Rose, D. B., 'Jesus and the Dingo', in T. Swain and D. B. Rose (eds), *Aboriginal Australians and Christian Missions*, Australian Association for the Study of Religions, Bedford Park, South Australia, 1988, 361–75.

Rose, D. B. and S. Sharon D'Amico, *Country of the Heart: An Indigenous Australian Homeland*, Aboriginal Studies Press, Canberra, 2002.

Rose, F. G. G., *Classification of Kin, Age Structure and Marriage amongst the Groote Eylandt Aborigines: A Study in Method and a Theory of Australian Kinship*, Akademie, Berlin, 1960.

—— 'Australian marriage, land-owning groups, and initiations', in R. B. Lee and I. DeVore (eds), *Man the Hunter*, Aldine, Chicago, 1968, 200–8.

Rose, S., 'Escaping evolutionary psychology', in H. Rose and S. Rose (eds), *Alas, Poor Darwin: Arguments Against Evolutionary Psychology*, Harmony Books, New York, 2000, 299–320.

Rowland, M.J., and N. Franklin, 'Rock Art Sites in the Cape York Peninsula Biogeographic Zone. Overview and Recommendations', in *Rock Art Sites in the Cape York Peninsula Biogeographic Zone. Overview and Recommendations*, Report to the Australian Institute of Aboriginal and Torres Strait Islander Studies, Canberra and Department of Environment and Heritage, Brisbane, 1992.

Rubel, P. G. and A. Rosman, *Your Own Pigs You May Not Eat: A Comparative Study of New Guinea Societies*, Australian National University Press, Canberra, 1978.

Rudder, J. C., *Introduction to Yolngu Science*, Galiwinku Adult Education Centre, Galiwinku, NT, 1977.

—— 'Yolngu Cosmology: An Unchanging Cosmos Incorporating a Rapidly Changing World?', PhD diss., Australian National University, Canberra, 1993.

Rumsey, A., 'Kinship and context among the Ngarinyin', *Oceania*, vol. 51, no. 3, 1981, 181–92.

—— 'Language and territoriality in Aboriginal Australia', in M. Walsh and C. Yallop (eds), *Language and Culture in Aboriginal Australia*, Aboriginal Studies Press, Canberra, 1993, 191–206.

—— 'Aspects of native title and social identity in the Kimberleys and beyond', *Australian Aboriginal Studies*, no. 1, 1996, 2–10.

Rumsey, A. and A. Redmond, 'The Northern Kimberley as a Socio-cultural Region', Department of Anthropology, Research School of Pacific and Asian Studies, Australian National University, Canberra, 1999.

Sackett, L., 'Indirect exchange in a symmetrical system: Marriage alliance in the Western Desert of Australia', *Ethnology*, vol. 15, no. 2, 1976, 135–49.

Sahlins, M. D., *Social Stratification in Polynesia*, University of Washington Press, Seattle, 1958.

—— *Stone Age Economics*, Aldine-Atherton, Chicago, 1972.

Samuelson, P. A., *Economics: An Introductory Analysis*, McGraw-Hill, New York, 1970.

Sansom, B., *The Camp at Wallaby Cross: Aboriginal Fringe Dwellers in Darwin*, Australian Institute of Aboriginal Studies, Canberra, 1980.

—— 'A grammar of exchange', in I. Keen (ed.), *Being Black*, Aboriginal Studies Press, Canberra, 1988, 159–77.

Satterthwait, L., 'A Comparative Study of Aboriginal Food-procurement Technologies', PhD diss., University of California, Berkeley, 1980.

—— 'Socioeconomic implications of Australian Aboriginal net hunting', *Man (n.s.)*, vol. 22, no. 4, 1987, 613–36.

Schebeck, B., 'Dialect and social groupings in north-east Arnhem Land', Australian Institute of Aboriginal Studies, MS 351, MS 352, 1968.

Scheffler, H. W., *Australian Kin Classification*, Cambridge University Press, London, 1978.

Schneider, D. M., *A Critique of the Study of Kinship*, University of Michigan Press, Ann Arbor, 1984.

Shapiro, W., 'The exchange of sister's daughter's daughters in northeast Arnhem Land.' *Southwestern Journal of Anthropology*, vol. 24, no. 4, 1968, 346–53.

—— 'Residential grouping in northeast Arnhem Land', *Man (n.s.)*, vol. 8, no. 3, 1973, 365–83.

—— *Social Organization in Aboriginal Australia*, Australian National University Press, Canberra, 1979.

—— *Miwuyt Marriage: The Cultural Anthropology of Affinity in Northeast Arnhem Land*, Institute for the Study of Human Issues, Philadelphia, 1981.

Sharp, L., 'People without politics', in V. F. Ray (ed.), *Systems of Political Control and Bureaucracy in Human Societies: Proceedings of the 1958 Annual Spring Meeting of the American Ethnological Society*, American Ethnological Society, Seattle, 1958, 1–8.

Shaw, B., *East Kimberley Aborigines: Their Traditional Past, Colonial Experience and Present Vitalisation*, Darwin Community College, Darwin, 1978.

Shott, M., 'Technological organization and settlement mobility: An ethnographic examination', *Journal of Anthropological Research*, vol. 42, no. 1, 1986, 15–51.

Smith, E. A., 'Risk and uncertainty in the "original affluent society": Evolutionary ecology of resource sharing and land tenure.' in T. Ingold, D. Riches and J. Woodburn (eds), *Hunters and Gatherers, Vol. I: History, Evolution, and Social Change*, Berg, Oxford, 1988, 222–51.

Smith, L. R., *The Aboriginal Population of Australia*, Australian National University Press, Canberra, 1980.

Smyth, R. B., *The Aborigines of Victoria: With Notes Relating to the Habits of the Natives of Other Parts of Australia and Tasmania, Compiled from Various Sources for the Government of Victoria*, 2 vols, Government Printer, Melbourne, 1878.

Specht, R. L., 'An introduction to the ethno-botany of Arnhem Land', in C. Mountford (ed.), *Records of American-Australian Scientific Expedition to Arnhem Land, vol. 3, Botany and Plant Ecology*, 1958, 479–503.

Spriggs, M., 'Early agriculture and what went before it in Melanesia', in D. R. Harris (ed.), *The Origins And Spread of Agriculture and Pastoralism in Eurasia*, Smithsonian Institute Press, Washington D.C., 1996, 524–37.

Stanner, W. E. H., 'The Australian Aboriginal Dreaming as an ideological system', *Ninth Pacific Science Congress, 1957–Proceedings*, vol. 3, 1963, 116–23.

—— *On Aboriginal Religion*, (Oceania Monographs No. 11), University of Sydney, Sydney, 1964.

—— 'Aboriginal territorial organisation: Estate, range, domain and regime', *Oceania*, vol. 36, no. 1, 1965a, 1–26.

—— 'Religion, totemism and symbolism', in R. M. Berndt and C. H. Berndt (eds), *Aboriginal Man in Australia*, Angus & Robertson, Sydney, 1965b, 207–37.

Stearns, K., *Gippsland Regional Environmental Study: Overview Report, 1984*, Department of Conservation, Forests and Lands (Victoria), Melbourne, 1984.

Steward, J., 'The economic and social basis of primitive bands', in R. H. Lowie (ed.), *Essays in Anthropology Presented to Alfred Louis Kroeber*, University of California Press, Berkeley, 1936, 331–50.

Strathern, M., *The Gender of the Gift: Problems with Women and Problems with Society in Melanesia*, University of California Press, Berkeley, 1988.

Sturt, C., *Two Expeditions into the Interior of Southern Australia, During the Years 1828, 1829, 1830, and 1831, with Observations on the Soil, Climate, and General Resources of the Colony of New South*, vol. 1, Smith, Elder & Co., London, 1833.

—— *Narrative of an Expedition into Central Australia* (2 vols.), T. & W. Boone, London, 1849.

Sullivan, S. M., 'The traditional culture of the Aborigines of north western New South Wales', MA diss., University of New England, Armadale, 1970.

Sutton, P., 'Wik: Aboriginal Society, Territory and Language at Cape Keerweer, Cape York Peninsula, Australia'. PhD diss., University of Queensland, St Lucia, 1978.

—— 'Some questions about adjudication, customary law and land', *Anthropological Forum*, vol. 5, no. 3, 1986, 489–91.

—— 'Material culture traditions of the Wik people, Cape York Peninsula', *Records of the South Australian Museum*, vol. 27, no. 1, 1993, 31–52.

—— 'The robustness of Aboriginal land tenure systems: Underlying and proximate customary titles', *Oceania*, vol. 67, no. 1, 1996, 7–29.

—— *Native Title and the Descent of Rights*, Commonwealth of Australia, Native Title Tribunal, Perth, 1998.

—— 'The system as it was straining to become: Fluidity, stability, and Aboriginal country groups', in J. D. Finlayson, B. Rigsby, and H. Bek (eds), *Connections in Native Title: Genealogies, Kinship and Groups*, Centre for Aboriginal Economic Policy Research, Australian National University, Canberra, 1999, 13–58.

Sutton, P. and B. Rigsby, 'People with "politicks": Management of land and personnel on Australia's Cape York Peninsula', in N. M. Williams and E. S. Hunn (eds), *Resource Managers: North American and Australian Hunter-Gatherers*, Westview Press, Boulder, Colorado, 1982, 155–71.

Swain, T., *Interpreting Aboriginal Religion: An Historical Account*, Australian Association for the Study of Religions, Bedford Park, South Australia, 1985.

—— *A Place for Strangers: Towards a History of Australian Aboriginal Being*, Cambridge University Press, Cambridge, UK, 1993.

Tamisari, F., 'Body, names and movement: Images of identity among the Yolngu of northeast Arnhem Land', PhD diss., London School of Economics and Political Science, 1995.

—— 'Body, vision and movement: In the footprints of the ancestors', *Oceania*, vol. 68, no. 4, 1998, 249–70.

Taplin, G., *The Narrinyeri*, E.S. Wigg, Adelaide, 1873.

Terray, E., *Marxism and 'Primitive' Societies: Two Studies*, Monthly Review Press, New York, 1972.

Thieberger, N., *Handbook of Western Australian Aboriginal Languages South of the Kimberley Region*, Department of Linguistics, Research School of Pacific Studies, Australian National University, Canberra, 1993.

Thomas, W., 'Thomas papers', Museum of Victoria, Box 14, 1849–60.

Thompson, D. A., 'Distribution of dialects along the east coast and hinterland of the Cape York Peninsula, Queensland' (Typescript), PMS 1825, Australian Institute of Aboriginal Studies, Canberra, 1975.

—— *Lockhart River 'Sand Beach' Language: An Outline of Kuuku Ya'u and Umpila*, Summer Institute of Linguistics, Darwin, 1988.

Thomson, D. F., Papers, Museum Victoria, MV Files 27, 164, 175, 189, 190–2, 195–6, 206, 213, 215, 256.

—— Photographic collection, Thomson collection, Museum Victoria.

—— 'Ceremonial presentation of fire in North Queensland. A preliminary note on the place of fire in primitive ritual', *Man*, vol. 32, no. 198, 1932, 162–6.

—— 'The hero cult, initiation and totemism on Cape York', *Journal of the Royal Anthropological Institute*, vol. 63, no. 2, 1933, 453–537.

—— 'The dugong hunters of Cape York', *Journal of the Royal Anthropological Institute*, vol. 64, no. 1, 1934, 237–63.

—— 'The joking relationship and organised obscenity in north Queensland', *American Anthropologist*, vol. 37, no. 3, 1935, 460–90.

—— 'A new type of fish trap from Arnhem Land, Northern Territory of Australia', *Man*, vol. 38, no. 216, 1938, 193–8.

—— '[Northeast Arnhem Land population]', *Report of the Administrator of the Northern Territory for the Year Ended 30th June, 1937–8*, Commnwealth Government, Darwin, 1937–8, 11.

—— 'The seasonal factor in human culture, illustrated from the life of a contemporary nomadic group', *Proceedings of the Prehistoric Society*, vol. 5, no. 10, 1939, 209–21.

—— 'An Arnhem Land adventure', *National Geographic Magazine*, vol. 93, no. 3, 1948a, 403–30.

—— 'Arnhem Land: Explorations among an unknown people', *Geographical Journal*, vol. 112, 113, 114, 1948b, 53–67; 146–64; 1–8.

—— *Economic Structure and the Ceremonial Exchange Cycle in Arnhem Land*, Macmillan, Melbourne, 1949.

—— 'Some wood and stone implements of the Bindibu tribe of Central Western Australia', *Proceedings of the Prehistoric Society*, vol. 30, no. 17, 1964, 400–22.

—— *Kinship and Behaviour in North Queensland*, Australian Institute of Aboriginal Studies, Canberra, 1972.

—— 'The concept of marr in Arnhem Land', *Mankind*, vol. 10, no. 1, 1975, 1–10.

Thorpe, W. W., 'Water supply of the Aborigines', *The Australian Museum Magazine*, vol. 3, no. 7, 1928, 233–7.

Tindale, N. B., 'The little people of our rainforests [north Queensland]', *Sunday Mail*, 16 June 1962, 25–6.

—— 'The Pitjandjara', in M. G. Bicchieri (ed.), *Hunters and Gatherers Today*, Holt, Rinehart & Winston, New York, 1972, 217–68.

—— *Aboriginal Tribes of Australia: Their Terrain, Environmental Controls, Distribution, Limits and Proper Names*, Australian National University Press, Canberra, 1974.

Toner, P. G., 'When the Echoes are Gone: A Yolngu Musical Anthropology', PhD diss., Australian National University, Canberra, 2001.

—— 'Ideology, influence and innovation: The impact of Indonesian contact on Australian Aboriginal Music', *Perfect Beat - The Pacific Journal of Research into Contemporary Music and Popular Culture*, vol. 5, no. 1, 2000, 22–41.

Tonkinson, R., 'Egalitarianism and inequality in a Western Desert culture', *Anthropological Forum*, vol. 5, no. 4, 1986, 545–58.
—— *The Mardu Aborigines: Living the Dream in Australia's Desert*, 2nd edn, Holt, Rinehart & Winston, Fort Worth, 1991.
—— 'The Mardu Aborigines of Australia: Resolving conflict within the Law', unpublished manuscript, Discipline of Anthropology, University of Western Australia, n.d.
Torrence, R., 'Hunter-gatherer technology: Macro- and microscale approaches', in C. Panter-Brick, R. H. Layton and P. Rowley-Conwy (eds), *Hunter-Gatherers: An Interdisciplinary Perspective*, Cambridge University Press, Cambridge, 2001, 73–98.
Turner, D., *Australian Aboriginal Social Organization*, Humanities Press, Atlantic Highlands, and Australian Institute of Aboriginal Studies, Canberra, 1980.
Tyers, C. J., 'Letter re Aboriginal population in Gippsland, 25th February 1857', State Library of New South Wales, 10/57, 1857.
Viesner, F., 'L'Institution des "hommes medecine" dans l'Australie Aborigene Contemporaine', PhD diss., Université Bordeaux 2, Victor Segalen, 2000.
Vigilante, T., 'Aboriginal landscape burning in the north Kimberley, 1999–2001', Australian Institute of Aboriginal and Torres Strait Islander Studies, XX(340002.1), 2002.
Von Brandenstein, C. G., 'Aboriginal ecological order in the South-West of Australia—meaning and examples', *Oceania*, vol. 47, no. 3, 1977, 169–86.
Von Sturmer, D., 'Rights in Nurturing: The Social Relations of Childbearing and Rearing amongst the Kuku Nganychara, Western Cape York Peninsula, Australia', MA diss., Australian National University, Canberra, 1980.
Wagner, R., 'Are there social groups in the New Guinea Highlands?' in M. Leaf (ed.), *Frontiers of Anthropology*, Van Nostrand, New York, 1974, 95–122.
Walker, M., *Come Wind, Come Weather: A Biography of A. W. Howitt*, Melbourne University Press, Melbourne, 1971.
Walsh, F., 'An ecological study of traditional Aboriginal use of country: Martu in the Great and Little Sandy Deserts', *Proceedings of the Ecological Society of Australia*, vol. 16, 1990, 23–38.
Warner, W. L., *A Black Civilization: A Social Study of an Australian Tribe*, 1st edn, Harper, New York, 1937.
—— *A Black Civilization: A Social Study of an Australian Tribe*, 2nd edn, Harper, New York, 1958.
Waters, B., *Djinang and Djinba: A Grammatical and Historical Perspective*, Dept. of Linguistics, Research School of Pacific Studies, Australian National University, Canberra, 1989.
Watson, P., *This Precious Foliage: A Study of the Aboriginal Psycho-active Drug Pituri*, (Oceania Monographs No. 26), University of Sydney, Sydney, 1983.
Webb, T. T., 'The making of a marrngit', *Oceania*, vol. 6, no. 3, 1936, 336–41.
Weiner, A., *Women of Value, Men of Renown: New Perspectives in Trobriand Exchange*, University of Texas Press, Austin, 1976.
—— *Inalienable Possessions: The Paradox of Keeping-while-Giving*, University of California Press, Berkeley, 1992.
Wesson, S., 'Yiruk plant use' (Report to Central Gippsland Aboriginal Health and Housing Co-operative), MS3557 Australian Institute of Aboriginal and Torres Strait Islander Studies, Canberra, 1991.
—— 'Australian Alps oral history project 1994: Aboriginal histories' (Report for the Australian Alps Liaison Committee), MS3397 Australian Institute of Aboriginal and Torres Strait Islander Studies, Canberra, 1994.
—— *An Historical Atlas of the Aborigines of Eastern Victoria and Far South-Eastern New South Wales*, School of Geography and Environmental Science, University of Melbourne, Melbourne, 2000.
West, A. L., 'Australian Aboriginal Cordage and Single-Element Fabric Structures', MA diss., La Trobe University, Bundoora, 1980.
West, L. M., 'Progress report on the processing of data since return from the field' 1st March 1962–1st April 1962, PMS 4424, Australian Institute of Aboriginal Studies, Canberra, 1962.
White, I., 'Aboriginal women's status: A paradox resolved', in F. Gale (ed.), *Woman's Role in Aboriginal Society*, Australian Institute of Aboriginal Studies, Canberra, 1970, 21–9.

White, J. P., 'New Guinea and Australian prehistory: The "neolithic problem" ', in D. J. Mulvaney and J. Golson (eds), *Aboriginal Man and Environment in Australia*, Australian National University Press, Canberra, 1971, 182–95.

White, L., 'Energy and the evolution of culture', *American Anthropologist*, vol. 45, no. 3, 1943, 335–56.

White, N., 'A preliminary account of the correspondence among genetic, linguistic, social and topographic divisions in Arnhem, Australia', *Mankind*, vol. 10, no. 4, 1976, 240–7.

White, N., B. Meehan, L. Hiatt and R. Jones, 'Demography of contemporary hunter-gatherers: Lessons from Arnhem Land', in B. Meehan and N. White (eds), *Hunter-Gatherer Demography: Past and Present*, University of Sydney, Sydney, 1990, 171–85.

Wild, S., 'Rom in Canberra', *Australian Aboriginal Studies*, vol. 1, 1983, 55–9.

Williams, C. J., 'Yuwaaliyaay and Yuwaalaraay: Dialects of North-Central New South Wales', BA Honours diss., Australian National University, Canberra, 1976.

Williams, N. M., *The Yolngu and their Land: A System of Land Tenure and the Fight for its Recognition*, Australian Institute of Aboriginal Studies, Canberra, 1986.

—— *Two Laws: Managing Disputes in a Contemporary Aboriginal Community*, Australian Institute of Aboriginal Studies, Canberra, 1987.

Winterhalder, B., 'Diet choice, risk, and food sharing in a stochastic environment', *Journal of Anthropological Archaeology*, vol. 5, no. 4, 1986, 369–92.

Wolf, E. R., *Europe and the People Without History*, University of California Press, Berkeley, 1982.

Wolfe, P. *Settler Colonialism and the Transformation of Anthropology: The Politics and Poetics of an Ethnographic Event*, Cassell, London, 1999.

Woodburn, J., 'African hunter-gatherer social organization: Is it best understood as a product of encapsulation?' in T. Ingold, D. Riches and J. Woodburn (eds), *Hunters and Gatherers 1: History, Evolution and Social Change*, Berg, Oxford, 1988, 31–64.

Woodgate, P. W., W. D. Peel, K. T. Ritman, J. E. Coram, A. Brady, A. J. Rule, and J. C. G. Banks, *A Study of the Old-growth Forests of East Gippsland*, Department of Conservation and Natural Resources, Melbourne, 1994.

Worsnop, T., *The Prehistoric Arts, Manufactures, Works, Weapons, etc of the Aborigines of Australia*, Government Printer, Adelaide, 1897.

Yallop, C., *Australian Aboriginal Languages*, Andre Deutsch, London, 1982.

Yengoyan, A. A., 'A comparison of certain marriage features between the Pitjandjara and other groups of the Western Desert with the northern groups: Also some comments on the red ochre ceremonies', *Journal of the Anthropological Society of South Australia*, vol. 5, no. 4, 1967, 16–19.

Zorc, R. D., 'Functor analysis: A method of quantifying function words for comparing and classifying languages', in *The Fifth Lacus Forum*, Hornbeam Press, Columbia, 1978, 510–21.

—— *Yolngu Matha Dictionary*, Darwin Institute of Technology, Darwin, 1986.

Glossary

affinal network

The network of relations to a person's spouse's kin.

affines, affinity

Relatives and relationships based on marriage ties. In Aboriginal societies, spouses already had kinship relations before marriage, but many kin terminologies included separate terms for affines that came into play once a particular individual was designated as a spouse or after marriage.

agnatic

Relationships traced through father–child links; see *patrifilial* and *patrilineal*.

alienable possessions

Possessions whose ownership can be transferred from one person or group to another as a gift, through barter, or (in market economies) by sale. See also *inalienable possessions*.

Aranda-like

A mode of kin classification named after the system used by Aranda (Arrernte) people; it differentiated four terminological 'lines of descent' traced from four sets of kin in the grandparents' generation.

asymmetrical marriage

A pattern of marriage in which women of one group marry men of another, but the marriage is not reciprocated; the pattern usually arises from matrilateral cross-cousin marriage in which a man marries a cousin on his mother's side but not his father's side.

band

A group of hunters and gatherers living together and exploiting the same land and waters for food; referred in earlier anthropology as a *horde*, and in this book as a *residence group*.

biomass

Calculated as the dry weight of organic matter of a group of organisms in a particular habitat.

camp

In this book a 'camp' comprises a small group of relatives who occupy a discrete area within a larger *residence group*. A camp, usually referred to as a 'household' or 'hearth-group', has one or more hearths and one or more shelters.

clan

A group of people with a common identity. A person becomes a member of a patri-clan through *patrifiliation* or *patrilineal descent*, and of a matri-clan through *matrifiliation* or *matrilineal descent*. Members of a clan are not necessarily all linked by descent from a common ancestor. See also *lineage*, *local group*, *matrifilial group*, and *patrifilial group*.

complementary filiation

The link to the mother's patri-group that 'complements' membership of a group through the father and father's father, or the link to the father's patri-group that complements membership of the mother's and mother's mother's matri-group.

corporate

A corporate group is one whose existence endures beyond the membership of any one individual; it has some kind of internal organisation and usually owns common property such as land. Aboriginal *clans* have often been described as corporate groups.

country

In this book 'country' refers to the land and in many cases waters (such as coastal waters) accorded the identity of a *country group* that 'held' or 'owned' the country. Countries were often defined with reference to a focal site or sites, such as lagoons or wells, given ancestral significance. Anthropologists often refer to a group's country as its *estate*.

country group

A group, often with a proper name, which 'held' or 'owned' one or more defined *countries* and the associated myths, ceremonies, and sacred objects. Anthropologists often refer to such groups as *clans*. In many areas country groups were *patrifilial* groups (or *patrilineal descent* groups).

cross cousin

A relation traced through the opposite-sex sibling of the linking parent—a person's mother's brother's child and father's sister's child are his or her cross-cousins. Aboriginal systems of kin classification extend the category applied to a first cross-cousin to many other more distant relatives. See also *parallel cousin*.

cross grandkin

A grandparent or grandparent's sibling of the opposite sex to the linking parent—father's mother, mother's father, father's mother's sibling, mother's father's sibling. See also *parallel grandkin*.

dependency ratio

The ratio of food-producers to dependants in a group.

descending kindred

A cognatic network traced through father–child and mother–child links from an individual or from a group of siblings or cousins.

descent group

A group defined by descent from a common ancestor. See also *lineage*, *matrifilial group*, and *patrifilial group*.

dialect

A variant of a language whose speakers understand and are understood by speakers of other dialects of the same language.

dialect group

Bernard Schebeck's term for nine language varieties recognised by Yolngu people, and named by the characteristic word for 'this/here'—*dhuwal, dhuwala, dhangu, djangu*, etc.

dispersed affinal alliance

A pattern of relationships between groups in which each is linked to many others by marriage ties that shift at each generation; see *shifting web*.

division

A.W. Howitt's term for a Kŭnai *country group*; in his scheme, a division consisted of several family groups, and several divisions comprised a 'clan' (*regional identity*).

ecotone

The transition zone between two distinct plant communities, such as rainforest and sclerophyll forest.

effective rainfall

The rainfall that remains in the soil, taking run-off into account.

endogamous, endogamy

'Marrying in': a person must marry a person of the same group or category, such as a *generation moiety* or *patrifilial group*. One can also speak of a 'tendency' to endogamy in a statistical sense even where endogamy is not required (e.g. of a language identity).

estate

See *country*.

ethnographer

A writer of *ethnography*.

ethnography

The description of one or more aspects of the culture, customs, or way or life of a people or community. During the nineteenth century and early twentieth century most ethnographies of Aboriginal societies were written by non-specialists, such as missionaries, administrators, and farmers; more recently, most ethnographies have been written by professional anthropologists.

exogamous, exogamy

'Marrying out': a person must marry someone of a different group or category, such as a *patrifilial moiety* or *patrifilial group*. One can also speak of a 'tendency' to exogamy in a statistical sense even where exogamy is not required (e.g. of a language identity).

genealogical

Relations based on links between parents and children. Many anthropologists argue that genealogical ties are the basis of *kinship* relations. *Patrifilial groups* vary greatly in genealogical depth (the number of generations people remember in oral tradition).

generation moiety

See *moiety*.

generational terminology

A mode of kin classification in which kin terms distinguish relatives of different generations but merge all one's relatives of the same generation under one or two terms, differentiating them only by gender and perhaps age.

Hawaiian terminology

A *generational* kin terminology, named after the Hawaiian system.

hegemony, hegemonic

Political domination of one class or group by another; in the sense Gramsci gave to the term, 'hegemony' refers especially to subtle ideological means of domination—for example, through education or religious doctrines.

home base

A place from which people move to hunt and gather food and to which they return to share it. This book refers to the group occupying a home base as a *residence group*.

horde

An early term for a group of hunters and gatherers living together and exploiting the same land and waters for food; referred to later as a *band*, and in this book as a *residence group*.

inalienable gift

A gift of an item that maintains its connection with the donor, so creating or reinforcing the relationship between donor and recipient; a lover's gift of a lock of hair is an example.

inalienable possessions

Possessions which cannot or should not normally be exchanged; in Aboriginal societies, these have included land and waters and some ancestral things, such as sacred objects and designs. See *alienable possessions*.

increase rites

Procedures, usually conducted at an ancestral site, believed to increase the numbers of or revive a particular food species.

institutional field

A broad domain of social practice (such as kinship or ancestral religion) that defines and sets the context for certain social relations and activities, or aspects of them.

isogloss, isoglossic

Words with equivalent meanings in different language varieties are *isoglosses*; examples in European languages are 'dog', 'chien', 'hund', and 'perro'. Aboriginal people have often used words such as those meaning 'no', 'yes', and 'come' to assign identities to people and country.

Karadjeri

A Karadjeri-like system of kin classification, named after the system of the Karadjeri (Karajarri) people, is characterised by the differentiation of cousins on the mother's and father's side, and is associated with *asymmetrical marriage*.

Kariera

A Kariera-like system of kin classification, named after the system supposedly (but not in fact) used by Kariera (Kariyarra) people, is typified by having two broad categories of grandkin and two terminological 'lines of descent' traced from them; cross cousins are distinguished from siblings and parallel cousins.

kinship

The system of relationships based on, but in Aboriginal kinship not restricted to, *genealogical* links.

language family

A group of languages with similar general characteristics.

language variety

A way of speaking that is recognised as distinctive by the speakers and others of the same community, but that is not necessarily a distinct dialect or language from the point of view of a linguist.

laterite

A red ferruginous soil, often pebbly, formed from the decomposition of the underlying rock and characterised by the formation of a hard crust.

levirate, leviratic

The marriage of a widow to the brother of her deceased husband, often a matter of rights in Aboriginal societies.

lineage

A group of people tracing descent from a common ancestor through either the male or female line; a lineage may be part of a larger group, the several lineages of which need not be linked by common descent.

local group

An anthropological term, no longer in common use, equivalent to *country group* as used in this book. Earlier anthropologists assumed that the local group was a *descent group* or *clan*; hence 'local descent group'.

local organisation

That aspect of social organisation concerned with relations to and ownership of land and waters.

logistical movement

Movement to and from a *home base* for the purpose of hunting, gathering, and collecting fuel and water.

mallee

Species of eucalypts characterised by many trunks springing from a common root system.

matrifilial

The link between mother and child; see also *matrifiliation*.

matrifilial group, matri-group

A group of people with a common identity gained from mother and mother's mother. Matri-groups of Yuwaaliyaay people and their neighbours were differentiated and related by *totemic* associations and the ownership of related sacred objects, but probably not land and waters. The anthropological literature refers to these as a variety of *clan*.

matrifilial moiety, matri-moiety

See *moiety*.

matrifiliation

The use of the mother–child link to assign identity, membership of a group, or a relationship to another group. See *matrifilial* and *complementary filiation*.

matrilineal

A series of links from mother to child forming the basis of identity or group membership; see also *matrilineal descent*.

matrilineal descent

Descent from a common ancestor traced through women; see *matrilineal*.

matrilocal residence

Residence after marriage with the wife's and wife's parents' people; see also *uxorilocal residence*.

moiety

The division of people and often of other creatures, places, and things into two kinds. In the case of *patri-moieties*, a person takes the identity of their father's moiety, usually opposite to their mother's, and in the case of *matri-moieties*, the person takes their mother's moiety identity. *Generation moieties* group people of a person's own genealogical generation with those of his or her grandparents' and grandchildren's generations. People of adjacent generations are in opposite moieties. Patri-moieties and matri-moities are usually *exogamous*, while generation moieties are normally *endogamous*.

naming system

A system of sections, subsections, or semi-moieties in which one of a set of names (four or eight, or sixteen with gender variants) is assigned to an individual on the basis of their mother's or father's name. Naming systems are also associated with marriage rules.

non-Pama-Nyungan

A number of diverse Aboriginal language families of the Kimberley and adjacent regions, most of which are prefixing languages. Many linguists group all other Aboriginal languages, most of which are suffixing languages, into a single family, *Pama-Nyungan*.

Omaha skewing

A feature of kin terminologies in which terms for mother and mother's brother are extended to mother's brother's children, replacing cross cousin terms. Omaha skewing is associated with the prohibition of marriage between close cross cousins who are classified as 'mother' or 'mother's brother' to 'woman's child' or 'sister's child'.

Pama-Nyungan

Linguists group the many languages of most of Australia into this one family, named after the Paman languages of parts of Queensland and the Nyungar languages of the southwest. The family does not include languages of much of the Kimberley and adjacent regions, which are *non-Pama-Nyungan* languages.

parallel cousin

A relative traced through a sibling of the same sex as the linking parent—one's mother's sister's child and father's brother's child are one's parallel cousins. Aboriginal kin terminologies classify these as siblings ('brother' or 'sister'), usually distinguished by gender and relative age.

parallel grandkin

A grandparent or grandparent's sibling of the same sex as the linking parent—mother's mother, father's father, mother's mother's sibling, father's father's sibling. See also *cross grandkin.*

patrifilial, patrifiliation

The relation between a father and child, taken as the basis for the child's identity and/or group membership; see also *agnatic* and *patrilineal.*

patrifilial group, patri-group

A group of people with a common identity in which a person gains his or her identity from their father and father's father. Patri-groups vary in *genealogical* depth and *lineage* structure. Patri-groups in Australia are usually associated with the ownership of land, waters, and ancestral things (such as sacred sites, ceremonies, and sacred objects). The anthropological literature often refers to the patri-group as a *clan*, sib, *local group* or local descent group.

patrifilial moiety, patri-moiety

The division of people and often of other creatures, places, and things into two kinds. People gain their moiety identity from their father; it is normally the opposite of their mother's moiety identity.

patrilineal

A series of links from father to child forming the basis of identity or group membership; see also *patrilineal descent.*

patrilineal descent

Descent from a common ancestor traced through men; see *patrilineal.*

patrilocal residence

Residence after marriage with the husband's and husband's parents' people ('virilocal residence' strictly speaking). In the anthropology of Aboriginal culture and society the term implies residence on the husband's patri-group country, a practice once thought to be universal in Australia.

phratry

A group consisting of two or more *clans.* A person is a member of their mother's or father's phatry. K. Langloh Parker uses the term to refer to Yuwaaliyaay *matri-moieties* which in that case cut across 'clan' identities.

polyandry

See *polygamy*.

polygamy

Marriage to more than one spouse concurrently; *polygyny* is the marriage of a man to more than one wife, *polyandry* the marriage of a woman to more than one husband. *Serial polyandry* is the marriage of a woman to more than one man, but not concurrently, and is related to the *levirate*. Serial polyandry was common in Australia, as a widow normally remarried. See also *levirate* and *sororate*.

polygyny

See *polygamy*.

regional identities

The identification through proper names of broad regions of land and waters and the people associated with them through birth, residence etc. Regional identities were typically rather open and context-dependent, and a person might take dual or multiple identities (see *shifters*). Regional identities are often treated as *tribes* in the older anthropological literature.

relational triangle

Relations between three people such that two people can compute a 'kinship' relationship to each other through their respective kin relationships to the third person; also called 'mediated kinship'.

residence group

A group of hunters and gatherers living together and exploiting the same land and waters for food; referred to in earlier anthropology as a *horde* and more recently as a *band*. Both terms imply an enduring social entity, whereas the expression 'residence group' leaves the duration of the group open.

residential movement

The movement of a residence group to a new *home base*.

samphire

A salt-tolerant plant species.

sclerophyll

The formation of thickened and hardened cells in the leaves of plants, reducing water loss as an adaptation to aridity.

serial polyandry

See *polygamy*.

shifter

A linguistic sign whose meaning is dependent on the linguistic and pragmatic context— the word 'this' in English is an example. Many Aboriginal markers of social identity, such as language identities and *regional identities*, had something of this character.

shifting web

A social network in which each group is linked to many others by marriage ties that shift at each generation; see *dispersed affinal alliance*.

skewing

See *Omaha skewing*.

social boundary defence

The regulation of access to land and waters and their resources through the differentiation of an owning group from non-owners, and the requirement that non-owners get the permission of the owners to gain access.

socialisation

The inculcation in an individual of dispositions to conform to social norms, rules, and expectations, achieved through informal education and formal procedures such as initiation.

sociocentric

A sociocentric classification scheme is one that looks the same from all points of view— a person's *section* identity was sociocentric, whereas kin categories were relative to a person's point of view and were 'egocentric'.

sororate, sororatic

The marriage of a man to two or more sisters, often concurrently.

spirit conception

According to the doctrines of many Aboriginal people, the conception of a child took place when some kind of 'spirit' entity entered the mother, typically coming from a waterhole. In some areas this belief was linked to doctrines of reincarnation.

talion

From Latin *lex talionis* (the law of talion): retaliation for an offence or injury in which the injured party inflicts punishment of the same kind and degree as the original offence or injury—'an eye for an eye, and a tooth for a tooth'. Aboriginal people referred to this form of retaliation as 'payback' in English; its application resulted in enduring feuds.

totem, totemic

An element in a system of totemic classification, in which the identities of individuals and groups are marked by the names of non-human entities, typically species of plants, birds, animals, insects, and fish, celestial bodies such as the sun and moon, and terrestrial entities such as rock and water. In Aboriginal cosmologies totemic classification schemes were often linked to *naming systems* and to *totemic ancestors*.

totemic ancestor

In Aboriginal cosmologies, beings who lived long ago, who were the ancestors of the people of a region in general or of specific groups, and who had the identities and characteristics of species of animals and plants, celestical bodies, etc., as well as having human attributes. Some ancestors had predominantly human attributes, although with greatly enhanced powers. See also *totem*.

totemic identity

The identification of a group and its individual members in terms of a *totem* and/or a *totemic ancestor*.

use rights

An individual or group's rights to use and exploit a group's land, waters, and resources; the bases for Aboriginal use rights included membership of a group, being the child of a woman of the group, conception or birth on the group's country, and marriage to a member of the group.

uterine

A synonym for *matrifilial* and *matrilineal*—a connection traced through the mother–child relationship. The complementary term is *agnatic* (*patrifilial* or *patrilineal*).

uxorilocal residence

Residence after marriage with the wife and her parents, but not necessarily on the wife's and wife's father's country (assuming countries were owned by patri-groups); see also *matrilocal residence*.

variability index

A measure of variability in annual rainfall, calculated by comparing the degree of variability to the median rainfall.

variable

Any trait or characteristic, such as rainfall or modes of kin classification, to which varying values or specifications can be assigned and that is used in a study that compares the values or specifications of two or more variables.

Index